D1070422

GALATIANS
RE-IMAGINED

For Roger. In Friedship.

Br Br

Aug 2010

PAUL IN CRITICAL CONTEXTS

*The Paul in Critical Contexts series offers cutting-edge reexaminations
of Paul through the lenses of power, gender, and ideology.*

GALATIANS RE-IMAGINED

READING
WITH THE EYES
OF THE
VANQUISHED

BRIGITTE KAHL

Fortress Press
Minneapolis

To Jan,
and to our children.
And to the wounded warriors of many wars.

GALATIANS RE-IMAGINED
Reading with the Eyes of the Vanquished

Cover image © Erich Lessing/Art Resource, NY.
Cover design: Laurie Ingram
Book design: The HK Scriptorium, Inc.

Library of Congress Cataloging-in-Publication Data

Kahl, Brigitte.
Galatians re-imagined : reading with the eyes of the vanquished / Brigitte Kahl.
    p. cm. — (Paul in critical contexts)
Includes bibliographical references and index.
ISBN 978-0-8006-3864-1 (alk. paper)
1. Bible. N.T. Galatians—Criticism, interpretation, etc. I. Title.
BS2685.52.K34 2009
227'.406—dc22

                                                    2009033988

13 12 11 10   1 2 3 4 5 6 7 8 9 10

Contents

Figures and Maps

Acknowledgments

Many people have assisted me in the long gestation of this book, which was conceived on two continents, somewhere between the fall of the Berlin Wall and the attack on the World Trade Center in New York. It reflects two decades of migration from East to West, from Europe to the United States, from socialism to capitalism, from German to English, and it is heavy with history both ancient and contemporary, secular as well as biblical. It also bears the indelible mark of a unique moment in history when the Bible became, if entirely on the margins, a liberating "third space" between the conflicting forces of conservative church dogma and dogmatic state Marxism of pre-1989 East Germany. It took a long journey with countless departures, transitions, and arrivals until I was able to see how much the apostle Paul needs to be counted as a fellow citizen and cofounder of such a heterotopian space, even in the crisis and war-ridden world of post-1989 global capitalism. I am grateful to those who have become teachers, companions, and contestants on that journey. I cannot name them all but I hope they will recognize their part and remember the community and practice we shared, a seminal conversation late at night, a text or an image we exegeted together, a dispute of minor or even unbridgeable dimension that eventually pushed us both further ahead.

I am deeply indebted to my students, at Berlin, Paderborn, and most of all at Union Theological Seminary in New York, who over these years have been indefatigable listeners, critics, and contributors. They were enthusiastic about re-imagining Paul when I was fainthearted about never getting close to a full picture; they asked all the thorny questions; and they even graciously conceded to semiotic squares. From among the participants of the doctoral seminar in New Testament, Davina Lopez, Jae Won Lee, David Sánchez, and Stamenka Antonova need to be mentioned in particular; as well as Liz Theoharis, who, together with Willie Baptist from the Poverty Initiative at Union, helped me relocate Paul's theology in the present-day context of poor people's movements. Grace Lewis, Maia Kotrosits, and Celene Lillie generously offered, in addition to their scholarly contributions, their expertise for technical help.

I want to say my thanks to many colleagues and friends inside and outside the field of New Testament who have supported this project in numerous ways and at various stages, mostly by reading parts of the manuscript or other related material and giving their comments, counsel, encouragement, or stern criticism: Elisabeth Schüssler Fiorenza, Luise Schottroff, Louis Martyn, David Balch, Annette

Weissenrieder, Mark Nanos, Angela Bauer, Angela Standhartinger, Sharon Ringe, Daniel Patte, Helmut Koester, Alan Segal, Mary Boys, Paul Knitter, and Roger Haight. Neil Elliott, as my editor and distinguished expert in the field of Pauline studies, did a lot to improve the manuscript. Moreover, I need to thank two colleagues at UTS whose scholarly companionship and friendship have been a vital resource over the past years: Hal Taussig, who was more than generous in donating time and energy to promote my writing, and Janet Walton, who unfalteringly kept a space on her bookshelf and in her imagination for this book to materialize.

From the disciplines of ancient, Jewish, and art history I received helpful advice and feedback from William Harris, Seth Schwartz, and Natalie Kampen. The director of the Staatliche Antikensammlung Berlin, Volker Koester, was most supportive during my numerous explorations of the Great Altar at the Berlin Pergamon Museum, and Holger Schwarzer gave me a memorable tour. They all taught me more than they may have realized and I hope they will not see this interdisciplinary "hybrid" as an alien intrusion into their domain.

Among those who materially sponsored my project I owe thanks in particular to the Lilly Foundation, which enabled me to take a full year sabbatical at the early stage of the work, and to Union Theological Seminary, which generously supported my research over the years. Fortress Press was a reliable partner and I am very thankful for the cooperation with Marissa Wold Bauck, who expertly steered the book through the final stages of its production. Furthermore, I am profoundly grateful to Bill and Barbara Cox, who openhandedly provided me with a beautiful space in which to read and write during numerous summer retreats I spent in their house in the woods of Connecticut, and to Dan and Tracy Hayhurst, who on these occasions would let me share the fruits of their amazing CSA-Farm and even do some digging in the dirt if I needed grounding. The traces of earth spirituality in this book are rooted in that soil.

I do not know how to thank my family for their sustenance and for what they went through with me, with Paul, and with the Galatians: to Sigrun, Thurid, and Jakob, who patiently endured their mother's enthusiasm, endless delays, and absorption by this work that they never believed I wouldn't finish, and who furthermore in several instances loyally followed me through museums, took photos, fixed diagrams, and commented on my writing. And finally to Jan Rehmann, my partner in life and work, to whom I owe my first introduction to theories of ideology when we were still communicating across the Berlin Wall, and without whose insights, dedication, and support I could not have completed this book.

Abbreviations

AGJU	Arbeiten zur Geschichte des antiken Judentums und des Urchristentums
ANRW	*Aufstieg und Niedergang der römischen Welt: Geschichte und Kultur Roms im Spiegel der neueren Forschung.* Edited by H. Temporini and W. Haase. Berlin: de Gruyter, 1972–.
Appian	
Bell. civ.	*Bella civilia*
Hist. rom.	*Historia romana*
ArchAnz	*Archäologische Anzeiger*
Aristotle	
Eth. Nic.	*Nicomachean Ethics*
Arrian	
Anab.	*Anabasis*
ASV	American Standard Version
BBE	Bible in Basic English
BMC	*Coins of the Roman Empire in the British Museum.* London: Trustees of the British Museum, 1923–.
Caesar, Julius	
Bell. civ.	*Bellum civile*
Bell. Gall.	*Bellum Gallicum*
Cicero	
Att.	*Epistulae ad Atticum*
Fam.	*Epistulae ad familiares*
Phil	*Orationes philippicae*
Pro Font.	*Pro Fonteio*
CIG	*Corpus inscriptionum graecarum.* Edited by A. Boeckh. 4 vols. Berlin: Ex Officina Academica, Vendit G. Reimeri Libraria, 1828–77.
CIL	*Corpus inscriptionum latinarum.* Berlin: de Gruyter, 1968–.
CPJ	*Corpus papyrorum judaicarum.* Edited by V. Tcherikover. 3 vols. Cambridge, Mass.: Published for Magnes Press, Hebrew University, by Harvard University Press, 1957–64.
EvT	*Evangelische Theologie*

FGH	*Die Fragmente der griechischen Historiker.* Edited by F. Jacoby. 3 vols. in 15 parts. Leiden: Brill, 1954–64.
Hesiod	
Theog.	*Theogony*
Horace	
Carm.	*Carmina*
IGR	*Inscriptiones graecae ad res romanas pertinentes.* Edited by R. Cagnat et al. Paris: E. Leroux, 1906–27.
ILS	*Inscriptiones latinae selectae.* Edited by H. Dessau. 3 vols. Berlin: Weidmann, 1892–1916.
IvP	*Die Inschriften von Pergamon.* Edited by Max Fränkel. Berlin, 1890–95.
JHS	*Journal of Hellenic Studies*
Josephus	
Ant.	*Antiquitates judaicae*
Ap.	*Contra Apionem*
B.J.	*Bellum judaicum*
JRS	*Journal of Roman Studies*
JSNT	*Journal for the Study of the New Testament*
JSNTSup	Journal for the Study of the New Testament Supplement Series
JSOTSup	Journal for the Study of the Old Testament Supplement Series
Juvenal	
Sat.	*Satirae*
LCL	Loeb Classical Library
LIMC	*Lexicon iconographicum mythologiae classicae.* Edited by H. C. Ackerman and J.-R. Gisler. 8 vols. Zurich: Artemis, 1981–97.
MAMA	*Monumenta Asiae Minoris Antiqua.* Manchester: Manchester University Press; London: Longmans, Green, 1928–93.
Martial	
Spect.	*Liber de spectaculis*
MEFRA	*Mélanges de l'Ecole française de Rome. Antiquité*
NTS	*New Testament Studies*
OGIS	*Orientis graeci inscriptiones selectae.* Edited by W. Dittenberger. 2 vols. Leipzig: S. Hirzel, 1903–5.
Ovid	
Fast.	*Fasti*
Pausanius	
Descr.	*Graeciae descriptio*
Philo	
Flacc.	*In Flaccum*
Leg.	*Legum allegoriae*
Leg. Gai.	*Legatio ad Gaium*

Migr. Abr.	*De migratione Abrahami*
Vit. Mos.	*De vita Mosis*
Pliny the Elder	
Nat.	*Natural History*
Plutarch	
Cam.	*Camillus*
Mar.	*Marius*
Marc.	*Marcellus*
Mor.	*Moralia*
Quaest. Rom.	*Quaestiones romanae et graecae*
Rom	*Romulus*
Polybius	
Hist.	*Histories*
Res Gest. Divi Aug.	*Res gestae divi Augusti*
Sallust	
Hist.	*Historiae*
Sib. Or.	*Sibylline Oracles*
SNTSMS	Society for New Testament Studies Monograph Series
ST	*Studia Theologica*
Suetonius	
Aug.	*Divus Augustus*
Claud.	*Divus Claudius*
Dom.	*Domitianus*
Gram.	*De grammaticis*
Tit.	*Divus Titus*
Tacitus	
Agr.	*Agricola*
Ann.	*Annals*
Hist.	*Historiae*
USQR	*Union Seminary Quarterly Review*
WUNT	Wissenschaftliche Untersuchungen zum Neuen Testament

Timeline

Note: Following customary usage, this outline generally uses the term *Galatia(n)* for the Celtic inhabitants of Asia Minor (contemporary Turkey) and *Gaul/Gallic* for the Celts of Western Europe north and south of the Alps (Gallia Transalpina and Gallia Cisalpina). As the text makes clear, however, ancient Greek and Latin authors usually did not make this differentiation with any consistency but tended to refer to a single coherent civilization using either term. This timeline therefore also uses the hybridized term *Gauls/Galatians* or Celts.

B.C.E.

387   *Rome is sacked.* Gauls in migration from beyond the Alps (the tribe of the Senones), searching for new land to settle on the east coast of Italy, conquer and destroy Rome (with the exception of the Capitol) and temporarily occupy the city. The attack, which follows a severe offense given by Roman emissaries at Clusium, is led by Brennus. It is preceded by a disastrous Roman defeat in a battle near the river Allia.

295   *Battle of Sentium (Italy):* After a century of clashes with the Romans, the Senones are subdued and driven out of their territory in Italy. Possibly they form part of the vast Celtic migration that pushes into the Balkans and Macedonia from the fourth century onwards.

Ca. 280   *Celts across the Balkans.* In the power vacuum following Alexander's death, several Celtic armies make incursions into Paeonia, Thrace, and Macedonia; they defeat the newly installed king of Macedonia, Ptolemy Keraunos.

279   *Attack on Delphi:* A sizable contingent of Celtic warriors under a second Brennus suffers heavy losses by a joint Greek coalition in the Battle of Thermopylae. They nevertheless march on against the sanctuary of Apollo at Delphi, a revered religious and political center of Greek civilization. The Celts are defeated and have to withdraw; a section of their force settles in Thrace and founds the kingdom of Tyle. The Greeks join Gallic shields to the trophies from the Persian wars displayed at Delphi.

279/78   *Galatian settlement in Asia Minor*: After Delphi, three tribes (the Toli-
          stobogii, Trocmi, and Tektosagi) cross to Asia Minor, invited by King
          Nicomedes of Bithynia as military allies and settlers in the central part
          of Anatolia around Gordium, Pessinus, and Ancyra.

270s   *Anti-Galatian battles of the Antigonids, Ptolemies, and Seleucids:* Anti-
          gonos Gonatas defeats a Celtic army at Lysimacheia and is installed as
          king of Macedonia in 277, establishing the Antigonid dynasty. King
          Ptolemy II of Egypt crushes a mutiny by his four thousand Galatian
          mercenaries in 275, his victory being hailed by Callimachus as an arche-
          typal triumph over "Titans." The Seleucid King Antiochus I wins the
          first decisive victory over the Galatians in Asia Minor in 270 (the "Ele-
          phant Battle"), presenting himself as the "savior" of Asia Minor.

240   *Pergamene-Galatian battle at the Caicus sources:* Attalus I of Pergamon
          defeats the Galatians and takes the title of "king"; he sponsors victory
          monuments of *Dying Gauls/Galatians* in several variations at Perga-
          mon, Athens, and elsewhere.

228   *First Galatian live sacrifice at Rome*: On instruction from the Sibylline
          books, a Galatian/Gallic man and woman (together with a Greek cou-
          ple) are buried alive at the cattle market in the centre of Rome (Forum
          Boarium), after a lightning strike close to Apollo's temple.

225   *Battle of Telamon (Italy):* Last great defeat of the Gallic Boii, Insub-
          res, and Gaesatae; Roman superiority in Italy is no longer threatened
          by Gallia Cisalpina (although fights continue until about 190). Roman
          thank offerings are devoted to the Delphic Apollo.

218–01   *Second Punic War.*

216   *Second Galatian live sacrifice at Rome:* Another Galatian/Gallic couple
          and a Greek couple are buried alive after Romans suffer a disastrous
          defeat by Hannibal in the Battle of Cannae.

190   *Roman victory over the Seleucids at Magnesia* ends both Seleucid rule
          and Galatian independence in Asia Minor.

189   *Anti-Galatian campaign of Manlius Vulso in Asia Minor:* Following
          Magnesia, the Romans carry out a wholesale massacre among the three
          tribes at Mount Olympus (near Gordium) and Mount Magaba (near
          Ancyra); about forty thousand victims are recorded. Manlius's "disci-
          plinary" and "pre-emptive" action earns him great booty and a trium-
          phal procession at Rome.

188   *The Peace of Apamea* lays the foundation of Roman hegemony in the
          eastern Mediterranean. The kingdom of Pergamon, faithful ally and cli-
          ent of Rome, rises to great power; the Greek cities of the region hail
          Rome as "savior" for ending Galatian terror.

183   *Pergamene victory:* Eumenes II defeats a coalition between Prusias I of Bithynia (host of the exiled Hannibal of Carthage) and the Galatian chieftain Ortagion. Hannibal commits suicide; Eumenes adopts the title "savior."

Ca. 180–160   *The Great Altar of Pergamon* is erected by Eumenes II to commemorate the Attalid conquest of the Galatians as the triumph of civilization over primeval chaos/giants.

168   *The Battle of Pydna:* Rome, supported by Pergamon, defeats the Antigonid dynasty and subsequently turns Macedonia into a Roman province (148); Galatians fight in both the Pergamene and Macedonian armies.

167   *Last Galatian revolt against Pergamon*

165   *First Galatian embassy to Rome*

133   *Kingdom of Pergamon is bequeathed to Rome* by Attalos III; it becomes the Roman province of Asia with Pergamon as its capital.

121   *Gallia Narbonensis:* Rome establishes its first Gallic province in the West around the Greek colony of Marseille (southern France).

113   *Third Galatian/Gallic live sacrifice at Rome* carried out during the invasion of the Cimbri and Teutoni.

86   *Mithridatic massacre at Pergamon:* Mithridates VI of Pontus, at war with Rome in Asia Minor, invites all tribal leaders of the Galatians to a banquet and treacherously murders about sixty of them.

59   *King Deiotaros is installed as client of Rome.* The Galatian tetrarch, survivor of Mithridates's plot and loyal ally of Rome in the three Mithridatic Wars (88–63) and other affairs relevant to Roman rule, is officially installed as king. In 47 he holds authority over all Galatian tribal territory and remains sole Galatian ruler until his death in 40. Deiotaros is on friendly terms with Cato, Pompey, Caesar, Crassus, Cicero, and Brutus. His army consists of two legions trained in Roman fashion; a Roman legion will later be named after him (Legio XXII Deiotariana).

58–52   *The Gallic Wars:* Julius Caesar subdues the entire territory of Gaul up to the Atlantic and makes an incursion into Britain; two million Gauls are killed or enslaved. He wins final victory over Vercingetorix in the Battle of Alesia in 52.

49   *Caesar crosses the Rubicon,* the boundary between Cisalpine Gaul and Italy proper, indicating that he has gained sufficient military power and wealth to move towards the violent transformation of the Roman Republic into an empire.

47   *King Deiotaros hosts Julius Caesar in his palace at Blucium* after the Battle of Zela in Pontus ("veni, vidi, vici"). Subsequently arraigned in Rome on charges of a murderous plot against Caesar, he is passionately

defended by Cicero in 45 in a speech "On behalf of king Deiotaros." He is found not guilty.

46	*Caesar's Gallic triumph* in Rome precedes his assassination by only two years.

40–25   *Galatian nobility rules in Asia Minor.* Under Marc Antony and Augustus, several Galatians of aristocratic descent are entrusted with client kingdoms in Asia Minor. Deiotaros's successor Amyntas shifts the power center from the tribal areas in the North to the Taurus region in the South. A loyal client ruler of Rome, he subdues the independent tribes of the Pisidians and Isaurians but perishes in combat against the insurgent Homonadeis. Amyntas bequeathes his kingdom to Rome.

31   *Octavian's decisive victory at Actium* over Antony and Cleopatra makes him sole ruler.

29   *Imperial cult is established at Pergamon.* The city, together with Nicomedia in Bithynia, installs the first provincial imperial temple, thus inaugurating imperial worship in Asia Minor (and throughout the Roman Empire).

25   *Province of Galatia is founded by Augustus.* Ancyra becomes the capital and chief seat of imperial religion. Massive road building includes the Via Sebaste; Roman colonies are established especially in the South.

12   *The Imperial sanctuary at Lugdunum (Lyons) in Gaul* is jointly dedicated by the three Gallic Roman provinces of Gallia Belgica, Aquitania, and Gallia Lugdunensis.

Ca. 10   *A list of thirty-six Roman soldiers from Alexandria* shows strong Galatian recruitment from Ancyra (ten names) and other places formerly under Galatian rule like Tavium, Sebastopolis in Pontos, Pompeiopolis, or Gangra in Paphlagonia (ten more names); it includes even Lugdunum (Lyons), the capital of Gaul in the West (two names).

10 B.C.E.   *The imperial temple at Ancyra is erected*, dedicated to the deities of Roma
to 20 C.E.   and Augustus; an inscription of Augustus's *Res Gestae* in Latin and Greek is set up on its exterior (the Monumentum Ancyranum). Ancyra is seat of the Provincial Council (*koinon*) of Roman Galatia.

6 B.C.E.   *The Homonadeis are extinguished* by Publius Sulpicius Quirinius (the Qui-
to 4 C.E.   rinius of Lk 2:2).

4 B.C.E.   *Herod dies; his bodyguard of four hundred Galatian warriors*, originally belonging to Cleopatra of Egypt and handed over to Herod by Octavian after Actium, walk in his funerary procession.

C.E.

20–40   *A list of imperial priests engraved at the Ancyra temple* records donations from "Priests of the Galatians serving the divine Augustus Sebastos and the Goddess Roma" to the public within the system of imperial euergetism that includes banquets, gladiatorial shows, bull and wild animal fights, and games.

Ca. 48   *Emperor Claudius makes Gauls eligible for membership in the Roman senate.*

49   *Jews and Gallic Druids are expelled from Rome.* Claudius punishes both groups for their un-Roman activities and disturbance of Roman order.

41–54   *Imperial presence in Roman Galatia under Claudius:* Several cities adopt the Emperor's name (Claudiconium, Claudioderbe); the imperial sanctuary at Pisidian Antioch is completed, its entrance bearing a dedication to Claudius. *Paul's Galatian mission takes place during these years.*

50s   *Julia Severa of Acmonia/Phrygia,* a Roman woman of Galatian aristocratic descent, serves as a high priestess of imperial religion under Nero; at the same time she sponsors the local Jewish synagogue. Her son becomes one of the first Roman senators from the East during Nero's reign and some of her descendants will rise to the highest offices in the imperial administration.

54   *Corbulo conducts military conscription in Roman Galatia* in preparation for campaign in Armenia; *Paul writes his letter to the Galatians around the same time.*

64   *Great Fire and Neronian persecution of Christians at Rome:* Paul possibly among the victims.

66–70   *Jewish War against Rome*

68   *Uprising of Vindex in Gaul:* Nero commits suicide, bringing the end of the Julio-Claudian dynasty. Another major Gallic/German uprising against Rome under Civilis follows in 69–70, heralding the "Empire of all Gaul."

69   *Civil War at Rome:* Three Emperors compete for power within one year; the Capitol, with the temple of Jupiter, goes up in flames. Finally Vespasian seizes power, beginning the Flavian dynasty.

70   *Destruction of Jerusalem:* Titus conquers the city, desecrating and razing the temple to the ground. Hundreds of thousands of inhabitants and refugees are killed or enslaved. The Roman triumph of Vespasian and Titus is celebrated in 71.

75   *Vespasian dedicates the Temple of Peace at Rome.* Jewish spoils of war are prominently exhibited in the sanctuary together with images of *Dying Gauls/Galatians.*

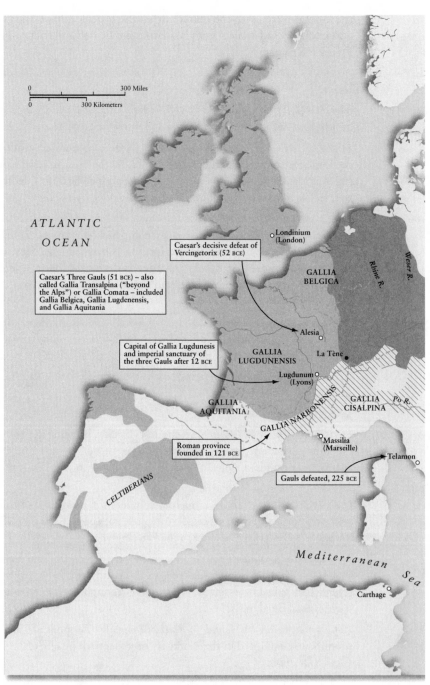

Caesar's decisive defeat of
Vercingetorix (52 BCE)

Caesar's Three Gauls (51 BCE) – also
called Gallia Transalpina ("beyond
the Alps") or Gallia Comata – included
Gallia Belgica, Gallia Lugdenensis,
and Gallia Aquitania

Capital of Gallia Lugdenesis
and imperial sanctuary of
the three Gauls after 12 BCE

Roman province
founded in 121 BCE

Gauls defeated, 225 BCE

ATLANTIC
OCEAN

Londinium
(London)

GALLIA
BELGICA

Rhine R.

Weser R.

Alesia

La Tène

GALLIA
LUGDUNENSIS

Lugdunum
(Lyons)

GALLIA
AQUITANIA

GALLIA NARBONENSIS

GALLIA
CISALPINA

Po R.

Massilia
(Marseille)

Telamon

CELTIBERIANS

Mediterranean Sea

Carthage

0   300 Miles
0   300 Kilometers

Galatians/Gauls/Celts: History and Settlements

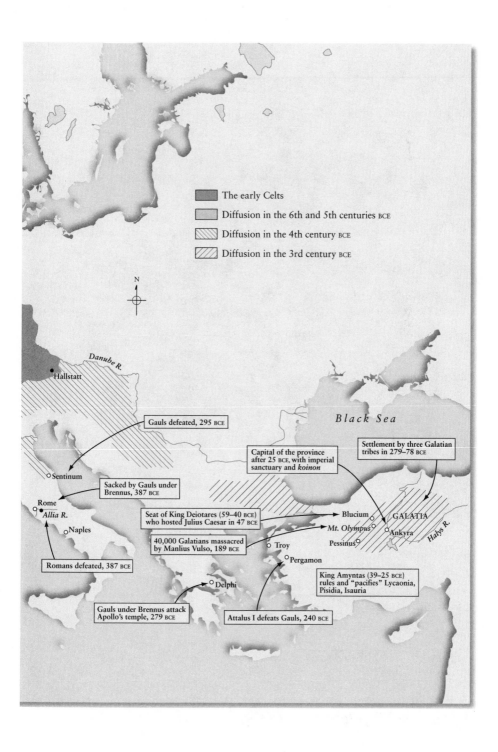

The early Celts

Diffusion in the 6th and 5th centuries BCE

Diffusion in the 4th century BCE

Diffusion in the 3rd century BCE

N

Danube R.

Hallstatt

Black Sea

Gauls defeated, 295 BCE

Capital of the province after 25 BCE, with imperial sanctuary and *koinon*

Settlement by three Galatian tribes in 279–78 BCE

Sentinum

Sacked by Gauls under Brennus, 387 BCE

Seat of King Deiotares (59–40 BCE) who hosted Julius Caesar in 47 BCE

Blucium

GALATIA

Rome

Allia R.

Mt. Olympus

Ankyra

Halys R.

Naples

40,000 Galatians massacred by Manlius Vulso, 189 BCE

Pessinus

Troy

Romans defeated, 387 BCE

Pergamon

King Amyntas (39–25 BCE) rules and "pacifies" Lycaonia, Pisidia, Isauria

Delphi

Gauls under Brennus attack Apollo's temple, 279 BCE

Attalus I defeats Gauls, 240 BCE

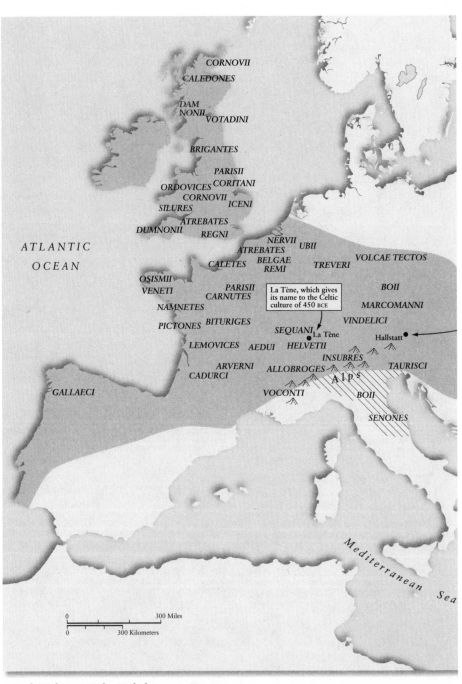

CORNOVII

CALEDONES

DAM
NONII
VOTADINI

BRIGANTES

PARISII

ORDOVICES CORITANI

CORNOVII
ICENI

SILURES

ATREBATES

DUMNONII REGNI

NERVII UBII

ATREBATES

CALETES BELGAE VOLCAE TECTOS

REMI TREVERI

ATLANTIC
OCEAN

OSISMII BOII

VENETI PARISII

La Tène, which gives MARCOMANNI

CARNUTES its name to the Celtic

NAMNETES culture of 450 BCE VINDELICI

PICTONES BITURIGES

SEQUANI La Tène Hallstatt

LEMOVICES AEDUI HELVETII

INSUBRES

ARVERNI ALLOBROGES TAURISCI

CADURCI Alps

GALLAECI BOII

VOCONTI

SENONES

Mediterranean Sea

0   300 Miles

0   300 Kilometers

Gauls/Galatians/Celts: Tribal Areas in Europe

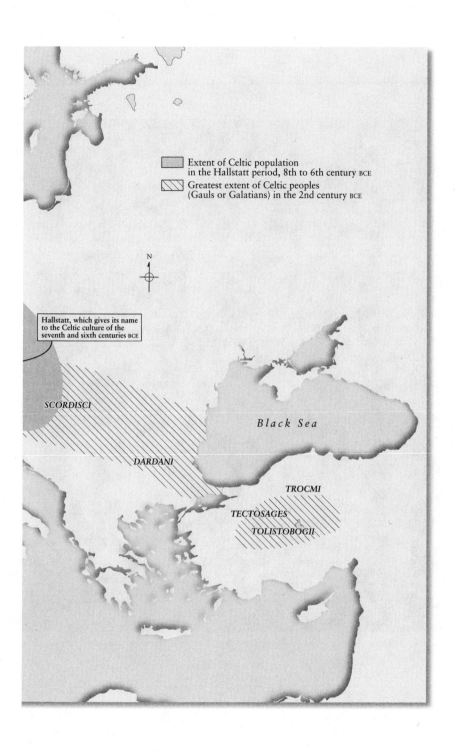

Extent of Celtic population
in the Hallstatt period, 8th to 6th century BCE

Greatest extent of Celtic peoples
(Gauls or Galatians) in the 2nd century BCE

N

Hallstatt, which gives its name
to the Celtic culture of the
seventh and sixth centuries BCE

SCORDISCI

Black Sea

DARDANI

TROCMI

TECTOSAGES

TOLISTOBOGII

Defeated Britons are trampled by Roman cavalry. National Museums Scotland/Licensor www.scran.ac.uk.

INTRODUCTION

The Critical Re-Imagination of Paul and of Justification by Faith

... cum adnotasset insculptum monumento militem Gallum ab equite R. oppressum trahi crinibus, ad eam speciem exsiluit gaudio caelumque adoravit.

... for he [Nero] noticed a monument on which was sculpted the defeat of a Gaul warrior by a Roman cavalryman, who was dragging him by his hair; at which sight he was filled with joy and praised heaven. (Suetonius, *Nero* 41.2)

In 68 C.E., Gaul was once again in an uproar. The message reached Caesar Nero in Naples. Gaius Julius Vindex, the provincial governor, a man of senatorial rank whose name revealed his impeccable Roman heritage as well as his Gallic descent, was leading the rebellion. After days spent in denial and indecision, the emperor returned to Rome, panic-stricken. On his way back, however, an *auspicium* lifted his spirits. The sight of the sculpture of a Gallic warrior crushed down by a Roman horseman and being dragged by his hair cheered him greatly, and he now expected a victorious outcome of his military campaign against the treacherous Gauls.

Within the broad canon of established exegetical approaches to Paul's Galatian letter, this little episode told by the imperial biographer Suetonius appears distinctly foreign, a strangely misplaced snippet of reality. But in fact, it is directly relevant for interpretation. Gaul in the West and Galatia in the East were more closely linked in the first-century C.E. mind than we realize. The rebel governor of Gaul, Gaius Julius Vindex, would have been called a Galatian (*Galatēs*) in the *koinē* in which Paul communicated with his congregations in Asia Minor; the Greek word refers to both "Gauls" and "Galatians." Conversely, the people whom Paul bluntly scolds as "You stupid Galatians" (*Galatai*) in Gal 3:1 would have been "Gauls" to Nero (*Galli* in the Latin master tongue). Indeed, the terms "Galatia" and "Galatians"—curiously, the only two concrete names and contextual markers Paul employs throughout his epistle—are not sufficient for efforts even to locate the recipients securely in Roman Asia Minor, today's Turkey: From a strictly lexical perspective, the whole letter that Paul addresses to the "assemblies of Galatia" (*ekklēsiai tēs Galatias,* Gal 1:2) could as well have been directed to the

1

Roman province(s) of *Gallia*, contemporary France, some fifteen years before the rebellious Julius Vindex would ascend to power there.[1]

As we shall see, from Nero's perspective in the West, Galatians (or Gauls), Jews, and Christians as well had one thing in common: all were suspected of subverting law and order. The iconography evident in Roman artworks and monuments—like the Dying Trumpeter on the cover of this book, or other masterful sculptures of Dying Gauls or Dying Galatians such as the one Nero saw on his way from Naples to Rome, or (an object that will receive more sustained attention below) the Great Altar at Pergamon— makes clear that in Roman eyes, Gauls/Galatians were objects of beauty precisely in their agony as they succumbed to the disciplinary blows of their imperial masters. This is how Paul himself and many of his brothers and sisters would eventually see death at Rome, about a decade after the Galatian controversy and less than ten years before Rome struck the final blow against the Jewish insurgency.

Beyond the complex meanings and identities conveyed in Greek or Latin, the universal language of images was clear and consistent with regard to Galatians/Gauls. Visually, they long occupied the Roman imagination as archetypal enemies, quintessential barbarian intruders, remaining dangerous even after their defeat. They were the favorite subject of a whole genre of victory art conveying a single message, the same message that had so reassured a troubled emperor in 68 C.E.: the inevitability of unconditional surrender to Rome.

This, then, is the common ground between the Jew Paul and the Gaul Vindex: the land of Gauls and Galatians seen as contested space under Roman supremacy. We can no longer keep first-century Gauls and Galatians as neatly separated from each other as we have long been accustomed to do. Both were Celtic peoples. And although throughout the centuries of Christian interpretation they have mostly been confined to a scriptural and dogmatic existence alone, Paul's Galatians had a life outside the New Testament, a quite turbulent life that has been widely ignored by their theological interpreters. Because the imperial representation of this people and the ideology that informed that representation will be focal topics of this study, it will be necessary to trace some of the dramatic history of the Roman-Gallic (Galatian/Celtic) encounter. The terms *Galatēs* (Galatian) and *Galatia* were crucial building blocks in the ideological construction and justification of empire; they were used with a range of meaning that is usually missing

Fig. 1. Coin struck by Gaius Julius Vindex, Roman governor of Gaul, during his rebellion in 68 C.E.; the inscription "The Genius of the Roman People" expresses Vindex's claim to represent the best interests of his subjects (see epilogue below). British Museum; photo by Werner Forman/Art Resource, N.Y.

from our theological dictionaries. Nevertheless, this "surplus" of meaning is crucial for making sense of Paul's exchange with his Galatian congregations.

My purpose here is not to relocate the Galatian correspondence to Gaul, or to add one more opinion to the perennial debate about whether its addressees inhabited the North or South of the Roman province in Asia Minor. Rather I seek a more comprehensive understanding of the letter by locating Gaul/Galatia in the Roman imagination, in the world of the *eidos* (form, shape) and *eidōlon* (image, idol)—that is, at the intersection of ideology and idolatry. On the ideological map of the Roman Empire, Gaul and Galatia were twin provinces, clearly recognized by their common Celtic origin as *antitopoi* of Roman law, order, and religion. Like the Greeks before them, the Romans knew the land inhabited by the Celtic peoples as barbarian territory par excellence. It was populated by a particularly hostile race who, after five centuries of godless and irrational onslaughts against the sacred shrines and foundations of Greco-Roman civilization, had at last been subdued and assigned their place within the god-willed system of worldwide Roman rule, whether in Italy or Spain, Britain or France, Greece or Asia Minor. Nevertheless, Galatians/Gauls retained a notoriously indomitable tendency toward lawlessness which lurked always just beneath their newly civilized demeanor, as the example of Gaius Julius Vindex shows.

Roman authors frequently used the Latin term *terror* when they discussed Gauls/Galatians. We should understand the Gallic War not as a singular event under Julius Caesar but as part of an ongoing, multistage Greco-Roman campaign against a Galatian "global terrorism," an archetype that has informed later occidental warfare as well. The allusion to contemporary realities is meant to point to the enduring legacy of the Roman representation of barbarian peoples. As we have now entered into a new era of worldwide crusading against *terror*, these historical precedents are chilling reminders of an unresolved past.

We must also ask at last about the appearance of Paul on the highly charged battlefield of imperial representations, ancient and contemporary alike. Given that the ancient theater of war set the stage for subsequent wars down to our own day, what exactly is Paul's position and role on that stage? How do we see him, how do we read him on the blood-soaked terrain of Western war-making history?

Re-Imagining Paul

This book is a new effort to set Paul in the context of his world. It engages in the scholarly endeavor of a *critical re-imagination* that pays attention to two issues still widely neglected in Galatian studies. First is the power of Rome and the representation of that power in images, most notably the images of vanquished Galatia(ns) that have their most influential prototype in the imagery developed at Pergamon (Asia Minor) in the third and second centuries B.C.E. The scope of this inquiry is necessarily much broader than is common among historical introductions to the Galatian correspondence.[2] It draws into the dialogue between biblical text and its historical context a range of disciplines and research areas that often are not in communication: art history and exegesis, classical studies and New Testament scholarship, Celtic (Galatian/Gallic) studies and Jewish history, theories of ideology and theology, feminist criticism and postcolonial and empire-critical approaches.[3] The major burden of this exploration is the *visual* reconstruction of the Galatian world behind Paul's letter through the lens of ancient sources, images, buildings, spaces, and performances.

Second: this book seeks to re-imagine the historical context in which Paul and the Galatians met, not as an end in itself but as an element of a comprehensive historical-critical rereading (*relectura*) of the letter that has been handed down through history as the material imprint of their encounter. Though space does not permit a comprehensive exegesis of the letter, such a rereading of Galatians drives, informs, and molds the contextual inquiry throughout.[4]

Galatians is arguably the most influential letter Paul wrote. It became the core document of the Lutheran Reformation. But in the "history of ideas" it has also played a formative and often lethal role with regard to dominant constructions of self and other, of identity and opposite, of ally and enemy, throughout Western civilization and war making. The figure of Paul is deeply implicated in the collective conscious and unconscious heritage of the Christian occident. The patriarchal and "kyriarchal" slant (Elisabeth Schüssler Fiorenza) of the social master code as represented in Pauline interpretation and its firmly established hierarchies of dominating and dominated, insiders and outsiders, normative and heretic have been rightly exposed by feminist, liberationist, queer, and postcolonial critics of Paul over the past decades.[5] Women and slaves, in particular, have often been told in the name of Paul to submit to their masters and to know their place in the order of things. It is Paul of Tarsus, rather than Jesus of Nazareth, who is most often quoted to confirm the political status quo and to silence voices for social change as faith-less and dogmatically incorrect.[6] Perhaps more than any other letter, Galatians has contributed to the image of Paul as the theological protagonist of a triumphant Christian Self on the archetypal battleground of Galatia; the fierce fighter engaged in relentless dogmatic struggle with a hostile and inferior Other, his "Judaizing" opponents; and as the authoritarian spokesperson of a normative world order.

Is there a new way to read and hear Paul as we have not read or heard him before? Can we re-imagine a "liberating (of) Paul," in contrast to his prevailing representation as a misogynistic, homophobic advocate of a disembodied social conservatism and anti-Judaism—a representation firmly rooted in two millennia of Christian-occidental interpretation? Are we at a moment in history when we need to turn "scripture" against "tradition" again, holding the text over against its normative received reading?[7]

And what part in that new reading do the "historical" Galatians and their ideologically driven representations have to play? *Critical re-imagination* seeks to recover the precious seeds of an alternative meaning that never took root within the dominant history of occidental Pauline interpretation, especially after the emperor Constantine set in motion a history that would convert the Roman Empire to Christianity and conform Christianity to the empire.[8] By tracing the lines of horizontal social networking, economic mutuality, and nonviolent resistance that were prophetic enactments of Paul's missionary practice, one attempts to retrieve an image of Paul that was buried beneath the weight of post-Constantinian interpretation, and with that image, the visionary imagination of an alternative world order and a nonimperial way to make peace.

Over the past decades, Pauline interpretation itself has become a battleground. The challenges posed to traditional paradigms have been formulated from various vantage points, but principally move in two directions: toward an uncompromising deconstruction of hitherto established Pauline readings and of Paul himself, on the one hand, and, on the other, toward a more adequate historical-critical reconstruction of Paul in his historical context. While the latter in one way or another tries to liberate Paul from the "iron cage" built around him by occidental and Christian frameworks of interpretation—the legacy of Aristotle, Constantine, Augustine, Luther, and the Enlightenment—the former has analyzed and exposed the principles by which that "cage" is constructed. Not infrequently such analysis has indicted the figure of Paul himself as a co-architect of the oppressive binaries between Self and Other.[9] Though both impulses in different ways have substantially shaped my own work on Paul and are reflected in it, I lean undeniably toward the "reconstructionist" side. As I am convinced that scripture is re-imaginable outside the confines of the occidental pattern, that history matters, and most of all that *Paul* matters, I am vulnerable to being accused of a measure of "neo-orthodoxy"; but I alert the reader that the following re-imagination of Galatia(ns) and of Paul will yield some quite unorthodox results.[10]

Law Criticism and Empire Criticism

A major point of departure from the prevalent paradigm of Pauline studies was the emergence in the early 1990s of empire-critical studies, under the guidance of Richard Horsley, from within the Paul and Politics Group of the Society of Biblical Literature.[11] Drawing on the pioneering work of Dieter Georgi, Robert Jewett, Neil Elliott, and others in the United States and of forerunners like Adolf Deissmann and Klaus Wengst in Germany, this new exploration contributed invaluable groundwork to reveal the Roman context and the Rome-critical implications of Paul's theology and practice. The contextual framework of Paul's letters was fundamentally reconceived, culminating in the landmark publication of Robert Jewett's monumental Hermeneia commentary on Romans (2007), a volume that represents the first verse-by-verse effort to integrate the best of historical-critical and empire-critical scholarship in interpreting Romans.[12]

The letter to the Galatians up to now has not been subjected to a thorough exegetical exploration that considers the Roman Empire as a major textual and contextual factor. However, recent reevaluations of imperial religion and civic obligations by scholars such as Bruce Winter and Mark Nanos have provided helpful historical insights and impulses with regard to Gentile-Christian circumcision in the context of a concrete first-century Eastern civic setting (see chapter 5 below).[13] Aside from such studies, however, the exegetical "fine print" of Paul's combative rhetoric of "faith versus law" has yet to be understood in its correlation to a Roman imperial environment. The primary focus of empire-critical studies so far has been much more on Paul's world than on his words, on history rather than on theology. The result has been that Galatians and the doctrine of justification by faith have remained relatively untouched as the traditional strongholds of Protestant dogmatic theology, both being understood predominantly in abstract and timeless language far above any concrete historical realities. The reconstruction of Galatia that I present here, setting Paul's letter within the framework of the Roman Empire, is necessary groundwork for the larger critical task of reinterpreting justification by faith through an empire-critical lens.

This is a task driven as much by contemporary urgency as by historical interest. We live in a precarious time, when imperial globalization extends its grip ever more rigidly and destructively upon the planet, imposing a de facto martial law on whole populations, often under the aggressive auspices of nominal Christianity. War and peace, competition or solidarity, poverty and wealth, consumption and pollution have become questions of the very survival of humanity. Whether Paul's theology can (again) become a source of spiritual, social, and ecological restoration, whether the "universalism" of his world mission can be reconceptualized in terms of border-transgressive peace building and justice seeking rather than the aggressive justification of the Western Self and a mentality of conquest, has become a pressing theological question.[14] Pursuing that question requires first and foremost a reexamination of the core concept at the center of everything Paul says and does: justification by faith rather than by works of the law.

Jewish Torah or Roman Nomos?

To trace the historical meaning of Paul's criticism of the law, and thus of justification by faith, in the hermeneutical framework of Roman imperial language and representation is a rarely taken path, and it radically changes the way we read. We all know how much our interpretation of a text depends on how we imagine its context. Traditionally, what we had imagined as the context of Galatians was a dispute between Jews and Christians (or, more precisely, between Jewish Christians and non-Jewish "Gentile" Christians) as to whether circumcision was a religious requirement for non-Jews among the Jesus followers. Paul's "opponents" propagated Jewish law and works of the law (= circumcision), and against them Paul offered his passionately polemical countermessage as an advocate of Christian freedom and the Christ-gospel of justification through faith and grace (see fig. 2).

This imagined contextuality, which has so profoundly shaped our understanding of Galatians, illuminates one isolated segment of a larger historical picture but leaves the rest in the dark, thus rendering the fuller meaning of the letter practically invisible. The Roman Empire, in Paul's time the most basic reality of life for both Jews and non-Jews of all kinds, is programmatically obscured in this theological reading. Yet long before

Fig. 2. Anti-Judaism in the traditional reading paradigm of law and justification by faith

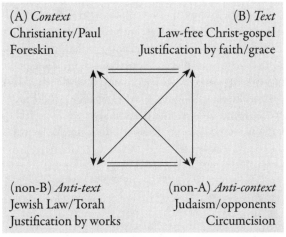

(A) *Context*
Christianity/Paul
Foreskin

(B) *Text*
Law-free Christ-gospel
Justification by faith/grace

(non-B) *Anti-text*
Jewish Law/Torah
Justification by works

(non-A) *Anti-context*
Judaism/opponents
Circumcision

Note: In this diagram, lines of opposition show that the positions of A and non-A, like B and non-B, are opposed to each other. Double lines indicate that A and B complement each other, as do non-B and non-A. Thus A is opposed to non-B and B to non-A. For a more thorough explanation of this "semiotic square" see p. 18 below and chapter 2.

Paul argued with the Galatians about law and freedom from the law in the Jewish "key" of circumcision, the polarity of *law versus lawlessness* was firmly established in the Greek, then Roman rhetoric of civilized warfare against the barbarians, and especially against the Gauls/Galatians. Such rhetoric permeated the public discourse in which Paul, in his own way, took part in his letter. This wider field of discourse must not be ignored when we venture to evaluate the hermeneutical framework of Paul's passionate criticism of the law. In starkest terms: What if Paul were targeting Greco-Roman imperial *nomos* much more than Jewish Torah?

A crucial result of the critical re-imagination offered here will be insight into the inseparability of the political, the ideological, and the theological threads that are interwoven in Paul's confrontation with the Galatians and his rejection of "law." I argue that it is not even plausible historically to imagine Jews and Galatians in Paul's time freely discussing and disagreeing about law and lawlessness in a secluded religious space, "Jewishness," without any political implications involving "Romanness." A strongly law-critical letter addressed to the "civic assemblies [*ekklēsiai*] of Galatia" (Gal 1:2) would hardly have been read in exclusively Jewish terms by the majority of non-Jews in the audience. Wherever Galatia was—South or North, East or West—it was a *Roman* location, as much as were Jerusalem or Judea. To perceive these places only as sites of "Judaism" is historically naive. And whatever the subject of contention between Paul and his "stupid Galatians" regarding *Jewish* law and *Jewish* affiliation, it was *Roman* law that ultimately defined and enforced what was licit or illicit.

Law as Power Construct (F. Nietzsche)

That Paul posed a challenge to Roman law and order is, in fact, not an entirely new discovery. Already toward the end of the nineteenth century, Friedrich Nietzsche, raised in the Protestant tradition and passionately enthusiastic about the Roman Empire, had fiercely indicted Paul as an anti-Roman rebel and rabble-rouser. The law, according to Nietzsche in his *Antichrist,* is in place to sanction the basic inequality between high and low in society, to safeguard the place of a small elite at the top of a pyramid of status and power with a middle level and the broad segment of the underclasses beneath them. This hierarchical split of humanity is justified by nature, Nietzsche declared; it is a natural and therefore sacred law that defies any demands for "equal rights" as lawless:

> The order of castes, the order of rank, merely formulates the highest law of life. . . . The inequality of rights is the first condition for the existence of any rights at all. (aphorism 57)[15]

This *nomos* of inequality, according to Nietzsche, is safeguarded by "noble warriors, and above all the king as the highest formula of warrior, judge and upholder of the law." Religion, on the other hand, is in place to proclaim, or actually to pretend, that this law has been installed by the gods and kept since ancient times—a kind of "holy lie" utterly necessary to maintain the proper order of things. In sum: "The source of wrong is never unequal rights but the claim of 'equal' rights" (aphorism 57).

Within this framework, Paul, in Nietzsche's view, represents the epitome of disorder and lawlessness, the mastermind behind the great upheaval from below that would eventually topple the grandiose structures of Roman power. His theology of the cross glorified the weakness, nothingness, and inferiority of the underclasses and outcasts. Paul thus subverted the natural social distinctions and political hierarchy, encoded as sacred law, that were necessary for life to prosper: the *nomos* underlying the Roman power structure. Christianity thus was the "vampire of the *imperium Romanum.*" Nietzsche saw the early Christian communities as a "cowardly, effeminate, and saccharine pack" that step by step alienated "those valuable, those virile noble natures" from Rome. Paul was this movement's distasteful and shrewd spokesperson.

> Then Paul appeared—Paul, the chandala [despised caste] hatred against Rome, against "the world," become flesh, become genius, the Jew, the eternal Wandering Jew par excellence. What he guessed was how one could use the little sectarian Christian movement apart from Judaism to kindle a "world fire"; how with the symbol of "God on the cross" one could unite all who lay at the bottom, all who were secretly rebellious, the whole inheritance of anarchistic agitation in the empire, into a tremendous power. (aphorism 58)

Profoundly knowledgeable about ancient history and the Roman Empire, Nietzsche never doubted that Paul was thoroughly "Jewish" and that the primary target of his law criticism was Roman law and order. He understood that in Paul the faith act—what happens between "me" and God—cannot ever be separated from its concrete social relevance, namely, its scandalous egalitarianism and concern for the Other, the weak, the sick, the excluded, the "feminine" and "unmanly."[16] Nietzsche was thus one of the most insightful proponents of re-imagining early Christianity as a gender-transgressive and empire-critical resistance movement from below—and at the same time, its fiercest antagonist.[17]

Law as Imperial "Compromise Formula" (J. Taubes)

In 1986, one hundred years after Nietzsche, Jacob Taubes, a Jewish philosopher at the Free University of Berlin and a student of Gershom Sholem, delivered shortly before his death a few seminal lectures on Romans. Despite their sketchy nature, these lectures again profoundly challenged the traditional understanding of Paul. A rabbi himself and thoroughly immersed in his own Jewish tradition, Taubes saw Paul not only as a "radical Jew" of the first century C.E., but also as a radical critic of Roman law and order(ing). The Pauline term *law*, according to Taubes, belongs in the realm of political theology and is "a compromise formula for the Imperium Romanum."

> All of these different religious groups, especially the most difficult one, the Jews . . . represented a threat to Roman rule. But there was an aura, a general Hellenistic aura, an apotheosis of nomos. One could sing it to a Gentile tune, this apotheosis—I mean, to a Greek-Hellenistic tune—one could sing it in Roman, and one could sing it in a Jewish way. Everyone understood law as they wanted to. See Philo, see Josephus: law as hypostasis.
> . . . I am not qualified (it's not so easy, I think) to sort out what Paul means when he says "law." Does he mean the Torah, does he mean the law of the universe, does he mean natural law? It's all of these in one.[18]

Taubes's insight is one of the decisive impulses behind the assumption of this book that in Galatians Paul does not abandon Jewish law but, on the contrary, wrestles, from a rigorously Jewish perspective, with a practice of Torah that has at least partly been "hijacked" and desecrated by Roman imperial law and religion.[19] Paul, as Taubes sees him, breaks out of the prevailing political compromise between patriotism and religion when he rejects the "consensus between Greek-Jewish-Hellenistic mission-theology" in terms of law. For Paul is "a zealot, a Jewish zealot" and radically "illiberal."[20] I decipher this "zeal" and "anti-liberalism" as Paul's radical commitment to the first and core commandment of Torah: the Oneness and Otherness of the God of the exodus whose "universal singularity" (to borrow a term from Alain Badiou) opposes the universal oneness of the divine Caesar.[21]

For Taubes, Paul's response to the "great nomos liberalism" he encounters is a protest and a "transvaluation of values." And as in Nietzsche, to whom Taubes explicitly refers, it is again the cross that subverts, or "transvalues," the established law:

It isn't *nomos* but rather the one who was nailed to the cross by *nomos* who is the imperator! . . . This transvaluation turns Jewish-Roman-Hellenistic upper-class theology on its
head, the whole mishmash of Hellenism. Sure, Paul is also universal, but through the "eye
of the needle" of the crucified one, which means: transvaluation of all the values of this
world.[22]

Torah Criticism as Affirmation of Roman Nomos

The idea of a Roman contextuality for Paul's theology of law, or of its empire-critical
implications, has not yet entered into the mainstream discourse of New Testament studies or of systematic theology. Rather, attention to Paul's theology in these disciplines
has been fixated more on the questions of Paul's Jewishness or anti-Jewishness, Greek-
ness or non-Greekness, and on the purely theological or anthropological nature of the
law debate in Galatians and Romans. That is understandable, given how central the
doctrine of justification by faith has been to the construction of Christian dogmatics.
Paul's declaration that "a person is justified not by the works of law but through faith
in Jesus Christ" (Gal 2:16) has been read predominantly either as a statement regarding individual faith, directed against Jewish "works righteousness," human "boasting,"
or religious self-righteousness in general (in the older Protestant and evangelical paradigm), or in contrast to Jewish "ethnocentrism" (in the New Perspective).[23] It has hardly
ever been seen in antithesis to Roman law and *its* self-justification through war, victory,
and power, or through meritorious "good works" attributed within the system of benefactions and euergetism that depended so heavily on competition for honor and social
distinctions based on shame.[24] Paul's generally positive attitude toward Roman law and
order was deemed to be sufficiently substantiated by casual references to Luke's book
of Acts, where Paul's Roman citizenship is asserted (though Paul never mentioned it in
his own letters). Furthermore, Romans 13 played a crucial role as proof-text of Paul's
allegedly pro-Roman stance.

The eclipse of the Roman context of Paul's text has inevitably channeled the full
force of his law criticism to Judaism alone. This substitution of an anti-Jewish Paul
for a Rome-critical Paul already starts in the New Testament itself, in the Acts of the
Apostles.[25] Arguably, such concealment of the empire-critical implications of Paul's
gospel was the only way it could survive in a canonized form agreeable to a Christianized empire. Yet the pro-Roman Paul needed an anti-Jewish double to be sustainable,
to "absorb" and politically neutralize the critical statements about law that are so prevalent in Galatians and Romans. The implications of this observation are vast. It means
that Paul more or less fell prey to a major "identity theft" and that the concepts of law
and disorder, of Self and Other, and of male and female that we have come to conceive
and confess, or to criticize and condemn as Pauline are highly deceptive. Instead, our
misconceptions of Paul's gospel depict the world as ordered in the image of Caesar, the
eidos (form, shape) and *eidōlon* (image, idol) of a master order that the historical Paul
himself opposed as idolatrous.

Long after his encounter with the risen Christ on the road to Damascus, Paul underwent a second "conversion" in the Christian imagination, one that turned him posthumously into the mouthpiece of the very imperial order that had originally executed him as enemy and Other. Only four years before he rushed into battle against Gaius Julius Vindex in 68 c.e., the same Emperor Nero had in the aftermath of the Great Fire in Rome publicly declared the *Chrestiani* to be arsonists and state enemies. In a carefully staged super-spectacle he cruelly punished them for an alleged "terrorist" plot against the city of Rome, a plot that had probably sprung from his own head. Paul, in all likelihood, was among the victims. Whether he was beheaded "according to the law of the Romans" during a trial or at Nero's personal decree, as stated in the second-century *Acts of Paul*, or whether he died anonymously with his Roman sisters and brothers during the Neronian massacre, it was for his transgression against Roman law and order that he eventually had to pay with his life.[26]

Re-Imagining Justification by Faith

The pro-Roman Paul's concern with order and the theological Paul's opposition to Judaism belong together in a kind of murky twin existence that eventually made the apostle to the nations admissible among the founding fathers of Western civilization. The theological price to be paid for this political makeover was high. At the heart of a gospel proclaimed and practiced "from below" as a message of global reconciliation among the vanquished nations of the Roman Empire, another message, a universal declaration of war "from above," was anchored. Justification by faith and grace, the innermost core of Paul's teaching, was turned into the Magna Carta of Christian anti-Judaism. Once expressed in the deadly binary logic of Us versus Them, this doctrine could resurface with a ghostly versatility as a powerful ideological weapon in subsequent warfares conducted by the Christian occident against its "Others," including the "other" religion, the "other" race or class, the "other" sex or sexual orientation, the "other" faith regarded as "deviant" in its social vision or way of life.

Constructing the Protestant Other (M. Luther)

It is instructive to consult Martin Luther on this point. Luther lectured twice on Galatians, in 1519 and 1531; his imprint on the interpretation of Galatians has proven momentous. His self-confessed love affair with Galatians as his "dear epistle" proved seminal for the Reformation.[27] Yet his description of the theology of justification in the introduction to his 1531 commentary appears less as a love message than as a sword irrevocably and irreconcilably dividing humanity into two categories: proper (Protestant) Christians, on the one hand, and, on the other, everyone else, aligned with Satan, law, works, and sinfulness.

For if the doctrine of justification is lost, the whole of Christian doctrine is lost. And those in the world who do not teach it are either Jews or Turks or Papists or sectarians. For between these two kinds of righteousness, the active righteousness of the Law and the passive righteousness of Christ, there is no middle ground.

. . .

We see this today in the fanatical spirits and sectarians, who neither teach nor can teach anything correctly about this righteousness of grace. . . . To be sure, they invent new names and new works: but the content remains the same. So it is that the Turks perform different works from the papists, and the papists perform different works from the Jews, and so forth. But . . . the content remains the same, only the quality is different. . . . For they are still works. And those who do them are not Christians, they are hirelings, whether they are called Jews, Mohammedans, papists, or sectarians.[28]

In Luther's perception, the Galatian antitheses of righteousness by law and works versus righteousness by Christ and grace obviously merge into a single universal dichotomy that splits the world into a battlefield with clearly defined hierarchical oppositions. A superior Christian (Protestant) Self as "in-group" is opposed to an inferior Other as "out-group," the latter encompassing such diverse antagonists as Jews, Muslims ("Turks/Mohammedans"), Catholics ("Papists"), and socioreligious movements from below (the "fanatical" sectarians).

It is striking that, for Luther, the highly diverse social practices and identities of completely disparate antagonists—like Jews, Catholics, or heretics (including the rebellious commoners of the German peasants' war)—became entirely irrelevant when measured against the supreme criterion of faith versus works. Read with contemporary eyes, the appearance of "Mohammedans" (Muslims) among the collective body of faith's opponents is particularly troublesome, as we now face the global emergence of a new, militant, Western anti-Islamism obsessed with the superiority of Christianity.

The almost limitless versatility by which Luther's construction of an "enemy" can be made to generate an even broader variety of "adversaries" is based on philosophical rather than theological assumptions. Once Paul's antithesis of grace-and-faith versus law/works righteousness was taken out of its concrete historical context and turned into a totalizing construct, justification by faith could be transformed into an abstract idea, a disembodied principle of "universal truth" behind and above contingent reality. It could be applied in diverse situations yet always embedded in a structural dichotomy between Self and hostile Other.

To be sure, Western idealism, with its inherent bifurcation between a higher, absolute realm of immutable ideas and pure essence over against inferior material phenomena, is older than Luther's appropriation of Paul. Indeed Luther could rely on the prior marriage of Paul and the Platonic/Aristotelian tradition in his own polarization of faith over against the combined mass of Jews, Turks, "Mohammedans," and sectarians under the categories of works and law. Western appropriations of Paul have extended the ancient dichotomies of spirit/flesh, good/evil, and active/passive to incorporate such diverse groups as Jews, women, savages (whether "natives" or "foreigners"), slaves, people of color, the lower classes, and homosexuals under the broad rubric of Otherness, construing all these groups alike in terms of their inferiority, their materiality, their passivity, their sheer differentness, as measured against the dominant Christian male.[29] Daniel Boyarin has shown that through this construct of Otherness, for example, "Jewish" and "female" could come to be paradoxically equated:

> Throughout the history of Christian Europe, Jews and women have been vilified in many of the same terms. The (male) Jewish body has been feminized: male Jews menstruate in the folklore of much of Europe, and circumcision has been repeatedly blamed for the femaleness (weakness, passivity) of the Jew.[30]

The accommodation of Paul to the Platonic and Aristotelian tradition happened after the apostle himself. As we shall see, the philosophical and theological constructions that have marginalized historical reality as much as they have stigmatized the position of the Other are not what Paul's theology of justification by faith in Galatians is about.

"Final Solution"

Despite—or because of—its privileging of the "disembodied" over the embodied, the pattern of constructing an enemy Other just described has had very corporeal and tangible effects on the lives and bodies of peoples through history. Paul's fierce wrestling with the "apostasy" of circumcision in Galatia has provided the paradigm that informed crusades, conquests, witch-hunts, and religious wars of all kinds. And twenty centuries after Paul, this paradigm eventually played a role in what was called the *final solution* of the *Judenfrage*, the Jewish question, a solution implemented with technological perfection in a Christian nation as the six-million-fold murder of Jewish men, women, and children.

Six million. Children. Women. Men.

At this point a detour through my own life experience is in place. I grew up in East Germany post World War II. My family lived in one of the sizable industrial towns in Lutheran Saxony, not far from the historic sites of the German Reformation that were the destinations of numerous family and church excursions. The story of Martin Luther throwing an inkpot at Satan during his stay at the Wartburg castle vividly captured my imagination as a child. The tour guide at the castle would gesture dramatically at a dark spot, surprisingly visible on the white wall of Luther's cell some four hundred and fifty years after the Reformer translated the New Testament into German in that same room.

But another childhood story bears recounting, a story my mother told over and over again. It was nothing more than a vague memory, a puzzled question that somehow never quite faded away. My mother had been an elementary student in the 1930s. Not long after Hitler seized power, she was invited to a birthday party where she was surprised to see the face of a classmate, a girl named Ruth, gazing through a fence from a neighboring garden. Had Ruth not been invited to the party? My mother did not understand why Ruth was on the other side of the fence and not at the party with all the rest of her classmates. Nor did she ask. Not long afterward, Ruth disappeared from the class altogether. Again, no one asked after her.

But my mother carried the question with her for years as if something hidden, something unspeakable, was driving her. She would only hint darkly at that something as she retold the story over the years. It took me some time to understand what had probably happened to Ruth and that the question was not the stuff of childlike innocence as I had first heard it. We learned about the Holocaust at school and went as a class to the Buchenwald concentration camp at Weimar, the town of Goethe and Schiller.

After the Berlin Wall fell in 1989, my hometown started an inquiry about the Jews who once had been its citizens. My mother donated a small pencil drawing from my grandfather's sketchbook to the newly opened synagogue. An avid painter, my grandfather had documented with a few strokes various scenes he encountered on his daily walks through the streets. As it turned out, this tiny piece of paper was the only preserved depiction of the remains of the old synagogue, drawn the day after the Nazis vandalized and burned the synagogue in 1938.

In the course of the inquiry my mother also found out something else. Ruth was alive, at an address in New York only a few blocks away from where my mother's grandson was going to school. She wrote Ruth a letter and received a reply. The two women started to correspond and, at last, decided in 2002 to meet. I will never forget the two of them, both over eighty years old, sitting one evening at our dining table on the Upper West Side in Manhattan. They talked for hours. They exchanged childhood memories, tentatively, searchingly: the name of a teacher, of a classmate, of a pastry shop, of an acquaintance who didn't "make it out." My mother fell silent, overwhelmed with unspoken relief, when Ruth declared that she didn't remember the birthday party when they were twelve. She had no recollection of the fence.

She told a long and dramatic story of escape and survival. At last she and her family had resettled in New York. She and my mother sat and talked intensely, without pause, in German, their conversation carrying them beyond the Holocaust, across half a century, beyond the Iron Curtain, from Europe to America.

I regard that evening as one of the moments when I have come closest to the miraculous, healing presence of the *ruach* in my life, the mending power of the Spirit that transcends murderous boundaries and deadly wounds. It was not long after the World Trade Center towers had fallen and any dream of worldwide reconciliation that might have been nurtured after 1989 was suffocated in a nightmare of war and violence. Since that evening it has become more urgent for me to re-imagine my Lutheran heritage—and to revisit Paul's Galatia in search of his "true" story. Part of the energy in this scholarly exploration is a desire to find out whether, after all and against all odds, the dream of peacemaking and justice seeking between East and West, North and South, those inside and those outside the "fence"—Jews and

Christians, Christians and Muslims, poor and rich, civilization and nature—might have a chance with the apostle.

Galatians and the Occidental Semiotics of Combat

The most serious challenge that a present-day re-imagination of Paul and his signature doctrine faces is to confront the apostle's role—specifically, the role of "the *Protestant Paul*"—in what Emilie Townes has called the "cultural production of evil."[31] Irreconcilable polarities—between law and faith, between Jews and Christians—seem inextricably woven into the fabric of justification theology and mark the heart of the problem. Galatians is not only the most influential but also the most polemical letter Paul wrote. On the one hand, it contains the outstanding declaration of unity in Gal 3:28, a declaration that programmatically bridges the gap between One and Other—Jew and Greek, slave and free, male and female—and that has had a lasting influence on egalitarian movements throughout church history. On the other hand, Paul consistently develops his argument in Galatians by means of antithetical binaries: faith versus works; grace versus law; Christ versus law; justification by faith versus justification by law or works (see Gal 2:15-21).

This dichotomizing aspect of Paul's arguments is tied to an overt hostility and rhetoric of rejection that surface already at the outset of the letter as Paul hurls an *anathēma* against his opponents (1:9).[32] Their demands on the Galatians to accept circumcision (6:12) seem so clearly marked as "Jewish" that Paul's insistence on "foreskin, not circumcision" has almost inevitably been read as anti-Jewish. Galatians and its advocacy of justification by faith rather than law have come to appear as the foundational event in the history of a Christianity defined by its aggressive negation of its Other, Judaism (see fig. 3). The Galatians themselves—or rather, their circumcision-preaching renegade teachers—have become the raw material for countless dogmatic remakings, being transplanted and re-embodied innumerable times. Like stones of an ancient building site, Paul's debates were reused, reshaped, reconfigured in the countless battles of the Christian occident. After his adversaries in Galatia had become "Jews" opposed to the "Christians," starting not long after Paul in the second century with his most enthusiastic (and troublesome) disciple Marcion, they later became "pagans" opposed to the faithful, or savages opposed to the civilized, or social rebels opposed to the "orderly," or heretics of all kinds opposed to the orthodox. Despite their striking diversity, all these identities had one feature in common: they represented the "wrong religion" and the Other. Throughout church history, Galatian faces can be traced behind the face of the enemy, the inferior, the outsider. Wherever "Galatia" was, it was inhabited by the antagonists who contended against proper Christian faith.

This pattern, however, is the invention neither of Martin Luther nor of Paul, nor of the Platonic-Aristotelian tradition in general. Rather it has a very concrete, "pagan," and most "unholy" precursor. Already in antiquity, images of Galatians (Gauls) were

Fig. 3. Protestant reading of justification by faith and its "opponents"

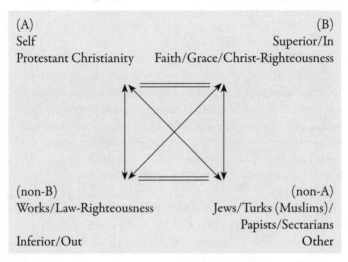

(A)   (B)
Self   Superior/In
Protestant Christianity   Faith/Grace/Christ-Righteousness

(non-B)   (non-A)
Works/Law-Righteousness   Jews/Turks (Muslims)/
                                                        Papists/Sectarians

Inferior/Out   Other

prolifically exploited for the perennial ideological (re)production of the hostile Other. They were represented as foes to be conquered and assimilated by the Hellenistic or Roman Self. Their image could effortlessly be switched back and forth between primeval "Giants" and the most recent reincarnation of the enemy, between the cosmogonic arch-battle against Chaos and the battlefields of the here and now. One of the crucial questions posed by the investigation that follows is how and to what extent the codification of justification by faith derived from Galatians came to be reabsorbed into this older, pre-Christian pattern of enemy construction, and thus turned upside down. That is, how did Paul's messianic justification of the vanquished Galatian Other become the justification of the victorious occidental Christian Self?

In terms of iconography, the imagery of Galatians as Giants, as Enemies, and as Others found its most powerful expression at the Great Altar of Pergamon. The Great Altar will provide the visual focus and anchor of this investigation. Showing the heavenly triumph of the Olympian gods in their cosmic battle with the rebellious Giants (the "Galatian" sons of Mother Earth), it exhibits the victory of order over chaos, law over rebellion, religion over blasphemy. These are the primordial elements of an occidental religion of conquest that glorifies and justifies the triumphant Self in its "sacred" right to subdue and vanquish the weak, the inferior, the ungodly, and Earth itself. The imagery and symbolic universe of the Pergamon Altar represent precisely the bifurcated "semiotics of combat" that has molded the structures of Western thought and that, despite its profoundly idolatrous origin in a primeval world war of the Olympic gods, has come to serve as the prevailing interpretational framework of Paul's theology of justification as the justification of Self over against the Other.[33]

Pauline Binaries Revisited

Philosophically speaking, this antithetical way of framing the world as Self over against the Other is based on the ancient conception of binary opposites. Tables of opposites as a device for explaining the deep structure of the cosmos were introduced into philosophical discourse already by Pythagoras and were used by Plato and Aristotle (*Metaphysics* 986a 22-25). They were typically organized in two oppositional columns, of unequal weight and value. The items listed on one side were complementary to each other in some way and, at the same time, opposed and superior to their counterparts in the other column:

superior—inferior
finite—infinite
odd—even
one—many
right—left
male—female
rest—motion
straight—crooked
light—darkness
good—evil
square—oblong[34]

Within this framework, a polarity like *male versus female* is embedded into several other sets of hierarchical dichotomies like *one versus many* or *good versus evil*. On the other hand, the terms on the dominant side, like *male, one*, and *good*, are linked to and complementary with one another. In the same way, terms on the inferior side, *female, many*, or *evil*, are also bound together as complementary. On this pattern, any of these polarities could be linked to other sets of dualisms, for example, *form versus matter*, *soul versus body, active versus passive, substance versus accident. Male* thus became tied to *form, soul, active*, and *substance*; on the other hand, *female* to *matter, body, passive*, and *accident*.

This structure of hierarchical dualisms was seen as the innermost building principle of the world in its entirety, the foundational order of *kosmos* itself. According to the Alexandrinian Jew Philo, a contemporary of Paul, the very act of creation was the division of everything into opposite contraries: First the heavy (or thick) was separated from the light (or subtle), and then each of these two opposites was divided again into the four elements of fire, air, earth, and water (*Quis Rerum Divinarum Heres* 133–34). That means that air and fire belong together under the rubric of *light* or *subtle*, whereas earth and water can be grouped under *heaviness* or *thickness*. At the same time, air and fire are opposed to earth and water.[35]

This quadrinomial pattern underlies my (slightly modified) use of the Greimasian "semiotic square," which I will employ as an exegetical tool in this investigation.[36] The semiotic square represents the meaning or semantic inventory of a text (in the widest sense) through oppositional and complementary relationships between the terms or concepts present in it. In so doing it thus provides a basic structure of signification. For example, if we try to arrange the four elements of the *kosmos* in the order described by Philo, the following diagram emerges:

Fig. 4. Elements of the cosmos

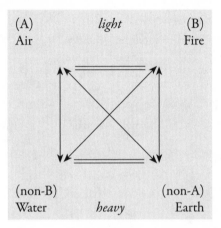

Air, fire, water, earth are grouped into the four categories of A, B, non-A, and non-B that are related to one another in three different ways. First, the A term, air, stands in opposition to non-A, earth, and B, fire, to non-B, water. Second, A, air, aligns with and is complementary to B, fire, as both are defined as "light" or "subtle"; similarly, non-A, earth, aligns with non-B, water, as they are gathered under the rubric of "heavy" or "thick." Third, A, air, is also in opposition to non-B, water, as B, fire, is in opposition to non-A, earth. Thus we see that there is a hierarchy between the two pairs of opposites: Water and earth are "lower" and secondary; air and fire are "higher" and superior.[37] I have used this model of a semiotic square with regard to the Pauline pairs of opposites in figs. 2 and 3 already and will return to it in chapter 2.

Starting already in the Pythagorean tablet of opposites, the upper and superior side of the binary structure is associated with the essence and univocity of the One, which is unchangeable, and "Sameness," or "identity," whereas the inferior counterpart represents difference, diversity ("many"), and therefore Otherness.[38] As we have seen already, this not only meant the degradation of the bodily and material world per se; it also led to the perception of truth as "one" and universal, residing in the world of ideas above and beyond all concrete material realities, strongly opposed to any dissidence or aberration looming in the difference and apparently accidental diversity of the material world.[39]

What made this ontology so damaging was that it inevitably implied a hierarchical, power-oriented anthropology and sociology as well. The dominant side was always linked to the male as belonging to the higher world, active and form-giving, whereas the female was assigned the inferior and passive counterpart linked to the body and materiality (as the linguistic relationship between matter and mother, in Latin *materia* and *mater,* betrays).

Superior:	*Male—form—soul—active—substance—One/same/Self*
Inferior:	*Female—matter—body—passive—accident—Other*

Already Aristotle had supplemented the *male-female* hierarchy by other power relations related to the order (*nomos*) of the household (*oikos*) or city-state (*polis*). These relations included, for example, the rule of masters over slaves or parents over children—but also the overarching superiority of Greeks over barbarians, a relationship directly relevant for the development of the constructed identity and representation of Galatians/Gauls/Celts as well.[40] At this point the philosophy of dominant principles turns out to be the principle of domination itself (see fig. 5).

This worldview, which orders everything and everyone into a series of binary polarities, undeniably has become the substructure of occidental Christian philosophy and civilization. Consequently it has had a profound impact on biblical interpretation as well. But how should we position Paul on this hierarchical and dualistic conceptual battlefield?

The Annihilation of the Antinomies (J. Louis Martyn)

In his exegetically and theologically momentous commentary on Galatians, J. Louis Martyn has tried to decipher the complex relationship between law, "elements of the

Fig. 5. Aristotelian binaries

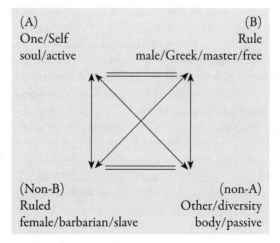

cosmos" (*stoicheia tou kosmou*), enslavement, and the pairs of opposites in Gal 4:1-11. He comes to the threefold conclusion that the "elements" in this text are synonymous with law and that the phrase *stoicheia tou kosmou* refers specifically to air, fire, water, and earth, or more precisely to these four elements in their oppositional structure, which is seen as the foundational order of the world. Martyn contends, however, that Paul wipes these binaries out and, with them, the old cosmos.[41]

This is a groundbreaking insight that has substantially advanced our understanding of Paul's theology. With Paul, according to Martyn, the philosophical and theological core presuppositions about the nature of the world/cosmos, of religion and of the religious Self are invalidated. The new creation that is the centerpiece of Paul's apocalyptic theology is "marked by anthropological unity in Christ . . . [it] does not have pairs of opposites."[42] This statement refers in particular to the oppositions between law and not-law, circumcision and foreskin. "The gospel of the cross announces the end of the *elemental* antinomy that formerly consisted of the law/not-law. What is gone, then, is the elemental pair of opposites that stood at the foundation of the entire cosmos of religion."[43]

My purpose here is to explore further this apocalyptic subversion (or, to use Martyn's term, "invasion") of the old cosmos by a nonbinary "new creation." What are the implications of such a subversion or invasion for the overall political, social, and military framework of Paul's world—not just the "religious"? For the hierarchical oppositions of Self versus Other or law versus lawlessness form the "cosmic" substructure not only of religion per se but, in particular, of Roman religion too. Neither are these oppositions restricted to religion; rather they comprise Roman law and order(ing) as well. The "slavery" involved in these binary oppositions is both spiritual and physical, since it results from a systemic politics of conquest and is based precisely on the nexus between Roman religion, Roman law, and the Roman construction of Self and Other.[44]

This insight brings us back to the question of identifying Paul's opponents and to the specific binary relation that has governed Pauline interpretation throughout its history, namely, *Christians versus Jews.* If (following Martyn's suggestion) we regard Paul as having abandoned oppositional binaries, whom or what shall we say Paul still needs to oppose and even anathematize in this letter? The answer definitely cannot be "the Jews" per se. One of the most fundamental insights for our investigation is the recognition that the supposedly "Pauline" semiotics of Christianity versus Judaism that has so powerfully shaped the identity of Western Christianity and its constructions of power is, in fact, not a part of Paul's language at all: it did not even exist at his time. Throughout his letters Paul never calls himself or his congregations "Christian." Simple as this observation seems, it was a seminal discovery on the part of Krister Stendahl only a generation ago.[45] Both Paul and his uncircumcised, Christ-believing Galatians were still *part of Judaism.* In particular, the Paul of Galatians thinks in terms of *Jews versus Gentiles/nations* (*ethnē*), not Jews versus Christians. And he talks about integration of these other nations rather than juxtaposition.

While in this matter I agree with proponents of the New Perspective, I diverge from it in insisting that we must take account of how disturbing the Roman imperial repercussions of just the integration that Paul advocates would have seemed to some of his contemporaries. The Galatian turmoil was *not* caused by a Jewish "ethnocentrism" or particularism that stubbornly insisted on the circumcision of Gentiles for the sake of religious purity per se. Rather, Paul's "international" inclusiveness of Jews and Gentiles/Galatians created a problem *beyond* Judaism, a challenge to the overarching civic setting of the *polis*. The mixed messianic communities claimed an exempt status from public and imperial religion and thus behaved as if they were fully Jewish—yet they were not. Their behavior ignored and transgressed the firmly drawn religious and political boundaries between Self and Other and thus defied the established taxonomy that ordered society into high(er) and low(er), insider and outsider. That taxonomy of innumerable configurations was based on the "law" of binary oppositions. As we will see, the Paul-opposing circumcision party in Galatia was driven much more by concrete sociopolitical concerns than by purely religious anxieties. What *appears* as "Torah-rigorism" is, at least from Paul's perspective, primarily a matter of political accommodation, religious assimilation, and civic prudence within the dominant Roman framework of law and religion. It is Paul, not his opponents, who attacks the religious-political "compromise formation" of this law and its God(s), and it is Paul, not his opponents, who speaks from the standpoint of strict Torah obedience focused upon the "one God alone."

The Politics of the New Creation

At this point, the colorful picture of Paul as primeval Christian warrior, defending the purity of the Christian gospel against the onslaught of Jewish law and otherness, begins to fade. Another oppositional configuration emerges, however, in which the oneness of Abraham's God is posed over against the idolatrous oneness of the divine Caesar. The conquest-based alignment of the nations under Rome is now called by its proper name, *slavery,* opposed to the liberating unity of the nations in Christ, which is named *freedom* in a new, universal exodus event.[46] But this means that Paul's gospel is not the erasure of just any polarity, but is rather the emergence of a new polarity that marks the simultaneous existence of old cosmos and new creation in the time "that remains." And just here we touch on the most complicated problem in re-imagining Paul.

Again, I agree with Martyn that an apocalyptic antagonism between old and new, slavery and freedom, "flesh" and "Spirit" fuels the militancy of Paul's language and the performative power of the curse he pronounces (*anathēma,* 1:9). Yet despite its antagonistic structure, Paul's apocalyptic theology is *not,* as other scholars have suggested, essentially a restatement of the old binaries with their "kyriarchal" and belligerent dynamics.[47] New creation and old cosmos, Spirit and flesh are opposed to each other, but not as dominant Self and inferior Other; nor are they engaged in a war of conquest, properly speaking.[48] To the contrary, Paul's "war" against the existing world order that has crucified the Messiah is an "anti-war," a war of the wounded warriors and thus a war not to be fought in the old way. Instead of heroes, it mobilizes, as Nietzsche already perceived, the losers, the crippled and limping, the never-victorious, who are branded on their bodies and souls with the stigmata of the Dying Gauls/Galatians—or of a dying Jew like Paul himself (Gal 6:14-17). And even if it uses martial language and has an apocalyptic background, it is not the messianic reprise of the primeval world battle as represented at Pergamon. If one needs to call this "war," one must add that this conflict subverts any established semiotics of war-making. The powerful and all-pervasive hierarchical polarities of the imperial cosmos remain as the "last enemy" to be conquered (see 1 Cor 15:24-28), but their erasure means the erasure of the principle of enmity itself.

It is thus an evil order, one "already" and "not yet" disempowered by the new creation, that needs to be confronted, not an evil Other: for this evil order is located primarily in the dominant representation of the Self over against the Other. In this way the abandonment of the old binaries does not create a new "Christian" binary but produces a nonbinary space where the old cosmos and its meanings, including the old Self with its identities, prides, antagonisms, and alliances, is put to death and turned into Nothingness. The "battle cry" that Paul voices in the greeting formula and at the end of Galatians, as in every other letter, is "peace"; and his peculiar form of war-making he calls love, love of the Other (the brother) as oneself (5:13-15).

Because our very language and logic are shaped by the binaries of the old cosmos, the transformation Paul perceives is difficult for us to grasp and to articulate. Paul himself perhaps saw the messianic transformation much more in terms of an embodied spiritual discipline and practice than in terms of dogmatic discourse. If this transformation implies the loss of cosmos and of Self, it hurls the individual, to quote Martyn again, "into an abyss with no dimensions," as though a "fissure had opened up" under one's feet.[49] This unfathomable *terra incognita,* where the old meanings and identities are void, is the unconquered and unconquerable territory of the Messiah. It is marked by the nonimperial semiotics of a messianic faith-praxis and faith-act (rather than a faith-statement) that perpetually subverts the binaries of domination and the dominant Self. Much more than a new theory or theology, it is a new relationship and a new community practice, created out of "Nothingness"—*ex nihilo.* It is the practice of Selves who no longer try to vanquish their Others. This is a transformation that "works" only so long as it is won and occupied, not through a war against an Other, but through a radical transformation of the Self in solidarity with the Other: "Faith working through love" is the only thing that counts (Gal 5:6).[50] We will return to consider this almost "mystical" oneness between Self and Other—and its relationship to Albert Schweitzer's discussion of a Pauline "Christ-mysticism"—in chapter 6.

We see, then, in Paul's often paradoxical language what we might call a semantic invasion by the (nonbinary) "new creation" into the existing structures of meaning.

This language confuses established definitions of One and Other, while at the same time converting and reincorporating the concrete mutual relationships implied. For example, Paul may argue apodictically and in a seemingly "binary" fashion for freedom versus slavery among the Galatians, urging them to not submit again to the yoke of slavery (5:1). This might look like a restatement of the old social dichotomy of free versus slave, especially in the context of the allegory of Sarah and Hagar in 4:21-31.[51] A few lines later, however, he pronounces that this freedom to be defended means nothing else than slave service to one another (Gal 5:1, 13). This kind of speech renders the old ways of meaning making literally senseless.[52] It implies a specific "rhetoric of annihilation," or rather an embodied "poetics of subversion," and a complex communal transvaluation of the values and social practices underlying it. These features are often neglected and misrepresented when the focus of analysis and criticism is on Paul's "kyriarchal" or binary language as such.

Fig. 6. Imperial order/law versus messianic order/law

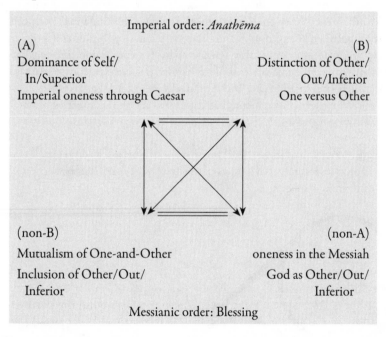

Imperial order: *Anathēma*

(A)
Dominance of Self/
  In/Superior
Imperial oneness through Caesar

(B)
Distinction of Other/
Out/Inferior
One versus Other

(non-B)
Mutualism of One-and-Other
Inclusion of Other/Out/
  Inferior

(non-A)
oneness in the Messiah
God as Other/Out/
Inferior

Messianic order: Blessing

Paul gathers the conquered nations, who lie at the bottom of the Roman conquest order as "others" opposed to the dominant Roman self, through a nonbinary practice of mutuality as one-an(d)-otherness. This not only requires a permanent discipline of self-othering that makes the Self abandon its privileged position and embrace the Other. It also remains itself other to the dominant order. For Caesar meanwhile continues powerfully to embody the superior self, claiming to be the sole force entitled to unite and capable of uniting and ruling these same vanquished nations of Jews and non-Jews "from above." Such unity "in Caesar" is achieved solely within the confines of the imperial logic of combat, an order that turns Self against Other in endless spirals of violence, competition, and oppression. This ongoing antagonism must be marked clearly and not erased in our interpretation: it is the "setting in life" of Paul's *anathēma*. It is not an antagonism between Judaism and Christianity, however, but an antagonism between a messianic way of life and an imperial order that claims to bless while it curses. Rather than the emergence of a new triumphant "world-religion," Paul's gospel means the rethinking of God and of religion(s) as such—that is, of all cultural representations of the sacred order in their world-shaping power—from the perspective of the Other (see fig. 6).[53]

Figure 6, on the one hand, is profoundly self-contradictory as it shows the messianic order, in "inferior" position, within an imperial binary and hierarchical construction of Self and Other. On the other hand, it demonstrates how this imperial construction is logically dismantled and annihilated as it depicts the messianic One/Self and God on the "wrong" and "inferior" side of the Other. The figure depicts the logical paradox of one-*and*-otherness, rather one-*versus*-otherness. From this "inferior" perspective, the opposition between A and non-A and between B and non-B thus collapses, and with it the cultural spaces of domination opened up by that opposition. The tensions inherent in this figure represent the real-life situation of a messianic existence within the old order. This same tension can, and should, also be depicted as an exodus-movement out of the old order, a movement that leaves behind the "combat semiotics" of the

Fig. 7. New creation as messianic transformation of Self and Other.
(The transformative dynamics of this messianic order will be further explained in chapter 6.)

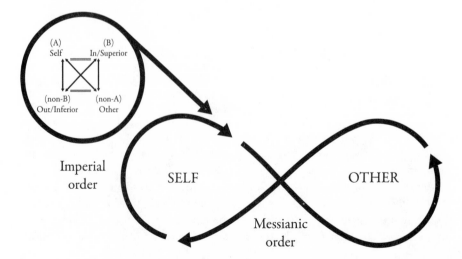

imperial binary cosmos. Such a movement establishes the messianic body in its "mystical" oneness of self and other, reflecting the oneness of the biblical God as otherness (see fig. 7).[54]

This discussion prompts a return once more to the "root" binary of Jews versus Christians that has so dominated scholarship on Galatians. The terminological insertion of "Christians," defined as properly justified selves in antithesis to improperly justified Jewish others, has permanently falsified and obscured the meaning of Paul's discourse and has reinfiltrated it with the imperial logic of battle, the "combat semiotics," that Paul's gospel implicitly dismantled and subverted. As a reminder that the term "Christian" is, with regard to Paul's time, an anachronism and, furthermore, that it now carries implicit connotations of self-justification that distort the other-directedness in Paul's thought, I will in what follows use instead the term "messianic," derived from the Hebrew word *mashiach*, anointed one, which was translated into Greek as *christos*, "Christ."[55]

Overview of the Book

Reopening the debate about the letter to the Galatians through a more comprehensive understanding of its Roman context, the following argument proceeds in five steps of principally historical and ideological deconstruction and reconstruction. Each chapter has a substantial introduction and conclusion that can be read on its own to become familiar with the overall plan. A final exegetical survey of the letter in chapter 6 relies on the critical re-imagination of the Galatian context accomplished in chapters 1–5 to decode the letter as a critique of empire and of the idolatrous imperial religion. This part, too, can be read on its own.

Chapter 1 addresses the visual presence of Dying Gauls/Galatians in classical antiquity. It confronts the "Christian" construct of Galatia and Galatians with a historical exploration that traces the ancient perception of the Gauls/Galatians—and the ideology behind that perception—over half a millennium. Substantial clashes with Greco-Roman civilization resulted in the Greco-Roman representation of Gauls/Galatians as prototypical barbarians, lawless and hostile others. Starting with the fateful Gallic/Galatian attacks at Rome in 387 B.C.E. and at Delphi in 279 B.C.E., and leading into a sequence of major conflicts with Pergamon and with Roman power in Asia Minor up to 189 B.C.E., these perpetual confrontations between civilized self and barbarian other paralleled the rise of Rome as an imperial power. Galatia is a crucial location on the ideological "construction site" of the Roman Empire: images of Dying Galatians/Gauls signified the empire's cosmic ideological justification.

Chapter 2 presents a semiotic analysis of the Great Altar of Pergamon as a paradigmatic image of the Dying Galatians/Gauls within the imperial law and religion of Western civilization. In imperial ideology, the identity of the superior self was constructed in symbolic "combat" with an antithetical and inferior other. This self drew its legitimacy to conquer, rule, and exploit others from the sacred power of its god-given victory over vanquished "barbarians," most prominently in the Roman case, the Galatian other. In Paul's time, the Great Altar had become an image of Roman law, world order, and imperial religion; at a somewhat later time this very altar was probably the target mocked as "Satan's throne" by the author of Revelation (2:13).

Chapter 3 deals with Roman imperial religion. Contrary to the prevailing description of that religion in terms of "polytheism" and religious tolerance, I trace a peculiar Roman "monotheism" that integrated polytheism but always (and often tacitly) placed the emperor and Rome at the center of the civic and religious cosmos as expressed, for example, in architecture or religious and political ritual. In my reading, this new type of universal imperial "world religion" is the main target of Paul's critique of idolatry (that is, we should say, of ideology). The imagery of Aeneas's shield in Virgil's *Aeneid* and the public spectacle of the Roman arenas are explored as "Pergamene" reperformances of the primeval battle against the Giants, fused with the battle against Galatians and Orientals that lay the foundations of cosmic order through the salvific deeds of the godlike victor. The arenas, for their part, functioned as "megachurches" of the empire, where, in a quasi-sacrifial act, the blood of the vanquished other was collectively consumed to establish the superior self as a social body, divinely sanctioned and legitimized.

Chapter 4 turns to the province of Roman Galatia in Paul's time, the actual destination of his letter. It explores the imperial "resurrection" of the Dying Gauls/ Galatians as *Sebastēni Galatai* (that is, "Augustan" Galatians) through a whole set of devices that reinscribed the Galatian body. These included the building of imperial roads, cities, temples, and dynastic power structures among the vanquished, the integration of the Galatians as soldiers into the war machine of empire, and most of all the performances and public rituals of imperial religion centered around the *koinon*, the provincial assembly, and the temple to Rome and Augustus at Ancyra, the provincial capital.

Chapter 5 deals with the specific issue at stake in Paul's letter, the issue of circumcision and foreskin. I decipher Paul's messianic community practice as a radical subversion of those Roman principles that governed the "ordering" of associations among the vanquished nations through relation to Rome. Nonimperial models of unity and practices of nonallegiance to imperial religion emerge as the two core issues signified by Galatian "foreskin." The clash between God-in-Christ and the divine Caesar was the focal point of conflict in Paul's letter—not primarily a confrontation between law-free Christianity and law-abiding Judaism; rather, we might say, the core conflict of Galatians was between messianic law and imperial law.

Chapter 6 moves at last from context to text and offers a "critical re-imagination" of the letter at the foot of the Great Altar of Pergamon. The first lines of Paul's letter in particular are read, on the one hand, in terms of a *visual* intertextuality with the Pergamene imagery and, on the other, in terms of *scriptural* intertextuality with the biblical root narratives of exodus and exile. This chapter establishes a basic exegetical model for decoding Galatians and justification by faith as an intervention into the imaginary construct of Roman imperial ideology and idolatry. The first commandment of Torah, with its anti-idolatrous emphasis on God's oneness and singularity, emerges as the key issue behind Paul's fierce attack on an "other gospel." Imperial "monotheism" and its "combat order" appear as the ultimate other rejected by Paul's theology of unity and construction of a new self. His inherent criticism of law is interpreted as the embodied practice of an alternative community based on love as self-othering, that is, the "loss" of the self as privileged and dominant, now in solidarity with the other.

An epilogue considers the two decades following the Galatian correspondence. It traces visual and textual clues that establish the imagery of Dying Gauls/Galatians, dying Jews, and dying "Christians" (including the image of "Christ crucified") as three strands of Roman imagination woven together into a single fabric during the Neronian massacre and the carnage that ended the Jewish War. In the context of the three Great Fires—first the burning of Rome (64 C.E.), then the burning of the state sanctuary of Jupiter Capitolinus (68 C.E.), and finally the defeat of Jerusalem (70 C.E.)—we see how the dying of both messianic and nonmessianic Jews came to serve as a cultural icon, urgently needed and willingly consumed to provide assurance to the Roman self. This icon perennially bolstered the ideology and idolatry of Roman peace through victory, just as the display of Dying Galatians/Gauls has done since ancient times. Paul's martyrdom is a part of this phenomenon.

A Methodological Postscript

Critical re-imagination is a method that supplements the traditional set of historical-critical and ideological-critical methodologies. It draws on images and other visual or written sources—including spaces, buildings, performances, and rituals—to deconstruct and reconstruct our perception of the ancient world in its interaction with the "word(s)" of the text. In stark methodological contrast to the prevalent hermeneutical pattern of a dematerialized and disembodied theological reading, *critical re-imagination* seeks to restore Paul, his Galatian congregations, and their dissention about justification by law or faith to their specific material, sociopolitical, and historical context.

Allowing Paul to be part of his "real world" changes the way we imagine him. It is a profound irony that, as I have suggested above, the perception of Galatia as a formative Christian battleground reflects much more of Roman imperial ideology than of Pauline messianic theology. Historically speaking, the Galatia of Paul's time was not first and foremost the place Christianity had to conquer from Judaism, but a region where Galatians and other nations had already been conquered by Rome. Firmly under Roman dominion, it was an ethnically diverse territory where Galatians, Jews, and other vanquished peoples had to come to terms with one another and with the omnipresent realities of Roman colonialism. When Paul wrote to the "assemblies of Galatia" sometime in the middle of the first century C.E., Roman power had already succeeded in molding the world in its image, Greeks and barbarians, Jews and nations/Gentiles alike, and in very special ways the Galatians as well. Historical recontextualization is therefore a prerequisite and essential part of re-imagination.

Critical re-imagination is a slow process that requires patience until we are able to see Paul and his world differently. For re-imagining Galatians in the light of images, most notably Pergamene and Roman images of Dying Gauls, is not an "illustration" of something we have already seen and read. Rather, it implies a "symptomatic reading" (Louis Althusser), aiming at an "illumination" to reveal the not-understood, the unheard, the unread in this text by opening our eyes, often in a sudden flash of recognition, to the vanished everyday realities behind the written words.[56] The defeated Gaul who turned up on Nero's way from Naples to Rome may help us see something of which we were not aware. He shows us that Romans and Galatians/Gauls were not on equal terms at Paul's time; he also communicates a core message about law and lawlessness as construed by the dominant. But the "law" of the dominant might have substantially differed from the worldview of the vanquished.

Here we are immediately involved in a fervent "clash of images." Images are, to use an expression of art historian Natalie Kampen, the "mental wallpaper" of the ancient world that shows what was before everybody's eyes—but what we unfortunately can no longer see when we read an ancient text. Images are also the medium that in any culture portrays how the world *should* be perceived. They are not simply natural: rather they represent what is normative *as if it were* natural and obvious. The *eidos* (shape, form) of the images is the visualization of ideology (not accidentally, both terms are semantically related to the Greek verb *idein,* "to see").[57] Nero's relief as he sees the depiction of a victorious Roman equestrian cherishing his triumph over the crushed Gaul was the comfort of seeing the world mentally restored to its proper appearance and "lawful" image, even as he was preparing to face the still pending military task of restoring the rebellious and lawless Gaul to its proper state of peace and submission. Again, from the perspective of the Gaul being dragged along by his hair beneath the Roman's horse, the world and its dominant law must have looked very different. But this, of course, was precisely the "forbidden" and "wrong" perspective. The display of the heroic scene was meant to serve both to reassure victors and to infuse the conquered with shock and awe—nothing else. Dealing with images and imagery to re-imagine Galatia and Galatians requires that we reflect on the politics of seeing and of making something (un)seen.

With whose eyes, then, did Paul see—from above the horse or from beneath it, with the eyes of the vanquished or of their conquerors? This is the essential question that runs through the present study like Ariadne's thread leading through the labyrinth. The classical image in Christian art of Paul having fallen from his horse, traditionally linked to his pivotal transformation at Damascus, might itself point to an unseen reality beneath the surface of the all-too-familiar icon. As we leave the well-trodden paths between South and North Galatia and move to less-explored trails from East to West, trails that all merge at last on the road map of the Roman Empire, we are looking for signposts redirecting our imagination. What were a law-critical Jew called Paul and his circumcision-leaning Galatian communities *really* wrestling with and quarreling about, in their own world and at a time when the dominant civilization and religion were not yet Christian but Roman?

Surrounded by Roman conquerors, Gallic/Galatian warriors flee in panic; one is trampled beneath the horses of a chariot. Fragment of a terracotta frieze from a Roman temple, early second century B.C.E. Museo Civico Archeologico, Bologna. Photo: Erich Lessing / Art Resource, N.Y.

CHAPTER ONE

Remapping Galatia

In Search of a Displaced Context

It was hardly a coincidence that Nero, on his way back to Rome at the beginning of the great uprising in Gaul, could come across that monument of a defeated Gaul that so immediately communicated victory to him. Visual representations on Roman monuments of debilitated Gauls or Galatians were widespread all over Italy and throughout the Roman Mediterranean. Anyone who traveled as much as Paul did as he carried out his mission among the nations would have encountered these representations.

As we shall see, from the beginning of the Celtic presence in the Mediterranean region in the fourth century B.C.E., Gauls had become a topic of visual art. Their images appear in various settings, in different materials, styles, and thematic representations: adorning temples, urns, and sarcophagi, cast in stone on triumphal arches or painted on vases, hardly visible on tiny coins or physically overwhelming in monumental marble sculptures set up in lavish Roman villas. All these depictions had one thing in common: In one way or another they deal with the Gauls in the context of war and victory.[1]

Whether depicted as enemy invaders or as robbers and plunderers of sacred sites, the perennial pose assigned to the Gauls/Galatians in ancient iconography is the same as Nero saw on that monument: they are failing and falling, dying or dead. Their depiction never leaves any serious doubt as to whether in their contest with other peoples the Gauls were the winners or the losers. Some of the representations, most notably the sculptures of the so-called Dying Galatians/Gauls, are of outstanding artistic quality and very famous. The Dying Trumpeter, which appears on the cover of this book, or the Suicidal Galatian who kills himself and his wife to avoid capture by the Romans, have with their superior beauty and eminent pathos captured Roman and Western imagination over a span of more than two millennia.

These two images of "Large Gauls," like their more numerous and less sizable counterparts, called "Small Gauls/Galatians" by art historians, are believed to have originated from Pergamon in Asia Minor in the third and second centuries B.C.E.[2] Geographically, then, we might regard them as representations of the direct ancestors of Paul's Galatians. None of the Pergamene originals has survived, however, and the copies we can see today are exclusively Roman. Judging from the sheer quantity of Dying Gauls/Galatians that are gathered today in museums all over Europe, the images enjoyed great popularity in the Roman world, and their visual presence in

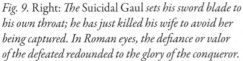

Fig. 8. Top: *The* Dying Trumpeter *or* Dying Gaul, *marble; commonly described as Roman copy of a Pergamene original from 230 to 220 B.C.E.; Musei Capitolini, Rome. Photo: Erich Lessing, Art Resource, N.Y.*

Fig. 9. Right: *The* Suicidal Gaul *sets his sword blade to his own throat; he has just killed his wife to avoid her being captured. In Roman eyes, the defiance or valor of the defeated redounded to the glory of the conqueror. Roman copy of a Pergamene original. Museo Nazionale Romane, Pallazzo Alltemps, Rome. Photo: Scala/Ministero peri Beni e le Attività cultural; Art Resource, N.Y.*

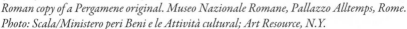

public and private spaces must have been both massive and arresting. Nero himself had taken statues of Dying Gauls/Galatians from Julius Caesar's gardens on the Esquiline Hill and placed them in his "Golden House."[3] Similar sculptures were probably set up in the Baths of Agrippa in the Field of Mars to commemorate Caesar's victory over the Gauls;[4] and when Vespasian celebrated his triumph in the Jewish War by erecting a temple of peace, he placed those statues there together with the spoils from the Jerusalem temple.[5]

None of these images has played a role in traditional theological reflections on the context of Galatia or Paul's letter to the Galatians. Although the monumental evidence shows that official Hellenistic and Roman representations of Galatians as a people were virtually omnipresent in Paul's world, New Testament scholarship has almost completely elided the presence and the imperial contexts of these representations (even as Western theology has tacitly relied on their negative valency regarding the barbarian other, as discussed in the introduction). Yet these artistic representations and their historical contexts are crucial for re-imagining Paul's world and for correcting what has all too frequently been a decontextualized reading of the letter.

Our starting point is the uniformly negative image of Galatia and Galatians as the epitome of barbarian lawlessness that we encounter not only in visual depictions but in ancient written sources as well. These indicate a very specific and complex semantic range for the words *Galatian* and *Galatia* in Paul's time—a range that has usually been neglected in contemporary theologically driven hermeneutics. The complexity of the conflicts between Gauls and the peoples they encountered and the compact library of historical and ideological narratives evoked by the first-century terms *Galatians/ Gauls* require an exploration of the history behind the words and images. Focusing on the three pivotal locations of Rome, Delphi, and Pergamon, I will trace four centuries of dramatic clashes between the Greco-Roman world and its Galatian Other that culminated in the establishment of the Roman Empire and Roman law across the Mediterranean.

As we will see, *Galatia*, a Greek term widely used in the ancient sources as synonymous with Latin *Gaul*, is not a neutral geographical or ethnic description. Neither can the term's reference be confined to any specific location, either north or south, in Asia Minor, where it has been traditionally (dis)placed. Rather Galatia stretches between west and east and up to the extreme north of the entire *orbis terrarum*, the Roman-dominated world. From a Roman point of view, it was the region populated by the Celtic "counternation," that is, a peculiar species of "universal barbarians" who, after centuries of struggle, had at last been forced into compliance with the "world-saving" power of Roman victory, at the threshold of the era of Jesus and Paul. This chapter's task is to establish and visualize Galatia as a focal *topos* on not only the geographical but also the ideological map of the Roman Empire. It is important first to note just how different that topology is from the conventional imaginary location of "Galatia."

Galatia as Primeval Battleground in the Christian Theological Imagination

Historical Galatia is virtually *terra incognita* in Christian imagination. While the Galatians themselves have over the centuries been preached from many pulpits and recruited for countless theological battles, they still seem to be much more at home in Martin Luther's Wittenberg and in the dogmatic mindscapes of Paul's modern or postmodern interpreters and critics alike than in the cultural and political environment where Paul first met them. A whole century of exhausting debates regarding just how we should locate and identify the addressees of Paul's letter has not led us very far; rather it has obscured the very contextual question it purports to address.

Unfortunately, the letter itself appears more secretive than other Pauline writings in terms of contextual markers. Giving away no concrete names or locations, it barely meets the minimal requirements of a standard letter opening: "To the assemblies [*ekklēsiais*] of Galatia" (Gal 1:3) sounds more like a conspiratorial concealment of the intended recipients' location than a proper address! But this is all we have to work with regarding the letter's destination. The apostle's angry outburst two chapters later, "You stupid Galatians" (3:1), does not clarify much in terms of either topology or ethnicity. So where is Galatia, and who are the Galatians?

Beyond North and South

Both questions have been extensively discussed in New Testament scholarship, with remarkably inconclusive results. Geographically, Paul's Galatia appears to be clearly located in central Asia Minor, today's Turkey, though its exact coordinates have been the subject of century-long debates. Even now the old alternative of a "South Galatian" versus a "North Galatian" destination is still the predominant contextual choice dividing scholars of Galatians, with well-established and well-known arguments on each side.[6] The proponents of the *North Galatian,* or *territorial, hypothesis* argue that in Paul's time the term "Galatians" (Gal 3:1) would be exclusively applied to ethnic Galatians inhabiting the old territory of three Celtic tribes that migrated into the central part of Asia Minor, around Ancyra, Pessinus, and Tavium, in the third century B.C.E. Advocates of the alternative claim that the reference is to the wider framework of the Roman province of Galatia that was established by Augustus in 25 B.C.E., which also included areas farther south around the cities of Pisidian Antioch, Iconium, Lystra, and Derbe and comprised a number of different ethnicities. This *South Galatian,* or *provincial, hypothesis* has the advantage of matching certain archeological data more satisfactorily;[7] it would also fit better than its counterpart the Lukan account of Paul visiting all these "southern" cities during his first missionary journey (Acts 13–14) and revisiting all of them again after the Jerusalem council, on his second journey (Acts 16:1-2). Only Acts 16:6-8 and 18:23, which give a summary statement of Paul's traveling through Phrygia and "the region of Galatia" (*Galatikēn chōran*), could be read as supporting the idea that Pauline congregations might have existed in North Galatia, on the assumption that these were founded during the second journey but not named in Luke's account of that journey.[8]

The geographical problem of "north" or "south," discussed with almost ceremonial zeal in the prefaces of all standard literature on Galatians, probably cannot be resolved on the basis of the literary and archeological information accessible to us so far, and is not the subject of this chapter. Rather I wish to inquire about the ideological scope of a question that has produced such scholarly fecundity and kept generations of exegetes passionately engaged. The debate about North or South Galatia is at best relevant for the data of Paul's biography and his missionary itinerary, but its impact on the actual interpretation of Galatians as a text and the much-needed clarification of its sociohistorical context has been marginal. More pointedly, one could perceive it as a model case of a self-contradictory research strategy in which, in the very effort to "contextualize" Galatians, scholars have produced the remarkably decontextualized reading that has become prevalent. Reviewing the standard literature on Galatians, one is struck by how little the question of north or south occupied attention once the introductory exercises were completed and exegetical attention could be turned to issues of more presumed importance for theological interpretation (that is, issues other than concrete sociohistorical reality).

Once transferred to a purely theological realm, the "Galatians" could be imagined dwelling far above worldly circumstances, wrestling with more transcendent questions regarding human sinfulness and whether they could be justified by faith in Christ alone, rather than by Jewish circumcision and "works" as well. Conspicuously absent in this imagined geography of religious spaces and counterspaces have been the Romans, the masters of the world in which Paul traveled and preached "among Jews and Gentiles" and in which the Galatians were presumably preoccupied with the sole question whether they should get themselves circumcised. It is surely ironic that we have entertained discussion of a "provincial hypothesis" as an introductory question but with very little concern for the Roman province of Galatia as a sociohistorical context for the letter's actual interpretation. That is, those who have asserted a southern location for Paul's Galatia have generally refrained from a closer look at the material and spiritual conditions under which his Galatians must have lived there or at the political setting that would have shaped their theological debates. One would not know from the standard New Testament textbooks that the Galatians paid taxes and tributes to Rome, or walked on Roman roads, or assembled at Roman temples; nor that they fought in the Roman legions or attended Roman meals and games. Were they concerned with how they might feed their children or fulfill their civic obligations? Did they fear punishment? Were they obligated to negotiate political compromises? None of this mattered to discussions of their "faith" (or their impending apostasy toward circumcision). Pale and abstract figures, they remained faceless and disembodied—except for the one striking male physical feature at the heart of the whole debate: their foreskins.[9]

Seen on these terms, the whole debate about North or South Galatia appears effectively to have filtered the historical data in such a way as to eclipse their theological relevance, or (to put the matter conversely) to suppress the historical relevance of the theological argument, thus neatly separating textual from contextual work, theological from social concerns. This seems a case of what Robin Scroggs has elsewhere referred to as an unreflective "methodological docetism" in New Testament scholarship,[10] an "idealism" that has shaped the interpretation of Paul and of Galatians until today. One concern in the present work will be to challenge that implicit docetism by emphasizing the concrete historical-material contextuality of the Galatian correspondence.

If the North–South controversy was not primarily about interpreting Galatians in its sociohistorical context, the dominant concern to reconcile Galatians with the apostolic itinerary of Acts, on the other hand, has allowed for Lukan themes to influence our perception of Paul and Galatia even more than Paul's letter itself. Luke's protrayal of Paul and his travel narrative in Acts has seeped almost imperceptibly into what has subsequently become the dominant image of the apostle. Thus, Paul has been turned into an entirely agreeable and politically correct model Roman citizen; his core teaching of justification by faith and the cutting-edge struggles around a new association of the conquered nations (*ethnē*) under Roman rule were cut off from the social and political realities of conquest as experienced by those very nations. And while Roman imperial realities became gradually obscured as the primary context of Paul's "disorderly conduct" (even Paul's execution by Rome is carefully sidestepped by Luke), another "target" of Paul's incisive polemics was brought to the fore: the rabble-rousing Jews.[11]

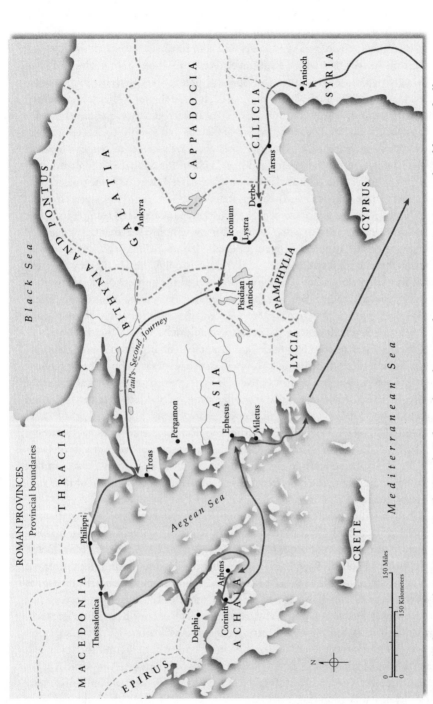

Roman Galatia and Asia Minor: On the North Galatian hypothesis, Paul writes to communities populated by specifically Galatian (Gallic) ethnic groups in the north of the Roman province; on the South Galatian hypothesis, he writes to the cities in the south that Luke places on his mission itineraries in the book of Acts.

The ideological pro-Romanization of Paul went hand in hand with his theological de-Judaization and historical decontextualization. Not all of this can be blamed on the narrative in Acts, of course. But the ultimate result is that Galatia is usually not seen as part of Caesar's empire. In New Testament scholarship it remains a well-defined *exegetical* territory, an eminently important *dogmatic* province in the theological history of the Christianized empire after Constantine, but nevertheless a politically unmarked space. Galatia became the primeval religious battlefield in the struggle between "Christianity" and "Judaism." And Paul, understood as a kind of archetypal hero in that struggle, could be readily mustered for many more battles that the imperial occidental civilization took up against its "Others."

Beyond East and West

The British scholar Sir William Ramsay at first sight appears as to be an example to the contrary. He is one of a group of scholars who thought that the Roman context of Galatia and Paul within the early empire was of great importance. Ramsay was quite knowledgeable about the historical and political background of Paul's Galatian churches. Based on firsthand experience from his own extensive travels and archeological research in the Roman province of Galatia, Ramsay's *Historical Commentary on St. Paul's Epistle to the Galatians* (1899) and his other books on Asia Minor still offer valuable contextual insights not easily found elsewhere.[12]

Yet for Ramsay there was not the slightest doubt that Paul not only spoke within a Roman imperial setting but also spoke as its uncompromising advocate and ally. The point at which Paul is most aligned with the Roman Empire is the battle of Occident against Orient. Whenever he speaks of Galatia and Galatians, as Ramsay categorically declares, Paul "speaks as the Roman." This means that Paul does not speak to ethnic (North) Galatians but to the "men of the Roman Province Galatia," an *ethnically mixed* group of people who have been elevated from their previous "Asiatic" ignorance and native superstition into a new and superior order: that is, they have been civilized by Rome and are now collectively called "Galatians."[13]

Thus, when Paul addressed his churches as "stupid Galatians" (3:1), he meant (according to Ramsay) to remind them of what they owed to their newly won "occidental" identity. He meant to warn them that they were about to abandon their privileged status as "Roman Galatians" in favor of their old selves as characterized by the "worthless spirit of Orientalism, of stagnation, of contented and happy ignorance, of deep-rooted superstition."[14]

Asia Minor is the Debatable Land in which Orientalism and Occidentalism have often striven for mastery. Under the early Roman Empire [that is, in Paul's day] and again at the present day, a vigorous Occidentalism is striving, apparently with every prospect of success, to subdue the plateau. The groundstock on the plateau is not antipathetic to Western organisation and order, though it is strongly antipathetic to the Western barbarian.

But it is far more sympathetic to Orientalism; and whenever it seems to have assimilated Occidental thoughts and ways, it tends to remould them to an Oriental form. The deep lying Orientalism always recurs. The Western conquerer triumphs, and before he is aware, when he turns his back for a moment, his results have melted into the old type. . . . Such was Paul's experience. . . . Such was the experience of every century in the Christian time. Every heresy in Anatolia recurred to a more *Oriental* and *specifically Judaistic* type; and at last Phrygia and Galatia reverted to *Semitic Mohammedanism.*[15]

Ramsay's remarks on the intellectual superiority of the Western civilization over Eastern "stagnation," of Rome (and Roman Christendom) over Judaism and "Oriental" barbarian ignorance, is a vivid illustration of the points Edward Said has made in his fundamental work on "Orientalism," a book that was instrumental in the emergence of postcolonial criticism.[16] His comments show how closely Paul had become tied into the Western imperial system as proclaimer of a gospel linked to the propagation of superior culture, and how his mission could be understood as securing the colonial submission of ignorant and superstitious "natives" for the sake of their cultural and intellectual advancement. It is precisely this kind of scriptural interpretation by colonial master races that is at the center of postcolonial critique today.[17]

It is striking to observe how readily Ramsay uses the terminology of combat and imperial conquest when describing Paul and Galatians, and how much the viewpoints of British Empire and Roman Empire merge as he turns Paul into the primeval warrior of the "Occidental" Galatian battle against "Orientalism." Again we see the smooth flow of one construction of "the enemy" into the next, a phenomenon we explored above in the introduction, made possible here within a surprisingly pliable general category of "Orientalism." This interpretive pattern deserves specific attention today, not least as it ultimately takes a rigidly anti-Islamic turn: After Ramsay declares the "Oriental type" as manifested in the "Judaistic type," its final metamorphosis manifests in "Semitic Mohammedanism."[18]

In the end, however, according to Ramsay, Paul prevails over all his enemies. The Galatian mission is a success story, or rather, a great victory:

The great struggle was won; the religion of the first Roman province on the road to the West was determined as free and non-Judaistic; and that meant that the religion of the Roman Empire was determined. Can we doubt that this struggle was critical and decisive? If Paul had been vanquished in the first Province he entered, and in the first Churches that he founded, he would have been vanquished definitely.[19]

The unreflective triumphalism that interprets Paul's letter to the Galatians within the framework of occidental victory, whether explicitly stated as in Ramsay or only implicit in arguments about Paul's de-Judaized and law-free gospel of faith, is the first major obstacle to our critical re-imagination of the "apostle to the nations." Within the great occidental battle narrative, the historical Paul has been strategically "displaced." His social and political location in the world where he lived, preached, and practiced his gospel was not alongside the victorious but among the vanquished nations of the empire, and he shared their common lot when he was executed by Nero.

The second challenge to a reinterpetation of Galatians (as observed above in the introduction) is the "combat semiotics" itself that appears so pervasive that it seems inscribed in the theological core of the letter. Paul's harsh polemic against his "opponents" and the strongly antithetical structure of his argument seems inevitably to turn every reading of Paul's letter into a weapon to be used against the "Other," whether the Jew or (later) the Muslim or barbarian. A third challenge is that it seems always to be the "Other" *as defined by imperial culture* that is the object of Paul's most passionate polemics—not the empire itself. Thus, it has come to seem almost self-evident that Paul is at once anti-Jewish and pro-imperial. This, too, is a myth of Pauline interpretation in need of revision.

A Depoliticized Geography

What I have called the "battle semiotics" that governed interpretation for both Luther and Ramsay no longer goes unchallenged in scholarship. Half a century after Ramsay and three decades into the post-Holocaust era, Krister Stendahl's small but seminal publication *Paul among Jews and Gentiles* (1976) reframed the debate on Galatians and "justification by faith." Stendahl, who would later become the Lutheran bishop of Stockholm, made two observations that set a new research agenda for all subsequent Pauline intepretation: first, that the proper historical context and hermeneutical key to understanding Paul's justification by faith is not the desperate struggle of an individual with sin, but Paul's practical concern with holding a community of Jews and Gentiles together; and, second, that Paul's Damascus experience was not a "conversion" to a new religion, Christianity, but a prophetic "call" to a new mission *within* Judaism *toward* the Gentiles. Paul subsequently did not fight against Jews or Judaism but worked to justify the status of uncircumcised Gentiles as "honorary Jews."[20]

Stendahl's theses, though sketchily drawn, had a profound impact: they unhinged the dominant paradigm of Pauline interpretation. Stendahl began the dissociation of the scriptural Paul from the Lutheran Paul, showing that Luther's question of the individual's standing before a just God was not Paul's. Unlike Luther prior to his "tower experience," the pre-Damascus Paul had not been tormented by a sense of inescapable sinfulness and the impossibility of keeping the law, but had rather experienced a "robust conscience."[21] Stendahl showed that the issue of individual sinfulness and the impossibility of justification as primary theological problems had been imposed on Paul by Augustine, three hundred years after the apostle, and subsequently by Luther, himself an Augustinian monk; the imposition revealed the individualistic and self-absorbed concerns of the "introspective conscience" of the West.[22]

With impeccable Lutheran credentials, Stendahl turned Luther's "scriptural principle," once set as a bulwark over against "Catholic tradition," against Lutheran tradition itself, asking what the Lutheran doctrinal pillars of faith alone, grace alone, and Christ alone would look like in light of "scripture alone," that is, in the form of the Pauline text restored to its first-century context. The scriptural Paul was thus read "against the grain" of the Lutheran Paul.[23]

Furthermore, Stendahl pointed out with prophetic clarity the problems inherent in traditional Protestant interpretation, namely, its stereotyped anti-Judaism, its narrow individualism, and its dogmatic disengagement from concrete social realities. Paul had been at first—*and remained even as an apostle*—thoroughly Jewish; "Christians" did not yet exist. In the place of a "combat semiotics" pitting Christianity against Judaism, Stendahl insisted that Paul's concern was how Jews and Gentiles could live together in a new community. Reconciliation, not combat, was central.[24]

Stendahl's insights, and the comprehensive argument of E. P. Sanders in *Paul and Palestinian Judaism* (1977), became the cornerstones of the "New Perspective."[25] Stendahl had pointed out that the Lutheran understanding of sin, law, and the futility of striving for "works righteousness" was not present in Paul. Sanders showed that it was not present in Judaism contemporary with Paul either. The point had been made earlier by other scholars, including George Foot Moore (1921), Albert Schweitzer (1911 and 1930), W. D. Davies (1948), and Johannes Munck (1954), but without changing the fundamental presuppositions of Christian scholarship. By the mid-1970s, thirty years after the Holocaust in Europe, a new theological climate called for Jewish–Christian dialogue and Christian repentance and renewal, and Christian theology was to an extent more willing to face the question of its own complicity in anti-Judaism. These concerns provided the environment in which a fundamental reorientation of scholarship, a "paradigm shift," could take place under the aegis of the "New Perspective."[26]

Sanders demonstrated that the traditional Protestant understanding of Judaism as a religion of "works righteousness" was not an accurate description of Judaism at Paul's time. As an alternative he proposed a model of Jewish "covenantal nomism" that rests on God's covenant and requires human obedience as a response, not a prerequisite.[27] His arguments made a reacknowledgment of Paul's Jewishness possible. In the wake of this "paradigm shift" brought about by Stendahl, Sanders, and others,[28] some scholars argued that Paul's theological concern was *only* for the *Gentiles,* who were to be admitted to the community of the saved without law, and did not in any way challenge the *Jews'* covenantal relationship to God through the law (L. Gaston, J. G. Gager).[29] From a slightly different angle, Paul's polemics were seen to be directed not against Judaism as such but *only* against a narrow form of Jewish particularism and ethnocentrism that relied on circumcision and other social boundary markers to establish and reinforce a distinctive identity (J. D. G. Dunn).[30] Or else, perhaps, Paul's polemic was not aimed at any inherent insufficiency in Judaism; it was directed *only* at the fact that Judaism "was not Christianity" (E. P. Sanders).[31]

While these arguments seemed to relieve Christian scholars of the onus of demonstrating some inadequacy on the part of Judaism in Paul's day, some of them have been criticized for rendering Paul fundamentally incoherent, and others for replacing traditional "Lutheran" critiques of Judaism with subtler but still pejorative characterizations of Jewish "exclusivism," or for "redeeming" Paul by driving a conceptual wedge between "good" Judaism (in which particular practices that maintained a social boundary were a matter of indifference) from "bad" Judaism (in which the distinctiveness of Jewish identity was required). What if, from a Jewish perspective, "boundary-maintaining" practices were not and are not marginal, but are decisive? Is the Gentile-inclusive "universalism" of the New Perspective then just a more veiled version of the old Christian anti-Judaism?[32]

These questions bring us back to the concern at the heart of this book: What is it that Paul opposes as "law" and "works"? Valuable as the insights of the New Perspective are, they do not go far enough in contextualizing the argument of Galatians in its real-life world. While the rediscovery of Paul's Jewishness by the New Perspective was a decisive breakthrough, it has addressed only a part of the contextual problem. Still obscured is the *Roman* context of Paul's Jewishness and his wrestling with the community of Jews and Gentiles/nations under the watchful eyes of a colonial superpower.

An important step out of the scholarly stalemate over geography (South versus North Galatia) has been taken by James M. Scott in his innovative investigation of the Galatian topology. Scott considers both Paul's Jewish and Roman historical contexts. He argues that Paul's missionary journeys were guided by the Table of Nations in Genesis 10 so that Paul focused his apostolate on the territory of Noah's third son, Japhet—that is, on Europe and Asia Minor.[33] Scott notes that Josephus, in his *Jewish Antiquities,* identifies Gomer, the firstborn of Japhet, and his three sons as the contemporary "Galatia" (*Ant.* 1.123, 126). The tripartite territory of "Gomer," from Josephus's point of view, was coextensive with the Roman province of Galatia. "For Josephus, the Roman Empire was the ruling world power; therefore, he naturally identified the Table of Nations [of Genesis] in terms of Roman nomenclature."[34] Scott concludes that within a Jewish geographic and ethnographic framework, Paul would have understood "Galatia" as the Roman province of Galatia (thus the southern, "non-ethnic" Galatia), which coincided with one part of the overall territory of "Gomer."

While Scott's study is highly original and insightful regarding historical data and sources, it also illustrates the problem of mental and political geographies, often implicit or subconscious, that is at the center of our investigation. Scott's straightforward alignment of a Jewish scriptural conception of the world (Genesis 10) and an imperial understanding of "Galatia" as a Roman province—though demonstrable in Josephus—still raises the question with regard to Paul himself. Scott rightly warns that geography is more than physical location; it is embedded in "worldviews" and mental (or ideological) maps as well.[35] But he nevertheless seems to assume that Paul, based on a spatial construct in Genesis, rather "naturally" would adopt the worldview and political perceptions of space that Josephus shared with his Roman patrons, that is, the worldview and perceptions of the dominant class. This assumption is questionable. Furthermore, as we shall see, the Roman perception of "Galatia" and "Galatians" was far more complex than Scott's discussion suggests[36]—and so was the spatial and theological imagination that Paul drew from the scriptural "maps" of exodus, exile, and promised land. That imaginative geography will be explored in chapter 6 below. We next turn to a more in-depth investigation of the *Roman* topology implicit in Paul's Galatian text.

Lawless Barbarians: The Representation of Galatians/Gauls in Imperial Ideology

For it has been their ambition [*zēlousin*] from old to plunder [*lēsteuein*], invading for this purpose the lands of others [*allotrias*], and to regard all men with contempt [*kataphronein hapantōn*]. For they are the people who captured Rome, who plundered the sanctuary at Delphi, who levied tribute upon a large part of Europe and no small part of Asia, and settled themselves upon the lands of the peoples they have subdued in war, being called in time Greco-Galatians [*Hellēnogalatai*] because they became mixed with the Greeks, and who, as their last accomplishment, have destroyed many large Roman armies. And in pursuance of their savage ways [*agriōtēti*] they manifest an outlandish impiety [*ektopōs asebousin*] also with respect to their sacrifices; for their criminals they keep prisoners for five years and then impale them in honor of the gods.... Captives also are used by them as victims for sacrifices in honour of the gods. (Diodorus 5.3, trans. C. H. Oldfather, LCL)

Diodorus's statement illuminates a topic closely related to Paul's Galatian letter and the circumcision controversy: law and lawlessness. Both terms are firmly established rhetorical topoi in designating barbarians, in particular Galatian/Gallic barbarians. As Edith Hall has pointed out, in Greek thinking barbarian lawlessness (as opposed to the "righteousness," *dikaiosynē*, and "law" of civilization) can refer to a variety of vices: disrespect of Greek democracy, irreverence toward civic law and legal processes, and finally the violation of social taboos or of the "laws of all mankind" in particularly abhorrent crimes. If such violations are directed against sacred institutions, lawlessness (*adikia*) turns into impiety (*asebeia*), the "flouting of the laws of heaven."[37] In every one of these aspects Diodorus's Galatians appear as shocking personifications of vicious transgression. It is not just their insatiable appetite for new lands, booty, and conquest (in other places paralleled by their uncontrolled sexual and covetous desire) that stigmatize the Galatians as lawless; they also violate fundamental religious taboos. They sacrifice humans and have at least twice transgressed the most sacrosanct political and religious boundaries of the Greco-Roman world: they sacked not only Rome, the city protected by inviolable and sacred walls, but also one of the symbolic centers of Greece and of humanity, the sanctuary of Apollo at Delphi. They were without respect for human and divine order, blasphemous, greedy, and cruel: in a phrase, lawless barbarians.[38]

The descriptions of Galatians/Gauls in ancient sources, on the one hand, express this lawlessness that the Greeks and the Romans saw in them, a lawlessness that needed to be punished. On the other hand, authors like Diodorus and Livy point out that Roman law from now on would legitimately rule the world and the Galatians. This theme is a key subject of Greco-Roman historiography and ethnography in dealing with Galatians/Gauls.

Reports in Colonial Texts

In stark contrast to the somewhat nebulous Christian imagination of Galatians, the Greco-Roman world at Paul's time had a surprisingly vivid, if hostile, picture of how Galatians/Gauls looked and behaved. Authors like Polybius, Diodorus Siculus, Pompeius Trogus (as known from excerpts by Justin), as well as Livy, Strabo, Appian, Pausanias, and many more, write about them. We know that other reports existed but have been lost, for example, the work of Posidonius.[39] We must remember, however, that all the extant written material is *about* the Galatians/Gauls, not *by* them. As history in general is written by the victors, the ancient historians, geographers, ethnographers, and artists dealing with Galatia and Galatians approached their subject from the position of the conquerors, not the vanquished. It might well be that Paul is the rare exception to this rule, though the deep gulf that has generally divided academic departments of New Testament from Classics has prevented this possibility from being explored or even noticed. As if they were living on a different planet, the Galatians studied by New Testament scholars are usually not a topic for ancient historians, art historians, or ethnographers, and vice versa.

Seen through the eyes of their Greek and Roman conquerors, the image of the Galatians hardly appears favorable. Karl Strobel has performed the most recent major research and reevaluation of the Galatians of Asia Minor and observes how massively occidental scholarship has been shaped by the ancient stereotypes.[40] Such stereotypes are dominant, for example, in Felix Stähelin's groundbreaking and still influential German dissertation of a century ago, and they continue up to the present.[41] The standard depiction of the historical Galatians/Gauls as wild, war-mad hordes of robbers and plunderers, violent but unsteady, strong yet intellectually inferior, still widely prevails, not least in Pauline studies. In a seemingly natural fashion, the ancient perspectives of a dominant, "civilized" worldview have been uncritically assumed.[42] As Strobel contends, however, the real history of the Galatians in Asia Minor involves a far more complex account, on the one hand, of migration, settlement, ethnic identity preservation, acculturation, assimilation, and, on the other, formation of power structures and rule than the ancient commentators convey. Unfortunately, our knowledge regarding the material history of Galatian Asia Minor is very sketchy, as archeological research so far has not focused much on the Galatians in rural Anatolia and is deplorably underdeveloped, especially regarding their pre-Roman history.[43] The excavations undertaken by the University of Pennsylvania at Gordion represent a notable exception.[44] While the documentary record of Anatolian history has been extensively explored, as Stephen Mitchell states, "archaeologically most of the region remains *terra incognita*."[45]

Only in recent decades has the paradigm shift in postcolonial studies begun to challenge our perceptions of the Galatians. Edward Said's *Orientalism* has sparked an academic discourse that focuses on the various ways in which the West has codified knowledge about the colonized Other who stands under its control.[46] Although the Galatians of Asia Minor would seem to provide a model example of an ethnic identity, indeed, of an "oriental" identity constructed by a dominant imperial discourse and, furthermore, would seem a prolific subject for exploring issues such as migration, ethnicity, and hybridity in an ancient imperial context, the Galatians have not yet been "discovered" by postcolonial studies.[47] Karl Strobel's work in this regard offers a new point of departure toward a fundamental reevaluation of Galatia and the Galatians.[48]

On the other hand, with regard to the Gauls/Galatians of western Europe the situation looks more favorable. The contemporary search for a European identity that does not rest exclusively on Greco-Roman, Christian, or even Germanic predominance and that moves away from colonial and Eurocentric perspectives has led to new inquiries into the ancient Celtic roots that most European nations hold in common. To a certain extent, the Celts recently have become a prominent and even fashionable topic. This development, in which the great exhibition on the Celts in Venice in 1991 was a hallmark event,[49] certainly does not protect the Celts from new kinds of ideological reconfigurations—that is, from being romanticized or glorified, or popularized, as in the famous comic heroes Asterix and Obelix by René Goscinny and Alberto Uderzo. Nevertheless, on the whole the revival of Celtic studies is a chance to review the traditional (mis)representations of Galatians in New Testament scholarship and to turn to less biased notions of who the Galatians/Gauls were. With all this in mind we turn our attention to the image of the Galatians as it emerges from ancient literary sources.[50]

Fig. 10. The Celtic chieftain Vercingetorix surrenders to Julius Caesar after the Battle of Alesia in 52 B.C.E. in this nineteenth-century engraving by Lionel Royer (1852–1926). Such depictions show the continuing romantic appeal of Celtic defiance and ferocity. Musée Crozatier, Le Puy-en-Velay, France. Photo: Bridgeman-Giraudon/Art Resource, N.Y. (See pp. 70–71.)

Diodorus's Galatians

In an extensive excursus in the fifth book of his *Library of History*, Diodorus of Sicily (80–29 B.C.E.), a Greek contemporary and admirer of Julius Caesar as well as of Augustus in the early years of his rule, gives a detailed and pictorial description of the Galatians:

> The Galatians [*Galatai*] are tall of body, with rippling muscles, and white of skin, and their hair is blond, and not only naturally so, but they also make it their practice by artificial means to increase the distinguishing colour which nature has given it. For they are always washing their hair in lime-water, and they pull it back from the forehead to the top of the head and back to the nape of the neck, with the result that their appearance is like that of Satyrs and Pans, since the treatment of their hair makes it so heavy and coarse that it differs in no respect from the mane of horses. (Diodorus 5.28, LCL)

The whiteness of their bodies for Diodorus by no means implies any trace of a superior race. Rather the Galatians' light hair color and the peculiar styling treatment with lime-water can appear to his civilized gaze only as indicators of the wild, alien, and untamed. Why? Because this is simply what the Galatians are, from Diodorus's point of view: savage barbarians, blond beasts of some sort. As he will further explain in the famous Galatian excursus in book 5 of his *Library of History*, they also drink unmixed wine without moderation (5.26), they covet gold and heavy golden jewelry of which they own a great deal (5.27), and during their meals they suddenly enter into single combat, for trivial reasons and without fear of death (5.28). Some of them go into battle naked and they cut off the heads of their defeated enemies, later nailing them as trophies to their houses (5.29). They practice human sacrifice and some of the most beastlike of their tribes living far in the north and on the borders of Scythia probably even eat human beings (5.31, 32). They are also sexually promiscuous and transgressive, men and women alike. The men "rage with lust, in outlandish fashion, for the embraces of males," and they do not see it as a dishonor to prostitute themselves freely to one another (5.32).

Diodorus has to admit that he finds some of Galatians' institutions and attitudes rather impressive. For example, they are not ready to give away their enemies' heads taken as trophies for either money or gold (5.29), which displays, as he concedes, a certain "barbarous greatness of soul" (*barbarōn tina megalopsychian*). But though he admits that the refusal to sell the insignia of one's excellence and distinction (*syssēma tēs aretēs*) is a mark of nobility (*eugenes*), Diodorus also points out that clinging to their gruesome trophies means that they continue the fight against "one of our own race" (*homophylon*) beyond death, which is simply beastlike (*thēriōdes*).

Another of these "mixed" observations follows in 5.31. After Diodorus has stated that the Galatians are "terrifying in aspect and their voices are deep and altogether harsh," he turns to their intellectual capacities. The language they employ is pompous and hyperbolic; they speak in riddles (*ainigmatiai*) and use one word when they mean another (*synekdochikōs*); they boast and threaten, yet "they have sharp wits and are not without cleverness of learning" (*dianoia, mathēsis,* 5.31). Their poets, called bards, sing songs of praise or obloquy (*blasphēmousi*) to the accompaniment of instruments that look like lyres. And their Druid priests, described by Diodorus as "philosophers" (*philosophoi*) and "theologians" (*theologoi*), as well as these "chanting poets" (*melōdousi poētais*), the bards, have enough authority to step out between two armies ready to fight each other and to cancel the battle, "as though having cast a spell over certain kinds of wild beasts [*thēria*]. In this way, even among the wildest barbarians [*agriōtatois barbarois*] does passion [*thymos*] give place before wisdom [*sophia*], and Ares stands in awe of the Muses" (5.31).

Constructing the Galatian Barbarian

The conceptual framework of Diodorus's description of the Galatians is the polarity between Greek and barbarian, civilized and wild, human and beast. While the term *barbarian* originally referred to the puzzling language of foreigners, which sounded like an incomprehensible "bar-bar" to the Greek—Diodorus's complaint about the harsh voices and the strange communication of the Galatians still has overtones of this meaning—it had by the beginning of the fifth century B.C.E. developed into a far more comprehensive construct of non-Greek "otherness." Edith Hall has proposed that the invention of the barbarian "as the universal anti-Greek against whom Hellenic—especially Athenian—culture was defined" reflects the concrete historical context of the Persian wars. The combined military efforts of the Greeks against the Persians, under Athenian leadership, were the catalyst that "first produced a sense of collective Panhellenic identity and the notion of the barbarians as the universal 'other.'"[51]

According to Hall, it was particularly the Athenian stage and the medium of the Athenian tragedy where the image of the barbarian was propagated. This image, which was later canonized through the definition of the cardinal Hellenic virtues (and their corresponding barbarian vices) in fourth-century Greek philosophy, opposed barbarian stupidity (*amathia*) to Greek wisdom or intelligence (*sophia*), cowardice (*deilia*) to manliness (*andreia*), abandonment (*akolasia*) to discipline and restraint (*sōphrosynē*), lawlessness (*adikia*) to justice (*dikaiosynē*). (See fig. 11.)

Each one of these four features of barbarian otherness in antithesis to the civilized self is clearly traceable in Diodorus's ethnographic excursus on the Galatians. If the Galatian barbarians fail with regards to *dikaiosynē*, the observance of custom and law, as we have already stated, they also fall short in the three other cardinal Hellenic virtues of intelligence, courage, and self-restraint either by lacking them or having them in excess.

As regards their *sophia,* or intelligence, although they do show signs of a sharp mind and learnedness (*dianoia, mathēsis* as opposed to *amathia,* 5.31), their culture is obviously inferior, as their alien ways of communicating show. Their intellectuals, the Druids, exercise their authority not in a rational, civilized manner, but as if they could "cast a spell over certain kinds of wild beasts" (5.31). Second, as for their *andreia,* or

Fig. 11. Greek virtues vs. barbarian vices

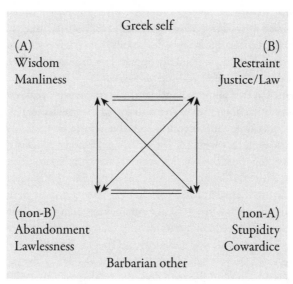

manliness, Diodorus admits that they are strong warriors and eager to fight, but, on the other hand, their courage is as irrational as their habit of keeping the heads of their dead enemies (5.29). It is stupid to fight naked and without armor (5.29), or for trivial reasons (5.28). Furthermore, the sexual promiscuity mentioned by Diodorus was, from a Greek point of view, a deficiency with respect to ordinary patriarchal household structures and thus showed a lack of true manliness.[52]

Most of all, what undermines the Galatians' manhood in Diodorus's account is that they are totally lacking the third and decisive virtue of Greek civilization: temperance and moderation (*sōphrosynē*), which, according to Hall, perhaps was the most important of all since "it tempered *all* the passions and made possible the observance of measure (*mesotēs*) in all actions, and the avoidance of extremes."[53] Like the tragic fifth-century characters presented in Athenian theater, Diodorus's Galatians are extreme personalities who do everything in excess (*kath' hyperbolēn*, 5.26.2, 3; 5.27; *en hyperbolais,* 5.31). They drink too much wine and drink it too strong, they are too fond of gold and jewelry, they talk in superlatives, and they are sexually unrestrained and uncontrolled (5.32). They are certainly no cowards, but they are boasting and overeager to fight. Courage not tempered by prudence was for the Greeks as much a barbarian feature, indicating a lack of manliness, as was timidity. (Distinguished fourth-century philosophers like Plato and Aristotle might have argued that Celtic rashness was not equal to Greek courage, as it ignored dangers and lacked endurance.[54]) As their passion and impulsiveness was only occasionally tamed by reason and wisdom (*thymos* versus *sophia,* 5.31), the Galatians appeared as uncivilized savages (*agriōtatois barbarois,* 5.31) who are something in between animals (*thēria*) and full human beings (5.29; 5.31). Human sacrifice and cannibalism fit into these categories of bestiality and wildness (*agriōtēs*) as well.

Note that in this construction, the opposite of one barbarian extreme is also perceived as barbaric. Cowardice and brainless heroism are *both* contrary to true manliness, as are wildness as well as excessive love of luxury—the latter closely tied to the "East" and often linked to effeminacy—deviations from proper self-restraint. Similarly, stupidity or extreme cunning are equally opposed to the adequate exercise of wisdom (*sophia*) and moderation (*sōphrosynē* and *mesotēs*).

We should pause at this point to consider the hermeneutics of an exchange between conquerer and conquered. Diodorus's description of the intellectual culture in Galatia, with its passion for riddles and incomprehensible allusions, might as well indicate a degree of sophistication that is simply "other" than the norm established by those who declare themselves superior: the Greeks. As his remarks in 5.31 demonstrate, he seems unable to follow what the Galatians/Gauls are saying, and this is neither a pleasurable nor an acceptable experience in the encounter between a dominant and an "inferior" culture. To slander barbarian intellectual refinement as being too smart, and thus simply as the mirror vice of barbarian stupidity, is the established pattern by which the civilized Greco-Roman mind responded to the challenge of dominating what it did not comprehend.

On the other hand, the "riddles" of Diodorus's Galatians, who "use one word when they mean another" (5.31), might also hint at a phenomenon that James C. Scott has called the "backstage discourse of what cannot be spoken in the face of power," the "hidden transcripts" of speech among the conquered that are illegible to the hegemonic semantic system.[55] This observation might be of interest regarding the "Galatian" hermeneutics of Paul's letter as a discourse among the vanquished. It should definitely alert us to the possible existence of linguistic codes and figures of speech that Paul employs in order to exclude unwanted conversation partners, codes, and figures of speech that hide rather than reveal their true meaning. The question to what extent Galatians as a text contains "hidden transcripts" that are incomprehensible from the perspective of the conquerors is profoundly troublesome in light of the established Christian reading of the letter, in which the vanquished are never seriously considered to be subjects.[56]

Gauls, Galatians, Celts: Who Is Who?

Rome and Delphi, Europe and Asia are the main stages on which the Galatians were represented as ruthless predators and invaders of the civilized world—the prototypical barbarian Other. Before we review the history and ideology behind these representations we should consider the term *Galatian* for a moment. So far, we have used it in ways that differ from standard English use. The third edition of *Webster's New College Dictionary*, for example, defines *Galatian* as, first, "a native or inhabitant of Galatia in Asia Minor," and, second, the name associated with the Pauline epistle in the New Testament that contained "a message from the Apostle Paul to the Christians of Galatia." Thus, in contemporary English, the term *Galatians* has a precise connotation and is definitively and unambiguously located geographically in Asia Minor (contemporary

Turkey), and theologically in the New Testament. This is clearly much less and something other than what Diodorus had in mind. For him, Galatians were a worldwide ethnic group that included the European Gauls and the Celts in general. Throughout his Galatian excursus in book 5 he talks about Galatians (Greek *Galatai*) and Celts (Greek *Keltai*) and about the land they occupy, Celtica (Greek *Keltikē*) or Galatia (Greek *Galatia*), using the terms interchangeably. These Celts/Galatians include a large number of different tribes (*ethnē*, 5.25.1) and live in the harsh climate of the north— from beyond the Alps north to the ocean, along the Rhone, Rhine, and Danube Rivers, and east of the Pyrenees as far as Scythia (5.32.1). They are described in different places as both European and Asian. At one point Diodorus briefly tries to differentiate between Celtic and Galatian territories in Europe, but concludes with the statement: "The Romans, however, include all these nations [*ethnē*] together under a single name, calling them one and all Galatians [*Galatas hapantes*]" (Diodorus 5.32.1).

This confronts us with a serious translation problem. Diodorus here quotes the Romans as if they were speaking Greek. It is quite clear that the Romans themselves in their own language would have called these Greek *Galatai* by the Latin equivalent, *Galli*, the term from which the English *Gauls* is derived, the people we normally would locate in contemporary France. In the Loeb translation of Diodorus, however, all the Greek *Galatai* are rendered as English "Gauls." This is problematic insofar as it may obscure the ancient meaning of the terms, the Greek *Galatians* as well as the Latin *Gauls*. Both terms were used interchangeably during Paul's time; that is, the *Galatians* were not described as restricted to Asia Minor but covered the entirety of "Galatia," throughout Europe and beyond, wherever the Celts had appeared over the course of centuries of migration. Nor are the Latin *Gauls* a phenomenon of the western and northern part of the Roman Empire alone, where we are used to locating them; rather they inhabited the East and South and Asia as well.

When Livy, for example, in his monumental Roman history (*Ab urbe condita*), talks in Latin about the decisive Roman triumph of Manlius Vulso over the Galatians in Asia Minor in 189 B.C.E., he calls them "the *Gauls* who inhabit Asia" (*de Gallis qui Asiam incolunt triumphavit*, 39.6.3). Conversely, when the *Greek* historiographer Polybius writes about the Gauls who in 387 B.C.E. attacked Rome and for seven months occupied the whole of that city except the Capitol, he uses the term *Galatai* (1.6.2). *Gauls*, again according to Livy (38.48), were the ones who in 279 B.C.E. had attacked and despoiled Delphi, the common oracle of the human race (*humani generis oraculum*), and then subsequently imposed their rule and empire (*Gallorum imperium*) over Asia Minor north of the Taurus—that is, over what we usually think of as *Galatia*.

Not surprisingly, the Greek-speaking historiographer Polybius, on the other hand, calls these same people who first marched against Delphi and then crossed over to Asia *Galatians* (1.6.5). But *Galatians* are in his report also the fierce and dangerous tribes who, after the sack of Rome in 387 B.C.E., settled in Italy south and north of the Po River and were gradually vanquished by the Romans over the next two hundred years. In this grand Celtic war, which, for Polybius, was "second to no war in history" (2.35.2), the enemy territory is named *Galatia*, covering regions both on "this" (that is the Roman) and the "other" side of the Alps, that is, what we (using Latin terminology) are accustomed to identifying as *Gallia Cisalpina* (2.21.9) and *Gallia Transalpina* (2.22.4). *Galatia* for Polybius was at the same time the land directly bordering the Roman sphere of influence in Italy (2.21.9 and 2.24.8) and a land far away beyond the Alps, from which at the end of the third century B.C.E. the Cisalpine Galatians of Italy (Insubres and Boii) would summon a huge force of formidable warriors to support their war against the Romans. Subsequently, Polybius recounts, an army of *Galatai* from *Galatia* on both sides of the Alps suffered the decisive final defeat of Cisalpine Galatia in the Battle of Telamon in 225 B.C.E. (2.33).

One could add many more examples from Roman and Greek historiography of traces left by the Galatians/Gauls. One would arrive again and again at the same result: Greek (and English) Galatians are called *Gauls* in Latin, Latin (and English) Gauls are in Greek called *Galatians*. Both may be called *Celts,* a name given as the original or indigenous name of the Galatians by Pausanias (*Descr.* 1.4.1), by Strabo (4.1.14), and by Caesar (1.1.1). There may be an occasional effort to locate and define more precisely the tribal affiliation or geographical location of the Galatians/Gauls/Celts, such as the "Galatians called Senones" (Polybius 2.21.7), "the Galatians dwelling among the Alps and near the Rhone" (Polybius 2.22.1), or, for Latin-speaking Pliny, the "Tolistobogii of the Gauls" in Asia Minor—one of the three tribes of our New Testament Galatians (*Nat.* 5.42.146). In addition, the Galatians of Asia Minor may be called *Gallo-Graeci* in Latin (Livy 38.17.10) or *Hellenogalatai* in Greek (Diodorus 5.32) because they became somehow mixed with the Greeks. There may even be a rare occasion where the Greek *Galatia* appears in a Latin text to refer to the Galatia in Asia Minor that is most familiar to New Testament readers (Pliny, N*at.* 5.42.147). Likewise, the Latin *Gallic* can turn up as a loanword in a Greek text, as in Strabo:

> The whole race which is now both called "Gallic" and "Galatian" [*ho nyn Gallikon te kai Galatikon kalousin*] is war-mad and both high-spirited [*thymikon*] and quick for battle . . . (4.4.2, LCL)

Strabo here makes exactly the point that there is no distinction between *Gallic* and *Galatian* and that both terms refer to a "whole race" (though in the following description of the Gauls/Galatians he clearly deals only with Gaul beyond the Alps, which he calls Transalpine Celtica: *hyper tōn Alpeōn Keltikēs,* 4.4.6). He repeats much of what we already heard from Diodorus in his Galatian excursus (book 5), though with several new additions, one of them major: Strabo declares that the "war-mad race" has been pacified at last:

> At present time they are all at peace, since they have been enslaved [*dedoulōmenoi*] and are living in accordance with the commands of the Romans who captured them. (Strabo 4.4.2)

Strabo, a native of Asia Minor who died in the early years of Tiberius's reign (20 C.E.), here summarizes the history of Galatia. It is the history of both Gauls and Galatians who, after countless battles, were finally conquered, that is, enslaved, by Rome, in the West as well as in the East.[57] It would have been easy for the Greeks and Romans to use different terms for the Celts in Europe and in Asia, as we do when we speak about "Gauls" and "Galatians." *But this is precisely what the ancients in general did not do.* Rather, they used terms that made clear that the Gauls/Galatians were *one and the same* phenomenon in the history of the world that Rome now dominated: a single people of warlike and uncivilized barbarians who had ultimately been tamed and subjugated by Rome.

This leaves us with a substantial hermeneutical problem. Spatially and ideologically, "Galatia" in the language of Paul's day means something other than what our theological translations imply. We must realize that the English *Galatians* are derived from the Greek word that basically includes rather than excludes the English *Gauls* and the Celts in general. The Galatians/Gauls/Celts, wherever they were physically located, cannot be dealt with on the level of geographical, historical, or ethnic-cultural description alone. In New Testament scholarship, the preoccupation with North and South Galatia and with the theological Galatians has prevented us from seeing that *Galatia* in antiquity is not a single carefully bounded geographical location, nor does it refer to a single ethnic identity standing neutrally among others, of any kind anywhere. It is a term soaked with memories, fears, and aggression that are completely absent from our New Testament dictionaries. Firmly established on the ideological map of the Roman Empire as barbarian territory par excellence, it is a worldwide topos that inscribes the history of a dramatic and paradigmatic encounter between Rome and its enemies, the history of the conquest of lawlessness by law. This is the historically adequate meaning we must recover before we are able to read Paul's letter, and to this historical reconstruction of the terms *Galatia* and *Galatians* we next turn.

Gauls/Galatians Marching against Rome, Delphi, and Pergamon (387–189 B.C.E.)

For the Romans, the Galatians became a myth. That is, they played a constitutive role in a colonial/imperial discourse centered on war and victory, order and counterorder, Self and Other in the battle of civilization versus barbarism. This observation requires some historical explications.

Sketched briefly, the historical picture looks as follows. The Celts/Gauls/Galatians comprised a wide variety of different tribes of Indo-European origin, linked by a common language family. It was not until Caesar in the middle of the first century B.C.E. that we find a distinction made between Germans and Celts, the Germans living east of the Rhine, the Celts on the west of it.[58] Before then, the two groups were mostly seen as one and the same. The Celts never established a unified empire but nevertheless occupied huge amounts of European territory. Originally settling in central Europe, in numerous migrations they conquered new dwelling places as far west as Iberia in Spain, as far north as Britannia (Scotland and Wales), as far south as the Po Valley in Italy, and as far east as Macedonia, Thrace, and Asia Minor, covering large parts of today's Balkans and Turkey. In the proto-Celtic period (1800–1200 B.C.E.) they are found in what today is southern Germany, gradually extending their areas of settlement farther to the west until they appear in southern France and Spain between 1200–750 B.C.E. (the *Hallstatt period*). Around 650 B.C.E. Celts and the Mediterranean culture meet for the first time around the Rhone Valley and Massalia (Marseille), a city founded by Greek colonists. During the *La Tène period,* from the fifth century B.C.E. onward, they are known as highly skilled metalworkers and fierce warriors, with a growing tendency towards military expansion and service as mercenaries. Most probably, external factors such as climate deterioration and overpopulation forced them to leave their territories. Searching for new land, they appeared already in the sixth century B.C.E. in the Po region in Italy, and more massively in the fifth and fourth centuries as settler-warriors in huge migration waves pressing toward the northern borders of the Greco-Roman world.[59]

Rome and "Lawless" Conquest (387 B.C.E.)

The first major encounter took place in Italy. Probably as early as the sixth century B.C.E. Celts had invaded the areas south of the Alps, gradually chasing the Etruscans out of the region of the Po Valley, which then became known as *Gallia Cisalpina*, and establishing settlements there. In the early fourth century, the Celts clashed dramatically with Rome in a battle that would later become a foundational element of the Roman imperial state myth. Livy, the historiographer of the Augustan age, mentions that before they marched on Rome in 387 B.C.E., the Celtic tribe of the Senones under Brennus had been negotiating peacefully for land on which to settle. On Livy's account, the Celts started military action only after being seriously offended by the arrogant and "lawless" behavior of the Roman emissaries at Clusium (Chiusi), who, according to Livy, violated the "law of the nations" (*ius gentium*) by breaking the peace and thus behaved not as true Romans should but as if they were Celts themselves (Livy 5.35). This twisted logic confirms the principle that it is barbarians who are lawless and Romans who keep the law—even when they do not.

The insult to the Celts by the Roman Fabii at Clusium, reinforced by an unjust cover-up of the whole matter on the part of the Roman senate, led to a military clash and a devastating *dies ater* ("black day") in Roman history, the Battle of the Allia (387 B.C.E.). The Romans suffered a horrendous defeat, and the way to Rome was opened up to the Celtic army. The city was conquered in 387, destroyed, and burnt to the ground. The Capitol itself was saved from being reduced to ashes only by the famous geese of Juno, whose honking during a Celtic night attack warned the Roman garrison. After seven months of siege, the invaders, according to Livy, had lost their sense of purpose and were content to withdraw with a ransom of a thousand pounds of gold (Livy 5.48.8).

The Law of the Strongest

It is striking to observe how hard Livy works to establish Roman righteousness as opposed to Galatian lawlessness at this juncture, when the future of the Roman people lay in the hands of the barbarians for seven months and could be ransomed only by gold. Livy's discourse on right and wrong is quite fragile and shows the extent to which "law" is presumed to be the right of the victorious and superior people, however disguised by nonpartisan and universal justifications. Law is perceived to be naturally on the side of the Romans, although their own aberrations from this fundamental Roman righteousness may have tragic consequences, as the case of the emissaries and the events after Clusium show. That the desire for new land made the Celtic conquests in no way different from Greek and Roman colonization is a conclusion that Livy does not draw. Interestingly enough, this crucial insight is explicitly stated only through the inferior voice of a Gaul in another subsequent report on these same events. Plutarch, writing about a century after Livy and in Greek, presents a fully developed speech of the Galatian/Gallic leader Brennus exactly at the moment when the Roman ambassadors are trying to defend the city of Clusium against the foreign invaders and their demand for land.

> When they [the Galatians] were asked [by the Romans] what wrong they had suffered at the hand of the Clusians that they had come up against their city, Brennus, the king of the Galatians, burst into a laugh and said: "The Clusians wrong us in that, being able to till only a small parcel of earth [*gēn kai chōran*], they yet are bent on holding a large one, and will not share it with us, who are strangers, many in numbers, and poor. This is the wrong which you too suffered, o Romans, formerly at the hands of the Albans, Fidenates, and Ardeates, and now lately at the hands of the Veientines, Capenates, and many of the Faliscans and Volscians. You march against these peoples, and if they will not share their goods with you, you enslave them, despoil them, and raze their cities to the ground; not that in doing so you are in any wise cruel or unjust [*adikon*], no, you are but obeying that most ancient of all laws [*presbytatō tōn nomōn*] which gives to the stronger the goods of his weaker neighbour, beginning with the God himself and ending with the beasts. For these too are so endowed by nature that the stronger seeks to have more than the weaker. Cease you, therefore, to pity the Clusians when we besiege them, that you may not teach the Galatians to be kind and full of pity towards those who are wronged [*adikoumenois*] by the Romans." (Plutarch, *Cam.* 8.2–4, LCL, slightly modified)

To whom does the earth (*gē*) belong? How much land (*chōra*) does a city need to support itself? What is the law of God (*nomos*) that defines justice and injustice, righteousness and unrighteousness (*adikon*) in the relationship between the strong ones and their weaker neighbors? What if the Gauls/Galatians were to become a force that united resistance against Rome? Plutarch provides no answer to the unpleasant and, again, overly clever questions that he places in Brennus's mouth in a rhetorical move bursting with irony. It suffices that Brennus is morally and culturally disqualified as a barbarian and therefore by definition lawless and wrong.

This point is vividly illustrated by an incident related to the final act of the Galatians' departure from Rome. The greedy Gauls, as Livy reports, could not refrain from shamelessly cheating the Romans by using false measures in weighing the thousand-pound ransom. Nor does Brennus even try to hide the blatant injustice and depravity of this act: rather he adds to it when he throws his sword onto the scale and exclaims: "*Vae victis*" ("Woe to the vanquished": Livy 5.48.8).

Their leader's proud exclamation would haunt the Gauls/Galatians over the next several centuries. For ultimately the questions To whom does the earth belong? and What is right or wrong? were decided by precisely that law of the strongest to which Brennus had appealed in Plutarch's report—except that the Romans would turn out to have the superior forces. After the disaster of 387 B.C.E., it took the Romans about thirty years to regain their domination over the Latin cities and a whole century finally to tame the Galatian/Gallic Senones in Italy. Several Roman–Celtic clashes took place in 367, 365–363, and 348 B.C.E. Livy's account focuses on a set of duels that are staged in a David-versus-Goliath way: The giant Celtic leader with his boastful arrogance, loud battle cries, and war dance is killed with cool elegance by his much smaller but more efficient Roman opponent (Livy 6.42; 7.25). In 295 B.C.E., the Senones suffered a decisive defeat in the Battle of Sentium. After another invasion in 284 B.C.E., the Romans finally broke the resistance of this Celtic tribe by a last punitive expedition and laid the foundation of the Roman colony of Sena in tribal territory near the mouth of the river Po.

The strong Boii, however, continued to pose a threat to Roman superiority in Italy for another hundred years. Together with the Insubres and Gaesatae, they were defeated in three years of war beginning with the Battle of Telamon (225 B.C.E.). Forty thousand Celts were killed. Of the ten thousand prisoners taken by the Romans, a large number ended up as slaves. The Romans decorated the Capitol with the golden insignia and torques of their enemies (Polybius 2.31). One may regard the war of 225 B.C.E. as the last great venture of the Cisalpine Gauls, though other uprisings were to follow and the resistance of the Boii was not finally broken until 190.[60]

Punic and Gallic Fear: Galatians Sacrificed at Rome

At this same time, the Romans had to deal with another crucial challenge. Shortly after Telamon, Hannibal of Carthage, the most powerful rival of Rome in the western Mediterranean, appeared south of the Alps, threatening the city of Rome with conquest in 218. Within two years he conquered almost all of Italy. The Romans suffered a major defeat at Cannae in 216, another day labeled as *dies ater* in their memory. Three times during these years, Rome was threatened by conquest before the Romans managed to regain what they had lost, winning a decisive victory over Hannibal in 201. The threat of Carthage was effectively ended, even though the city itself survived another half century until it was finally destroyed by the Romans in the Third Punic War (149–146 B.C.E.).

Ideologically, the events around Telamon and the Second Punic War mark a decisive paradigm shift in the construction of the Galatian/Celtic Other. Its external sign is the invention of an exceptional ritual that was performed twice, before Telamon (228) and after Cannae (216). In order to make atonement to the gods and to save Rome, a Galatian man and a Galatian woman, together with a Greek man and woman, were offered as live sacrifices at the Forum Boarium, the cattle market in the heart of Rome.

How should this horrendous act be understood? In 228 Rome faced a twofold danger threatening its very existence. A military conflict with Carthage was imminent. On the other hand, the Cisalpine Galatians were in an uproar because their land, starting with the *ager Gallicus* of the Senones, was being divided up among Roman citizens. It seemed that only extraordinary events and measures could save the Republic. Therefore, when lightning struck near the temple of Apollo at the Capitoline Hill, the *decemviri sacris faciundis* searched the Sibylline books for a means to pacify the gods. The answer came promptly: Rome had to beware of the Galatians and had to bury a Galatian man and a Galatian woman (*Galatai dyo*) alive at the Forum Boarium, along with a Greek man and woman (Cassius Dio frg. 47 and 50.1).

Why and whether a Greek couple had to be added to this gruesome ceremony is controversial. Apparently there was an ancient oracle that one day Rome would be seized by Greeks and Gauls (Cassius Dio frg. 47).[61] Emma Dench refers to the "potent symbolism of Gauls and Greeks as archetypal enemies" in the late third and second centuries.[62] But the immediate thrust of the ritual is clearly anti-Gallic. Rome, according to the Sibylline books, had to beware of the *Galatai*, the Galatians (Cassius Dio frg. 50.1.4). The inclusion of a male and a female victim for live burial is a brutally stark symbol for the wholesale destruction of the enemy as an ethnic entity; by comprising men and women it symbolically destroys the possibility for reproduction.[63] Plutarch, who gives the precise location of the ceremony as the Forum Boarium (*Marc.* 3), admits that it could easily remind one of barbarian practices—as we have seen, human sacrifices were among the standard features listed to establish the barbarian nature of the Celts/Galatians—but tries to explain it in the context of exceptional and deep-rooted Roman fear of the Gauls. The present sense of danger is fueled by historical memories of the Galatians sacking Rome. According to Livy (5.48.3; 22.14.11), it was at the Forum Boarium, at a spot called *ad busta Gallica*, where the Gauls who died during the siege of Rome in 387 B.C.E. were burnt and buried.

> Nevertheless, the Romans were greatly alarmed by the proximity of their country to the enemy, . . . as well as by the ancient renown of the Gauls [*Galatōn*] whom the Romans seem to have feared more than any other people. For Rome had once been taken by them. . . . Their alarm was also shown by their preparations for the war (neither before nor since that time, we are told, were there so many thousands of Romans in arms at once), and by the extraordinary sacrifices which they made to the gods. For though they have no barbarous or unnatural practices, but cherish towards their deities those mild and reverent sentiments which especially characterize Greek thought, at the time when this war burst upon them they were constrained to obey certain oracular commands from the Sibylline books, and to bury alive two Greeks, a man and a woman, and likewise two Gauls [*dyo de Galatas*], in the place called the "forum boarium," or cattle market; and in memory of these victims, they still to this day, in the month of November, perform mysterious and secret ceremonies. (Plutarch, *Marc.* 3, LCL)

Present and past danger merge and lead to an unprecedented military mobilization. This outstanding psychological and military effort, supported by diplomatic activities that delayed Hannibal's invasion, helped the Romans defeat the Galatians. The triumph of Telamon (225), in a way, showed that the sacrifice of the Galatians in 228 had obviously been favorably accepted by the gods, who had given victory in return.

Thus, while there appears to be some rationale behind the Galatian sacrifice in 228, its repetition twelve years later following the defeat at Cannae in 216 seems puzzling. Why are *Galatians* sacrificed if the threat is posed by *Hannibal* and *Carthage*? The answer is both political and ideological. Politically, Hannibal counted on Celtic resistance as a natural ally in his war against Rome. Livy (21.52) reports that he presented himself as liberator of the Italic Galatians/Gauls from the yoke of Rome. He could recruit large numbers of Celtic mercenaries, possibly about fourteen thousand,[64] who marched in his army when he defeated the Romans at Cannae (216) and later threatened Rome again in 211 and 207. But while this Gallic–Punic alliance is an important element of the overall picture, it cannot sufficiently explain the extraordinary fact that in order to obtain divine intervention against Hannibal, again two Galatians had to be made ritual scapegoats instead of a Carthagian man and woman.

Imperial State Myth and the Archetypal Galatian Enemy

In fact, the Galatian sacrifice of 216 might indicate that the Roman construction of the Galatian/Celtic enemy had undergone a profound metamorphosis. It had been universalized, on the one hand, and been made part of Roman state religion, on the other. The Galatians had grown in the Roman imagination into an enemy of mythological stature who represented the primeval threat to Rome per se. It is interesting that the Galatian sacrifice in 216 was linked to an accusation of unchastity against the Vestal virgins (Livy 22.57.1–6), who with their ritual purity embodied the security and inviolability of Rome: like the Galatians and the Greeks, the Vestals were buried alive, though not in the marketplace, but in the liminal *campus sceleratus* ("Field of Desecration").[65]

The *metus Gallicus*, the fear of the Galatians/Gauls, was historically rooted in the traumatic conquest of the city in 387 B.C.E., but it grew into a kind of ideological matrix that for centuries to come could assimilate multiple other fears and threats. Heinz Bellen has shown how this process started with connecting the *metus Gallicus* to the *metus Punicus* in the Second Punic War and was closely linked to the ideological justification of Roman imperial expansion. The *metus Gallicus* was revived on several occasions right into the first century C.E., including the disastrous defeat Varus suffered from the Germans in 9 C.E., under Augustus, and the rebellion of Vindex in 68 C.E., under Nero.[66] According to Karl Strobel, no other nation ever represented such an archetypal threat to the Romans, the "enemy per se," as did the Galatians.[67]

How naturally any serious emergency or danger could be perceived as essentially "Galatian," that is, as a *tumultus Gallicus*,[68] again became obvious when the invading Cimbri and Teutoni threatened Rome at the same time that the Scordisci, a Galatian tribe in Thrace, defeated a Roman army in 114 B.C.E. Although the migrating tribe of the Cimbri, originally from the region of the North Sea, were not Celtic but German, they were assimilated into the prototypical image of the northern barbarians with their Celtic features of fierce aggressiveness, love of war, extreme cruelty, irrationality, greediness—into the brute forces of anti-civilization who had already once plundered Rome and raided Delphi as well as Asia.[69] Again—and for the third and last time in Roman history—a Galatian couple (and a Greek couple) were buried alive at the Forum Boarium in 113 B.C.E. (Plutarch, *Quaest. Rom.* = *Mor.* 284 B–C). And once again, as before Telamon and after Cannae, the sacrifice worked, in the official Roman perception, and brought the Romans victory. After severe defeats—the Battle of Arausio (Orange) in 105 became the worst military disaster since Cannae in 216 and another *dies ater* on the Roman calendar[70]—Marius gained two decisive victories, at Aquae Sextiae (Aix-en-Provence) and at Cisalpine Vercellae in 102/101. Having preserved the city from a traumatic catastrophe similar to the Gallic conquest of 387 B.C.E., he is celebrated as the third founder of Rome, in line with Romulus (Plutarch, *Mar.* 27.9).

The Galatians, as these developments show, are intimately linked to the rise of the Roman Empire. If the Punic fear in the second century B.C.E. stimulated and legitimized Roman world conquest—on the argument that Rome could not tolerate any external power such as Carthage again threatening its very existence—the same can be said about the Galatian fear. And if the three Punic Wars are to be perceived as the first decisive victory of Rome in the battle for world rule,[71] then the symbolic linkage between Gaul/Galatia and Carthage has programmatic implications for Rome's ambitions as well. From the second century onward, the Romans gradually moved "out of area" to defeat the Celts both in the East and the West. In 189 B.C.E., Manlius Vulso marched against the Galatians of Asia Minor in his glorious, cruel, and highly disputed anti-barbarian crusade, which ended in a disastrous defeat for the Galatians. In that case, however, it was no longer Rome alone that he claimed to defend, but also Greece and the whole of humanity.

Delphi under Attack (279 B.C.E.)

For the Greek world, the encounter with the Celts is interwoven with the rise and fall of Alexander's empire. Although the Greeks had met Celts before as mercenaries, the grand opening act took place when a delegation of Galatians approached Alexander the Great around 335, during his military campaign in the Balkans and the area of the Lower Danube. The Celts at that time had already moved into this region.[72] Apparently the Galatian emissaries wanted to reach an agreement about friendly mutual relations with the Macedonian invader who was about to embark on the long march of conquest against Persia that would make him the ruler of the known world. Legend has it that Alexander asked the Galatians what they feared most on earth. They replied that they feared nothing on earth except that the sky might fall down on them (Strabo 7.3.8; *FGH* 138 frg. 2; Arrian, *Anab.* 1.4.6–8).

Again we encounter the barbarians using a figure of speech that puzzles the civilized. We are reminded of Diodorus's complaint that the Galatians speak in riddles and exaggerations, talking about one thing when they mean another, boastful and fearlessly disrespectful (Diodorus 5.31). Again, the combination of Galatian courage and fear appears to the invader as irrational and excessive: it does not fit Greek categories of manliness, restraint, and wisdom. Here again, it seems, the Galatians are cloaking elements of resistance in their public discourse with the conqueror, concealing what cannot be said openly, as it were.[73] They clearly are not without wit, intelligence, and sophistication, but they demonstrate once more that they are, in a barbarian manner, "overly clever" and irreverent. According to Arrian, Alexander had of course expected the Celts to praise his greatness and show their respect to his power in one way or another. But this submission to the dominant order is exactly what they refused to do.[74] Half a century later, this innate "lawlessness" would allow the Greeks to portray the Galatians' defeat at Delphi as an archetypal victory won in the holy war of civilization versus anti-civilization.

Historical and Ideological Galatians

Thirty-three years old and at the zenith of his success in 323 B.C.E., Alexander died unexpectedly in Babylon, the city he had intended to resurrect as the metropolis of his world empire. He left an enormous power vacuum, with his generals struggling among themselves to become his successor. When the last of these Diadochi was murdered in 281, no universal heir to Alexander's empire was yet in sight and the Hellenistic world had sunk into the chaos and confusion of endless power struggles. The Celts seized this moment of weakness. Around 280, several Celtic armies made independent incursions into Paeonia, Thrace, and Macedonia.[75] The newly installed king of Macedonia, Ptolemy Keraunos, was defeated and the Galatians put his head on the point of a spear as a trophy.[76]

While some of the Galatian troops must have withdrawn from Macedonia after this, or were eventually pushed back by military force, the Galatian leader Brennus (that is, another Galatian bearing the name of the earlier foe of the Romans) urged a campaign against Greece (Pausanias 10.19.7–8). According to Pausanias, Brennus's army, mustering some 152,000 men and 24,000 horses, marched farther south toward Delphi. The Athenians, though greatly exhausted by the Macedonian conquests and warfare since Alexander, took the leadership in defending Thermopylae against the barbarian invaders. Their heroic resistance, still following Pausanias's report, was broken, however, when the Galatians managed to pass the famous Gates of Thermopylae on a secret path that the Persians had used in their legendary war against the Greeks two hundred years earlier (Pausanias 1.4.1–2). Brennus reached Delphi in 279.

What happened at Delphi is not exactly clear.[77] If we trust Pausanias's account, the main source for these events, it was Apollo himself who took over. The god told the terror-stricken Delphians not to be afraid and promised to defend his sanctuary himself (10.22.12). The earth started to shake violently under the Galatian army; heavenly signs like thunderbolts and lightning terrified the Celts with fire that fell on them, and a cacophonous noise made them unable to understand any orders. Ghosts of ancient heroes appeared, great rocks were hurled toward the barbarians from Mount Parnassus, and finally severe frost and snow set in. In the end a "panic" seized the Celts at night. They heard the trampling of horses and imagined an attack. Rushing to their arms, they started to kill one another, no longer able to identify friend from foe or to understand their own mother tongue, instead hearing Greek all around them. The "madness" sent by the god led to a great mutual slaughter and enabled the Greeks to defeat them. Brennus, already wounded, committed suicide (Pausanias 10.23).

For the Greek world, the Battle of Delphi in 279 held as much importance as the Celtic attack a hundred years earlier had held for the Romans. It does not seem coincidental that the leader of the Celtic incursion, at both Rome and Delphi, was named Brennus, possibly a ceremonial title with a kingly connotation.[78] In fact, both events became tightly interwoven in the "mythopoietic process" that turned the Celts into the archetypal enemies confronting gods and rulers of the Greco-Roman universe, in both the West and the East. Undoubtedly the sanctuary of Apollo at Delphi was one of the most important and revered religious and political centers of Greek civilization, holding the *omphalos* stone that symbolized the world's navel. Kings from all over the world asked questions of the famous Pythian oracle, which the priestess, the Pythia, answered while sitting on the tripod of Apollo; the temple guarded extraordinary wealth from the numerous dedications it received and the treasures kept in its precinct.

We do not know whether Delphi was actually occupied and plundered by the Celts or managed to remain immune. In a statement that appears almost "Jewish" in its fierce rejection of idols made in the image of humans, Diodorus reports (22.97) that Brennus mocked the anthropomorphic gods of the Greeks when he entered the temple. There are enigmatic reports about a "Delphic" treasure of gold turning up at Tolosa (today Toulouse), in Narbonese Gaul in the West, at the time of the invasion by the Cimbri and Teutoni around 105 B.C.E. Strabo (4.1.13) believed that the Galatian tribe of the Tectosages had sent the sacred objects stolen from Delphi to their native lands in the West where they had been sunk in sacred lakes. Nevertheless, it is probable that the Celts did no serious damage to the temple precinct.[79] But inevitably their attack was represented as a heinous crime of sacrilege and blasphemy. It was Apollo himself whom the barbarian invaders had attacked and who in person had appeared on the battlefield to defend his sanctuary against desecration. From this time onward, the Galatomachy—the battle against the Galatians/Celts—took on a profoundly religious dimension as an event that reestablished and safeguarded human and cosmic order. The games of the *sōtēria*, a festival of "salvation" subsequently installed at Delphi by the Greek cities, commemorated the rescue not only of Apollo's temple but also of Greek civilization itself, as well as of the whole divinely sanctioned order of the world.[80]

Galatian Battle and World Salvation

The ideological effect of assimilating the Galatians to the image of an archetypal enemy, as godless and lawless antagonists of civilization, was represented visibly when the Greeks decided to hang up the shields of the defeated Celts next to those of the defeated Persians in the temple of Apollo at Delphi.[81] The message thus sent was powerful: As the Greeks had once overcome the barbarians from Persia, civilization had now won another crucial triumph over those who sought to overthrow it. In fact, Pausanias's description of the great Celtic War in 279 is strongly modeled after Herodotus's account of the Persian wars two hundred years earlier, including the Athenian leadership at Thermopylae, the indescribable atrocities committed by the barbarian invaders, and the claim of the Delphic god to defend himself.[82]

One may well ask how far this emerging "Galatian myth" reflects historical reality. Were the Greeks being confronted with a foreign invasion more barbaric and devastating than they had ever experienced, either before or after the Persian wars? To what extent were the Greek cities under ideological and political pressure to construct an extraordinary enemy in order to restore their damaged self-image through a spectacular victory? Since the Macedonian takeover of Greece and the troublesome period after 321, when Alexander the Great's successors struggled to divide up his empire, Greek self-assurance had proven elusive. Nothing could be more welcome than a Galatian triumph, to be celebrated as a new Panhellenic victory over the evil forces of barbarism and a return of Greek power and glory. Not only the victory of Delphi itself but also relatively minor subsequent victories over the Galatians functioned in that way.

The issues were not self-esteem and honor alone, but these were intimately linked to the fierce power struggles of the post-Diadochian era as well. The newly emerging Hellenistic dynasties of the Antigonids in Macedonia, the Seleucids in Asia and Mesopotamia, and the Ptolemies in Egypt needed an ideological framework within which they could authorize their power. The Galatian threat was nearly ideal material to construct systems of legitimization in which the defeat of barbarians could be transformed into supreme benefactions provided on behalf of civilization itself, and the charisma of the conquerors could be reconfigured as trustworthy and well-earned rulership.

In an extensive study of this phenomenon, Karl Strobel has shown that, in the scramble for power after Alexander's death, no fewer than five rulers (Antigonos Gonatas, Ptolemy II, Antiochos I, Attalos I, Prusias I, and Eumenes II) derived their legitimacy from a Galatian victory, establishing their claim to power on their glory as *euergetēs* (= Latin *benefactor*) of Greek civilization and *sōtēr* (savior) from the barbarian (= Galatian) threat.[83] Antigonos Gonatas, who defeated a Celtic army two years after Delphi at Lysimacheia in 277 B.C.E., was hailed as king of Macedonia and was thus able to establish the Antigonid dynasty.[84] The Seleucids and Attalids in Asia Minor, as we will see, followed the same logic.

The ideological effect was at work even as far afield as Alexandria. Around 275 B.C.E., King Ptolemy II crushed a mutiny by his four thousand Galatian mercenaries by trapping and starving them to death on an island in the Nile. The act may not appear a particularly heroic victory. Nevertheless, his court poet Callimachus celebrated the event in the context of Apollo's battle at Delphi and as part of the common Hellenistic fight against the insane and warlike tribes of the Galatians, who act like their mythological doubles, the Titans, in their blasphemous ravaging against divine and human order.[85]

Pergamon's Triumph (240 B.C.E.)

After Delphi in 279 B.C.E., Asia Minor and Pergamon become the next momentous stage where the Galatians/Gauls enter history's limelight. Following their final defeats in Greece and Macedonia, the Celts split into two groups and either returned north to the Danube or went farther into Thrace, where, on the western shore of the Black Sea, they founded the kingdom of Tylis, which lasted until 213 B.C.E. Three tribes (the Tolistobogii, Trocmi, and Tektosagi) crossed over the Hellespont to Asia Minor in 279/278 B.C.E.

Settlers or Robbers?

The tribes were hired as *symmachoi*, that is, allies of King Nicomedes of Bithynia, who had begun a dynastic fight with his brother and at the same time wanted to muster military support against his Seleucid rivals, who aspired to bring all of Asia Minor under their control. The Galatians thus, according to Karl Strobel, entered Asia Minor not as lawless invaders but on a negotiated basis and to find new areas for settlement. In addition to their soldier's pay and share of the booty, King Nicomedes granted them territory in which to settle. The Tolistobogii (or Tolistoagii) received the western part of central Asia Minor, which included the ancient town of Gordium and the temple of the Great Mother of Pessinus (which remained independent, however); the Tectosages took their residence in the area around Ancyra; and the Trocmi in the eastern part. [86] Historically, this is the starting point of Galatia and of the Galatians who later became key players in the context of the New Testament and Pauline Christianity.

Strobel sees the acquisition of land as the Galatian tribes' primary goal and contends that they took over possession of the territory granted to them, rather than being forced to give up their nomadic lifestyle, only because of harsh military measures and disciplinary actions by the Seleucids, Attalids, or Romans.[87] Maybe for the Galatians the agriculturally rich region between Sangarios and Halys resembled the fertile areas in their original central and southern European homelands; in the power politics of the day, however, the Galatian lands in Asia Minor primarily served as a buffer zone between the kingdom of Nicomedes I and the sphere under Seleucid control.[88]

This version of the Galatian genesis in Asia Minor differs notably from the story told by the surviving ancient sources—written by the victors—which portray the Galatians not as warrior-settlers in search of new land but as nomadic robbers and habitual brigands, a view that still widely prevails in contemporary scholarship. Stephen Mitchell, in his magisterial work on Anatolia, concedes that land was at most an ultimate goal but not an immediate priority: what the Gauls were really looking for in his opinion was primarily "money or booty."[89]

From this perspective, the narrative of the Galatian settlement in Asia Minor is told as the century-long drama of a peaceful, advanced civilization under attack by hordes of ravaging and marauding barbarians. The Celtic newcomers wanted not to plough fields but to rob cities. From the beginning they divided Asia into "raiding areas" among the three tribes, demanding "protection money" from communities and even kings; plundering sanctuaries, cities, or the countryside; desecrating shrines, abducting women, committing atrocities. A third-century B.C.E. relief found in Cyzicus commemorates Heracles as helper of the city in the fight against the Gauls; inscriptions from the rich shrine of Didyma report a Galatian attack; three girls from Miletus commit suicide after being captured by Galatian warriors; another woman from the same city is carried away as far as Massalia (Marseille) in Gaul; inscriptions from Priene talk about substantial amounts of money and hostages that had to be sent to the barbarians to gain "protection." Other examples could be added. Eventually, following this logic, only harsh military force against the Galatians could make them settle down on their land and farm it peacefully.[90]

It is hard to tell what the "true story" of the first century of Galatian settlement in Asia Minor was behind this official story. But the clearly ideological nature of the "Galatian myth" told by their enemies and conquerors should at least caution us against taking it entirely at face value. Such an ideological-critical approach to the interpretation of ancient sources coincides with what Peter Wells describes as the necessary deconstruction of the dominant bias and stereotypes that shape these texts.[91] The more terrible the Galatians as the "scourge of Asia Minor" were portrayed, the more credible the power and territorial claims of their victors could be presented as "salvation" from Galatian terror.

This ideological potential of a Galatian victory was successfully exploited both by the Seleucids and by the Attalids of Pergamon to build up their rival dynasties. The Seleucid king Antiochus I won the first decisive victory over the Galatians in Asia Minor in the famous "Elephant Battle" around 270 B.C.E., which according to the established opinion turned the Galatians from marauding bandits into settled farmers and at the same time into the Seleucids' allies. But the most immediate success was that Antiochus could present himself as "savior" of Asia Minor and subsequently assumed the title *Sōtēr* to establish his dynastic and power claims.[92]

The Birth of the Dying Galatians

Nevertheless, the Galatians seem to have remained a menace, especially to the Greek cities and Pergamon. By paying some kind of tribute or "blackmail," the Pergamenes obviously managed to live for about three decades in peace with the tribes while they were busy fighting the Seleucids. When Attalus I succeeded Eumenes I in 241, however, he made a bold anti-Galatian gesture by refusing to pay the levy imposed on him. In the war that ensued, he beat the tribe of the Tolistobogii at the sources of the river Caicus around 240 B.C.E. (Pausanias 1.25.2).[93] This victory is featured as a major and groundbreaking anti-barbarian triumph in the defense of Hellenism and becomes the foundational event in the political mythology surrounding Pergamon's rise to power. Celebrated as a new ideal victory comparable to the great triumphs of the Greeks over the Persians in 490/480 or the mythological battles against the Giants and Amazons, it granted Attalus charismatic legitimacy as savior and benefactor of Pergamon and the Greek cities of Asia Minor, thus providing an overarching foundation and justification for the Attalid kingdom. Polybius (18.41) reports that after this victory over the Galatians, the "most formidable and warlike nation in Asia," Attalus assumed the title of king for himself and his dynasty. He ruled for forty-four years (241–197).[94]

This specific connotation of subduing the Galatian Other as an act of salvation subsequently emerges as a trademark of the Attalid kingdom and its two most notable cultural productions, the Great Altar and the famous sculptures of the Dying Gauls.

As victory monuments that Attalus both erected at Pergamon and sent elsewhere, the Dying Gauls in their numerous variations became ambassadors to the Greek world of Pergamon's triumph against barbarians, as, for example, at the acropolis in Athens, where Attalus displayed them together with dying Giants, Amazons, and Persians in a monument mentioned by Pausanias (1.25.2).[95] We will retrun to this subject in the following chapter.

The political function of the Galatian construct that features them as an archenemy of civilization within the framework of the competing Hellenistic power claims, is so obvious that one should make a clear distinction between the historical Galatians and their "ideological double" shaped by the dominant historiography. One can assume that the Galatians were probably ethnically "different," that is, more archaic and "savage" in their way of fighting and in aggressive explorations for new land to settle[96]—but essentially not more cruel, greedy, evil, and warlike than everybody else. They did not build city-states but adhered to their habit of building fortified hill castles; they kept their Druidic priesthood and Celtic religion—all this despite clear tendencies toward assimilation.[97] It might be that they continued to sacrifice humans.[98] Although they were more widespread than any other ethnic group at that time and had considerable military power, which at some points seriously interfered with Roman, Pergamene, and other interests, the Galatians obviously never had any intention of building a unified kingdom or empire of larger dimensions. In Asia Minor they maintained their tribal structure and became a ruling caste on top of the indigenous population. Strabo in his *Geography* (12.5) describes the Galatian society as a confederation of three tribes that assembled in a council (*boulē*) called the Drynemeton. Each of these tribes of "Gallo-Graecia" or "Galatia" was divided into four tetrarchies under a tetrarch, a judge, and a military commander. All of them spoke the same Galatian language, which coexisted with the widespread usage of Greek. [99]

Overall, the Galatians appear to have been quite ordinary players in the post-Diadochian political constellations of Asia Minor. Their transition into Anatolia and their settlement were not a brutal invasion and takeover but a negotiated move; at different stages they were employed by and helpful to virtually all involved parties as settlers, mercenaries, allies, counterbalancing agents, and participants in the dramatic power struggles of the third and second centuries. They were used, but, like every other player in the politics of ancient Asia Minor, they themselves tried to make use of favorable conditions to their own advantage. Nevertheless, the myth of the Galatians as prototypical enemies and barbarians persisted and flourished, but the myth conveys more about the civilization that produced, nourished, and needed it than about the Galatians themselves.

In an interesting study, Jane Webster has challenged the ahistorical and decontextualized reading of ancient sources on "innate" Celtic aggression and endemic warfare. She points out that, with the exception of Polybius's *Histories*, the main literature on Celts—like Caesar's *Gallic War,* Diodorus's *Bibliotheca* or Livy's Roman history—is historically contingent and embedded in the history and ideology of Roman imperial expansion, which employed the Greek colonial discourse of Celtic barbarism and used it for its own ends.[100]

The literature of Celtic warrior society is the literature of Roman territorial ambition, aggression, and conquest, which has far more to say regarding Graeco-Roman attitudes to Celtic peoples, and Rome's need to justify territorial expansion, than it does regarding Celtic warfare.[101]

This brings us back to Rome once again. The mytho-political web and ideology spun by the Greco-Roman world around the Galatians as universal agents of disorder and rebellion establish the semantic universe into which the Roman sacrifice of a Galatian man and woman in 228 inscribes itself. The elements of its initial staging—a lightning strike close to Apollo's temple and the Sibylline books of Apollo declaring that the Galatians posed a dreadful threat—are reminiscent of the Celtic sack not only of Rome in 389 but also of Delphi in 279, where Apollo had acted similarly through thunderbolts and taken leadership in the battle with the Galatians. Delivering a Galatian couple to an extremely slow and cruel death at the Forum Boarium brought together not only Rome and Delphi but also Rome and Pergamon, where around this time probably the first sculptures of Dying Galatians—among them the astonishing image depicting the suicidal death of a Galatian couple—were emerging.

Apart from its immediate significance within the crisis on the Italian peninsula, did the dramatic act of human sacrifice signify on a more general level that Rome's fight against the Galatians and Carthaginians *also* had a symbolic universality? That a new powerful player had entered into the arena where Alexander's empire was the ultimate prize to be won? This "global" perspective can be traced to the time when the Romans, after their victory over the Galatians at Telamon in 225, not only granted Marcellus a glorious triumph and the rarest spectacle of personally offering the armor of the defeated Galatian king Britomartus to Jupiter Feretrius, but also sent a precious gift to the Delphic Apollo as a thanks-offering (Plutarch, *Marc.* 8), a gesture that drew on the already established role of Delphi as the symbolic center of the great Panhellenic triumph over barbarians/Galatians.[102] The message thus conveyed is powerful: Rome's victory is not Rome's alone, but part of a worldwide struggle against the Galatian agents of godless and lawless disorder. Rome was now ready to defend civilization on a global scale, with Pergamon as its most faithful ally in Asia Minor.

Universalized Galatian Barbarians and the Worldwide Roman Savior (189 B.C.E.—25 B.C.E.)

If we consider the sources and historical events outlined so far, it becomes obvious that the Galatians/Gauls/Celts achieved something in the realm of ideology that had a much greater impact than their deeds on the battlefield. They were an enemy that Rome repeatedly encountered, in more places around the Roman world and throughout more centuries than any other antagonist. And like no other ethnic group, they united Romans and Greeks in grizzly tales of a monstrous adversary they had in common, as well as in proud memories of heroic victories won over the titanic forces of evil and barbarism. The centuries-long shock waves of Celtic migration and activity throughout the Mediterranean world thus became the ideal breeding ground for the political myth of a world-saving superpower that could serve as a bulwark against the chaos embodied by the Galatian invaders.[103] It is striking to observe how closely the process of empire building and the gradual defeat of the "universal" Gauls/Galatians are tied together. Rome will make sure that it can eventually claim both: the final victory over the Celts in the East, West, and North, as well as world rule.

When a Roman force under Manlius Vulso entered Asia Minor for the first time, it not only defeated the Seleucids at Magnesia in 190 B.C.E.—the "official" pretext for its interference—but swiftly proceeded, with unsurpassed brutality and contempt for legal objections from Rome, to settle Galatian affairs in the East once and for all. After Vulso devastatingly defeated the Galatians in 189, Galatia officially became obliged to follow Pergamene orders—and to submit to Rome. The year of 189 B.C.E., two hundred years after the Celtic sack of Rome, marks a decisive moment in Roman history. Manlius Vulso struck the death blow to Galatian independence in Asia Minor at about the same time that Rome more or less vanquished the Celts in Italy and took back whatever territory it lost in the Second Punic War. The next 150 years would be the decisive period in the gradual buildup of Rome's worldwide empire. Carthage and the successor states of Alexander's empire were one after the other subdued or annexed—the Antigonids of Macedonia first, then the Attalids of Pergamon, and later the Seleucids and Ptolemies. Simultaneously, the Gauls/Galatians all over the world were forced step by step into compliance with Roman rule.

Hannibal, the much-feared Punic opponent who tried to muster Celtic resistance against Rome in Cisalpine Italy, can be taken as a starting point. The fact that Macedonia allied itself with the Carthaginian in the Second Punic War (218–201 B.C.E.) in his quest against Rome is one of the pretexts for Roman interference in the East. In the name of Greek freedom and in close alliance with Athens as well as Pergamon, Rome fought against the Antigonids, who suffered a decisive defeat in 197 B.C.E. and were finally dismantled in the Battle of Pydna in 168 B.C.E. The dynasty that had built its royal power on Antigonus Gonatas's deed of "salvation" from the Galatian terror a hundred years earlier ceased to exist. Once Macedonia became a Roman province in 148 B.C.E., the homeland of Alexander the Great and the first of the post-Diadochian kingdoms were conquered, the power it had claimed over Greece was gone forever. The meaning of Greek freedom within a Roman framework, however, becomes clear when the rebellious city of Corinth was razed to the ground by Rome shortly afterwards in 146 B.C.E., the year that also saw the final destruction of Carthage in the Third Punic War. Greece from then on was firmly under Roman control.

During this same period, Rome was able to establish its rule in Asia Minor as well. The victory over the Seleucid Antiochus III was in part owed to the strong support by Attalid Pergamon. The Pergamene king Attalus I had already maintained a policy of close alliance with Rome in dealing with the power claims of Philip V of Macedonia. When Attalus's successor Eumenes II (197–159) took over, he was confronted with the Seleucid attempt to regain control over western Asia Minor and to deny any

Roman rights to interfere in this area. Faced with the decision whether to side with Antiochus or the Romans, Eumenes maintained his father's policy of alliance with the Romans and urged the senate to declare war on Antiochus. After defeating Antiochus at Thermopylae, the Romans for the first time crossed the Hellespont and won victory in the Battle of Magnesia in 190, which forever ended Seleucid rule in Asia Minor. As Eumenes had granted Rome considerable military assistance throughout the campaign, he was awarded the lion's share of the conquered Seleucid territory, which the Romans divided between their main allies, Pergamon and Rhodos. Pergamon increased its territory more than tenfold and thus became the most powerful kingdom of western Asia Minor designed to rule in the interest of Rome—it was, as Polybius states, now "inferior to none" (21.22.15). Rome itself at this point did not want to take direct responsibility but made sure that Asia Minor was governed in accordance with Roman interest.[104]

The Campaign of Manlius Vulso in 189 B.C.E.

Even before the campaign against the Seleucids was concluded by the peace conference of Apamea in 188 B.C.E., the Romans turned against the Galatians who had served among the Seleucid forces of Antiochus III at Magnesia. The punitive expedition in 189 B.C.E. of Manlius Vulso, who was assisted by Eumenes' brother, Attalus of Pergamon, led to a disastrous defeat for the Galatians and the "greatest slaughter of them known in the historical record."[105] At the approach of Manlius's army, the three tribes tried to take hasty refuge with their women and children in two camps at Mount Olympus near Gordium and the hill fortress at Mount Magaba southeast of Ancyra. But they had no chance to protect themselves against the brutal assault carried out by a professional army with more powerful weapons. Livy reports the events as if he were watching an arena spectacle. The Gauls from the outset were marked as losers. Ill-prepared for the Roman onslaught, they appeared vulnerable even in their most ferocious response. At one point they hurled far-too-small rocks at the enemy (an image of desperate futility we will encounter again at the Great Altar of Pergamon):

> Stones—but not of suitable size, since they had made no preparations in advance, but took each what happened to come to his hand in his hasty search—they did use, but like men untrained in their employment, with neither skill nor strength to add effectiveness to the blow. (Livy 38.21.6)

Wounded by arrows, sling-bullets, and darts from all sides, their naked white flesh, exposed for the battle in Celtic manner, was black with blood, and their famous shields could not protect them. As the Galatians were driven into panic, they sought refuge with the unarmed crowd of the women, children, and the elderly in the camp. Livy does not fail to mention that "they had brought with them their whole population of every class and age, like a people in migration rather than setting out to war." Amid the screams of women and children being butchered, the Roman victory took its course.

The massacre's carnage "went on far and wide over all the outlying parts of the mountains," and the "number of the casualities could not easily be calculated." At Mount Olympus alone, 40,000 were slain or captured and subsequently sold into slavery (Livy 38.23.8–9). The booty that Manlius Vulso exhibited in Rome during his triumph comprised "212 golden crowns, 220,000 pounds of silver, 2,103 pounds of gold, 127,000 of Attic four-drachma pieces, 250,000 cistophori, 16,320 gold Philippei; there were also arms and many Gallic spoils [*arma spoliaque multa Gallica*] transported in carts, and fifty-two leaders of the enemy led before his car" (Livy 39.7).

There is no doubt that Manlius Vulso's attack on the Celts of Galatia was, even within the framework of Roman law, an entirely unprovoked war of aggression that was waged without the permission of the Roman senate and moreover violated the "law of the nations" (Livy 38.44–49). Rumors spread that it was mostly an act of "personal robbery" (*privatum latrocinium*) by a man who craved the fame of an unprecedented victory as well as the considerable wealth of the Galatian tribes. It is interesting to observe that contemporary scholarship in general is aware of these issues, but nevertheless maintains an unfaltering loyalty to the righteousness of the Roman cause, treating the massacres of Mount Olympus and Mount Magaba as a kind of "collateral damage" that is deplorable but inevitable in pursuit of the higher goal of Roman security and domination.[106]

This mirrors the attitude of the Greek cities of Asia in 189 B.C.E., who hastened to appear before Manlius Vulso at Ephesus in order to praise him for his victory over "Galatian lawlessness" and "barbarian fear" (*barbarikon phobon kai tēs Galatōn paranomias;* Polybius 3.3.5). Manlius is honored with golden crowns because "all inhabitants of the country on this side of the Taurus" declare themselves to be overjoyed at the release from the "ferocity of the rude barbarians" and Galatian *terror*. "And while the Roman victory over King Antiochus had been more glorious and splendid [*clarior nobiliorque*] than that over the Gauls, yet the victory over the Gauls afforded the allies more satisfaction than that over Antiochus" (Livy 38.37.1–2). Rome was now officially hailed as savior (*sōtēr*) by the Greeks. For the battle's contemporaries, the political implications of this were clear. According to Polybius (21.16), emissaries of Antioch came to praise the victory that had made the Romans "masters and rulers of the whole world" (*archēn kai dynasteian tēs oikoumenēs*) and to ask what they had to do in order to have peace and alliance (*philia*) with Rome. The peace of Apamea one year later in 188 B.C.E. effectively reduced the Seleucid Empire to Syria, Cilicia, and its eastern parts. Another post-Alexander dynasty that claimed a Galatian victory as a salvific foundational event (and meanwhile had enlisted Celts in its army) had felt the emerging power of Rome, though it would still take a century and a quarter until Rome in 64 B.C.E. conquered Seleucid Antioch and turned Syria into a Roman province.

One detail of the agreement of 188, a treaty that required high compensation to be paid to Rome, is worth mentioning in particular: The Romans demanded the extradition of Hannibal. The dreaded Carthaginian who had challenged Rome in Italy for sixteen years with his undefeated Punic-Celtic army was now in exile under Seleucid protection. After Rome demanded his life from Antiochus, he found refuge with

Prusias of Bithynia, but not for long. In an effort to reclaim territory lost to Pergamon in the peace of Apamea, Prusias entered into an anti-Pergamene alliance for which he could also muster the Galatian chieftain Ortagion, who had survived the campaign of Manlius Vulso and was apparently still able to mobilize forces. For a last time Hannibal and the Galatians confronted Rome together. Prusias and Ortagion were defeated by Eumenes II of Pergamon in 183. But the actual peace was negotiated by Rome; it confirmed Pergamon's power and, moreover, required Prusias to turn over Hannibal, reproaching the king that he had given shelter "of all living men to the one who was most dangerous to the Roman people" (Livy 49.51). Hannibal committed suicide. One might speculate whether the title of "Savior/*sōtēr,*" which Eumenes took after this victory—following the example of his predecessor Attalus I after the Galatian triumph at the Caicus sources around 240—specifically reflects the double nature of a victory over Hannibal and the Galatians, the two archenemies of the Roman order.

The relationship between the Galatians and Rome from then on began to change, while the linkage between Rome and Pergamon, so far the closest ally of Rome and facilitator of Roman order in Asia Minor, seems to have suffered from some disturbances. The events of the next two decades, which saw more battles between Pergamon, the Galatians, and other kings in the area are not transparent in every detail. Galatians appear on different sides and in quickly changing coalitions. In the Roman war with Perseus of Macedonia (179–168 B.C.E.), the Galatian chieftain Cassignatus appears as commander in Eumenes' pro-Roman cavalry (Livy 42.47). On the other hand, Perseus also has Galatians in his army, though he, in an ill-advised move, refused to pay them properly, so they withdrew. Livy admits that if the Macedonians had not foolishly offended the Celts, their army would have caused great difficulties for the Romans in the Battle of Pydna (168 B.C.E.), which sealed the fate of the Antigonid dynasty.

While Eumenes was engaged in combat with the Macedonians, the Galatians used this distraction to revolt against Pergamon in 168 B.C.E. (Livy 45.19; Polybius 29.22; 30.1). Again the details are not exactly known, but at one point Eumenes himself was personally threatened and miraculously saved. The Romans negotiated with the Galatians at Synnada in 167, while King Eumenes sent his brother Attalus to Rome for help—but Rome this time appears to have been reluctant to grant support to Pergamon (Livy 44.20), distrusting Eumenes' loyalty with regard to the Macedonians and thus rather willing to side with the Galatians. At the same time, Prusias II of Bithynia turned up in Rome and claimed overlordship in Galatia (Livy 45.44; Polybius 30.30). When Eumenes himself went to Rome in person to demand a Roman army to bring the Galatians to heel, the Roman senate passed a law forbidding the presence of any foreign kings in Rome (Polybius 30.18–19, 30; Livy 45.44). Unable to meet his overlords, Eumenes returned home and defeated the Galatians by himself. [107]

The somewhat turbulent events around the seemingly incessant stream of embassies moving between Asia Minor and Rome are noteworthy insofar as they indicate that Rome after 189 is generally recognized as the supreme mediator of conflicts and in firm control of the affairs of Asia Minor. On the ideological plane, one can see it as another great victory for Rome, when even the Galatians finally acknowledge this undisputable fact by themselves sending an embassy to Rome in 165 B.C.E. to appeal for more independence. The senate decreed that Galatia should be seen as autonomous, but that it must stay within its borders (Polybius 31.2; also 31.32 and 32.2). It is a matter of scholarly debate to what extent the agreement of 165 indicates a diminished role for Pergamon and a strategic move by Rome in favor of the Galatians to keep Pergamon from becoming too powerful.[108]

The end of this story and of the Attalid dynasty is somewhat puzzling. In 133, Pergamon handed itself over to the Romans voluntarily and peacefully. The last Attalid ruler officially bequeathed his kingdom to Rome, which turned it into the Roman province of Asia.

The same would happen with Galatia roughly a hundred years later when Amyntas, the last Galatian king, died in combat for the establishment of Roman order in the Pisidian mountains and left his domain to Augustus, who turned it into the Roman province of Galatia in 25 B.C.E. The century leading to this event saw the emergence of a pro-Roman Galatian ruling cast in Asia Minor and the merger of both the Seleucid and Ptolemaic dynasties into the Roman power structure—Pompey makes Syria a Roman province in 64 B.C.E.; Augustus, Egypt in 30 B.C.E. after the defeat of Antony and Cleopatra at Actium. At the same time, the major Gallic/Galatian nations were conquered and pacified both in the East and the West. While we will deal with the post-189 B.C.E. history of the Galatians in Asia Minor more specifically in chapter 4, we want to conclude this chapter with a brief glimpse at the development of Gaul in the West and the role it played in the process of empire building.

Caesar's Gallic War and the Foundation of Empire

The first Galatian province had been founded in the West in 121 B.C.E. With the Greek colony of Massilia/Marseille as its main settlement, it was called Gallia Transalpina or Provincia Nostra ("our province") and gave its name to today's Provence in the south of France. A colony of Roman military veterans founded at Narbo in 118 B.C.E. secured the new province, which was later called Gallia Narbonensis. Rome now had stable communication lines as far as the Iberian Peninsula and control over the important trade route between the Rhone Valley and Marseille. Rankin states that thus the foundation was laid for Caesar's conquest of Gaul seventy-five years later. At this earlier time, however, Rome still showed reluctance to become entangled in the affairs of wild *Gallia Comata*, that is "long-haired Gaul."[109]

When, in the middle of the first century B.C.E., Julius Caesar set out to become sole master of Rome and the ancient world, his venture, with much inner logic, began in Gaul. In 59 he received the consulship and command of Cisalpine Gaul, Illyricum, and a little later Transalpine Gaul as well. A new mass migration of Celtic tribes gave him the pretext for military intervention. The Boii had been displaced from Dacia and pushed back toward Noricum and the territory of the Helvetii in 60. Under pressure from Germanic tribes, the Helvetii themselves, living in modern-day Switzerland, had decided to abandon their old territory and look for new settlement areas in southwestern Gaul. They asked Caesar for permission to pass peacefully through Roman-controlled territory. Caesar refused and under the pretense of protecting Gallia Narbonensis, he crushed the Helvetii at Bibracte. The battle became a wholesale slaughter, and of the 370,000 Helvetians on march with their women and children, 260,000 were killed and another large number sold into slavery.[110]

This operation set the pattern for eight years of Gallic wars (58–52/51 B.C.E.) fought between Rome and the peoples of Gaul, culminating in the Battle of Alesia in 52 B.C.E. In his own description of the campaigns, the famous *De bello Gallico*, Caesar draws the picture of a series of noble and entirely defensive Roman actions that were all either in support of friends crying out for help or legitimate punitive measures against rebellious and insurgent tribes not content with the rapid extension of Roman rule. Caesar presents himself as an ingenious military leader as well as an eminent ethnographer who with scholarly inquisitiveness examines and debates the ways of the Gauls while he defeats and without mercy wipes out a great number of their tribes.[111] After the final victory over Vercingetorix in 52 B.C.E., Caesar had not only subdued the whole country of the western Galatians/Gauls up to the Atlantic coast but had also crossed into the farthest and most "savage" territories beyond—Celtic Britannia in the North and Germany across the Rhine river in the East. Caesar's commentaries about the "Gallic war," a brilliant piece of imperial propaganda and, until fairly recently, the standard teaching text in modern Latin classes, leave no doubt that the price the war-mad barbarian Gauls had to pay for their pacification and integration into Roman civilization was not to be a matter of concern to the victorious. All together, over one million Gauls were killed and a similar number enslaved. According to Adrian Goldsworthy, "every soldier in the army was given a prisoner to sell as a slave."[112] Of the original estimated population of Gaul, only one-third remained. As Plutarch (*Caesar* 15) observes in a summary statement about the achievements of Caesar in Gaul—in Plutarch's Greek, "Galatia":

Fig. 12. Denarius issued by Julius Caesar showing the armor and weapons of a defeated Gaul. Photo: Bildarchiv Preussischer Kulturbesitz/Art Resource, N.Y.

For although it was not full ten years that he waged war in Gaul [*peri Galatian*], he took by storm more than eight hundred cities, subdued three hundred nations [*ethnē*], and fought pitched battles at different times with three million men, of whom he slew one million in hand to hand fighting and took as many more as prisoners. (trans. Bernadotte Perrin, LCL)

Indeed, after he had secured the regions of Gaul for Roman control and exploitation, Caesar had gathered enough symbolic and monetary capital to take over Rome. Refusing to disband his powerful army and to submit to the orders of the Roman senate, he, in a move that became legendary, crossed the Rubicon, the boundary between Italy and Gaul in 49 B.C.E. and thus sparked a new civil war. After defeating Pompey at Pharsalus in 48 B.C.E., annihilating Pharnaces of Pontus in 47 B.C.E., gaining control of Egypt and crushing the last remnants of the senatorial opposition in Africa and Spain, he celebrated his final triumph in Rome in 45 B.C.E. The senate proclaimed him dictator in perpetuity. He now had the supreme *imperium*, that is, undivided authority in all civil and military matters. This moment can be seen as the first decisive event in the birth of the Roman Empire under a single ruler; his successors, starting with his adopted son, Octavian/Augustus, would bear the name Caesar as one of their titles. Julius Caesar himself, however, was murdered by a group of senatorial opponents only one year later in 44 B.C.E. in a last attempt to restore the Republic.[113]

Caesar, according to Rankin the "first Roman thoroughly to exploit *Gallia Comata* as a source of power and wealth,"[114] survived his most formidable adversary Vercingetorix, the chieftain of the Gallic/Galatian tribe of the Aedui by only two years. Vercingetorix had managed to unite all of Gaul in the last decisive battle at Alesia. After his magnificent surrender in 52 B.C.E. (see p. 44, fig. 10 above), he was kept prisoner in Rome for six years before he was publicly displayed at Caesar's Gallic triumph in 46 B.C.E. and then ceremonially strangled or beheaded (Plutarch, *Caesar* 27). It seems noteworthy that the birth of the empire and the death of its last grand-style Gallic/Galatian opponent—whose victory would have prevented Caesar's triumph in Gaul and thus his takeover of Rome, reversing the course of history—happened simultaneously. While Caesar irresistibly took the last fast strides to world power between 51 and 46 B.C.E., the Galatian/Gaul, with predestined necessity, was slowly approaching his death at the Tullianum, the Roman state detention center. Vercingetorix's final execution within the ritual framework of Caesar's triumphal procession appears as the climax of the three Galatian life sacrifices at earlier stages of Rome's ascension to world rule. One might see in him a live version of a Dying Gaul/Galatian, whose death was the symbolic military and economic precondition for Rome's magnitude.

After Caesar's sudden death at the hands of the senatorial conspirators, his adopted son and designated heir, Octavian, moved with due caution, using admirable skill and utmost determination to make sure that all the power Caesar had held at the end of his life was transferred step by step to himself, while maintaining the appearance of a republican system and thus avoiding Caesar's fate. The year of 27 B.C.E., when the senate granted him the titles of *Augustus* ("the elevated and revered one") and *Princeps* is usually seen as the final point of transition from the Roman Republic to the Roman Empire.

Again it is intriguing and perhaps not entirely accidental that only two years later a major achievement in Rome's dealings with Gauls/Galatians can be reported: the founding of the Roman province of Galatia in Asia Minor in 25 B.C.E. We will return to this matter in chapter 4.

Rome's Global War on Galatian Terror

It is worthwhile to turn once more to Manlius Vulso's campaign in 189 B.C.E., which was Rome's first step beyond Italy in the worldwide defeat of the Gauls/Galatians and the decisive historical act that shaped Galatia in Asia Minor for the next centuries, into the time when the apostle Paul encountered its inhabitants, now firmly integrated into the Roman provincial system and fully under Roman control. In the political state myth of the newly established Roman Empire, Manlius Vulso's anti-barbarian crusade, not surprisingly, emerges as a landmark event. We will take a brief look at Livy's Roman history (*Ab urbe condita*), a core text of imperial ideology.

As Augustus's historiographer, Livy (59 B.C.E.–17 C.E.) gives an extensive report about the campaign of 189 B.C.E. The passage in books 38 and 39 is not only interesting regarding the first and formative Roman–Galatian encounter in Asia Minor, but even more as it shows how this clash was presented two hundred years later during the transition from the Roman Republic to the Roman Empire.[115] Livy's narrative does not try to hide the fact that, somewhat similar to the configuration of the first great historical encounter between Rome and the Gauls in 387 B.C.E., and not unlike Julius Caesar's conquest of Gaul, the law is not entirely on the side of the Romans. As we have already mentioned, after the victory over the Seleucids in the Battle of Magnesia (190 B.C.E.), Manlius Vulso had no legitimate reason to make war against their equally defeated Galatian allies. The Roman senate had not approved of marching against Galatia and intended to refuse Manlius Vulso his official triumph after he returned to Rome. It is interesting to see how Manlius, in Livy's words, manages to convince the Roman senate of the necessity of his attack on Galatia/Gaul and the integrity of his conduct.

> "The Gauls," they [Manlius's opponents] say, "were not enemies, but you attacked them while they were peaceful and obedient to our orders." I shall not ask you, conscript fathers, to believe about those Gauls also who dwell in Asia what you know in general about the barbarous character of the people of the Gauls and their most deadly hatred of the name of Rome [*odium in nomen Romanum*]; setting aside the ill repute and ill fame of the race as a whole, judge them by themselves. Would that King Eumenes were here, would that all the cities of Asia were here, and that you could hear them complaining of rather than me accusing the Gauls. (38.47)

A standard list of barbarian Galatian crimes and vices follows, including devastation, plunder, human sacrifice, and in particular the sacrifice of children. Livy then turns to the Roman victory over the Seleucid Antiochus preceding and justifying Vulso's attack on the Galatians and continues:

> The farther Antiochus should be removed, the more uncontrollable would be the rule of the Gauls in Asia, and all the lands on this side of the ridges of Taurus you would have added to Gallic territory [*Gallorum imperium*], not to your own. Grant, if you will, what my opponents say is true; but even on one occasion, Delphi, the common oracle of the human race [*humani generis oraculum*], the navel of the world [*umbilicus orbis*

terrarum], the Gauls despoiled, and the Romans did not on that account declare war on them. For my part, I thought that there was some difference between that time, when Greece and Asia was not yet under your control and sway, as regards your interest and concern in what was happening in those lands, and this time, when you have fixed the Taurus mountain as the boundary of the Roman empire [*finem imperii Romani*], when you bestow liberty and immunity upon cities, increase the territory of some, deprive others of their lands, impose tribute on others, enlarge, diminish, give, take away kingdoms, and deem it your responsibility that they shall have peace on land and sea. (38.48)

If the campaign of Manlius Vulso clearly was a breach of the "law of the nations," it however was deemed justified because of the ill and "lawless" nature of the Galatians as arch-barbarians and arch-enemies of Rome, Delphi, and Pergamon—of the cities of Asia Minor, the Greeks, and the whole human race (*humani generis*). The existence of the undefeated Gauls is presented not only as a threat to Roman hegemony on the northern ("this") side of the Taurus Mountain (as Gallia Cisalpina had been a threat in Italy on "this" side of the Alps) but as a threat to the whole world (*orbis terrarum*), which was attacked by the godless and lawless Celts at Delphi in its innermost existence, at its "navel" and most sacred spot.

Vulso/Livy, however, makes a crucial distinction between past and present. "Then," in 279 B.C.E., the Romans did not act and interfere in Greece or Asia—but "now" they have taken over worldwide responsibility. They "bestow liberty and immunity upon cities, increase the territory of some, deprive others of their lands, impose tribute on others, enlarge, diminish, give, take away kingdoms and deem it your responsibility that they shall have peace on land and sea." Peace in this context clearly means first and foremost the establishment of Roman power over foreign cities and kingdoms. It requires merciless and preemptive military strikes against any enemy of the Roman order, which are then, however, portrayed as salvific deeds for the benefit of humanity. Thus, Rome's murderous and unlawful war of aggression against the Galatians in 189 B.C.E. is not only sanctified as a kind of late retaliation for the blasphemous attack on Delphi but becomes a purely defensive act in a worldwide mission of peacemaking and safeguarding human civilization and law.

This is the language of world rule under the disguise of world salvation—and the Galatians as universal barbarians are vital to it. As blasphemous and lawless invaders of Delphi and Rome, they are the ideal enemy, who after their conquest of Rome in 387 B.C.E. would renew their attack against the foundations of heaven and earth, law and order, gods and humans wherever they appeared. Presenting a Galatian triumph thus means appropriating not only enormous amounts of gold but also the much more precious ideological currency that could purchase the legitimacy to rule—as a godlike savior of civilization and benefactor of humanity worldwide. In this way the Celtic attack on Rome in 387 B.C.E. and Manlius Vulso's inititiave of 189 B.C.E. to defeat the Galatians as players on the global stage can be seen as two key events in the genesis of the Roman Empire.

In Livy's weaving of the Roman saga, Manlius Vulso embodies both the local and the global aspects of the Celtic myth. He counts among his ancestors Marcus Manlius and Titus Manlius (Torquatus). The former features as the famous savior (together with the holy geese of Juno) of the Capitol in 387 B.C.E. (Livy 5.47). The latter successfully fought against a Celtic Goliath in single combat in Italy in 362 B.C.E. He was called Torquatus after the torque he took from his enemy and placed, spattered with blood, round his own neck (Livy 7.9–10). When Manlius Vulso in Asia Minor addressed his soldiers before the campaign against the Galatians, he referred to both men who belonged to his *gens* (clan): "Titus Manlius, Marcus Valerius have shown how far Roman valor [*Romana virtus*] surpasses Gallic madness [*Gallicam rabiem*]. Then Marcus Manlius alone thrust down the Gauls as they climbed in close array to the Capitoline" (Livy 38.17).[116]

Yet it is clear that now the defense of the native Capitol alone is no longer sufficient. The heroic traditions incarnate in Manlius's distinguished pedigree call for international action, as "this fierce tribe travelling up and down in war, has almost made the world [*orbem terrarum*] its residence" (Livy 38.17). It is time to move out of the officially condoned operational area in order to pursue and conquer the terrorist Celts worldwide: the Latin term *terror* occurs frequently in Manlius's speech; often combined with *tumultus,* it is a standard expression of anti-Celtic rhetoric and often used to describe Gauls/Galatians in the context of imperial propaganda.[117] The senate of Rome, when they eventually granted Manlius his triumph, confirmed this new necessity of hunting down Galatians on a worldwide scale. A universal enemy requires a universal Roman engagement. Or, as we might invert this logic of universal self-defense and world salvation: A worldwide Roman power claim requires the construction of a worldwide terrorist enemy.[118]

What started as self-defense against the Galatian assault has tacitly mutated into a justification for worldwide aggression. The more monstrous, lawless, and ubiquitous the enemy is portrayed, the more salvific, justified, and universal its victor's power. If Brennus and his Celts who attacked Rome and Delphi, if the pillaging and ravaging Galatians of Asia Minor had not existed, one would have needed to invent them. Rome could not rule without them. Livy's report demonstrates that at the threshold of Paul's era the Celtic myth was very much alive and one of the foundational great narratives of the Roman Empire.

Conclusion: Galatia(ns) as Topos of Roman Law and of Imperial Justification

What Galatia and Galatians meant for the ancient world has long faded away in present-day English understanding, not least in contemporary theological debates. Our examination of the first-century language usage of both Latin and the Greek *koinē* used by Paul has unearthed Galatia as a much more complex, comprehensive, and controversial concept than New Testament scholarship has taken into account so far. In view of the ideological construction of ancient Galatia(ns) as revealed in the written sources of their conquerors, our critical re-imagination has exposed a dramatically colorful, antagonistic, and thoroughly Roman profile attributed to them. It is closely connected to the world-wide establishment not only of the Roman Empire but also of Roman law.

At two crucial points in history, the Celtic sack of Rome and the Roman conquest of Celtic Asia Minor, we have examined how the establishment of the lawful nature of Roman, rather than Celtic, claims to foreign lands was a matter of intense hegemonic struggles and was ultimately decided by military force and the power of victory. World-wide *Galatia* was the prototypical battlefield of the Roman ideology of domination that derived its law and legitimacy from the triumph over the barbarian Other, the quintessential topos signifying hostile and inferior barbarian Otherness that needs to be conquered. When entering the ancient world as readers of a letter to Galatia—north or south, east or west, wherever Paul's Galatians were situated geographically—we have to keep in mind that on the *mental* map of the first century C.E., *Galatia* was a well-defined territory: it was *Roman* territory and it was enemy territory, burnt earth and fertile ground where civilization—and the worldwide Roman Empire—could thrive on the ashes of barbarism.

This re-imagination of the Galatians through the linguistic lens of the terms *Galatia* and *Galatians* has far-reaching consequences for any interpretative strategy used to read Paul's letter. The entire vocabulary of Paul's justification theology we had so securely anchored in the semiotics of a Jewish–Christian controversy all of a sudden reveals an entirely different *Sitz im Leben* within the framework of the Roman–Galatian encounter and of Roman imperial ideology. The self-justification, self-righteousness, and law of the dominant Roman order are derived from the glory of victory, most notably the Galatian victory. It is the works of war and conquest that are supposedly good and salvific to the entire world, including the vanquished themselves. The defeat of the Galatians is a Roman act of political euergetism or benefaction, which literally means *good works*.

In the mind-set of the first-century world, Galatia is thus firmly inscribed not only as a Roman term but as a topic that is highly sensitive to issues of imperial law and order. Long before Paul confronted the Galatians with issues of Jewish law and messianic justification by faith and grace alone, they were already firmly and categorically condemned or justified by Roman law and power, and had been granted *grace* through *faith* as loyalty and allegiance to the Roman emperor. This observation, which will be further explored in chapter 3 below, does not yet answer the question of how Galatian foreskin fits into this overall panorama, an issue that will require further contextual re-imaginations throughout the remaining chapters. At this point we can simply say that law, justification, and works as key terms of a first-century debate with and about Galatians have a robust Roman semiotics that serious hermeneutical investigation cannot ignore. From a Roman perspective, the righteousness and justification of Galatians was nothing to be tampered with, and certainly not to be bestowed by anyone except Caesar.

A Giant/Galatian is crushed beneath Aphrodite's boot; marble relief from the Gigantomachy Frieze of the Great Altar of Pergamon, ca. 160 B.C.E. Pergamon Museum Berlin. Photo: Erich Lessing/Art Resource, N.Y.

CHAPTER TWO

Dying Gauls/Galatians Are Immortal

The Great Altar of Pergamon

The white marble sculpture depicted on the front cover of this book, commonly known as the Dying Trumpeter, stands in the Capitoline Museum in Rome and is among the most moving and significant pieces of Greco-Roman art that have survived into modernity and postmodernity. It shows a mortally wounded *Galatian/Gallic* warrior who has collapsed on his shield. His sword and a broken horn, or trumpet, have fallen from hands that can barely continue to hold himself in a seated position. The strong and muscular body is completely naked, except for a braided torque around his neck, and his hair stands up in short tufts from his skull. The mustache and the clean-shaven cheeks probably indicate a noble rank. The oval shape of his very large shield with the protruding central boss offers no more protection, but instead mercilessly exposes the dying warrior's body to the spectator's gaze.[1]

Sitting on the ground, the Gaul has his one arm propped up in a position between rising once again and final collapse. The same contradictory impulses are embodied in his feet. The left is still up, with his leg forming an arch over the broken horn underneath, the right has already collapsed. We can read in his slightly opened lips and downturned, furrowed forehead tension, pain, and the agony of death—but he also seems to possess a stubborn resistance that refuses to die. This man is still sufficiently alive to be truly menacing and to showcase the fortitude of his victor, but he is too injured to pose any realistic threat. The blood pathetically dripping from the wound on his right side in full view of the spectator indicates that his time is running out. Yet it is this very moment of dying, frozen in timelessness, that has made him immortal, encapsulating a message that was as vital for Greeks, Pergamenes, and Romans as for their Western imperial successors to communicate. It is a message about sacred violence and the basic order of the world, about victory and civilization: our civilization.

The visual semiotics of dying and dead Galatians is the overall topic of the present chapter. After an initial exploration of the Dying Trumpeter, we will turn to a much larger, though closely related monument that has been called "one of the most impressive sculptural projects of its (and any) time": the Great Altar of Pergamon.[2] Our exploration of the Great Altar in both its Pergamene context and in light of its Roman semiotics aims at establishing this unique piece of art as an essential background image, auxiliary context, and *intertext* for reading Paul's letter to the Galatians—"a complementary semantic system" for interpreting the text.[3] For with unsurpassed beauty and complexity, the Great Altar visualizes the dominant thought world in which Paul and his Galatians move, think, and argue, and the symbolic universe of the master order that ascribes them their place, identity, and rules of conduct.

In Paul's time, the city at the center of the universe was no longer Pergamon but Rome, and the preeminent dynasty that claimed both heroic origin and a destiny to rule the world was that of the Julio-Claudians, rather than the Attalids. But the glory of the Great Altar had not vanished, nor was its basic conceptual framework in any way outdated. In fact, the Great Altar was most probably as active as ever, now within the framework of imperial religion. And the Galatians? Despite their incessant dying on the monumental reliefs of the Great Frieze and elsewhere in the Galatian battle imagery of Greco-Roman art, in the real world of Roman Galatia they turned out to be quite alive, as Paul's correspondence shows. But there, as at the Great Altar, they were again involved ambivalently in matters of law and transgression. We will take a brief look at this lawlessness of the Galatians, and of Paul, in light of the Dying Trumpeter and then more extensively return to it in chapters 4 and 5.

——— The Lawlessness of the Dying Trumpeter—and of Paul ———

For centuries the Dying Trumpeter, one of the most famous pieces of occidental victory art, has captured the Western imagination and shaped the Western mind. He was rediscovered in the early seventeenth century in Rome during excavations in an area that had been the gardens of Sallust. After Pope Clement XII had acquired him for the Capitoline Mueseum, Napoleon carried the sculpture to Paris in a triumphal procession in 1798 under the terms of the Treaty of Tolentino. The Dying Trumpeter (often also called the Dying Gladiator) was copied innumerable times at European courts and elsewhere and "quickly entered an inner sanctum of the 'musée imaginaire' of educated Europe."[4]

Though the image is a strangely familiar sight, for a contemporary viewer the details of the depiction are not easily readable. Yet in the language of images that was current in the first century C.E., all his visual features would be markers of a well-established *koinē*: torque, oval shield, nakedness in combat, wild and spiky hair, moustache, strong and white body, warlike nature, heroic resistance, and inevitable defeat were the basic visual vocabulary denoting Celtic/Gallic/Galatian ethnicity and destiny within a common sign system of otherness.[5] The Dying Trumpeter is a Dying Galatian/Gaul, and his broken trumpet is the definitive Roman summary concluding the five centuries of Gallic/Galatian warfare throughout the Greco-Roman world that we studied in the previous chapter: the ear-splitting barbarian noise it produced on the battlefield is now silenced forever.[6]

The Dying Galatian has been depicted in numerous variations and is at home in many places of the ancient Mediterranean—Greece, Asia Minor, Pergamon, and Rome.[7] He is also an inhabitant of the New Testament, although scholars have rarely noticed this.[8] Paul and the Galatians of his letter, like everyone else in their world, would encounter these omnipresent images and have no difficulty reading them. And as the Dying Trumpeter is generally believed to have originated from the Pergamene victory over the "barbarian Galatians" of Asia Minor in the late third century B.C.E., he is specifically and intimately related to Paul's Galatians anyway. Representing de facto one of their forefathers, he holds a decisive clue to their history and identity. At the same time he is also and with equal right "Roman"; that is, the sculpture was found at Rome where it, like other Dying Gauls in their "small" and "large" versions, obviously enjoyed enormous popularity.[9] The Trumpeter thus simultaneously belongs to the contemporary context of Paul and the Galatians as well. As part of the dominant worldview, his image offers us a window into both the history and the current perception of Galatia(ns) in Paul's time. A contextual and historical-critical exploration of a first-century Galatian correspondence would certainly need to take a closer look at him.

This is, however, where the dilemma of a decontextualized theological Galatian interpretation starts. We have no clues about how to read Dying Galatians because we have rarely ever tried. The only markers of concrete Galatian contextuality that we have established and explored in our theological inquiry are Jewish circumcision versus Gentile "foreskin." Foreskin (*akrobystia*) is the exact term Paul uses in Gal 2:7; 5:6; 6:15, although its "naked" maleness and physicality have been mostly hidden under more "covered" translations like "uncircumcision" or "Gentiles."[10] Undoubtedly the conflict over circumcision is at the heart of the Galatian controversy, leading Paul to even coin a daring phrase like "gospel of the foreskin" (Gal 2:7), which is remarkably idiosyncratic and occurs nowhere else in the New Testament.

The Dying Trumpeter's foreskin happens to be in plain view, fully visible—but less clearly legible. Is there any relation between his foreskin and the mortal wound on his side? And who inflicted this wound? Who is the victorious opponent who stays out of the picture—and what was the combat about? From the viewpoint of our theological tradition we might be led to ask whether it is the Jews who have brought this man down because he believed the Pauline "gospel of the foreskin"—for no other "opponents" appear on the mindscape of the established interpretation. Is it Jewish law that has cruelly punished the dying man for not complying with the "works" of circumcision? Is he trying to hold himself up against the violent strikes of his Torah-observant and work-righteous antagonists, desperately trying to cling to "justification by faith alone?"

These are bizarre questions, of course, but the absurdity they imply unfortunately is not too far from the myopic selectiveness in traditional Christian perspectives on "Galatian foreskin" and Galatians in general. We urgently need to recontextualize the Pauline controversy about Galatian circumcision and foreskin, historically and politically, and the Dying Trumpeter may be a most helpful facilitator of this process. He is a "body of evidence" that something else is going on in Paul's Galatia than what we have previously "seen."

We should begin with his missing adversaries. The Dying Trumpeter, like the other Dying Gauls/Galatians, represents a piece of "victory art without victors."[11] Whoever defeated him remains invisible, but his presence is tangible. Someone must have dealt the decisive blow that pierced the Galatian's body right where the liver sits. And everyone in Paul's time, even the illiterate majority of his Galatian communities, would have known how to read the name of the victor printed in large letters all over the dying warrior: *Rome.* It is not Jewish particularism or ethnocentrism that has struck him down but Caesar's imperial universalism. It is the glory of the Roman conqueror that the vanquished Galatian proclaims in the solitude of his dying, the cold marble prolonging the perishing of his flesh into eternity.

The Galatians/Gauls as "lawless barbarians" and conquerors of Rome and Delphi, as we have seen in the previous chapter, played a constitutive role in an ideological worldview centered on war and the god-given victory of "law" in the fight of civilization against barbarism. They provided one of the most powerful, "universal" stereotypes of law-defying barbarian otherness and of its final, legitimate, and "world-saving" defeat by Rome. Portrayed as archetypal enemies of divine order, civilization, and civilized humanity, they delivered an ideal pretext for conquest and rule in general, and for Roman world conquest and world rule in particular. The "Galatian myth" as embodied in the Dying Gauls/Galatians is a major proof for the justification of Roman rule and law. It is the power of victory clad in religious garb that assigns "righteousness" to the victorious ones and "unrighteousness" to the vanquished others.

From this point of view, the sculptures of the Dying Gauls/Galatians are not only victory monuments but also powerful manifestations of Roman law and "righteousness." They showcase the lawless being lawfully punished for any past, present, or future transgression of human and divine order as these are defined and represented by Rome. They are vital to Rome as the perpetual image of rightful, merited death that makes Roman rule both moral and immortal. The rich, shining white marble of their dying shapes proclaims Rome as savior and benefactor of the world. The blood trickling down from the muscular bodies not only speaks of military might and relentless violence necessary to crush any "lawless resistance" but also, more indirectly, of the wealth, lifeblood, and life force now legitimately channeled from the Galatian provinces into the Roman capital, and the pockets of the governing Roman magistrates.[12]

Maybe these immortal images also speak, more quietly, of inevitable Roman nightmares that one day the dying but not yet dead Galatians might rise up and once more turn their swords against Rome, like the *simulacra* (images) of the nations in Pompey's theater did in one of Nero's haunted dreams around 68 C.E.[13] In their incessant dying, the Dying Galatians thus also embody a hidden magic of warding off evil. Yet on the surface they are Rome's powerful and omnipresent disciplinarians, meant to imbue living Gauls/Galatians with awe and a fear of rebellion, as well as an understanding that their very survival is a mere gift by the emperor's grace, a gift that must be reciprocated and justified by faith and loyalty toward Caesar alone. Such was the uncompromising lesson taught by the Dying Galatians to the living Galatians in Paul's time.

This changes the perception of circumcision and non-circumcision in Paul's Galatia. The Dying Trumpeter's foreskin clearly cannot be treated as an isolated piece detached from his overall physique; rather it belongs in a much larger and more dramatic "body picture" and "body politics" that we must decipher before the individual part makes sense. The disembodied reading of Galatian foreskin in theological interpretation inevitably implies its mis-reading. As we have seen in William Ramsay's battle construct, the non-circumcision of the Galatians, that is, the "defense" of their foreskin, was eventually turned into the decisive Christian-occidental victory over the Jewish and Oriental other. In Christian theology, Galatian foreskin represented non-Torah and therefore, at least as a dogmatic metaphor, has become the "trophy" and marker of a triumphant Christian self in combat with its inferior other. This is clearly not the image that Paul and his communities in Roman Galatia had "before their eyes" (compare Gal 3:1), judging from the evidence of our sculpture. The Dying Trumpeter represents Galatian foreskin as part of an overall sign system that strictly forbids any identification with a victorious self; rather in its entirety it signifies defeated otherness under the iron fist of a disciplinarian superpower (cf. Gal 3:24).

We must go a step further. None of what has just been said would have been different for the Jewish countermarker of "no foreskin." In the concrete body politics of Paul's time, Jewish circumcision and Galatian foreskin share the same social location: they both belong to the vanquished other of the dominant Roman order.

This has vast implications for a recontextualized reading of Galatians. Perhaps the Dying Galatian with his broken trumpet could help us spell out something we were not able to read in Galatians, a presence that is decisive despite its absence, namely, the omnipresent reality of Rome that invisibly pervades the whole letter as a discourse among the vanquished. The visual absence of the antagonist and victor in the Trumpeter's sculpture resembles, in a way, the shadowy figures of the circumcision-promoting "opponents" in the letter who never enter the scene in full view either. Yet, as everyone agrees, they are the most significant players in the Galatian foreskin drama.[14] Or are they? There is one point in the epilogue where Paul's text cracks open, for just a moment, to give us a glimpse of a "third party" looming in the background and behind the "opponents." Paul, writing this last passage with his own hand and "in large letters," points out that the whole controversy is really not about Jewish law, since his adversaries do not keep it themselves. Rather, their campaign is driven by something or someone else of whom they are genuinely afraid and with whom they therefore want to comply. It is fear of reprisals, not passionate Jewish piety, that urges these opponents to impose the decisive (and, according to Paul, self-glorifying) cut into the "flesh" of the Galatians.

See what large letters I make when I am writing in my own hand. It is those who want to make a good showing [*euprosōpēsai*] in the flesh that try to compel you to be circumcised, and only in order that they may not be persecuted for the cross of Christ. Even the circumcised do not themselves obey the law, but they want you to be circumcised so that they may boast about your flesh. (Gal 6:11-13)

A "good showing" in whose eyes? Who are the ominous "persecutors"? "Boasting" in front of whom? The invisible hand that struck the deadly blow against the Trumpeter—might it be the same one that makes Paul's opponents fearful of "persecution" and violence, forcing them into a compliance that shapes every twist of their argument, even where it seems entirely "Jewish"? It is true that Paul never mentions Rome explicitly. Would everyone have "seen" it nonetheless, understood the unsaid, connecting the dots between the words? The vanquished often choose not to talk directly or in plain words about their conquerors, even if this is what their conversation is about. Have we missed the allusions and codes of Paul's language, taking a "(semi-)public transcript" for the whole truth?

But then, why should Galatian foreskin have mattered to Rome? It certainly was irrelevant for the Roman soldier who struck the Trumpeter with the deadly blow, or for the horseman on Nero's sculpture who dragged the Trumpeter's kinsman along by his hair. This is the main challenge a "Roman" reading of Galatians faces. There is nothing we know that might indicate that the Romans would bother about Galatian circumcision per se. Or perhaps, at some point, they did. The whole of this book tries to re-imagine and reconstruct a contextual framework where Galatian (and "Gentile") foreskin indeed becomes an offense to Rome.

────── **Reading Self and Other at Pergamon's Great Altar** ──────

Nowhere has the death of the Gauls/Galatians been depicted and celebrated with more artistic perfection and beauty than in Pergamon. In ideological terms, nowhere has it been more carefully staged; from a political viewpoint, nowhere has it been more efficiently exploited. And today, nowhere can one get closer to its breathtaking magnitude and chilling mercilessness than in the exhibition space of the Great Altar in the Berlin Pergamon Museum. It is there that the most stunning large-scale version of dying and dead Galatians ever created in antiquity, rediscovered by nineteenth-century German archeology, has been preserved and restored in a spectacular setting.

The Great Altar summarizes the Greco-Roman construct of the universal Galatian other. At its center is the same basic logic of a salvific victory over lawless barbarians as essential foundation of rule and order that we have seen at work in different historical configurations in the previous chapter. Yet compared to the individual sculptures of Dying Galatians we have seen so far, the layout of the Great Altar is much more comprehensive and puts the Galatians' death within a very complex visual and conceptual framework. Visually, it offers a whole colorful panorama of combat with more than one hundred larger-than-life-sized fighting bodies on display, and it places this panorama of battle within the overall spatial arrangement of a richly decorated, highly structured composite cultic building where it becomes a signifying element in a multidimensional semantic system. Conceptually, the Great Altar presents the war against the Galatians/ Gauls as the primeval cosmogonic battle against the Giants. This universal world war is the originating event that establishes the totality of world order, a universal religion, and divinely sanctioned kingship with cosmic overtones, all of which are embodied in the city of Pergamon and its ruling dynasty.

A Polymorphous Altar and the Question of Impact

Pergamon certainly did not invent the image of the Galatians as the barbarian other of the Greco-Roman world, but it made an indelible contribution to it. The city was among the most impressive in the ancient world. Situated in northwestern Asia Minor, close to the Aegean coast and opposite the Greek island of Lesbos, its majestic acropolis was dominated by the temple of Athena, the theater of Dionysus, the royal palaces, and the Great Altar, all situated on a dramatic hill rising over the valley of the Caicus River. Rivaling Athens and Alexandria, Pergamon was famous for its monumental architecture and spectacular art, as well as its renowned library, which housed two hundred thousand scrolls and functioned as a prestigious center of scholarly study and activities, not to mention the invention of a new writing material called parchment (etymologically derived from *Pergamon*), which originated there.[15]

As a relative latecomer among the powerful and famous Greek cities of the Aegean coast, Pergamon became important only under the Diadochian dynasty of the Attalids (283–133 B.C.E.). Haunted by rumors of treachery and their previous marginality among the Greek Aegean coastal

Fig. 13. Model of the Pergamon acropolis. The Great Altar is surrounded by the Upper Agora to its left, the theater of Dionysus at its front, slightly to the right, and the sanctuary of Athena with the library to its right. Further up are the royal palaces and the imperial temple of Trajan that was added in the early second century C.E. Photo © Trustees and Fellows of Harvard University.

Fig. 14. The Great Altar at display in the Berlin Pergamon Museum today. The staircase leading toward the upper level with the Telephos court opens up to the West. It is flanked by the Gigantomachy Frieze that runs around the whole structure. Photo © Trustees and Fellows of Harvard University.

cities, the Pergamenes from the very beginning of their dominance, as Erich Gruen has pointed out, attributed a decisive role to their *Kulturpolitik* and were determined "to cast into shadow their dubious origins with a blaze of cultural glory."[16] The Attalids vigorously developed Pergamon, their royal city, into a center of arts, literature, and science that soon claimed a leading role among the Hellenistic cities of Asia Minor. As the "Athens of Asia," Pergamon, like Delphi and Olympia, organized celebrations of Athena. Throughout the Greek world, the city cultivated its image as a generous donor-benefactor and true defender of Hellenistic culture. The Galatians and their defeat played, as we have seen, a major role in these endeavors to demonstrate cultural and political preeminence. This is the background of Pergamon's most distinguished cultural accomplishment, the Great Altar.

Towering on the Pergamene acropolis immediately next to Athena's temple, the shiny white marble square of the Great Altar, approximately ten meters high on a foundation of some thirty-four by thirty-six meters, was an imposing sight and visible from afar.[17] Since its (re)discovery by the German road-building engineer Carl Humann in 1871, the exact date of its construction, dedication, and precise function have been and still are widely debated among scholars, and so are an infinite number of more specific issues regarding the arrangement, placement, and interpretation of individual elements.[18] For the purpose of our work, none of these questions needs to be decided; the common ground reached by art historians so far is sufficient to generate an operative model for our semiotic approach.[19]

It is generally acknowledged that the Great Altar was built under Eumenes II (197–158 B.C.E.), more precisely after the peace of Apamea in 188 B.C.E. had brought the Roman-

Pergamene wars against the Seleucids and the Galatians to a conclusion. The latest date would be the mid-sixties after the Roman-Pergamene victory over Macedonia in 168 B.C.E. and Eumenes' final triumph over the Galatians, won without Roman assistance in 166 B.C.E. If one dates the altar in the 180s B.C.E., it reflects the alliance between Rome and Pergamon in the campaign against the Galatians; alternatively, if it belongs in the 160s, it probably mirrors some of the tensions between Pergamon and Rome in the wake of the Third Macedonian War and the Roman refusal to take a clear pro-Pergamene and anti-Galatian stance. For our reading of the Great Altar, however, it is the *overall* political configuration of these two decades with Pergamon, Rome, and the Galatians as major players that provides the crucial historical background information.[20]

As far as the dedication of the Great Altar is concerned, scholars have made a wide range of suggestions: to Zeus, to the Pergamene city goddess Athena Nikephoros and Zeus together, to all gods, to Telephos, Agathe Tyche, to Queen Apollonis, or others.[21] Again we do not need to decide on any one of these alternatives; rather, we want to observe how each of these options participates (and can claim its relative right) in a multifunctional and multidimensional event of meaning making through architecture and sculpture.

The functional term *altar* needs a few words of explanation at the outset, because for a modern-day visitor this is not the most obvious description of the Great Altar. In antiquity, an altar was a sacrificial site that could vary greatly in size, shape, style, and location. Architecturally, the Great Altar belongs to the category of large monumental altars that developed in Greece from the seventh century B.C.E. onward. These altars

Fig 15. Relics of the Great Altar structure at its original site in Pergamon, today's Bergama on the west coast of Turkey, across the island of Lesbos. Photo: Erich Lessing/Art Resource, N.Y.

could feature raised platforms, an external flight of stairs ascending to the sacrificial space, and walls or columns around that space. They were usually erected, as was the Great Altar, as freestanding buildings within a sacred district or in connection with a temple that housed the cult image.[22] Though spatially linked to the Athena temple, the Great Altar was an independent structure and was, in fact, four times as big as the Athena temple, which could have fit into its inner court.[23]

In contrast to our notions of an altar, the actual sacrificial altar table thus was only one part of the Great Altar's overall structure. It is generally assumed that the Great Altar functioned as a burnt-offering altar for animal sacrifices.[24] Leading the animals to the site in a solemn procession, slaughtering them, burning special parts on the actual altar table to nourish and honor the god(s), and distributing the rest of the meat for a festive meal among the ritual participants was all part of the sacrificial ritual. Where exactly the slaughtering, the burning, and the feasting took place, however, has spurred a debate as lively as the question of what other functions the Great Altar might have fulfilled. This debate has been recently fueled by the numerous architectural quotations that link the Great Altar not only with the Parthenon at Athens but also the Mausoleum of Halicarnassus and other royal tombs, as well as with palatial, triumphal, or cultic architecture dedicated to heroic ancestors, dynastic values, royalty, and victory.[25]

We will return to the issue of function. The primary concern of our exploration, however, is not so much with single descriptive categories such as sacrificial altar, victory monument, site of worship for rulers or heroes, and so on, that are under discussion and need the expert knowledge of art historians. Rather, our focus here is on the question of visual impact: How do different elements of this visually and architecturally complex building synergistically produce a coherent semantic system of meaning making that is readable even for the illiterate and generates an effect on those who came (and still come) to visit the altar?[26] Andrew Stewart has pointed out that the precinct of the Great Altar obviously enjoyed great popularity with the people of Pergamon. Numerous honorary statues were found on the altar terrace that were almost all dedicated by or to the *demos* (people) of Pergamon.[27] What, then, did the people of Pergamon see when they visited the Great Altar? How were they affected? And what were they *meant* to see, how were they *expected* to respond?[28] It is widely acknowledged that the Great Altar is a very carefully crafted structure with a most sophisticated philosophical background and a complex political message. Almost nothing of its effects on the viewer is unplanned and unintended. We are going to focus first on the spatial semiotics of the Great Altar and develop a basic reading model for the construct of self and other; it may later assist us in our "critical re-imagination" of Paul's Galatian correspondence.[29]

Spatial Semiotics: High and Low, In and Out

In its basic spatial structure, the Great Altar can be perceived as an enormous cube that functions on two levels: a ground level and an upper level, with a connecting staircase as a third decisive element. The upper level of the six-meter-high altar podium carries a colonnaded superstructure and can be reached by climbing up the staircase. The base or ground level of the cube is accessible only by walking around its outside; it does not have an inside, unless one perceives the Great Frieze with its battle imagery as a metaphorical window into its innermost core. Displaying the war of the gods against the giants, the Gigantomachy, the Great Frieze ran around the entire lower and outside part of the altar podium, 2.3 meters high and at a length of 113 meters.

With the uninterrupted flow of images on the east, north, and south sides, the only inlet to the sacred precinct was to the west, where the altar base dramatically opened up to make room for a magnificent staircase that was part of the altar podium. Flanked by two projecting wings that had the Great Frieze narrow in an upward pointing movement, the staircase was twenty meters wide and led up to a platform that supported the colonnaded and abundantly adorned upper level. There, at an inner court accessible through an impressive porch of columns, the actual sacrificial altar was presumably placed. This inner, upper space is adorned by a second smaller frieze that tells the story of Telephos, the mythological city founder and ancestor of the Attalids.

Even this most cursory description draws our attention to two polarities in the Great Altar's spatial semiotics that are a key to the strong impact it makes on its spectators, even today: *inside* and *outside, high* and *low*. Passing the Upper Agora on their way up the Pergamene acropolis, with the royal palaces of the enclosed citadel visible farther ahead on the mountaintop, ancient visitors would turn to the left in order to enter the altar terrace through a *propylon* (gate) from the east. Through this entrance arrangement, the Great Altar presents itself first from the back as a relatively high,

Fig. 16. Left projecting wing of the Great Frieze at the staircase, showing deities of the sea in combat with Giants. Pergamon Museum Berlin. Photo: Jakob B. Rehmann.

compact, enclosed structure. Without any door or opening to the inside, it might have reminded its ancient viewers of a fortress well guarded against hostile invaders, mirroring the impenetrable walls of the immediately neighboring citadel. At a closer look, this impression is intensified by the Great Frieze's combat imagery. As one walks around the complex along either its south or north flank, scene after scene of battle unfolds slightly above one's eyes in an incessant flow of images, making the massiveness of the walls below more tangible—in stark contrast to the relative openness and lightness of the richly decorated colonnaded facade and roof structure high above on the upper level.

Only when one arrives on the western side of the Great Altar do the static spatial elements suddenly break open. The Great Staircase appears somewhat like a startling gash that dramatically disrupts the Great Altar's enclosed structure, providing both a way *in* from out and *up* from below. It is one of the great advantages of the Berlin Pergamon Museum's arrangement today that it has made the staircase accessible to the public. Its height is dizzying, but the impulse to climb up and enter the platform above is irresistible to most visitors, despite signs warning against the hazards of the stairs. In the spatial semiotics of the Altar, the Great Staircase is the magic territory where *out* can become *in*, *low* is transformed into *high*—and vice versa.[30]

In order to provide us with a visual aid to represent these spatial relationships on paper, we are borrowing a tool usually utilized by structural semiotics for the analysis of texts, the so-called *semiotic square*.[31] First we may arrange the four spatial terms that emerged from our first reading of the Great Altar as the four corners of a square:

High/Up   In

Out/Down   Low

In this square clearly not all corners are equal. *High* and *In* are, in the construct of the Great Altar, the two privileged spatial locations, what we look up to, where we want to be, and where we are visually led. They are different but appear together and cannot be separated; in other words, they somehow correspond to each other. We express this complementary relationship of implication as *High == In*.

In a similar way, *Out == Low* correspond to each other. In stark contrast to *High == In*, they denote the space where we start but do not want to stay; they represent the two affiliated elements of the nonprivileged level. If *High* is A, *Low* is non-A. And if *In* is B, *Out* is non-B. In our culturally framed spatial perception, the nonprivileged side would be normally seen as low, and the privileged part as high. This obviously mirrors the way in which the Great Altar situates them.

But *High == In* and *Out == Low* do not yet make a proper space, either in architecture or in semiotics; they are just two horizontal layers, with one lying on top of the other. The force that is able to create the second dimension of space is the vertical and diagonal repulsion between the four categories: the power of opposition, of contradiction and contrariety[32] that has the one category push against the other category, thus opening up a field of tension between them: *In* ↔ *Out* and *High* ↔ *Low*, as well as *High* ↔ *Out* and *In* ↔ *Low*. Or: A versus non-A and non-B, B versus non-B and non-A. This now creates the complete shape of a semiotic square.

Fig. 17. Spatial Semiotics of the Great Altar: High and In versus Low and Out

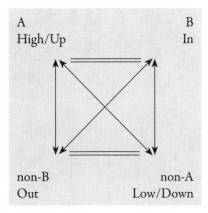

The horizontal, vertical, and diagonal forces of complementarity and contrariety/contradiction, of holding together and pushing against are the innermost forces that constitute the Great Altar as an architectural space and a space that represents and constructs meaning. The Great Staircase is the topos where this spatial structure and structure of meaning are disclosed. As it offers the "outsider" a way in and the "underling" a chance to climb up, at least metaphorically, it causes the whole edifice to become transparent as a construction of these oppositions, *Up* ↔ *Down*, *In* ↔ *Out*. The staircase is the place where *In* and *High* are presented as an object of desire, and the liminal space where the boundary between *In* and *Out, High* and *Low* becomes fluid and negotiable, thus revealing the innermost categories that constitute its meaning, and the meaning of the Great Altar as a whole.[33] Verticality and horizontality, integration and exclusion, boundary and boundary transgression are the elements of the core spatial grammar of the Great Altar. These elements, and the negotiation between them, are the focus of our Pergamene reading of Paul's letter to the Galatians as well.

It is notweworthy that the high–low polarity of the Great Altar is frequently noticed in scholarship. The inside–outside spatiality, however, is rarely discussed.[34] This might be linked to the way the Great Altar is exhibited in the Berlin Pergamon Museum today. Whereas the experience of high and low is very well conveyed to the visitor who is looking and moving up or down the exceptionally steep and high stairs of the altar, the sensation of an outside–inside tension was probably much stronger in the original setting and is now somewhat lost. It is nevertheless crucial for understanding how this space produces social and cultural meaning.[35]

Fig 18. Visitors at the Great Altar in the Berlin Pergamon Museum today. Photo: Wikimedia Commons.

"Locating" Good and Evil, Self and Other

Height was not just an architectural feature of the Great Altar but, through its dominant position on the Pergamene acropolis and its visibility from afar, also a natural marker. This has been widely observed and occasionally linked to the ancient Near Eastern, Israelite, and particularly Anatolian imagery of deities and kings residing on mountain thrones.[36] The linkage between High = mountain = throne = power is a perfect reminder that space naturally constructs meaning, though in a somewhat abstract way. What do *In* and *Out*, *High* and *Low* as the four cornerstones in the spatial semiotics of the Great Altar mean more specifically? That is, what do they stand for? This is evidently spelled out through the visual language of the two friezes at the inside and outside of the Great Altar.

Unfortunately the precise narrative behind them, for example, in terms of a hypothetical Pergamene "court epic," is lost and a matter of guesswork.[37] Like probably the majority of the illiterate ancient spectators, we are thus left with what was meant to be the primary medium of communication anyway: the powerful visual impression of the images themselves, in combination with their overall spatial arrangement. Apart from the basic spatial impression of being down (and somewhat small) at the bottom, and outside of a monumental, closed inside that is reaching up to the skies high above, what thus would we "read" when approaching the Great Altar?

Fig 19. The Zeus-scene on the East Frieze of the Great Altar. The father of the gods (second from left) is flanked by three Giant opponents. His eagle (only partially preserved) attacks the snake-legs of his bearded enemy, possibly Porphyrius, to the right. To the left, Zeus's lightning bolt has struck a giant to the ground. Pergamon Museum, Berlin. Photo: Bildarchiv Preussischer Kulturbesitz/Art Resource, N.Y.

Prompted by the entrance design, we face the East Frieze at the back of the altar first (see fig. 19, p. 91). An extraordinary scene slightly decentered to the right is instantly eye-catching: Zeus, the supreme Olympic god and ruler of the world, his masculine body in heroic motion, is defending himself against three savage fighters to the right and left who are ferociously attacking from below.[38] One of them is already nailed to the ground by a powerful lightning bolt that shoots across Zeus's thigh. The other is on his knees but still aggressively pursuing the assault. The third opponent, bearded, with wild hair and mad eyes, is apparently the most dangerous of the three, perhaps the leader of the whole gang, with only his muscular back and profile visible. His athletic, slightly twisted torso radiates raw violence and untamable hatred. The spontaneous response of fear and terror he evokes turns into sheer horror when we take a look at his legs: two thick monstrous snakes are growing out of his knees, coiling themselves upward in a slithering motion against the father of the gods. Yet Zeus seems entirely in control, even somewhat remote from the scene. The spatial distance between his location above and the ground below from where his attackers have risen appears somewhat reassuring, though this one enemy comes menacingly close. Zeus's eagle, however, is already coming to the rescue, vigorously attacking the sinister snake-legs from above. We can sense some relief in our own bodies. The world we are staring at is terrifying but maybe not entirely out of our hands.

As spectators, we have seen what we are meant to see: not just a gruesome fight among four combatants, but the struggle of an innocent, noble victim against three hideous assailants. Even if we were not able to read the names of Zeus or any other deity that were engraved on the cornice above the frieze, or the names of the antagonists written below, we can immediately identify who represents the good side and who are the evil forces. We know exactly who defends himself and who attacks, and who deserves our compassion and should gain victory, and who not. Evidently the good are located *High* at the top, defending the *Inside*, whereas the bad belong to the *Below* of the bottom and need to be kept *Out*. The spatial semiotics is linked to most basic moral judgments. By making a decision between *High/In* versus *Low/Out*, we have taken sides for the good cause.

All of this seems natural. Indeed, the worldview into which the altar has drawn us has been deeply ingrained in Western civilization since ancient times. It is the occidental construct of self and other—enemy and friend, us and them, rebellion and order—that the Great Altar has set in stone with irresistible plausibility and beauty for millennia to come. [39]

The Semiotics of Victory and Defeat in the Gigantomachy Frieze

Perhaps if someone had told us that we were watching the battle between Pergamenes (or Romans) against Gauls/Galatians/Celts, we would have paused and pondered the historical facts with their less-than-clear assignment of right and wrong. Yet even though Zeus's three gigantic naked adversaries, ferocious in appearance and mad in their attack, vividly resemble Galatians/Gauls as we have encountered them in the description by Diodorus Siculus above (see chapter 1), we know that this is not what they are—at least not on the surface. The Great Altar has transposed the historical struggles of the Pergamene kingdom into the timeless realm of myth, and the language it speaks is the renowned vernacular used to convey stories of origin and universal truth far above any concrete reality. The war presented to us on the panels of the Great Frieze does not need to be dated or disputed in any of its tedious historical details, for it is a primeval event: the battle of the gods against the Giants. The Giants are the agents of primordial chaos, disorder, and rebellion. Rising from below, they have attacked the divine realm and are trying to dethrone the deities, thereby destroying the world. This requires a brief look at the mythology behind the Great Frieze. What, actually, is the story of the Giants and the mystery of their relationship to the Galatians?

The Archetypal Myth: Gaia/Earth and Her Insurrection

Immediately next to Zeus on the East Frieze, his daughter Athena wrestles with Alkyoneus, the youngest and favorite son of Gē/Gaia, the earth goddess. This scene is the

Fig. 20. The Athena-Gaia scene from the East Frieze of the Great Altar. Athena, the daughter of Zeus and city-goddess of Pergamon, tears the double-winged Alkyoneus away from his earth-mother Gaia (bottom right) who holds up her cornucopia, pleading in vain for her son's life to be spared. Winged Nikē/Victory is about to crown Athena from the right. Pergamon Museum Berlin. Photo: Wikimedia Commons.

most pathetic of the Great Frieze and the only one featuring a female opponent of the gods and goddesses above (see fig. 20, above). Reaching out from the ground, which covers her body up to her breasts, Gaia raises her arms in a desperate plea for mercy. Her cornucopia, the horn-shaped vessel overflowing with a bounty of fruit, appears at her left hand. With her right hand she tries to hold on to her Giant son Alkyoneus, who remained invulnerable as long as he could keep contact with the motherly ground. But Athena's elegantly draped leg intervenes between the two of them, from above; her arm and his own large wings seem to lift him up without resistance. As he is about to lose the life-preserving connection, the deadly poison of Athena's snake already penetrates into his chest and his face is torn in pain and despair. Directly above and unmoved by the tragedy of Gaia and her son, the winged goddess of victory, Nikē, is approaching to adorn Athena with the crown of triumph.[40]

Gaia is the mother of all the evil that has come upon the deities of the Great Frieze. The Giants in an uproar against the Greek pantheon are her seditious sons, and it was she who started the rebellion. If we use Hesiod's *Theogony* to fill in the narrative behind the sculptures, as Erika Simon has proposed, the contours of a dramatic cosmogonic myth emerge.[41] According to Hesiod (*Theogony* 154–87), the Giants were born of the blood that dripped on the ground after Uranos/Heaven was castrated by his son Chronos/Time (138). The gender and generational conflict behind this bloody birth story is startling. Uranos—not only the partner but also the son of Gaia/Earth—hated the powerful and monstrous children to whom she gave birth and forced them back into her womb, not allowing them to see the light of the day. This caused the Earth Mother great pain and she eventually made an iron sickle and gave it to her sons, asking them to revolt against their evil father. Yet only Chronos dared to rise against the primeval patriarch and mutilated him. Uranos's blood impregnated the Earth Mother again and became the seed of the Giants, who sprang to life as aggression incarnate, already wearing armor and carrying spears.

If we follow Hesiod's story, the Giants are directly and very physically—literally speaking, with their "blood-line"—linked to antipatriarchal and antiheavenly rebellion. Only Apollodorus in the first century C.E. will tell how they themselves later attacked the Olympian gods, combining that battle with Hesiod's battle of the Titans and Typhoeus, which establishes the victorious Zeus as world ruler (*Library* 1.6.1–2).[42] The topic of the Gigantomachy, the divine battle against the Giants/Titans/Typhoeus as a unified heavenly counterattack to preserve heaven and earth from chaos, was familiar throughout the Greco-Roman world. From the sixth century B.C.E. on, it became a well-established iconographic theme. It occurred on vases, and in Athens was depicted on the east metopes of the Parthenon frieze.[43] It was also woven into Athena's *peplos*, that is, the newly made cloak that was annually presented to and draped on the goddess's statue. The famous artist Phidias also depicted it on the inside of Athena's shield, where for the first time the deities and Giants are arranged in a firm spatial order of above and below that resembles the Great Frieze of Pergamon. Depiction of the Giants as snake-legged, as encountered in the Zeus scene, became a standard iconographic feature from about 450 B.C.E. onward. Similarly, Athena and Apollo as well as Heracles are usually the dominant protagonists in the battle, under the victorious leadership of Zeus.[44]

Yet the Giant battle also had powerful literary counterparts in many other ancient Near Eastern mythologies.[45] Its popularity matched its ideological relevance. The Gigantomachy was essentially a political creation myth showing how cosmic order was (re)established against chaos, how universal law defeated anarchy and lawlessness on a worldwide scale, and how culture/male vanquished nature/female. It was also, and substantially, a myth of power that explained the establishment of autocratic rule out of an individual's extraordinary deed of salvation from mortal threat to the divine community. In the Babylonian creation epic of *Enuma Elish*, Marduk's victory over the primeval mother goddess Tiamat makes him king of the gods and humans, and so too does Zeus's eventual triumph over the Giants/Titans/Typhoeus establish his position at the top of the Olympian hierarchy and as ruler of the world.[46] The creation (or salvation) of the world is thus primordially linked to political power. Kingship is both a divine institution and a cosmic survival necessity; and it has its earthly representation in the human king.[47] The victorious leader on the battlefield of the Gigantomachy is always the leader and lawgiver of peaceful times as well, both among gods and humans—and he is "naturally" male.

The gender puzzle of the Great Frieze has already been briefly mentioned. On the surface the Great Frieze is strikingly inclusive: According to Andrew Stewart, goddesses outnumber male deities 3:2, and divine mothers fighting together with their divine children outnumber divine fathers 2:1.[48] Yet whether this strong presence of female characters, together with Hera's focal position at the East Frieze, expresses a diminution of the ancient patriarchal gender hierarchy needs more careful reflection. A very masculine Zeus clearly has the dominant position over all the deities. There is no doubt that the core of the whole construct is the primordial defeat of a rebellious female, Gaia/Earth, by a superior male who represents law and order—although this defeat is implemented through another female, his daughter Athena. From the perspective of ecological and feminist criticism, this is a highly troublesome configuration, especially in light of Athena's mother-eclipsing birth narrative, which makes her the "ideal" daughter that will never rebel against Zeus' rule.[49]

There are profoundly colonial implications as well. Though many issues in the interpretation of the Great Altar are controversial among art historians, the point most pertinent to our study is largely undisputed. The Gigantomachy, as the primeval battle of the gods against the Giants and Gaia, mirrors the Galatomachy, the historical battles of the Attalids against the three barbarian tribes of the Galatians at various stages of Pergamon's history. How is this stunning metamorphosis of Galatians into giants to be explained?

Colonial Imagination: Giant Battle and Galatian Battle

Edith Hall, in her study about the Greek "invention of the barbarian," has demonstrated that the Gigantomachy in Greece was early on linked to battles against other mythical enemies of abnormal, monstrous, half-beastly appearance such as Amazons and Centaurs and that it became part of the process that gradually defined the barbarian other.[50] Amazonomachies, Centauromachies, and Gigantomachies were, already in the archaic thought world, mythical conflicts with species of super- or subhuman barbarians. Historically, the Greeks encountered foreign people in the process of colonization, in war, or internally as slaves (as slaves were to a large extent prisoners of war). Then, during the Persian Wars in the fifth century B.C.E., in a situation of utmost threat, the Persians as historically "real" enemies were assimilated to the primeval agents of disorder. At the same time they became a universal antitype of all Greeks, that is, barbarians. The equivalency of Giants/Amazons/Titans/Centaurs =Persians and their arrangement as non-Greek/barbarian/chaotic in a dichotomous opposition to Greek/civilized/lawful evidently produced an ideologically very powerful enemy construct in the joint battle of the Greek cities against the Asian invaders.[51] It laid the foundation for some of the most fundamental polarizations that have shaped occidental identity constructs and Western worldviews until today.

Represented as a semiotic opposition as discussed above, four of the polarities mentioned by Hall are of particular interest for this study:

Civilization   ↔   Primitivism
Self   ↔   Other
Law   ↔   Lawlessness
Colonizers   ↔   Colonized

Even before "Greek versus barbarian" became the cardinal antagonism in the fifth century B.C.E., the archaic thought world, according to Hall, was concerned with the opposition of civilization versus primitivism, because "the struggle to conceptualize the nature of civilization is as old as civilization itself." For Hall, this is a process whereby the civilized define themselves in "comparison with their former selves." The journey of the self from the former to the present stage is perceived as an upward movement from an inferior to a superior state ("a chaos from which society rose")—a spatial metaphor of *Low* and *High* that immediately reminds us of the Great Altar. However, as an inevitable by-product of this (upward) "evolutionary journey toward new levels of culture and technology," the former self is turned into an "other." Prior to the Persian crisis, this is not (yet) an ethnically, non-Greek other, but rather a monstrous, supernatural, nonhuman other like the Titans defeated by Zeus or the Giants and other monsters killed by Heracles as the "great civilizer."[52]

The rationale and moral justification for these Herculean deeds of defeating and slaughtering a whole range of differently shaped others is not just their strangeness as such. It is true, as Homer's Odysseus finds out, that, for example, the Cyclopes eat dairy products and the Lotus-eaters fruit (*Odyssey* 9.219–23.84), while the civilized and cultured rely on a diet of bread, meat, and wine.[53] But at the core of the others' deviant "primitivism" is something more severe: their lawlessness. As Hall states, "The most distinctive sign[s] of civilized life are however the imperatives and taboos it constructs for itself."[54] The key oppositions that "lie at the heart of the archaic thought world," inseparably linked to one another, are "civilization against primitivism, order against chaos, observance of law and taboo against transgression."[55]

Amazons are matriarchal, Titans violent, and Centaurs savage; Giants disrupt order, Cyclopes do not have laws and political institutions, and the "inhuman communities" Odysseus visits on his journeys are shockingly neglectful with regard to the most basic performance of proper sacrifices. They also refuse to treat guests in a civilized manner, not to mention the threat to the hero's patriarchal status. There may even be incest and cannibalism present, defined as the two most severe markers of pre/anti-civilization in virtually every culture.[56]

None of these mythical encounters and battles with lawless Amazons, Centaurs, Titans, and Giants happens in a historical vacuum, nor is the legitimacy of fighting and subduing the primitive other a purely mythological construct. Rather, according to Hall it mirrors the "age when Greek cities were beginning to expand self-confidently all over the Mediterranean and the Black Sea,"[57] the age of Greek colonization. What the *Odyssey* reflects are the "aspirations and experiences of the Greek colonizers." It presents a "validation of the colonists' subjection of indigenous tribes on hostile shores," though admittedly a very sophisticated one: "The resistance the Greek colonizers must have encountered in foreign lands informs the poem, but it is highly mediated by the vocabulary of myth: it is embodied in supernatural creatures, monstrous Cyclopes or gigantic Laestrygonians."[58]

Hall's study thus has located the Giant battle within the framework of colonization myths that express the conflict between colonizers and colonized by giving the enemy a monstrous appearance. This type of myth survived well into the age of Christopher Columbus and the last great wave of European colonization in the nineteenth century;[59] it has become foundational to the self/other construct of occidental civilization.[60] Each one of the polarities of civilization versus primitivism, self versus other, law versus transgression, and colonizers versus colonized adds a crucial layer of meaning that is critical not only for our understanding of the semiotics of combat that pits gods against Giants at the Pergamon Altar, but also of the fight between Paul and his opponents in the letter to the Galatians.

This brings us back to the correlation of Gigantomachy and Galatomachy. To perceive the Giant battle as a colonization myth shows how fluid the boundaries between myth and history were, and how easily new monsters and historical agents of disorder and primitivism could be assimilated to their mythical archetypes: the Persians in fifth-century Greece—or the Galatians in second-century Pergamon. Though Hall's study does not deal with Galatians or Gauls, it offers an excellent conceptual framework to understand why and how Galatians could become Giants on the Great Frieze of Pergamon. The assimilation of mythological and historical enemies and their totalizing subsumption under the rubric of an ethnically defined, non-Greek barbarian other that the Greek invented during the Persian Wars, was simply replicated by the Attalids with regard to their Gallic/Galatian Wars.

Clear evidence for this Attalid *reinvention* of the barbarian is provided by an artistically and ideologically elaborate monument that was sent from Pergamon to Athens somewhere between the end of the third and the middle of the second century B.C.E. Pausanias (1.25.2) saw it still in place in the second century C.E. and describes it as follows: "Toward the south wall, Attalos has dedicated the famous war of the Giants, and the Battle of the Athenians against the Amazons, and the deed [*ergon*] at Marathon against the Persians, and the destruction of the Gauls in Mysia; and every figure is two cubits high."

The linkage between Gigantomachy, Centauromachy, and Amazonomachy was exhibited already in the depiction of these three arch-battles on the east, south, and west metopes of the Parthenon frieze. Attalus with his dedication adds the Galatians as a fourth element, establishing an explicit connection between Giants, Amazons, Persians, and Galatians, thus putting the Pergamene dynasty into the glorious tradition of great Panhellenic victories over prototypal enemies.[61] In the previous chapter, we have seen this merging of Galatians and Giants/Titans, Galatians and Persians, Galatians and Carthaginians already at work in Alexandria, Delphi, and Rome. The Galatian myth was used as a powerful ideological construct in both the East and the West. Not only could Galatians substitute for other ruthless invaders (such as the Carthaginians in Rome's Punic Wars against Hannibal or Titans in third-century B.C.E. Alexandria), but because of their ubiquity they had a quality the fifth-century Persians were lacking: they represented a special category of *universal* barbarians that brought them particularly close to the archetypal barbarians, the mythological Giants. Defeating them therefore was an act of salvation and benefaction that again and again substantiated dynastic power claims in the turbulent world after Alexander the Great. By using the Great Altar to inscribe itself into this preexisting pattern of the Hellenistic mythology of victory, Pergamon not only articulated and reinforced its own leadership claims but also substantially reformulated and developed it into a comprehensive worldview of monumental impact and outstanding aesthetic and ideological refinement.

Cosmic Combat Order and the Victorious Self

If we proceed from the Zeus group on the East Frieze of the Great Altar either to the right or left, we encounter many similar combats scenes. After passing Athena and Nikē/Victory in their confrontation with Gaia, the next of the heavenly fighters is Ares/Mars in his chariot and, opening up the North Frieze around the corner, his companion Aphrodite (Venus) with their son Eros/Amor, farther down on the north side, followed by the Moirae, the Gorgons, and finally Poseidon with his seahorse, who appears at the beginning of a series of battle scenes featuring sea gods and goddesses around the corner on the West Frieze, to the left of the staircase. All of these divine fighters are engaged with human or half-beastly enemies, and so are their heavenly allies on the other side of the Great Frieze. Returning in this way to the East Frieze and moving to the left of Zeus, after passing Heracles and the quadriga of Hera, we come across Zeus's children Artemis and Apollo with their mother Leto, then Hekatē, then farther down the South Frieze, the deities of Day and Night—Asteria, Phoebe, Uranos/Heaven, Selenē/Moon, Helios/Sun, Eos/Dawn; in the last part on the south side, finally the Anatolian mother goddess Cybele/Rhea appears riding on a lioness, at the corner to the west where Dionysus and his followers occupy the space of the West Frieze on the right side of the staircase.

Michael Pfanner has analyzed the compositional and conceptual principles underlying the Great Frieze and discovered a very complex system of symmetries.[62] The movement patterns on the North Frieze, for example, are mirrored on the South Frieze, the two parts of the West Frieze (sea gods and Dionysus) correspond to each other, and so do the left half of the East Frieze (Zeus-Athena group) and the right half (Apollo-Artemis group). This symmetric composition seems to strengthen the notion of an overall coherence that bridges polarities represented by the deities and spatially creates strong links where the six corners threaten to interrupt the continuity of the frieze. It is one continuous movement leading from east to west via north or south, comprising the whole of the world, of nature and cosmos alike. The deities of night and day at the center of the South Frieze represent the order of time and of cosmos; their corresponding counterparts are the dark forces of chthonic and underworld deities ruling over fate, life, and death in the middle of the North Frieze.[63] Both of these highly diverse groups are linked to and through the Olympic deities, that is, the extended family of Zeus, who occupy the whole East Frieze and the easternmost parts of the North and South Frieze,

Fig. 21. *Aphrodite pulls a spear from a defeated Giant, her foot on his face (see image facing the beginning of the chapter); her son Eros assists Dione (to the right) in defeating another snake-legged foe. North Frieze. Photo: Bildarchiv Preussischer Kulturbesitz/Art Resource, N.Y.*

Fig. 22. *One of the Gorgons defeats a scale-legged Giant, leading into the scenes of sea-combat on the North and West Frieze. Photo: Wikimedia Commons.*

Fig. 23. Left side of East Frieze: Hekate to the left, goddess of ways and witchcraft, fights with torch, sword, and lance against a snake-legged, bearded giant; in the center, Artemis the huntress, sister of Apollon, charges over a dying Giant caught by her ferocious dog (see p. 290 below) to attack a Greek-looking adversary; to the right, Leto, the mother of Artemis and Apollon thrusts a blazing torch at a fallen, hybrid Giant with animal features: wings, talons, and a tail. Photo: Wikimedia Commons.

Fig. 24. Selenē the moon goddess rides on a mule over a fallen Giant on the South Frieze. This part of the gigantomachy depicts the order of time (day and night) under attack. Photo: Erich Lessing/Art Resource, N.Y.

Fig. 25. On the westernmost corner of the South Frieze Cybele/Rhea, the powerful mother-goddess of Asia Minor, sits astride a lion and beneath Zeus' eagle. Nyx/Night is in combat to her right. Photo: Bildarchiv Preussischer Kulturbesitz/Art Resource, N.Y.

Fig. 26. An unidentified deity on the South Frieze (possibly Aither) strangles a snake-legged Giant with lion's head and paws. Photo: Erich Lessing/Art Resource, N.Y.

thus connecting with their southern and northern allies. Similarly, the two parts of the West Frieze and the adjacent westernmost ends of the North and South Frieze represent another polarity: the water-bound sea gods to the north relate to the more earthly *thiasos* (festive procession) of Dionysus and his mother Semelē, and the local Anatolian Magna Mater Cybele/Rhea as their counterpart to the south.

Pfanner's study has reconstructed some of the compositional master plan underlying the Great Altar and revealed what the ordinary visitor to the Great Altar would only intuitively sense: that the panorama of the Great Frieze deliberately evokes the imagery of a huge heavenly alliance uniting the main deities of the Greco-Roman pantheon in a common quest—a cosmic battle that leaves nothing and no one out. As the Giants' attack is directed against all spheres of divine rule, against the most elemental principles that hold the world together in time and space, the whole cosmos is in an uproar. The totality of nature and every deity participate in the struggle for survival. The message of the Great Altar is framed in the most universal and cosmic way possible.[64]

The gods and, even more so, the goddesses fight gracefully. The Giants die beautifully. The artistic refinement of the sculptures is exceptional. In particular, the goddesses show an amazing variety and care regarding the details of their hairstyle, dress, and especially footwear. The shoes of the goddesses are exceptional. No one would ever believe that lines, textures, and drapery could be carved out of marble with such subtlety and precision. There is no doubt that the Pergamene masters must have been the most talented of their time.[65] This breathtaking artistic skill shows in every scene of the Great Frieze, which in an enormous panoramic visual synopsis exhibits the various moments of the battle simultaneously: images of utmost danger, yet persistence, fortitude, and strategic efficiency as concerns the deities, and of furious uproar, brutal attack, yet defeat, dying, and death on the side of the enemies. The iconographic program comprises an astonishing variety in staging the different combat scenes. Its semiotics, however, stays within a clearly legible sign system to denote good and evil, superior and inferior, self and other.

On the one hand, the vertical spatial code of the Great Altar as a whole strongly dominates the Great Frieze as well. The upper sphere belongs to the deities, who defend it against the Giants' attack from below: *High* ↔ *Low*. As the Giants are attached to the lower sphere and pushed back there, the battle, according to Andrew Stewart, literally is their *kata-strophē* (downturn).[66] This spatial order, emphasized through the oppositional inscription of the two sets of names on the upper (deities) and under (Giants) sides of the frieze, is translated into dramatic visual polarities as well. Whereas the deities above fight in a calm, focused, and composed manner without showing any unbalanced emotion that would signal their lack of control, the Giants below are depicted with distorted facial expressions showing pain, rage, and despair, and with aggressively realistic details like pulsing veins and armpit hair (see the image on p. 290). The list of physical abnormalities and half-beastly deformities comprises animal ears, the head of a bull or a monstrous lion, birds' claws, wings, and, most prominently, snake legs as displayed on Zeus's chief enemy. The Giants also fight naked and instead of proper weapons use brutish teeth, fists, viper's fangs, or simply primitive clubs and boulders for their attack on the cultured bodies of the goddesses and gods. (See figs. 21, 22, 23, 25, 26.)

Within the framework of ancient rules of perception, all this would have been seen as the epitome of repellent ugliness and foreignness that marks the inferior as well as civilization's outcast: the barbarian. The different bodily features of gods and Giants express precisely the dualism of Greek virtue against barbarian vice that we examined in the previous chapter: rationality versus stupidity, true manliness and courage versus self-destructive fearlessness and rashness, moderation and self-discipline versus excessive emotion and brainless action, righteousness versus lawlessness, including the lawlessness of blasphemy, which defies the rules of proper religion and reverence toward the gods.[67]

That is why none of the sacrilegious attackers, altogether an army of about fifty male bodies, has a chance to survive. Even if the battle is not over yet, even if it is terrifying in its gory details, the spectator gets a strong sense of eventual triumph for the deities. The gods and goddesses are on the brink of victory. Some of the Giants are already dead; some are dying, painfully and agonizingly as they are burned, impaled, speared, stabbed, mauled, bitten to death, trampled down by the divine forces and their fierce animal allies—hunting dogs, lions, horses, snakes. But the pain and agony of the Giants are not a matter of concern or compassion; rather, they are to be seen as rightful punishment for their lawless attack, imposed on them by the superior power of the deities, who, in the well-established semiotic system of the battle with the Giants, represent the law and the rightful order of things. Though fighting with all their strength, the gods and goddesses are mostly unaffected by physical or emotional pain and act calmly and determinedly, neither seriously wounded nor overwhelmed by fury and despair like their foes. Again, in the language of the ancient images, this spells out as *mastery* and as a *civilization* that is destined to rule over crude barbarians.[68]

If we attempt to draft a semiotic square to depict the visual semiotics of the Great Altar discussed so far on the analogy of its spatial semiotics, we now are dealing with many more than four categories. The simple *In-Out, High-Low* square seems to split into a multitude of relationships of the type A ↔ non-A:

beauty	↔	ugliness
good	↔	evil
cosmos	↔	chaos
order	↔	anarchy
civilized	↔	barbarians
gods	↔	Giants
virtue	↔	vice
righteousness	↔	lawlessness
moderation	↔	excess
rational	↔	irrational
rule	↔	rebellion
religion	↔	blasphemy

Every one of these polarities and its linkage to the others is a vital component in the overall process of decoding the Great Frieze. They are the building blocks for many different semiotic squares we could construct, and all are valid for our interpretation. Nevertheless, for the sake of clarity, we will try to focus on the two most basic polarities, an admittedly somewhat subjective choice. If we nonetheless try to discern what among the many things we have seen so far seems to matter most, we focus on the core event of the Great Frieze itself: the battle.

As we have seen above, the combat of the gods against the Giants is presented with so much visual power that we were drawn into it almost instantly. Staring at the monstrosity of the Giants, their falling and fallen bodies almost level with our eyes and visually engulfing us the moment we face the Great Altar, we look up to the fighting deities and hope for their victory, for this seems the only way to restore peace, order, normalcy. Hans-Joachim Schalles rightly talks about feelings or primordial fears (*Urängste*) that are mobilized by the Great Frieze and prevent any distanced reflection. The threat is imminent, the enemy cold and alien: who would ever sympathize with the snake-legged figures depicted here?[69] But as we align ourselves with the noble battle of the gods as *our* cause as well, as we turn ourselves against "them" as the foreign and hostile other, the Great Altar constructs our identity. While we refuse our allegiance to those dying in front of our eyes, our self emerges and rises triumphantly, forever entangled into the victory over the hostile and inferior other.

Fig. 27. Combat Semiotics: Self and Victory versus Other and Defeat

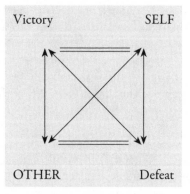

This is the basic shape of a "battle square" as the core semiotic construct of the Great Altar. The polarity of *Victory* ↔ *Defeat* establishes the war-based hierarchy between dominant *Self* ↔ vanquished *Other*: *High* versus *Low*, *In* versus *Out*. All the other polarities we have listed above can be assimilated to this semiotics of conflict. As the Self declares itself in alliance with the deities' good or *righteous* causes, including the law and order of the cosmos, righteousness and rationality, beauty and virtue, civilization and universal salvation in general, the Other is moved to the positions of inferiority

(= *Down*) and not belonging (= *Out*), which are defined as blasphemous, lawless, rebellious, criminal, ugly, evil, barbarian.

Aesthetics of Resistance and the Pain of the Other

Even today in the Pergamon Museum the evidence of these polarities has lost nothing of its power to define *us* and *them*—no tour guide, and hardly any visitor, would bother to wonder how the beauty of this unique work of art relates to the cold-blooded cruelty of the mass slaughter depicted at its base and core; it is as if the pain of the Dying Giants did not exist. Yet it is there, plainly before everyone's eyes, even if it remains unseen by those same eyes. One of the rare counter-readings of the Pergamene Giant battle from the perspective of the vanquished, set in the dramatic context of European resistance to Nazi Germany in the 1930s and '40s, is offered by Peter Weiss in his *Aesthetics of Resistance*. Its introduction displays the Great Frieze in a monumental panorama that evokes with visceral intensity the history and fate of the conquered and enslaved—those who simultaneously became the subjects, producers, and victims of Pergamon's art.

> In the marble quarries on the mountain slopes north of the castle the master sculptors had pointed their long sticks at the best blocks while eying the Gallic captives toiling in the sultry heat. Shielded and fanned by palm branches, squinting in the blinding sun, the sculptors took in the rippling of the muscles, the bending and stretching of the sweating bodies. The defeated warriors, driven here in chains, hanging from ropes on the rock faces, smashing crowbars and wedges into strata of glittering, bluish white, crystalline-like limestone and transporting the gigantic ashlars on long wooden sleds down the twisting paths, were notorious for their savagery, their brutal customs, and in the evenings the lords with their retinues passed them timidly when the stinking prisoners, drunk on cheap rotgut, were camping in a pit. Up in the gardens of the castle, however, in the gentle breeze wafting up from the sea, the huge bearded faces became the stuff of the sculptors' dreams. . . . Slowly they scraped forth the limbs, felt them, saw forms emerge whose essence was perfection. With the plundered people transferring their energies into relaxed and receptive thoughts, degradation and lust for power produced art.[70]

Peter Weiss's three-volume novel, masterfully translated into English by Joachim Neugroschel and with a foreword by Frederic Jameson, is one of the most demanding works of twentieth-century German literature. It interlinks the history of anti-fascist resistance in Spain, in the cities of exile, and in the Berlin underground with an ongoing interpretation of the Great Altar. The author is keenly aware of the harsh polarity of rulers and ruled that the sculptors translated into aesthetic perfection, making its merciless violence disappear under the veil of arresting beauty and timeless law:

> Historic events appeared in mythical disguise, enormously palpable, arousing terror, admiration, yet not understandable as man-made, but endurable only as a more-than-personal power that wanted enthralled, enslaved people galore, though few at the top,

who dictated destinies with a mere stirring of the finger. The populace, when trudging by on solemn days, scarcely dared to glance up at the effigy of its own history. . . . The initiates, the specialists talked about art, praising the harmony of movement, the coordination of gestures; the others, however, who were not even familiar with the concept of the 'cultured,' stared furtively into the gaping maws, felt the swoop of the paw in their own flesh. The work gave pleasure to the privileged; the others sensed a segregation under a draconian law of hierarchy.[71]

As Weiss reads the Great Altar "from below," he subverts its inscribed aesthetics of compliance and the "draconian law of hierarchy" it imposes; in a similar fashion the protagonists of his novel are standing up against the most draconian law and order enforced by Nazi Germany. This resistant reading in the context of a resistant practice—a model for our reading of Paul's Galatian letter—clearly turns the intended message of the altar upside down. For with its emotional intensity, unheard of in classical Greek art,[72] and the almost unbearable aliveness embodied in the defeated in their dying, the Gigantomachy frieze aggressively constructs and cultivates its model reader as self detached from the suffering and misery of the other, and ready to fight the wars of civilization against its respective barbarians. This interactive and transformative power of the Great Altar was as appealing to the Attalids as later to the Romans, and after almost two millennia had passed, its propagandistic spell would again be exploited by the ideologues of the German Empire, followed a few decades later by the masterminds of fascist architecture.[73]

The transformative function of the Great Altar aims at conformity. When we have finally walked down to the right or left side of the Zeus group, south or north, and turn around the corner to face the western part of the altar, we are not supposed to arrive as neutral observers of a foreign war, nor, even worse, to fraternize with the dying and dead Giants. We are meant to see this war as our own in a proper manner—the war of the gods and goddesses. Arriving at the front of the Great Altar, where the continuous band of images suddenly splits in the middle to make room for the staircase, we should have become partisans ourselves, and it needs no more thought as to which army we would join. This is the decisive transition that brings forth the superior occidental self as victorious, disconnected from the defeated, barbarian, inferior other; we are now at least symbolically allowed to go *Up* and *In*. We will first take a look at the upper room and then turn to the Great Staircase.

Telephos's Upper Room: The Religion of Rule(rs)

The upper level of the Great Altar is defined by three basic elements: what we presume was the sacrificial altar at its center, the colonnades that surrounded it, and the Telephos frieze that adorned the walls behind the columns on three sides. Not all of it has been preserved, and the story it tells is not entirely transparent.[74] But the main points are sufficiently clear:

Telephos was the son of Heracles and Augē, a priestess of Athena in Arcadia/Greece, who after long and numerous journeys back and forth eventually became king of Mysia/Asia Minor and the founder-father of the Pergamenes. The space in the upper room thus is designated as a symbolic representation of "city," more precisely a colonizing city of Greek origin in non-Greek territory. Even before Pergamon is established, Telephos's mother, Augē, installs the worship of Athena there. Telephos's city therefore is built appropriately on the foundation of religion, a supreme civic value in antiquity. Proper performance of sacrifices, as we have seen, is a marker of civilization as such, a lack thereof signals barbarian lawlessness and blasphemy. On a plate to the right, Telephos himself introduces the cult of Dionysus. This cultic dimension of the Frieze would connect well to the sacrificial altar in the middle of the room as the innermost and most sacred point of the Great Altar. Through the open roof the smoke rising from its table creates a direct link to the divine above.

Heracles, Telephos, and the Genealogy of Power

A third signifying element next to city and piety requires further explanation: rule and kingship. As Telephos is the ancestor of the Attalid dynasty, the Telephos saga as portrayed at the Great Altar certainly represents a genealogy of power.[75] Whatever deity the Great Altar was dedicated to, it was undoubtedly also dedicated to the royal cult of the Attalid house and its preeminent heroic ancestors. Holger Schwarzer has drawn attention to the Attalid ruler cult that was in place since Attalus I (241–197 B.C.E.) had adopted the title *Sotēr*/Savior after his victory over the Galatians at the sources of the Caicus. Royal worship, according to Schwarzer, was further developed by Attalus's son Eumenes II (197–158 B.C.E.), who strengthened its dynastic aspects when he had his father divinized as *theos*/god and promoted the mythological roots of the Attalid dynasty. Eventually, he built the Great Altar as a monument dedicated to the ruler worship of the Attalids.[76]

The focus of the Great Altar on the Attalid ruling dynasty and its ancestors has been strongly supported by Ann Kuttner, who, like Schwarzer, draws on the Telephos myth but adds another element: the clear resemblance that links the Great Altar to "dynastic heroa of non-Greek Anatolia, like the Mausoleion of the Karian Halikarnassos, and the Nereid Monument at Lykian Xanthos," as well as the Tomb of Lysimachos at Belevi.[77] In her view, pilgrims entering the *temenos* (sacred district) of the Great Altar from the east side first "saw the contour of an Asiatic podium tomb for a heroized king, with temple-like colonnaded crown. . . ." The Telephos courtyard, on the other hand, in her opinion imitates the shape of Lykian royal heroa.[78] This brings the overall arrangement of the Pergamene acropolis back into the picture: the palace citadel immediately neighboring the Great Altar recalls the notion that divine and political power are linked to the topology of mountain heights in Anatolian and Middle Eastern thought. The space of and around the Great Altar is marked by royal power. Kuttner concludes: "At palatial sites there is one essential star of any spectacle: the living dynasty. The Altar was a stage set for kings in ceremonial performance."[79] Where the narrative of the frieze plates stops with the death of its hero Telephos, subsequently King Eumenes II, his family, and his court thus would provide its contemporary continuation.

Fig. 28. Telephos-Frieze: A boat is built to cast out mourning Auge, mother of Telephos, from Arkadia/Greece. Photo: Jakob B. Rehmann.

Fig. 29. Left: Heracles discovers his abandoned son Telephos, suckled by a lioness.

Fig. 30. Right: King Teuthras in Mysia/ Asia Minor hurries to meet and welcome the stranded Auge. Photos © Trustees and Fellows of Harvard University.

Yet the foundation of Attalid rule at the Great Altar is not just an issue of architectural quotations of monumental structures from elsewhere. Rather, it is woven into the very fabric of the Telephos and Giant battle friezes themselves. We need to start with the birth of the founder himself. Apparently Augē's father, King Aloeus in Arcadia, had been warned to beware of her son, who would threaten his or his sons' rule. Augē was therefore made a virgin priestess of Athena to stop her from producing offspring. Heracles came to Arcadia and seduced her, but King Aloeus was not ready to accept the new family. Expelled onto the open sea in a small boat, Augē, however, miraculously survives her father's intended punishment of death, and after a long sea journey finds a new home in Mysia in Asia Minor at the court of King Teuthras, who warmly welcomes her. Her baby son, Telephos, cruelly abandoned by his grandfather as well, is saved in a similarly spectacular way. Next to the moving scene that shows Augē mourning her father's verdict, the frieze depicts Heracles, who has obviously rediscovered his exposed infant son. Leaning on his club and draped with his signature lion skin, he looks down at baby Telephos, who is suckled by a lioness at his feet.[80] In the next scene we see how the child is given into the care of nymphs by his devoted father. Telephos and his mother are later reunited in Mysia, where Telephos wages war with the Greeks on their way to Troy and takes over the kingdom of Teuthras, becoming the forefather of the Attalids and the founder of Pergamon.[81] (See figs. 28–30.)

An unwanted royal descendant from Greece is spared from death by divine providence and receives a friendly welcome by a king in Asia Minor, to be finally installed as ruler himself. This story is certainly impressive but not entirely exceptional. What makes it really outstanding is only its second half, which is not depicted in the Telephos frieze but needs to be deciphered from its inscription on the Great Frieze and the Great Staircase. This more comprehensive visual narrative starts with Zeus. Zeus, the father of the Gods, had also fathered Heracles with a mortal woman, provoking family disturbances with his divine spouse, Hera, somewhat comparable to those at the birth of Telephos in Arcadia. Heracles, however, will become a key player in the survival battle of the gods against the Giants. According to Apollodorus, an oracle had informed the gods that they could win the battle only if a mortal entered their ranks and fought together with them (*Library* 1.6.1). Heracles fulfills this task with superior commitment and efficiency. On the Great Frieze he was originally depicted at Zeus's right hand, next to Hera, though his figure, except for the paw of the lion's skin he is carrying, has not been preserved. Heracles is the only mortal among all the divine combatants. He will be deified after his death, a pattern that the Pergamene ruler cult adopted, as Holger Schwarzer has shown.

Heracles is also the most conspicuous mediator between the *Outside-Below* and the *Inside-Above* of the Great Altar. A fierce fighter on the battlefield of the Great Frieze located at the underside and outside of the altar, he is depicted as a lovingly caring father for his little son on the upper and inside level of the Telephos room. Heracles discloses the real foundation of city, piety, family, and dynasty: victory over anti-civilization by allegiance to the superior divine forces.[82] All that constitutes city and civilization in its

Fig. 31. The Semiotics of the Telephos Room

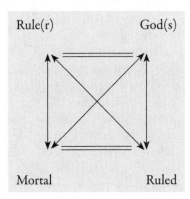

Rule(r)   God(s)

Mortal   Ruled

entirety emerges from the battlefield, but most of all the divine entitlement and commission to rule. Rule, the hard core of the Giant battle myth, is bestowed on Telephos not just as a result of his fortunate encounter with King Teuthras, but as his true legacy and sacred birthright because he is the son of the most eminent and successful human/ divine Giant-fighter that ever existed: Heracles, the son of Zeus. As semidivine progeny of Heracles/Telephos and as famous Galatian/Giant-fighters, the Attalids are destined to rule as well.

The diagram shown in figure 31 marks the upper room, and the altar as a whole, as a space dedicated to political religion. Through Heracles/Telephos, and through their own "herculean" deeds on the battlefield of civilization versus barbarism, Pergamene rulers and the gods are closely affiliated, no matter whether the living Attalids tended to see themselves as gods or merely as godlike, no matter whether the offerings on the sacrificial altar were burnt to Zeus, Athena, the pantheon, present or past rulers, or to all of them. In a strange inversion of "heaven" and "earth," the order established by the Pergamene kings *up here* in the Telephos room mirrors and upholds the order defended and safeguarded by the gods and Heracles *down there* at the bottom of the Great Altar. Attalid rule is a pillar of divine rule on earth.

The lower level of the semiotic square we have drawn links *Mortal == Ruled* as non-A and non-B. Both categories mark the *dēmos*, the people of Pergamon, who are in a clearly subordinate position—unlike the rulers/kings, and unlike the immortal gods. Still, the non-negotiable hierarchy and polarity between *Ruler* ↔ *Ruled, Divine* ↔ *Mortal* seems somewhat less intense compared to the strict boundaries between *Up* and *Down, In* and *Out* that we have encountered in the antagonistic battle order of the Great Frieze where it related to enemies of a most alien and terrifying nature, rather than citizens. Civic cult as worship of the gods has a unifying, non-dichotomous aspect; it unites rulers and ruled in common devotion to the deities, pointing to the mortality and nondivine nature of the rulers themselves and their subordination to the gods, which makes the rulers appear similar to everyone else.

Inclusiveness rather than Polarities? An "Asianizing" Reading

This leads to the most fascinating question recently raised by Ann Kuttner. The somewhat programmatic title of her essay "Do You Look Like You Belong Here?" points to the core issue of polarities and alignment represented by the Great Altar: Could it be that the Telephos frieze breaks up and even subverts some of the clear-cut self/other dichotomies of belonging and not belonging that are linked to the combat order of the Gigantomachy/Galatomachy? Indeed, while Telephos is shown as a brave warrior on the frieze, there are some confusingly heterodox elements that seem entirely out of place. It is Greeks with whom Telephos fights and wrestles, not barbarians—and it is an Amazon of outstanding beauty whom he marries as his first wife and who is killed by the Greeks. The iconographic focus is no longer exclusively on battles but rather on royal court scenes, sacral and royal domestic banquets, bedroom and funerary scenes, all related to a palatial setting, on the one hand, and to sacrifices and cultic practice, on the other.[83]

Moreover, did the specific model of worship drafted by the Attalids try to embrace a fundamental inclusivity, an ecumenism of Greek and non-Greek (Anatolian) gods, Hellenistic and Asiatic civilization, in order to integrate and acknowledge local peoples and their rulers? This anti-dichotomous and anti-vertical argument, which recalls Pfanner's support for the Great Altar's dedication to the pantheon, has Kuttner suggest that "Pergamon's Kunstpolitik proclaimed horizontal lines of kinship as much as or more than vertical, patriarchal power," aiming at a "culture of collaboration" that transcended ethnic lines.[84] The Gigantomachy of the Great Frieze thus for her is not just about victory and domination/colonization, Hellenic versus barbarian, but "it depicted royal hegemony over loyal subjects and freely federated allies, joined in common defense. The frieze does not just damn rebellion; it rallies the Attalid federation." In Kuttner's Asianizing interpretational model, the Telephos frieze in particular expresses this fundamental inclusiveness, as it does not show good Greeks versus bad Asians, but the defense of Asian Mysia "against bad Greeks, by good Asians and good Greeks."[85]

Yet, despite such horizontal and inclusive allures, the upper room is undeniably, simultaneously vertical and exclusive. For the rulers are also fundamentally dissociated from the equation of *Ruled* == (ordinary) *Mortals,* as even the briefest look at their walled and impregnable citadel further up on the Pergamene acropolis shows. They physically have divine blood and seed in them; they are immortal in their dynasty and rule; and they are the chosen and victory-confirmed allies of the gods and goddesses in the battle against the Giant/Galatian other. As such, they have crossed the boundary between *Down* and *Up, Human* and *Divine, Ruled* and *Ruler.* If they show themselves to the crowds, they also stay distant from them. As the gods in the primordial battle saved the world from annihilation through chaos and lawlessness, the king is the supreme present-day savior (*sōtēr*) and benefactor (*eurgetēs*) who in return for his royal benefactions deserves gratitude, reverence, worship— together with the gods.

The Telephos court thus may have united rulers and ruled in front of the gods, or perhaps the rulers were up in the court and the ruled down on the altar terrace.[86] The issue is not so much how modest or inclusive the Attalid rulers were (or their propaganda).[87] The link of Telephos to Zeus as his grandfather is a subtle, or not so subtle, reminder that in the world after Alexander, victory and salvation from the gigantic Galatian threat meant royal-divine rule and divine royal power, and it always implied the dimension of world rule and world ordering as well.[88] Yet whoever the Attalids were, and whatever their ambitions, the full political and ideological potential of this power construct was realized only by the legal heir of the Pergamene kingdom: Rome.

The Law and Magic of the Great Staircase

This brings us finally to the magical space of the Great Staircase, where *Out* becomes *In* and *Down* is transformed into *High*—or maybe not. Not everyone, as we have seen, is admitted *In* and *Up*. Starting to ascend from the altar terrace below, after a few steps we are at the same level as the Giants to our right and left side. Standing on the battlefield among the fighting and falling Giants, we ourselves have now entered the war zone. Like them we have risen from below, for we are mortals, not gods. Is there an impulse to join those who are earth-born like us, against those *up there*? Shall we rise in reverence

or rebellion? As allies or enemies of the gods? Literally, no one can pass here without taking sides.

But as we continue to climb, we make a striking discovery: the lower level of the Great Frieze has started to move up, following the ascent of the staircase. The Giants now metaphorically try to climb a mountain, or the citadel of the Olympians, as the Giant myth maintains they did. Or maybe they are now attacking the Pergamene acropolis itself? Perhaps even *our* city? Yet as we stand watching them, anxiously, reluctantly, we notice suddenly that their space is starting to shrink. The higher they

Fig. 32. Left wing of the Gigantomachy at the Great Staircase: A fallen Giant grabs a stone, moving out of the Frieze into the space of the stairway. Photo: Jakob B. Rehmann.

climb, the more they lose ground. The sharp rise of the base to their feet inevitably crushes them against the upper cornice of the frieze, which stays with stony immovability on a horizontal plane. The building, architecture, and space all collaborate with the gods to push away and crush the Giants. Their fatal way toward the *Up* and *In* destroys them with innermost, elementary necessity.

But there is no time for contemplation. Suddenly a Giant appears next to us on the left, right at the stairs. With the further narrowing of the frieze, he has been forced to his knees and literally squeezed out of the relief, almost a freestanding figure with no more than loose ties to the relief plate at his back left. He has entered our space, and he threatens us with a stone that he has grabbed in a desperate convulsive motion. Whether we want it or not: he is now taking us on as an enemy. Myth is turning into history.[89] (See fig. 32.)

Is it hardly possible even for a split second not to draw back in revulsion, dread, and rejection. We have already seen and made a decision about him before we entered the staircase. And things are now moving quickly. Another grisly snake-shape is penetrating into the stairwell, menacingly coiling itself upward. It appears to be using its curved back to hold up the kneeling, staircase giant. Monsters and snakes, primeval fears and traumas are there again, together with the feeling of being unjustly attacked, attacked for no obvious reason. We must run for safety.

Subject Formation under the Eagle's (C)laws

As we are heading for the upper platform, the battle frieze and its nightmares are miraculously vanishing. The spot where the upper and lower bases of the Great Frieze meet in a sharp angle is the most sensitive point of the passage between *Down* and *Up*. The two triangular Gigantomachy panels to the left and right seem to melt into the staircase and disappear. It is the magic boundary where *they* stay behind and *we* go on. It

Fig. 33. Right wing and uppermost corner of the Gigantomachy-Frieze at the Great Staircase: A snake-legged giant is repelled by Zeus's eagle. Photo: Jakob B. Rehmann.

will take us only one more step before we have made it *Up* and *In*. Is it over? Not quite yet. A most vigilant border patrol protects the precarious threshold on both sides of the stairs, a Giant-fighter with even more preeminent credentials than Heracles: Zeus's eagle.

On the right side of the staircase this last and climactic corner of the frieze and its eagle imagery are especially well preserved. We can see how the combative eagle, which is the standard attribute of the supreme divine father, vigorously strikes its left claw into the open mouth of an upward-crouching monster serpent. *Down* there at the East Frieze, the eagle had defended Zeus himself against a similar monster. *Up* here at the staircase it defends the order and well-being of Zeus's city and her god(like) king, Zeus's great-grandson, Eumenes—and us. Spatially, the eagle acts as the turnstile between *Up* and *Down*, *In* and *Out*. It is obvious that in the symbolic order of the Great Altar it serves as a guard; it sets the rules of admission and secures the preservation of the cosmic order, established by the fighting deities at the mythological bottom, in the upper space of contemporary history as well. In other words, Zeus's eagle represents cosmic law, divine law, universal law. The eagle also represents human law enforced or even embodied by the Pergamene kings.

In lines 1–6 of the Stoic *Hymn to Zeus* by Cleanthes from the third century B.C.E., Zeus is addressed and praised as being the all-powerful, first cause of nature and humans and the supreme king of everything in eternity, who rules nature and universe with his law (*nomos*).[90] He is assisted by the thunderbolt he holds in his "invincible hands" (lines 7–11); its stroke guides "all works [*erga*] of nature" and also directs the universal reason (*logos*, line12).

> Noblest of all immortals, many-named, always all-powerful
> Zeus, first cause and ruler of nature, governing everything with your law [*nomos*],
> greetings! . . .
> This whole universe, spinning around the earth, truly
> obeys you wherever you lead, and is readily ruled by you;
> such a servant you have between your unconquerable [*anikētois*] hands,
> the two-edged, fiery, ever-living thunderbolt.
> For by its stroke all works of nature <are guided>.
> with it you direct the universal reason [*koinon logon*], which permeates
> everything. . . .[91]

Logos and law are almost synonymous in this concept, and both have an external dimension related to the cosmic and natural order and an internal one that underlies the moral and ethical behavior of "good" humans in contrast to the "evil ones" (lines 17, 22–32). As Johan C. Thom states, "In the *Hymn*, however, the difference between *nomos* and *logos* is only one of emphasis: 'law' indicates the principle or order on which Zeus' rule is based, and which also should be honored and obeyed by human beings (cf. lines 2, 24–25, 39), while 'reason' refers to the principle of orderly and rational arrangement in nature, which humans should make the basis of their own decisions (lines 12–13, 20–21, 22)."[92]

In line with Cleanthes' Stoic framework,[93] one could interpret the eagle at the Pergamene staircase as a representation of all three modalities of Zeus's rule: (1) of law as the principle of order as such that determines who belongs *In* and *Out*, *High* and *Low;* (2) of *logos* as the rationality and goodness of this order, based on the commonsense idea that irrational and terrifying monsters with ophidoform legs should not get *In* and *Up*; and (3) of the thunderbolt as the eagle's metaphorical claws, that is, the instruments of Zeus's justice and law enforcement and an extension of Zeus's "unconquerable hands," which have created order and uphold it on both a cosmic and a social level.

The Great Altar's eagle-controlled staircase is thus the space where the city's symbolic order is established and protected on the basis of supreme divine and human law. The staircase functions as an entry way, a liminal space where outsiders are elevated to the rank of insiders, but only after they have been checked for admissibility and searched. Comparable to the tunnel-like gates leading through the compact walls of ancient cities—the famous Ishtar Gate of Babylon is displayed not far from the Great Altar in the Berlin Pergamon Museum—it is a well-guarded space. *Law* as represented by Zeus's eagle marks the *In*, and *Lawlessness* embodied in the Giants the *Out*. *Law* in our semiotic square thus could be defined as B and *Lawlessness* non-B. This requires the other polarity of A and non-A to be defined. If *Law* is the ultimate criterion of admission, what else is necessary to gain access from a deep *Down* to the high *Up*? If we reconsider our way up the Great Staircase, it appears that there was one decisive choice that made our passage through the haunted space of transition successful: *Submission.*

Fig. 34. Subject formation as submission to the Law

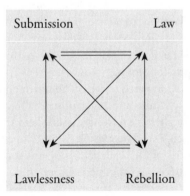

While climbing up, we had to make a conscious or unconscious decision not to join the rebellion against the gods, thus submitting to their rule and law and becoming worthy of admission. Rather than talking to the Giants or even befriending them, we were terrified and threatened by them. The very fact that Zeus's eagle graciously admitted us saved us; consequently we are entering the courtyard (and the realm of city and civilization it represents) with gratitude and reverence toward the gods and the ruler who kept and keeps this space safe. There is nothing we have in common with the Giants, the species of inferior, alien, and monstrous (sub)human beings who commit incomprehensible acts of madness and evil as they try to destroy all that makes the world good.

We have chosen our allegiance. In submission to, or even alliance with, the heavenly forces, we are admitted to the upper level. In other words, we have become proper subjects under Pergamene rule, in the double sense of this term. According to philosopher Louis Althusser, the constitution of a subject requires that an individual is "interpellated" as *you = subject* by a higher authority such as God, and becomes *I* and *self* through the answering act of subjection to this higher *Subject* (with a capital S) and its law, *logos,* or commandments. This mechanism of subjection that, for Althusser, marks the core and essence of ideology implies the universal mutual recognition of subjects and Subject, of each other and self, as well as the absolute guarantee that "everything will be all right" for the "good subjects" in contradistinction to the "bad subjects," who require repressive intervention.[94]

Here in the upper room of Telephos at this point, probably no one would talk about repression and subjection in terms of ruled, vanquished, conquered, or colonized, but rather about subjects as allies or confederates or grateful citizens who have been saved and liberated into true civilized subjectivity, all united in joyful worship of the gods and the royal family, in subjection to their beneficial law. These are the ideal *Ruled* <non-A> of the Telephos court who as *Mortals* <non-B> accept the *Godlike Rule* <A> of the king, which corresponds to the *Kinglike Rule* of the god(s) <B>.[95] (See fig. 31.) This is the law, both cosmic and political, to which *we* as "good subjects" have submitted at the Great Staircase, and which holds the world, nature, and civilized society together. It is in constant need of being defended against the Giant forces of destruction from outside, a world inferior to ours.

It might seem strange that submission, literally putting oneself under someone else, here appears as a superior category of the *Inside-Above.* This change of perspective is precisely part of the magical transformation that happens at the Great Staircase. There is another metamorphosis. Compared to the environment of the Great Frieze, the Telephos sanctuary is a relatively calm and peaceful space. Yet, if the noise of battle has faded and the images of slaughter are no longer visible here, they are not gone; symbolically the battlefield has been, and always is, the entrance to city and civilization, palace and sanctuary. The semiotics of the battlefield—the way it constructs order, rule, law, identity, and even god(s)—is entirely built on victory, and so is its religion.

The Order of Civilization and the Sacrifice of the Other

This requires a last look at the sacrificial table, the actual altar whose appearance, function, and very existence at the center of the Telephos court are highly disputed. Scholars such as Andrew Stewart have been puzzled by the very practical problem that the steep staircase and the relatively narrow colonnaded entrance to the upper platform would have made it quite difficult to bring bovine victims up there to be sacrificed, especially the relatively large number of animals required to feed the long list of potential guests for the "obligatory sacrificial feast."[96] He therefore suggested that the actual slaughter

*Fig. 35. Wolfram Hoepfner's model of the Great Altar as victory
monument, with figures of Dying Gauls/Galatians placed in the
innermost sanctuary. Photo: Jakob B. Rehmann.*

and butchering of the animals took place at the altar terrace and then the portions
reserved for the gods were carried up for immolation on the altar. Taking up an earlier
suggestion by Wolfram Hoepfner that the palatial architecture of the Telephos court
would match its use for royal feasting, Stewart imagines, "Sheltered from the wind,
surrounded by the Telephos Frieze, and overlooked by the Olympians [the *akrōtērion*
sculptures on the roof] this court would have been a perfect venue for an outdoor banquet celebrating the prosperity of city and state under the Attalid's benevolent rule."[97]

Hoepfner's more radical proposal concerns the altar itself. Its table top shows
marks that seem to indicate that objects, such as sculptures, were attached to its surface. Hoepfner, whose model of the Great Altar traveled in an exhibition through
the United States in the 1990s, came to a striking conclusion: he believes that the
Great Altar did not have sacrificial functions at all, but that statues of the so-called
Lesser Attalid dedication were placed on the altar table instead. With the figures of
dying and dead Amazons, Galatians, Giants, and Persians on display at its innermost
center, the Great Altar, for Hoepfner, is primarily a victory monument rather than
a sacrificial altar in the traditional and literal sense. The vanquished are "sacrificed"
metaphorically.[98] This idea has again been modified by Stewart, who thinks that the
irregularity of the marks would be much more fitting for trophies of weapons taken
from vanquished enemies, most notably Galatians.[99] The Athena sanctuary next to
the Great Altar shows a whole frieze that displays such primarily Gallic spoils as oval
shields (see Pausanias 1.4.6).

The most far-reaching rearrangement has been suggested by Ann Kuttner, who
challenges the idea that the colonnaded upper court contained a sacrificial altar or any
structure resembling it at all; instead, she places the sacrificial site on the much more
spacious altar terrace around the Great Altar. Royal feasting and hospitality, however,
would remain the primary function of the Telephos court: "The palace eventually

present from below was a simulacrum—Telephos' lofty courtyard, an extensive medi-
tation on royal hosting. . . . Perhaps suggestions that the Altar court hosted ritual
banquets for ruler cult are true." Kuttner insists, however, that the necessary couch
arrangements for such a symposium would require removing the sacrificial altar from
the Telephos court. In this model, the altar terrace below the Telephos court would
provide space not just for the sacrificial altar but also for hosting "big crowds of lower-
ranking feasters." This would also solve another problem, namely, "the vexed issue, how
did the restricted extant Attalid palaces hold the big formal palace banquets which
were necessary to all Hellenistic courts."[100]

Again, we do not have to make any decision here. But no matter where the sacrificial
site was placed or what it looked like, all four options are equally valid descriptions of
the Great Altar: worship of gods, victory monument, ruler cult, regal hospitality/ritual
banquets. Stewart summarizes this as the "aggressively ecumenical multi-functionality" of
the Great Altar: "For it served, *inter alia*, as a ritual focus for king and people, a celebration of divine power and benevolence, a monument to royal triumph and civic prosperity, a grandstand for Pergamene heroic *aretē*, and a showcase for the fruits of victory."[101]
Victory seems focal to all of these functions. The altar as a religious site is entirely based
on victory, and this victory translates into the praise of rule(r), of the gods, and of the
people's well-being. Whoever and whatever were worshiped at the Great Altar, it was a
worship of victory and power translated into salvation and benefaction.

From this perspective, Hoepfner's controversial proposal to put the Dying Galatians,
Giants, Amazons at the surface of the sacrificial table, irrespective of historical factual-
ity, points to a basic truth at the core of the images. We saw it already materialized in
the life sacrifice of the Galatian and Greek couples in Rome in 228, 216, and 114 B.C.E.
The death of the savage, barbarian, hostile other celebrated at the Gigantomachy frieze,
in the Attalid dedications and the countless copies of Dying Gauls/Galatians all over
the Greco-Roman world is, in the deep structure of the Great Altar and the civilization
it represents, linked to the sacrifical ritual. It constitutes the righteous, justified self of
the civilized and the lawful well-being of the city in communication with its gods. Like
the sacrifice of beasts, the "sacrifice" of the beastlike and subhuman others rechannels
the life-blood of the inferior into the bloodstream of the dominant order to cleanse,
nurture, and sustain it. The bloodshed of the battlefield and the bloodshed of the sacrifice both represent sacred violence, which legitimately destroys and consumes the other
at the altar of civilization for its own higher ends.

Satan's Throne: The Great Altar
as a Roman Monument

In Paul's time, the Great Altar was two hundred years old, but its beauty was still spell-
binding, and the normative power of its underlying concepts more relevant than ever.
The Romans had "inherited" the altar together with the whole kingdom of Pergamon

in 133 B.C.E.;[102] as a visually condensed representation and legacy of the Attalid and Diadochian age, it provided one of the aesthetically and philosophically most brilliant visual anticipations of the emerging Roman world order and a new type of imperial world religion.

To employ a Roman reading of the Great Altar seems awkward at first and strangely out of sync with well-established reading patterns, which traditionally have strongly focused on its uniquely Pergamene character and the intricate affiliations with the Hellenistic world it embodies.[103] The Great Altar, to be sure, is the most stellar and genuinely Pergamene achievement Pergamon ever brought forth, and a monument of strong Attalid self-confidence. Yet it is also part of the competitive post-Alexander discourse about power, and even world power. As such, it sends a message to Rome, as it sends messages to the Greeks and non-Greeks. The hesitation to apply a Roman semiotics to Pergamene images may be rooted in a deeply ingrained reluctance to mix the sublime subject of Greek/Hellenic art with anything as pragmatic as Roman politics. Or, as the previous chapter showed, it might also stem from an over-compartmentalized approach that separates Latin Gauls and Greek Galatians, that is, the Roman, Delphic, and Pergamene sections of one and the same history into disconnected research areas and mental boxes. Partly linked to this overall problem might be the long-standing tradition in art history to perceive of anything looking "Pergamene" in Italy, such as depictions of Dying Gauls/Galatians, as per definition nothing else than a "Roman copy" of a "Greek original" and thus without a Roman semiotics of its own.[104]

Rome as Owner of the Pergamene Acropolis

The Galatomachy that is so beautifully laid out on the Great Altar was a Roman topic before it became a Hellenistic subject, as we have shown in our historical outline in chapter 1. It never ceased to belong to Rome even as it belonged to the Antigonids, Seleucids, Ptolemies, and Attalids as well—and it became a joint venture of Rome and Pergamon when the brother of Eumenes II aligned his forces with Manlius Vulso in the Galatian massacre of 189 B.C.E. Whatever political fine print the Pergamenes wanted to communicate about their Galatian victory to Rome, Greece, Asia, and themselves, the Great Altar's overall historical context is marked by the crude military imprint of Manlius Vulso, which already foreshadows the political dissolution of the Pergamene kingdom into the Roman Empire in 133 B.C.E.

Altogether, the Pergamenes owned the altar for a maximum of fifty years, and maybe just for two or three decades. They were never able to finish it. As Pergamon's final statement before leaving the stage of world history, the Great Altar visually represents the most triumphal victory in the arena of a centuries-long Diadochian competition. It was a victory achieved through the power not of arms but of images; as such it would never be surpassed. It was only one more century until this victory was fully accomplished militarily, and Caesar's armies in Gaul had won him the rank of

the ultimate Giant/Galatian slayer. When Rome subsequently needed to conceptualize and visualize this triumph within the framework of empire, the Great Altar was
there with the images perfectly modeled, prearranged, and ready to be fit into the
one large image of imperial ideology. Rome won the final victory over the Gauls/
Galatians as the universal barbarian other of the ancient world, but the communication of this triumph as a natural rationale for universal power, global order(ing), and
an imperial world religion was already masterfully and comprehensively delineated
at Pergamon and its Great Altar.

The traces of a Roman appropriation of the Great Altar, however, are patchy and
indirect, though more clearly readable when seen against the broader background
of Pergamene–Roman cultural exchange.[105] Ever since Attalus I had assisted Rome
in the transfer of the Magna Mater Cybele from Mount Ida/Troy to Rome in 204
B.C.E., the "elective kinship" between Rome and Pergamon was an established fact.
At a moment of relative political weakness, the move of the goddess to the Palatine
Hill helped Rome strengthen its credentials in the Hellenistic world through a spectacular symbolic transaction that involved not only the highly respected Great Earth
Mother Cybele but also the Sibylline books, the Delphic Oracle, Hannibal, and the
Pergamene kingdom. It featured the emerging great myth of Rome's Trojan origin, its
formidable descent from Aeneas and from the battle at the center of Homer's *Iliad*—
and it conveniently emphasized both Rome's non-Greek roots and identity and its
original claim to the Greek East and Asia Minor. Pergamon, on the other hand, at
that time the political suzerain of the territory of Mount Ida and the Troad, had
much symbolic capital to gain from the transfer, and it may even have provided the
idea, as Erich Gruen muses. Subsequently, Pergamene intellectuals and artists further elaborated the mythological and genealogical links between Pergamon, Rome,
and Troy. [106]

As a result of the political alliance between the two unequal friends, Pergamene culture and philosophy played a strong role in Rome both before and after 133 B.C.E.[107] Its
influence, according to Kuttner, was partly mediated through Athens as Rome's favorite university city, which in turn was under Pergamene patronage as a major center for
Stoic, Academic, and Peripatetic studies. In Rome, on the other hand, visiting scholars
from Pergamon were a constant and influential presence. The Stoic philosopher and
head of the Pergamene library Crates of Mallon, for example, potentially the mastermind or one of the masterminds, behind the Great Altar, appeared before the senate in
Rome as an Attalid emissary in 169/168 B.C.E. (Suetonius, *Gram.* 2).[108] How relevant
the cultural and philosophical symbiosis between Pergamon and Rome still was at the
threshold of the Augustan era is shown in that Julius Caesar in the forties of the first
century B.C.E. appointed a Pergamene tutor for his adopted son Octavian/Augustus,
the rhetorician Apollodorus.[109]

Rome's close interest in Pergamon is also reflected in the archaeological record of
the city itself. When the Attalid kingdom turned into the Roman province of Asia
after 133 B.C.E., Pergamon became its capital. The Pergamene citadel, now Roman state
property, probably housed the Roman magistrates, as Kuttner suggests. For this group

of Roman officials and their activities, more republican and Augustan monuments are documented in Pergamon than "for any other site in the Greek East, especially after 133," and "their portrait dedications cluster for attention in the zones of the Athena precinct, theater and Great Altar terrace. The Roman governing class took care to preserve these royal monuments, as we know they preserved the royal library."[110]

Augustus at the "Throne" of Zeus

If the Romans thus maintained the Great Altar, if they monumentalized themselves at its terrace, what did they use it for? Though the answer to this question is a matter of guesswork, it is not entirely hypothetical to assume that the altar continued to play the role it had played under the Attalids: a sacred site for worship of the god(s), of victory commemoration and thanksgiving, and especially for ruler cult in the new imperial setting under Augustus. In light of Pergamon's well-established tradition of and superior expertise in political religion, it seems almost the next logical step that the Pergamene initiative would become a catalyst for the establishment of imperial worship under Augustus. In 29 B.C.E., only two years after his decisive victory over Antony and Cleopatra at Actium had made Octavian sole ruler and emperor-to-be, Pergamon, together with Nicomedia in the province of Bithynia, applied to be the first city to install a provincial temple dedicated to the worship of Rome and Augustus.

Though the details of the overall arrangement are not entirely clear, this was, in fact, the inauguration of imperial religion in the Roman Empire. As Steven Friesen states, ". . . the cult in Asia, along with the lesser known cult in Bithynia, became the starting point for an expanding phenomenon of provincial imperial worship throughout the empire. With the establishment of the cult of Rome and Augustus, new symbolic resources entered public life."[111] The speediness of this move was clearly related to the fact that Asia had sided with Antony and Cleopatra before Actium and needed to make up with Octavian; nevertheless, it does not seem accidental that it was Pergamon from where Rome was offered these "new symbolic resources" that bore the potential to be shaped into one of the most efficient elements of imperial ideology and governance: imperial religion.[112]

Again, we do not know with certainty what role the Great Altar played in this context. That it in all likelihood became a site of Roman imperial worship is a conclusion drawn by Holger Schwarzer after careful consideration of the archeological evidence.[113] Curiously, the strongest piece of evidence for the Roman takeover of the Great Altar within the framework of imperial religion is preserved in the New Testament. In the Book of Revelation, dating from the nineties of the first century C.E., the exiled seer John of Patmos strongly criticizes Pergamon as the dwelling place of "Satan" and the place where "the throne of Satan is" (Rev 2:13). In the apocalyptic thought world of John, *Satan* is a code word for emperor, or the cosmic power behind him. Reverence toward Satan/emperor, as implied in the term *Satan's throne* thus means emperor worship in opposition to the proper worship of God. This is laid out in the strongly polar images of the "throne" of the beast/Satan/emperor that is worshiped in Rev 13:2-4 versus the heavenly "throne" of God as center of eternal worship in the celestial throne vision of Revelation 4.[114]

Following an old suggestion of Adolf Deissmann,[115] Adela Yarbro Collins has convincingly shown that "Satan's throne" at Pergamon in Revelation 2 probably refers to the Great Altar (in connection with the adjacent temples of Zeus and Athena). As the current emperor Domitian was represented as Zeus, and Zeus as the antagonist of Israel's God, the Great Altar's (co)dedication to Zeus, in Yarbro Collins's opinion, could easily have sustained John's subversive reading of the Great Altar as dwelling place and "throne" of the emperor = Zeus = Satan. Furthermore, as discussed above, the spatially and visually exposed position of the Great Altar at the height of the Pergamene acropolis would naturally have lent itself to seeing it as (mountain)-throne of the supreme human and divine power.[116] If the "throne" of Satan = dragon = beast = Zeus = emperor in Rev 13:2–4 solicits universal worship, this would be a piece of literary evidence for the Great Altar as a site of emperor worship.

It is not exactly clear how the presence of Augustus/Caesar on this Pergamene "throne" should be envisioned. A fragmentary inscription found on the altar precinct praises Augustus (*Sebastos*) as emperor (*autokrator*), Caesar, god (*theos*), and son of god, as well as "ruler of sea and land."[117] Was there a statue of Caesar or Zeus = Caesar added to the Great Altar, perhaps comparable to the colossal seated statue of Zeus that Mary Sturgeon envisions as having been placed on a real throne directly in front of the sacrificial altar in the Telephos court?[118] Indeed, such a sitting Zeus/Jupiter surrounded by two emperor statues would eventually become the center of imperial religion on the Pergamene acropolis under Trajan (98–117 C.E.), when a huge temple dedicated to emperor worship was built on top of the Great Altar and the Athena sanctuary. But this was long after Augustus and after Paul, and even John of Patmos did not yet know the imposing sight of the Trajaneum when he wrote about the "throne of Satan" at Pergamon.[119]

What we do know about the time of Augustus, however, is that a striking transformation took place in the immediate neighborhood of the Great Altar, in the precinct of the Athena sanctuary in 20 B.C.E. On a round base in front of the temple, King Attalus I (241–197 B.C.E.) in the thirties of the third century B.C.E. had erected a statue of Athena in gratitude for his victory over the Tolistoagian Galatians at the sources of the Caicus River. Two hundred years later, in 20 B.C.E., Augustus regained the Roman standards and eagles that had been lost to the Parthians by Crassus in 53 B.C.E. Though this was mainly a diplomatic and not a military success, it was celebrated as a Roman victory of key importance and a prerequisite for the beginning of the golden age.[120] When Augustus, on a journey through the eastern provinces in 19 B.C.E., visited Pergamon, he was presented with a statue of himself that had replaced the Attalid Athena in front of her sanctuary. According to Wolfgang Radt, the old dedication by Attalus was simply covered with a bronze band running around the base; the new dedicatory inscription to Augustus was placed underneath it. It said that the people (*dēmos*) of Pergamon and the Romans living there dedicated this statue to God Augustus Caesar (*theos/Sebastos/Kaisar*), the ruler/overseer of land and sea. Augustus responded to the extraordinary gesture by arranging a number of trophies, presumably of Parthian origin, on the uppermost of the three stairs surrounding the monument base and by dedicating them to Athena, as another inscription reports.[121]

The symbolic relevance of this episode is striking. The Pergamenes made a bold move to represent Augustus as a present divine reincarnation of all past triumphs over Galatians, barbarians, and Persians won by Attalids and Greeks under the leadership of Athena, the city goddess for both Athens and Pergamon. Not only did Augustus now "share the smoke of sacrifices at the altar of Athena Polias Nikephoros," as Kuttner states, but he also "dominated the precinct's victory portraits of Attalid kings and generals, with a monument visible from anywhere in the city."[122] Augustus, in return, humbly honors the battle-leading (*promachos*), victory-bearing (*nikēphoros*) city goddess (*polias*) Athena; through the dedication of his Parthian spoils, he ties his own victory to hers.

The way that Rome here acquires a place at the temple of Athena models the Roman takeover of the Great Altar—in fact, it is the imperial reappropriation of the altar as well. Since S. R. F. Price's landmark study, it is widely acknowledged that the Roman imperial cult in the Greek East did not create an entirely new symbolic system but rather inserted itself into the existing religious universe shaped by the Hellenistic ruler cult. One could say that emperor worship changed the established semiotics by leaving it intact per se, but added a new dimension.[123] What was left intact on the surface, however, in its deep structure became profoundly transformed, as it was redirected toward the emperor's own divine self as supreme one. The replacement of the Athena statue by Augustus as divine embodiment of all past and present victory automatically changed the semiotics of the neighboring Great Altar as well. The archetypal victory over the Giants/Galatians won under Zeus and Athena is now a Roman victory.

In general, imperial religion would not demolish or replace any of the established deities, nor destroy existing architectural complexes; rather, it preserved sacred and civic sites and simply inserted a new imperial component, which, however, rearranged the whole space.[124] As Kuttner has pointed out, for example, at Athens the prestigious and famous old ensemble of the Attalid Stoa facing the Stoa of Zeus was kept in its original shape; the only change made was the supplement of an added *exedra*-space for Rome and Augustus next to Zeus. Where Attalus had previously talked to Zeus, Augustus and Rome were now talking back to Attalus and Pergamon.[125] In a similar way, Augustus and Rome now "talked back" through the deities of the Great Frieze and the Great Altar in general. Rome was the new city of Athena, the city at the center of civilization that stood against barbarian lawlessness and giant rebellion. As Augustus appears behind or with Athena and Nikē/Victory on the Great Frieze after his takeover of the Athena precinct, his wife Livia now becomes Hera,[126] or he himself is shown in close relationship to Apollo, Aphrodite, and Mars. Moreover, both dedicatory inscriptions to Augustus found at the altar terrace and at the Athena temple, as we have seen, address him as the supreme god-Ruler and overseer of land and sea. At the Great Altar this position is owned by no one apart from Zeus alone.

Augustus's divinity not only rules land and sea—and thus redefines space on a global scale—but also time. We have observed how on the North Frieze this most sensitive realm of day and night, of months, years, and seasons, where cosmic order intersects the course of history and individual life, was attacked by the Giants. The victory of the gods and of Zeus restored the order of time. Since the establishment of the first temple to Rome and Augustus in Pergamon in 29 B.C.E., the imperial calendar increasingly ordered the course of time.[127] Imperial games, the *Sebasta Romaia,* were probably installed at Pergamon already in 29 B.C.E. to take place annually or bienni-ally, providing popular entertainment and climactic social events.[128] The birthdays of Augustus and Livia, and of later emperors, were celebrated annually and even monthly, with imperial choirs (*hymnodes*) playing a key role. An entire month was named after Augustus. Finally, in 9 B.C.E., the provincial assembly of Asia declared that the birthday of Augustus on September 23 thenceforward would mark New Year's Day.

The reason given for this exceptional symbolic action is impressive and revealing. The birth of Augustus marks the "beginning of all things," the restoration "of the form of all things," the bringing of "order to all things," and "the beginning of life and exis-tence" as such—in short, the renewal of the whole world, which was about to accept its own destruction. The allusion to the primeval battle against the forces of chaos and destruction—traditionally linked to the celebration of the new year—is evident. Cae-sar is the beginning of time, the creator-restorer of cosmic and social order: in other words, he is the one god who has performed a new creation, including the creation and salvation of human life. Every human being owes him gratitude without limits. Again Augustus here talks back through Zeus, as well as through the North Frieze deities who safeguard the order of time.[129]

Yet this emergence of a Roman Genesis narrative that bestows supreme cosmic power on Augustus is carefully counterbalanced by demonstrations of Augustus as a model of humble piety. As chief deity of an imperial new creation at the same time, Augustus submits to the gods in worship and reverence. On the new monument in the Athena sanctuary, he thanks Athena for granting him the victory that made him ruler of the world. On the Ara Pacis at Rome, he is shown as he leads a procession to per-form a sacrifice to the gods. This remarkable versatility, fluidity, and adaptability were the core assets of imperial religion that made it one of the most successful ideological constructs in human history. Augustus is with the many deities of the pantheon as they are with him; he appears behind and in all the other gods, as well as under them; he is the one human princeps coequal with others while no human is coequal with him. And he is also the one god on whom everything and everyone depends. Seen on a strictly functional level, imperial religion here appears to oscillate between imperial polythe-ism and a new kind of imperial monotheism. This is a topic we will further explore in the next chapter.

A brief look at further developments in Pergamon might support this idea of an inherent tendency toward imperial monotheism. Under Emperor Trajan (98–117 C.E.), an enormous imperial temple complex was constructed on the very top of the Pergamene acropolis, where Trajan and his successor, Hadrian (117–138 C.E.), were worshiped with—or as—Zeus Philios (the friendly) or Jupiter Amicalis, respectively.[130] The cult images, as already mentioned, included a colossal seated statue of Zeus/Jupiter, and the two emperors standing next to him. Fragments of an eagle's head at the top of a marble scepter and winged Victories/Nikēs standing on the globe now spell out in plain language that Zeus's world power—the power that belonged to him alone and that originated from the battle against the Giants and chaos as shown at the Great Altar—now and forever is the power of the ruling emperor alone. Yet the emperor cult is also visibly pointing to its continuity with the Pergamene rulers. Two monuments to the north of the temple, now lost and only traceable though a dedicatory inscription of Attalus II (159–138 B.C.E.), were most likely related to the Attalid dynasty.[131]

At this point we have returned to where we began. The erection of the Trajaneum in the most dominant position in Pergamon marked the final act in the physical and conceptual appropriation of the Attalid inheritance by Rome, a process that took centuries to be completed and was still in progress in the time of Paul. So far we have looked mostly at external and general aspects of this development, searching for material evidence of the lasting significance of the Great Altar in the first imperial century. As we have seen, the Great Altar in all likelihood was not an antiquarian monument in Paul's time but created a vibrant link between the ruler worship of the Attalid and the Julio-Claudian dynasties. This answers a very basic question concerning our own project. To read Paul's letter in light of the Great Altar does not construct an anachronistic contextuality; rather, it places the Galatian debate squarely in the middle of its germane first-century contemporaneity.

Conclusion: The Great Altar as a Mirror of Paul's Galatia and the Occidental Self

The Great Altar as a core monument of Western civilization models the *imago mundi*, the image of the world that has stayed pervasive and powerful throughout the ages of occidental rule, crusades, colonial expansion, and imperial or nationalistic war making until present times. The way it depicts order and chaos, self and other is key not only to seeing the dramatic clash between Paul and his Galatian communities in the fifties of the first century C.E. with new eyes, but also to understanding the ongoing challenge his messianic countervision poses with regard to the established perceptions of self, world, and religion within the dominant framework of Christian occidental hermeneutics, including Pauline hermeneutics.

The altar presents the world as it is meant to be perceived from above and below. To the conquerors, it makes the righteousness and glory of their victory evident, while it confronts the conquered with the unbending divine law that required their defeat. Highly complex and of unsurpassed beauty, it is also strikingly monodimensional and aggressive in imposing, performing, and ritualizing normative modes to perceive self and other. It shows the image of the Galatia(ns) through the eyes of their overlords, as the Galatians themselves, Paul, and everyone else were supposed to see it, and it offers incorporation into city/civilization through submission to the conquering gods and rulers, including a deliberate act of self-distancing from the ungodly, unruly other. Every single element in this construct of divine and human order, the nature of god(s) and the nature of community, will be challenged by Paul in interaction with Galatian communities in the first century C.E. His letter is a unique document in the "war of perceptions" that offers a critical re-imagination of God, self, and other through the eyes of the conquered, and a passionate plea for the vanquished (as well as for their conquerors) to retrain and refocus their seeing through the lens of a crucified and resurrected God.

As seen in both the previous and present chapters, in the formation of the great narrative of ancient Mediterranean civilization, the Galatians/Giants have been set up as the archetypes of lawlessness and rebellion who needed to be ruled (out) by law and order, of barbarian foreignness irreconcilable with culture and civilization, and of all blasphemy, superstition, and areligiosity, which marks the wrong religion in contrast to proper piety and right religion. Drawing on this narrative, the Great Altar, created between approximately 180 and 160 B.C.E., represents not only the crown jewel of the Attalid dynasty of Pergamon but also the most significant monument of the Galatians' history, as codified by their conquerors and colonizers: Pergamon, Greece, and Rome. The imperial imprint of Rome, Pergamon's close ally, had already forcefully marked Asia Minor and Galatia when the Great Altar was built. Its intensity increased after the Roman takeover of the Pergamene kingdom in 133 B.C.E., and well into the first century C.E. when the Great Altar functioned in all likelihood as a site of imperial religion and when the history of the Galatians, at least on the surface, had become an entirely Roman history—two aspects that we will further explore in the next two chapters.

The appearance of the Galatians at the Great Altar under the guise of Giants, that is, the mythological forces of evil in rebellion against the lawful rule of the Olympian gods, has added an important dimension to our search for the meaning of Galatia(ns) in the cultural and political dictionary of Paul's time. It has shown the inner mechanics of ancient meaning making, which derives its power and plausibility from oppositional polarities. A conquest-based culture en route to world power in the post-Alexander era portrayed the Galatians/Gauls as the historical reincarnations of the prototypical evil other, which stands in contrast to the righteous self of city and civilization. As the dark and subhuman forces of destruction, the Giants/Galatians evoke primeval fears, justifying war and violence as a means of self-defense. In their mythological disguise, the Galatians represent all the rightly vanquished, acceptably vanished, appropriately enslaved, lawfully subjugated and exploited others over whom the Attalid, Roman, and occidental self rises toward legitimate domination and mastery through god-given victory.

None of this functions without an elaborate semiotics of polarities and analogies. Our brief tour of the Great Altar has established a reading model that is based on a modified version of Greimas's semiotic square and uses the oppositional and complementary spatial concepts of *High* and *Low*, *In* and *Out* to constitute the architectural core grammar of the Great Altar. This matrix generates multiple and interconnected layers of a dualistic *combat semiotics* in constructing the world and self. The strictly antithetical character of the semiotic square as a conceptual *battle square* corresponds to the primary importance of the Gigantomachy as the architectural and ideological basis for the Great Altar's overall organization. The irrevocable tension and permanent negotiation between verticality and horizontality, integration and exclusion, boundary and boundary transgression, law and lawlessness under the dictatorship of a victory-defined godlike self are key elements in the semantic system of the Great Altar. They will resurface as focal points in our reading of Paul's Galatian letter, which turns the Pergamene combat semiotics upside down by offering righteousness to the undeserving and envisioning, through the eyes of the vanquished, a new city and civilization of peacemaking.

The Gemma Augustea, a cameo gem dating from ca. 10 C.E. The goddess Roma is seated in the center; next to her, the Emperor Augustus, posing as Jupiter, with the eagle at his feet and personifications of Land, Sea, and Oikoumene to the right. The imperial world is carefully segregated from the space of the vanquished nations underneath it where soldiers erect a trophy to which a barbarian couple is tied. (See also fig. 43.) Photo: Wikimedia Commons.

CHAPTER THREE

Creating the World Out of Dead Gauls

Imperial Monotheism, Virgil, and the Arena

The transition from Republic to Empire under Julius Caesar's successor, Octavian (styled "Augustus" by the senate), saw an explosion of images and works of architecture that exhibited the new ideology and power arrangements. None of these images was a replica of the Great Altar of Pergamon, yet there are plenty of visual echoes. The Forum of Augustus, which constructed the whole of Roman history and identity, past and present, around the temple of Mars Ultor, the god of war; the impressive architectural arrangement on the Field of Mars, which integrates Augustus's Mausoleum, the *Res Gestae,* the sundial obelisk, and the Altar of Peace (Ara Pacis) in a monumental interactive display of the new cosmic order of time and space, under the imperial world savior; the temple of Apollo on the Palatine, next to Augustus's palace, where the God and the divine ruler became housemates: all these images, as well as single artifacts like the Prima Porta Statue, the Boscoreale Cup, and the Gemma Augustea, are in intense communication with the imagery of the Great Altar.[1] Rome certainly did not imitate the Great Altar in a single image. Yet the longer one looks at Roman and Pergamene images comparatively, the more one realizes that the Great Altar was creatively reinvented in multiple ways and appears in indirect allusions and quotations throughout Roman art and architecture under Augustus.

This chapter tries to answer a few basic questions vital for reading Paul's letter and the Great Altar *synoptically*. First, if the Great Altar had become a Roman monument at the time of Paul, how exactly should we imagine the shifting of Pergamene images into Roman images? How were the divine combat scenes of the Great Frieze and the royal court and sanctuary scenes of the Telephos room seen with Roman eyes? How can we understand the sacrificial and political functions and the overall architectural and visual semiotics of the Great Altar within the framework of Roman imperial hermeneutics?

We ask these questions not simply because of a general interest in Roman history and ideological formation, but because their answers address the issue at the heart of our overall historical investigation. What does the transformation of Pergamene images into Roman images show us that we have not yet been able to see about the world in which Paul and the Galatians lived? In other words, how can the images become a visual aid for deciphering the untold story behind the Galatian correspondence, those parts of the argument that were not said or written down because they were assumed and clearly understood within the world that Paul, the Galatians, and the Romans shared?

In the previous chapter, we traced some of the material evidence for a Roman appropriation of the Great Altar. In order to obtain a more in-depth understanding, we now want to examine closely two sets of Roman mirror images of the Great Altar: first, the Shield of Aeneas in the foundational imperial myth, Virgil's *Aeneid,* and, second, the Roman arena. Widely different in style and setting, genre and texture, the two at first seem too incongruent to be compared as images. As we shall see, however, both the literary images described on the Shield and the living images of death produced in the arena share a strikingly similar visual program with each other and with the marble images of the Great Altar.

This comparison will help us understand how such key themes as law and order, rule and religion, city and civilization, self and other were reconceived and re-imagined within the framework of empire. Reading Pergamene and Virgil's Shield imagery synoptically, we will pay specific attention to the cosmogonic, legitimating function of the Giant/Galatian battle and the core concepts of city, piety, rule, and genealogy that they both have in common. That will lead us into a more detailed investigation of the twin construct of imperial world rule and imperial world religion as it is reflected on the Shield, most notably the concept of an *imperial monotheism.*

Overall, this chapter once more tries to get a step closer to seeing the world of Paul's time more clearly—at least the dominant image of the world that was being inscribed on the totality of cityscape, mindscape, and landscape, all throughout the Roman Empire and wherever Paul went on his missionary journeys. What we will also see more sharply is how little this official image of the world "in the likeness of Caesar" had in common with the way the world looked for Paul or for the Galatians, and how it inevitably had to clash with the other image Paul had made visible to the Galatians. They, as we know from Gal 3:1, however, were no longer able to see it.

Aeneas's Shield: Roman State Myth Re-Imagines the Great Altar

In 19 B.C.E. Virgil's *Aeneid* appeared, the grandiose imperial myth of Roman origin that covers the mytho-historical events leading from Troy to Rome in twelve books. As part of this literary work of art, the Shield of Aeneas at the end of book 8 does not exactly fall under the category of a visual monument. However, its nature as an artifact, that is, a piece of art that has been most skillfully made in order to be seen, is so vividly described by Virgil that we are going to deal with it as a piece of quasi-visual art.[2] As a multilayered text-image the Shield reflects not only an imperial appropriation of the Pergamene images in general but also in particular the complex exchange in which the

Great Altar's imagery shaped Roman imagination and was itself reshaped by Roman ideology until it became an adequate expression of the dominant first-century C.E. worldview.

The Foundational Battle: Conquering Giants, Galatians, Orientals

After a dramatic escape from the fall of Troy and long and dangerous journeys, Aeneas and his companions in book 7 of the *Aeneid* arrive in Italy and face the final battles that will establish Rome on the newly won territory.[3] Aeneas's mother, Venus/Aphrodite, who bore him from a human father (Anchises), talks her husband, Volcano, into providing weaponry for Aeneas in exchange for sex. Immediately the following morning, the fire god and divine smith Volcano/Hephaestus, who is in charge of the military supplies needed by the gods, stops all production in his underground workshop caves beneath Mount Etna to let his Cyclops assistants deal with Aeneas's armor. Even Zeus's lightning and thunderbolts have to wait (8.370–453).

The shield in particular turns out to be a unique masterpiece of art (8.630–728). It recalls the shield that Hephaestus had made for Achilles in Homer's *Iliad* (18.478–608) and depicts a select sequence of scenes foreshadowing Roman history from Aeneas to Augustus's victory at Actium (31 B.C.E.). The relation between text and images is intriguing. At the outset Virgil calls the scenes depicted on the shield a "text that can't be told" (*non enarrabile textum*, 8.625), as if visual communication in this case was more telling than verbal narration. Furthermore, Virgil numerous times refers to the fact that Volcano "made" (*fecerat*) and "made visible" (*videbatur*) this or that particular detail. There is no doubt that the author is familiar with the question of how images need to be presented in order to show the world the way it is meant to be seen.[4]

The affinity between the Great Altar and the Shield of Aeneas (and Virgil's *Aeneid* in general), first explored by Philip Hardie, is remarkable.[5] Like the Great Altar, the Shield represents a piece of victory art and a type of victory religion with cosmic overtones that is strongly geared toward ruler legitimation and worship. The core event in both cases is the Great Battle. Its nature is strikingly similar: a battle where the gods fight with *us*, or *we* with the gods, on the one hand, a battle against Gauls/Galatians/Giants, on the other. In a short introduction, Virgil announces at the beginning (8.626–29) that the shield contains the history of Italy, the triumphs of the Romans, and the wars that were fought. But at a closer look there are only two wars that dominate the scene: the battle against the Gauls/Galatians in 387 B.C.E. and the Battle of Actium against Antony in 31 B.C.E.

While some of the conflicts in the earlier history are briefly mentioned (8.635–51), by far the most extensive description is given to the attack of the Gauls/Galatians and Manlius's brave defense of the citadel in the fourth century B.C.E. (8.652–62). The depiction, which is situated on the very top of the shield, is very spatial: Manlius stands guard "high above" (*in summo custos*); the Gauls/Galatians have secretly approached and encircled the citadel in the darkness of night; they are already in the liminal space between *out* and *in* at the gate (*porticibus Gallos in limine adesse*), pushing in (*adesse/ aderant*); by implication they have also come from *below*. The spatial semiotics of this scene is familiar from the Great Altar: Manlius defends the *High* and *In* of the citadel mountain on which sits the temple of state god Jupiter and the house of city founder Romulus (a rather modest building covered by straw).

The scene immediately following Manlius's victory (8.663–70) depicts a religious celebration in Rome. As Hardie notes, the "preservation of Rome from the Gauls is seen to accord with the universal divine order of things; . . . and is itself met by the proper observation of religious ceremony on the part of a grateful city."[6] The last scene in this sequence is an underworld tribunal. While lawless criminals are punished, like the traitor Catilina, who hangs on a rock and is tormented by Furies, law-abiding and *pious* people are rewarded. On the whole, the polarity of piety (*pius*) and law (*iura*) versus blasphemy and lawlessness, a core constituent of the Pergamene semiotics of combat, ties Manlius's Galatian triumph firmly together with the Roman worship and final judgment scenes that on the Shield mark the transition from the Capitoline to the Actium battle.

That the battle with the Galatians thus in a way summarizes the whole pre-Augustan history between 387 and 31 B.C.E. should not come as a surprise—it is not just any battle, but the quintessential battle, as the Great Altar has set it in stone. What we encounter here is, as Hardie rightly states, clear evidence for a Roman "mythologization of the Galatians" that has its prototype and is visible "most magnificently in the remains of the Great Altar at Pergamon." Through its association with the cosmogonic giant battle, the Galatian battle becomes a "symbol of the divine guarantee of the continued existence of Rome." The miraculous preservation of the Capitol thus foreshadows the victory at Actium.[7]

The symbolic value of the Galatian *Sacco di Roma* ("sack of Rome") is even more far-reaching. It also substantiates a claim made in the name of supreme law and justice/ righteousness: the claim to world rule. In this respect, the unspecified name of Manlius on the Shield has a quite complex background and semantic range; it evokes the other Manlius called Torquatus in Italy, who once heroically won a blood-spattered torque in single combat from a Goliath-like Galatian enemy. It also evokes Manlius Vulso in Asia Minor who marked the beginning of Rome's anti-Galatian warfare on foreign territories in the East.[8] The glaring unrighteousness of Manlius Vulso's brutal campaign in 189 B.C.E. disappears behind the triumphant righteousness of the generic Capitoline Manlius in 387 B.C.E. As Rome's miraculous salvation from the Galatian threat demonstrates, it is Rome that has not only the gods but also the law on her side, but Rome's enemies who by definition violate the law and therefore must be punished and subdued—worldwide.

This leads right into the Actium scenes on the Shield that cover its central part (8.671–728), roughly two-thirds of the overall textual-visual space. Within the semiotic system of the Great Altar, a Galatian battle must be linked to a Giant battle. As it turns out, Virgil's overall setting of the battle of Actium is indeed strongly modeled after Gigantomachy motifs and themes.[9] It is not simply a naval battle between two armies that unfolds at Actium; rather, the whole cohesion of the cosmos and the rule of the Olympian gods is threatened—and miraculously restored when Augustus through the help of Apollo wins world power. As in the sea storm in book 1 of the *Aeneid*, and reminiscent of the Great Frieze, all elemental forces and the whole of nature have entered into cosmic combat. Moreover, like the Giants at the Great Altar the enemy gods are depicted as bestial, alien, and monstrous (*omnigenumque deum monstra*, 8.698), including the dog-headed Egyptian Anubis, who is slandered as "barker" god. As in the Great Altar, the underlying polarity is between ugly and beautiful, perverted and proper divinity, barbarism and civilization, chaos and cosmos. In the end, the restoration of the superior order needs a divine intervention by Apollo. It simultaneously establishes the Roman imperial world order.[10]

The historical counterparts of the mythological giants at Actium, however, are no longer Gauls/Galatians, as at the Great Altar, but rather Egyptians. They are part of a huge "Eastern" army of different nations mustered by Antony *ab Aurorae*. They are "Orientals" (*virisque Orientis*); they are "barbarians" (*barbarica*) of various kinds; and they are all fighting under one woman, the Egyptian queen Cleopatra, who is simply "shameful" (*nefas*). She is also the wife of Antony, at that time still the legal coruler with Octavian/Augustus within the triumvirate forged after Caesar's death (8.685–88, 696, 705–6). Not Antony, however, but the abhorrent female figure of the militant enemy queen dominates the battle scene and at least implicitly seems to suggest some Amazon connotations.

Obviously, another assimilation of historical enemies to mythological Giants has happened. As the Greeks had defined barbarians = Giants = Amazons = Persians, and the Attalids had added Galatians to that equation, Virgil now presents a new variation of the same semiotics of otherness: barbarians = Giants = Amazons = Galatians = Egyptians/Orientals. Trained in the school of images, we by now know what iconographic markers such a paradigmatic gathering of enemy otherness would be matched with: the dying and the dead. And indeed, with remarkable descriptive detail, the Egyptian queen is "made visible" (*videbatur*) in 8.705–13 as she loses control and sinks into demise after the decisive shot from Apollo's invincible bow that turns the battle. Two vipers that have appeared behind her back (8.697) signal her imminent suicide—a truly Galatian death. Surrounded by her terrified army of Egyptians, Indians, Arabs, and Sabaeans, Volcano has "made" (*fecerat*) her in the midst of all slaughtering "pale, expecting her approaching death" (*morte futura*). In a way, she appears like a hybrid "quotation" of all the Dying Gauls, Dying Amazons, and Dying Giants we have seen already.

Historically, Octavian's victory over Antony at Actium in 31 B.C.E. made him single ruler and emperor. In the Virgilian imaginary world, however, the birth of empire is a supremely and almost exclusively religious event—the gods have granted victory to their ally Octavian, who had led the battle of the Romans and their gods (8.679); in gratitude and reverence to them, on his triumphal march back to Rome, he vows to dedicate no fewer than three hundred temples all over the city. A huge public feast in the streets of Rome follows, with joy and games and praise for the victor and for the gods (8.714–19).

In the final scene of the Shield, Augustus is shown as he sits at the threshold of the newly built temple of Phoebus/Apollo on the Palatine, which is "shiny" and "white" (*niveo candentis*) (8.720–21). As Hardie notices, the emphasis on *light* in this scene hints at both the spectacular sight of the glistening marble and the association of Apollo (and Augustus) with the universally present power of the Sun. Augustus, apparently seated below the pediment of the temple, which according to Propertius 2.31.11, carried an image of the sun-god Sol in his chariot, is receiving the gifts of foreign peoples from all over the world and has the "long row of vanquished nations" (*gentes victae*) march past him (8.722–28). "The combination of allusion to sun-god, sitting in review, with a catalogue of peoples points to the common Roman *topos* of universal empire as comprising all the lands that the sun beholds in his daily passage from east to west."[11]

The mention of different tongues and dress and arms in the description of the defeated peoples, their strangely exotic names, and the puzzling geographical terms signal that the battle won is not just a victory over "Egyptians" but a worldwide victory taming even the most remote and savage races like the "undominated" (*indomiti*) Dahans, and the most distant, inaccessible territories (*extremique hominum*). Notoriously noncompliant agents of nature like the un-bridgeable river Araxes, the Rhine, and the "already mollified" (*iam mollior*) Euphrates have surrendered to Augustus, pointing to the cosmic dimension of his rule. He is now ruler of the world and at the center of the universe; both natural and social forces of terrifying destructive potential, symbolized by the tsunami-like upheaval of the sea during the battle itself, are made submissive and rebalanced through his victory. Augustus's cosmic *imperium* is a *new creation* of both society and the world as a whole.[12]

Augustus Meets Telephos: The Divine Pedigree of World Power

If the Shield's battle narrative strikingly resembles the Gigantomachy-base of the Great Altar, the post-battle setting in Rome that Virgil describes in 8.714–28 in many ways evokes the symbolic order and the political ritual of the Pergamene Telephos court and its popular counterpart at the altar terrace downstairs. The emphasis is on city and piety, on the ruler himself, and the gods.

City. The precarious transition between *outside/inside* the city, carefully marked and monitored at the Great Altar through the Great Staircase, is conspicuous on the Shield as well. Upon his triumphant return from the battlefield, Caesar Augustus enters "into the Roman walls." The walls (*moenia*) are the foundational element that establishes a city, and the term is often used by Virgil as synonymous with Rome/city, for example, in 1.276, when Romulus is envisioned as founder of the "walls (*moenia*) of Mars," that is, the city of Rome. In the same text, the famous Jupiter prophecy, it is foretold that Aeneas will destroy "savage peoples" in Italy and establish "laws and walls" (*moresque viris et moenia ponet*) (1.263–64). In mythological narration, the disrespectful attitude of Remus toward the freshly marked walls of Rome causes his brother Romulus to kill him.[13] Remus's "leap" is a transgression that threatens both the foundation of the city and Romulus's primacy. On the Shield, the walls of Rome have been violated by the Gauls/Galatians. Augustus's global victory over the barbarian/Oriental other has finally made Rome and her walls safe, protecting the civic *Inside* against the lawless and hostile *Outside*. In this perspective, Augustus's triumphal entry into the city equals an act of refounding the city. The securely founded city/inside emerging from victory in the world battle outside is a topos that creates a strong link between Telephos son of Heracles at the Great Altar and Augustus as "new Romulus" in Virgil's Shield vision.

Piety. The same holds true for the notion of piety as the core value on which the city is built. The Telephos frieze at the Great Altar shows the erection of the main shrines of Athena and Dionysus as foundational acts for the city of Pergamon. Similarly, on the Shield Augustus's first concern, upon reentering his newly established city, is the deities. He immediately pledges the dedication of no fewer than three hundred mighty temples to the gods of Italy all over the city as his "immortal votive gift" (8.715–16). While the figure of three hundred seems somewhat overstated—at the end of his life Augustus will report in the *Res Gestae* the no less impressive number of eighty-two temples rebuilt or restored (*Res Gestae* 20)—it makes a crucial statement: piety and religion are foundational practices for Augustan Rome.

Pietas, as Paul Zanker states, "was to become one of the most important leitmotifs of the Augustan era. Ever since Cato the Elder, the dissolution of tradition and of the state, as the self-destructiveness that threatened to destroy Rome, had all been ascribed to a neglect of the gods. 'You will remain sullied with the guilt of your fathers, Roman, until you have rebuilt the temples and restored all the ruined sanctuaries with their dark images of the gods, befouled with smoke' (Horace, *Carmen* 3.6)." Therefore, Augustus already in 29 B.C.E., very shortly after Actium (and the same year Pergamon applied for an imperial temple), proclaimed a program of religious rebuilding.[14]

Piety is embodied in Augustus himself[15] and also pervades the life of Rome and her citizens. On the Shield the whole city joins Caesar Augustus and rejoices with him in the triumphal celebration that is primarily an act of worship. While the "streets" are filled with joy, play, and applause (*laetitia ludisque viae plausuque fremebant*), "mothers" (*matrones*) sing hymns in "all temples." And "all altars" (*omnibus in templis . . . omnis arae*) are smoking, the ground in front of them covered by slaughtered bulls (8.714–19). The setting somewhat resembles the lower space at the Pergamene altar terrace, where the people are feasting, incorporated into the collective body of the city through a huge and joyous sacrificial meal. Choirs and sacrifices are the key ingredients of a citywide ceremony of "communion" between rulers and ruled, gods and humans, where "mortals" irrespective of social status show their gratitude and reverence to the immortal gods for the victory won. In a seemingly horizontal and nonantagonistic way, they are united in worship with the victorious emperor. Again, piety as a supreme value of the Augustan Age dominates the scene.

Monarchy/supreme rule. The sense of horizontality is deceptive, however. While the people celebrate in the streets, Augustus is shown in front of the temple of Apollo, looking at the "gifts of the peoples" and the march of the vanquished nations. No *High–Low* polarity is explicitly mentioned, but it would be obvious to anyone familiar with the Roman topology that the temple of Apollo is located on the Palatine Hill and thus *above* the streets of Rome. If the ritual of communion in the Roman streets and temples resembles the layout of the Pergamene altar terrace *below*, the Palatine setting would correspond to the *upstairs* of the Telephos courtyard. The stage is set for the display of supreme rule and power, and of the emperor himself. The gifts of the (nonvanquished) peoples that are fixed to the doorposts of Apollo's house represent the tokens of voluntary compliance,[16] whereas the march of defeated nations shows the fate of those who needed to be forced into submission.

The scene represents the same peculiar mix of palatial and temple settings that we already observed at the Great Altar. While the location is explicitly given as the threshold (*limine*) of Apollo's temple, it is clear that the diplomatic protocol of receiving the ambassadors of foreign nations with their gifts would rather fit into a royal court. Yet this is an arbitrary problem: For the house of Apollo on the Palatine and the immediately neighboring house of Augustus are almost one and the same—both are architecturally and conceptionally most closely linked. The relatively modest palace of Augustus on the Palatine is practically built as an annex to the temple of Apollo, directly connected to the temple forecourt by a ramp.[17] If this architectural multivalence strongly reminds us of the Great Altar, which had the double connotations of royal court and sacrificial site inscribed into its upper room, one needs to add that the entire complex of Apollo's temple and Augustus's house on the Palatine, including its library, probably is meant architecturally to quote Eumenes II and the Pergamene acropolis.[18] Both imitating and reinventing, mirroring and creatively re-imagining the Pergamene model, the setting of the last scene on Aeneas's Shield thus perfectly blends palace and sanctuary, ruler and religion, political and priestly contexts. If one imagines Augustus to be seated on a metaphorical throne in front of Apollo's temple, this throne, similar to the Great Altar, symbolizes both supreme divine and human power.

Dynasty and genealogy of power. One focal element of the Telephos frieze at the Great Altar, as we remember, is the establishment of the Attalid dynasty's divine lineage. Genealogically, the parallels between the Virgilian and the Pergamene power construct are most obvious, even though the pedigree of Augustan rule is not fully legible from the Shield alone but also requires a brief look at the rest of the *Aeneid*, most notably the famous Jupiter prophecy (1.257–96).

The Augustan age enthusiastically embraced the concept of a divine pedigree of world rule that had already been staged at Pergamon with the lineage Zeus → Heracles → Telephos → Attalids. Yet the lineage developed in the *Aeneid* is much more complex than its Pergamene precursor. It links the Julian house (starting with Julius Caesar) via its Trojan ancestor Aeneas to Venus/Love, the daughter of Zeus, on the one hand, and via Aeneas's Roman descendant Romulus to Mars/War, also the son of Zeus, on the other. Venus and Mars are the divine parents mothering and fathering the first imperial dynasty, whose name—*Julians*—is derived from Troy = Ilion = Ilus/Julus/Ascanius (son of Aeneas) and Ilia (mother of Romulus and Remus).[19]

On the Shield, this more comprehensive genealogy is only alluded to, but the most important ancestors of Augustus are made clearly visible: Venus and Mars, Ascanius

(Julus) and Romulus/Remus, as well as Julius Caesar. Venus is the one who commissions the divine armor for Aeneas and hands it over to him. Mars's fatherhood is evoked when Romulus and Remus are shown in the "green cave of Mars," where the mother wolf is lying, with the two twin boys suckling and playing "without fear" (8.630–34). "Mars' green cave" is the closest allusion to the war-god ever taking care of his two baby boys; it faintly reminds one of the Pergamene scene where Heracles finds his exposed son Telephos suckled by a lioness and gives him to the nymphs to be raised. (See fig. 29.)

Other key motives of Virgil's genealogical narrative, however, much more prominently resemble the Pergamene Telephos myth of the Great Altar. The Attalids and the Julians not only share divine ancestors ultimately leading back to Zeus. The journeys of Aeneas from Troy and the travels of Telephos from Arkadia to establish the city of destiny—Rome by Romulus and Pergamon by Telephos—echo each other; the young princess (Ilia/Augē) forced into priesthood and chastity to prevent dynastic claims by her son, her (enforced) pregnancy through a god or demigod (Mars/Heracles), the exposure of the children born (Romulus and Remus/Telephos) and their suckling by a wild animal (she-wolf, lioness), and finally the emergence of these boys (Romulus/Telephos) as founders of city and dynasty—all of these are so clearly related to the same narrative pattern that the fictive kinship between the Attalids and the Julio-Claudians can hardly be overlooked.

In both cases these outstanding genealogies are meant to bolster power claims by presenting two of the most esteemed credentials: ancient and divine origin of a ruling dynasty—and of rule itself. And in both cases the ultimate source of power is Jupiter/Zeus and the victorious Giant/Titan battle. Heracles, the father of Telephos, fights with Zeus and the other gods against the Giants at the Great Altar. The *Aeneid* has the supreme god Jupiter declare at the outset of its hero's journey in book 1 that Rome is destined to rule "without end" (*imperium sine fine*) and that Augustus is going to establish that rule "without boundaries in space and time" (1.278–79, 286–89); on the Shield Virgil then shows the actual fulfillment of this prophecy by staging the Battle of Actium as a cosmogonic Giant battle that indeed establishes Rome's global rule and the Romans as "masters of the world, the toga-clad people" (1.282).

This is the point, however, where Pergamon and Rome part ways. Augustus, unlike Eumenes II, after Actium indeed has won sole world power. The march of the defeated nations as a symbol of universal victory on the Shield does not have a counterpart on the Great Altar. Augustus refounds Rome both as the "eternal city" with walls secure forever, and as a world-city: the city (*urbs*) at the center and apex of the inhabited world, which receives taxes, soldiers, and other tributes from the provinces *in concrete historical reality*. Augustus himself is not just any ruler, but ruler of the world. This shift in the actual range of power that makes the Julian Caesar Augustus different from the Attalid kings leads to a subtle but decisive transformation in the overall construct of rule and religion, king and gods as laid out on the Great Altar. The emperor is not simply a ruler deriving his legitimacy from the world-ruling god and the world battle; rather, he is world ruler himself—and world god too.

This transformation is reflected in the genealogical pattern. Compared to the relatively simple Attalid pedigree with one semidivine ancestor (Heracles) linking back to the Gigantomachy and Zeus, the Virgilian genealogy of Augustus's power is marked by an "overload" of divine elements. Not only does the Julio-Claudian dynasty have both a fully divine father (Mars) and mother (Venus), but Augustus himself is heavily embedded in a double layer of divine fatherhood/sonship. As he is standing high in the stern of his battleship leading the war against the Giants/Gauls/Egyptians/Orientals at Actium, the "paternal celestial sign" (*sidus patrium*) emerges above his head in 8.681. This term refers to the comet that appeared in 44 B.C.E. and was interpreted by Augustus in a bold move as a visible sign that his adoptive father (and great-uncle) Julius Caesar had indeed ascended to heaven and was now a god among gods—a proof of Caesar's apotheosis, which turned Octavian himself into a "son of god" (*divi filius*).[20]

Similarly, one might wonder whether the privileged relationship between Augustus and Apollo is linked to the birth myth that had Augustus fathered by Apollo, who, in the form of a snake, impregnated his mother (a similar story was told about the mother of Alexander the Great).[21] This thick cluster of divine markers attached to the person of Augustus points to the core message of the Shield and the *Aeneid* as a whole: Augustus is the center and climax of everything: victor in the cosmogonic world battle, world ruler who implements law and order on a global level, the one who establishes the world city—and the founder, prime devotee, and supreme god of an imperial world religion.

The New World God among Mortals and Immortals

The climactic scene of the Shield with Augustus sitting in front of Apollo's temple looking at the gifts of the nations and watching the march of the vanquished not only signals the dawn of the Roman imperial world order, but also the birth of a new imperial world religion. Both are inseparably interlaced. The hybridity of the setting—temple and palace at the same time, the palace being an extension of the temple and vice versa—is matched by the hybridity of Caesar: both human and divine, housemate of the god and god himself. The triumph at Actium was the triumph of Apollo, but the triumph of Apollo is the triumph of Augustus, the divine son of Julius Caesar and of Apollo himself, born out of the divine seed of Mars and Venus. This triumph bestows primordial power, for the fight with Antony was not an ordinary war against a political rival, but the cosmogonic battlefield where the gods and one chosen human fight together against the universal chaos embodied in the Giants. It is a sacred war that makes Augustus the most distinguished warrior fighting with the Gods and for the Gods, even as a leader of Gods and of humans (8.679).

Although Apollo in the end shoots the decisive arrow from his almighty bow, it would be obvious that the god merely supports the transhuman superhero in the cause that is the most noble for them both: Rome's and Pergamon's century-long fight against the barbarian other of Gauls/Galatians and Apollo's Delphic battle of 279 B.C.E. against these same blasphemous Galatians merge at Actium and with Apollo's battle-turning arrow, which brings down the army of the barbarian Egyptian/Orientals. This connection, though, is not made verbally, but through the parallel sign system of the images. Apollo's battle against the Galatians at Delphi was one of the two big scenes depicted on the doors of his temple, which form the background of the whole scene.[22] In his victory, Augustus emerges as Apollo's anti-Galatian and anti-Giant standard-bearer on earth.[23] The emperor sitting at the threshold of Apollo's temple, the depiction of the universally powerful sun above him and the Delphic battle against the Gauls at his back, is thus made visible as the living image of the god, the embodiment and representation, or incarnation, of Apollo. As such, he is fully divine through his distinguished pedigree. The nations of the world parading in front of him are submitting both to the Roman world order and to Roman world religion.

Imperial Monotheism and the Camouflage of (Un)traditional Religion

The issue of Caesar's divine/human nature is a matter of controversy among scholars. It is traditionally assumed that imperial religion in the Latin-speaking West tried to avoid direct worship of a living emperor as god in order to honor traditional religion, whereas in the Greek East the tradition of religious honors for present rulers (and thus their divinization) was well established since Alexander the Great. Simon Price argues that even in the East, however, the difference between emperor and god was mostly upheld, for example, by sacrificing not "to" but "on behalf of" the emperor.[24] Other scholars have challenged this assumption. Steven Friesen points out that the epigraphic evidence shows "no hesitation in assimilating the emperors to the gods," even within sacrifical contexts. [25] Or, as Philip Harland states: "In Asia Minor it became common in various contexts, including provincial cults, to refer to a given emperor as 'god *Sebastos*,' and to refer to the emperors (and some members of the imperial family) collectively as the '*Sebastoi* gods,' the 'revered gods.'"[26] As the Greek *Sebastos* is the translation of the Latin *Augustus,* Harland uses the term "imperial gods" to render the phrase "*Sebastoi theoi.*"[27]

The question is not so much where and to what extent Augustus was really believed to be a god and was worshiped as such. The issue is that, under Augustus and in conjunction with the now universal scope of Roman rule, a comprehensive system of imperial religion emerged that is much wider than emperor cult alone. It comprised traditional religion as well, which was both left intact on the outside and reshaped from the inside, as it was inserted into a new framework of reference where Caesar de facto held the exclusive position of supreme human and divine power. In its essence, this was nothing less than a functional imperial monotheism that operated, however, on the basis and under the disguise of traditional polytheistic religion.

A statement by Price might illustrate the difficulty in coming to terms with imperial religion's remarkable mimicry and hybridity. Wrestling with the ambiguities of prayers and sacrifices being made both "to" the emperor and "on behalf of" the emperor to the gods he observes:

> This range of ritual practices and language expressed a picture of the emperor between human and divine. This intermediate position is in no way indicative of a breakdown of the old divide between people and gods. There was still a clear distinction between human and divine honors . . . and the traditional civic cults of the gods were not threatened or superseded by the new ruler cults. . . . The emperor might have been slotted into the intermediate category of hero, but this was not appropriate. The emperor's overwhelming and intrusive power had to be represented not in terms of a local hero but of a universal god. Standing at the apex of the hierarchy of the Roman empire the emperor offered the hope of order and stability and was assimilated to the traditional Olympian deities. But he also needed the divine protection which came from sacrifices made to the gods on his behalf. The emperor stood at the focal point between human and divine.[28]

Price's description in its first part very adequately renders what imperial religion wanted to communicate about itself: a new element of imperial ritual is added; it may look somewhat strange and occupy a space between the established categories, but on the whole it is perfectly compatible and blends in with the established system of "traditional civic cults of the gods" and "the old divide between people and gods." In substance, thus, nothing much seems to change. The second half of the statement, however, makes it clear that everything has changed. While the emperor is truly human and an intermediary between human and divine, he is much more than that. If the "intermediate category of hero" does not fit him but rather that of a "universal god" who is "assimilated to the traditional Olympian deities"—what else does this mean than that he is fully god himself? This is what we have essentially already observed in the Virgilian pedigree that substitutes the semidivine heroic forefather Heracles for two fully divine Olympic ancestors and a deified father. With this, nothing stays as it was. In fact, the divide between mortals and gods does break down as traditional religion has to come to terms with a new chief deity that completely remodels the old religious universe, though under the pretense that everything stays the same.[29]

This incoherence between appearance and essence, image and reality, or several images and realities coexisting, seems to be a core issue throughout Augustan propaganda. It is deeply ironic that the transformation of the victorious Octavian into the imperial Augustus in 27 B.C.E.—the date usually given as the beginning of the Roman Empire—happened precisely at the moment when he officially returned all his power to the senate and thus nominally restored the Republic. Well aware of the disaster that had come upon his deified father Julius Caesar, murdered when he made himself dictator, Augustus very carefully maneuvered between a Republican-looking Principate, where he posed modestly as "first among equals" (*princeps*), and an imperial-style autocracy, where a complex system of special offices, privileges, and authorities effectively made him sole ruler.[30]

This profound ambiguity is expressed also in the term *Augustus* (Greek *Sebastos*) itself, which after Octavian would become generally synonymous with *emperor* or *imperial*, mostly with regard to the reigning emperor (and his wife). It clearly communicates the unique position of the emperor as sole ruler, yet it avoids any explicit statement that would contradict the "restoration of the Republic." It can denote the emperor both as revered God and as reverent human. As Zanker states:

> *Augustus* was an adjective with a broad range of meanings, including "stately," "dignified," and "holy." It could also be connected with the verb *augere* ("increase"). After all, had he not made the Empire grow? Alternatively, it could recall the *augur,* the priest who interprets omens. . . . As a honorific title, Augustus was a brilliant choice, for, even as he officially relinquished power, it surrounded him with a special aura, "as if the name alone had already conferred divinity upon him" (*Florus* 2.34.66).[31]

The bestowal of this title on Octavian thus right from the outset comes close to a kind of deification; it implies supreme piety and supreme power at the same time. Cassius Dio points out that "Augustus" signifies that "he was more than human; for all the most precious and sacred objects are termed *augusta.* Therefore they addressed him also in Greek as *Sebastos,* meaning an august personage, from the passive of the verb *sebazo,* to revere" (53.16). The astonishing variation and versatility in the various aspects and *personae* of Augustus—republican and monarchical, *princeps* and emperor, human and divine, high priest (*pontifex maximus*) and highest god, god and son of god[32]—may be logically incoherent but were essential for the hegemonic power and survival capacities of Augustan ideology and rule. There was no need to harmonize or organize things on a conceptual level—no unified system of imperial theology that required the conundrum of Augustus's two natures to be settled in a coherent and orthodox manner as an ontological problem;[33] rather the different images were made to coexist in practice. On a functional level, however, the contradiction almost dissolves if one considers that as both human and divine being, Augustus holds supreme power that is derived from his universal victory in the imperial cosmogonic world battle and makes both gods and humans submit to him as their savior and benefactor.

This might be illustrated by another look at the Shield. Augustus's monumental donation of three hundred new temples for the gods of Italy appears to be an extraordinary act of human piety that puts the emperor into the position of the humble human being expressing his gratitude and reverence toward the gods. He acts as a mortal in submission to the immortal gods, upholding traditional religion. But on closer examination, the picture gets more blurred. The gift is as extraordinary as the donor. Its sheer size requires funds that could not be won except through a global victory, a victory that was as vital for the survival of the traditional gods as the rebuilding of their temples: the victory in the battle of the gods against the god-hating Giants. As supreme protector and patron of the gods, Augustus in fact acts as supreme god himself, a configuration that vividly resembles Marduk's position in the *Enuma Elish.*[34] Receiving his grant means acknowledging him and his exclusive authority and benevolence, that is, submitting to him. If the traditional gods accept Augustus's donation, they also accept his status as victorious commander-in-chief of the giant battle and thus supreme god, or at least as the supreme god's representative.[35]

Further, the grant dedicated to the deities is taken from the spoils of the Egyptian/ Oriental victory over inferior and barbarian gods like the "barker" Anubis. Even though there seems to be an unlimited inclusiveness that integrates no fewer than three hundred different shrines, in fact a strict hierarchy of *In* and *Out*, right and wrong religion comes attached to the donation. As recipient of Augustus's extraordinary gift, traditional religion does not remain the same but receives the imprint of imperial order and imperial religion.

This is confirmed by a brief consideration of the actual distribution principles of Augustus's donation. In terms of concrete funds allotted to the different cults and deities, there is a clearly pre-set hierarchy and exclusivity, as Paul Zanker has observed: deities like Apollo, Mars, Venus, and Jupiter that are most closely linked to the emperor received shining marble temples that integrated the finest traditions of Greek temple building with some specific Roman and Italic features. The old temples, on the other hand, often got not much more than a symbolic makeover. And Egyptian or Oriental gods such as the extremely popular Isis were widely left out of the religious rebuilding program altogether.[36] "The varying levels of expenditure in the building of so many temples created in the popular mind a vivid impression of the different status of each divinity. The dominant ones were clearly those to which Augustus felt closest."[37]

This process of religious ranking and selection demonstrates that the heavenly order perfectly mirrors the earthly one. Both are dominated by Augustus. The divine and human power pyramids are remodeled in such a way that they intersect in the person of Caesar as the supreme power in both realms. Every deity is placed further up or down, in or out in relation to the top and center position of the emperor. This illustrates the double-faced interaction between traditional and imperial religion. While on the outside Augustus appears as a pious protégé of the gods rendering his thanks and reverence for the victory they granted, on the inside he is the almighty protector of the deities who not only sustains and guards but also ranks and orders them. Within an entirely polytheistic framework, this appears as an operative imperial monotheism. (See fig. 36 below.)

Caesar as or with Zeus/Jupiter?

The construct of an *imperial monotheism* is not without precursors. The idea of the Giant battle as cosmic event of universal (re)ordering and creation through an all-powerful monarchical leader/ruler-god established the supreme power and singularity of Zeus already in Hesiod and at the Great Altar. Zeus's predominance as universal ruler in Stoic thinking led to a kind of Zeus monotheism that becomes especially tangible, for example, in Cleanthes' *Hymn to Zeus*.[38] It did not deny other gods but rendered them less significant. According to Walter Burkert, Zeus was "the only god who could become an all-embracing god of the universe."[39]

Fig. 36. Imperial Monotheism and Traditional Religion

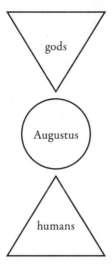

Explanation: Both human and divine spheres are hierarchically ordered as pyramids of power. The gods (= the pyramid on top) hover above the human sphere (= bottom pyramid) and are technically also above Augustus. This reflects traditional religion. Yet as both pyramids intersect in the person of Augustus, who acts as intermediary between both spheres and "ranks" the gods, the emperor de facto holds not only the top position of the human but also of the (now inverted) divine pyramid. This gives him a quasi-monotheistic position as sole ruler-god.

It would be easy to claim that this Zeus monotheism, once it became affiliated with the political realities of Roman universal world power under a single god-ruler somewhat seamlessly merged with Augustan imperial monotheism. Yet things seem to be more complicated. While Zeus/Jupiter held the main state temple on the Capitoline Hill in Rome and his monarchical position among the Olympian gods, he does not become active on the Shield of Aeneas, but rather is defended by Manlius against the Galatian attack. The most prominent fighters in the Actium battle are Apollo and Augustus, not Jupiter/Zeus and Augustus. It is Apollo's temple on the Palatine where Augustus appears as world ruler and world god, not Jupiter's temple on the Capitol. According to Rufus Fears, Jupiter after 27 B.C.E. was "relegated to a position of honored insignificance," which Fears sees as a result of his strong ties to the traditional (republican) order, which were inconvenient for Augustus.[40] One could also say that Jupiter/Zeus as active principle of the cosmos has in reality been replaced, or displaced, by Augustus, who acts as the present defender of Rome and the whole world against Giants, Galatians, and Orientals of all sorts.

It is of profound symbolic meaning that the eagle, representing the law, *logos*, and relentless force of Zeus at the Great Altar, now is the sign on the standards of the Roman legions; its retrieval from the Parthians in 20 B.C.E., as we have heard, inaugurates the golden age. The event was depicted on the famous Prima Porta statue of Augustus, where the eagle, returned by a subservient barbarian to a superior Roman soldier, is the focal point directly in the center of the emperor's breastplate. Two mourning women, one of them representing the vanquished Gaul, form the immediate background of the scene that is embedded in a cosmic panorama comprising Heaven/Uranos and Earth/Gaia as well as the deities of day and night.[41] This is about as explicit, in the language of the images, as Augustus could be about himself being the embodiment of Zeus.

A similar image is rendered on the Gemma Augustea, where Augustus clearly is represented as earthly counterpart of Jupiter and triumphant world ruler enthroned together with the goddess Roma and the eagle at his feet. (See image on p. 128.) He is flanked by the divinities of earth and sea, with Oikoumene as the personification of the inhabited world crowning him from behind with a *coronoa civica,* which is usually awarded for acts that save the life of citizens. Augustus thus appears as the universal savior, protector, and benefactor of the whole united, civilized world, which, according to John Pollini, has merged into "one great *polis* (city-state) governed by one *nomos* (law)," in line with early Stoic thought. The emperor is placed in the center of the scene, with the long scepter and the eagle showing his "hegemony over the Roman world as the vice regent of Jupiter on earth." His seated pose and seminudity reflect "no doubt the cult worship of Roma and Augustus in various parts of the Roman world."[42]

The imagery of the Great Altar is intensely mirrored in the Gemma, including the basic spatial polarity between *High* and *Low.* The vanquished nations as the object of Jupiter's/Caesar's world rule, one of their male representatives wearing a Gallic *torque,* are located on the lower level of the image, bound to a trophy or still in the process of being forced into submission. The boundary between their *under*-world and the triumphant scene *above* is, as Pollini notes, "a symbolic line of demarcation separating the rational and ordered world of the Augustan State from the peripheral and chaotic world of barbarism." The allusions to the Pergamene Gigantomachy and its "binary composition of oppositional forces" for Pollini are evident, although the battle itself is no longer on display. Rather, in a neoclassical rather than baroque style, the victory is embedded in the "almost harmonic calm," "balanced forms," and "symphonie" of the new imperial world order.[43]

The association of Jupiter and princeps, present in Virgil and other Augustan writers as well, according to Rufus Fears "contained the seeds of a theocratic monarchy . . . based . . . upon the eternal image of the emperor as the divinely chosen vice regent of the supreme king of gods and men."[44] Closer to Paul's time, the assimilation emperor = Jupiter, strongly shaped the rule of Caligula and especially of Nero, when it reentered "the mainstream of official imperial ideology."[45] This supports one of the basic presuppositions of our investigation into the ideological and political backgrounds of Paul's Galatian correspondence. The de facto imperial monotheism of the 40s and 50s C.E., which celebrated Caesar as the dominant divine figure through the various channels of imperial religion and ideology, constituted a fundamental challenge that Paul confronted in his Jewish-messianic theology of the One God—a god who is Other than Caesar.[46]

Virgil's Staircase: Emperor Religion, Faith, and the New Subject

So far we have left the third element of the Great Altar out of our synoptic comparison with Aeneas's Shield. If both the Gigantomachy base and the upper room of the Pergamene Altar are present in Virgil's vision of Roman imperial order and religion, what about the Great Staircase, where on the way *up* and *in* the individual is turned into an imperial subject? We found that at Pergamon this act of subjection implied submission to the imperial law by purging oneself from any connection with the lawless and rebellious other of the Giants. As it turns out, on the Shield this fundamental act of dissociation of self from other, and of submission to the rule of the supreme imperial Subject, plays a key role as well.

Virgil, to be sure, does not present any visible stairway like that of the Great Altar, nor feature a last encounter with an almost defeated enemy throwing stones—at least not on the surface of the sumptuous victory celebration that on his Shield unites the religiously and socially diverse multitudes of Rome after Actium. Yet underneath the festive surface of horizontal civic oneness and traditional religious celebration, an invisible staircase nonetheless reorders the world in the image of imperial religion, imposing its iron rules of vertical integration on old gods and new subjects alike.

This requires another brief reflection on the issue of imperial religion. Prior to S. R. F. Price's influential study of rituals and power, scholars tended to describe the Roman emperor cult primarily in terms of its shortcomings compared to proper religion. It was seen mostly as only a ritual, political, and external observance without deeper religious meaning in terms of true individual faith and religious feelings. Based on the work of Clifford Geertz, Price strongly challenged this concept and its underlying—mainly Protestant—individualistic and antiritualistic presuppositions.[47] The first great merit of Price's work was that it showed how inseparably religion and politics, "ritual and power" were linked in an imperial context like that of Asia Minor. Imperial ritual was seen as a powerful way to "conceptualize the world" in public and for the public, most notably with regard to the position of the emperor and the relationship between emperor and subjects.[48]

Imperial ritual, second, not only reflected the political reality of the Roman Empire; it also constructed it by universally inscribing it on time, space, and concrete human bodies: "The ritual was also structuring; it imposed a definition of the world. The imperial cult, along with politics and diplomacy, constructed the reality of the Roman Empire."[49] As a public "cognitive system,"[50] imperial rituals permeated the whole of society, functioning both through the still images of art and architecture, and their living counterparts at civic celebrations, sacrifices, meals, processions, prayers, and other ceremonies. The core issue was not primarily what someone really believed but what was embodied, depicted, monumentalized in stone and marble, and collectively practiced by concrete human actors. As Price states, "A Christianizing theory of religion which assumes that religion is essentially designed to provide guidance through the personal crises of life and to grant salvation into life everlasting imposes on the imperial cult a distinction between religion and politics." This distinction, however,

obscures the basic similarity between politics and religion: both are a way of systemati-
cally constructing power. . . . The imperial cult, like the traditional cults, created a relationship of power between subject and ruler. It also enhanced the dominance of local
élites over the populace, of cities over other cities, and of Greek over indigenous cultures.
That is, the cult was a major part of the web of power that formed the fabric of society.[51]

Price's emphasis on imperial cult as sociopolitical construct and collective cognitive
system was a vital contribution to a better understanding of its inner mechanics and
function. For example, social macro-management, by having imperial religion orches-
trate the "dominance of local élites over the populace," was a key factor of Roman rule
in the province of Galatia, as we will see in the next chapter. However, the way imperial
religion spread its "web of power" needs further consideration. For Price, imperial cult
basically exists alongside traditional cults, leaving them widely intact and unchanged.
As our study of Aeneas's Shield has shown, however, it seems preferable to use the term
imperial religion as a much wider framework that integrated both imperial cult and traditional religion, essentially by tacitly subordinating the old gods to the new world god
Caesar. No matter how modest the disguise under which Caesar attached and assimilated himself to existing temples, festivals and cults, he was the chief deity.

Another aspect of imperial religion and its "web of power" seems important: the
hierarchical polarity of self and other. The emphasis on the social dimension of emperor
religiosity rightly emphasized by Price should not obscure the fact that the individual
self played a vital role in it as well. If the manifold practices of sacrifice, worship, feast,
and commemoration of imperial cult were not "empty rituals" but communicated and
established the new worldview, created meaning and cohesion, identity and reassur-
ance, they did so both collectively and individually.[52]

Within the framework of imperial religion, an individual's understanding and
acceptance of the way the world was built and functioned would start with an indispensable faith act on the most personal level. The term *faith/faithfulness* here renders
the notion of Greek *pistis* and Latin *fides* as defined by the socioreligious and political
dictionary of Paul's time—namely, as a mutual bond of responsibility between rulers
and ruled. Its essence is the same on the Shield as it is at the Great Altar: with a faithful
pledge of allegiance, an act of subjection in the Althusserian sense,[53] the "small" individual self submits to the "big" victorious Self of the divine power(s) and their human
representative(s). In return for this faithful subjection, the dominant promise faithful protection. For example, in his *Res Gestae* (32), Augustus can proudly announce
that under his principate "many other nations" (*alla ethnē/aliae gentes*) with whom the
Romans had no connection before, have experienced the "faith of the Roman people"
(*pistis/fides*).[54]

This vertical self-alignment inevitably implies or is driven by a dis-alignment from
the evil and defeated other. Within the symbolic and spatial order of the Great Altar,
as we have seen, this was the decisive step away from and over and against the Giants at
the Great Staircase; it was followed by the upward and inward movement of the new
subject, in acknowledgment of victory-based law as the righteous, divinely ordained,

and cosmic order that is embodied in the legitimate ruler. This act of submission elevates the ones/us far above the rebellious and lawless others/them that stay *out* and *down* as dying and dead, while the compliant self can move in and up to partake in the life of the city of the civilized.

This imperial self–other construct as a polarity of chaos versus order, death versus life is strongly present on the Shield as well. The whole description—or depiction—of the battle ends with the term *victis*—"vanquished." In sadness, "father Nile" receives back and welcomes home the dead Egyptians, the lifeless bodies of the defeated, the chaos on the under-/outside of order (8.711–13). The next sentence/image (8.714) is introduced with a word that in Latin signals a strong contrast: *at* ("yet/but"). "But Caesar entering in triple triumph the Roman walls . . ." (*At Caesar triplici invectus Romana triumpho moenia*). According to the perception rules that had been crafted by the divine arms-smith Volcano when he created the Shield (8.710), we are now required (and allowed) to turn away our attention abruptly from events and people that no longer matter to the victorious. He has let us see our enemy, the forces of chaos, in all their ugly and terrifying foreignness as dying and dead in a grand scene, but before we can get involved with any messy details we are shown something else. The enemy vanishes, replaced by "good people" surrounding us as we enter the city. This parallels exactly our experience in the transitional space between Great Staircase and Telephos court at the Great Altar.

Caesar's triumphal entrance into the city also matches the semiotic order of the Great Staircase in other ways—it is an entry that was refused to the hostile other of the Gauls/Giants who had tried to find access to the Roman citadel earlier (8.652–62) but were thrown back through the vigilance of Juno/Hera's geese and Manlius's bravery. Admission is granted only to the superior self that embodies righteous law and order of victory: Roman law and Roman victory. Caesar's (re)entrance ticket into the Roman walls (*Romana moenia*) is his triple triumph (*triplici triumpho*); it converts the suffering and mourning among the dead and dying at the outside and underside of city/civilization into the joy and feasting of those inside and above. As we submit ourselves to him and his law we enter into the family of the civilized under god-father Caesar.[55] A new master race stands in irreconcilable opposition to the seditious counter-race below that violates the law and order of patriarchy: lawless outsiders like Gaia's fatherless Giant-sons at the Great Altar or the *Oriental* forces under Cleopatra, the barbarian Egyptian Amazon queen in the Shield.

This means that the merriment of the feasting community in the streets of Rome is not as innocent as it first seemed; it is pierced by the march of the defeated nations in "long rows" (8.722) through these same streets. This scene, however, is made not to disturb but instead to enhance the pleasures of the celebrating self—a self that has cut itself off from the suffering of the other in order to partake in the collective "we" of the dominant race, city, civilization. The defeated nations, especially the Egyptians, are going to become the source of the bread and games Augustus will shower upon the city of Rome, and of all the wealth that he will channel from the periphery to the center.[56] Each sacrificial act performed at the altars of victorious Rome on the Shield confirms that this is the divinely ordained order of things, each religious hymn sung by the mothers in the temples reinscribes the violence of the imperial self into each new generation of Romanhood,[57] each slaughtered bull spread out in front of the altars recalls the human sacrifice necessary to perpetuate the triumph of empire. Yet the space where this emerging imperial worldview in its totality and in every single one of its individual aspects would unfold its most formative and transformative power among the masses of the empire, was not the books of the writers nor the temples and altars of imperial religion, but the arenas. There we will turn next.

Human Beings in the Image of Caesar: Arena, Self, and the Other's Blood

If imperial religion spells out imperial order, performances of imperial order, on the other hand, also represent imperial religion. This is particularly true of the public games (*ludes*) that are explicitly mentioned on the Shield in 8.717 as part of the victory celebration. Although we are inclined not to see any political or religious implications connected to this term, games in the Roman Empire were neither secular nor nonpolitical events. The sequence joy–games–streets–applause and temples–mothers' choirs–altars–sacrificed bulls (8.717–19) should alert us to the fact that games, soon to be housed in Augustus's newly built amphitheaters, were embedded in the larger framework of creating social consensus and applause for the emperor, a setting they shared with the rituals of imperial religion. While the games were enthusiastically embraced as a source of public entertainment and joy (*laetitia*) by the people of Rome, they were also a powerful medium of mass communication that shaped Roman subjects in the image of empire throughout the provinces. The arenas were the training ground for an imperial worldview and self-perception that restaged the order and *piety* of the Great Altar with enormous visual effect and propagandistic efficiency.

Augustus's New Game

One of the great innovations that Augustus and his successors brought to the sphere of mass entertainment was a new way to stage hunts, executions, and gladiatorial combats, next to the ongoing conventional pleasures of chariot races, athletic games, and plays. Public displays of animals, animal fights, and executions had existed before, and hunts since ancient times had been seen as demonstrations of the superior royal power to protect civilization against the savage forces of nature.[58] Similarly, single combats (*munera*) had been known officially in Rome for more than two centuries; they had originally been linked to private funerary rites in honor of deceased persons of high rank.[59] In her study on the Roman arena, Alison Futrell examines the historical records of gladiatorial combats throughout the first three centuries B.C.E. and finds increasing size and numbers, growing use of political manipulation, and a connection to times of crisis and transition.[60] Something fundamentally changed, however, when Augustus came to power.

In the first two centuries C.E. amphitheaters were built throughout the empire, with the Colosseum in Rome eventually emerging as the most famous. The arenas, that is, the sand-covered round or elliptical space at the bottom,[61] became the space where in every part of the Roman world more or less the same sequence of events would unfold: wild beast hunts and fights (*venationes*) in the morning, involving the display and slaughter of fierce and exotic animals; public execution of criminals by animals, fire, or crucifixion around noon; gladiatorial contests (the actual *munera*) in the afternoon. When games took place over a longer period, this same sequence was probably followed every day.[62]

Augustus not only restructured and reappropriated but also strongly controlled and monopolized the games, organizing *munera* and *venationes* on a larger scale than ever before.[63] The provision of eight gladiatorial shows with no fewer than ten thousand men confronting each other in single combat, as well as twenty-six fights with "African wild beasts," which left thirty-five hundred animals dead, was proudly proclaimed by the emperor when he listed his lifetime achievements in the *Res Gestae* (22–23). It seems that the *zeitgeist* of the new imperial order found its ideal expression in the arenas. The amphitheaters that subsequently appeared not only in the major cities of the Roman Empire, including Pergamon, but also in rural centers and very prominently in the Celtic/Galatian provinces of the Three Gauls, were closely linked to the imperial cult and were seen as a superior way for the provincials to express their newly won Romanness and loyalty to the emperor.[64] We will look more closely at this phenomenon when we turn to Roman Galatia. Many of the amphitheaters accommodated thousands of spectators, but none was surpassed by the Colosseum in Rome, which was finished in 80 C.E. and could seat at least fifty thousand people; counted among the events and topics it monumentalized was Rome's final conquest of Jerusalem and defeat of the Jewish rebellion.[65]

Unlike a theatrical performance, the suffering, fighting, and killing in the arena were real and occurred much more massively. But, though authentic, the spectacles were staged, choreographed, and made for "seeing" as well. Sometimes theatrical elements were borrowed that turned executions into a public reenactment of common myths or contemporary legends around famous robbers and highwaymen.[66] Amphitheater literally means *double theater*, or *theater from both sides*—and the word *theater* is derived from the Greek verb for *seeing* (*theaomai*). The arena was one of the most compelling places where imperial ideology was generated and enacted through the power of images: living images that were images of dying and of imposing death. Again, as at the Great Altar, we need to ask about presentation and reception. What was it that was shown and propagated through these mass performances of death, and what was expected to be seen and understood?

The Oneness of the Nations and Caesar's "Good Works"

The inauguration of the Colosseum in Rome in the year 80 C.E. was an event that surpassed, in terms of the magnitude and splendor, all of the Roman games up to that time. The poet Martial in a set of epigrams dedicated to the Roman emperor under the title *Liber de spectaculis* ("About the shows/games") celebrated the Colosseum as the most wonderful of all the wonders of the world, more magnificent than the pyramids of Egypt, the walls of Babylon, the temple of Artemis at Ephesus, or the Mausoleum at Halicarnassus (*Spect.*1). On a single day, five thousand animals were killed in a hunt (Suetonius, *Tit.* 7.3; Cassius Dio 66.25). Over a period of no less than one hundred days, Emperor Titus presented thousands of animals and humans to fight to the death. In a kind of lottery, small wooden balls were thrown into the audience, which could be redeemed for a wide variety of gifts: clothes, food, animals, and even slaves (Cassius Dio 66.25). The emperor's generosity was matchless, the greatness of Rome as the capital of the world unequaled, and the gratitude of the people(s) of Rome insuperable.

Martial (*Spect.* 3) gives a vivid description of the arena as a huge melting pot of the *oikoumenē*. Spectators from all over the world are present in Caesar's city and amphitheater, even members of the most remote and barbarous races. The arena integrates and creates unity. All the different languages of the nations (*vox diversa sonat populorum*) become "one" (*una est*) when the emperor is acclaimed as "father of the country" (*pater patriae*). The material structure of the amphitheater, or stadium, with its circular or semicircular shape would reinforce this sense of social cohesion. Arranging thousands of bodies in a circle, with everyone facing the inside, together for one or more days in an emotionally intense atmosphere—shouting and shivering, betting and applauding together—in itself must have created a powerful sense of unity across all borders of social, gender, ethnic, or religious diversities.[67]

Status became fluid, too. All the drama and excitement, the opportunity to step out of ordinary life, the presents and free food distributions that were added as a bonus from time to time, were a *gift* from the emperor to the people. *Dedi* ("I gave"), and *populo dedi* ("I gave to the people") are the two phrases used when Augustus talks about the mass slaughtering of gladiators and African animals he organized (*Res Gestae* 22–23). Rich and poor, high and low, powerful and powerless not only share the same circular seating arrangement, the same gaze and perspective, but they are also honored as recipients of the emperor's *benefactions*, a term that, like its Greek-derived counterpart *euergetism,* literally means "good works." We have to pay attention to this term, as *works,* as well as the question of unity and community building "among the nations" are key issues in Paul's Galatian letter. The good works of the emperor in this case are his donation(s) of the game(s) to the populace, including the expensive gifts of human and animal victims for public slaughter.[68]

Another aspect of seemingly horizontal civic "Oneness" created in the arena is the communication between low and high. During the games, the small and powerless people are granted an opportunity to interact directly with their superiors, which in Rome would include Caesar whenever he was present. Social and political barriers were dissolved, at least partially, as Futrell states: "For this moment or day or week, the government was not an impersonal and impervious body, distanced from the average person, but a fellow-spectator, practically within reach, one with the Populus Romanus."[69] Moreover, in this surrogate political assembly, the function of the games as a substitute for meaningful political activity and participation becomes obvious: "Deprived of any voice in government during the Principate, the plebs exchanged their traditional forum for a form of expression in the amphitheater."[70]

For Martial, the oneness of the arena ultimately is embodied in the person of Caesar, who receives unisonous praise as "father of the fatherland" (*Spect.* 3).[71] His "sacred power" (*potestas sacra*) and divinity are recognized even by wild beasts (*Spect.* 33)—including an elephant, who "also feels our God" (*nostrum sentit et ille deum, Spect.* 20). Obviously, the divine nature of the emperor for the elephant is beyond doubt. This shows how closely political acclamation and imperial religion indeed became linked in the arena and how subtle nuances regarding Caesar as "fully god" or just "god's vice-regent" probably got lost in this context. The recognition of the person at the top of the human power pyramid, with unlimited power over life and death, is the recognition of his divinity too. This phenomenon is not restricted to Rome and the Colosseum. As we will see when we turn to Roman Galatia in the next chapter, the arena is firmly and prominently tied to the rituals and observances of imperial religion in the provinces as well.[72]

Yet the religious dimension of the arena is not only attached to the godlike person of the emperor, but also is established through the events that take place at the center of the arena itself. Neither Caesar's presence nor the elbow rubbing and camaraderie among the audience would by itself have had the power to integrate social diversity and polarities into the new imperial one-self, if it were not for the magical object that drew all eyes to the sand-covered circular floor at the center and that was collectively consumed: the blood of the Other.

It was the sight of killing and being killed that was the focus of the common gaze, the center of everyone's attention, giving high and low the same perspective and making them magically see the world, the emperor, and themselves with eyes no longer different. It was the collective excitement created through the "live performance" of death, with all its most crude or sophisticated variations that transformed them into one body and miraculously gave them one language that they all understood, no matter what their native tongue (*Spect.* 3). However, there was more to this than just seeing—the arena was no space for passive spectators. Rather it was about becoming involved, committed, and transformed by actively participating as players in Caesar's games. It was as agents and partakers in the supreme sacrifice that all were becoming one and self: the life of the Other.[73]

The Other and the One-self

Before more closely examining the sacrificial dimension of the arena in the next section, we first need to identify precisely who the victims of the arena were and what made them an appropriate object to be violently and publicly destroyed through elemental and human forces, fire and water, lions' claws and tigers' fangs, sword and spear, and countless other inventions of lethal creativity. What justifies their death and makes it lawful and enjoyable? Corresponding to the tripartite structure of the Roman games, the victims in the games fall into three basic categories:

Nature to be subdued. Exotic and savage beasts such as lions, panthers, and elephants, as well as domesticated bulls shown and killed in the *venationes* of the morning exemplify the other of raw nature as such and the power to subdue it. Since ancient times in the Near East the king's prowess as hunter had signified his social and military power.[74] At the same time, these wild beast fights also proclaim the triumphant message of victory over faraway lands like Africa, where these animals were caught, to be subsequently transported over long distances in costly and complicated transactions.[75]

Lawless criminals and "liminals" to be punished and eliminated. The criminals entering the arena around noon to be disposed of by fire, beasts, or cross (or a mix of any of these three) are other in terms of social status and transgression of the law. They are slaves or low-class persons, that is, *humiliores.* They are executed for crimes such as murder and robbery, as well as rebellion against their masters or the Roman order. The mass executions of prisoners of war in this context are solely based on their identity as *enemies.* They are seen as representatives of hostile and noncompliant nations who have committed barbarian, lawless acts of sedition against the emperor and Roman world rule.[76]

A special category of *dis-order* was presented by liminal people who did not fit into established standards and therefore were publicly executed. Suetonius and Cassius Dio, for example, report about special events when people seen as abnormal were forced to fight to the death in the arena: women against dwarves under Domitian (Suetonius, *Dom.* 4.1; Cassius Dio 67.8.4) or people of black color from Ethiopia—men, women, and children—under Nero (Cassius Dio 62.3).

Gladiators. Another assembly of universal outsiders/others with similar features appears again, but in a new role, in the afternoon. Gladiators are mainly prisoners of war, criminals, or slaves sold into gladiatorial schools as punishment for certain (less severe) offenses. They could include freeborn people as well who sold themselves voluntarily either because of poverty, to escape military service, or because they lusted for battle. All of them were considered social outcasts.[77] However, the rules of the game are different this time, as a few of the bravest and most fortunate of the gladiators have a chance to leave the arena alive and even in triumph.[78] This turns their fight against the other into a *real* fight for survival, enhancing its entertainment value as a restaging of the universal order of combat and victory and showing that even the vanquished adhere to it.

Every single aspect of the arena that we have thus far observed seems reminiscent of the Great Altar. The Giants on the Great Frieze and the victims of the arena share the same markers of beastly, barbarian, rebellious, hostile, criminal, and liminal otherness that makes them archetypal and prototypical enemies of the Roman imperial city and of civilization as such.[79] Both have a ritual of dying and death imposed on them that functions as a triumphal celebration of victory, superiority, and a (re)foundation of the city. Furthermore, the rules of perception to be followed when one contemplates the combat scenes in the arena and at the Great Altar are virtually identical too. It is through approvingly looking at the bloody and torturous suffering, killing, and dying of all these different, universally threatening others that the individual self is supposed to bond irrevocably with the victorious power and the power of victory: the ruling imperial power. To see like that also means visibly to distance oneself from the vanquished other, who literally vanishes. The blood that had been publicly shed disappears as fresh sand is spread out over the arena after each act of dying. This individual and collective (dis)alignment is the decisive production of the arena, as at the Great Altar: the production of imperial subjects. It was supposed to elevate the civic body to Roman selfhood throughout the empire, be it in Rome, Gaul, or Galatia.

The "undeserving" other. The first rationale of the arena, as already described in 1922 by Ludwig Friedlaender, is the division of humanity into deserving and undeserving.[80] The arena makes clear that humanity is irrevocably and irreconcilably segregated into two parts—us and them, superior and inferior, human and subhuman, winners and losers, self and other. The decision to attach oneself to the victorious ones, against the vanquished others, is presented as natural, moral, and without alternative.

Therefore, the most cruel and perverse ways of killing exhibited in the arena were seen as a righteous performance of law and order and a kind of ethical test. Squeamishness at the sight of blood, raw flesh, exposed intestines was a sign of moral weakness.[81] The death shown in the arena was death required by law and therefore right; watching it with approval meant moral steadfastness and submission to law and emperor. Compassion toward the suffering fellow creature was to be avoided at all costs and was instead to be rechanneled into the fun of watching and participating in the lawful events of a slaughterhouse.[82] It was only through the destruction of *them*, the subhuman, worthless, harmful non-us, that we could live—their suffering therefore did not matter except as a celebration of life. The segregation of humanity and the dehumanization of the other was at the core of the arena production.

The enemy other. The unconditional acceptance of a predetermined other as enemy and the readiness to fight him/them constitute the second goal toward which the audience is trained. The whole sequence of arena performances in endless variations presents war and combat as an innate law of cosmos, nature, and humanity. What counts most is the willingness to perceive the unknown other exactly as it is made known by the imperial order: not as a human being whose suffering matters but as a bestial, criminal, dangerous, and threatening foe to be destroyed, a faceless mass of disposable life. The *righteous* brutalization of the civic body in the arena is an essential requirement of warfare and is reflected in the cruelty of cities plundered and their people tortured, slaughtered, and raped.[83] The mass consumption of the emperor's games, together with his bread, was metabolized into political compliance with the rules of battle and victory, conquest and subjugation, competition and violence, domination and distinction as codified and sanctioned by Roman law both for the inside and toward the outside of the Roman Empire.

By exhibiting the frightening image of the *other-than-us* at the center, and by staging the Great Combat, the arena not only exposed but also veiled, covered, softened with its bloody sand all the deadly tension, violence, and injustice that in reality were at the core of Roman society itself. It transformed privileged and nonprivileged members into a common Roman subjectivity of one-self, lifting up even the lowest ranking members of the plebs, the socially others inside society, by putting them above someone lower—the outcast other dying in the arena.[84] It also justified and purified the audience by defining them as Not-other, that is, not lawless, not uncivilized, not barbarian, not seditious—and therefore not doomed to die. None of these operations of exorcism, purification, and justification could have been performed without visually consuming the blood of the other.

Again this translates effortlessly into the language of the Great Staircase: everyone participating in the arena's combats as a compliant spectator was allowed to move symbolically *Up* and *In*; everyone willing to see what was meant to be shown by the carefully orchestrated spectacle was elevated in status and honor and became an accepted insider of the imperial order. In this way everyone was personally profiting from the death of the other. The celebration of oneness and community by the imperial body over and against the lawless counter-body reached its climax when the crowds were allowed to participate in the decision over life and death in a gladiatorial combat. Being asked whether a defeated gladiator should be killed or allowed to live—the famous thumbs up or down—gave even ordinary people for a short moment the precious sovereignty of being lord over life and death like the emperor himself.[85]

In this overall arrangement, social oneness and selfhood are established through the carefully staged, quasi-ritual death of the other within a firmly decided order of *Inside* versus *Outside*, *us* over and against *them*. The blood of the other drenching the sand of the arena becomes the magical substance that gives birth to the civic self.

The Rules of the Game

If the games contained an element of horizontal social integration, there was an even stronger moment of vertical stratification. We came across this same dialectic already on the Great Altar and Aeneas's Shield. As the arena converted the tensions within the social body into oneness and selfhood through the most violent ways of othering, it at the same time and with the same brutal force reinsribed the hierarchical segregation of one and other in itself. Being transformed into the likeness and oneness of the imperial body, the participants of the games also had to accept domination and subordination as constitutive of this body—for it reflected cosmic law and order.

Since the world had been saved, newly created, and established through Octavian's victory in the Gigantomachy with Antony, there was no doubt that a strictly hierarchical order with an imperial pinnacle was essential for safeguarding the universe against its chaotic underside. And as the arena metaphorically and in a controlled setting restaged the primeval combat against chaos and otherness, it also had to re-present and implement the one order of civilization and city that stood against chaos (and that at the Great Altar was represented at the staircase and in the upper room): the imperial order.

And it did. Augustus issued a very precise legislation, the *Lex Julia Theatralis,* which determined the entrance everyone had to use and the place everyone had to take in the amphitheater: women and low classes/slaves were high up in the outer areas of the auditorium; the emperor, and the vestal priestesses were immediately next to the arena at the bottom. Everyone else—senators, boys and their tutors, married men—had to sit in precisely determined areas and rows according to social ranking.[86] This seating plan applied to all kinds of spectacles, not only gladiatorial and animal fights, and demonstrated the reestablishment of the proper social order by Augustus in its idealized form. Every row and the whole sophisticated system of structured space and regulated admission provided the different levels of society with their very specific location, entrance, and exit. It thus gave symbolically to everyone their exactly defined place in the social hierarchy—in fact, the Latin word for *row* (*ordo*) is the root of the English word *order.*

Unity in diversity was established, indeed, but within a vertical framework. Everyone saw what happened to those who did not comply with their assigned place in the imperial order. The amphitheater thus as a whole demonstrated, inscribed, and reinforced the perfect state of social order and hierarchy—which was made even more visible through a new dress code introduced by Augustus that prescribed white togas for Roman citizens and stolas for married women with woven stripes that indicated their social status.[87] Social order was publicly shown and performed by the audience as law and submission in juxtaposition to the unruly chaos at the bottom of the arena that represented lawlessness and rebellion. As Paul Plass observes, referring to the meaning of *ordo* as both a "row of seats" and "social rank": "The precise geometry of the arena's architecture and blocks of spectators wearing clothing of the same color helped draw sharp lines of status among the 50,000 or so spectators of the Colosseum, who represented the body politic secure from the actual carnage down on the sand, though deeply involved in the symbolic defeat or victory they had assembled to view."[88]

Following the rules of a public seating order and dress code was the outside aspect of submitting to the law and order of empire within the framework of the arena, and to the rules of the game in general. In the deep structure of identity formation it meant something else no less carefully regulated and implemented: becoming a compliant subject and, at least metaphorically, a soldier of empire through the development of a proper imperial self-consciousness that was shaped by the image of the other as enemy, rival, threat, and as unrighteous, inferior, and subhuman.

The arena taught people that this strictly hierarchical, competitive, and violence-obsessed order of inclusion and exclusion is not only universal but also beneficial: after a day of games even the lowest ranking and most marginalized spectator had been elevated above someone more inferior and outcast: the victims of the arena.[89] And even the highest ranking person had paid reverence to someone higher in status—the emperor to the gods and everyone else to the emperor, the supreme donor of the games. After a day in the arena, everyone was not only fellow spectator but also a coexecutor of law and coconqueror of uncivilized nature, animals, and state enemies. This is how the imperial order of conquest and victory, of subordination and economic exploitation inscribes itself on the bodies of its subjects. The law and rules taught and learned in the arenas were the law and rules of the imperial game played in the world as a whole.

Cross, Creation, Sacrifice: The Arenas as "Megachurches" of Imperial Religion

In the sequence of bloody events at the inauguration of the Roman Colosseum reported by Martial, an episode involving a robber called Laureolus receives special attention. Laureolus himself was long dead, but after he had been caught and crucified, his figure became the legendary subject of popular plays. Now he and his cross have their theatrical return in the arena as well. The cross that is erected for his execution, however, is no fake cross as on the theatrical stages (*non falsa pendens in cruce*; *Spect.* 7). Nor will Laureolus ever play his part in this superperformance again—for the agony of his dying body and the blood on display are real. He is no actor but a criminal condemned to death.[90]

Before the eyes of the Roman audience gathered in the Colosseum, Laureolus is crucified. After he has been hung on the cross, his naked flesh, as Martial lets us know, is exposed to a Caledonian bear that tears him into pieces. Yet the dying takes time: "His lacerated limbs lived on, dripping gore, and in all his body, there was none." Martial hastens to add that the utmost brutality of this execution, after which the human body was no longer recognizably human, was well deserved. But strangely, it does not seem to matter precisely what this man had done; rather, Martial gives a list of capital crimes he *could* have committed: cutting the throat of his father or master, robbing a temple, trying to set Rome afire. Obviously every single one of these offenses would justify the torture this man had to suffer, for every single one of these crimes is a most severe transgression of the divine and civic order that needs to be punished without mercy.

This reminds Martial, well versed with Greek myth, of Prometheus. The prominent ancient hero of Titan origin, in an act of primeval insurgence for the sake of humanity, stole fire from the gods and therefore was punished by Zeus, who had him bound to a rock and sent an eagle to eat away his liver, which grew back overnight (Hesiod, *Theog.* 521–25). Laureolus hanging on the cross and giving up "his defenseless entrails to a Scottish bear"—this for Martial is like Prometheus who "chained on a Scythian crag, fed the tireless bird on his prolific breast."[91]

Cross and Arena

Since Martin Hengel's landmark 1977 study *Crucifixion* we have been alerted to the fact that the cross in antiquity was not primarily a Christian theological construct but a virtually omnipresent, terrifying, and ferociously brutal reality with an overwhelming visual effect. Crucifixion, according to Hengel, was a penalty of extreme cruelty, originally widespread among numerous peoples of the ancient world, but newly formulated by the Romans. Under Roman rule crosses were introduced on a mass scale and given a fairly precise social location and political connotation. Crucifixion was "a political and military punishment," and it was "inflicted above all on the lower classes, i.e. slaves, violent criminals and the unruly elements in rebellious provinces, not least in Judaea."[92]

The crosses, often T-shaped or consisting simply of a vertical pole, were prominently erected at places where most people could see them: at crossroads, on high ground, before the walls of a besieged city like Jerusalem in 70 C.E. Crucifixion was the deliberate public display of naked victims who were slowly tortured to death over several days. Outlawed from society as transgressors of order and disturbers of Roman peace, they were exposed to extreme suffering and humiliation. They were often denied ordinary burial, which exposed their cadavers to wild beasts and birds of prey.[93]

Some of the most spectacular crucifixions in the Roman era demonstrate their social and political context. Over a distance of about two hundred kilometers the six thousand survivors of Spartacus's army were nailed to crosses on the road between Capua and Rome after the defeat of the gladiators' rebellion in 71 B.C.E. (Appian, *Bell. civ.* 1.120); collective slave executions, often by crucifixion, were performed in Rome if the head of a household was murdered (Tacitus, *Ann.* 13.32);[94] two thousand crucifixions took place in Judea under Varus to quell unrest after the death of Herod the Great in 4 B.C.E. (Josephus, *B.J.* 2.75); during the anti-Jewish pogroms in Alexandria in 38–41 C.E. Jews were crucified in the theater after public scourging and torture on the occasion of the emperor's birthday celebrations (Philo, *In Flaccum* 10.83–85); to demoralize the enemy, five hundred Jewish fugitives were crucified per day in front of besieged Jerusalem under Titus in 70 C.E. so that "there was not enough room for the crosses and not enough crosses for the bodies" (Josephus, *B.J.* 5.449–51).

Though Hengel does not draw the connection between crucifixion and the wider context of the Roman games, it is quite obvious that cross and arena were conceptually, and often also factually, linked, as Laureolus's example shows. Death through crucifixion alone, however, would normally take time, while the fast-moving pace of the arena required speed and "spectacular appeal." This is the reason why crucifixions in the arena would often be combined with other means of execution such as burning or exposure to savage beasts, as in the case of Laureolus.[95] At the same time, they were staged on a large scale in public spaces outside the arena, as the examples mentioned above demonstrate.[96] But no matter where a crucifixion took place, it shared its (per)formative and transformative visual effect with the other spectacles of the arena.[97]

It is noteworthy that this aspect of the cross as public "show" in the New Testament is explicitly rendered in Luke's passion narrative, where the crucifixion of Jesus is called a *theōria,* that is, a *spectacle* (Luke 23:48). The Greek term *theōria* can be used for public visual events at games and processions; like *theater* it is derived from the word *theōreō* ("to look at, behold, perceive"). The actual object to be displayed on a cross is revealed by Martial when he spontaneously associates Laureolus's crucifixion in the Colosseum with Prometheus "crucified" on the rock. It matters little whether an eagle eats the perpetrator's liver or a Caledonian bear tears his body to pieces. Underneath the countless variations of how it is staged and performed, the core visual program of a crucifixion is quite stable. What needs to be shown is not just the execution of a criminal but the elimination of a rebellious, transgressive other and the restoration of the proper order of the world.[98]

This is vividly demonstrated by Martial. Obviously, he is well trained and ready to see what he is supposed to see when looking at dying Laureolus: someone who either cut the throat of his father or master, robbed a temple, or tried to set Rome afire. The case's details and the precise offense do not matter. All four of these crimes are contemporary versions of the primeval Giant/Titan uprising against the patriarchal order, the political and social order, the divine order, and the order of the godlike city/citadel Rome, which rules the world. Laureolus's crucifixion thus in its essence is a reenactment of the primordial battle against the Giants;[99] it is not human cruelty played out but the sacred violence of divine retribution. A fundamental threat to the divine and human order of the world is eliminated, for everyone's benefit.

To view a crucifixion as Martial viewed it was the proper worldview expected from Roman subjects and continuously redeveloped and reinforced in the arena. Fifteen years earlier, Emperor Nero had counted on precisely this proper perception mode among the Roman public when he blamed the Christians for the great fire of Rome in 64 c.e. and hung them on crosses (*crucibus adfixi*) to be burned alive, or wrapped them in animal skins to be torn by wild dogs (Tacitus, *Ann.* 15.44.4). Their "folly" and "mad" way of perceiving one crucified (cf. 1 Cor 1:18) made them "ideal victims" of crucifixion themselves, as well as of other deadly performances in the arena. Hengel aptly summarizes this point, especially with regard to the perceived lawlessness of Paul's theology of the cross:

> In Roman times, crucifixion was practiced above all on dangerous criminals and members of the lowest classes. These were primarily people who had been outlawed from society or slaves who on the whole had no rights, in other words, groups whose development had to be suppressed by all possible means to safeguard law and order in the state. Because large strata of the population welcomed the security and the world-wide peace which the empire brought with it, the crucified victim was defamed both socially and ethically in popular awareness, and this impression was heightened still further by the religious elements involved. . . . In this context, the earliest Christian message of the crucified messiah demonstrated the "solidarity" of the love of God with the unspeakable suffering of those who were tortured and put to death by human cruelty.[100]

Martial's gruesome description of Laureolus's crucifixion in the Colosseum in 80 c.e. thus also displays something about the cross of Jesus of Nazareth in 30 c.e. that we do not normally see. It shows that Golgotha is not an insular Jewish or New Testament topos that was first understood by Paul in its universal theological implications for *all the nations/Gentiles* of the world. Rather, it already had a salvific and global connotation within the overall framework of Roman imperial world order, world law and world religion. Crucifixion represented an inter-national event, ubiquitous among the vanquished nations under Roman rule, both at Rome and in the provinces, inside and outside the arena, and was as universal as the Roman Empire itself. It was Paul, however, who radically redefined this universalism and the law it imposed, and who gave the notions of salvation and peace that came from the cross an entirely new meaning.[101]

Arena and Cross as Re-performance of the Great Altar

We need to return to the Great Altar of Pergamon once again. Arena and cross share the threefold dimension of public mass entertainment, punishment of capital crimes against divine and human law, and restoration of public—and ultimately cosmic—order against transgression as their common ideological background. As highly power-ful "mass media" and means of social control, both are at the same time mythological events in the primeval battle of "order against chaos" that reinscribe the law of victory and submission, especially in the provinces of the Roman Empire. The Caledonian bear devouring the crucified perpetrator Laureolus under the gaze and gasp of the watching audience, in Martial's imagination shape-shifts into Zeus's eagle, which embodies and enforces the triumph of supreme divine law and rule by merciless punishment. Behind Laureolus, the rebellious Titan Prometheus emerges. The images of both arena and crucifixion are steeped in the mythic world of Gigantomachy and Titanomachy. They are therefore intimately linked to the cosmogonic combat imagery of the Great Frieze.

Visually, the animals and humans dying under unspeakable torture on the bloody sand of the arenas are strikingly close to the stony figures of the Pergamene Galatians/Giants, as if these were coming to life again to face their death once more. And after training our perception in the school of Roman images, we can see how even the con-tours of the cross, though materially absent from the Great Frieze, start to emerge as virtually present among the different means of discipline and punishment imposed on the Giants by the deities of the Great Altar. If crucifixions are not depicted at the Pergamene Battle Frieze, they nonetheless belong conceptually there: they are the specifically Roman *re-imagination* of suitable weaponry for the divine battle against chaos, insurrection, and barbarism. At a second glance, the Pergamene images indeed resemble the torture of the cross more closely than it might seem at first. Arms spread wide in agony, immobilized legs, naked and defenseless bodies exposed to the brutal force of wood, fire, savage animals' teeth; the goddess on the East Frieze who is about to penetrate the body of her enemy with a torchlike post of wood; above all the grisly slowness of dying that is the signature of the cross and that the relief plates of the Great Frieze have frozen into eternity—the images of crucifixion, like the show of the arena in general, have their marble prototype in the images of the Great Altar.[102]

Furthermore, the appearance of Zeus's eagle under the guise of a Caledonian bear as agent of supreme law enforcement in Martial's arena diary points to the religious dimension of the arena. The eagle is well known from the Great Frieze as the supreme Giant fighter. As current reenactments of the Giant battle, arena and cross are inherently political and religious at the same time. Imperial and divine law are one and the same. Arena and crucifixions are more than a public show that performs and generates social and political order—they are also part of imperial worship. In this way the arena indeed can be seen as the "political temple" of the empire "that housed the mythic reenactment of the cult of Roman statehood," as Alison Futrell states.[103] One might as well use a more contemporary term and call the amphitheaters the "megachurches" of imperial religion.

Salvation and justification, damnation and moral exhortation, communion and excommunication, law and *works*—all the theological and ecclesiological concepts that we have come to perceive as part of a largely disembodied and dehistorized discourse in Paul's Galatian correspondence were alive in the arena, embodied in images of flesh and blood rather than words. And even Paul's cruciform theology and ethics need to be understood against the backdrop of this primary context. For no matter whether it was actually placed in the arena, the cross belonged to the same production of a coherent imperial worldview and world religion, staged in the same way and meant to be seen with the same eyes as the rest of the performances of death in the amphitheater as a whole. Paul and his communities, however, were not compliant spectators and coactors, neither in the Roman arena nor in the Great Battle of Pergamon.

Arena, Enuma Elish, and the Imperial Creation Myth

Spatially, the comparison between the arena and the Great Altar is most intriguing. Both share an underlying obsession with space and place, structuring *High* and *Low*, *In* and *Out* as carefully as the placement of bodies within this order. Both have meticulously regulated entrance rituals and requirements. Constructing a spatiality that assigns to different groups their precise location above or below, both the Great Altar and the arena embody law and order per se. The establishment and affirmation of a privileged inside space against the outside and underside are another element that links the arena to the altar, most notably to the magical transformation happening at the Great Staircase.

The process of civic identity (trans)formation, which is key to arena and Great Altar alike, functions slightly differently in the arena than at the Great Altar. Whereas at Pergamon the representation of city and civilized *Inside* is architecturally placed at the *In/Upside* of the whole altar structure, the arena is designed to express a sort of reverse spatiality. It was on the carefully segregated *Inside* of the amphitheater, though *Down* at the bottom, where the outcasts and aliens were placed. The audience, as the civic *Inside*, was watching from the *Outside*, though from *Up/Above*. Through the seating order of the amphitheater, the highest representatives of society were at the deepest point down, yet at the front, whereas the lowest members were high up, but at the far back of the funnel-like architectural arrangement.[104]

This partial reversal of the semiotic order of *In==High* versus *Out==Low* might support the thesis of liminality embodied in the arena and acted out through the games. In the light of the work of Arnold van Gennep and Victor Turner, Plass sees *munera* as a quasi-ritual, liminal process where spectators are separated from normal outside activities by being gathered inside the arena, where they experience "vicarious participation in lethal combat" and afterwards are reintegrated into society with an enhanced "sense of solidarity." The gladiator, for example, is expelled in his function as "dangerous stranger," outsider, alien-victim, and loser.[105]

Thomas Wiedemann supports this idea, with a strong emphasis on the aspect of social integration and identity formation through othering: the arena served to integrate people into Roman society and also "symbolically divided off what was Roman from what was not." It was the "limit" where Roman civilization confronts nature (animals), societal justice has to deal with wrongdoing (criminals), the empire meets its enemies (gladiators), and the passage from life to death and death to life takes place.[106] By entering the secluded space of the amphitheater, which, according to Wiedemann, often was placed at the edge of the city or even formed part of the city wall,[107] one thus encounters the forces of chaos set lose in a controlled way, that is, when animals or elemental forces such as fire or water are allowed to kill humans. The ordinary structure of the world reverts—in order to be reestablished and re-created.

This element of a *new creation* again directly links to Paul, who too sees the order of the entire cosmos suspended and reverted through the cross (Gal 6:14-15). Yet the profound transformation of world and self that he in the dramatic final (dis)closure of his Galatian letter calls *kainē ktisis* is worlds apart from Caesar's "new creation."[108] What precisely constitutes the difference? And if the arena, like the Great Staircase, features the (re)establishment of the ordered world as well as of city and civilization through combat and victory, and through self-distancing from the vanquished other, how exactly does this primordial act of imperial creation function? Another brief look at one of the most influential and ancient imperial creation myths, which we began to explore in chapter 2 above, the Babylonian *Enuma Elish*, might be helpful for understanding the deep structure of the cosmogony that unfolds in the arena.

The *Enuma Elish*, dating from the early second millennium B.C.E., focuses on the legitimate ascendancy of state god Marduk to supreme rulership over the Babylonian deities, and of Babylon itself to political supremacy.[109] This is a configuration that mirrors the Augustan age. At the same time, the *Enuma Elish* parallels the Greco-Roman Gigantomachy in many ways. The gods are threatened by a coalition of insurgent gods and monsters led by the primeval mother goddess Tiamat. In order to win the battle, they install Marduk as supreme leader and king. The creation of the world and of humanity follows after Marduk's triumphant victory. He uses the maternal body of the brutally slaughtered and butchered Tiamat as matter out of which he forms the physical world of heaven and earth. After this, humankind is created, not out of earthly dust as in the biblical creation narrative, but out of blood. The blood belongs to Kingu, the partner of the defeated arch-mother and commander-in-chief of her divine-monstrous rebel army; he had to be handed over by the vanquished gods now held in captivity as prisoners of war. Through this treacherous act of scapegoating and extradition, they are allowed to win their freedom, purged of the sin of rebellion by Kingu's blood. It is humanity, however, created specifically for this purpose, that has vicariously to bear the serfdom that had been the legitimate punishment of the pardoned loser gods.[110]

> Kingu it was who created the strife
> And caused Tiamat to revolt and prepare for battle.
> They bound him and held him before Ea;
> Punishment they inflicted upon him by cutting (the arteries of) his blood.
> With his blood they created mankind;
> He (Ea) imposed the services of the gods (upon them) and set the gods free.
>   (VI.29-34)

The political theology and anthropology of this combined combat-creation myth that in Babylon was regularly recited on the fourth day of the New Year festival, shed more light on the logic of the arena and the Great Altar.[111] Creation is perceived as creation-out-of-battle and creation-out-of-victory. It is not a *creatio ex nihilo* (creation out of nothingness) by the power of the divine word, as in the biblical Genesis, but a most bloody *creation out of annihilation*. A merciless act of divine retaliatory violence establishes the order of *Above* and *Below*, conquerors and vanquished, free and slave as primordial foundation of the cosmos. It is also a highly patriarchal creation that has a superior male God perform creation as the chillingly brutal submission and slaying of the primeval female, described with strong connotations of rape. Tiamat is penetrated by Marduk's evil and raging winds, which he drives into her open mouth so that they fill her swollen belly. He then shoots an arrow through her mouth that tears her interior apart and cuts through her inner parts, splitting her heart. After he has subdued her, he casts down her carcass and stands upon it triumphantly. Later he will split her open to form heaven and earth out of her (IV.96–104, 137–138). The flesh and blood of the defeated (female) enemy/other are not just there to be shown and seen, but they become literally the magical substance out of which heaven, earth, and human beings are formed—a world and a humanity in the image and likeness of the imperial order and in subservience to its gods.

Like the later Giants at Pergamon, humanity in the *Enuma Elish* physically embodies the "bloodline" of defeated rebellion, with the law of enslavement and the religion of compliance, both gender-encoded in a female downfall, primordially inscribed on its collective body.[112] So also is the murder/sacrifice of the (br)other as birth of the self. The defeated and socially "dead" enemy gods are only allowed to become self by vicariously sacrificing one of their own, that is, Kingu, as other.[113] The general mechanism of city/civilization collectively defeating, punishing, sacrificing, and "consuming" the vanquished other at the Great Altar, as we have stated, could be perceived as the deep structure linking the Dying Giants/Galatians at its *Under-/Outside*, sons of the rebellious arch-mother Gaia, to the victims sacrificed at the altar on the *In-/Upside*.[114] In a similar way, on Virgil's Shield of Aeneas, the dead Egyptians, Oriental monster gods, and their army, together with the defeated barbarian queen and her shameful lover Antony, would be connected to the slaughtered bulls in front of Rome's sacrificial altars.[115] Both images have their prototypes in the *Enuma Elish* and establish the totality of cosmos, civilization, and universal city—Babylon, Pergamon, Rome—on strikingly similar foundations of primeval matricide, fratricide, and ecocide. World battle and world city, triumph and sacrifice in this profoundly occidental version of the creation myth share the same dark secret, which is hidden on their underside and ritually enacted in the liminal space of the arena: the collective consumption of "mother" nature, and of human flesh and blood.

Arena Ritual as Human Sacrifice

The sacrificial dimension of the arena is a matter of debate among scholars, strongly rejected by some, much affirmed by others.[116] While the link between ritual sacrifice and archetypal combat is quite obvious in the Great Altar of Pergamon, the arena is clearly not a proper sacrificial site marked as sacred space. There is no altar directly involved; the victims are not offered by priests; the cultic connection to deities who need to be pleased or reconciled in order to reintegrate the community is less obvious. On the other hand, the arena does embrace undeniably sacrificial elements: it is a carefully segregated space; the events taking place are precisely regulated and publicly staged with ritual, religious, and mythological overtones; blood is the key component, with the slaughter of animals and humans occurring within the framework of public ceremony and festival, and with profound implications for the protection and reconstitution of community. Further, the games can be seen to have a cathartic effect by vicariously eliminating violence and evil dwelling not only outside but also inside the social body, for example, in terms of slave or gladiatorial rebellions, treachery, and civil wars. The social body is purified through the sacrifice of victims that represent specific types of threat and dangerous otherness. Violence and rebellion endangering social cohesion from within are redirected against the outside and neutralized through presenting a scapegoat other as target.

Keith Hopkins therefore states that "in gladiatorial contests and in wild beast shows, the Romans came very close . . . to performing human sacrifice."[117] Coleman observes a link between sacrificial atonement, scapegoat rituals and arena executions that are staged as mythological role-play. The death of the victim expelled from his/her community achieves "the reintegration of that community as a homogenous group that has expiated its guilt."[118] Plass, drawing on René Girard and R. G. Hamerton-Kelly, points to the protective function of the arena, which helps to manage deadly violence and conflict inside society by projecting it on scapegoat-outsiders who vicariously process and exorcise it in a controlled environment.[119] Plass also sees a connection between the arena and mass human sacrifices, for example, in the Aztec culture, which were performed for public entertainment, intimidation, and power display and in response to the perceived threat of instability and chaos. According to Aztec myth, the universe would perish if the sun did not receive the required amount of blood. Like the Aztecs, the Romans made "raw energy . . . available to deal with the threat of disorder" when they publicly spent and collectively consumed human blood, human life, and human pain on a mass scale to reestablish cosmic and social order. [120]

> In the scale and focus on physical danger, *munera* have few parallels and seem most comparable as an institution to the mass human sacrifice practiced in ancient Mesoamerica. At the tops of pyramids, victims, sometimes by the thousands, had their chest slit open and their hearts torn out in a spray of blood to be offered, still throbbing, to the sun. The bodies were then tumbled down steep, blood smeared steps running to the ground, where they might be skinned and have parts taken for consumption at banquets.... Next to the pyramids stood great racks containing thousands of skulls from previous sacrifices, to register, as the scale of games at Rome did, the importance of extraordinary violence publicly consumed.[121]

Alison Futrell, following Hyam Maccoby, puts specific emphasis on another aspect crucial for our focus on city and civilization: the connection between human sacrifice and the "foundational events" in the history of a city, nation, tribe, or religion when the community needs to be "reborn" and reassured through the offering of human life.[122] Reminded of the early association of the *munera* with state crises, Futrell sees the ritual combat of the arena as a kind of (subconscious) reenactment of the archetypal slaughtering of Remus by his brother Romulus, which she interprets as a "foundational sacrifice" for the city of Rome.[123] In the critical time at the end of the Republic when Augustus acts as a new founder of Rome, the reinvention of this primeval sacrifice on a much larger scale both reflects and protects the emerging empire. The pattern of the Roman *munera* thus "can be identified with the mythic foundations of the Roman State and with the fundamental institutions of the Roman Empire. The regular refounding of the state through gladiatorial sacrifice would be a source of renewal for the empire. ... The arena was the embodiment of the empire."[124]

Strange as it may sound for today: from a Roman perspective the most barbaric rites of death and torture in the arenas were a highly sophisticated and efficient (from the standpoint of mass psychology) school of civilizing the city, inspiring imperial piety, and celebrating Roman victory and the new worldwide family of Caesar's offspring. In the arena everyone became a worshiper of imperial religion under the divine Caesar, and everyone participated actively in the resurrection and new creation of the well-ordered imperial world out of dying enemies and the life-giving spirit of unconditional struggle and ultimate victory. In the arena everyone was born again him- or herself as a participant, subject, and soldier of the empire, in Rome as well as in Gaul or Galatia.

Conclusion: Paul and the Messianic Clash of Monotheisms

This chapter has dealt with the images and concept of imperial religion, seen through the lens of Virgil's Shield of Aeneas and the Roman arenas, and their "archetypes" in the

Great Altar and *Enuma Elish*. Our exploration of the amphitheater has revealed how the Roman games as mass medium of imperial ideology constructed civic self(hood) and oneness by immersing their spectators in powerful flesh-and-blood images of the other as enemy to be lawfully humiliated and eliminated, dehumanized, tortured, punished, and fought against. This is linked to a fundamentally religious dimension of the arenas as "megachurches" of the empire where the blood of the other/them was collectively consumed in a quasi-sacrificial public ritual that created, educated, justified, and united *us* as the one-self of the imperial civic body, compliant with Roman law, order, and religion. In particular we have noted how crucifixions are firmly embedded in the overall framework of the arena performance, and how they are (at least virtually) present in its marble counterpart at the Gigantomachy frieze of Pergamon.

Roman religion, as it turns out, is not just an isolated aspect of Paul's reality but permeates the whole of the social fabric and is omnipresent as a decisive cultural, political, ideological factor wherever he moves. It is not and not even primarily restricted to the emperor cult but comprises the entire conceptual system of a universal religion and ideology that construct god(s), the world, and humanity in the likeness of the imperial world order. Imposing its image of victory and power, self and other, imperial salvation and new creation universally on cosmos and human society, leaving nothing and no one out, Roman imperial religion functioned, on the one hand, as a totalizing and aggressively missionary world religion, while at the same time tolerating and protecting the wide variety of different cults and religions already in place in the empire.

Drawing on the legitimating power of the cosmogonic Giant battle myth, imperial religion bestowed supreme divinity on Caesar as sole world creator, single world ruler, and the *one* world god. Within an entirely polytheistic framework, and the undeniable mortality of Caesar as human being notwithstanding, it thus operated in a quasi-monotheistic manner. As it left the traditional plurality of polytheistic religions intact, it simultaneously impregnated them with a new logic and a new chief deity, Caesar, and thereby became a hybrid meta-religion of high flexibility and adaptability. It meticulously maintained the discourse of "traditional religion" and showcased Caesar's piety and submission to the gods, yet on the operational level it practiced a "functional monotheism" with Caesar at its center. It generously tolerated and integrated diverse cults and gods in an efficient syncretism from above, as long as they were compliant with the imperial superstructure—an issue that made certain outsider religions appear suspicious again and again, for example, Celtic/Galatian Druids, Jewish believers, and Christians.

Nowhere does the "clash of images" between Paul's messianic and Caesar's imperial theology, both of them sharing an astonishing amount of common terminology, become more tangible than in the Roman amphitheater. A most powerful show event, the arena is not only the liminal space where the empire rehearses its "new creation" of world and humankind; it is also the social and symbolic space where Paul's most subversive image is located: the image of God-Self being crucified as lawless and worthless other or, conversely, of a crucified lawless and worthless other being resurrected, vindicated, enthroned as God-Self. With this, the imperial image of the world, of god(s), and of human is turned upside down. From a Roman perspective, Paul's preaching of "Christ crucified" is an act of unprecedented iconoclasm that makes the Dying Gauls/Galatians all of a sudden "un-dying," as if the Pergamene Giants were set loose against city and civilization again.

The images and conceptualizations of an imperial gospel, an imperial new creation, an imperial world God and savior, an imperial divine benefactor of humanity at the turn of a new age take Paul's dispute in Galatia into a context where it has rarely been located thus far. It seems that the theological semiotics of Jewish law versus Pauline gospel, which has been foundational for Christian and especially Protestant readings of Galatians throughout the centuries, is in urgent need of revision. What if the primary clash took place not between Christ and the Jewish God in Galatia, but between Paul's Jewish God-in-Christ and the imperial god-in-Caesar? What if the target of Paul's universal and inclusive gospel is not the partial exclusivism of Jewish law, but the universal exclusivism of an imperial world order and world religion under the divine Caesar? If criticism of "works of the law" was directed not at Jewish works and Jewish law but rather at the competitive, combative, and consumptive logic of self versus other inscribed in the innermost core of imperial law in all its "workings," including the "good works" of Caesar's euergetism? What if the Galatian controversy does not primarily concern Jews and Christians at all, but rather Jewish-messianic monotheism disputing the claims of imperial monotheism?

As we shall see in chapter 6, Paul's argument in Galatians is indeed strongly shaped by a passionate argument for the oneness of the biblical God alone, an argument that has been widely neglected exegetically as it did not fit into the reductionist hermeneutics of Paul-against-Judaism. Yet it owns a striking plausibility when read in the context of a dispute with the oneness and singularity of the divine Caesar. The clash of monotheisms, however, is not predominantly based on an abstract concept of biblical monotheism as such. What seems to concern Paul much more than dogmatics are the concrete images of heaven and earth, human and divine that Caesar imposes, and the concrete practices that are embedded in them: not only the image of the world created out of blood and battle but also the split of humanity into deserving and undeserving as core of the new imperial Genesis narrative. This is where Paul's wrestling with a new type of oneness and community has its setting in life: concrete everyday life practices that transform the blood-drenched oneness of the nations *in Caesar* into a messianic mutuality and solidarity of weak and strong, insiders and outsiders, Jews and Gentiles/nations *in Christ*.

With this, we have anticipated core elements of our reading of Galatians in chapter 6. Before we can explore these textual issues further, we must take another close look at the historical context of Paul's Galatians and his Galatian letter. The amphitheater as surrogate political assembly was the place where the Roman pledge of allegiance and civic code of conduct were collectively recited through images. In their function as the political temples and "megachurches" of the empire, the arenas visualized, memorized, and confessed the credo of imperial religion in multimedia shows all over the world before tens of thousands of audience members, or perhaps—dare we say?—*congregants*.

Yet no one needed to read letters, as the letters became flesh and blood and spelled themselves out in images of "righteous" triumph over deviant life to be consumed for the higher ends of Roman survival, in the arenas of Gaul as well as Galatia.

But how did this "baptism" into the body of Caesar concretely function in Roman Galatia in Paul's time? What were the images there that interacted with his letter, trying to make it unreadable? In the next chapter we will turn to the province of Galatia in order to get a clearer understanding of how the resurrection of the Dying Gauls/Galatians functioned on Caesar's terms, that is, what the lawful and orderly subject formation and integration of Paul's Galatians into the imperial body would have looked like.

Gaia (Gē) with her cornucopia. The earth-goddess, half-buried in the ground and pleading in vain for the life of her son Alkyoneus, is subdued by Nikē and Athena, the victorious deities of city and civilization who will reap the fruit of her fertility. Detail of the scene on the East Frieze shown on p. 93. Photo: Jakob B. Rehmann.

CHAPTER FOUR

Roman Galatia

The Imperial Resurrection of the
Dying Gauls/Galatians (189 B.C.E.–50 C.E.)

At this point we turn from Rome to Roman Galatia and to the native country of the Dying Gauls/Galatians. The concrete circumstances of Paul's first stay there are completely unknown, though the overall setting must have been somewhat dramatic, as Gal 4:12-15 indicates. At some point in the 40s of the first century C.E., a Jewish foreigner in deplorable physical condition receives Galatian hospitality far beyond the measure to be expected. Subsequently, messianic communities emerge in Galatia. In the early 50s Paul writes them a letter that addresses them as "assemblies/churches [*ekklēsiai*] of Galatia" (Gal 1:2). We continue to focus on these Galatians who welcomed the stranger Paul. All the enigmas that cloud our perception of the Galatian congregations notwithstanding, there are at least two things we can say about them with certainty: they live in a Roman province (Gal 1:2), no matter whether in the north or south, and they are called by a name that at this time no longer simply indicates Celtic ethnicity but has become a universal moniker for defeated and rehabilitated barbarians, as well as the official political designation for a number of different nations or tribes (*ethnē*) united as *Galatians* in this very province of Galatia (Gal 3:1). And we can say something else: that Paul is furious at recent developments among the messianic followers in Galatia and thinks they are now being "stupid" (3:1).

The provincial *Sitz im Leben*, rather than being eclipsed or depoliticized into a matter of merely geographical location, as in standard theological readings, needs to be taken seriously as the primary sociohistorical context of the Galatian correspondence in a much more comprehensive way. Who are the people addressed as "You stupid Galatians" (3:1) in the concrete environment of a Roman province named after them, and why would the fairly marginal events around their encounter with Paul at some point grow into a serious challenge to the empire? This chapter focuses on a reconstruction of facts and facets that are part of this overall contextual framework and that may help us to re-imagine the larger picture implicitly reflected in Paul's quarrel with the Galatian communities over circumcision: pieces of their day-to-day reality under Roman rule that give the Judaizing circumcision demands and Paul's messianic counterproposal a relevance far beyond the scope of Jewish law and Jewish religion. At the center of this exploration is the complex process of an imperial acculturation that exposes the Galatians of Paul's time to multiple imperial interventions and pressures, benefactions and rewards, hierarchies and obligations that are gradually transforming their existence, imprinting the grammar of Roman rule on their bodies and minds. What we are going to examine is nothing less than the astounding metamorphosis that eventually resurrected, over a period of about 250 years, the lawless and barbarian Dying Galatians of Asia Minor as law-abiding subjects, servants, and soldiers of the Roman Empire.

The Pergamene imagery in this exploration is crucial as an auxiliary context and looking glass that may help us to visualize the conceptual world that descended on Galatia in the process of its Romanization—the symbolic universe thrown as a web of new meanings, honors, rituals, practices, deities, identities, and affiliations over what used to be enemy territory. For the law and order that were established when the Romans remodeled the client-kingdoms of Deiotaros and Amyntas into one of their provinces were precisely the law and order exhibited at the Great Altar of Pergamon in all its beauty and mercilessness. In other words, the four most notable supports of Roman civilization and peace to be constituted among the former barbarians of Galatia exactly mirror the values defended in the ancient Giant battle and celebrated in Telephos's upper room: victory, dynasty, city, and piety.

In the first section, we will look at the genesis of Galatian Romanization between 189 and 25 B.C.E., with a focus on the establishment of dynasty, genealogy, and power, on the one hand, and military formation, on the other. Next we will explore the crucial importance of cities and imperial piety for the process of an imperial "repatriation" of the fatherless Giants/Galatians in the period immediately following the foundation of the Galatian province in 25 B.C.E. The third part will be a case study of imperial religion that investigates the public banquets and games donated by the imperial *koinon* at Ancyra. As works of imperial piety and euergetism (beneficence), they implanted the *In/Out* and *High/Low* structures of the Roman order into the provincial body of Galatia, a transformation that again had its prototype in the Great Altar and, in a sense, represents its ongoing performance.

The notion of these benefactions as works of law—no less than the overall process of a corporate genealogical realignment, rehabilitation (or "justification"), and repatriation of the Galatian nations/tribes within imperial law and order—steers our interpretation of Paul's critique of "works of law" and his theology of justification and faith into new and still uncharted territory.

Dynasty and Military: The Giants' Transfiguration into Subjects and Soldiers of Rome (189–25 B.C.E.)

How did the Galatians as prototypical Giants/outsiders and evil other of Greco-Roman civilization eventually make their way *up* and *into* the imperial order, as it was symbolically represented in the Great Stairway and Telephos's upper room at the Pergamon

Altar? Certainly this process was started much earlier than the provincial foundation in 25 B.C.E.[1] And except for a small Galatian ruling caste, for the majority of the
Galatians getting *in* meant accepting their place at the bottom of the Roman order
with obligations in terms of subjugation, or servitude, including the duties of paying
taxes and military service. The imposition of order on the barbarian chaos through the
buildup of dynasties and power structures, on the one hand, and military formation,
on the other, are two key mechanisms for assimilating the lawless Galatians to Roman
law that we will study first.

Barbarians, Hybrids, Noble(wo)men: The Galatians Turn Roman

In the early decades of the first century B.C.E., another one of Rome's most frightening
archenemies had risen in Asia Minor: Mithridates VI of Pontus. Residing in Pergamon, he was hailed as king and liberator of Roman Asia. Plutarch, whose account we
will follow, reports an interesting incident (*Sulla* 11). In order to pay their reverence
to the new emerging superpower, the Pergamenes decided to honor Mithridates with
a crown of victory. The event was planned as a spectacular performance in the great
theater on the slope of the Pergamon acropolis, immediately next to the Great Altar.
Special machinery was built and designed to lower the goddess Nikē/Victory herself
so that she could place the crown on Mithridates' head from above. The setting mirrors
the Athena-Nikē scene on the Great Frieze above the theater, where Nikē flies in to
bestow the token of triumph on the victorious Giant-slaying city-goddess Athena (see
chap. 2, fig. 20). But this time a terrible accident takes place. Through some failure of
the technical equipment, Nikē breaks into pieces the moment before she touches the
usurper, and the crown goes tumbling down from her hand to the middle of the theater.
One could see this scene not only as a gloomy portent for Mithridates, then at the apex
of his power, as Plutarch does in retrospect. Nikē refused him the symbolic capital of a
victory in the Giant battle, that is, the license to power. Yet off stage and implicitly, this
incident also conveyed a message about the Galatians and their changing relationship
to Rome, in which Mithridates had some stake. Roughly a century after Manlius Vulso's
devastating campaign of 189 B.C.E. and the erection of the Great Altar, Mithridates
had made the city of Pergamon the site of another large-scale Galatian massacre in Asia
Minor. In the initial phase of his three wars against Rome (89–63 B.C.E.), Mithridates
invited sixty leading men of the Galatian tribes to a banquet in Pergamon in 86 B.C.E.,
where he attempted to murder them all. Only three of the intended victims escaped.
In his account, Appian says that Mithridates distrusted the Galatians as potentially
being pro-Roman (*Hist. rom.* 12.46).[2] Galatian loyalty was apparently undergoing a
transformation.

Two years before, in 88 B.C.E., Mithridates had organized the slaughter of all Romans
and Italians in the cities of Asia, who obviously welcomed him as liberator from the
Roman yoke, including Ephesus and Pergamon. Appian reports frightful scenes and
atrocities. Women, children, and slaves of Italian origin were not spared, nor was the

sacred right of temple asylum respected: "The Ephesians tore away the fugitives, who had taken refuge in the temple of Artemis, and were clasping the images of the goddess, and slew them. The Pergamenes shot with arrows those who had fled to the temple of Aesculapius, while they were still clinging to the statues" (*Hist. rom.* 12.23). The number of Roman victims is usually given as eighty thousand. This shows that during forty years of Roman rule, many business-minded people must have found it profitable to move to Asia.[3] Yet the harsh exploitation imposed by the Roman tax-farming system after the transferal of Pergamene sovereignty to Rome in 133 B.C.E. and the accumulation of wealth in the hands of Roman tax gatherers, merchants, and bankers had become intolerable for the inhabitants of the newly founded province of Asia. Mithridates therefore won support among the lower and disenfranchised parts of the population by offering freedom to slaves and cancellations of half the debts to debtors if they slew their Roman masters and creditors (*Hist. rom.* 12.22).[4]

The Galatians initially were divided in their allegiance. Galatian troops fought in the army of Mithridates before the Pergamon massacre (*Hist. rom.* 12.41), and even at the end of his life, betrayed by all and surrounded by enemies, there was a faithful Celtic officer named Bituitus who was entrusted by Mithridates with the assistance in his suicide (*Hist.rom.* 12.111). But overall, the year 86 B.C.E. marks a decisive turning point with far-reaching consequences. Mithridates' bloody banquet turned the Galatians almost naturally into allies of Rome. Thus, if the mass execution of the Galatian nobility at Pergamon and in the tribal territories visually evokes the scenes depicted on the Great Frieze, there is also a decisive difference. This time the Galatians die not as enemies but as supposed allies of Rome.

Nikē's reluctance to crown Mithridates in Plutarch's episode symbolically points out that victory, that most precious gift from heaven, belongs to Rome alone, the lawful ruler of Pergamon and Asia, the legitimate heir of the Attalids and of Heracles, as well as the worthy ally of the gods in their fight against chaos and destruction. Yet Nikē implicitly also demonstrates that slaughtering Galatians is no longer entirely necessary to prove a ruler's legitimacy and the righteousness of his cause. Mithridates made the Galatians die side by side with the Romans, to whom victory rightfully belonged. In terms of the Great Altar, they have thus undergone a miraculous metamorphosis, moving metaphorically, and by virtue of their bloody sacrifice, from the *underside* and o*utside* to the *inside* and *upside* of city and civilization. Now it is Mithridates who faces his downturn and shameful expulsion, like the Giants/Galatians of the Great Altar, whereas the Galatians somehow belong *in*. The anti-citizens are on their way to citizenship.

This tendency is reflected in Plutarch's book about brave and virtuous women, which movingly reports the heroic deed of a Pergamene woman who dared to bury her Galatian lover, one of the victims of the Mithridatic massacre (*Mor.* 259). Yet already in Livy's account of the Roman victory over the Seleucids and Galatians in Asia Minor, the simple stereotype of Galatian, as barbarian reversal of Greco-Roman civilization, is no longer universally applicable. Reporting about the campaign of Manlius Vulso in 189 B.C.E., Livy offers three categories of enemies—the barbarian, the hybrid, and the noble Gaul/Galatian. This triple typology reflects a complex dialectic between subjugation and co-optation.

On the one hand, Livy has Manlius Vulso justify his action, as we have seen in chapter 1 above, by referring to the standard barbarian vices of the Gauls. Their irreconcilable otherness is uncompromisingly affirmed: their uncivilized character and deadly hatred of the name of Rome, their reign of terror over Pergamon and the cities of Asia, their practice of human sacrifice, their sack of Delphi (the common oracle of the human race and the navel of the world), and the intolerable threat a persistent Galatian strength would present to the newly won Roman control over Asia Minor (38.47–48).

Yet this well-known standard repertoire of anti-barbarian/Galatian rhetoric is significantly expanded and supplemented. When addressing his soldiers before the campaign against the Galatians, Livy's Manlius reassuringly, though somewhat self-contradictingly, tells them that their opponents are no longer real Celts, but a hybrid and mixed race called *Gallograeci*. They are less dangerous, as they have degenerated into something like "Phrygians" (seen as proverbially effeminate and slavish), losing their fierceness and being tamed by the pleasantness of Asia, which Romans as the "men of Mars" must avoid—obviously one of Livy's favorite subjects (38.47).[5]

Even more surprising is an anecdote Livy adds a little later, while still narrating the campaign in Asia Minor. He provides the example of an outstandingly beautiful and dignified captive Galatian woman who happens to be the wife of the Tolistobogian chieftain Ortagion. Raped by a Roman centurion and subsequently allowed to return home for a large sum of money, she orders the two Galatian emissaries who brought the ransom to kill the centurion. She takes his head, wrapped in her garment, back to her husband as token of her marital fidelity (38.24).[6] Even more than Chiomara, as her name is given by Polybius (21.38) and Plutarch (*Mor.* 258*)*, her husband is praised. He obviously not only survived the massacre of Manlius Vulso but was the first who (unsuccessfully) tried to unite the Galatian tribes in Asia Minor under a single ruler and ignite resistance to Pergamon even after the peace of Apamea (188 B.C.E.). Nevertheless, Ortagion is considered properly hellenized and no longer barbarian. Polybius (22.21) reports that he was a man of remarkable charm, intelligence, humanity, and martial prowess.

The introduction of Ortagion and his wife as the first officially *good* Galatians in Asia Minor is not accidental. As Stephen Mitchell states, they "are the earliest aristocratic couple to produce a son whose name is known and who held a position of influence in Galatian society." Before that, there is no evidence "for elaborate genealogies, indeed even the parentage of most Galatian chieftains is unrecorded."[7] We here touch on a key element in the imperial transfiguration of the former Giants into subjects and soldiers of the Roman order. What obviously counts more than the murder of a Roman officer is that Chiomara and Ortagion are the representatives of an incipient model of proper hereditary dynasty and power. It is first through developing a stable and predictable indigenous power structure that the barbarians become civilized.

Deiotaros: Rule and Dynasty as Entrée into City/Civilization

As we saw in our semiotic analysis of the Great Altar, the way *up* at the Great Staircase and *into* the upper room requires submission in contrast to rebellion, and the acceptance of law rather than lawlessness. The core issue is the existence and acknowledgment of a divinely ordained hierarchy that sets rulers above the ruled (*High* versus *Low*). A first step toward the imperial "resurrection" of the Dying Gauls, and their admission to the *upside* of city and civilization, thus is their transformation into subjects of a native monarchy. To implant and secure its own power structures as efficiently as possible, Roman rule abroad generally needed a reliable, indigenous power base with a well-defined hierarchy that possessed long-term stability granted through hereditary rule.

From this perspective, Mithridates' decapitation of the Galatian hierarchy served Roman interests very well in the long term. The three Celtic tribes entering Asia Minor in the third century had probably been led by a fluid, charismatic warrior aristocracy that consisted of numerous chieftains who divided authority among themselves without long-term dynastic claims.[8] This archaic and to some extent anarchic tribal structure would not have been suitable for Roman purposes. The extent to which it was barbarian is quite a different question. Strabo, a native of Asia Minor, in his famous account on the political organization of the Galatians in book 12 of his *Geography* describes the Celtic constitution "of the old days" as a very well structured entity. The three tribes were each ruled by four tetrarchs, with each of these twelve leaders being assisted by a judge, a military commander, and two junior commanders. These sixty leaders gathered in a larger council of three hundred men at the so-called *Drynemetos*, where matters of common importance were discussed and murder cases judged. Strabo also mentions that in his own time—he was born around 70 B.C.E.—"power has passed to three, then to two and then to a single ruler, namely Deiotarus, and then to Amyntas who succeeded him" (Strabo 12.5.1).

This traditional political system of the Celts in Asia Minor had, undeniably, been a well-ordered and highly complex one. Mitchell sees this sophistication chiefly as the result of the "civilizing influence of Pergamum and the other kingdoms of Asia Minor," yet also adds the slightly contradictory observation that the overall structure "was a feature of all Celtic societies," including the Helvetii in the Alps and the Cantii in Britain.[9] However, according to Mitchell the transition from sixty to only three leaders, as mentioned by Strabo, probably reflects the effects of the Mithridatic massacre that destroyed the traditional Celtic system of rule. This transformation was also propelled by the ambitions of the three surviving chieftains, who entered into a fierce power struggle. The ensuing dynamics clearly helped Rome establish its own power within Galatian society. For Rome, "now more seriously involved in Anatolian politics than ever before, had a vested interest in a strong and coherent leadership."[10]

No one among the Galatians of the first century B.C.E. was able to represent the strength and coherence of a pro-Roman leadership more aptly than the Tolistobogian Deiotaros, one of the three surviving Galatian chieftains after Mithridates' slaughter.

With remarkable shrewdness, prowess, and brutality, he managed in the next four decades to become the sole ruler of all Galatian tribes and an indispensable pillar of Roman rule, similar to the Pergamenes earlier. Rome gradually built him into a client ruler and finally granted him the official title of king in 59 B.C.E. Twelve years later, in 47 B.C.E., he had all Galatian tribal territory under his authority. After his death in 40 B.C.E., Amyntas became the last significant Galatian ruler in this area.

At the same time, other descendants of Galatian nobility were entrusted with governing kingdoms in Asia Minor. This reflects the overall process of gradual Galatian self-colonization that replaced the former pluralistic warrior aristocracy with a more permanent and centralized form of power. Ruling dynastic families now established themselves, taking over the position of the traditional warrior leaders whose "chief claim to authority had been their personal prowess."[11] In the course of the first century B.C.E., Rome began to rely heavily on these indigenous leading families of an emerging Galatian dynastic nobility. Mitchell observes that one of the most striking features of the political rearrangement of Anatolia under Mark Antony and later Augustus was the prominence of Galatian chieftains.[12] Apart from a few exceptions, "virtually the whole of central and north-eastern Anatolia was ruled by Gauls."[13] It is obvious that the term *Galatians* had become synonymous with loyalty to Rome and was no longer restricted to a specific tribal area. But one has to be careful: it was the Galatian upper caste, not the commoners, on which Roman rule relied, especially after the foundation of Roman Galatia.

When Galatia became a Roman province in 25 B.C.E., the leading families continued to be vital to Roman provincial administration. However, this family-based character of Roman rule under Augustus had two sides. As William M. Ramsay observes, on the one hand these families' political power was broken insofar as it rested on priesthood in the service of the traditional gods, including the supervision and exploitation of the large temple estates. "The supreme god was the Emperor; and the power and the lands of the local god belonged to the Emperor, who was the manifestation of the divine power."[14] But, on the other hand, the local nobility was by no means impoverished or doomed to insignificance. They became imperial priests, served as magistrates in the cities, and could maintain their economic power if they collaborated with Rome. In short, Augustus "enabled them to retain their honors and wealth in the services of the Empire."[15]

Later, we encounter high-ranking officials who claimed descent from this old Galatian nobility, for example, Paul's contemporary Julia Severa or the Ancyran C. Julius Severus in the second century C.E.[16] But the dynastic principle meanwhile took an interesting twist. It integrated the royal houses not only of Galatia but also of the former archenemy Pergamon. C. Julius Severus, Roman senator under Hadrian, is called a descendant of King Deiotarus and of King Attalus, and so were his relatives C. Antius A. Iulius Quadratus and C. Iulius Bassus, who under Vespasian were the first Galatians to became Roman senators.[17] The precise origin of this dynastic link between Galatians and the Attalids is unclear; one possibility is that King Deiotaros's wife, Stratonike, was a member of the Attalid house.[18] At any rate, Pergamene records for the late Roman

Republican era in Pergamon testify to close connections of the city with Galatian royalty.[19]

Legio XXII Deiotariana: "Dying Giants" Revived

King Deiotaros undoubtedly succeeded in establishing the new category of the "civi-lized" Gaul/Galatian—the barbarian transformed to fit Roman categories and inter-ests—on the Roman stage. He could read and quote Greek; a statue of him was erected at Athens; and his palace at Blucium was comfortable enough to host Julius Caesar upon his return from Pontus in 47 B.C.E.[20] The extent of his Hellenization and Roman-ization—and that of the rest of the Galatian aristocracy—is shown in a grand speech delivered by Cicero in the house of Julius Caesar in 45 B.C.E. The content and context of this oration are remarkable. Following the stay of Caesar in his palace, Deiotaros is accused by his grandson Castor of plotting to murder his most distinguished guest. Cicero makes a magnificent speech of defense that obviously has the desired effect. Deiotaros leaves Rome a free man and, upon his return home, puts Castor's father, the tetrarch of the Tectosages, and his mother—Deiotaros's own daughter—to death, thus becoming effectively the single ruler of all Galatia.[21]

In an astonishing catalogue of virtues and achievements, Cicero's speech "In favor of King Deiotaros" (*Pro rege Deiotaro*) praises the Galatian as a most trustworthy friend and close ally of the Romans who represents all virtues of the civilized, especially mod-eration and temperance (26, 37) as well as unfaltering loyalty (*fides;* 16), who received manifold honors from the Roman senate, including his royal rank as king (14, 27, 36), who is a very close friend of the empire (*huic imperio amicissimus;* 11) who would never have thought of extinguishing Caesar as "the fairest light of all nations" and the "van-quisher of the world" (*omnium gentium clarissimum lumen; victorem orbis terrarum;* 15). The stark contrast to an earlier oration is noteworthy; in *Pro Fonteio* Cicero had mounted a series of hateful attacks against Gauls/Galatians as entirely untrustworthy barbarians.[22] There, they are described as the notorious enemies of Rome, the gods, and the law of civilized humanity, whereas the Galatian Deiotaros now is presented as fully devoted to waging the wars of the Roman people (6), as he deems Caesar's enemies his own (15).

The latter remark is of particular concern. The prototypical enemy combatants now are officially acknowledged as soldiers of the empire. This points to a second core requirement in the Galatian "resurrection" as subjects of Rome, next to rule and dynasty building. If Mithridates basically made the Galatians die side by side with the Romans, this was a concrete portent for future Roman–Galatian relationships: the Dying Galatians are allowed to live once they are ready to die at the right side and for the right cause. They are admitted as subjects of Caesar when entering his legions and auxiliary forces to subject the world to him.

A few examples may illustrate how Deiotaros's power becomes a virtually inex-haustible resource of soldiers, administrative and financial assistance, military and diplomatic support, and money for Rome. When Lucullus leads his five legions against Mithridates in 72 B.C.E., he can count on thirty thousand Galatians to carry grain for his soldiers (Plutarch, *Lucullus* 14.1; Appian, *Mith.* 78). During his time as governor of Cilicia in 50–51 B.C.E., Cicero not only became a close friend of Deiotaros, conversing with him about religious matters and entrusting his two young children to him, but he also had twelve thousand Galatian infantry and two thousand cavalry led by Deiotaros at his disposal during the Parthian threat (Cicero, *Att.* 6.1). Brutus was assisted by Deiotaros when he tried to recover debts from Ariobrazanes of Cappadozia (ibid. 6.1). At the battle of Pharsalus in 47 B.C.E. against Caesar, Pompey had about one thousand Galatian soldiers and King Deiotaros himself at his side (Caesar, *Bell. civ.* 3.4.5). Fortunately, after Pompey's defeat, Deiotaros was backed by Brutus and managed to be pardoned by Caesar, getting away with a comparatively small penalty, thus remaining the most powerful ruler in Anatolia.

It is interesting that Deiotaros's troops, which proved so invaluable to the Romans, presumably were no longer fighting in the traditional Celtic way but were trained in the Roman manner and were organized in two legions. King Amyntas, Deiotaros's successor, probably took them over, and after him Augustus. With Amyntas's rule, the actual center of power moved from North Galatia south into the Taurus region, which was inhabited by rebellious tribes that were a major concern to Rome. As a loyal client king and ally of Rome, Amyntas set out to subdue the independent mountain settlements of the Isaurians and Pisidians. His contemporary Strabo vividly describes the villages of Isauria as "settlements of robbers" and a source of much trouble to the Romans (12.6.2). We are reminded of earlier reports on the Galatian settlements in Asia Minor themselves.

Amyntas conducted several successful campaigns in these areas and captured many places previously believed to be impregnable, for example, Isauria, which he turned into his massively fortified capital.[23] In the middle of these intense efforts to wipe out resistance among the intransigent mountaineers, however, after only five years of full power, Amyntas lost his life in a fight against the large and fierce tribe of the Homonadeis, shamefully vanquished by a woman, the wife of the chieftain he had killed.[24] This unfinished war of the last Galatian king was later, after the province of Galatia had already been established, completed by Publius Sulpicius Quirinius ("Cyrinius"). Between 6 B.C.E. and 4 C.E. he exterminated the Homonadeis as a tribe.[25] His success in Pisidia was hailed as a victory of great importance and earned him the insignia of the purpel toga and laurel wreath in Rome.[26] Only a little later, as governor of Syria, this same Quirinius who had already brought the wild Berber tribes of Libya under Roman rule would order the census in Palestine (6/7 C.E.) that plays a prominent role in Luke's birth narrative of Jesus (Luke 2:2).

With a Galatian king and Galatian soldiers sacrificing their lives in the Roman battle against "Giant" barbarian forces of chaos and disorder, Galatia once more is symbolically transferred from its *Underside/Outside* location in the spatial order of the Great Altar. It has moved *up* and *in* and become a full member of the Roman world. When Augustus directly steps in after Amyntas's death and turns the Galatian client kingdom into the Roman province of Galatia, already three Roman legions show strong recruitment from the former areas of Amyntas and other Galatian chieftains.[27] In addition, Augustus inherits from Amyntas the Roman-trained forces of Deiotaros, which are integrated into the *Legio XXII,* which soon would be called *Deiotariana.*[28] The bestowal of this name upon a Roman legion is not only an official acknowledgment of King Deiotaros's crucial role in the process of military and political integration but also the triumphant proof that four centuries of Greco-Roman warfare against "Galatia" have indeed been crowned by ultimate victory.

Although archeological evidence is widely lacking, Mitchell assumes a strong impact of Rome's military presence all throughout Anatolia. Basically, the communities had to supply soldiers, food, housing, equipment, and services to the army on a very large scale so that "dues and taxation in kind, to provide the armies with their daily needs, weighed heavily on all the country districts. Military recruitment was an institution that directly affected remote mountaineous areas, the main source of new soldiers, and cities, which often commuted their obligations into cash payments. Few communities were not directly affected by the multifarious demands of the Roman army."[29] Tacitus mentions a conscription conducted in Galatia and Cappadocia in preparation for Corbulo's campaign in Armenia in 54 C.E. (*Ann.* 13.35.1), that is, very close to the time when Paul wrote to the Galatians.[30] Enlistment was usually not voluntary but forced, even though military service offered an opportunity to acquire higher status and privileges such as citizenship.

The integration of the Galatians into the legions and auxiliary forces not only served military but also educational and political purposes. It trained a whole class of new citizens who were now proudly bearing their Latin names, and who had risked their lives for and made a living on the Roman order, being stationed for twenty or more years of their lifetime in different places of the world. The army in itself with its strictly hierarchical command structure and internal organization was an image of the Roman order.[31] If the recruits returned to their former countries as veterans, they held a privileged status and usually would continue to propagate and protect the Roman way of life.[32] As Ramsay observes, "They became all loyal Romans, entering the service at an impressionable age, and owing to the Empire their education, experience, skills in the use of weapons, discipline, amusements. . . . A new social class was created gradually by Rome for Rome."[33] In this way the Legio XXII Deiotariana models how "lawless Galatians" could win symbolic entrance through the Great Staircase: embodying supreme order with their own lives, they are now confronting the chaos of rebellion from *outside* and *below,* fighting like Heracles at the Great Frieze under the Roman eagle and on the side of the officially acclaimed deities against whoever is declared an enemy of Roman law.

The price, however, for the Galatians to be allowed into the civilized universe was accepting their own defeat, as well as the order of victory and defeat itself. Whenever a Galatian was permitted to climb up the Great Staircase, he or she had to accept the boundary between *In* and *Out, High* and *Low* that was set in stone. The Galatian self had to negotiate its own way *up* and *in* by stepping symbolically on the others at the underside and outside who were opposing Rome, turning against the contemporary "Giants" of whatever ethnicity and location—the Galatians' own former self now emerging as hostile and evil other. The contradictory mechanism of this self-subjection is challenged, according to Tacitus, by the Batavian insurgent general Civilis, who united Gallic and German tribes in the West against Rome in 69/70 c.e. Tacitus has Civilis address his rebel forces with the following incendiary statements:

> What if the Gallic provincials should throw off the yoke? What forces are there left in Italy? It is by the blood of the provinces that provinces are won. Do not think of Vindex' battle. It was the Batavian cavalry that crushed the Aedui and Averni, among the auxiliary forces of Virginius were Belgians, and if you consider the matter aright you will see that Gaul owed its fall to its own forces. (Tacitus, *Hist.* 4.17)[34]

With great clarity, Civilis here points to the paradox of a double self-subjugation that has the Gauls/Galatians bear the yoke of Rome and at the same time help to enforce this yoke on others who are Gauls/Galatians themselves. Arguing for a unity of the vanquished "from below," one might see the rebel leader as trying to contradict and reverse the very metamorphosis from enemy to subject/soldier that the Great Staircase of Pergamon had staged with so much visual power and persuasive force.[35]

Repatriating the Fatherless: Provincial Foundation and the Role of Imperial City and Piety (25 B.C.E.–50 C.E.)

When Caesar Augustus inherited the Galatian kingdom of Amyntas in 25 b.c.e., in much the same way as Rome had been bequeathed the kingdom of Pergamon a century earlier,[36] he immediately turned the newly won territory into an imperial province, named Provincia Galatica.[37] The first governor was Marcus Lollius, who held office as *legatus Augusti pro praetore* until 22 b.c.e.[38] Ancyra, the chief settlement of the Tectosagian tribe and a great crossroads in the north of Asia Minor, was chosen as capital.[39] It became the seat of a new temple of Roma and Augustus and of the imperial *koinon* (provincial council or congregation). Initially, the province covered the domain of Amyntas. The center of his kingdom had been in the South, but he had controlled most of central Asia Minor, including tribal Galatia in the North and, to the south, parts of Pisdia, Phrygia, Isauria, Lycaonia, and Pamphylia.[40] In 6/5 b.c.e., the kingdom of Paphlagonia was added after the death of its monarch Deiotarus Philadelphus, a great-grandson of King Deiotaros. Pontus Galaticus to the northeast became part of Roman Galatia in 3/2 b.c.e., and the temple state of Comana Pontica, in 34/35 c.e.[41] The province now reached from the mountains bordering the Black Sea to the Taurus region and the Mediterranean Sea in the South. In Paul's time it thus comprised a diverse mix of regions and ethnicities—Paphlagonians, Pisidians, Lycaonians,

Isaurians, and Pamphylians, along with ethnic Galatians, Jews, and Roman colonists. All of these territories had one thing in common: they had been under the rule of a pro-Roman Galatian elite before. This obviously made "Galatia" a compelling name for the new province.

There is sufficient evidence that the province as a whole was called "Galatia"—a point that has been traditionally emphasized by the proponents of the South Galatian hypothesis. An honorary inscription from Iconium, for example, mentions L. Pupius Praesens as "Procurator... of the Galatian Province" *(epitropos... Galatikēs eparcheias)* in 54 c.e., and another governor, C. Rutilius Gallicus, is known as *legatus provinciae Galaticae* under Nero.[42] Furthermore, the provincial congregation was called *koinon (tōn) Galatōn* or *koinon (tēs) Galatias*, that is, "provincial congregation (or council) of the Galatians/of Galatia."[43] It is important to note that this terminology exactly parallels the destination given by Paul in addressing the "assemblies of Galatia" in Gal 1:2 and the "Galatians" in 3:1 *(tais ekklēsiais tēs Galatias/Galatai)*. For the purpose of our exploration, this terminological clarification is important not necessarily in order to locate Paul's Galatians in the southern part of the province, but to point out that wherever they lived, they were primarily defined as inhabitants of a multiethnic "Celtic" Roman province in Asia Minor.

Via Sebaste: *A Holy Imperial Road*

After the disastrous end of King Amyntas on the battlefield of Roman order, the stabilization of the Taurus region in the south as site of his defeat became a primary focus of Roman policy in the first decades of Roman Galatia. On the one hand, Augustus had Qurinius avenge the death of his faithful client through a bloody retaliatory "pacification" that rendered the Homonadeis extinct. On the other hand, direct military interventions alone were not sufficient to subdue the rebellious tribal south of Roman Galatia. Two important long-term strategies in imposing Roman law and order in this unstable area were the establishment of colonies and the building of roads.

Colonies were military settlements on provincial land that was confiscated from the original owners and given to veterans of the Roman army and other immigrants from Italy who were granted the privilege of Roman citizenship. As strongholds of Roman order and culture on foreign territories, colonies far from Rome represented or even imitated Rome and protected Roman interests through military, political, and economic means. Their internal organization was not Greek but Roman and "preserved much of the hierarchy of the legions from which the settlers were drawn."[44] Most of the colonies founded by Augustus in provincial Galatia, not fewer than thirteen altogether, were in Pisdia, Isauria, and Lycaonia to the south of the province, including Cremna, Comama, Parlais, Olbasa, Lystra, Iconium, and, most prominently, Pisdian Antioch, the latter three playing a prominent role in Luke's report on Paul's missionary journeys in Acts 13–14. Furthermore, colonists were settled in existing communities at Apollonia, Neapolis, Isauria, and Attaleia.[45]

Another decisive measure to stabilize the region was the building and improvement of a functioning road system that connected cities and colonies, making possible a smooth flow of military and nonmilitary traffic. The most famous of these roads, dating back to Augustus, was the highway of the *Via Sebaste,* which ran from Pisidian Antioch as its head city (*caput viae*) to Iconium and Lystra in the East and to Apollonia, Comama, and the coastal cities of Perge and Attaleia in the Southwest.[46]

A milestone on this road found at Comama, 140 miles from Pisdian Antioch, bears the following inscription: *Imp. Caesar divi f. pont. maxim. cos. XI, des. XII, imp. XV, tr. pot. XIXX, viam Sebasten, curante Cornuto Aquila leg. suo pro preatore, fecit.* Emperor Augustus as "Imperator Caesar, son of the divinized, and High Priest" (*Imp. Caesar divi f. pont. maxim.*) thereby proudly proclaims that he made (*fecit*) this holy imperial road, the Via Sebaste, through the help of "his" *legatus pro praetore,* the provincial governor Cornutus Aquila (*viam, Sebasten curante Cornuto Aquila leg. suo pro praetore fecit*).[47] According to Mitchell, this text "simply demonstrates imperial authority, the presence of his [the emperor's] agent as provincial governor, and the existence of a road which was at the same time a visible symbol of Roman dominion and an essential requirement of the military presence which could enforce it. At a basic level this spells out what it meant for a region to become a province."[48] The milestone, erected in 6 B.C.E., thus demonstrates how Roman power inscribed itself on provincial territory and on the minds of those who traveled or had to deal with the travelers on this road, for example, representatives of the imperial administration, soldiers, businesspeople, slaves, grain suppliers, traders, villagers, and private citizens. At some point probably Paul himself moved along this road as well.[49]

While the system of roads is both a practical requirement and a symbol of Roman control in a conquered land, it is striking to see how much emphasis is put on the religious character of this achievement. The message of the Comama milestone shows the close linkage of imperial piety and imperial administration as a key feature of romanizing Galatia. Emperor Augustus Caesar, as metaphorical builder of the road, does not fail to mention his divine status as "son of God" (*divi filius,* that is, son of the divinized Julius Caesar), as well as his office as high priest of the Roman state religion (*pontifex maximus*), which he had held since 12 B.C.E. Even more important, this road bears his own name: Via Sebaste is a hybrid that links the Latin term for "road"(*via*) and the Greek term for "Augustus" (*Sebastos*).

Augustus/Sebastos, however, as we have seen, is in itself a term loaded with political and religious connotations that intersect and interact so intensely at every level that piety and power, divinity and humanity are always hiding one behind the other. *Augustus/Sebastos* means imperial, and it also means divine and holy, the divine connotation being even stronger in the Greek *Sebastos,* which is linked to *eusebeia,* "piety." This conflation and confluence of concepts are a constant reminder that the imperial order is divine and holy, and the divine order is imperial.

Sebastēni Galatai: *Holy Imperial Galatians*

The milestones on the "holy imperial road" of Augustus/Sebastos had a propagandistic power not unlike that of coinage in communicating key messages about Roman rule and religion.[50] The milestones were a palpable manifestation of Roman control in the South of the province. In the North of Galatia, imperial piety and power were inscribed in slightly different ways. There were no more wars to wage here, where a pro-Roman government had been in place at least since King Deiotaros. The territory to be conquered was not a physical space like the Taurus mountains. Rather, what the Romans needed to colonize was primarily the minds and bodies of the Galatians themselves, namely, traditional tribal mentality and way of life.[51]

If we continue to trace the "inscription" of the term *Sebastos/Augustus* in the context of North Galatia, we find a highly illuminating, complex interaction between imperial piety, cultural transformation, and subjugation of the colonized subjects. Strikingly, the most prominent places where the adjective *Sebastos/Sebastēnos* occurs in tribal Galatia after 25 B.C.E. are in references to the Galatian tribes themselves. In the official language they are now called *Sebastēni* Tolistobogii, *Sebastēni* Trocmi, and *Sebastēni* Tectosagi. Furthermore, each one of these tribal affiliations is firmly linked to the respective cities of Pessinus, Ancyra, and Tavium. In "politically correct" imperial language, the Galatians are now addressed as Sebastēni Tolistobogii Pessinuntii, Sebastēni Tectosages Ancyrani, and Sebastēni Trocmi Taviani.[52]

The term *Sebastēni* in this context is a Latinism and means "belonging to the *Sebastos/Augustus.*" The Latin equivalent would be *Augustiani,*[53] using the suffix *-ianus/-ianos,* which is usually connected with names, as, for example, in "Herodians" or "Christians"(*Christianoi;* Acts 11:26; 26:28). The Galatians as *Sebastēni* have a new corporate identity and a name that connects them to Caesar Augustus/Sebastos who (re)founds their cities Pessinus, Ancyra, and Tavium and to whom they owe gratitude, reverence, and worship (*sebēma*).[54]

The term *Sebastēni Tolistobogii/Trocmi/Tectosagi* again is a hybrid. On the one hand, it acknowledges a strong non-Greek and non-Roman element of still existing Celtic tribal affiliation and, on the other, signals that the Galatians as *Sebastēni/Augustiani* are no longer those wild, blasphemous, half-beastly subhumans of the Great Frieze who attack the gods and goddesses of civilization from *outside* and *below,* trying to destroy the very foundations on which the city is built.[55] Rather, they act and worship now within the framework of proper civic—that is, imperial Augustan—religiosity and order. Belonging to Caesar Augustus/Sebastos, the *Sebastēni Galatai* have irrevocably crossed the sacred borderline that kept their blasphemous and temple-robbing ancestors at the Altar of Pergamon *down* and *out;* as their aristocracy did before, the Galatians now as a collective entity have adopted a new ancestry and family that links them via Augustus to his divine father Julius Caesar and the noble lineage of the Julians back to Romulus and Aeneas, Mars and Venus.

Augustus now, in a way, is their new father. He has legally inherited not only their territory from Amyntas but also supreme patriarchal power over them, which defines, names, and rules them. As Sebastēni, the Galatian Tolistobogians, Trocmi, and Tectosagi are members of the worldwide Augustan "super-tribe," sons of the universal imperial father and his fatherland. The title of *pater patriae* (father of the fatherland) is adopted by Augustus in 2 B.C.E., an event he reports at the end, and as the climax, of his achievements (*Res Gestae* 35). He notes that this designation was first inscribed in the vestibule of his house, secondly in the senate house, and thirdly under a triumphal quadriga that was erected in front of the new temple of Mars Ultor (the Avenger) in the Forum of Augustus. The linkage of house–senate– forum as topoi of this inscription points to the political and all-inclusive dimension of Augustus's fatherhood over his family, the Roman people, and the *oikoumenē*. In particular, his universal fatherhood over the nations—in other words, world rule—is communicated with impressive power in the new Forum of Augustus, at which we will take a brief look.[56]

It was not a random coincidence that this magnificent space, Augustus's own Forum with the temple of Mars the Avenger as centerpiece, was inaugurated the same year the emperor became the Roman "father. " Its architecture and images represent the pedigree of imperial Romanhood and of the emperor himself set in stone and marble. A carefully selected range of Rome's human and divine ancestors—Venus and the divinized Julius Caesar, Romulus and Aeneas, the kings of Alba Longa, the Julians, and the heroes of Roman history (*summi viri*)—are on display, while the nexus between Mars as "father" of Augustus and Augustus as "father of the father- land" is spatially and visually the backbone of this grand re-imagination of Roman genealogy and world rule. Mars has the center position both in the group of cult statues inside his temple (next to Venus Genetrix and the deified Julius Caesar) and at the pediment outside standing in line with Augustus, to whom the triumphal quadriga with the inscription *pater patriae* in front of the temple is dedicated.[57] The arrangement speaks of war and victory as the necessary prerequisites for the birth of the Roman Empire. In his description of the Forum, Ovid renders this aspect very succinctly:

> The Avenger (Mars) descends himself from heaven to behold his own honours and his splendid temple in the forum of Augustus. The god is huge, and so is the structure: no otherwise ought Mars to dwell in his son's city. That shrine is worthy of trophies won from giants [*Giganteis*]; from it might the Marching God [*Gradivus*] fitly open his fierce campaigns, whether an impious foe shall assail us from the eastern world or whether another will have to be vanquished where the sun goes down. The god of arms surveys the pinnacles of the lofty edifice, and approves that the highest places should be filled by the unconquered gods [*invictos deos*]. He surveys on the doors weapons of diverse shapes, and arms of lands subdued by his soldiery. On this side he sees Aeneas laden with his dear burden, and many an ancestor of the noble Julian line. On the other side he sees Romu- lus carrying on his shoulder the arms of the conquered leader, and their famous deeds inscribed beneath the statues arranged in order. He beholds, too, the name of Augustus on the front of the temple, and the building seems to him still greater, when he reads the name of Caesar. (*Fasti* 5.551–68, LCL)

Velleius Paterculus (2.39) reports that the names of the nations Augustus vanquished and made tributary to Rome, including Spain and Egypt, were recorded at his Forum.[58] Furthermore, the business conducted there manifested Augustus's universal fatherhood. According to Paul Zanker, it made the Forum a showplace of Rome's foreign policy:

> Here young men when they came of age would put on the toga and were inscribed in the military lists. In the Temple of Mars the Senate officially proclaimed war, peace, or triumphs. From here provincial governors departed on campaign, and here returning victorious generals laid down the insignia of victory. Here barbarian princes swore their friendship and allegiance to Rome. The Temple of Mars thus took over certain distinctions that had previously been reserved for the Capitoline Temple of Jupiter.[59]

Among these distinctions one should probably also list the title *pater patriae* itself, which is clearly reminiscent of Jupiter/Zeus, the "father of God and men." As Claude Nicolet states, "The title of *Pater Patriae* could, by an explicit analogy to the Father of the Gods, suggest a universal terrestrial domination."[60]

Ovid's comment, quoted above, that the building is a worthy monument to the victory of the gods over the Giants, points in the same direction. As supreme Giant slayer, Augustus "fathers" the world and humanity out of chaos and nothingness through the supreme divine and cosmogonic power of his victory. This concept of imperial fatherhood is obviously relevant for the Galatians as ex-Giants. Monumentalizing, as Ovid states, the "unvanquished gods" and the mythological "war against the giants" (including all its contemporary rewrites), the Temple of Mars and the Forum of Augustus implicitly make a powerful statement about the identity of the Sebastēni Galatai as well: they are the newborn or adopted "sons" of Sebastos/Augustus, no longer Gaia's unruly children.[61] They have to show their filial "piety" to him by submitting to his paternal body and by defending the corporeality of the *patria* Rome against other mutineers who want to mutilate it, as Chronos once mutilated his father Ouranos/Heaven. This type of *pietas* was modeled by Aeneas, Augustus's noble ancestor, who "piously" saved his father and son, as well as his country, from the ruins of Troy. Augustus had practiced it toward his own deified father Julius Caesar with a large-scale "revenge" that wiped out his assassins and other enemies of Rome, and he sealed this achievement with the temple of Mars Ultor (the Avenger).[62]

In this framework, "piety" as a Roman core value means a "relation of respect that should equally bind together members of the family, members of society, and man and god"; it is religious and political at the same time, individual and collective, holding both society and family (as the analogy of society at the micro-level) in balance.[63] Piety, in short, is the mind-set and practice directly opposed to the Titan and Giant rebellion against the heavenly father. When the Galatai finally become "pious" as Sebastēni, Sebastos/Augustus has finally repatriated the fatherless rebel sons of Gaia that were born out of the great matriarchal uprising.[64] Their new name is his name—or the name of his successors, his provincial governors, army recruiters—and their collective passport into the *inside* of Roman peace and city/civilization.

How this "imperial fatherhood" and its renaming practices concretely functioned can be illustrated by another brief look at the list of thirty-six Roman soldiers from Alexandria/Egypt that dates from about 10 B.C.E. and shows a strong Galatian recruitment from Ankyra and elsewhere.[65] As the Roman legions had to be formed by Roman citizens, the Galatian provincials who entered received citizenship and a Latin name, for example:

M. Lollius M. f. Pol. Ancyr. (Marcus Lollius, son of Marcus, tribe Pollia, from Ancyra) and *L. Longinus L. f. Pol. Ancyr.* (Lucius Longinus, son of Lucius, tribe Pollia, from Ancyra). Marcus Lollius shares his name with another Ancyran on the list. Both are named after the first Roman governor of Galatia, Marcus Lollius, under whom they obviously entered the army. They are distinguishable only by the different names of their centurions, that is, Servatus and Maternus. The centurion's names are given for each of the thirty-six soldiers on the list in the line immediately above his name; they are thus de facto part of the soldier's identity. As Ramsay points out, Galatian soldiers might also take their entire Roman names from the officers under whom they served.[66]

Even more striking is another observation. Marcus Lollius is called the son of Marcus, Lucius Longinus the son of Lucius. This pattern persists without a single exception for all the soldiers on the list. Yet it is hardly the case that every father and son shared the same name. Apparently all the thirty-six names of the "real" non-Roman fathers of the legionaires have been erased and fictively replaced by the Roman *prenomen* of the renamed soldier-citizens.[67] The Roman claim to have officially "fathered" and newly created these men "out of nothing," shaping them uniformly in the image of empire (and of the god Mars), could hardly be made more tangible. It is Galatians themselves who are now embodying the imperial victory over Galatia, reborn through the war machine of the empire and renamed after their proper father, who has resurrected them from their well-deserved dying by gracefully forgiving their rebellious birth defect. To the one name behind all the fictive naming, they owe faith, loyalty, and worship—God and Father Augustus.[68]

The "Koinon" of the Holy Imperial Galatians

The three tribes of the "Holy Imperial Trocmi, Tectosagi, and Tolistobogii" are united into a common body of "holy imperial Galatians" through the institution of the provincial congregation, the *koinon Sebastēnōn Galatōn*. The term *koinon* is derived from the Greek word for "common" and in this context means something like council, congregation, assembly, league, federation, or union of the Augustan Galatians. Ramsay translates it as "commune," thus rendering the aspect of togetherness particularly well. David Magie chooses "commonality." We use the terms *council* or *congregation*. "Council" corresponds to the Latin equivalent of *koinon,* namely, *concilium,*[69] which also relates to the Celtic precursor institution of the *koinon,* the *Drynemetos.* "Congregation," on the other hand, emphasizes the element of union, community, and "commonwealth," and makes the term *koinon* a reflection of Paul's "assemblies of Galatia" (*ekklēsiai*) in Gal 1:2.

As Emin Bosch points out, the establishment of the *koinon* probably goes back to the foundation of the province in 25 B.C.E. The first inscriptional evidence, however, which was found at Ancyra, dates only from the middle of the first century C.E., that is, from Paul's time, when the term *koinon Galatōn* also appears on coins. In the Ancyran inscription, the *koinon* of the Augustan Galatians honors a certain Gaius Iulius, son of Quintus, whose Latin name (and that of his father) indicates Roman citizenship dating back to either Augustus or Caligula: *To koinon Sebastēnōn Galatōn eteimēsen Gaion Iulion Kointou hyion.*[70]

The *koinon* of the Augustan Galatians had its chief seat at Ancyra, the new capital city, and was the leading body of the provincial subjects. Though the term *koinon* was widely used for federations of cities in Greek history, the provincial councils created by Augustus throughout the provinces of the Roman Empire, which survived until the third century C.E., were something new. Jürgen Deiniger has shown that these *koina* were more or less uniformly established with representatives elected from among the leading citizens of each province. They met once a year under the leadership of the provincial priest. The *koina* were strictly separated from the Roman provincial administration and its power, and their two main tasks were organizing imperial religion on a provincial level and representing local interests to the provincial governor or, through embassies, directly to Rome. Both duties were so demanding financially that only the wealthy members of the elite class could become members of the *koinon*. The *koinon* thus co-opted and controlled the indigenous ruling classes by giving them a prestigious but politically very restricted sphere of influence and making them the chief instruments of self-Romanization.[71]

The responsibility of the *koinon* for imperial religion included the building and maintenance of temples for Caesar and Roma, honorary inscriptions for Caesar, and public celebrations with processions, prayers, sacrifices, and games. As we will see, all of these political demonstrations of the leading provincials on behalf of the emperor and the well-being of the Roman Empire are well attested in Roman Galatia. A huge and magnificent Hellenistic temple of Augustus and Rome was erected at Ancyra between approximately 10 B.C.E. and 20 C.E.[72] At Pessinus, the tribal territory of the Tolistobogians and, at Pisidian Antioch in the South, two other major temples dedicated to the imperial cult were built. Major inscriptions were produced, the most famous among them the *Res Gestae*, the "Acts" of Augustus. Much of this building program was still under way in Paul's time.[73] Wherever he traveled in Galatia and wherever his Galatians lived, imperial architecture was omnipresent as one "of the most notable examples of the transformation of civic space, whereby imperial buildings literally took over and dominated the urban landscape, thus symbolizing unequivocally the central position that emperor worship occupied in city life and the overwhelming manner in which the emperor dominated the world view of his subjects."[74] Further, the age of Emperor Claudius (41–54 C.E.), contemporaneous with Paul and his Galatian mission, brought an intensification of imperial presence in Roman Galatia. Several cities, for example,

Claudiconium, Claudioderbe, Ninica Claudiopolis, Claudiolaodicea, Claudioseleucia, and Claudiocaesareia Mistea adopted the emperor's name, and his legate, M. Annius Afrinus (49–54 c.e.), was particularly active.[75]

To illustrate the function of the *koinon,* a short glance at Gaul in the West might be helpful. In 12 b.c.e., the imperial sanctuary of the three Gallic provinces Gallia Belgica, Aquitania, and Gallia Lugdunensis was dedicated at Lugdunum (Lyon), a city that became the capital of Roman Gaul and the major city of Roman Europe, with an important imperial mint. At the *Condate* Altar of Lugdunum, representatives of the Celtic tribes would meet for an annual imperial festival and council to celebrate, worship, and express their loyalty to the goddess Roma and the divine Augustus. The imperial sanctuary of Lugdunum combined three key institutions of the Augustan age: a provincial council (*koinon*) of the tribal elite, reminiscent of the traditional Celtic council but reduced to the manifold manifestations of emperor religion and without any real political power; an amphitheater, where games were held; and an imperial temple and altar for the observances of the imperial cult, whose high priest was also the head of the provincial council.[76] Strabo reports that the altar carried an inscription with the names of the sixty tribes, in addition to their images, representing "all of the Gauls/Galatians in common" who built and dedicated the temple to Caesar Augustus (*to de hieron . . . hypo pantōn koinē tōn Galatōn Kaisari tō Sebastō;* 4.3.2). The expression *koinē* (in common) in this inscription points to its sister-term *koinon* and highlights its unifying function.[77]

The example of Lugdunum/Lyon to some extent might illustrate the situation in the newly founded Galatian province of Asia Minor in the East, where around this same time the building of the great temple to Rome and Augustus must have begun. As in western Gallia/Galatia Lugdunensis, imperial worship was linked to the imperial council (*koinon*) and to games and other public donations. To express and organize imperial piety was the main task attributed to the provincial council, which acted as the official institution of the Roman emperor religion in the province of Galatia and played a leading role in adapting the Galatians to the "common" standards of Roman rule and order. Imperial religiosity, as we will see in the next section, united North and South Galatia in a new way, not only in terms of architecture but even more in terms of civic activities: religious festivals and processions, commercial gatherings, horse races, games, public banquets, and donations as an expression of the benefactions that Caesar made to the Galatians through the priests and other local representatives of his cult. At least ten cities in both North and South Galatia at the time of Paul are known to have sponsored the imperial cult on either the provincial or local level.[78] Through the work of the *koinon,* the term *Galatian* thus became inclusive of all inhabitants of the province of Galatia, describing the new "commonality" and makeover of their original ethnicities. As Sebastēni they all become Galatai, at least ideally. Phrygians, Lycaonians, Pisidians, Isaurians in the same way as Celtic Trocmi, Tolistobogians, and Tectosagi were collectively reshaped in their identity and allegiance as Sebastēni Galatai through the manifold expressions of imperial religion.

That means that in the official language and performance of imperial domination, a wider, multiethnic use of the term *Galatai* existed. The native Galatians in this arrangement were the exemplary barbarian race demonstrating the transformation from previous super-rebels to current model citizens. This, at least subconsciously, may have been another reason why their name was given to the whole mixed bunch of peoples living in the Roman province of Galatia, all of them now united in common imperial observance and obedience, "reborn" into a common subjectivity as Sebastēni Galatai represented and propagated by the collective congregation (*koinon*) of the Galatians. Just as the mythological Giants/Galatians at the Great Altar of Pergamon were universal yet multiethnic in the "*a-sebeia*" (blasphemy) of their unified attack on the gods of the Greco-Roman pantheon,[79] the Sebastēni Galatai were multiethnic in their universal reverence for the one divine Caesar Augustus/Sebastos, who together with the goddess Roma embodied the worldwide peace of the universal Roman city and civilization.

It was the joint reverence for Sebastos/Augustus Caesar that unified the Galatians of all tribes and nations, and this very identity of theirs as Sebastēni/Augustans was what they truly and legitimately had "in common." Again we are reminded of the Great Staircase at Pergamon and Louis Althusser's concept of subjectivity as subjection that is created through interpellation of the small subject by the *one* big Subject.[80] In an interesting twist, Clifford Ando has applied Althusser's critique of Christian religion to Roman imperial religion:

> The image of the emperor as "one among many of the same kind as himself" was ultimately supplanted by a much more powerful and longer-lasting image, that of an emperor over many who were equal in their subordination to him. The power of this rhetoric lay in its seduction of the provincial population: to use Althusser's term, it interpellated individuals as concrete subjects and encouraged them to view other provincials as well as imperial officials as similarly concrete subjects. In effect, to adapt Althusser's critique of Christian ideology, this aspect of imperial ideology sought "to obtain from [its subjects] the recognition that they really do occupy the place it designates for them as theirs in the world," with the implicit condition "there can only be such a multitude of possible subjects on the absolute condition that there is a Unique, Absolute, *other subject*, i.e. [the emperor]."[81]

This is exactly the phenomen of a "functional imperial monotheism" that we have tried to describe in chapter 3 above. It is important to understand the clash with imperial religion and its *koinon* that was provoked by Paul when his model of worship and *koinōnia*/community turned out to be based on a quite different concept of the one God and the oneness of humanity.

Galatian City and Roman Civilization

It is obvious that this whole process of transformation through piety had its center in the cities. Next to imperial religion—and as its prerequisite—urbanization was a basic requirement of Roman administration, dominion, and integration. "The Empire rested on the cities," as Ramsay states.[82] Since the bureaucratic apparatus that the Romans imposed for governing their empire was actually surprisingly small, the cities, with their traditional Hellenistic institutions and structures of self-governance, were indispensable tools of Romanization, which culturally in many ways was Hellenization.[83] Rome needed cities. In Galatia, however, in contrast to the more southern regions of the province, there were few cities in the ethnic territory of the North. Strabo talks about several fortified castles (*phrouria*) of the Tectosagi and Trocmi, among them Ancyra and Tavium, as well as the two Tolistobogian strongholds of Deiotaros at Blucium and Peium. Famous ancient Phrygian cities like Gordium and Gorbeus meanwhile had become villages. Pessinus with its renowned shrine of Cybele, however, was a still strong temple state.[84]

At the beginning of the provincial era, the Romans substantially transformed this settlement pattern of North Galatia. A hybrid term such as *Sebastēni Tectosagi Ancyrani* not only signals the new imperial (trans-)"ethnicity" and identity of the Galatians as "Augustan," but it also indicates their transition from a tribal to a Hellenistic model of city-centered life dominated by Augustus/Sebastos. With the refoundation of Pessinus, Tavium, and Ancyra as cities by the "holy imperial" Caesar Sebastos, and with their three tribes now being defined as Sebastēni as well, the Sebastēni Tolistobogii of Pessinus, the Sebastēni Trocmi of Tavium, and the Sebastēni Tectosagi of Ancyra were supposed to "melt" into their respective cities. This process included not only a far-reaching redistribution of ancient tribal territory, thus weakening the tribal structures, but as a whole it was meant to replace tribal organization with urbanization.[85] We might assume that the overall procedure was met with some reluctance or even resistance on the part of the tribal population well into Paul's time. Coinage until Trajan shows that the *koinon* and the tribes, rather than the cities themselves, minted coins, thus indicating their predominance over an obviously still underdeveloped *polis* system that was not enthusiastically accepted by the native people.[86] It was only several decades after Paul that the cities in North Galatia could actually assume their proper role as "the primary institutions of local government in the provinces."[87]

Urbanization was not only a political, cultural, and administrative necessity but a key economic requirement. The "law of the city," maintained by a police force, in general implied the subjugation of rural areas and their village communities, which were required to feed and sustain the city.[88] This was the basic structure within which the Roman system of taxation could function. This, after all, was the core rationale of conquering foreign nations and organizing them into provinces.

According to Stephen Mitchell, cities in the Roman world included dependent rural dwellers at an average ratio of one to ten, which means that a city like Ancyra had hundreds of villages in its territory.[89] Typically, the leading citizens would own much of the surrounding land and take away from the peasants large portions of the harvest as a kind of rent. This transfer from country to city probably happened for the most part on a nonmonetary basis, which means that large parts of Anatolian society were not integrated into the monetized economy of the wider Roman world.[90] In the urban market, however, agricultural produce was sold to the city dwellers, which produced the cash that was the source of taxes for the Roman state, on the one hand, and of disposable income for the wealthy elites, on the other. Mitchell points out that these elite citizens/landlords would also pay the poll tax (*tributum capitis*) for their peasants, because "communities (usually cities) were held collectively responsible for paying the tax bill for their inhabitants."[91] The extra money raised from these transactions would enable rich citizens/landlords to act as benefactors within the euergetic system, financing public buildings and honorary inscriptions, big festivals, games, and civic and imperial worship in the widest sense.

This model of redistributing large parts of the land's harvest to the city and the Roman state, including various tributes to feed the Roman army, left the countryside impoverished and often unable to retain what they needed for their own subsistence. According to Mitchell, the average per capita amount of grain that remained for peasant consumption was 225 kilograms, as opposed to 720 kilograms for city consumption.[92] This resulted in poverty and often starvation among the peasants. Moreover, large tracts of land in the province of Galatia were either possessed by the Roman state as *ager publicus* and could be given to the veterans of the Roman army through the foundation of colonies or turned into imperial estates that were managed by imperial procurators, freedmen, and slaves supervising the peasant *coloni* working the soil. Romans or Italians, including the tax collectors (*publicani*), who used slaves and freedmen to extract the required tithes from the local harvest were often able to buy land themselves from native owners who were no longer able to pay the property tax (*tributum solis*).[93]

Galen of Pergamon, the famous physician and philosopher, lived in the second century C.E., but his description of the urban–rural relationship is definitely illuminating for the time of Paul as well:

> For among many of the peoples who are subject to the Romans, the city-dwellers, as it was their practice to collect and store enough grain for all the next year immediately after the harvest, left what remained to the country people, that is, pulses of various kinds, and they took a good deal of these too to the city. The country people finished the pulses during the winter, and so had to fall back on unhealthy food during the spring; they ate twigs and shoots of trees and bushes, and bulbs and roots of indigestible plants; they filled themselves with wild herbs, and cooked fresh grass. [94]

Again the imagery of the Great Altar seems to come to life, more precisely the moving figure of the earth goddess Gaia on the East Frieze (see chap. 2, fig. 20 and p. 168 above). Presenting her overflowing cornucopia to the city goddess Athena, she seems to offer the abundance of fruit in exchange for the life of her son Alkyoneus and his brothers. Her appeal for mercy has in one way been heard, yet in another way remains unheeded. Gaia's Galatian children in Paul's time are no longer exterminated and slaughtered in combat, at least not in Asia Minor. But as imperial and pious "Augustan" Galatians, they have become tied to the city in subservience, deep down on the ground. Gaia and her horn of plenty belong to the emperor now—on the famous Prima Porta statue

Fig. 37. Gaia reclines at the bottom of the Emperor's breastplate in a statue of Augustus from Prima Porta. Braccio Nuovo, Museo Chiaramonti, Vatican Museums, Vatican State. Photo: Alinari/Art Resource, N.Y.

of Augustus, for example, she is depicted with two children reclining in the groin part of the imperial armor, the body area where imperial virility and fertility are located.

A similar image of Gaia/Tellus surrounded by vegetational abundance is depicted at the Ara Pacis of Augustus and in many other places. What Gaia's motherly fertility brought forth and what is linked to her, that is, her earth-grown children and crops, are expropriated and exploited by the superior race of the civilized city-dwellers, taken away from the primeval mother by the supreme law of the all-powerful god-father who generates abundance out of victory and blood. Athena/Minerva and Nikē/Victoria on the upper side of the Great Frieze, the motherless goddess of the city and the victory goddess, are boundless in their triumph, the triumph of "culture" over "nature." And so is Roma, the worldwide mother city, the unsatiable divine *metropolis,* who is worshiped alongside the deified Caesar at Ancyra and elsewhere.

The Emperor's "Good Works": Imperial Meals and Games as Reinscription of the Galatian Body

We move to the 20s and 30s of the first century C.E. in Galatia. Roman rule has been in place for more than fifty years. Tiberius is Caesar in Rome. Metilius, Fronto, Silvanus, and Basila serve as provincial governors in the rank of *legati Augusti pro preatore*.[95] It is the time when in Roman Palestine a marginal figure called Jesus of Nazareth causes trouble and is subsequently executed under the Roman procurator, which no one in Galatia under ordinary circumstances would ever notice. Another Jew from Tarsus in the neighboring province of Cilicia, well trained in Jewish law, tries to erase the emerging Jesus movement and then, in an unexpected reversal, starts to propagate it on a worldwide scale, which will eventually bring him to Galatia. But this would be some ten to twenty years later. Right now, around 30 C.E., in the Galatian capital of Ancyra, a Roman governor by the name Fronto is in charge (29–33 C.E.), having basically the same duties as his colleague Pontius Pilate in Judea. Under his administration, as always, the leading families of the Galatian nobility take great pride in representing Roman rule, and their own, as beneficial and salutary to all. The way to accomplish this was well established among Romans, Greeks, and Celts. One of the most proficient channels of ancient mass persuasion and mass control was the spending of large sums of private money on public entertainment and donations. A unique document has survived that reflects a small but significant example of this practice and may give us a rare glimpse at such details of life: the Ancyran list of imperial priests and their donations under Tiberius.[96]

Res Gestae and the "Acts" of the Imperial Priests at Ancyra

At the imperial temple of Ancyra, an honorary inscription was found that commemorates nineteen leading priests of the imperial cult in Roman Galatia over a period of about twenty years. Cut into the narrow vertical strip of stone on the *anta* surface left of the entrance, a list of names and donations catches the approaching visitor's eyes. The exact number and nature of gifts made by every one of the imperial priests are reported; presumably this acknowledgment was added to the list every year after the regular term of an officeholder was over.[97] It is quite obvious that these men who acted as heads of the Galatian provincial congregation (*koinon*) between 20 and approximately 40 C.E. showed eminent generosity in sponsoring, among other things, a formidable sequence of public feasts. Banquets (*dēmothoiniai*), sacrifices of multiple animals (*hekatombai*), and an impressive number of gladiatorial shows— hunts, bull or wild animal fights—are listed. The individual contributions vary, depending on the personal assets available. Only one officeholder has no donation at all reported, but most of the others gave several items and must have had considerable resources. Pylaemenes, son of King Amyntas, was by far the most generous and presumably wealthiest man on the list.

Before we reflect further on the specifics of these donations, we have to think a bit about the system of euergetism/benefactions as such. Why did these high-ranking representatives of the Galatian nobility—many of them still identified by their names as Celts, some as Roman citizens with Latin names, and others bearing Greek names often making the precise ethnicity hard to identify[98]—invest so much in public donations, and how was that related to the imperial cult they were appointed to implement? Why are different kinds of entertainment (the most frequent being at least twenty-two dona-tions of public feasts/banquets, closely followed by spectacles [*thea*], and gladiatorial and animal fights) so much more prominent on the list than purely "religious" gifts of more obvious relevance for imperial religion, such as the erection of imperial statues, which is recorded only twice, or the one-time gift by Pylaemenes, son of Amyntas, of the actual place for the imperial temple (*Sebastēon*) and the adjoining space for festive assemblies (*panēgyris*) and horse races?

One answer to these questions can be found in another, much more extensive text inscribed behind the priest list a few steps farther inside the entrance hall (*pronaos*), readily presented for a "synoptic" view: the *Res Gestae Divi Augusti,* the "Acts of the Divine Augustus." The comprehensive twenty-five-thousand-word record of the emperor's accomplishments, written by Augustus himself, covers political achieve-ments, nations conquered, buildings erected in Rome, donations made, and honors received. The original document was supposed to be engraved on two pillars in front of the Mausoleum of Augustus on the Field of Mars in Rome, that is, as part of the overall architectural ensemble that included the Mausoleum itself, the Horologium with the Egyptian obelisk, and the Ara Pacis, the Altar of Peace. This Roman original of the *Res Gestae* has not been recovered so far, however, and the wording of the monumental inscription must be restored from its bilingual copy at the imperial temple of Roma and Augustus at Ancyra, as well as two less well preserved versions from Galatian Apollonia and Antioch.[99]

The *Monumentum Ancyranum,* as the *Res Gestae* are sometimes called after their most prominent location, were carved in stone in two languages on the walls of the imperial sanctuary at Ancyra around 14 C.E., probably at the initiative of the *koinon.*[100] The "common" Greek translation of this remarkable text, lauded as the "Queen of ancient inscriptions" (Theodor Mommsen), is found on the long sidewall of the rect-angular temple *cella* to the right. Compared to the placement of the Latin version, this is clearly a less prominent and more "public" location, which communicates with the Greek-speaking *Outside.* The Latin *Res Gestae,* on the other hand, were carved in three columns on each side on the wall of the *pronaos* (Greek: pre-temple), the covered vestibule or hallway that leads to the actual temple *cella,* the enclosed inner part, which usually housed the divine statue(s) and represented the sacred *Inside.* Comparable to the Great Staircase at the Pergamon Altar, this liminal area of the *pronaos* is the most prominent outside spot where the transition between *Out* and *In* is negotiated and performed. Upon entering this space, one is immediately immersed in the presence of Caesar, who "speaks" from the two sidewalls right and left in a stereophonic manner. His voice is recorded in the Latin master language that renders the original tongue of Augustus himself, who throughout the document speaks in the first person singular: I did, I made, I gave. Brought to life through the magic of the stony letters, the imperial self that resides at the *urbs* (city) of Rome thus visibly and tangibly claims this faraway Galatian space as part of the Roman *orbis* (world). Only an infidel or an insane person would hear this as the voice of a dead man speaking from his tomb on the Field of Mars:

the inscription as such is ample proof that Augustus has been resurrected perpetually into a powerful worldwide presence.

It is tempting to draw a comparison between the milestone on the Via Sebaste and the Ancyran temple of the Sebastos himself. Though the contrast in size and function is considerable—a relatively inconspicuous distance marker on a road or a huge cultic building inside a city—both resemble each other as spatial objects that are turned into "writing tablets" in order to communicate a message about the Roman order and the emperor. Both inscribe the perennial lordship of the imperial self on conquered provincial land, making Augustus manifest and alive as the "I" that "did." Evidently, the "deeds" of Augustus are much more comprehensively recorded at the temple than on the milestone, which gives only a condensed summary. But the message is similar. The sanctuary, however, carries so much writing on its walls that it seems to be as much "scripture" as it is architecture and temple.[101]

What is even more striking is that the different inscriptions of the temple seem to talk vividly to each other. A brief look at the headlines, or "titles," of the three documents is interesting. In the Latin version of the *Res Gestae* at the entrance hall, the deeds of Augustus are titled "Acts of the deified Augustus by which he subjected the whole world to the empire of the Roman people, and the expenditures he made for the republic and the Roman people" (*Rerum gestarum divi Augusti quibus orbem terrarum imperio populi Romani subiecit, et impensarum quas in rem publicam populumque Romanum fecit*). This is the plain and unembellished language of conquest and Romanhood colonizing foreign land. The fact that this is laid down in the *pronaos*—the two inner "front pages" of the temple/script, as it were—adds to its weight and strategic importance. Not many people at Ancyra, however, would be able to read Latin. It is interesting that in the more accessible Greek version (the "back cover" maybe) the headline is considerably shorter and much less offensive and blunt: It has a definitively positive ring as it simply announces the "Deeds/Acts and gifts of God Augustus" (*praxeis te kai dōreai Sebastou theou*)[102] as the content of the six columns of text that are inscribed underneath it.

The third inscription, the imperial priest list, could be seen as a mediation between the two faces of Augustus, the Greek and the Latin. Its position at the outermost part of the entrance makes it the "front cover" of the "script," in a way. As such, it "translates" the Latin language of the conqueror into the Greek of the conquered, setting the politically correct tone for the vanquished to speak within and about the empire. In large letters its title announces the nineteen dignitaries as "priests of the Galatians serving God Augustus/Sebastos and Goddess Roma" (*Galatōn hoi hierasamenoi theō Sebastō kai thea Rōmē*). What in the Latin "fine print" of the *Res Gestae* inside is a proud proclamation of the deified Augustus and his "deeds" of worldwide conquest becomes, in the Greek "forefront" inscription, the pious announcement of Galatian worship to "God Sebastos/Augustus" and "Goddess Roma." What the Latin text reports about the spoils of conquest being donated as "gifts" exclusively to the Roman people and proceeds spent on buildings in the city of Rome alone, in the priestly document of the Galatian province, is transformed into an incessant sequence of donations and gifts made to the Galatians on behalf of the emperor by his imperial priests. The imperial conquest of

Galatia, it seems, has become an act of euergetism itself; the "geographic imperialism" of an entirely Romanocentric discourse in the *Res Gestae*[103] vanishes behind the veil of genuinely "Galatian" feasting and merriment.

This "synoptic" intertextuality of the two inscriptions becomes even more obvious through a quick comparison of the actual donations featuring prominently in both of them. In the report of the *divus Augustus* about his lifelong achievements and gratuities, the following, among other things, are mentioned: large gifts of money and grain to the population and soldiers of Rome (*Res Gestae* 15); eight large gladiatorial shows (*munus gladiatorum/monomachia*) with no fewer than ten thousand fighters involved; athletic competitions (*spectaculum athletarum/athlēthōn gymnikou, agōnos thean*); six large games (*ludi/ thea*), including the secular games of 17 B.C.E.; twenty-six fights with wild African beasts (*venationes bestiarum Africanarum/*[Greek lost]) in the circus, forum or amphitheaters, with thirty-five hundred animals killed (*Res Gestae* 22).

These items are replicated, on a much smaller scale, on the list of the donations of Augustus's Ancyran priests, which uses the same vocabulary: Seven games (*thea*) and one athletic competition (*agōna gymnikon*), which included a horse and chariot race, are arranged; four priests donate altogether 145 pairs of gladiators (*monomachōn zeugē*); eight hunts and bull or wild beast fights are mentioned (*kynēgion, tauromachia, taurokathapsia, thēromachia*); and a grain allocation of five *modii* is made, which looks like a copy of the free corn distribution at Rome.[104]

This striking parallelism between the benefactions made by the representatives of the imperial *koinon* and by the "divine Augustus" shows that the generosity of the imperial priests at Ancyra was meant to appear as the Galatian micro-reflection of the over-powering Roman example of the emperor himself. Through the priests, the emperor was incessantly showering the general accomplishments of the Pax Romana—peace, stability, prosperity—on the whole inhabited world, at least propagandistically. The placement of the Galatian priest list within the physical context of Augustus's report of achievements on the temple walls makes it function like a mirror or replica of the emperor's euergetism and "good works."

This linkage has a strongly hierarchical structure. The priests' submission to and representation of Caesar's rule, already eye-catching in the inscription of the "small text" (priest list) in front of and within the framework of the "big text" (*Res Gestae*), is most tangibly embodied in the act of replicating the emperor's superior generosity. For those able to read, the text leaves no doubt about the social hierarchy implied. The inscription of the priest list gives, in slightly larger letters than the rest of the body, the names of the particular governors (Metilius, Fronto, Silvanus, and Basila) "under" (*epi*) whom each priest had his term, thereby structuring the list in four or five groups of three to five priests.[105] The structure is somewhat similar to the list of the thirty-six Roman soldiers in Alexandria discussed above, each of whom is named with his centurion's name listed before his own. In Althusser's terminology, in each case (though at different levels of the political hierarchy) provincials are interpellated as "small" subjects of the "big" Subject—the imperial father, patron, god speaking through the presence of his centurions and provincial governors—and are assigned their place in the social order. Although the imperial priests of the Galatians are thus clearly in a position of subordination with regard to the divine Augustus/goddess Roma and the provincial administration (as the centurions and governors are subordinate to their superiors and the emperor), they represent and reinforce Roman authority toward the Galatians, who are subordinate to them. The close nexus between imperial religion and the inscription of imperial power and order could hardly be made more obvious.

Imperial Euergetism as "Works of the Law"?

The Ancyran priest list as a case study enables us to take a brief look at a core component of social interaction in Paul's time that is still widely underestimated in its implications for Pauline justification theology—the practice of euergetism or benefactions. Closely affiliated with the code of honor and shame, as well as firmly embedded in the distinctly Roman master system of patronage and clientship, this practice represents one of the most fundamental social patterns of the ancient world, forming an all-pervasive cluster of relationships and mechanisms that both structure and integrate society as a coherent whole.[106] A focal question of our exploration is whether Paul's criticism of "works of the law" (Gal 2:16) needs to be first recontextualized within the framework of Greco-Roman euergetism—a term that, like the Latin-derived *benefactor/benefaction,* literally means "doing of good works"—before its specific relationship to circumcision or purity as *works* of Jewish law (Torah) can be understood. One aspect of euergetism in particular is most relevant to our topic, namely, the social "alchemy" that transforms a horizontal mutuality of exchanging "gifts" among coequals into a hierarchical reciprocity that mirrors and cements domination and subordination.

The Ancyran priest list on the surface might give the impression that the free distribution of certain goods to the inhabitants of Galatia was nothing other than a noble gesture of some high-ranking individuals on behalf of the civic community, meant simply to enhance the public standing and recognition of the donors, that is, their "honor." Yet, as a more critical reading in the context of the *Res Gestae* and with regard to the provincial governance inscribed in it has indicated, it also reflected and reaffirmed social hierarchy and submission, on the local, provincial, and imperial levels. The "vertical" and hierarchical nature of the benefaction system, however, is also inscribed in its very mode of operation as an essentially asymmetrical and competitive exchange that is closely tied to imperial religion. The gratifications masked and glorified the basic inequality and power relationship that made them possible and that they strengthened; the gratitude and reverence they evoked on the side of the inferior recipients ("the people") translated directly into social compliance with and acquiescence to the local and provincial structures, as well as into devotion to the imperial divinity that was behind and above all donations received.

1. *Asymmetrical nature.* According to Seneca's treatise on benefactions (*De Beneficiis*), beneficence or euergetism as exchange of favors and services "binds together human society" (1.4.2). On the side of the beneficiary it requires, as a matter of honor, gratitude and return in kind (1.10.4).[107] Following the rules of honor and mutual

obligation, the gift inevitably establishes a debt that needs to be paid back. Yet directly returning a "favor" such as the organization of a public banquet or gladiatorial fight, two of the donations listed on the Ancyran inscription, would have been impossible for most of those partaking in the feast, but they had at least to be grateful for the gift received. The inability of a person to requite adequately a benefaction thus "naturally" established the lower status of the recipient and the social superiority of the generous donor/patron, as well as political complicance with this order (that was the political expression of the required gratitude). As Peter Garnsey and Richard Saller point out, this stabilized not only social cohesion but also the social power structure, and especially the imperial power pyramid with Caesar at the top:

> Augustus sought to establish his legitimacy not only by restoring the social order, but also by demonstrating his own supremacy in it through the traditional modes of patronage and beneficience. Much of the *Res Gestae,* his own account of his reign, was an elaboration of the staggering scale of his benefits and services to the Roman people. . . . Since subjects could not repay imperial benefactions in kind, the reciprocity ethic dictated that they make return in the form of deference, respect, and loyalty.[108]

2. *Imperial religion.* Euergetism, as it was practiced after Augustus, was closely connected with imperial religion. In this realm the reciprocity between donation and gratitude was by definition vertical and unequal, sustaining the pyramid of power with the local aristocracy as immediate and the divine Caesar as superior benefactor of the empire. Richard Gordon analyzes the linkage between priesthood and euergetism among the provincial elite in Asia, in particular sacrificial euergetism. The donation and performance of sacrifices by the elites fulfilled a primary need, namely, to maintain proper relationships with the gods, on which the well-being of the city rested. He points out that the "fusion of the euergetic with the sacrifical system within civic priesthood" (which was strongly modeled after Augustus's own pious example as *pontifex maximus*) not only veils and naturalizes but also sanctions the underlying social hierarchy and inequality as beneficial and divinely ordained. It "evokes both the divine necessity and the social responsibility of the existing social order. The relationship proposed by the sacrificial system between god and human beings (inferiority; reciprocity between unequals; providential beneficence; changelessness) is implicitly offered as a model of the relationship between the elite and the rest of the community."[109] In light of these considerations, it is important to note that sacrifices *(hekatombē)* are mentioned explicitly no fewer than six times on the Ancyran priest list.[110]

3. *Competitiveness.* Euergetism was also highly competitive. Giving to the public and the city established a superior status in general; giving more than another established a higher status in the contest for honor, immortality, and ultimately power. As Stephan Joubert states, "The *agonistic* ancient Mediterranean culture turned most forms of social interactions, from invitations, meals, public debates, recitals, business transactions, right up to gift-exchanges, into agonistic contests for honour."[111] In the Ancyran list, one can find indications that the imperial priests tried hard to outshine each other or at least not give less than their predecessors. In the donation of oil, for example,

the second most frequent item of the list after banquets,[112] a significant change happens when Pylaemenes, son of King Amyntas, serves for the second time in 30/31 c.e. After three previous donors had provided for a term of only four months, Pylaemenes switched to providing for a whole year and included all three tribes (*ethnē*). After that substantial increase, not only every one of his eight followers gave oil, but they did not fail to give it for a whole year rather than four months only. And four among the eight now mention either tribes or cities as recipients as well.

A conclusion to be drawn from this very cursory look at the benefaction system is the insight that in spite of "munificent forms of assistance by nobles to their communities, generally, most of them used their benefactions to increase their own honour and not so much to alleviate the needs of others."[113] Moreover, the efficiency of the benefaction system was based largely on the extent to which it veiled the underlying power relations that were fortified through acts of euergetism. "Mask and veil here coincide: for the true purpose of giving is not to receive honor, but to maintain the power and wealth of the elite."[114] Commenting on an honorific inscription for a local civic priest/benefactor in Cyme (Aeolid), Gordon states that "the wealth of Cleanax almost certainly derived from his dominant roles in reproducing the very social relations that his activity as euergetes serves to veil."[115]

This mechanism shows up on the Ancyran list as well. It is noteworthy that the term "give" (*edōken*) occurs no fewer than thirty-one times—next to the word "and" (*kai*) it is the most frequently used single expression. The imperial priests of Galatia "gave" in order to express their gratitude, reverence, and submission to "god Sebastos/Augustus" whom they served, and in order to receive in return the gratitude, reverence, and submission of the people—but it is also from these same people that the wealth spent on the gift was originally taken. The word *take,* of course, is absent from the list, as the social reality behind the gift is at the very core of what the inscription tries to hide. On the side of the recipients, expressions of gratitude and honor toward the priestly donors and benefactors would affirm and reinscribe the basic inequalities and divisions on which the provincial society rested, presenting them as the essential prerequisite for common welfare. And as the headline of the inscription states, these are the "priests of the Galatians serving God Augustus/Sebastos and Goddess Roma." Therefore, the Roman conquest of the world, monumentalized through the background inscription of the *Res Gestae,* appears as the beneficial divine order for the conquered and constitutes what is truly at the core of proper collective Galatian worship and celebration.

Thus, euergetism is part of an efficient Roman micro-management of power structures in which local and imperial rulers support each other, thus minimizing the need and quantity of direct Roman interference and more violent forms of repression.[116] The priest list, with its double message to those above and below—giving honor to Caesar by donating to his subjects, evoking their submission in return—is a model of this principle. Whatever tribal and royal hierarchies had been structuring Galatian life before were now inserted into the overarching vertical order of the worldwide imperial system with Caesar at the top and the imperial priests as benefactors, the mediators of the process that confirmed their status as well.

In the chapter on the Roman arenas above, we briefly reflected on imperial euergetism/benefactions as the doing of "good works" and its relation to Paul's concept of "works righteousness." Our investigation raises the basic question whether this type of "good works," modeled after the hierarchical, competitive, and combative construct of imperial euergetism, might not be at the core of the problem that Paul is targeting when, in Gal 2:16 and 3:2-5, he opposes "works of the law" with faith. Later, in 5:4-6, he will state that in the context of faith righteousness (as opposed to law righteousness) neither circumcision nor foreskin counts as a marker of distinction but only "faith working through love." This points toward a transformed concept of "works" and "faith." It does not reject social practice as irrelevant, as Protestant interpretation has traditionally assumed, but rather projects an entirely new quality of social interaction that is not mirroring the honor, benefaction, and patronage of the divine Caesar but the "shameful" counter-hegemony of a crucified one.[117] Its thrust is not toward status distinctions, upward mobility, and agonistic giving but toward solidarity, the true needs of the poverty-stricken, and a new world order other than the Roman conquest scheme: the order of the new creation (Gal 6:14-15).[118]

That the "works" of benefactions indeed are "works of the law" is not difficult to establish. In general, one might say that the system of euergetism, in conjunction with patronage and the codes of honor/shame, represented and inscribed the imperial law and order of *In/Out* and *High/Low* on the provincial body. The different forms of benefactions molded imperial self-constructs and the *habitus* of submission each in its own specific way. From among the most prominent items on the Ancyran list we will take a closer look at two concrete examples of how this "social engineering" through the good works of imperial law and order happened: meals and arenas/public spectacles.

At first glance, these two donations of the imperial priests to the provincial public do not seem to have much in common. Nevertheless, both of them are forms of mass entertainment intended to "resurrect" the death-bound body of the Galatians and transform it from an outsider to an insider mode. While the public banquet integrates through placing, ranking, and feeding the invited *ones*, the arena divides through segregating, exposing, fighting, and executing the undeserving *others*. Yet, as we have seen, the arena also "places" and occasionally even feeds people, and banquets always necessarily exclude, and sometimes even execute others.[119] Both common meals and public amusement through "games of death" thus contain a significant element of ordering and played an important role in imperial Galatia between 20 and 40 C.E., and presumably thereafter. Moreover, they resonate intensely with two of the core issues of Paul's letter to the Galatians: table community and public death spectacles, that is, crucifixion.

Public Feasts and Banquets Sponsored by the "Koinon"

On the list of priestly benefactions, the dominance of public feasts and banquets (*dēmothoiniai*) is noteworthy. They were "given" by all the priests except one, and there were at least twenty-two such occurrences over the two decades. In five instances, the list specifies the recipients of the imperial priests' hospitality:

> Pylaemenes, son of King Amyntas: for the three tribes (*ethnē*)
> M. Lollius (?): in Pessinus
> Seleucus, son of Philodamos: for the two cities *(polesin)*
> Pylaemenes, son of Menas: for the two tribes (*ethnē*)
> Iulius Aquila (?): for the two tribes (*ethnē*)

The mix of Greek/Roman and Celtic flavor in this summary of invitees is significant—two dedications are to a *polis*, while three are tribal dedications to some or all of the Galatian *ethnē*. This clearly shows the dynamic that was key to Roman colonization. Romanization took place by gradually hellenizing and urbanizing the "alien" tribal matrix over a period of time where *polis* and tribe as social core structures coexisted. The term *ethnē*/tribes in itself is also interesting, as it plays a key role in Paul's letter to the Galatians but is usually translated in an exclusively Jewish reference framework as "Gentiles" (= non-Jews), without any consideration of its political connotations with regard to the vanquished nations/tribes of the Roman Empire.[120]

We do not know exactly who would normally take part in these meals sponsored by the chief priests of the *koinon*. The delegates of the annual celebration of the provincial council? The public of Ancyra? The tribes in their entirety? All of these or a mixture of some sort? It is unlikely that all three (or even two) tribes would have been invited, so some kind of representative tribal meal may have taken place, perhaps in conjunction with the annual meeting of the *koinon*.[121] Nevertheless, the mention of the tribes as such is interesting. It is well known that common meals were of great importance in Celtic societies. Social dominance and leadership were demonstrated by the capacity to give lavish feasts for as many people as possible.

One of the most famed and legendary Celtic super-banquets, for example, was the huge celebration hosted by King Loverius of the Averni in the second century B.C.E. in Gaul, where everybody took part, and even a bard who had arrived too late for the meal was still given a bag of gold.[122] With regard to the public meals organized by the Ancyran *koinon,* Mitchell states that

> it is difficult to resist the conclusion that these feasts perpetuated the well-attested traditions of the Celtic nobility, for whom public banquets offered to the whole tribe were part of their culture. The ethnographic sources which describe Celts both in Gaul and in the eastern Mediterranean make it clear that an important part of the leader's prestige and status depended on his ability to offer unstinting hospitality to his own kinsmen and even to all comers. The public feasts of the Galatian *koinon* fulfilled a comparable function and it would be surprising if they did not preserve some elements of distinctive Celtic tradition.[123]

While meals as sharing of goods in a "potlatch" type of (re-)distribution have an equalizing and "horizontal" dimension, the overall dynamic in such banquets reveals a vertical structure as well. As Dennis Smith, Matthias Klinghardt, and Hal Taussig have shown in their work on Hellenistic meals, horizontal concepts such as equality/*isonomia*, social bonding/*koinōnia*, and friendship/*philia* were vital to the ancient dining protocol and "had the potential to break down social barriers." However, social equality always stood in tension with social stratification, as equality meant that everyone received in accordance with their social status.[124] On the one hand, the donation of a meal within the twin systems of euergetism and patronage increases the authority of the donor and his symbolic capital, obliging the recipients to some kind of reciprocity in terms of support and subservience. On the other hand, a similar hierarchical mechanism works among the participants of the meals themselves. The seating order and the distribution of the different qualities of meat, or in the Greco-Roman culture the permission to recline or not to recline, all indicate a "ranking" of the individual.[125]

This means that the feast itself became the space where social order was demonstrated and established or, on the other hand, challenged and renegotiated, for example, in the Celtic culture through the infamous single combats between rivals that frequently broke out during meals when the "junior elites competed for the choice cut of meat."[126] This is one of the points Greco-Roman authors like to make about the barbarianism of the Celts (for example, Polybius 2.19). But, as Alison Futrell states, this sort of fighting during public meals in Celtic culture was probably a much more ordered and regulated performance that affirmed or transformed the status and standing of the individual and aimed at order and balance. "The feast was thus an articulation and performance of one's place in the Celtic world and cosmos; it was also a dynamic venue for the resolution of tensions within the group, not only through differential access to food items but also through spatial relations."[127]

The function of the Celtic feast as a prominent place to verify or transform one's position in the overall social and even cosmic order would make it an almost ideal vehicle for the transition from a tribal to an imperial/civic way of life in the Roman province of Galatia. That may be the reason why at the time of Tiberius public banquets were so prominent on the Ancyran priest list. Merging Greco-Roman and Celtic features, the festive meal was able to inscribe the new *In/Out* and *High/Low* basics of the Roman order on the social body of the Galatians right at the spot where it was traditionally open to reconfiguration. Mitchell observes that this type of public feast disappears in the late first century and the beginning of the second from among the benefactions of imperial high priests in Galatia. This might support the notion that the *dēmothoinia* of the Ancyran priest list were a Greco-Romano-Celtic hybrid that lost its importance after the initial stage of transition had been accomplished.[128] The public meals of the imperial *koinon* helped to reshape and integrate the Galatian community into the imperial sphere; they replaced the tribal leaders with imperial priests as donors of food, drink, status, and fellowship, and, in the ideological superstructure, ultimately with Caesar himself as supreme host. The potential relevance of this development for Paul's wrestling with issues of table community in Galatians is evident. Taussig has suggested viewing early Christian meals in the framework of social experimentation as resistance to Rome.[129] If Rome used meals to inscribe its law and order on provincial bodies, as the

Ancyran model shows, then we indeed might imagine that segments of the vanquished nations practiced table community as embodiment of a countervision.[130]

Gladiators, Hunts, and Games

The second most frequent item on the Ancyran list of public benefactions made by the *koinon* were games and spectacles. Already in the first readable entry from 20 C.E., Castor, son of King Brigatus, "gives" gladiatorial combats with thirty pairs of gladiators, and at the end of the list Pylaemenes, son of Menas, again offers thirty pairs. Throughout the list, shows (*thea*) in general are mentioned seven times. This may refer to gladiatorial combats but could also mean chariot races, animal hunts, or theater performances.[131] Although an athletic competition (*agōn gymnikos*) and a chariot and horse race are mentioned only once, the overall number of gladiators that were donated by four of the priests amounts to 135 pairs. Furthermore, three of the priests gave wild animal or bull hunts and fights (*kynēgion, tauromachia, taurokathapta, thēromachia*), some of them several times. It is noteworthy that the most generous (and obviously most wealthy) donors of these items came from among the former Galatian royalty. Castor, son of King Brigatus, apart from a public banquet and oil, gave both gladiatorial fights and wild beast hunts; so did Pylaemenes, son of King Amyntas, who even served twice. With the exception of the unknown Rufus, who served between 21 and 22 C.E., bull or beast fights and hunts are mentioned only for these two kingly descendants, who are also the only ones who give both animal as well as gladiatorial fights.

The prominence attributed to public entertainment through "games of death" is obvious. The question of a specific Celtic "barbarian" predisposition toward the arena, refuted with the help of inscriptional evidence by Louis Robert already in 1940,[132] has more recently been raised again from a slightly different angle, drawing attention to the western relatives of the Galatians. In her study on the sociopolitical function of amphitheaters in urban and rural Gaul, Alison Futrell came to the conclusion that the deadly games were introduced by Rome not only for troop management and population control in notoriously rebellious Celtic territories, but also for the unique role they played in assimilating the traditional Celtic way of life to Roman power interests. Concepts that were key to the Celtic worldview were integrated and transformed at the same time: myths of primeval battle and universal struggle, a sense of liminality and natural distinction, the role of single combat and feasts as a public forum for establishing or challenging social hierarchies, and, last but not least, the practice of human sacrifice—all this prepared the Celtic community, according to Futrell, for the arena.

> The Celtic community was predisposed toward the arena; the performance of ritualized combat played an important role in Celtic religious practice and constituted a "tournament of value" in the Celtic social economy, even prior to the coming of the Romans. Into this environment Rome introduced the amphitheater, an institution charged with meaning in Roman politics and cult but also an institution readily susceptible to a Celtic

interpretation of authority and the sacred. The Celtic rural amphitheaters could thus serve as a venue for the symbolic reconstitution of the status quo on the mortal and the cosmic level, a syncretization of Celtic and Roman symbolic systems.[133]

Futrell observes how closely in the Gallic West the amphitheater was linked to the activities of the *koinon* at the imperial Celtic sanctuary at Lugdunum, the capital of the three Gauls that was set up in 12 B.C.E. The annual celebration of imperial religion at the beginning of August—traditionally the festival of the supreme Celtic god Lug after whom the city of Lugdunum was named but now the beginning of the newly defined "month of Augustus"—probably included games of the *koinon*. The amphitheater where they would have taken place still contains traces of inscriptions that determine a tribal seating order. As an integral part of the holy imperial precinct at Lugdunum, the amphitheater, in Futrell's view, may have been the end point of a festive procession of state gods, priests, magistrates, and combatants that started at the imperial altar with the inscription of the sixty Galatian tribes. The close linkage between imperial altar/sanctuary, assembly of the *koinon,* and amphitheater can be shown most clearly at Lugdunum, but it is traceable in other imperial cult complexes around the empire as well.[134]

These findings regarding the province of Gaul accord with the data of the Ancyran priest list and should not be ignored in our investigation of Roman Galatia. The close nexus of imperial cult, provincial congregation, and games is so clearly confirmed by this unique document of the Galatian *koinon* that it might even add evidence to Futrell's argument. Nevertheless, the precise details can be reconstructed only hypothetically. We do not know, for example, where exactly the games were held that are mentioned on the Ancyran list and how much of a distinctly Celtic flavor they had—whether all 135 pairs of gladiators and all the animals fought at Ancyra or whether small rural sanctuaries as in Gaul existed, maybe at former tribal strongholds.[135]

Another interesting question is whether the spectacles (*thea*) of the Ancyran *koinon* perhaps indeed included some kind of theatrical performance, not as an alternative to but in combination with gladiatorial combat. We have already seen that the Roman arenas integrated theatrical elements (see chapter 3 above). The same seems to have happened in Gaul. Futrell points out that the standard form of amphitheater in Gallia Lugdunensis was the so-called mixed edifice, which combined theater and amphitheater in a hybrid "multipurpose entertainment center," of which at least twenty-one have been found.[136] Were the games of death in their syncretized Romano-Celtic version both in Gaul and in Galatia perhaps a multidimensional performance where a gladiatorial fight was staged as a reenactment of Celtic warrior legends and Greco-Roman combat mythology? Was perhaps even Heracles—at Pergamon still the highest-ranking slayer of Giants/Galatians—on the new stage of the imperial (amphi)theater assimilated to the old Celtic heroes?[137]

Whatever the answer to these intriguing questions, one point is clear. The games of the imperial *koinon,* like the public meals, served as a kind of monumental crossroads and "turnstile" where Celtic civilization became incorporated into the dominant culture of the Roman Empire. To quote Futrell once again:

The amphitheater allowed a very large group of spectators to share in the affirmation of loyalty to the central authority, the confirmation of the ruler's divine nature and his concomitant justification as ruler, and the identification of the individual with the rest of the community. . . . The establishment of this sort of corporate identity in the provinces was a more important goal in the early Principate, when a whole series of such relationships, on many levels and involving many social groups, was first being established and codified. . . . The amphitheater accommodated and contributed to the establishment of the stable hierarchy necessary for maintaining order in the provinces.[138]

Those who had been enemies of Rome since ancient times received a new "corporate identity" as her subjects, servants, and soldiers. Ironically, the same enthusiasm for fierce fighting that had turned them into foes of mythological dimensions now made the Galatians prone to submission. Every time they consumed the entertainment and ideology of the arena, they pledged allegiance to the Roman emperor and his battle against chaos; every time they looked down at the agony of the *others,* they took on the orderly shape of their *new self* in accepting the Roman power structure with the tax burdens, wars, and everything else it imposed; and every time they cheered at a victory won on the sand of the arena, they celebrated the death of the Giants, their *old self,* as universal salvation.

This is a vivid illustration of what Ando describes as the *body politic* of empire, that is, the perpetual search of its rulers "to found their actions on the *consensus* of their subjects, making them active participants in their own subjugation by urging them to iterate the principles of the ruling order."[139] Maybe this is the "setting in life" where one of Paul's most authentic and uncensored exclamations in his Galatian correspondence gains immediate plausibility: "You stupid Galatians . . ." (Gal 3:1).

——— Conclusion: Imperial versus Messianic Justification ———

Paul continues his famous affront with a question of vision and eyesight: "Who bewitched you? It was before your eyes that Jesus Christ was publicly exhibited as crucified" (3:1). The image of Christ crucified appears to contest another way of "seeing" that is obviously more plausible to the Galatians and that Paul slanders as witchcraft and "evil eye." After we have looked in this chapter at the stunning metamorphosis of the Galatians from barbarian outlaws to imperial subjects and soldiers, the overall phenomenon of an *imperial re-imagination* offers itself almost irresistibly as the backdrop for Paul's passionate outcry against wrong modes of perception. For at the end of the day, when the great transfer of images was completed and the Dying Gauls had become "resurrected" as Sebastēni Galatai under Augustus, Galatians were no longer free to choose how to see the world, in particular the image at the core of the dominant worldview: the image of self and other. Is it possible that Paul, with his blunt attack on their "bewitched" vision, tries to remind the Galatians of the messianic countervision they had shared, and that he aims much more at the normative imperial master images than at perceptions of Jewish Torah?

To see the image of the crucified not as the image of an evil other to be lawfully destroyed but as the image of the world savior and divine life-giver, shatters all the images of power that were the embodiment of imperial ideology, most notably the dyadic icon at its center—the image of the defeated enemy/other that as its flipside held up the idol of the triumphant self. To substitute "works of the (imperial) law" by faith in the crucified, as Paul urges in the sentence immediately following, destroys the very foundations of warfare, victory, and the imperial power establishment built on it. It dismantles the self/other perceptions that are produced in the public spectacles of the arena as rigorously as the basic notions of godhead and supreme power ingrained in the observances of imperial religion. To exhibit the messiah and God-self as crucified and dying like one of the Dying Gauls, and to do so "publicly," is the most fundamental attack on the normative way of "seeing."

Yet, according to Paul's own report in 6:14-17, this was precisely the image he embodied while he was writing to the Galatians, being marked by the "stigmata" of the crucified in his own body. This image was the icon at the core of the counter-imperial messianic pedigree that Paul derived from the Jewish ancestor Abraham to give the vanquished nations their new identity and belonging, instead of renaming and "repatriating" them through the Julio-Claudian fathers Aeneas, Romulus, or Caesar (3:7, 16, 29). It also represented the image he himself depicted when he first met the Galatians in despicable weakness and agony, an image they embraced when they received him "like Christ/messiah Jesus himself" (4:13-14). They could as well have despised him and spit at him, as they were trained to spit at the suffering other in the arena, or during public triumphs and crucifixions. But they did not. This, from all we can know, was the beginning of the Jesus movement in Galatia, that is, of the Galatians' nonimperial identity transformation and messianic rebirth that is now in danger of being aborted (4:19).

Within an imperial imagination, everything about this image of Christ crucified and the mode of perception it creates is wrong. It tampers with at least three icons that are sacrosanct and literally as well as metaphorically set in stone everywhere: the image of the divine, the image of Caesar, and the image of the Dying Gauls/Galatians/Giants themselves. Like the Dying Galatians, the crucified Jew Jesus belongs among the transgressors of Roman law who are defined as unjust and unjustifiable enemies of imperial and divine order and whose dying therefore is righteous. By resurrecting Jesus, the one God of Israel has openly challenged the singular power of the divine Caesar to define law and to impose death, and to restore life and righteousness to the vanquished at his discretion. The centerpiece of the "monotheistic" imperial construct falls apart without the exclusiveness of the one imperial deity who claims to be the sole god capable of granting the mercy/favor/grace (Greek *charis*) of survival and justification to those who are doomed to die for their lawlessness.

Contemplating their dying forebears, the living Galatians of Paul's time were officially supposed to understand themselves and to act as grateful creatures of Caesar's grace, which had fathered and borne, justified and repatriated them, and given them their proper name, pedigree, identity, and faith. Attaching Galatian identity and genealogy, faith and righteousness, ultimate destiny and origin to an executed other of the Roman order rather than to the executing imperial self, as Paul does, is reversion and perversion at once—nothing less than an iconoclastic blasphemy and violation of Caesar's majesty, an attack of truly "giant" nature on the images and ideologies of Roman power. That the Dying Gauls/Galatians/Giants could be vindicated and raised from their divinely ordained death sentence by fighting the right enemies, cheering the right victories, serving the right masters—Roman masters, Roman victories, Rome's enemies—was the Roman idea of a "resurrection" of the vanquished nations. Their righteousness and life, established on another god's faith and grace alone, enshrined in the image of an (Un-)Dying Jew and without any works of imperial law, are what makes Paul's justification theology the dangerous messianic countervision of a nonimperial world order, the *new creation* of the kingdom of God (cf. Gal 5:21; 6:14-15). All this will be further discussed in chapter 6.

In this chapter we have explored several media and modes that over a period of several centuries integrated the Galatians as former model barbarians into the orbit of civilization and Roman order: dynasty and pedigree building, military formation, cities, and above all imperial religiosity, most notably meals and games as donations and benefactions of the emperor and his representatives, the high priests of the imperial *koinon*. The imperial resurrection of the Dying Gauls/Galatians in terms of their Roman rehabilitation and repatriation as subservient subjects of the empire was, on the surface, a success story.

Yet we do not know what happened behind the official facade. Did the "ordinary" Galatians under Augustus, Tiberius, Caligula, Claudius, and Nero dispute the extent to which the imperial benefactions were truly beneficial? Were there even pockets of resistance, efforts to maintain and return to old and more horizontal tribal affiliations and practices? Or was there rather some critical recognition of how their own venerable traditions of combat, competition, and victory were now "naturalized" and exploited by Rome, devouring and enslaving themselves (cf. 5:15)? Was there a reluctance to acclaim Caesar as world god?

None of this we know. But perhaps we might try to (re-)imagine Paul as he enters this conflicting field, raising these very questions and presenting an *other* option: the option of a peace on terms completely different from Caesar's Pax Romana; of a god who belongs to all *ethnē*/tribes/nations but does not speak with the voice of and fight on the side of their conquerors; of a "divine son" (*divi filius*) dying in solidarity with the vanquished and being resurrected by a power other than Rome's; of a local yet global life practice that functions horizontally instead of vertically, fundamentally subverting the imperial world order of self versus other by creating mixed communities that cultivate nonviolent conflict resolution and share mutual benefactions based on need rather than the hierarchical obligations endemic to the Greco-Roman codes of patronage, euergetism, and honor.

To find the traces of this messianic life practice, one has to focus attention at precisely those crucial parts of Paul's letter that have often been neglected in the name of "faith" versus "works." Alternatively, the ethical sections in Galatians 5–6 can be seen as a key to Paul's theology, as they give some indications what the "work(ing) of faith" as opposed to the "work(ing) of imperial law" (5:6) might concretely imply. Love as the "law of Christ" (6:2) has the one bear the other's burden; it has the self serve rather than consume the other as rival in the race for status, honor, power, and distinction. The competitive order that marks the core of imperial law surfaces in Paul's parenesis with astonishing power as the behavioral code and (by implication) *law* he opposes (for example, 5:13-15, 26). Love as the focal commandment and fulfillment of Torah (5:6, 16) is the decisive faith-work that manifests the inherent otherness of God's law from Caesar's law. This otherness of Torah, however, might have become blurred by the ways both Jews and Galatians believed they had to replicate the benefactions, grace, and "good works" of the emperor in order to be "justified."

This finally takes us to the core question of the letter: Why do the Galatians and their Jewish "teachers" think that they have to be circumcised, and why does Paul reject this move as a justification through works of the *wrong law*—not the law of Christ, nor the law of the Jews properly understood, but the law of empire? In order to get a clearer picture of the Galatian "apostasy" we must finally and as a last step take a look at licit and illicit modes of association among the conquered nations and tribes (*ethnē*) in a Roman province like Galatia that make the imperial entanglement of circumcision demands and "Judaizing" tendencies in Paul's congregations visible.

Gigantomachy scene on the right wing of the Great Staircase. In this uppermost corner of the Battle Frieze, Zeus's eagle strikes at a serpent-monster, symbolically protecting the entrance of city and civilization under his wings. Detail from the scene shown on p. 113. Photo: Jakob B. Rehmann.

CHAPTER FIVE

Under the Eagle's Wings and (C)laws

Messianic Insurrection among Dying Gauls and Jews

At some point toward the middle of the first century C.E., a man who plainly identifies himself as a Jew comes, under rather dramatic circumstances not altogether clear to us, to encounter a group of *Galatai,* "Galatians" (Gal 3:1), who unexpectedly step up as his helpers in his severe distress (Gal 4:13-14). One possible scenario is that he had run into trouble with agents of the civic establishment because of his "un-Roman" missionary activities and that the Galatians became his "Good Samaritans" as his life was on the edge, perhaps after he had suffered severe physical punishment. This encounter and his subsequent stay with them in "Galatia" (Gal 1:2) profoundly change who they are and who he is. In theoretical terms, their socioreligious self-perception and adherence shift toward what we might call an uncommon hybridity. They come to think of themselves in a way as Jews and yet in a way they stay non-Jews—"Gentiles," nations, too. Paul claims that "in Christ" they are as fully children of Abraham and his God as he is himself, but they are neither proselytes proper—that is, they are not circumcised—nor are they merely uncircumcised affiliates and sympathizers of the synagogue.

About developments after Paul's departure we are mostly in the dark, except for the arrival of other Jews who are concerned by what they encounter. These Jews strongly challenge the messianic identity of the Galatians and push them to clarify who they really are, either by being circumcised in order to become properly Jewish, or by staying uncircumcised and thus returning to the recognizable civic patterns of behavior shared by the rest of the non-Jews ("nations"). Paul vehemently opposes both options.

In this chapter we take up the questions that are most directly relevant for the reading of Galatians: Why is the messianic association of circumcised Jews and uncircumcised Galatians a controversial issue in Roman Galatia? Are Rome and its law in any way involved? Can we trace a discourse of nonconformity and resistance beneath the arcane language of Jewish ancestry, ritual law, and scriptural quotations that shapes Paul's argument in his Galatian letter?

We will begin with a brief look at Paul's fellow Jews as the other party, alongside Galatians and Romans, implied in his correspondence. Who, in the context of an eastern province like Roman Galatia, are they? And why do some of their representatives—Paul's ominous "opponents"—press for circumcision among the male

Christ-followers? To understand more fully the historical background of this demand and the inclinations of the Galatians to comply with it, we must look at established and acknowledged patterns of "proper" association between Jews and Galatians within the power structures of the Roman Empire—patterns evident, for example, with regard to Herod the Great's Galatian bodyguard, or the Roman-Galatian imperial priestess Julia Severa, a contemporary of Paul, and her favors to the Jewish synagogue of Acmonia.

Against this overall backdrop, the unspoken and unseen part of Paul's Galatian correspondence finally begins to emerge from historical oblivion. The letter reveals an irreconcilable tension between the law of the imperial order, on the one hand, and the construction of identity and community practice of Paul's messianic congregations, on the other—that is, between imperial *koinon* and messianic *koinōnia*.

Jews in Asia Minor as Insiders and Outsiders of the Roman Order

At the Great Altar of Pergamon, as we saw in chapter 2, the top of the staircase marks the sacred threshold from *Out* to *In* as the symbolic entrance to city and civilization, the magic divide between *Us* and *Them* and the spot most carefully guarded by the Roman eagle. The eagle at Hellenistic Pergamon was the personification of Zeus's supreme *logos* and law. In Paul's time, however, it had come to signify Caesar's *logos* and law, which determined who was *In* and who was *Out,* distinguishing self from other. Thus far, we have considered the history of the Galatians as lawless barbarians and dying others positioned symbolically at the *underside* and *outside* of the Great Altar, and the various modes of their "resurrection" into lawful indwellers of the Roman order. We have explored the building up of dynasties and power structures, of cities and roads, of the imperial war machine, and, most prominently, of imperial religion in Roman Galatia as the principal means of vindicating, integrating, and reinscribing the Galatian body in compliance with the laws of Roman selfhood (chapter 4).

The issue of circumcision, which is at the center of Paul's letter, somehow does not seem to fit into this framework. Why should foreskin or no foreskin matter in terms of imperial law in Roman Galatia? Galatian foreskin as such was surely of no interest to Rome; how much more far-fetched and awkward, then, to propose that the Galatians' motive in seeking circumcision might have been to make themselves acceptable to Roman law! Jewish circumcision certainly did not count among the physical markers of newly won Romanness that an ex-barbarian might present as a symbolic ticket at the Great Staircase. It was no valid passport for escaping the eagle's deadly claws in order to be admitted to the identity of a civic self under its protective wings. Or was it?

The concrete ways for colonized people to negotiate and uphold an alternative social space without risking direct and deadly confrontations with the colonizers are far more complex and murky than our usual constructs, often neat and naïve as they are, allow us to see.[1] Within a hermeneutics of resistance, the absence of any direct mention of the conflicts, fears, and pressures inhering in a colonial situation is more to be expected than an explicit argument against their powerful presence. Still, we are moving on hypothetical ground if we contend that there might have been one particular moment in history, one specific political configuration, when the decision to adopt Jewish circumcision for Paul's messianic Galatians appeared as a possible escape route from a dangerous confrontation with Roman law. To understand this proposal we have first to turn to the issue of Jewish law and the precarious *inside/outside* mode of Jewish existence within the Roman order.

Jewish Settlements and Their Unsettling Aspects

The foundation of the Jewish settlements in Asia Minor goes back to Antiochus III. Between 212 and 205/4 B.C.E., he sent about ten thousand Jews as military colonists from Mesopotamia to Phrygia and Lydia in order to maintain internal stability and thus safeguard Seleucid rule in the area.[2] Typically, such colonies were charged with protecting sensitive lines of communication, trade routes, or frontier zones and stopping insurgencies. The Jewish colonists were granted land and were allowed to live according to their own laws, that is, to have a degree of separate organization. According to Paul Trebilco, we know of Jewish settlements in over fifty places in Asia Minor during the imperial period, and "doubtless there were many more."[3] As regards Roman Galatia in particular, Jewish settlements in the provincial territory are somewhat unclear, especially in the northern tribal areas, but in Paul's time there was certainly a Jewish presence in the cities of the South such as Pisidian Antioch or Iconium, and probably elsewhere as well.[4] For the purposes of our study, which does not focus on the South or North Galatian location of Paul's addressees, it is sufficient to state that Judaism in general was a well-known, well-established, and relevant element in the overall ethnic and religious mix of Galatia, irrespective of provincial boundaries or extant epigraphic and archeological evidence.

The Jews had entered Asia Minor a little later in the same century as the Galatians, and under somewhat analogous terms. Their settlement, too, was in return for the political and military favors they had to render. Like the Galatians, the Jews were dependent on, subservient to, and used or abused variously by the "big players" of the power game, most notably the Seleucids and Rome. Their existence on the whole appears as less conspicuous than that of the Galatians, however, and more on the side of the established order. In Paul's time the Jews, like the Galatians, had by and large rather successfully gained an "insider" status and, for some of them, even an upper status in the eastern part of the Roman Empire. Jewish communities were relatively well embedded and connected within the overall framework of the Hellenistic cities and had achieved a widely successful modus vivendi.[5]

A profound ideological ambiguity never ceased to overshadow their demeanor as reliable and lawful subjects of the empire, however. Living in Diaspora settlements all around the Mediterranean, the Jews in a way were global players like the Gauls/Galatians, but on different terms. They had never attacked Rome, Delphi, or Pergamon, and their "lawlessness" was of a different order from that of the Galatians, who always retained a "shadow side" as mythological agents of barbarian chaos and upheaval. The Jews were known as the people of an ancient and sophisticated law; and anything of ancient origin was accorded high standing in the Roman world, which honored the "law of the ancestors" (*mos maiorum*) and "traditional religion" even among the conquered.[6] Yet the Mosaic law to which the Jews adhered with a kind of stubborn perseverance that often astonished and infuriated their masters had, from a Roman perspective, a decisive flaw. It made Judaism more resistant than other traditional religions to what we might call "imperial modernization."

Jewish Monotheism as Counter-religion

The crucial point was Jewish monotheism. It not only claimed that the God of the Jews was the one and only God, but from a Greco-Roman perspective it implied a whole range of offensive and even subversive practices that undermined city, civilization, and empire. In his famous Jewish excursus in book 5 of the *Histories,* Tacitus lists these practices simply as an inversion, a negation of the proper and familiar order upheld by Roman and any other "true" religion. Linked to its shameful origin as a religion of disease-ridden outcasts expelled from Egypt, Judaism was, in Tacitus's view, introduced by Moses as "a new cult, which was the opposite of all other religions [*novos ritus contrariosque ceteris mortalibus*]. All that we hold sacred they held profane, and they allowed practices which we abominate" (*Hist.* 5.4).

This "contrarian" (*contrarios*) existence and reversal of the established socioreligious consensus, as stated by Tacitus, made Jews antipatriotic, antisocial, and antireligious. Their law required them to stay separate from all other nations in terms of taxation, food, Sabbath, family, cult, and culture.[7] They practically formed their own "city within the city"—a city oriented toward Jerusalem as worldwide capital, whereas the civic communities at large were oriented toward the universal city of Rome. Although in reality Jewish separation constituted only one side of a broad conceptual and behavioral spectrum that also comprised assimilation, acculturation, and accommodation, this cultural and social antagonism stayed as a decisive identity marker.[8]

That the Jewish God did not allow his people to participate fully in the various observances of civic and imperial piety that represented and celebrated, safeguarded, and restored the order of the world posed a severe problem. Taking care of the very gods whose benevolence everyone saw as foundational for the well-being of the city and empire was rejected by Jewish law as idolatry already in its first commandment (Exod 20:1-3; Deut 5:6-7). This "atheism" made Jewish integration into the city always somewhat fragile, even where the Jewish community was solidly established, as it was in Asia Minor.[9] We should note that in their appearance as "godless" members of an "antireligion," the Jews were strikingly close to Gauls/Galatians.[10] There was an enduring potential to perceive them as enemies of the city and of the whole human race, as potential rebels and blasphemers, as superstitious foreigners whose otherness was likely to provoke the wrath of the gods and therefore required atonement—especially if any calamity such as drought, famine, or disease should befall the city.[11]

Circumcision

Jewish circumcision, according to Tacitus, was the external marker of this notorious Jewish otherness that found its expression in specific particularist regulations and practices, for example, with regard to table fellowship and food, Sabbath, the Jerusalem temple tax, intermarriage, and ritual calendar. Next to the separation from others "both in meals and in bed,"[12] circumcision in his text functions as the permanent bodily sign of difference:

> They have introduced circumcision to distinguish themselves from other people. Those who are converted to their customs adopt the same practice, and the first lessons they learn are to despise the gods, to renounce their country, and to regard parents, children, and brethren as worthless. (*Hist.* 5.5)

It is noteworthy that in Tacitus's construction of Jewishness as ultimate otherness and reversal of the Roman self, circumcision becomes a kind of shorthand for conversion to Judaism as separation from the community at large. It is a signifier of distinction linked to the signified of Jewish godlessness, nonpatriotism, and neglect of patriarchal and family ties.[13] This betrayal of the established value system and order naturally is perceived as even more offensive in proselytes, who actively decide to make a transition from *us* to *them* and who, according to Tacitus, are taught to "despise the gods, to renounce their country and to regard parents, children, and brethren as worthless."[14] The precarious notion of boundary transgressions, on the one hand, and the widely accepted "official" identification of circumcision = Jewishness, on the other hand, are crucial to understanding the context of Galatians.[15]

[handwritten margin note: This equation is what Paul is up against — yet radical Jonshu against Romanness]

Worship without Images

The Jewish ban on images of anything in heaven, on earth or "in the waters under the earth" and the prohibition against worshiping them—that is, the second commandment in the Mosaic Decalogue (Exod 20:4-5; Deut 5:8-9)—made things worse.[16] As we saw in chapter 3, the common practice among religious communities throughout the Roman Empire was to add the emperor's image as another cult image in the established temples. This, however, was taboo when it came to the Jews. As Josephus recounts, even a relatively modest gesture, like the golden eagle King Herod the Great put up at the entrance of the Jerusalem temple, led to massive protests that eventually cost the lives of thousands of Jews.[17] The import of an image that synonymously spelled out Zeus's (Jupiter's) rule and Caesar's "divine" supremacy over Judea was all too well understood and all too intolerable to the Jewish population.

A few decades later, Emperor Caligula (37–41 C.E.) tried to have a statue of himself as *Neos Zeus Epiphanēs* (Philo, *Leg.* 346) installed in the Jerusalem temple, an effort

that was sternly opposed by the Jewish community. Their resistance was about to esca-
late into a military confrontation, but the clash and its disastrous consequences were
eventually prevented by the moderation of the Roman legate of Syria and the emper-
or's assassination.[18] These events were preceded by a series of murderous outbursts
of anti-Jewish violence in the city of Alexandria, the capital of Roman Egypt, which
also included the forced erection of imperial images and statues in the synagogues, as
Philo reports (*Flacc.* 41–43). Even a brazen statue of Caligula borne on a four-horse
chariot was erected in the greatest and most conspicuous synagogue of the city (*Leg.
Gai.* 135–38). The images posed a severe dilemma; they were effectively desecrating the
synagogues for worship, yet they could not be easily removed, as this would be tantamount to political irreverence toward the emperor.[19]

Caligula's particular obsession with his image and deification brought to the fore
a problem that, slightly less conspicuously, had always been there. In a world where
the reality presented and created by the power of images mattered a lot, the imageless
religion of Israel came dangerously close to subversion.[20] On the one hand, no statue
of Israel's God was available to be placed into the Roman pantheon, where the gods
of the vanquished nations were housed to demonstrate the benevolence and religious
tolerance of the Romans toward the rites of the defeated nations (and, not incidentally,
their deities' consent to their conquest). On the other hand, the divine Caesar could
not as easily, as, for example, at Pergamon, Athens, or Rome, be presented as *synnaos*,
a housemate of the Jewish God in his Jerusalem temple or in the synagogues around
the Mediterranean.[21] Rather, the Jews insisted, according to Josephus, on their ancestral law, which prohibited "an image of God, much more of a man, not only in their
sanctuary but even in any unconsecrated spot throughout the country" (*B.J.* 2.195).
This posed a substantial problem since it blurred the representation of the carefully
constructed Roman worldview. Petronius, the Roman governor of Syria charged with
installing Caligula's image in Jerusalem through the force of his legions, tries to argue
the case in front of the noncompliant Jews:

> All the subject nations, he urged, had erected in each of their cities statues of Caesar,
> along with those of their other gods, and that they alone should oppose this practice
> amounted almost to rebellion, aggravated by insult. (Josephus, *B.J.* 2.194, LCL)

Interestingly, the question of images is the point where Tacitus as well, at the end of
his excursus on Jewish otherness in *Histories* 5, becomes most explicit about the incom-
patibility between the Jewish god and Caesar.

> The Jews acknowledge one god only, of whom they have a purely spiritual conception.
> They think it impious to make images of gods in human shape out of perishable materials.
> Their god is almighty and eternal, inimitable and without end. They therefore set up no
> statues in their temples, nor even in their cities, refusing this homage to their kings and
> this honor to the Roman emperors. (5.6)

Refusing the honor of images and statues to the emperor is dangerously seditious behavior.[22] This is something Tacitus does not need to mention explicitly at this point in his famous anti-Jewish digression in *Hist.* 5.2–5, for the whole excursus is framed by the report of Titus's siege of Jerusalem (5.1–13). The description of the religious deviance of Judaism thus becomes focal to Tacitus's account of the violent military and political clash between Rome and Jerusalem. At this point in his narrative, the Roman army is still stationed outside Jerusalem, the rebellious Jewish metropolis that it will finally conquer and destroy in 70 c.e., together with the temple of its alien and perverse religion. It is clear that the oneness and otherness of the Jewish God and the insurgence of his people, of which their refusal of images is an emblem, are, for Tacitus, two sides of the same coin: Jewish Torah. It is the law of the Jews with its subversive potential of "codified lawlessness" that from a Roman perspective requires drastic measures in order to pacify Jewish insubordination once and for all.

In light of these deliberations, we have again to turn back to the Great Altar. The imageless Jewish God is obviously not depicted among the deities of the Great Frieze as they fight their cosmic battle against chaos and rebellion "from below." This God was visually "not presentable" as part of the heavenly alliance under the victorious leadership of Zeus (or Jupiter or Caesar). The relevant question for our purposes is whether this absence is "only" an issue of forbidden images—so to speak, of single discrete ordinances in Jewish law concerned with ritual—or whether the problem is much more basic: namely, a fundamental disagreement between Israel's aniconic God and the imperial icons of law and order displayed at the Great Altar and elsewhere, especially the image of world and humanity that they project. Does the protest against the images target nothing apart from images per se or implicitly also the social and political realities of Roman rule that are sanctioned and sanctified by them? Could one imagine that Israel's God, though visually absent at the Great Altar, was nevertheless at least invisibly present, implicated as part of the imperial scheme of divine power that governs the world, smashes the losers, and validates the law of the victorious, the sacred divide between self and other? Some of Paul's fellow Jews like Flavius Josephus and the high-ranking Jewish power brokers he cites would probably find this acceptable in one way or another.[23] Others, however, would vehemently disagree, Paul among them. Yet within a broad spectrum of anti-Roman resistance that claimed Torah as a space of nonaccommodation to foreign rule and religion, his position was that of a tiny and peculiar minority. [24]

Torah in the Eagle's Clutches: Clashes and Compromises

A core concern of Roman diplomacy was to play down the profound difference between Jewish law (or the law of any colonized people) and imperial world law as nothing but ritual idiosyncrasies. Roman diplomacy aimed at conciliatory policies to promote a carefully controlled self-rule (meaning self-policing and self-jurisdiction) in conquered territories for the sake of order, stable tax payments, and the easy movements of soldiers. This type of limited autonomy meant that the Jews were given permission to live, within bounds, according to their own law.[25] A well-established "normalcy" of Jewish integration under Roman rule tolerated the ancestral traditions of the Jews and smoothed out the rough edges of anti-idolatrous zeal, especially in the cities of the Roman East.[26] Nevertheless, the demands of imperial religion, traditionally largely underestimated in New Testament scholarship, were probably quite imposing both in Roman Palestine and in the Diaspora, as recent research has shown, and required constant negotiation.[27]

With regard to civic and imperial sacrifices, for example, the mandatory mechanisms for securing the *pax deorum* (the well-being and benevolence of the gods), an empire-wide compromise helped to reconcile Jewish and Roman religion: twice each day, a sacrifice was offered on behalf of the Roman emperor in the Jerusalem temple, paid for by the whole worldwide Jewish community through their taxes sent to Jerusalem.[28] In addition to prayers on behalf of the emperor and honorary dedications, this substitute sacrifice served in lieu of the imperial sacrifices and celebrations at Pergamon, Galatia, and elsewhere, in which the Jews could not participate except very partially. It functioned as a lawful protective umbrella for the Jewish community in the Roman world.[29]

This does not necessarily imply that the Jews had a permanently acknowledged legal status as a "licit religion," yet it means that a flexible and relatively reliable mode of accommodation and inclusion had been found that usually allowed the Jews, metaphorically speaking, to enter the symbolic inside of the city (and of the civilization represented in the Great Altar) without directly submitting to the Olympic gods and father Zeus (or the divinized Caesar).[30] They did not need to use the Great Staircase, so to speak, but received tacit permission to ascend by a "back stair," as it were, circumventing but not resisting the controlling dominance and divinity of the imperial eagle. For even if the Jews did not worship the Olympic and local gods, there was no doubt that they had to submit to the dominant imperial order that was sanctioned by these deities. It was Roman power itself that granted the Jews a license to abstain officially from its worship by this "minimum acceptable act of allegiance"[31] acknowledging Rome's supremacy. This was a politically viable solution, though full of inherent contradictions and significant theological problems. The Torah of the one God who did not tolerate other gods had in effect become a favor granted by the supreme representative of idolatry, the *one other god,* Caesar.

The acceptability of this arrangement, however, was probably promoted by a long-standing tradition that preceded the Roman Empire. In an interesting study, Seth Schwartz has shown that both Torah and Temple, chief symbols of first-century Jewish corporate identity, owed a substantial part of their defining power to ongoing imperial support from the time of the Babylonian exile to that of the emperor Nero.[32] It was Persian sponsorship in the time of Ezra and Nehemia that had established the Second Temple in 515 B.C.E. and subsequently authorized the "Torah of Moses" as the "official law of the Judahites."[33]

Cyrus posed as a liberator, a restorer of gods and peoples following the depredations and deportations of the Babylonians, and this pose became a fixture of Persian imperial rhetoric. In practice, the Persians tended to patronize native oligarchies, preferably those with strong connections to temples, and encouraged them to regulate the legal and economic activities of their provinces. This last consideration may help explain the imperial patronage of the Torah. Though probably the work mostly of reformists and radicals, the Torah claimed to be the traditional law of the Israelites and was the only Jewish law code available. . . . The desired and sometimes attained result of the Persians' interventionism was a smoothly running, peaceful, and consistently profitable empire.[34]

Schwartz's reference to the "reformist and radical" origin of Torah sheds light on a basic contradiction in the use of the Jewish law code as one of the prime "repositories of power in Hellenistic and Roman Jewish Palestine." Schwartz describes this problem as a "mild tension between hierarchical and egalitarian principles" in the way Torah envisions society, that is, between vertical and horizontal elements.[35] I would go one step further. This "tension" was an irresolvable disparity between biblical monotheism and its social implications, on the one hand, and the religion and social order imposed by imperial conquerors, on the other, a dialectic inscribed on the innermost fabric of Torah.[36] This may help to explain why Jewish law could be claimed for Jewish causes at opposing ends of the social and political spectrum. If, as Schwartz maintains, the dominant interpretation of Torah was linked to temple and high priesthood, both tightly controlled by Rome,[37] it was also the case that a counter-interpretation of Torah "from below" could claim the authority of Israel's prophetic and exodus tradition, as well as of the Maccabean resistance to the violation and usurpation of law—of temple, land, and people of Israel—by the established power apparatus.

Paul, as we will see in the next chapter, undoubtedly perceived himself as a continuation of Old Testament prophecy, and he was also shaped by a profoundly "Maccabean" anti-idolatrous zeal within an exodus framework. To understand Paul's law criticism in Galatians, one of the most thorny issues of Pauline exegesis, as a prophetic, empire-critical reassessment of prevalent (ab)uses of Torah by Roman *nomos/lex* offers a far more plausible interpretational model than the traditional Christian antithesis of "law versus gospel" can provide. What Paul has in mind, then, is not an abandonment of Jewish law; rather, it is the law's faithful reclamation and liberation from a long "Babylonian" (but more precisely, Persian, then Roman) captivity that constitutes the core content of his gospel.

Paul, from this perspective, is part of an ongoing debate on the fundamental opposition between Jewish Torah and Greco-Roman *nomos,* an opposition only partially masked by a dominant ideology that presented them as pragmatically compatible. Tacitus's comments, quoted above, on the outcast origins and disorderly nature of Jews as such convey an irreconcilable conflict between imperial order and Torah. From the perspective of rebellious discourses among the conquered themselves, this same antagonism is asserted as the "lawful" (in terms of Torah) refusal to accept the subjection of land and people to Roman law and supremacy, the refusal to allow the one God of Israel to be held as Caesar's court hostage.[38] Paul's message must be situated in this debate, though without the resort to armed resistance among some of his contemporaries and with the surprising slant of reaching out to the non-Jewish nations in a new hybrid mixture of radical Torah particularism and all-inclusive Torah universalism.[39] His preaching of God's crucified and resurrected Messiah and of the nations being integrated into God's people, confronts imperial representations of law and order with countervailing assumptions and practices that signal a level of dissidence ultimately more difficult to control and crush than the violent uprising of 66–70 C.E.[40]

Not everyone was willing to see Roman rule as a permanent conflict between Caesar and Israel's God in which the core question of Torah—God or the idols? (Exod 20:1)—was constantly at stake. Not everyone was ready to pay the price for such a radical perception. Jewish Torah and Roman *lex* (or *nomos*) were inseparably linked wherever Jews lived under Roman domination, and there was no "Rome-free" zone in Judea, Galilee, or any part of the Mediterranean Diaspora. Even the Jerusalem temple was guarded by Roman soldiers watching from the Antonia garrison that overshadowed it (named after Marc Antony) as the visible embodiment of Roman law.[41] How to respond to this omnipresent encounter between Jewish Torah and Roman *lex* was nevertheless, and not accidentally, a highly contentious issue among Jews. The surprisingly broad spectrum of concrete Jewish practices that negotiated "inside" and "outside" with regard to the non-Jewish world at large raised the constant question of how far one could go in either direction without betraying one's Jewish identity and the oneness of Israel's God, on the one hand, and without jeopardizing Jewish security and the precious privileges of (semi-)autonomy in the precarious civic context, on the other.[42]

With its inherent tensions and irreconcilable contradictions, this compromise between Jewish Torah and Greco-Roman *nomos* was under constant challenge from all sides. It is no accident that a priestly refusal to continue with the "alien" sacrifice on behalf of the emperor in 66 C.E. sparked the Jewish War. Based on the "lawful" separation of Jews and non-Jews—according to Torah the sine qua non for the purity of the temple—it terminated the political modus vivendi that had persisted through all the turmoil of the preceding decades and inaugurated the open confrontation that would finally lead to the destruction of the temple by Titus five years later.[43]

Paul's letter and the trouble he faces in Galatia are located at the heart of these debates about accommodation and resistance and of all the conflicts and compromises that ensued.

Roman *Nomos*, Jewish Torah, and Galatian Foreskin as Point of Friction

We return to the image of the Dying Trumpeter. His torque, nakedness, rugged hair, and oval shield are iconographic markers of his rebellious Galatian/Gallic/Celtic identity, while the blood dripping from his sunken athletic body and the broken war trumpet signal his defeat. The pain in his face reflects the lawful and righteous judgment imposed upon a lawless barbarian race that has transgressed all divine and human order. Like a condensed version of the Pergamene Gigantomachy at the Great Frieze, the Dying Trumpeter embodies, in his eternal dying, the enduring triumph and the "works" of Roman *nomos* more powerfully and succinctly than any written law codex. As a representation of Roman worldview and world order, his image is sacrosanct, not to be tampered with. The Dying Trumpeter is a work of Roman law, or Roman law "at work": an *ergon tou nomou*.

Messianic Iconoclasm

In first-century Roman Galatia, the collective imagery of Dying Galatians is still normative for the perception of living Galatians, reminding them of their lawless past and their righteous condemnation and subjugation by an act of Roman law enforcement. Acknowledging their lawful death sentence, they nevertheless may redeem themselves by doing the works of Roman law that "resurrect" them, through Caesar's mercy and benevolence, as new Galatian people transfigured in the image of empire, embodying Roman order; fighting Roman wars; glorifying Roman victory; and rendering worship, gratitude, and subservience to the Roman god(s). Renamed and reidentified as Sebastēni Galatai, they are affiliated with civilized humanity through Caesar (see chapter 4).

Paul, steeped in the tradition of Jewish criticism of images,[44] refuses the images of empire. By implied consequence, we should expect his theological perspective also to resist and defy the imperial representation of Galatians as godless and idolatrous. Indeed, this is how one might describe in a nutshell the whole of his theology: a critical re-imagination of the Dying Trumpeter in which his shape/*eidos* is purged from any resemblance to the ideology and idolatry it was meant to represent. Two aspects of the way Paul pictures the Galatians in his letter immediately catch the eye: first, the complete lack of any rhetoric that acknowledges the Galatians' proper official identity as Sebastēni, reborn and redeemed by the father-god and the son of god, Caesar. Second, Paul makes the bold assertion that they as Galatians are fully legitimate children of Abraham and Sarah, calling the God of Israel their father, justified by *his* divine son, resurrected from their dying through *him* to be renamed and restored into a new universal and inclusive identity as messianic Galatians—that is, as people "in Christ."

Compared to their proper imperial "resurrection," this raising-up of Dying Galatians *en Christō* turns the normative worldview upside down and is a symbolic act of insurrection. At precisely this point, the question of circumcision becomes relevant and, in an unexpected turn, a matter of Roman law. Like the Dying Trumpeter, the Galatians "naturally" have foreskin, and although it is not a specific mark of Galatian or Roman identity, it nevertheless testifies with sufficient clarity that they are not Jews. Their (foreskin-bearing) images as defeated and dying Galatians/Gauls are meant to convey the triumph, righteousness, disciplinary power and life-giving mercy of the

Roman Empire alone, not of any other god whose empire is rumored among Jews, that is, a group that distinguishes itself through circumcision. When Paul declares that neither circumcision nor foreskin matters any longer because both circumcised Jews and uncircumcised Galatians belong to Abraham's seed and stand under the authority of Israel's God alone, that declaration smashes an icon of Roman law and order. And the Galatians' foreskin, never before of any significance, all of a sudden emerges as evidence of an illicit boundary transgression that claims for the God of the circumcised what lawfully belongs solely to the deified Caesar.

For the male members of Paul's Galatian communities, what had been a relatively inconspicuous part of their physique thus takes on significance as a marker of resistance, nonconformity, and refusal of subservience to the law and religion of the Roman world's god, the divine Caesar. That is, they are reincorporated, readopted, and "reclothed" (Gal 3:26-29) into a circumcised Jewish body that Rome had turned into a *Dying Jew,* but that Israel's God resurrected to life and power as divine Son and Messiah. On the symbolic level, this is again an act of fundamental subversion of Roman law; it becomes even worse if one assumes that the Galatians in their sociocultural practice then indeed began to act like Jews, that is, true children of Israel's monotheistic God. Only they are much worse, for their foreskin clearly defines them as *not* Jews and thus not "licensed" to be fully Jewish, for example, to behave publicly as enemies of the gods, of humanity, of the city—and especially of the emperor. It is in particular the withdrawal from previous participation in imperial religion that probably represents the actual storm center of the Galatian correspondence, an assumption that from various vantage points and within different interpretational frameworks more recently has been strongly supported by Bruce Winter, Mark Nanos, Thomas Witulski, and Justin Hardin.[45]

Before we can investigate the still widely unexplored theological implications of this new contextual construct, which entirely transforms the reading parameters of Galatians, we have to fill in some more historical detail. If the new existence of the uncircumcised Galatians "in Christ" included publicly noticeable demonstrations of an impious and irreverent neglect for their "real" father and god Caesar, Paul's messianic re-imagination of the Galatians would have made foreskin indeed a matter of life and death, giving the circumcision debate, traditionally perceived as a Jewish issue alone, a completely different spin. All matters considered, it is hard to believe that the conversion of the Galatians did *not* entail any of such conspicuous changes from a socially acceptable and conformist behavior to an unacceptable nonconformity. Paul's stance against idolatry is well enough attested throughout his correspondence and, as we will see in the next chapter, constitutes the theological core of Galatians.[46] In his dispute with the Galatians, he at one point very explicitly and with strongly anti-idolatrous zeal emphasized their transition (or "conversion") from a formerly polytheistic and enslaving worship to a new, liberating "knowledge" of Israel's sole God, whom they are about to betray:

Formerly, when you did not know God, you were enslaved to those who by nature are not gods [*physei mē ousin theois*]. Now, however, that you have come to know God, or rather to be known by God, how can you turn back again to the weak and beggarly elemental spirits, to which you again want to be slaves all over? You are observing special days, and months, and seasons, and years. I am afraid that my work for you may have been wasted. (4:8-10)

For the long-established reading of Galatians within an exclusively Jewish framework, this passage with its clearly "pagan" markers has always posed considerable difficulties. Relating relapses into idol worship with the apostasy of circumcision as part of the same "Judaizing" setting requires quite a stretch of the imagination.[47] But if one sees, as the target of Paul's criticism not simply paganism (or Judaism) in general, but in particular the observances of imperial religion, this offers a surprisingly effortless decoding of Gal 4:8-10, making these three verses at the same time the hermeneutical key for an empire-critical *relectura* of the entire letter.[48]

What Paul simply calls "those who by nature are not gods" (evoking a contrast with the God-who-is [Exod 3:14]), in the context of Roman Asia Minor includes not only the whole pantheon of Olympic and local and civic deities, all the heroic and victorious gods and goddesses of the Pergamene Great Altar, but also their supreme contemporary representative: Caesar. More concretely, it might be precisely the emperor and the imperial family who are derided by Paul in 4:8 as gods (or sons of gods) not "by nature," but simply by senatorial declaration and enslaving human convention.[49] As we have seen in chapter 3, civic and imperial religion are inseparable, with imperial religion being the dominant marker of every other religion. In Paul's opinion the Galatians must abstain from both, as did the Jews. Yet the special Jewish "back stair" to the inside of city and civilization, granting access to a zone of respectability without full recognition of Caesar's divinity, is—thanks to Caesar's own magnanimity and permission—open by definition to *Jews* alone, that is, to circumcised full members of the Jewish communities. This "back stair" is not open for Galatians or any other nations to establish their own status as lawful insiders.

What makes things even more complicated is that Paul's messianic "innovation" of inviting the non-Jewish other into oneness with Israel and Israel's God constitutes a double offense—against Roman law and Jewish law as well. From the perspective of the Torah, this innovation transgresses the boundary between God's chosen people and the rest of the Gentile world, marked by circumcision or foreskin; this is the familiar, well-traveled aspect of the Galatian controversy. What has usually been underestimated, however, if it has been recognized at all, is that within the framework of the compromise struck between Torah and Roman *nomos/lex*, a whole host of transgressions ensue from this boundary-crossing: the breach of ancestral (Jewish) law as safeguarded by Rome, undesirable missionary activity and expansion, illicit associations, and unlicensed "atheism." The latter accusation, in a way, summarizes the rest of them.[50] Paul shamelessly expands the carefully segregated territory of the conquered God of Israel—defying boundaries set by both Roman and Jewish law, though for different reasons—into the territory of the conqueror god, the divine Caesar, as if the law of victory did not exist and the demarcation line between triumphant self and defeated other no longer upheld the cosmic order. From the standpoint of Roman law and rule, this was intolerable.[51]

In the concrete situation of Galatia, foreskin or circumcision were no longer just the bodily markers of Jewish or non-Jewish but had become signifiers of political compliance or noncompliance. The fundamental either-or of *self* or *other* constitutes the "sacred" taxonomy at the heart of every construction of an imperial world, disclosed with beautiful mercilessness at Pergamon and elsewhere. By proclaiming the neither-nor of the new creation, asserting that there is "neither Jew nor Greek, neither slave nor free, neither male and female" (Gal 3:28), Paul negates the imperial order and its *nomos*—and puts the uncircumcised messianic Galatians on the spot.

Disorderly Identities: Neither Circumcision nor Foreskin?

The point requires more exploration. Why should Paul, while integrating the Galatians so clearly under "Jewish" terms into the community of Abraham's children, nevertheless so uncompromisingly refuse to allow them to seek circumcision? Paula Fredriksen has shown how this inclusion without circumcision depended on Paul's fundamentally Jewish apocalyptic framework, which anticipated an end-time pilgrimage of the nations to Jerusalem (Isa 2:2-3; Zeph 3:9), whereupon they would abandon their idolatry. As Fredriksen points out, within this vision there was no expectation that the nations should become Jews in terms of a full conversion (including circumcision).[52] The Galatians, seen from this point of view, represent the eschatological movement of the nations turning to God, the beginning of a new creation that has been triggered by the resurrection of God's crucified Son. Only if they keep their foreskin are they truly "nations." Only if they worship God alone, uncircumcised as they are, do they testify to the new creation that has started to transform the world.[53] Their circumcision would not be a return to Jewish orthodoxy (for they have never been Jews) but, on the contrary, a concession to imperial idolatry, that is, to a world ordered in the image of Caesar.[54]

Yet Fredriksen sees also the dilemma at the heart of this "inclusion without conversion." The existence of uncircumcised Gentiles who refuse idolatry as if they were fully Jewish is highly anomalous:

> By insisting both that they not convert to Judaism (thus maintaining their public and legal status as pagans) and that they nonetheless not worship the gods (a protected right only of Jews), Paul walked these Gentiles-in-Christ into a social and religious no-man's-land. In the time before the Parousia, they literally had no place to be.[55]

It is my contention that precisely this denial of any significance to legible identity markers in the age of the Messiah and the implied consequences—the replacement of the imperial worldview with what must have appeared a completely disorderly, lawless, un-Roman construction of self and other and, as a result, a threat of collective civic disobedience and nonconformity—was the core of the Galatian controversy, as it was of Paul's theology of justification. His reconceptualization of righteousness legitimizes the "lawless" Galatians as nonetheless justified through the grace of the supreme other, the nonimperial God of Abraham and Sarah. The conflict in Galatia is therefore far less a matter of Jewish religion per se than of the precarious status of Jewish and non-Jewish communities alike whenever they stepped outside of conformity with the law and religion of the Roman city and the Roman Empire. We have seen how strongly in Tacitus Jewish foreskin and Jewish otherness are linked. We have also seen how, for Tacitus, proselytism as full conversion to Judaism is signified by circumcision. Galatians who still have their foreskin are technically non-Jews and, consequently, "non-other"; they thus are expected fully to participate in the observances and ceremonies of imperial religion like everyone else. They have not the slightest excuse not to comply, as do circumcised Jews (though even that is granted rather grudgingly). Pagan sympathizers of the synagogue—no matter whether we perceive them as an established category of so-called God-fearers or a more loosely defined group[56]—could participate in the worship of Israel's God and keep aspects of the Jewish law in various ways, but they were not on that account exempt from their obligations with regard to civic and state religion. This point—which, for example, Mark Nanos has argued so forcefully—fundamentally changes our perception of Paul's opponents from advocates of Jewish law per se into "social control agents" of the established civic and imperial order.[57]

Paul dramatically disturbs the fragile civic equilibrium of Jewish–pagan conviviality by advocating, with an utterly Maccabean and at the same time missionary zeal, against idolatrous religion. This was at a time when not many of his contemporaries were willing to see a problem: few among non-Jews, who by (Jewish) definition were idolaters, and few among those Jews who believed they were perfectly in conformity with Jewish law in requiring the Galatians to be circumcised if they wanted to be "fully Jewish" and to refuse conformity with Roman worship. In practical terms, Paul destroys the flexibility pagan adherents to the synagogue would normally have enjoyed with regard to their civic obligations and requires them to observe what he sees as the chief commandment of Torah: not to worship any deity except God alone. But he refuses them circumcision because, for him, in the resurrection of Jesus as apocalyptic turning point, God has reclaimed his visible sovereignty over Jews and nations alike. What is called for is nothing less than a new type of "transnational" obedience, including Jews and non-Jews, self and other alike with all their differences, in *one* messianic community that worships God alone. Emperor Claudius might describe it differently: as "a general plague infecting the whole world."[58]

While this ultra-rigorous concept must have created severe problems for both Jews and their fellow citizens in any part of the Roman Empire, one might imagine that it was particularly troublesome in Roman Galatia and that it almost inevitably led into a showdown with imperial religion. For, as we have seen, within the framework of city and civilization, Galatians were a special case. Unlike someone from other nations, anyone called a "Galatian" was subject to particular scrutiny, required to pass a metaphorical test of loyalty under the eagle's watchful gaze at the staircase of the

Great Altar. Uncircumcised Galatians who behave as if they were circumcised Jews, not fully submitting to the observances of imperial religion or law, embodied lawlessness par excellence. In the symbolic order represented by the Great Altar, they have relapsed—*remutated*—into the godless outsiders and enemies of the Roman cosmos that they were before. Like the Giants depicted on the walls of the Great Altar in their blasphemous attack against the ruling Olympian deities, they are refusing to submit to the gods and the worldwide divine rule installed by the deities: against Zeus/Jupiter/ Caesar and against Athena/Roma. They suddenly again appear as chaos-bearing others, lawless outsiders who cannot be tolerated in the space of the city since they subvert the law and order of the imperial world. Like the Trumpeter, they are meant to embody dying rather than living.

Setting It Straight: Either Foreskin or Circumcision

Bruce Winter has made a strong case for the imperial cult as an all-pervasive provincial reality in Roman Galatia, spelling out in some detail the concrete obligations, practices, attractions and challenges this entailed for the inhabitants of the Galatian (or any other) province: a firmly established sequence of festivals, games, and competitions; occasional feasting and banqueting near an imperial temple; colorful processions with candles, torches, and flowers as highlights of civic life, where imperial images and statues were carried around, accompanied by speeches, musicians, choirs. Everyone was expected to take part in these events and to wear festive attire, notably crowns or wreaths and to adorn their houses with laurels and lamps. Wine and incense were distributed to the townsfolk so that everyone could perform personal acts of devotion to the emperor alongside the sacrifices that were performed to and on behalf of the emperor.[59]

It is clear that "opting out" of these social rituals and practices would not go unnoticed and would almost inevitably be read as a political statement.[60] Concerned neighbors of the Galatian congregation who had taken offense, those more inclined to play by the rules, might have signaled their disapproval.[61] Yet it is possible that the risky behavior of the Pauline groups was first noticed by Jews at a time when recent events in Alexandria, Jerusalem, and Rome[62] were still fresh in everyone's mind. Jews might well have been alarmed, since the possible consequences of any demurrals from the civic cult in the name of the God of Israel might have fallen on the Jewish community. Furthermore, as we have seen, despite ongoing pressures and dangers, portions of the Jewish population in Asia Minor negotiated rather successfully the compromise between Jewish otherness and civic and imperial integration, which brought them in some cases closer to the civic and imperial establishment in the cities.[63] We should expect that these Jews would have been extremely concerned about any aberrations from the established routines of coexistence between Jewish and Roman law that might have been interpreted as sedition. Such aberrations would have implied a risk that both Pauline communities and the Jewish communities at large would be held accountable for disturbances of civic and imperial order. Such a risk threatened the very basis of Jewish existence in the eastern Diaspora.[64]

Whether they were Jews or non-Jews, Christ-believers or not, those in the Galatian congregation who advocated circumcision likely sought a return to a more inconspicuous existence within civic and imperial religion. Their message was probably given serious consideration by the non-Jewish members of the congregation.

There were basically two ways to "regularize" the hybrid, in-between status of Galatians who were neither Jews nor non-Jews (see Gal 3:28): either return to what the outside world considered proper behavior by complying with at least the minimal requirements of public religion—that is, be properly Gentile—or become fully Jewish. Although circumcision and a complete proselyte conversion would not immediately silence the hard questions being asked by outsiders, these actions would mark a return to some acceptability in terms of law.[65]

1. *Resume the practice of civic religion.* From the perspective of Roman law and order the first option for the Galatians would be to reconsider that they owed their loyalty and faith to Caesar and should therefore submit themselves again to some basic observances of civic and imperial religion. This would have been in accordance with the usual practice of non-Jews who were attracted to the synagogues; they could stay in a loose affiliation, uncircumcised, and free from any expectation that they would fully keep the Jewish law, for example, by abstaining from public religion.[66]

This is strongly supported by our reading of Gal 4:8-11 within the framework of imperial religion as outlined above. If in this notoriously difficult passage the Galatians are accused of returning, or considering a return, to the idolatrous service of the "non-gods" to whom they were enslaved before, resuming the observance of "special days and months and seasons and years," this probably has nothing to do with keeping a *Jewish* calendar. Many of the interpretational difficulties of this passage can be resolved if we assume that the Galatians are accused here not of "Judaizing," but, on the contrary, of resubmitting themselves to the civic obligations of public and especially imperial religion.[67]

As we have seen in our discussion of the Priene decree (in chapter 2 above), Caesar had imposed his own calendar on the sequence of days, months, and years, marking the rhythm of political, individual, and cosmic life. The emperor was celebrated both as supreme "time giver" and as archetypical restorer of the order of time in a manner reminiscent of Zeus. Nonparticipation in the numerous periodic commemorations and celebrations of public life in a Roman city would have brought public visibility and potential shame on the messianic Galatians, singling them out from their customary civic environment. Stephen Mitchell has succinctly commented on this dilemma, using the example of Pisidian Antioch as a possible location of Paul's communities:

> One cannot avoid the impression that the obstacle which stood in the way of the progress of Christianity, and the force which would have drawn new adherents back to conformity with the prevailing paganism, was the public worship of the emperors. The packed calendar of the ruler cult dragooned the citizens of Antioch into observing the days, months, seasons, and years which it laid down for special recognition and celebration. Its sacrifices were the chief source of meat which the Apostolic Council had forbidden Christians to touch. In the urban setting of Pisidian Antioch where spectacular and enticing public

[handwritten margin note: Note this is what is referred to at Antioch]

festivals imposed conformity and a rhythm of observance on a compact population, where Christianity could not (if they wanted to) conceal their beliefs and activities from their fellows, it was not a change of heart that might win a Christian convert back to paganism, but the overwhelming pressure to conform imposed by the institutions of his city and the activities of his neighbours.[68]

2. *Circumcision.* The second option for the Galatians would have been to accept circumcision. The circumcision demand of Paul's opponents in Galatia is clearly stated and beyond doubt. The traditional interpretation, which turned Galatia into the primeval battlefield between a law-observant Judaism and law-free (and Jew-free) Christianity, is much less self-evident than is usually assumed, not only because Christianity as a separate religion did not yet exist but also because in the controversy Paul claims to be the voice of "proper" Judaism and law-observance, in contrast to the circumcision party.[69] In the context proposed here, on the other hand, for the Galatians to get rid of their foreskins and become fully Jewish proselytes would have been less an expression of faithful, theologically motivated Jewish Torah-obedience than of political realism. Only if they could pass as proper Jews would they be entitled, at least theoretically, to participate in the arrangement available only to Jews with regard to imperial and civic religion. Otherwise, they—and the Jewish communities along with them—would risk possible persecution and repression.[70]

This profile of Paul's circumcision-demanding opponents as advocates of a pragmatic solution to a complicated political problem is strongly supported by Gal 6:12-13:

> It is those who want to make a good showing in the flesh that try to compel you to be circumcised—only that they may not be persecuted for the cross of Christ. Even the circumcised do not themselves obey the law, but they want you to be circumcised so that they may boast about your flesh.

Paul's adversaries are concerned not primarily about Jewish law itself (6:13) but about the "persecution" they might suffer, from an unspecified third party, on account of the uncircumcised state of the Galatians. This "third party," I suggest, would have been the civic public and its magistrates, who would have been concerned about any group that openly challenged the normative observance of Roman imperial religion and order and thus provoked possible trouble with Rome.

That the circumcision advocates themselves did not keep Jewish law but were, in effect, instrumentalizing circumcision in order to "boast" (6:13), suggests a certain theological indifference on their part. Paul's use of the terms "boasting" and "making a good showing" (*euprosōpēsai*) in 6:12 points to a kind of public window dressing.[71] They were turning away from the troublesome and murky messianic identity of uncircumcised Galatian children of Abraham that Paul held out for them "in Christ," and toward the properly established and acknowledged categories of us and them, self and other, Jews and Galatians/Gentiles that aligned with the codes at the core of city and civilization. In Paul's view, their making a political demand under the guise of

Torah-obedience in fact twisted and bent God's will so that it would fit Roman imperial law. The term *nomos* in Galatians thus necessarily oscillates between a Jewish and a Roman connotation, the latter being the predominant one.

This double meaning of "law" in Galatians surfaces quite evidently in Gal 3:19-20. This is another infamous passage that has never been fully decoded within a frame of interpretation focused on Jewish Torah alone. The text points to the agency of a "mediator" (*mesitou*) who has "ordained" (*diatageis*) the law and is denounced as "not being of the one" (*henos ouk estin*), while "God is one" (*ho de theos heis estin*). This statement explicitly opposes the law and the act of lawgiving, as these pertain to Galatia, to the one and singular God of Israel. In the biblical grammar of Torah, the juxtaposition of "one God" and "not-of-the-one-God" clearly points to the opposition of God and the idols, or "other gods" (Exod 20:1-6; Deut 6:4). As Christian commentators, however, primarily read this passage as a wholesale rejection of Torah, its profoundly Jewish and Torah-centered thrust needed to be suppressed.[72] The implication of idolatry combined with the notion of "law" in this passage strongly supports the framework of imperial and civic religion, rather than Judaism per se, as the context for Paul's law criticism, and for the "law-abiding" motives and activities of his antagonists. The "mediator" and the authority they serve are no longer Moses and Israel's God but the emperor or his local agents who de facto define the adequate meaning and practice of God's will and law. To refute the famous formulation by E. P. Sanders, Paul's problem with Judaism is *not* that it is not Christianity, but that in the context of Roman Galatia Jewish Torah has become imperial law in disguise. The law Paul confronts is not Jewish law as such, but Jewish law in enforced servitude to Roman law.[73]

The question behind Paul's enigmatic reference in 3:19 to the "hand of a mediator" that "ordains" the law thus would be twofold. From Paul's side, to what extent could one allow the merging of Roman and Jewish law in this obscure middle ground, where Jewish law in essence becomes an allowance from Caesar or any other imperial ruler, given "through his hand," as it had always happened since the time of the Babylonian exile? From the side of his antagonists, the counter-question would be: To what extent can one *refuse* to receive Torah from the hands of the emperor, *refuse* to follow the law in the way the emperor expects, without putting Jewish law and existence itself at risk? Paul's demand to follow the law of Israel's God alone posed an extraordinary challenge to the order of the city as well as to the security of the Jewish and Galatian congregations who lived in that order, more or less by Caesar's grace.

One (or Other) "in Caesar": Lawful Jewish–Galatian Encounter

The *logos* and law of the imperial eagle at Pergamon not only watched over the boundary between *In* and *Out*, but with equal vigilance it also controlled lawful and lawless activities, specifically admissible and nonadmissible ways of affiliation and association, among those deemed *insiders*. No law stated this explicitly, yet our re-imagination of the Galatian situation through the lens of the Great Altar makes it evident that from the perspective of the Roman eagle, the way of life adopted by the uncircumcised messianic Galatians of Paul's communities would have been lawless and godless conduct.

Divide and Conquer

The problem, in Roman eyes, was not simply that the "imperial" Sebastēni Galatians had taken over an alternative identity as *Christiani,* an identity that cost them their imperial status as justified and caused them to appear again like those lawless, "Giant" outsiders of the Roman order who had never ceased to be their alter ego, their *other* barbarian self.[74] What is worse, the Galatians had banded together with Jews in ways completely antithetical to the terms and conditions under which the empire allowed the vanquished nations under its rule to associate.[75]

To understand the full weight of Paul's lawlessness from the perspective of Roman *nomos,* we must revisit the diagrams used in our exploration of the Great Altar. As we saw, the "combat" law of the Pergamene Giant battle frames the imperial hierarchical order. That order places a victorious self and its god(s) over a defeated other that has the blasphemous and lawless Giants as its mythological archetype.

Fig. 38. "Combat Order of Self and Other"

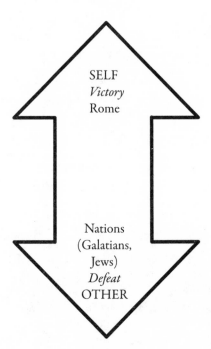

The dominant position of the superior self in this figure is assigned by virtue of victory. Whoever wins the battle enjoys the approval of the gods and represents divine law. This concept underlay the Roman world order and projected victorious Rome as the righteous, god-willed ruler of the defeated, colonized "nations," including Galatians and Jews.

The longevity of the Roman Empire over centuries owed much to the brute force of Caesar's highly proficient legions, exerted in conquest and discipline, but also to the skillful application of powerful ideological mechanisms. What prevented the conquered nations, the collective other of the Roman self, from uniting in resistance to Roman dominance was the fact that they had, in one way or another, internalized the imperial law of self versus other, which pitted the defeated others against one another, rather than against the Roman self.

That the Greeks thought themselves superior to "barbarians" (which would have included Galatians, Jews, and possibly even Romans), or that the Jews insisted on the outsider status of "Gentiles" (which would have included Greeks, Galatians, barbarians, as well as Romans), undoubtedly provided some irritation for Rome. By and large, however, such prejudices and imagined hierarchies served Roman interests very well, since they principally set the conquered against an other and prevented any unity "from below." Each member of a vanquished nation could in this way establish an imaginary superior self and thus restore some vestige of damaged honor and pride by cultivating the image of an inferior other. This mechanism—already discussed above with regard to the logic of the arena (chapter 3)—allowed members of subject peoples to participate, within certain strict limitations, in the perspective of the victorious self at the expense of other victims.

It is probably this self-elevation and self-distinction through "othering," a common enough practice among the conquered and distressed,[76] that Paul criticizes as "boasting" and "works (or workings) of the law." In both Galatians and Romans, *kauchēma* (boasting) and *erga tou nomou* (works of the law) are the two fundamental opposites of Paul's theme of justification by grace.[77] These opposites have traditionally been linked to Jewish law and the works righteousness it supposedly produces. Jewish law is indeed involved, but only as an auxiliary construct in support of the overarching dominance of Roman law. For as it establishes a hierarchical polarity between Jewish self and Gentile other, it indirectly imitates and reproduces the law and order of the victorious Roman self ruling over the other of the vanquished nations. The conquered take over the worldview of the conquerors. This allows us to understand, from yet another angle, why the lawful boundary between foreskin and circumcision, between Jews and Gentiles (and Galatians), though often a nuisance to Rome that held circumcision in contempt, nevertheless upheld Roman law, that is, the overarching hierarchy between Roman self and conquered other.[78]

Figure 39 shows how the construction of both Galatian and Jewish identity in terms of self versus other could support and be supported by Roman law and order—the one directly, the other more indirectly—and how their interaction is molded by a complex synergy between Roman law and Jewish Torah.

Fig. 39. Possible Galatian versus Jewish Constructions of Self and Other, in Complicity with the Imperial Self/*nomos*.

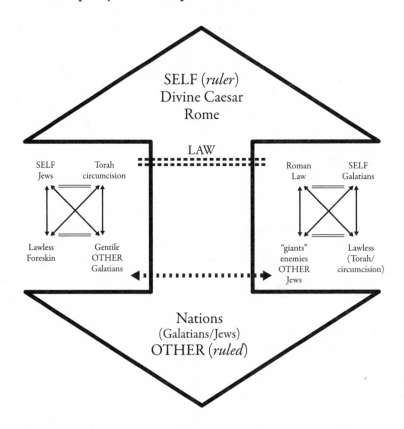

As the diagram indicates, although Jewish Torah has aspects that are (from the Roman point of view) undeniably "lawless," it has been tolerated, authorized, and thus domesticated by Rome as the defining authority in establishing Jewish identity and the Jewish self. Galatian identity, on the other hand, is expected to be more or less entirely defined by *Roman* law. On this "upper level," which constitutes the ideological superstructure of the Roman order, both Jews and Galatians in their lawful mode of being, submit to the imperial self of Caesar, though they show their allegiance in different ways. They are thus in a kind of peaceful coexistence strictly mediated by Rome. This is the ideal model of Pax Romana, Roman peace.

On the "underside" of this order, however—the location of the conquered nations—Galatians and Jews are mutually exclusive groups and can only be hostile to one another. Uncircumcised Galatians, on the one hand, are obviously Gentiles, and therefore *other* to the Jews. The reverse relation is more complicated. Circumcised Jews bear the mark of their "oppositional" law (as described by Tacitus and others); from the point of view of Romanized Galatians, they are therefore, at least potentially, chaos-bearing enemies of the sacred Roman order, like the mythological Giants. This order has "justified" and elevated the formerly barbarian Galatians who used to be lawless others themselves (and thus analogous to the Giants) to the position of an accepted self, on condition of their strict submission to Roman law. Thus, the Galatians are not only taxpayers but also soldiers of the Roman order, marching against enemies and lawless rebels of all kinds, including Jews. This imperial self-reconstitution of the Sebastēni Galatians sets up an unbridgeable gap between them and the heteronomous Jewish other.

That means that in the "belly" of the Roman order, where the imperial system extracts its power and wealth from all the conquered nations alike, Jews and Galatians are pitted against each other while being consumed together. Their respective self-constructs make them enemies of one another and prevent any unity and collective resistance. It is precisely this antagonistic, hierarchical self that is cultivated by and adopted into the Roman imperial order in a deceptive ritual of participation and co-optation "from above."

Four specific examples may offer glimpses into how these mechanisms worked: Judas Maccabaeus's Galatomachy; Herod the Great's Galatian bodyguard; the imperial toleration edicts for Jews at Ancyra/Pergamon; and, finally, the Galatian imperial priestess, Julia Severa, who sponsored the synagogue of Acmonia. These brief sketches illustrate the extent to which Paul's Jewish-Galatian communities and their "oneness in Christ" must have been perceived as a security risk according to the (unwritten) rules and laws of the imperial order.

Judas Maccabaeus and the Roman–Jewish Galatomachy

The first example comes from Jerusalem in the second century B.C.E., at about the time the Great Altar was under construction in the Pergamene kingdom of Eumenes II. In 167, the Seleucid king Antiochus IV Epiphanes ordered that the Jews under his rule abandon Torah by submitting to the laws of all other nations and having a cult statue of Zeus erected in the Jerusalem temple. This abhorrent act of unveiled imperial despotism ignited the Maccabean rebellion.[79] The deuterocanonical books of 1 and 2 Maccabees tell the story of the uprising.[80] It is in this context that two of the few references to Gaul/Galatia within the corpus of biblical literature occur outside of Paul's writings. Strangely, these two brief passages present the strikingly familiar imagery of an anti-Galatian combat ideology, including even the Jewish version of a Galatomachy.

1 Maccabees 8:2

In 1 Maccabees 8, Judas Maccabaeus contemplates enrolling Rome as an ally in the fight for Jewish identity and survival against the hated Seleucid overlords. Judas's deliberations eventually result in a treaty of mutual peace and military aid signed between the Jewish people and the Roman senate (1 Macc 8:17-32). The report of his deliberations at this point is noteworthy. The scene takes place some two decades after the Romans have defeated the Seleucids and the Galatians in Asia Minor. Judas weighs the strength and reliability that the Romans have reportedly shown in their dealings with their allies. Rome's impressive rewards for their anti-Seleucid ally Eumenes II of Pergamon after the Battle of Magnesia (190 B.C.E.) and the peace of Apamea (188 B.C.E.) are explicitly mentioned (1 Macc 8:8). This support stands in contrast to the irresistible power of Rome to crush any resistance worldwide, including "the kings who came from the ends of the earth to attack them" (8:4). The eulogy of Rome's invincibility comprises all of the noteworthy victories in the post-Alexander battles of the late third and second centuries B.C.E. over Carthage, Seleucids, Antigonids, and Greeks, which laid the foundations for Roman world rule.[81] It is somewhat astonishing that the first and foremost triumph mentioned on Judas's impressive list is the conquest of the Galatians/Gauls.

> Judas had heard about the Romans: that they were a great nation who welcomed all who wished to join them and established ties of friendship with all who approached them. As for their being a great power, Judas' informants told him of the Romans' valor in war: they had fought and conquered the Gauls [*Galatais*] and imposed tribute upon them (1 Macc 8:1-2, trans. Goldstein).

Again, the English translation of Greek *Galatai* as "Gauls" needs to be complemented by "Galatians." Judas's applause for the Roman conquest of Gaul/Galatia could refer either to Manlius Vulso's campaign in Asia Minor 189 B.C.E. or to the Roman victory over Italian Gallia Cisalpina in 190 B.C.E.[82] In light of our deliberations thus far, it seems likely that he hints in a generic way at both and, furthermore, at all the other major victories over Galatians, as historical proof for Rome's destiny to rule the world in accordance with the divine order. Within the overall semiotic framework of Galatian triumphs, the prominent position of Galatia on Judas's list does not appear to be an arbitrary or random choice; rather, this is carefully chosen political rhetoric that praises Rome's supreme power in saving the world from historical enemies and from prototypical evil. Judas himself wants to enlist this same invincible power for his own

Fig. 40. Roman and Jewish *Self* in Alliance versus the Galatian/Giant *Other*

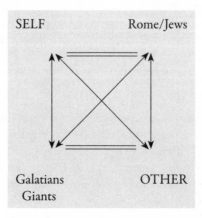

fight against the Seleucids.[83] Nothing else could describe Rome's greatness and trust-worthiness as powerfully as her conquest of Galatia.[84] Here we see exactly the "Pergamene" logic of self versus other at work: Judas seeks to enter into an alliance with the dominant and victorious force of Rome by declaring himself (and the Jewish self) an enemy of the Galatian other. (See fig. 40.)

2 Maccabees 8:20

This reading of 1 Macc 8:2 is sustained by the second Galatian passage, 2 Macc 8:20, which shows a similar pattern, though with less explicitly pro-Roman connotations. This time Judas Maccabaeus addresses his own rebel army, a force of about six thousand men (2 Macc 8:1) right before the decisive anti-Seleucid battle against Nicanor, the enemy general "in command of no less than twenty thousand gentiles of various stocks, with orders to destroy the entire people of Judea" (2 Macc 8:9). Nicanor has already organized a huge auction of Jewish slaves, which he plans to sell to help cover the two-thousand-talent tribute still owed to the Romans (2 Macc 8:10-11).[85] In order to boost the fighting spirit of his soldiers, Judas invokes the power of God's covenant and mentions two great victorious precursor battles that showed how Israel's almighty God fought on the side of the Judeans and achieved victory.

The first is the grand combat in 2 Kings 18–19, when, through the help of God, the much weaker Judean king Hezekiah, supported by the prophet Isaiah (see Isa 37:36-37), prevailed against the overwhelming, God-denying power of the Assyrian king Sennacherib. This is a biblically prominent and well-attested example of God coming to the rescue of the people, who were under siege by a foreign imperial "Goliath."[86]

This makes the second reference in the text even more puzzling. It is not a biblical event, and in fact it is so marginal in Jewish tradition that scholars are not sure where to locate it historically. Judas refers to a supposedly monumental battle in which a comparatively tiny number of Jews defeated a gargantuan army of "Galatians" in Babylonia. He reminds his men of

> the battle fought against the Galatians in Babylonia [*pros tous Galatas parataxin*]: all the Jews numbering eight thousand, had marched to meet the emergency in company with four thousand Macedonians, and when the Macedonians melted away, six thousand Jews destroyed one hundred twenty thousand through receiving the help of Heaven and took exceedingly vast quantities of spoils. (2 Macc 8:20, trans. Goldstein)

Why this vague and somewhat apocryphal account of a Jewish–Galatian battle is lined up next to the two grand past and present battles of Jewish survival—the one under Hezekiah and the other under Judas—appears mysterious at first glance.[87] It is probable that both Jews and Galatians in the "Babylonian" battle fought as mercenaries of competing powers, not for their own cause.[88] How does this fit with wars more central to Jewish identity, in which God intervened as a warrior against an overpowering foreign ruler (and his gods)? The most plausible explanation lies, again, in the symbolic power of the mythic battle against Galatians/Giants that Judas evokes, not only to encourage the

Jewish fighters but also to impress the Greco-Roman world. The text from 2 Macc 8:20 makes sense when read together with 1 Macc 8:2, as an effort to "translate" the Jewish anti-Seleucid fight into the common political and religious *koinē*: accordingly, the Jewish cause becomes part of a larger anti-chaos (= anti-Galatian) combat that secures not only Jewish Torah but the universal law and cosmic order as well.

The effort provides both supreme legitimacy and a "natural" alignment between the anti-Seleucid cause of the Maccabeans and the Roman struggle for world power against Galatians, Seleucids, and other enemies. If we express this in the language of the Pergamene imagery, Israel's God now indeed has symbolically entered the alliance of divine combatants on the Great Altar. Politically, this appears to be a brilliant move. Theologically, Israel's God has tacitly been substituted for Zeus in his rank as supreme heavenly Giant/Galatian slayer. This seems a metamorphosis that, on the surface at least, leaves Jewish monotheism intact, even strengthening God's position by declaring him the (co)creator of an anti-chaotic imperial order from the beginning of time. It is still the creator God of Genesis, the God of Israel, who is invoked, trusted, and defended as sole world ruler—or is it?[89] A less benign reading might claim that in reality it is Zeus who is now revered, or co-revered, under the name of Israel's God.

The question is relevant beyond the immediate context of the Maccabees. While Judas and his men fight to uphold Jewish law against a Gentile takeover, and the purity of the temple against its defilement by an image of Zeus, does the foregrounding of war against Galatians at the same time unwittingly also adopt imperial law and logic, however implicitly, by presenting the God of Israel in the role of Zeus, embodying the *nomos* and *logos* of the fight against the Giants? The implication would be a great irony: two of the most radically anti-assimilationist Jewish writings, 1 and 2 Maccabees, in their theological core-construct betray a subtle "merging" of Jewish and Roman law.

One might imagine this as one of the focal questions raised two hundred years later by Paul as he moves among his fellow Jews and non-Jews in a world profoundly shaped by the Roman imperial order: "What then is the law?" (Gal 3:19 ASV, BBE). Looking back at his pre-Damascus career as a "Maccabean" holy warrior who had been striving to defend the integrity of Torah in combat against Jewish dissidents, heretics, and "liberals" of various kinds, all of them representing the forbidden Gentile other (Gal 1:13-14), Paul is no longer sure whether this is really the adequate expression of God's will and law. Can one legitimately speak about the oneness of the biblical God and simply take over the "combat law" of one-against-other that so undeniably belongs to Zeus and the imperial order of Caesar? Is not the one God also *other* than the imperial idols and their law, *other* than Caesar in relating to the vanquished co-others of the empire, *other* than the Pax Romans in terms of peacemaking and reconciliation, of constructing self and other?[90] How can one uphold the "Maccabean" zeal for God's Torah as order of the messianic kingdom, without making it a mirror image of the Roman Empire? We will return to these questions in chapter 6.

Our study of the Galatians' presence within the two Maccabean texts 1 Macc 8:2 and 2 Macc 8:20 has indicated the semantic shift that happens as soon as the religion of Israel, like all other "traditional religions," must move and express itself within the emerging framework of Roman global imperial order and its semiotics of sacred combat. The "Maccabean paradox" of Jews and Romans united in a divinely backed victorious Galatomachy, on the one hand, points to the new meanings that the old biblical stories of God's divine assistance to an oppressed Israel may acquire when put into another context of domination. At the same time, we see that the officially acceptable way for the subaltern nations to interact with one another within the dominant Roman order implies two things: first, an unconditional acceptance of the world as a battlefield between self and other, and, second, an uncompromising acceptance of the "official enemy" as an enemy of oneself as well.

If the dominant order makes a Jewish self-presentation as anti-Galatian heroes suitable, a Jewish Galatomachy is produced; if the empire requires that Galatians fight against Jews, they must do so, too. Or if it demands peace, they must keep peace. Thus, what constitutes "lawful" relations between Jews and Galatians can vary greatly, but it is always dictated from above, never on the basis of an "illegal" peacemaking from below where the vanquished determine their own relation to one another without Caesar as supreme intermediary or authority. Some further examples may demonstrate this logic.

Herod the Great's Galatian Bodyguard

A century after Judas Maccabaeus, pro-Roman sentiment among the Jewish people had suffered a decisive blow, and the Jews had learned unwelcome lessons about the true meaning of self and other, friend and foe, alliance and nonalliance in the Roman vernacular. In 63 B.C.E., the Roman general Pompey, after reconquering Asia Minor from Mithridates and defeating the Seleucids as overlords of Palestine, "took" Jerusalem as well and desecrated the temple.[91] There was no military need for this brutal and traumatic violation of the sanctuary, yet we may detect a certain ideological necessity in terms of image production, for this act demonstrated visibly that imperial religion and the Jewish God could never negotiate on equal terms. When Pompey tore the temple curtain apart and entered into the Holy of Holies, the space that was reserved for the imageless God alone and that only the high priest was allowed to enter once a year on the Day of Atonement, something changed irreversibly in the fabric of Roman–Jewish relations. Although the innermost sanctuary was cleansed immediately afterwards (at Pompey's own order) and continued to be the space of the aniconic presence of Israel's God, it now invisibly but indelibly was shaped by the image of Roman imperial presence as well. If Judas Maccabaeus had tried symbolically to place the collective Jewish self into a strategic alliance with the victorious Roman self by presenting the Jewish God as co-combatant against the Galatian other (see fig. 40 above), Rome had responded, in the person of Pompey, that the Jews and their God themselves had first to accept their position as an other among the defeated nations, precisely like the Galatians.

And like the Galatians, the Judeans soon were ruled by a king appointed through Rome. At the Capitol in Rome, the site of the most dramatic anti-Galatian battle in the

Roman state myth, Herod the Great was made client king over Judea by Octavian, Antony, and the Roman senate in 40 B.C.E.[92] Herod was trusted in his capacity to pacify a tumultuous realm in accordance with Roman interests, and his rule resembled that of King Deiotaros in Galatia in many ways.

Ten years later, the situation looked different. After his victory in the battle of Actium in 31 B.C.E. made Octavian single ruler, the life and power of Herod were at great risk. Unfortunately, he had been an ally of the defeated Antony rather than of the victorious Octavian. In a spectacular scene, Herod puts himself at the mercy of Augustus, and he is pardoned and confirmed in his rule.[93] Augustus not only awards him territories and cities previously owned by Cleopatra, the last Ptolemaic queen and Antony's consort, but also her four hundred Galatian bodyguards (*phylakēn tou sōmatos tetrakosious Galatas*).[94] Twenty-five years later, at Herod's funeral in 4 B.C.E., these Galatians, in conjunction with Thracians and Germans, were mentioned as walking directly behind the family following the king's bier, "equipped as for war" (Josephus, *B.J.* 1.672).

This is another interesting turn in the relationship between Jewish self and Galatian other. The Galatian "gift" (*edōrēsato*) by Caesar Augustus has a complex symbolic meaning on several levels. The Galatians are a part of Cleopatra's power and physical presence that is allowed to survive in order to glorify the emperor's limitless triumph. As former guards of her royal body (*phylakēn tou sōmatos*) that so shamefully enticed both Augustus's own divine father Julius Caesar and his rival Antony, these Galatians are made a living monument to Cleopatra's punishment and death by being transferred to Cleopatra's archenemy Herod.[95] Augustus thus presents himself as supreme executor of the "barbarian queen." He has at last won power over her vile body that she denied him when she committed suicide. While Cleopatra herself could not be paraded through the streets of Rome together with the other defeated nations in Augustus's post-Actium triumph, the Galatians play a substitute role that comes close. Representing the emperor's idiosyncratic variation on the theme of Dying Amazons and Resurrected Galatians, they communicate his worldwide and ultimate conquest of formerly barbarian territory that includes, as we have seen in Virgil's Actium report, not only Egypt and its debased queen but also the Galatians/Gauls themselves as prototypical barbarian other. Doomed to die, they are allowed to live by Caesar's grace, an incarnate image of his invincible order.

To entrust these Galatians to Herod is an honor and recognition of his achievements, but also an expression of Rome's expectation that he will continue loyally and successfully to integrate *another* species of problematic foreigners into the orbit of Roman rule, namely, the Jews. The conspicuous presence of the Galatian bodyguards at Herod's funeral indicates that throughout the tumultuous years of Herod's cruel and power-driven reign, Galatians must have had some public visibility among the Jews as safeguards of Herod's rule, as well as of Rome's. If Judas Maccabaeus had boasted of the Roman and Jewish victory over the Galatians, now Rome boasted of Roman victory over Galatians and Jews, conveying a strong message that compliance with the imperial order was advisable for both. One might call this a model of Jewish–Galatian integration, but it is an entirely "vertical" integration, dictated by Caesar from above (see fig.

39 above). It is his relentless determination to "unite" and "pacify" the nations from above that forces them into conformity with the imperial order, even requiring that they police each other or fight each other if necessary (fig. 39). It is hard to imagine that this elite troop of Galatians, with their proverbial capacity to evoke terror among people now being mustered for Rome's cause, would have fostered much sympathy or solidarity between Jews and Galatians "below."

Jews, Galatians, and the Koinon *"at Ancyra"*

The next two examples are of a less warlike and more conciliatory nature, both involving imperial religion. We have already discussed the temple of Roma and Augustus at Ancyra, seat of the imperial *koinon* of Roman Galatia, which had the *Monumentum Ancyranum* and the imperial priest list inscribed on its outer walls. Both documents give a vivid impression of how the program of imperial unification and transformation, implemented by the *koinon,* worked to Romanize and de-Gallicize the disparate body of provincial subjects (chapter 4 above).

According to Josephus, there was one more interesting set of inscriptions on display in the same temple. In *Ant.* 16.162–65, he reports that the Ancyran temple of Roma and Augustus also housed Augustus's decree (*diatagma*) about protection and tolerance for the Jewish population (*ethnos tōn Ioudaiōn*), inscribed on a pillar in the most conspicuous part of the temple. The Jews of Asia had complained that they were mistreated by the cities and that their status of enjoying equal civic rights (*isonomia*) had been violated. In response to a Jewish embassy to Rome, the emperor restored Jewish rights.

In his letter to the provincials, he states that the Jews may follow their own customs and the laws of their fathers (*patriōn autōn nomōn*): this includes the collection of money sent to Jerusalem, the protection of Jewish sacred books and funds from thieves, and permission to abstain from civic duties such as court appearances on the Sabbath. Prior to this, the Jews had offered a resolution to Caesar honoring his "piety" (*eusebeia*), which he showed to all human beings, and on behalf of Gaius Marcus Censorius, the proconsul of Asia in 2–3 c.e.[96] Following the ancient custom of using temples as archives and exhibition sites for important legislation, Caesar suggests that this resolution of the Jews, together with his own edict, should be placed in the sanctuary that the federation (*koinon*) of Asia has assigned to him at Ancyra.[97]

Historically, it seems unlikely that an exchange between Caesar and the Jews of the province of Asia would have been published in the capital of Galatia; we should expect the city to be Pergamon rather than Ancyra.[98] But the basic setting would be similar anywhere in Roman Asia Minor. Augustus's decree certainly does not portray the whole reality and ambiguity of Jewish existence in the Roman Empire, but it demonstrates one important aspect of it: Roman law protects Jewish law (see fig. 39). The placement of the edict and the preceding Jewish honorary address to Caesar within the sanctuary of the *koinon* shows that the physical and ideological space where Jews and nations (Galatians or Asians) can interact and be integrated with each other safely is, in its entirety, created and safeguarded, defined and controlled by Caesar, and that it is Caesar who mediates and establishes the peace between the two parties.

Even as a fictive place of Augustus's decree, the temple of Ancyra once more opens up a window into the reality behind Paul's complaint in Gal 3:19-20 that the law is given through the hand of a "mediator" who is not a representative of the one God (*henos ouk estin*). The "law of their fathers" and of their singular God alone is in this case publicly confirmed, conferred, and conceded to the Jews by the divine Caesar in his own temple, in front of his own cult image, through the agency of his own universal imperial religion and in the presence of the written reports of his universal benefactions and divine achievements (as featured in the *Res Gestae* and the priest list). Again, Paul's question in Gal 3:19 gains plausibility as an exasperated exclamation in an absurd situation where the anti-idolatry of Jewish Torah is de facto "licensed" through the law-giving act of the supreme idol himself. Indeed: "What then is the law?"

The integration of the provincial body, that is, the "community" (*koinōnia*) created by the imperial commune or council (*koinon*), in the case of the (hypothetical) Ancyran edict is based on the common (though diverse) expression of reverence to Caesar on the part of both the Galatians and the Jews. The former maintain the sanctuary; the latter voice their gratitude to the emperor in the same sanctuary through a publicly exhibited letter of reverence (though without directly participating in the sacrificial acts of worship performed at this temple). This shows a pattern of compromise similar to what we saw already at work with regard to the imperial sacrifice in the Jerusalem temple. The devotion to Caesar and the practice of "piety" as subjection need to be stated as minimal prerequisites for the integration of the Jews among the Sebastēni/Augustan Galatians. The same pattern, Philip Harland maintains, underlay the widely positive interaction of Jews and non-Jews within the civic settings of Asia Minor, which rested on a strong component of civic and imperial piety, even if the concrete practices were remarkably flexible and able to accommodate Jewish concerns.[99] It is noteworthy that among the admirably broad range of sources Harland utilizes to illuminate the situation in Asia Minor, including a significant number of New Testament passages, a document that one should expect in this list is completely missing: the letter to the Galatians. Maybe that is not without reason. For it seems that the relationship of Paul's Jewish-Galatian associations to their civic and imperial environment was far more complicated than Harland's conciliatory picture suggests.[100]

Julia Severa of Acmonia

Our final example is embodied in a person rather than a set of inscriptions, although coins and epigraphic sources play a crucial role. Julia Severa lived in the 50s of the first century C.E. in the Phrygian city of Acmonia at the western border of the province of Galatia, thus very close to Paul's Galatians in terms of time and location. Although her name is quite familiar in scholarly literature, the full complexity of her triple Galatian-Roman-Jewish identity is usually only partly reflected, especially with regard to its ideologicial-critical implications.[101] Julia Severa was a Galatian who not only in an exemplary way represented the imperial admission of ex-barbarians to the inside/upside of the Roman order; she was also a Roman and modeled the lawful and publicly acceptable form of Jewish–Galatian association within the Roman province of Galatia. In these capacities, she is of immediate relevance for our attempt to re-imagine the contemporary frame of reference for Paul's Galatian controversy about the integration of Jews and non-Jews in the age of Caesar and of Christ.

Paul theoretically could have met Julia Severa at some point. Phrygian Acmonia was less than fifty miles into the province of Asia from the provincial border between Asia and (South) Galatia. And like Paul himself, she was active in the time of Emperor Nero. Although no visit of Paul to Acmonia is known, Julia would fit the profile of high-ranking women with noticeable public standing whom he encountered, according to Acts 13:50, in Pisidian Antioch. And not accidentally, these women resist Paul's project, as Julia Severa would probably also have been in severe disagreement with the community model of Galatians and Jews "in Christ."

We may, first, understand Julia Severa as the prototypical example of the Galatians' "resurrection" in imperial terms. She represents the process that rehabilitates formerly lawless barbarians into imperial civilization, a process involving dynasty, victory, city, and piety. An heiress of great wealth, she was a Galatian woman of no ordinary social status, with an outstanding aristocratic pedigree that linked her to King Deiotaros and other Galatian rulers in Anatolia, as well as to Pergamon. We know this from two inscriptions at Galatian Ancyra, where in the first half of the second century C.E. a kinsman of hers, Gaius Julius Severus, boasts of his descent from King Deiotaros and the Attalids, as well as other high-ranking kinsmen.[102] As a very distinguished Galatian noblewoman, Julia thus represents precisely the "genealogy of power" that was key to the transformation of "barbarian" into "civilized" and imperial Galatians. She embodies the formation of "lawful" indigenous rule and social stratification that the Romans saw as a basic precondition for successful colonization. Dynasty building and the firmly established networks of ruling families, as we have seen, tamed the potentially chaotic and egalitarian impact of unstable charismatic military leadership among the tribes. The merging of Galatian and Pergamene nobility, in particular, gave the ultimate proof of the Galatians' admissibility to the "upper room" of city and civilization.

Yet the genealogical "makeover" of Severa's family goes beyond the adoption of her Galatian ancestors, formerly representing the arch-barbarian and archenemy, into the civilized Pergamene pedigree that reached back to Heracles and Zeus. There is another metamorphosis, linked to the moment when her family received Roman citizenship, probably under Augustus.[103] We do not know the original Galatian name that was replaced in the act of renaming; we only know from her first name that she has become part of the fictive kinship of the Julio-Claudian dynasty that goes back to Aeneas, his son Julus, the grandson of Venus, and Ilia's twin sons Romulus and Remus, the offspring of the god Mars (see chapter 3). "Julia" thus is first and foremost a Roman woman, who in a very peculiar way also embodies Galatian and Pergamene history, presenting the "world-saving" Pergamene and later Roman victories over the Galatians/Giants as a matter of Galatian pride rather than shame.

Julia Severa therefore stands for the magic metamorphosis staged at the Great Staircase of Pergamon, which incorporates the defeated into the power construct of their conquerors: first, through military means in the murderous campaign of Manlius Vulso; second, through gradual self-colonization by an indigenous ruling class willing to celebrate its own defeat as Roman triumph; and, third, through all the victories that Rome and Galatia won together after Deiotaros, Amyntas, and other Celtic client rulers had integrated their Galatian subjects into the war machine of the Roman Empire. Becoming subjects and providing soldiers for the empire were among the decisive credentials that allowed admission to the upside and inside of the Roman symbolic order represented at the Pergamene Great Altar. In this way Julia and her ancestry, as well as her widespread family, which is tightly integrated into the local networks of power,[104] present an exemplary model of Galatian citizenship in the Roman order.

It is, second, entirely within the double logic of self-submission and self-advancement already set in stone at the Great Altar, that this woman of power also represents the civic piety that honors the supreme ruler, the divine Caesar. For as we know from coinage and epigraphic evidence, she is a high priestess of the imperial cult and director of games dedicated to the imperial (*Sebastoi*) gods at the time of Emperor Nero.[105] An important and wealthy city, her hometown Acmonia has built an imperial temple and made her, together with her husband, the local high priestly officials of the imperial religion, as well as presiders over games and competitions. She thus rose to one of the highest positions of power available within the imperial power pyramid in a province. Not accidentally, this achievement made her a hybrid figure, barely recognizable as Galatian any longer and almost fully Roman. Her son would become one of the first Roman senators from the East under Emperor Nero, and some of her descendants would rise to the highest offices in the imperial administration.[106]

Interestingly, Julia Severa not only integrates a Galatian and Roman identity; she also, third, models a licit interaction of Galatians and the Jewish community that is compatible with the ordering principles of Roman rule. As one of the highest representatives of the imperial religion in Galatia, she embodies the province's submission to Caesar in her own person and at the same time acts as its broker among the different groups and ethnicities living in her city. This task is promoted by works of euergetism that Julia performs both as priestess and as sponsor of public entertainment.

One of Severa's benefactions is of specific importance for our topic. An inscription with her name found at Acmonia, dating from the second half of the first century C.E., happens to be the earliest inscriptional evidence for a synagogue found in Asia Minor. Julia Severa apparently gave the money for the building of that local synagogue in her hometown.[107] There is a substantial debate among scholars concerning her *personal* relationship to Judaism, whether as a sympathizer, apostate, proselyte, or simply non-affiliated patron and benefactor, and to the other sponsors who are mentioned in the inscription.[108] This should not obscure that her donation makes sense as an *official* act of euergetism that is situated within the much wider framework of municipal imperial religion, irrespective of any direct or indirect religious affiliation with the synagogue. Though we do not know whether she made her grant to the Jewish community during her time as an officeholder of the emperor cult,[109] she is a functionary of imperial piety and loyalty no matter whether she held a formal office or not, and as such she is a benefactor of the synagogue.

Julia Severa's substantial contribution to the local Jewish community, reminiscent of the Roman centurion in Luke 7:1-5, is therefore in line with the benefactions of the imperial priests under Tiberius on the Ancyran list discussed above (chapter 4). As we have seen, such contributions are "neutral" only on the surface: what appears as a simple gift to a religious group active within the framework of the city in fact integrates that group into the realm of compliance with imperial religion and rule. Supporting different strata of a city's population facilitates their submission to Caesar. Within the asymmetrical and reciprocal structure of patronage and euergetism, the adequate response to such a substantial gift from a high-ranking benefactor requires gratitude and honor on the side of the beneficiaries, which subsequently translates into political conformity. When the synagogue publicly expressed its gratitude to Julia Severa in an inscription that has preserved her name and deed to this day, it not only announced its own social standing as a community well connected to the highest circles of the civic establishment but also indirectly pledged allegiance to the divine figure Severa served as priestess, Emperor Nero.

Again we might ask whether this kind of synergy or tacit syncretism between Judaism and imperial religion would have been seen as positively by all Jews as it was obviously seen by the synagogue leaders of Acmonia, who, some thirty or forty years after Paul, "monumentalized" Julia Severa in their inscription. In all likelihood, they would not have found any reason to monumentalize Paul. If our reconstruction is correct, his community practice stands in glaring contrast to the model of acquiescence adopted by the synagogue in Acmonia when it assumed "that people actively involved in pagan cults were acceptable associates."[110] Julia Severa perhaps might indeed be seen, as Philip Harland has suggested, as a type very close to the figure of "Jezebel" in Rev 2:20, whom John scorns immediately after his attack on the Pergamene "throne of Satan" in 2:12-17. Yet if she represents a widespread and "normal" Jewish (and Christian) compromise that "took honoring the emperors and other imperial representatives, as well as full participation in the economic life of the city, as appropriate activities," then not only the Seer of Patmos but also Paul from Tarsus might need to be listed among those who dissented.[111] The Galatian Julia Severa stands in glaring contrast to Paul's vision for his Galatian communities as he tries to challenge the smooth and prudent arrangement between the Jewish God and the imperial idols proposed by his "opponents."

Conclusion: Imperial *Koinon* versus
Messianic *Koinōnia*

Although both the imperial *koinon* of the "devout [*Sebastēni*] Galatians" and the messianic *koinōnia* of Galatians and Jews envisioned by Paul operate in the landscape of Roman Galatia, and although both names derive from the Greek words for "common," "communal," and "community," the two had very little in common. From the perspective of Pax Romana and its imperial *nomos*, Paul's peacemaking and community building (*koinōnia*) between Jews and Gauls/Galatians "in Christ" must have appeared as an upsetting irregularity that implied lawless conduct and disturbed the common (*koinon*) provincial reverence for the divine emperor. On the symbolic level, it looked like another blasphemous Gallic-barbarian attack on the core principles of Roman rule and order. The examples of Julia Severa, the pro-Jewish imperial decrees for Asia, Herod's Galatian bodyguards and Judas Maccabaeus's Galatomachy, which we have studied in this chapter, each in its own way highlights how the *appropriate* form of association and community between Galatians and Jews under Roman auspices is totally dependent on the imperial intermediary. The divine Caesar *alone* was entitled to set the terms and conditions for licit interaction between Jews and Galatians, not his crucified antagonist.

Messianic Galatians who still had their foreskins yet did not participate in civic and imperial worship because of their allegiance to a God other than Caesar were an anomaly that challenged the most fundamental principles of the imperial cosmos. Moreover, that these Galatians had established a *koinōnia* together with messianic Jews, apart from the properly pious multiethnic community of the imperial *koinon* and independent of the *grace* of imperial benefactions, constituted a symbolic act of insurrection among the conquered nations (*ethnē*), a gesture of mutiny on an international scale. The messianic *koinōnia* did not comply with any of the principles of integration, rehabilitation, or association that the imperial order had established, explicitly and implicitly, for vanquished barbarians. It came from "below" rather than "above," and it functioned without Caesar as mediator who acted, at his own discretion, as either supreme warlord or peacemaker to make Jews and Galatians *one* in himself (yet other to one another). The messianic *koinōnia* between Jews and Galatians created a civic and religious space where the colonized started to make peace with one another and declare a common cause on terms oblivious or even opposed to Roman interests and the policy of "divide and rule."

Uncircumcised Galatians, with circumcised Jews as their brothers and the Jewish rather than Roman God as their common father, constituted an identity, a community, and a model of worship that was ambiguous in terms of Jewish law but more importantly, was illicit in its civic consequences within the framework of Roman law. This community offered a unity and an affiliation beyond the power of Caesar to define or control; much worse, this community was defined by and subject to the authority of a crucified provincial rebel leader in Roman Judea. Such a "universalism from below" was incompatible with the principles of the imperial "universalism from above."

William R. Ramsay, with his astute sense of political realities within the Roman order and their ideological underpinnings, described the phenomenon aptly when he stated that the Christians with their "wide-reaching organisation" maintained "a unity independent of, and contrary to, the Imperial unity."

> Such an organisation was contrary to the fundamental principle of Roman government. Rome had throughout its career made it a fixed principle to rule by dividing; all subjects must look to Rome alone; none might look towards their neighbours, or enter into any agreement and connection with them. But the Christians looked to a non-Roman unity; they decided on common action independent of Rome; they looked at themselves as Christians first, and Roman subjects afterwards; and when Rome refused to accept this secondary allegiance, they ceased to feel themselves as Roman subjects at all. When this was the case, it seems idle to look about for reasons why Rome should proscribe the Christians. If it was true to itself, it must compel obedience.[112]

Ramsay's identification of a non-Roman primary allegiance and unity, and of a peacemaking with one's neighbors on terms other than Rome's, confirms the essential points of our re-imagination here of the Galatian controversy in light of its imperial context. The two core issues of Paul's letter are, on the one hand, the new messianic identity of the Galatians, who (from the Roman perspective) unduly refused emperor and civic worship as if they were circumcised, and, on the other, an irregular communal affiliation operating outside the mandatory subservience to Roman rule. That affiliation built up a horizontal network of communities that was based not on the principles of Roman ordering but rather on a quite disorderly narrative in which a crucified man had been raised from the dead and had found followers who commemorated and worshiped him, but not the divine Caesar. As associations of all kind in this period were strictly monitored by imperial authorities, as we have seen, such deviant behavior could hardly have gone unnoticed.

In the configuration outlined in this chapter, Gentile foreskin *does* matter to Rome, as it embodies nonsubservience to imperial idolatry. It thus becomes a highly contested sign in Roman Galatia. The circumcision party with whom Paul wrestles emerges as a proponent of a political "back-to-normal" approach. In the concrete context of Roman Galatia, the foreskin of the Galatians is not simply an other-than-Jewish marker but has become the other-than-*Rome* sign. It announces a new relationship between self and other that is based on universal solidarity rather than competition and warfare, thus not simply abrogating imperial religion but also subverting the logic of battle that is the foundation of imperial world order. It also announces the rule of the singular God who in a new way claims sovereignty over the nations. All this requires a more detailed textual exploration of Paul's Galatian letter, to which we finally turn.

The beginning of Galatians in Papyrus 46, ca. 200 C.E., is one of the oldest New Testament manuscripts known to exist. Photo provided by the Archivist of the Papyrus Collection at the University of Michigan.

CHAPTER SIX

ᴄAmēn and ᴄAnathēma

Galatians at the Great Altar of Pergamon

P aul's exclusive allegiance to God "the father" and Christ crucified implied the ridicule of the images of power so carefully set up and staged everywhere in the temples, marketplaces, arenas, roads, theaters, and execution sites of the empire. When the Christ-following Galatians declared that their identity was defined not by the imperial *koinon* established by Rome but by the new messianic *koinōnia,* they practically became nonpersons, nobodies themselves—anti-selves, like the barbarians they had once been, and symbolically homeless among the images of the city.

The historical explorations of the preceding chapters have opened up a new reading of Galatians through its implied "intertextuality" with the Great Altar of Pergamon, a monument in which the collective history and imagination of Roman Galatia are condensed. A comprehensive rereading of the whole epistle on the scale customary to theological commentaries is beyond the scope of this study. Nevertheless, we will draft an exegetical summary of Galatians 1–6, introduced by a more in-depth investigation of Gal 1:1-9. As Paul's opening statement, these first nine verses in a nutshell frame the focal concerns of his letter.

Throughout, we will review the text of Galatians in intertextual "synopsis" with the images of the Great Altar, on the one hand, and core themes of the First Testament on the other. This bifocal critical re-imagination step by step discloses a textual logic incompatible with traditional readings of Galatians in an exclusively Jewish, or rather anti-Jewish, key. Semi-hidden in scriptural codes of exodus and exile, curse and blessing, and in plain sight only when juxtaposed with the Pergamene imagery, it enables a new understanding of Paul's core theme of justification by faith, as nothing less than an intervention into the world of the *eidōla,* that is, the images, idols, and ideology of Roman imperial rule. In a somewhat dramatic hermeneutical "landslide," the intertextual re-imagination thus exposes the antagonistic *other* in Galatia—Paul's "opponents"—not as Judaism but rather its opposite, namely, idolatry as the paradigmatic "Gentile" sin of non-Jewishness.

In a ground-shaking act of divine iconoclasm, the God of Paul has broken the imperial world image and world rule of the Olympic gods, and most notably of the divine Jupiter/Caesar. This has political and ethical implications on every level of the imperial taxonomy and policy of ordering, as an examination of Galatians 1–6 demonstrates. It means liberation and deliverance of Israel and nations together "out of this evil age" (Gal 1:4)—a new exodus that at the same time signifies a new creation, leading into a transformed social corporeality within the "body of Christ." Love and mutuality become the new *nomos* of this alternative community and commonality, a *koinōnia* that is profoundly *other* than the imperial *koinon,* implying a "mysticism" of self-transformation into messianic One-an(d)-Otherness. A brief reflection on Albert Schweitzer and Dietrich Bonhoeffer as co-genial interpreters of this most crucial Pauline "conversion" to the Other concludes our textual investigation.

[margin handwriting: alternative community]

Paul's (S)word: Theology of Combat Dismantled (Galatians 1:1-9)

We cannot "hear" the imagery of the Great Altar of Pergamon as we would hear a text; but at the beginning of his magisterial work *The Aesthetics of Resistance,* Peter Weiss provides a description of the Great Altar that allows us to experience its three-dimensional textures through the verbal medium:

> All around us the bodies rose out of the stone, crowded into groups, intertwined, or shattered into fragments, hinting at their shapes with a torso, a propped-up arm, a burst hip, a scabbed shard, always in warlike gestures, dodging, rebounding, attacking, shielding themselves, stretched high or crooked, some of them snuffed out, but with freestanding, forward-pressing foot, a twisted back, the contour of a calf harnessed into a single common motion. A gigantic wrestling, emerging from the gray wall, recalling a perfection, sinking back into formlessness. . . . With mask-like countenances, clutching one another, clambering over one another, sliding from horses, entangled in the reins, utterly vulnerable in nakedness, and yet enrapt in Olympic aloofness, appearing indomitable as an ocean monster, a griffin, a centaur, yet grimacing in pain and despair, thus they clashed with one another, acting at higher behest, dreaming, motionless in insane vehemence, mute in inaudible roaring, all of them woven into a metamorphosis of torture, shuddering, persisting, waiting for an awakening, in perpetual endurance and perpetual rebellion, in outrageous impact, and in extreme exertion to subdue the threat, to provoke the decision.[1]

And here is how Paul begins his letter to the Galatians (1:1-9):

> Paul an apostle—sent neither from human beings nor through one individual human being, but through Jesus Christ and God Father, who raised him from the dead—and all the brothers and sisters who are with me;
> To the assemblies [*ekklēsiai*] of Galatia: Grace to you and peace from God our Father and the Lord Jesus Christ, who gave himself for our sins to set us free from the present evil age, according to the will of our God and Father, to whom be the glory into all ages to come forever. Amen.
> I am astonished that you are so quickly deserting the one who called you through the grace of Christ and are turning to a different gospel—that is not an other gospel, but there

are some who are confusing you and want to pervert the gospel of Christ. But even if we or an angel from heaven should proclaim to you a gospel contrary to what we proclaimed as gospel to you, let that one be accursed [*anathēma*]! As we have said before, so now I repeat, if anyone proclaims to you a gospel contrary to what you received, let that one be accursed [*anathēma*].

Amēn and *Anathēma:* Like a double-edged sword, these two words in Gal 1:5 and 9 impose themselves at the outset of Paul's letter, and at the onset of occidental Pauline interpretation as well, splitting the world down the middle—good and bad, condemnation and salvation, blessing and curse. Galatians is the most polarizing and angry letter that Paul wrote. After the epistolary prescript with the messianic greeting in 1:1-5, it takes him no more than two sentences—just forty-six words—to go from *Amēn* to *Anathēma* in 1:6-9. He makes not the slightest attempt to exchange a few friendly words with his addressees, the "assemblies [*ekklēsiai*] of Galatia," as he does elsewhere at the beginning of other letters. Instead the conflict immediately bursts open. He bluntly accuses the Galatians of betrayal, desertion, changing sides. Immediately the murky figures of "opponents" appear in the background who pervert (*metastrepsai*) the messianic gospel and lead the Galatians away from God, from Jesus, and from Paul.

Does this rhetoric not put us right back at the foot of the Great Altar in Pergamon? The terms "warlike gestures," "gigantic wrestling," "relentless rivalry," and clashes with one another are the terms in which Weiss describes the Giant Battle Frieze, but these phrases could as well summarize the opening of Paul's letter.

"Warlike Gestures" and the Accursed Other: Traditional Readings

A battlefield, it seems, unfolds before our eyes in the first nine verses of Paul's Galatian letter, with clearly drawn lines of demarcation between the camps, portending a fierce fight to the death against dissidents and enemies who have invaded Paul's missionary domain like a band of marauding assailants. And Paul strikes back. The curse formula of an *Anathēma* that he hurls at the never-named adversaries is more than just words. It "does" something: it functions as a weapon no less efficient than the deadly spears, arrows, and snake-pots that we see in action on the Pergamene Frieze. In Paul's world, a curse effectively engages the power to destroy someone and expel them from the community.[2] As preachers of an *other* gospel (*heteron euangelion*, 1:6), Paul's opponents are doomed at least to excommunication, if not extinction.

Further, as at the Great Altar, the combatants, to quote Weiss again, act "at higher behest." The fight we witness apparently transcends the human sphere, evoking the order of the whole cosmos: it musters earthly as well as heavenly forces, human and divine families of astounding complexity and numbers. It is not just Paul alone whom we encounter in hand-to-hand combat against the Galatians and their false teachers; rather a whole extended kinship group struggles with him, including "all the brothers [and sisters] with me" (1:2). All of them are declared family through the one figure whose paternity is mentioned imposingly no fewer than three times within the first four verses of the letter: "God our Father." The final and climactic mention of "our" God and Father in 1:4 authoritatively puts both sender(s) and recipients of the letter under a collective *paterfamilias*, as if to make alienated family members recognize one another again as belonging to the same family tree: Paul, the brothers/sisters, and the Galatians alike, comprising both Jews and Gentiles/nations.[3] The messianic genealogy that brings them all together as one human family out of Abraham's and the Messiah's seed, across all their differences, rivalries, and unfamiliarities, will be the dominant theme of Paul's grand rereading of the Genesis narrative in Galatians 3–4.

In this family, however, Paul obviously has a special status that distinguishes him from his brothers and sisters: he is an *apostolos*, literally, a "sent one." Neither humans nor any particular human has sent him, but the Messiah Jesus Christ and the divine Father. As an ambassador, Paul is entrusted with the highest heavenly authority to represent the sole ruler over this and all ages to come, the God who has the power to resurrect "out of the dead" and who wills our liberation out of "this present evil age." Yet simultaneously Paul acts as the authorized legate of the Lord and Messiah (*kyrios/Christos*) who "gave himself for our transgressions" in order to lead us out of this evil age (1:3-4).

Both God the Father and the Lord Christ, together with their envoy/apostle Paul, have entered into what seems to be a cosmic war of the messengers and messages: conflicting, mutually exclusive messages of salvation—on earth as in heaven. In 1:8, an angel from heaven is mentioned as a potential counter-messenger, alongside the human voices of an "other gospel" (*heteron euangelion*), who all pervert the "good message" of the Messiah Christ (*euangelion tou Christou*) and mislead the Galatians.

Who are these invaders? Who is launching the attack? As we know from the overall context, the *other gospel* requires the Gentile members of the messianic *ekklēsiai* to be circumcised. This has made the decoding of Paul's battle cry "No other gospel" appear deceptively easy in much of the Christian interpretive tradition. Since circumcision is Jewish, the holy war unfolding in Galatia surely was directed against the unholy other of Jewishness and against Jewish "particularism" as codified through Torah. By implication, it seemed indisputable that the opposed "good" message of the Messiah Jesus, the beleaguered "gospel of Christ" (1:7), was the *Christian* gospel of universalism. The argument was seductively straightforward. If Jewishness is *Anathēma*, the countervailing *Amēn* must affirm Christianity. This reading produced the birth of the Christian self out of, and in antithesis to, the Jewish other—a new variation on the Pergamene battle construct through which the self of civilization and power emerges from the victory over vanquished others, the godless Giants/Galatians/barbarians.

Similar to the curse, Paul's *Amēn* is also a speech-act, a performative utterance that transforms reality the moment it emerges as sound or written sign.[4] A familiar term in Christian liturgy, *Amēn* is actually a Hebrew word that in the Greek of the Septuagint was either kept in its original form and transcribed with Greek letters as in Gal 1:5, or translated into a phrase such as "truly" or "let it be" (*alēthōs/genoito*). *Amēn* is an affirmation of something that has been said in a prayer, a creed, a hymn, or a sermon. There are multiple terms derived from the Hebrew root *'mn,* which all converge around the basic meaning of being firm, steadfast, reliable, secure, permanent.[5] This stability may include the trustworthiness and faithfulness of God and the corresponding trust and faith of humans. The Greek translation of this aspect would use terms from the word group related to *pistis* (faith or trust). A prominent case for such a transfer from the Hebrew root *'mn* to Greek *pisteuein* is Abraham's faith act in Gen 15:6, which becomes the basis for Paul's argument in Galatians 3–4: "He *trusted/believed* [*episteusen*] the Lord, and he counted it to him for righteousness" (Gal 3:6).

In the overture to his letter, Paul thus alludes to faith or trust, his theological signature concept, while at the same time converting the epistolary prescript of his letter into a moment of liturgical performance. What would in other contemporary letters be merely an opening with sender, addressees, and greeting—"grace to you and peace"— here swells into the unfathomable grandiosity of a messianic confession, a liturgical doxology, which the Galatians are rhetorically prompted to join in by saying the faith-word *Amēn* together with Paul and all the brothers and sisters with him.

Amēn in this setting is more than simply an affirmation of the messianic event and of God's eternal glory. It has a participatory thrust, implying a conforming act of submission. As J. Louis Martyn states, this *Amēn* transforms congregants from observers into participants.[6] Traditionally, this was understood to involve dissociation from the old and incorporation into the new covenant, the transition from Judaism to Christianity that the Galatians are on the verge of reversing. The act of incorporation prompted by Paul's *Amēn* appears, in a way, as their "conscription" into allegiance to Christ, which annuls any allegiance to Judaism.

Read in these terms, Paul's clash with the "Judaizers" in Galatia irreversibly opens up the archetypal battleground of the Christian occident, wherein the Christian gospel of justification by faith stands as the superior religion of the righteous, dominant self in juxtaposition to the inferior Jewish other, marked by circumcision and Torah-based works righteousness. Thus *Amēn* versus *Anathēma* paralleled Christianity's exodus out of and in opposition to Judaism. If we condense this complex antithetical structure into a semiotic quadrangle, the figure 41 emerges (see below).[7]

This figure shows the classic semiotics of a "battle square" as we have derived it from the spatial order of Great Altar in chapter 2, wherein we see opposed the constructs of a dominant insider self versus an inferior outsider other, godliness versus godlessness. The similarity of the tensions at work in Gal 1:1-9 to those in the Pergamene combat panorama is as striking as it is disturbing. Anathematizing his false-believing Jewish opponents, Paul appears on this reading as the prototype of the holy warrior alongside God.

All too soon his words would indeed morph into swords in multiple Christian theaters of war, turned against pagans, Muslims, savages, and various inferior others of the most diverse range. Not accidentally, the sword would come to feature as the standard iconographic marker of the "apostle to the Gentiles" in Christian artwork.[8] In the making of the Western mind, is not Galatians thus the nodal point at which the war of the gods against the Giants, the mythological archetype of our civilization, becomes a "Christian battle"? Does not Paul's intolerant theology lay the foundation for the

Fig. 41. Semiotic "Battle Square I": Christianity versus Judaism

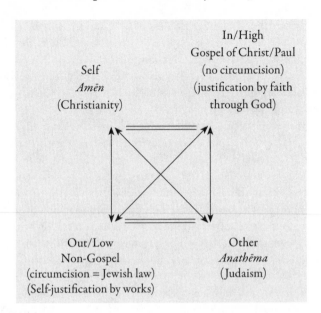

occidental-Christian construct of the enemy-other? Condensed into these opening lines, it seems that we can already foresee the whole post-Pauline history of Christian crusades, witch-hunts, pogroms, religious strife, conquests, and war making to come. And already in these opening lines, the whole interpretation of Galatians is at stake.

Critical Re-Imagination, Intertextuality, and "Coded" Language

Following the lead of a structural congruence in terms of western "combat order," we have entered into Galatians by simultaneously entering the Great Altar of Pergamon. Contemplating the symbolic world of the monument offers a frame of reference to understand the wider symbolic context of Paul's conversation with the Galatians in a "real world" that we no longer see before our eyes. The critical re-imagination proposed here is, in a wider sense, both a method of contextual and intertextual interpretation. Intertextuality in this case means more than the relationship between written texts. Rather, it includes images, spaces, and ritual practices too; it implies an understanding of the general "matrix of ideas" that is manifested in texts as well as in other cultural representations like sculptures and architecture, monuments or rituals.[9] Following Roland Barthes and Julia Kristeva, Richard Hays already in 1989 defined intertextuality as the "study of the semiotic matrix within which a text's acts of signification occur. All discourse in this view is intertextual as its conditions of intelligibility are given by and in relation to a previously given body of discourse."[10] To quote Jonathan Culler,

"Intertextuality thus becomes less a name for a work's relation to prior texts than a designation of its participation in the discursive space of a culture."[11] In our reading, images like the Great Altar of Pergamon or the Dying Gaul therefore are seen as (inter-)texts as well.[12] Whether Paul intentionally referred to them does not determine their relevance for the interpretation of his text.[13]

Given the history of interpretation of Galatians, however, we should also give an account of how this Pergamene *iconic* intertextuality relates to that other intertextuality that has so dominated Christian thought and that is more conventionally "textual" and much more widely explored: *scriptural* intertextuality. Jewish Scripture is obviously crucial to understanding Paul's letters in general, and Galatians in particular.[14]

In Galatians 3–4, Paul explicitly talks about Scripture (*graphē*) as a voice to be heard (4:30) or even as an acting character (3:22). These two chapters in their entirety are an intertextual retelling and reframing of the Genesis and Exodus narratives. There are no such obvious scriptural citations in the preceding two chapters of the letter, including the first nine verses (1:1-9). Nevertheless, as we shall see, the presence of Scripture is crucial for understanding this introductory section of Galatians as well. As recent scholarly debates have shown, biblical intertextuality is by no means a phenomenon restricted to explicit citations; rather, it can include a vast range of allusions, echoes, and resonances between texts.[15]

According to Richard Hays's criteria, an *allusion* would be primarily a *deliberate* evocation of Scripture by Paul. Identifying an allusion requires that Paul's readers would have recognized the allusion as such and would have shared with Paul the required "portable library," that is, would have known the texts to which he alludes. An *echo*, on the other hand (a term Hays takes over from John Hollander),[16] is a metaphor for an intertextual gesture the identification of which does not depend on establishing conscious authorial intention or on the capacity of the readers to identify the reference.[17] Both allusion and echo can bring up points of *resonance* between two texts that are not explicitly stated: "Allusive echo functions to suggest to the reader that text B should be understood in light of a broad interplay with text A, encompassing aspects of A beyond those explicitly echoed."[18]

The specific question for our exploration is, finally, whether such resonances and "whispered or unstated" intertextual correspondences are not only indispensable hermeneutical tools in general, but may also help us trace another message in Paul's text than the one we have heard so far. Or to ask a more pointed question: Is scriptural intertextuality a way for Paul to encode a message in an environment of external and internal censorship; and does it provide us a means to decode the prevalent occidental codification of Paul's theology as a "theology of the sword"? Can intertextuality help us to critically re-imagine Paul's "(s)word" as something else than an unbending weapon directed against the *other* of the dominant Western self?

We have mentioned this question of a "hidden transcript" already before and must raise it again at the outset of our textual investigation. If Roman law and imperial order, as we are trying to show, constitute the overarching context of his Galatian correspondence, why was Paul so cryptic about these issues, leaving them for us to arduously reconstruct and re-imagine, rather than addressing them more plainly and explicitly in his own text? In order to understand the conditions under which Paul was writing and communicating, we need rigorously to leave behind our own presuppositions about public speech and writing. In the discursive space controlled by the conquerors and shaped in conformity with imperial law and order, a letter like the one Paul is sending to Galatia can hardly talk in a straightforward manner about politically sensitive matters like civic nonconformity or disobedience. It requires encoded forms of speech and reading "between the lines," on the part of his hearers and of his contemporary interpreters alike.

In Gal 2:4, Paul refers—explicitly and probably not accidentally—to "spies" and "false brothers" who obviously serve as informants and thus, in whatever way, are linked to social control agents, the factor of "fear" plainly entering into sight in 6:12. The political implication of these terms is usually significantly downplayed. Yet they describe precisely the setting where we should expect the emergence of "hidden transcripts" of speech and social practice among the dominated that are noticeably different from their "public" counterparts.[19]

The dominated always know how to communicate in "other words" under the eagle eye of their censors, using abbreviations, allusions, omissions, and the camouflage of a "double tongue" to say what they want to say, without saying it. Only when the context changes and the rules of the (reading) game are no longer understood, the text produced by this matrix of force and coercion, caution and indirection becomes unreadable or ambiguous, as the semantic of its "hidden transcript" is no longer accessible.

This seems a much underestimated aspect of Pauline hermeneutics that might well account for some of the puzzlement surrounding his discourse on law and justification by faith. Our critical re-imagination of the Galatian letter will therefore treat this text as a semi-hidden (or semi-public) transcript circulating among the dominated that has an anti-Roman core message, without, however, displaying an overt and easily identifiable anti-Roman rhetoric.[20] We will consider its intertextual linkages with Hebrew Scripture as a means of revealing meaning, as well as hiding and encoding it within a "hermeneutics of conspiracy."[21]

To summarize these various aspects and dimensions of our methodological approach, we might describe "critical re-imagination" as a combination of several textual, intertextual, and contextual modes of operation:

1. On a literary level, critical re-imagination works with images (in the widest sense) to unlock layers and dimensions of meaning that have largely stayed inaccessible and invisible in traditional interpretations.

2. On a sociohistorical level, critical re-imagination uses images as keys to access, if only in a surrogate mode, the no longer accessible "real world" around Paul and his Galatian conflict. Visual art, like the Pergamon Altar or the Dying Gauls, represents a condensed version of the symbolic and political universe where Paul's text is located and thus may function as an "auxiliary context" for its interpretation.

3. Based on James Scott's work, critical re-imagination conceptualizes Paul's text as a "semi-hidden transcript" that is neither a replica of the official imperial propaganda (and of the corresponding discourse of subservience on the side of the colonized) nor an unfiltered and uncensored proclamation of resistance, but rather an indirect, concealed, and guarded mode of speaking about domination and liberation that partly hides and partly discloses its subject and that would be heard with different ears from "above" and "below," from "outside" and from the "inside."

4. Critical re-imagination uses scriptural intertextuality—a reservoir of meaning making that was widely unfamiliar to the dominant Greco-Roman culture and therefore fairly "safe" for Paul to employ—to "de-code" the semi-hidden transcript of resistance in his text.

5. Overall, critical re-imagination tries to retrieve and reclaim the *other* meaning of Paul's text that got lost when Paul's semi-hidden transcript was converted into the public scripture of a dominant Christianity after Constantine.

The Scriptural Code of Galatians: Anti-Idolatry and New Exodus

From the outset, the beginning of Paul's letter throws the Galatians in the middle of two opposing camps, both claiming their allegiance. Like the biblical Israel at the end of Deuteronomy, standing between the mountain of curse and the mountain of blessing, Paul metaphorically lines up the *ekklēsiai* of Galatia between *Amēn* and *Anathēma*, confronting them with a choice they have to make.[22] But is this choice really the alternative between Christianity and Judaism, as the Christian tradition has encouraged us to believe, or something else?

In a highly illuminating study, Roy Ciampa has explored the field of scriptural resonances with regard to Galatians 1 and 2—a generally neglected topic in scholarship to date—and has shown how intensely and coherently these chapters interact with First Testament material, most notably Deuteronomy, Second Isaiah, and Exodus.[23] According to Ciampa, the overall biblical pattern that shapes the conflict between Paul and his opponents in Galatia is the antinomy between exodus and restoration, on one side, and apostasy and exile, on the other, that is embedded in a strongly apocalyptic-messianic framework. True and false prophecy clash, as opposing messages and messengers confront each other.[24]

The Other Gospel: Apostasy and Golden Calf

Within the biblical narrative, Paul's double curse in Gal 1:8-9 echoes one of the most powerful condemnations used against those who succumbed to the treacherous and illusory attraction of the "idols," the other gods. In addition to Deuteronomy 27–30, the structure of the curse formula in Gal 1:6-9 is also reminiscent of Deuteronomy 13.[25] Both Galatians 1 and Deuteronomy 13 (LXX) feature conditional if-clauses dealing with false teachers who seek to seduce "you" into apostasy; and both use the *Anathēma* formula to describe a severe punishment.

Deut 13:   If . . . X (says) . . . "Let us go and worship other gods,"
              then: death/*Anathēma*
Gal 1:8–9:   If . . . X (proclaims) . . . another gospel . . .
              (then): *Anathēma*

Deuteronomy 13 constructs three such casuistic *if-* sentences around the idolatrous proclamation, "Let us go and worship other gods" (*poreuthōmen kai latreusōmen theois heterois*, 13:3, 7, 14 LXX), which is made first by false prophets, then by family members or friends, then by lawless men (*andres paranomoi*). In all three cases the death penalty is required: *Anathēma*.

The juxtaposition of texts from Deuteronomy and Galatians casts a new light on Paul's rejection of the "other gospel" that his opponents are proclaiming (1:6). Referring to this "other gospel," *heteron euangelion,* Paul declares boldly that "there is no other" (*ouk estin allo,* 1:7). In the biblical semantics of one versus other, this phrase is a standard expression for *the singularity of Israel's God* and the prohibition of subservience to *any other god* (Exod 8:10; 9:14; Deut 4:35; Isa 45:21, 22). In Mark 12:28-34, for example, when a scribe approaches Jesus in Jerusalem and inquires about the first commandment, Jesus replies with a citation of the *Shema Israel*, the everyday prayer of an Israelite, which begins with the words of Deut 6:4-5: "Hear, O Israel, the Lord our God, the Lord is one." The scribe approves of this answer and repeats it, adding the formula of Isa 45:21 (and using exactly the same phrase that Paul uses in Gal 1:7): "You are right, teacher, you have truly said that he is *one* and besides him *there is no other* [*ouk estin allos*]."

Paul's phrase, then, touches on an intertextual undercurrent involving idolatry and curse. This is reinforced by another scriptural echo that evokes Israel's most paradigmatic and prototypical act of apostasy/idolatry, which happened in the very shadow of the giving of the law itself, the golden calf episode (Exodus 32). Paul accuses the Galatians of having turned away "quickly" (*tacheōs*, 1:6): so, too, at Mount Sinai the Israelites fatefully turned away "quickly" (Exod 32:8; Deut 9:12; compare Ps 105:13 LXX, *etachynan*) while Moses received the tablets with the commandments and was absent for too long. A text like Judg 2:17 indicates that "quickly" formed part of a larger speech pattern with regard to apostasy.[26] Ciampa has carefully researched this connection and concluded that "turning away quickly" should indeed be heard as an echo of "Israel's first and classic apostasy from God, the creation and worship of the golden calf at the foot of Mount Sinai after the miraculous deliverance at the Red Sea."[27]

The juxtaposition should give us pause. If Paul is anathematizing idolatry, biblically the antithesis of Torah, the traditional reading that pits him against Judaism falls apart. As we have seen, in Paul's time the most overbearing and all-encompassing form of idolatry was the Roman imperial religion with its claim to integrate and dominate all other religions. In Exod 32:4, the golden calf was falsely named and celebrated by the

Israelites as the liberating "God of exodus." In a similar way, the supreme idol in Paul's day deceptively had himself hailed in Roman Galatia as the god of liberation from the *previous* "evil era," who had brought the world into the *present* age of golden prosperity and peace: the divine Caesar (see chapter 3).

Imperial versus Messianic Gospel: Exile or Exodus

The competing gospel message, the "other good news" referred to no fewer than five times in 1:6-9,[28] is thus much more likely the gospel of imperial salvation than any "Jewish gospel." *Euangelion* is a term firmly embedded in imperial propaganda; it celebrates, for example, the accession or birth of an emperor.[29] A text such as the Calendar Inscription from Priene in Asia Minor (9 B.C.E.) may illustrate this:

> Whereas the providence [*pronoia*] that ordains our whole life has established with zeal and distinction that which is most perfect in our life by bringing Augustus [*Sebastos*], whom she filled with virtue as a benefaction [*euergesia*] to all humanity; sending to us and to those after us a savior [*sōtēra*] who put an end to war and brought order to all things [*kosmēsonta de panta*]; and Caesar [*Kaisar*], when he appeared, the hopes of those who proceeded . . . placed, not only surpassing those benefactors [*euergetas*] who had come before but also leaving to those who shall come no hope of surpassing (him); and the birth of the god [*tou theou*] was the beginning of good tidings [*euangeliōn*] to the world [*kosmōi*] through him.[30]

Already in 1923, Adolf Deissmann pointed to Paul's use of "gospel," and of other key terms of imperial religion such as *kyrios,* as a "protest against the worship of Caesar" that was born out of the "passionate determination of the monotheistic cult of Christ."[31] Deissmann asserted a "polemical parallelism between the cult of the emperor and the cult of Christ, which makes itself felt where ancient words derived from the treasury of the Septuagint and the Gospels happen to coincide with solemn concepts of the Imperial cult which sounded the same or similar."[32]

But again, with this characterization the entire hermeneutical framework for reading Galatians shifts. If Paul's *Anathēma* refers to imperial idolatry in his day as prototypical apostasy, a *contemporary* "golden calf," so to speak, then the curse must apply to the violence of enslavement and coercion, exile and death that in biblical logic is the inevitable consequence of idol worship and of turning away "quickly" from the exodus commandments (Deuteronomy 27–30). The curse thus represents the current life realities of *conquered nations under Roman rule.* The *Anathēma* that Paul declares is not violence that he himself "creates" but a violence he voices and identifies by pointing to the deadly destructiveness inherent in the imperial system itself: the very same accursed system of oppression and colonization that requires that the vanquished hail its idols as salvific and all-powerful.

But for Paul, the curse is lifted through Christ. The universal event of divine justification by means of faith and grace takes away "our sin"—meaning the complicity of the defeated themselves, both Jewish and Galatian, that has kept Israel and the nations alike under colonial slave masters. This will be the core theme of Paul's theological argument in 2:15-21 and throughout chapters 3–4.

If, as the preceding observations suggest, the *Anathēma* in Gal 1:6-9 is speaking in coded language about the curse of Roman rule as the collective slavery and exile of Jews and nations alike, and no less about their complicity in a rule that keeps them down and in bondage, the *Amēn* in 1:1-5 is an encrypted message of redemption and liberation: the messianic gospel for Israel and the whole world according to Isaiah 40 and 52.[33] The antithesis of slavery and freedom that serves as the semantic backbone of Paul's entire argument from Gal 3:28 through 5:15 is then not simply projecting an otherworldly freedom, but is part of a coded discourse among the enslaved nations about the spirituality and practice of liberation from the Roman "yoke of slavery" (5:1).[34] This suggestion is indirectly supported by the fact that the "false brothers" (*pseudadelphoi*) who had infiltrated the Pauline community as "spies" and informants have precisely targeted the concept and practice of liberation that defined the new messianic identity, as Paul remembers in 2:4: "the freedom that we have in Christ Jesus."

Contesting the Supreme Idol: Caesar

It is the nature of intertextual allusions and echoes that they are not as easily "provable" as explicit quotations. Their existence is more a matter of likelihood, of intuition, of creative patchworking and listening, of being "tuned in" to a certain textual sound and imagery. Nevertheless, the exploration of intertextuality has fairly clear criteria of plausibility.[35] In the case of the opening lines of Galatians, the overall picture that emerges is too coherent to be denied: it involves a complex substructure of exodus imagery that underlies and shapes Paul's address to the Galatians.

Through these intertextual echoes and allusions, the whole of Galatians is configured within a bifocal biblical vision of apostasy, slavery, and exile, on the one hand, and of new exodus, redemption, and restoration, on the other—curse versus blessing, Roman world order versus God's new creation. God's new intervention in the course of world history as envisioned by Second Isaiah now comprises Israel and the nations alike. Both Jews and Galatians, both Israel and the Gentiles, are redeemed, made righteous by God, and both are liberated in a new exodus out of Roman exile. If the false gospel of imperial idolatry and apostasy is the focus of Paul's *Anathēma*, then the messianic gospel of universal redemption and restoration is the core of his *Amēn*.

These connections give our semiotic "battle square" an entirely different form (fig. 42). In this modified figure, Paul's gospel of Christ confronts the gospel of the idol(s), most notably the gospel of the one primary idol, the divine Caesar, whose proclamations are labeled "good news" and who is hailed as the ruler of the best of all possible worlds—but from Paul's viewpoint, of "this present evil age."

This may at last help us decode a strange phrase at the beginning of Galatians that has been puzzling to interpreters. In 1:1, when Paul somewhat enigmatically but with noticeable verve declares that he has "not been sent from human beings, *nor by a single man*," does he speak about the *specific* single man who should not be named explicitly but kept in mind as the antagonist of Paul's message throughout the letter, Caesar? Is

Fig. 42. Semiotic "Battle Square II": God of Exodus versus Idols of Exile

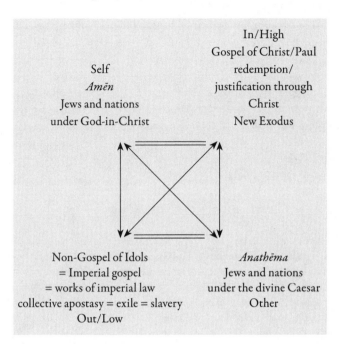

Self
Amēn
Jews and nations
under God-in-Christ

In/High
Gospel of Christ/Paul
redemption/
justification through
Christ
New Exodus

Non-Gospel of Idols
= Imperial gospel
= works of imperial law
collective apostasy = exile = slavery
Out/Low

Anathēma
Jews and nations
under the divine Caesar
Other

the somewhat clumsy and repetitive "not from a single man," which seems superfluous and which commentators tend to see as redundant, in reality a signal for the reader "to understand" (compare Mark 13:14) that the whole of the following letter needs to be read in an empire-critical key?[36]

Like the first-century censor, spy, informant, or control agent, we as twenty-first century visitors to Paul's Galatia cannot "prove" this other meaning of his words; it might, however, have been quite obvious to the Galatians themselves. For it was Caesar who had "sent" Jesus into the darkness of the dying and dead out of which he was then raised by God (*ek nekrōn*, 1:1); it was Caesar whose authority as universal father (*pater patriae*) was vaunted in terms rivaling that of Paul's God the Father and Lord Jesus Christ in 1:1-9; it was Caesar whose claims on the allegiance of individuals in the civic square was the ultimate source, as we have argued above, of the most pervasive contestation both of Paul's messianic message and of his status as authorized messenger of universal "good news."

This suggestion aligns with the argument in previous chapters that the principal antithesis behind Galatians is not Jesus Christ versus the Jewish God but instead the Jewish God-in-Christ versus the divine Caesar, the supreme idol of Paul's world. The law and religion that Paul primarily criticizes are the law and religion not of Judaism but of the Roman Empire. If idolatry and apostasy are the focus of Paul's *Anathēma,* and if messianic redemption and restoration constitute the core of his *Amēn,* then the otherness that he condemns with prophetic zeal is not Judaism but the scandal of Israel and the nations together being subject to and subjecting themselves to the idol(s) of empire.

Nonetheless, this empire-critical understanding of Paul's message, though radically different from the traditional anti-Judaistic interpretation, still seems to retain the established logic of the battle order, the dichotomous hierarchy between self and other. This logic is the logic of an imperial order, even where it is developed into an anti-imperial thrust. Its structure is still the hierarchical and dichotomous opposition inherent in any bipolar enemy construct. Is the messianic kingdom then just the upside-down version of Caesar's empire? Is Paul's messianic peace simply reinstalling under a new disguise the old pattern of holy war making? These questions require another "intertextual" return to the Great Altar of Pergamon.

The Pergamene Code: Confusing the Battle Order

> And so in the dim light, we gazed at the beaten and dying. The mouth of one of the vanquished, with the rapacious hound hanging over his shoulder, was half open, breathing its last. His left hand lay feeble on the forward-charging leather-shod foot of Artemis, his right arm was still raised in self-defense, but his hips were already growing cold, and his legs had turned into a spongy mass. We heard the thuds of the clubs, the shrilling whistles, the moans, the splashing of blood. We looked back at a prehistoric past, and for an instant the prospect of the future filled up with a massacre impenetrable to the thought of liberation. Heracles would have to help them, the subjugated, and not those who had enough armor and weapons.[37] (Peter Weiss, *The Aesthetics of Resistance,* 1:9)

> . . . who raised him out from the dead . . . who gave himself for our sins so that he might liberate us out of this present evil age . . . (Gal 1:1, 4)

Let us imagine that we stand again at the Great Altar of Pergamon, with the text of Galatians in our hands and scenes of combat before us. We are once more spellbound by an aesthetics of victory that holds so much beauty and monstrosity, unsurpassed throughout the history of human art. Almost instantly the power of these images begins to draw our minds into their orbit irresistibly, seductively, triumphantly. How might one hope to withstand the evidence of the self-evident, the sheer logic of the real, the magic of triumph, the aura of power, the tantalizing naturalness of combat and war radiating from the marble? Not the snake-legged ugliness of the fallen Giants, the "spongy mass" of the dying and dead. The steel-clad glory of the immortal deities attracts our desire; it is they with whom we strive to identify. We want it to be *our* cause they are fighting for. And indeed, in a divinely ordered world under the eagle's wings, we are entitled to rely on the presence of the gods-with-*us*, rather than with *them*, the undeserving others.

Paul's *Amēn* and *Anathēma* echo from the Great Frieze. Under our gaze, the Pergamene images that are so much part of our civilization's self-perception, deeply infused into our Christianity, tighten their grip on Paul's text and our effort at a counter-reading of it. The attempt to resist these images with no force other than that of the scriptural *logos* slackens and begins to feel strangely out of place. Surely it is the Galatian text, our very own text, that we see mirrored in the texture of the Great Altar. How could we not be lured into recognizing the correspondence between image and word? Does not the biblical dichotomy of blessing and curse, promise and conquest, us and not-us, *Amēn* and *Anathēma* seem to breathe in and out of these images of control and punishment, prosperity and war making, divine presence and massacre—a massacre, in the words of Weiss quoted above, truly "impenetrable to the thought of liberation"?

Then, just as these questions form, in a flash of historical anticipation, the emperor Constantine rises before our eyes, his sword raised. He grasps in the other hand the cross as the sign of Christian victory; he plants it on the top and at the center of the Great Altar. The Bible appears beneath it. The meaning of the vision is clear: the deities and doctrines of empire may change, but not the imperial battle order and its law of conquest and subjugation. Is this ultimately where our exploration leads us? Is this what Paul's empire criticism is finally about?[38]

But wait. Once we begin to read, once Paul and the Galatians appear around us, something strange happens. Before the first lines of the letter are finished, the flow of the words comes to a halt; they meet an unexpected resistance. They cause confusion and uproar, and the images begin to blur. It is as if an un-word has been pronounced, a forbidden term infused with a hidden magic: *ek nekrōn, from the dead*. The very moment the echo bounces back from the Great Frieze it produces tears in the densely woven fabric of the battle order; it deranges the fighting armies and disorders the symbolic universe. For nothing that is implied in this phrase is permissible or even imaginable within the confines of the Great Altar. Not that this one was raised from the dead; not that a Father God did this; not that he gave himself for our sins; not that a liberation out of this present evil age is thinkable, let alone possible (1:1-4).

Resurrection from the Dead

As both Paul and the Galatians knew only too well (for had Paul not insisted on its graphic representation before them in 3:1?), Jesus died the most violent and public death imaginable. Crucifixion destroyed the body under unspeakable torture; it usually meant that the corpse was left to the disposal of the elements and wild animals, until nothing recognizably human was left to be remembered, let alone "resurrected." Death by crucifixion was the large-scale public display of Roman capital punishment. As we saw in chapter 3, it was imposed on the rebellious territories of alterity, the inferior *others* on the underside of empire, as a brutal restatement of Roman law and its reinscription on the body of subject and slave.

In the pictorial "dictionary" of the Great Altar, crucifixion is synonymous with the punishment and "pacification" of the Giants at the bottom of the edifice, which represents the cosmos. Within both Pergamene and Pauline logic, crucifixion is the ultimate act of salvation accomplished by the Father God—except for one decisive difference. At the Great Frieze, the divine paternal deed of rescuing humanity means petrifying the transgressor into the stony immortality of the dead and dying. It could

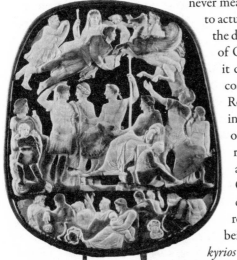

Fig. 43. Tiberius, portrayed as divine, sits enthroned; above him the deified Augustus is welcomed into heaven. The Grand Camée de France, ca. 23 C.E. Photo: Erich Lessing/Art Resource, N.Y.

never mean bringing a crucified delinquent back to actual, eternal life. Jesus' resurrection "from the dead" (Gal 1:1) thus is a spoken mockery of Olympic and Roman law enforcement; it clashes with the most sacred images of cosmic order. Though the Hellenistic and Roman world had no difficulty imagining how Caesars, divine sons, or victorious demi-gods like Heracles could be raised from the dead to heavenly glory and power, as for example on the Grand Camée de France (see fig. 43), neither could ever contemplate a *crucified* man representing the vanquished nations being raised to life—and to lordship—as *kyrios ek nekrōn.*

This is where every apparent parallel between the opening lines of Paul's letter and the imagery of the Great Altar collapses from within. In the symbolic universe of Pergamon and of Rome, the resurrection of Jesus could only be an abominable, blasphemous act of insurgence by the God of a subject people who has thereby aligned himself with the archenemy, betraying the common divine cause of power and victory. Translated into the language of the Pergamene images, Jesus' installation as Lord *from (ek) the dead* is an appalling "Giant-like" act of mutiny against divine supremacy as well as against imperial order, imperial logic, and imperial agency, which represent divine order on earth. God's appearance on the side of the *other* destroys the dominant image of God, of law, of the world, and, worst of all, it destroys the image of the enemy. This is divine iconoclasm on a cosmic scale. For Paul, however, it is the beginning of a new creation—or of an exodus out of the old world order, "from [*ek*] this present evil age" (1:4).[39] Only the "will of God the Father," the *true* God who is the primeval creator and who rules "unto the ages of the ages" (1:4-5), can inaugurate it—not the father god Zeus, or Jupiter, or Caesar. For Paul, Genesis and Exodus are inseparably intertwined.

God the Father

Before Paul talks about God as "our Father"(1:3, 5), he introduces God as the Father of Jesus Christ, a relationship both confirmed and defined by the act of resurrection (1:1). But the metaphor of God's fatherhood and the concept of resurrection resound with scriptural echoes as well that all converge in the exodus theme. While scholars like J. Christiaan Beker place the concept of resurrection squarely in the context of an apocalyptic worldview, where it points to the "transformation and recreation of all reality" in the new age to come,[40] Roy Ciampa detects in the proclamation of resurrection aspects of an analogy to Israel's deliverance from Egypt.[41] Paul's language of God's fatherhood, for example, according to Ciampa contains strong exodus connotations that are usually overlooked: "In the Old Testament references to God's Fatherhood are consistently found in contexts which refer to the exodus redemption or which anticipate a future redemption and restoration (second exodus) of God's people."[42]

These intertextual exodus echoes include Exod 4:22, where Moses is told to declare Israel God's firstborn *son* in front of Pharaoh, so that Israel should be allowed to go out of Egypt and serve God. In Deuteronomy 32, shortly before his death, Moses addresses Israel as God's children who rejected their *father* who has made them (32:6, 18) and cared for them in the desert (32:10-12). Moses warns that as the people turn to idols (32:15-18) and non-gods (32:21; compare Gal 4:8), they bring God's punishment upon themselves, enacted through triumphant and overpowering foreign nations (32:19-27), in a sequence of curse, enslavement, and exile (Deut 27:11—28:68). But finally Israel will find God's fatherly compassion again (32:36).

These scriptural resonances around resurrection, exodus, new creation, and fatherhood stand in stark contrast to the images of the Great Altar; they evoke an *other* image of cosmic order that subverts the archetype of supreme human and divine fatherhood in the Pergamene imagery. As we saw in chapter 2, the centerpiece of the Great Frieze is the heroic masculinity and barely covered sexuality of Zeus's semi-nude body. The father-god is depicted in combat with three attacking opponents and is flanked by his son Heracles and some of his most prominent other children: Athena/Minerva, Apollo, Artemis/Diana, and Ares/Mars, together with their mothers. (See figs. 18, 19, 24.) Both Zeus's official wife, Hera/Juno, and his mistress, Leto, are present as co-combatants. (Athena's mother, Metis/Wisdom, must stay invisible: fearing her power, Zeus had devoured her before she could give birth and then brought forth his daughter himself, motherless and perfectly loyal to her father.) The overall scene shows vividly how sexual potency as male power to give life is closely tied to the power to kill and conquer, subdue and master, discipline and punish, the power to triumph over rebellious women and insurgent nations alike.

But Paul's concept of divine fatherhood is radically different. It presents procreation as a new creation by resurrecting *from the dead,* thus undoing the imperial order of (pro)creation that has the murderous violence of conquest inscribed on the very act of giving life. At the core of this new (pro)creation is the rejection of victorious masculinity and subjugated femininity as the "genetic code" of humanity.[43] God becomes father not by imposing death like Zeus, but by undoing death. This Christo-genesis is the foundational procreative intervention that enables the rebirth of humanity as well. Truly transformed into the image of the *one* God (*heis*) who is other than Caesar (*henos ouk estin,* 3:20),[44] and made brothers and sisters out of *one* messianic seed (*henos,* 3:16), both Jews and Greeks, both slave and free, both male and female are reborn into the *oneness* of a new messianic universality and family genealogy (*heis,* 3:28) radically detached from the bloodline of empire.

In his messianic retelling of the Genesis story in Galatians 3–4, Paul establishes this new universal human family and genealogy as a counterimage of the universal family of the imperial *pater patriae* and his *domus*. (See fig. 43 above.) Presenting himself as a mother in labor, Paul poses in Gal 4:19 as intermediary of this cosmic rebirth, alarmed that the Galatians are about to lose their Christo-morphic shape (*morphōthē Christos en hymin*) and slip back into conformity with the imperial body, which in their specific case must either bear the mark of foreskin or be reincorporated into imperial and civic worship. The new creation, on the other hand, of which Christ is the firstborn, erases the inscription of conquest and violence from the collective and individual self and reshapes human beings in the likeness of Christ's solidarity and love.

Self-giving versus Works of (Imperial) Law

We touch here the core of Paul's opposition to "works of the law" (which we understand as works of imperial violence and competition). The fact that the divine Father, guarantor of cosmic law and worldwide patriarchal order, should now sympathize with the lawless and vanquished, with the unrighteous and punishable other, necessarily dissolves and dismantles the sacred hierarchy and segregation of self and other and all the violence and human sacrifice it justifies. If God neglects the works of imperial law fit for a supreme father (1:1), so does Jesus refuse what a son, especially a divine son, is supposed to do. That "he gave himself for our sins" and "leads us out" (1:4) radically defies every code of filial behavior exhibited at the Great Altar.

As we have seen, at the Great Frieze the divine father Zeus vigorously engages the *evil other* in combat, properly supported by his sons and daughters who join him in battle with equal fervor. Fighting in the image of the father, the emerging *self* of the "son" must establish its righteousness, power, privilege, and very identity by equally trampling down the unrighteous, the weaker and undeserving *other*. It is through condemning, overpowering, and killing that the self wins life—not through "giving oneself" on behalf of a sinful other. The transgressors and *their* sins need to be established as other and properly punished, not justified by an act of self-giving. There is no way out of this setting. The unbridgeable hierarchy that sets self, law, victory, and righteousness against other, lawlessness, defeat, and punishment expresses the primeval logic of combat, a logic set in stone on the Great Altar and reenacted by the everyday "works" of Roman imperial might. Jesus' act on behalf of *us,* and God's act on behalf of *him,* negate all the rules of this logic. This is the foundational move in the universal event that announces a new exodus and a new creation, the "good message" (*euangelion*) of humanity being restored from the likeness of Caesar's image into the image of God.

Here we detect another intertextual echo with Israel's Scripture. It has long been recognized that the statement about Jesus giving himself echoes the suffering servant of Isaiah 53. Ciampa suggests that the phrase "The Lord [God] gave *him* over for our sins" in Isa 53:6 was refashioned, already before Paul, into a christological affirmation that "the Lord [Jesus] gave *himself* over for our sins."[45] Paul repeats the theme, which stands at the core of his justification theology, in Gal 2:20. In Gal 3:13, this vicarious messianic self-sacrifice links Isaiah 53 and the curse traditions of Deuteronomy 27–30: Christ redeemed us from the curse of the law by becoming a curse for us (Deut 21:23 and 27:26).[46]

It is quite plausible that Paul was aware of the echoes with Isaiah 53. In Gal 4:27, he explicitly quotes Isa 54:1, the opening lines of the following chapter, which focuses on restoration. In Isaiah 52, the preceding chapter, Isaiah explicitly uses the language of "gospel" (*euangelizomenos*, 52:7), peace/salvation (52:7), and a new exodus (*exelthate*, 52:11, 12) to celebrate this restoration, which has universal implications for all the nations/Gentiles (*enōpion pantōn tōn ethnōn*, 52:10)—notes clearly struck in Galatians. Immediately after this statement, the passage about the suffering servant begins (Isa 52:13—53:12). In Second Isaiah, death "for our sins" is thus closely linked to exodus and restoration concepts, as well as to the wider world of the nations/Gentiles; removing the sins of (all) the people(s) is the prerequisite for God's new liberating intervention on their behalf.

This linkage of Jesus' self-giving to themes of exodus and restoration is vital for our exploration. The act of messianic self-giving on behalf of an *other* is focal to all the seminal passages that express Paul's theology of justification and rejection of law in Galatians (1:4; 2:20; 3:13). The exodus connotation reinforces the political implications of this antithesis. As the "undoing" of the works (or workings) of imperial law, rather than of Torah, justification by faith unhinges the established hierarchy and segregation between self and other that is built on precisely these competitive, combative, disciplinary, and consumptive "works." It annuls any "boasting" on the part of the self, which always celebrates its own superiority through the mirror image of an inferior and defeated other that is "consumed" on behalf of the self (Gal 5:25—6:4).[47]

Self-sacrifice on behalf of an other or the (br)other's "consumption" on behalf of the self are the two oppositional poles that mark the antithesis of new and old creation, of justification by faith or justification by works of the law. The *erga tou nomou*, the works of law, in this reading of Paul refer to the myriad ways of upholding and reproducing the "combat order" of the imperial world construct with the victorious self at the top. The double act of divine peacemaking and border crossing toward and on behalf of the other that is accomplished by God the Father and Jesus Christ the Son in Gal 1:1-4 is, then, the most comprehensive possible negation of the world *nomos*.

Exodus from an Evil Age

That Jesus "gave himself" for a sinful other (1:4) and that it was precisely as an inferior and unworthy other condemned to death, he was raised by God (1:1) to represent lordship (*kyrios*, 1:3) and universal power according to the true will and image of God the Father (1:4)—all this profoundly disturbs, confuses, and disorders the clear-cut constructs of enmity and antagonism, identity and alliance underlying the semiotic "battle square" of empire. That one might give oneself on behalf of another, and that the divine *One* should then intervene on behalf of this *other*, justifying rather than condemning the sinner, resurrecting the lawless instead of sanctioning their execution as a reestablishment of divine order: these affirmations leave nothing in the imperial world construct as it is supposed to be. It sends the hierarchical dichotomies on which the imperial cosmos rests into a boundless swirl of circular motion. (See fig. 44.)

Self-giving and resurrection. In this new figure below these two circular movements of human–divine transgression destabilize and disempower the all-powerful combat arrows at the center of the battle square. They lead into a universal mass exodus of Jews, Galatians, and other defeated nations out of this "present evil age," an age marked by

Fig. 44. Exodus and Messianic Dissolution of the Combat Order

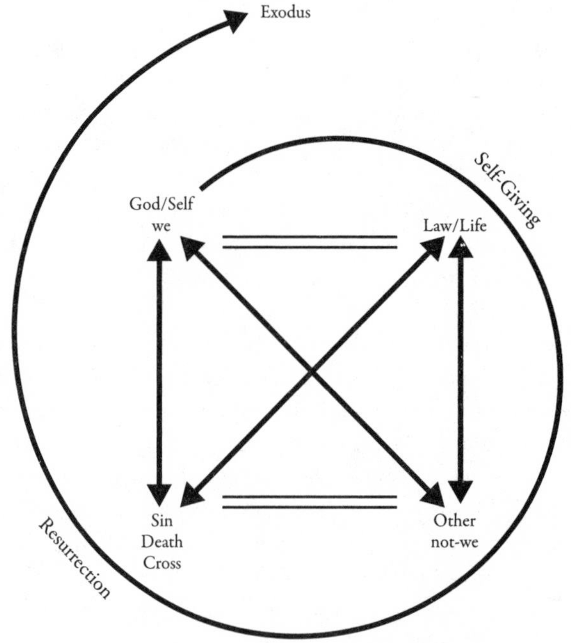

the combat order of Roman rule. The last and climactic messianic phrase in 1:4 is that Christ died for our sins to "lead us out of [*ek*] this present evil age." As stated above, this movement *out of* the battle order, "out of this present evil age," parallels the resurrection of Jesus "from [*ek*] the dead" in 1:1. Both phrases in their scriptural semiotics connote exodus, though—again—these intertextual echoes are widely neglected by theological dictionaries.

According to François Bovon, the term "lead out of" in 1:4, in Greek the middle voice of the verb *exairein* with the prepositional *ek*-phrase attached to it, is firmly rooted in the exodus tradition and in liturgical formulas reminiscent of it.[48] The construction typically refers to God's intervention in favor of his people and against their enemies, leading to a transition from one space (*ek/ex*) to another: from slavery/Egypt to freedom/promised land in its most basis sense. The phrase may be used with regard to the liberation from Pharaoh's power (Exod 3:8; 18:4, 8-10), as well as from Babylon (Jer 42:11 [49:11 LXX]), and with regard to a future, eschatological exodus (Isa 31:5; 60:16; Ezek 34:27). The underlying spatial or temporal dichotomy may be amplified into the symbolic order of death and life or of "this age" and an "age to come." In Daniel 3, a text that, like Galatians, deals with a fierce confrontation between the biblical God and coercion to imperial idolatry under conditions of captivity, *exairein* is used several times to describe the contested power of God to *deliver* Daniel and his companions from the "blazing furnace" of the Babylonian emperor whom they refuse to worship

(Dan 3:15, 17, 29), and ultimately from the power of death itself (3:88).[49] In Sir 51:11, the term is used, as in Gal 1:4, for redemption from an "evil age" (*kairos ponēros*). In these later texts, the exodus out of Egypt receives a new, cosmic, and apocalyptic dimension in terms of resurrection and universal eschatological deliverance.[50]

All these layers of meaning come together as Paul declares in Gal 1:4 the new exodus as *deliverance out of this present evil age,* that is, out of Rome's not-so-golden age and away from the power of its idols. This exit movement, however, leads not into a reestablished battle square under Christian auspices—at least not for Paul—but into a new corporeality that lives and practices a new way for the self to relate to an other. This different way of being within the body of Christ, embodying an ethics of mutuality, is the theological centerpiece of Galatians: the mystical community of one-and-other.

Love and the New Order of Noncombat (Galatians 5–6)

Heilmann's bright face . . . had turned to the demoness of the earth [that is, Gaia]. She had brought forth Uranus, the sky, Pontus, the sea, and all mountains. She had given birth to the Giants, the Titans, the Cyclopes, and the Furies. This was our race. We evaluated the history of the earthly beings. We looked up at her again, the demoness stretching out of the ground. The waves of her loosened hair flowed around her. On her shoulder she carried a bowl of pomegranates. Foliage and grape vines twirled at the back of her neck. The start of the lips, begging for mercy, was discernible in the raw facial plane, which veered sidewards and upward. A gash gaped from her chin to her larynx. Alcyoneus, her favorite son, slanted away from her, while dropping to his knees. The stump of his left hand groped toward her. She was still touching his left foot, which dangled from his stretched and shattered leg. His thighs, abdomen, belly and chest were all tensing in convulsions. The pain of death radiated from the small wound inflicted between his ribs by the venomous reptile. The wide, unfurled wings of the kingfisher, growing from his shoulder, slowed down his plunge. The silhouette of the burst-off face above him, with the hard line of the neck, of the hair, which was tied up and tucked under the helmet, spoke of the pitilessness of Athena.[51]
—Peter Weiss, *The Aesthetics of Resistance,* 1:6

For you were called to freedom, brothers and sisters; only do not use your freedom as an opportunity for self-indulgence [*sarx*], but through love become slaves to one another. For the whole law is summed up in a single [*en heni*] commandment, "You shall love your neighbor as yourself." If, however, you bite and devour one another, take care that you are not consumed by one another. (Gal 5:13-15 NRSV)

The force that ultimately breaks the power of the battle order, accomplishes the exodus, converts the "pitilessness of Athena," and makes the massacre "penetrable to the thought of liberation"[52] is as simple to name as it is complex in its "works": love, *agapē*. Love is the driving power that throws the combat square into an irreversible spin of messianic "revolution." It rotates the vertical into the horizontal and makes the out-cast our sister and brother; warlike gestures turn into hands offering support. This is the topic of Galatians 5–6, but it pervades the whole letter. At a crucial meeting in Jerusalem, a virtually irresolvable conflict between self and other that involved spying, conformity pressures, authority claims, anxieties, and distrust, was miraculously con-verted into a ritual of peacemaking and a practice of solidarity. When they extended the "right hand of community" (*dexias koinōnias*, 2:9), the leading "pillars" among the Jewish Jesus followers accepted, with a handshake, the *other* and alien gospel that Paul proclaimed in the non-Jewish world (2:7) and that did not require circumcision of the Galatians in order for them to be adopted as fully legal heirs of Abraham (Gal 3:29);[53] in return, they themselves asked for help from the Gentile congregations on behalf of their own poor—the famous endeavor of the Pauline collection as an international relief action of "them" for "us" (2:10). For Paul, this was a foundational *kairos*.

This messianic transformation is no longer imaginable within the confines of the Great Altar, which lacks the imagery to represent it. It is a metamorphosis that does not simply replace one empire with another empire, the kingdom of Caesar with a counter-kingdom of God; rather, it establishes an *other* order that is different. It dis-arms the combatants of the Great Battle, disables the combat law, and brings the per-petual war of civilization to a halt. For Paul this messianic "interruption" marked all the great moments in the early Jesus movement and his own journey: Damascus, Jerusalem, Antioch, and Galatia (Gal 1:11—2:21; 4:12-14). Each time, the messianic power of love embodied in Jesus Christ intervened in deep-rooted conflict settings and caused the death of the old self constituted as anti-other (Gal 2:20). Each time, an antagonistic self and other were thrown out of their battle order and discovered a new way of being together. And each time this alternative social practice of messianic peacemaking was fiercely contested.

Swords into Ploughshares: Heracles and Paul at the Great Altar

The Jerusalem handshake of *koinōnia* (community), the Antioch table community, the Galatians acting as the "Good Samaritans" of a helpless Jew—none of this has a representational space at the Great Altar. The Pergamene depiction of the world does not allow this "messianic revolution" of the imperial cosmos to become visible or even imaginable. It is a dangerous image that will not be represented in images of stone at all, but rather in images of the living bodies gathered in Paul's *ekklēsiai*. Still we might think for a moment what a messianic "re-imagination" of the Pergamene images, the prototypical images and nightmares of our own civilization, might look like in light of the new creation (Gal 6:15).

As Peter Weiss envisioned in his *Aesthetics of Resistance*, quoted above in a few frag-ments alongside our reading of Galatians, the awakening from the horror frozen and petrified at the Great Altar would begin with the transformative act of one single person on the upper side of the combat frieze. For Weiss, it would need the help of Heracles himself, the ancient popular hero co-opted by the Olympians.[54] In order to interrupt the scenes of massacre, Heracles would have to change sides in the Gigantomachy and become an ally of the vanquished. The gods could not gain victory without him, as mythological lore had fatefully pronounced.

With Heracles at their side, would thus the Giants on the underside of the Great Frieze win the world battle? This raises another crucial question. Would they, in their triumph, subsequently establish themselves as superior gods at Mount Olympus, subjecting the prior rulers to their own domination and punishment, as they themselves had been dominated and punished previously? Merely reversing the sides of the battle, turning upside down and downside up, making the former *other* the new victorious *self*, does not break up the battle order. Is there yet another solution to the primeval world war at the foundation of the imperial cosmos?

There is an empty spot on the eastern part of the Great Frieze where Heracles' figure is actually missing from the combat panorama (the stone never retrieved from the marble ruins of Pergamon); he must have been fighting to the right of his father, Zeus, with Hera's conquering quadriga somewhat menacingly racing toward him from the other side.[55] In the void we can see only the inscription of his name at the bottom and the paw of a lion's skin, his usual cloak, above. This unintended vacancy in a way holds the space for creative re-imagination and new creation alike.[56] Reminiscent of Walter Benjamin's famous quotation, it is like the crack or "narrow gate" through which the Messiah can enter into world history at any time.[57]

We might try to re-imagine the Pergamene Heracles in his "conversion" or "call" out of the imperial battle order through the lens of Paul.[58] If Heracles changed sides in the battle of the gods against the Giants, he would lose his position as a righteous *self* and divine son at the right hand of Zeus, the father of gods and humans, a position of privilege and power so impressively "monumentalized" at the Great Altar. He would appear instead on the dark underside of the dying *others* where the primeval mother goddess Gaia pleads, with both hands risen in a gesture of surrender, for her cursed sons. Paul sees this very downward movement of self-abnegation, foolish according to the established notions of self and other, as quintessential for the messianic event.

In a most vivid resonance with the Pergamene imagery, this counterlogic is expressed, for example, in the Christ-hymn in Phil 2:6-11, where Christ gives up the privilege of his "God-likeness" (*isa theō*, 2:6), emptying himself of his superiority to become coequal with the enslaved human other, including this other's death.[59] This same dynamic, however, is also emblematic of Paul's own descent from self to other, which happens in what is usually called the "Damascus event." The former persecutor of the lawless others, the blameless executor of God's will, suddenly "dies" to his selfhood of power and his entitlement as (symbolically) the "right hand" of God the Father; instead, he is sent to preach "good news" among the Gentile others (Gal 1:13-16).

The "victory" ensuing from this death and defeat of the dominant self, unlike imperial triumphs, defeats the combat order itself. It is tied into the exodus dynamic of resurrection, justification, and new creation, which does not lead upward into a new position of power but outward and downward: "out of this present evil age"(1:4) of competing empires into the messianic space where a different law and order are in place and where Torah is finally liberated from imperial restraints. We might imagine this messianic exodus as the transition into a new horizontal figure of being that opens up on the underside and outside of the battle square as the doubled circle of the sign of infinity. (See fig. 45.)

Fig. 45. The Messianic Order of One-an(d)-Other

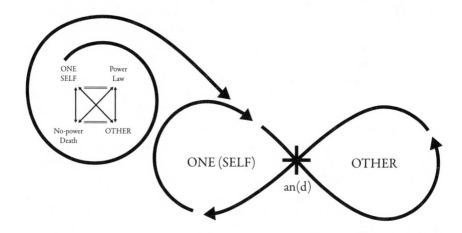

The circular arrows in this figure are vital. The messianic body is alive only so long as the movement from self to other persists as constant flow of love and solidarity. The cross becomes the central "joint" of this body; it is the junction where self and other continuously meet and reconcile in their respective downward movements, which makes the self other and the other self; it is the transformative space where inside and outside flip and verticality is dissolved into horizontality, thus turning antagonism and strife of the old combat order into the one-an(d)-other of the new creation.

The self in this messianic movement is constantly dying in self-giving and resurrected with and through the other: it sees the other invade its own space and ascend to the place of the self. Yet, because the self is moving meanwhile in the space of the other itself, this elevated and guarded position of self-against-other has been vacated, and the self experiences its own being resurrected by and alongside the other.

This is, in an nutshell, the description of Paul's own journey after Damascus, which we will explore further below. "Seeing" Jesus as the son of God revealed to him, and being sent out to the *other* of the nations (1:16), Paul entirely lost his well-established identity and superiority as a "persecutor" (1:13) of the unrighteous other. Dying to his own former self and living among the Gentiles, he became the target of persecution himself, precisely because of the "offense of the cross" (5:11). When the Galatians picked him up as a weak and wounded other and nursed him back to life (4:12-14), his dying was converted into resurrection and a new life. For Paul, in a way, this is the "proof" of the resurrection and the new dynamic it has injected into the old world order. The Galatians received him "like Christ" (4:14). Just as Jesus Christ was resurrected by God the father *from the dead*, the almost dead and dying Paul, who had himself become other on behalf of others—is brought back to life by those others and lifted up to a new type of self-with-the-other. The Christ mysticism of the individual dying and living with/in Christ is inseparably tied into the mysticism of the communal body of Christ where the co-crucified self is resurrected through the miraculous power of self-less mutuality, solidarity, and compassion.[60]

This, for Paul, is one of the moments where indeed the Messiah had visibly entered into human history, embodying a new face of human being and being humane, across cultural differences that need not be erased because they are no longer the breeding ground of hostility and superiority. Foreskin and circumcision can be *with* one another "in Christ," rather than *against* one another "in Caesar." Nor must differences be erased: they are the litmus test of whether a community is in Christ or in Caesar, and whether it is really the nations, the uncircumcised who are now participating, together with the Jews, in the new worldwide exodus "out of this evil age," the exodus of love.

The Politics of Love

One of the most succinct formulas Paul uses to describe this messianic transformation of love is the term *allēlōn* (one another), which is derived from Greek *allos-allos,* literally "other-other." It might be best rendered as one-anotherness or one-and-otherness. The term *allēlōn* occurs no fewer than seven times in Galatians 5–6 (5:13, 15, 17, 26; 6:2). It points to the key feature of the new human being and a truly humane order. In a constant revolving and "revolutionary" movement from self to other, the ego loses and retrieves itself in the other, for the other, through the other, with the other, constantly dying and being resurrected, living no longer as self but as the mystical body of Christ. This is "love of your neighbor as your-self," which is the complete (*pas*) fulfillment of Torah (5:14).

Love means continual mindfulness in discerning, disobeying, and unfreezing the antithetical *nomos* of self versus other that is set in stone and cast in iron everywhere; that imprisons and deforms every human being under the regimen of what Paul calls "sin." Love as messianic practice and permanent self-revolution is for Paul an indispensable "work of faith" in compliance with the "law of Christ" (*nomos tou Christou,* 6:2) and the Torah of God. "*Faith working through love*" (*pistis di' agapēs energoumenē,* 5:6) is the mandatory self-evidence of truly being in the body of Christ, not circumcision or foreskin (5:6). The "works" and body politics of love are the main topic of the parenetic part of Galatians 5–6 and the climax of the whole letter. This most crucial concluding section, however, was often neglected or treated as suspect by theological exegesis because it seemed to defy the established (Protestant) antithesis of faith versus works.[61]

Throughout Galatians 5–6, Paul deals with the reorganization of community in a nonhierarchical, nonantagonistic, nonexclusive way as horizontal mutuality and solidarity, as noncompetition, noncombat, nonconsumption of the other (see 5:15). Not surprisingly, the terms for self and other are very prominent. Alongside the sevenfold occurrence of *allēlōn* (one another) that we have mentioned already, *heteron* (other) is used in 6:4, *seauton* (yourself) in 5:14 and 6:1, while *heautou/heauton* (of oneself/oneself) is repeated no fewer than four times in 6:3-4 and 6:8. Nowhere else in Galatians is the language of messianic intervention into the relationship between self and other so pervasive.

Furthermore, a whole cluster of statements explicitly engages the vices of the dominant self and the ensuing community conflicts. The paradoxical claim of freedom to be enacted as mutual slave service through love stands against self-indulgence or "flesh" (*sarx*, 5:13). If love of "your neighbor as yourself" is the *one* fulfillment of Torah/law (*en heni logō*, 5:14), it stands in juxtaposition to "biting and devouring one another," which inevitably leads to the mutual destruction or consumption by one another (5:15).

While the antagonism between self and other is synonymous with what Paul calls *sarx* (flesh), the countersphere of messianic community is the space where the *pneuma* (spirit) is at work. The polarity of *sarx–pneuma* is fundamental for Paul and present throughout Galatians, but especially shapes the last two chapters.[62] The "works of the flesh" (*erga tēs sarkos*, 5:19) are spelled out in a list of vices (5:19-21) that show an exceptionally strong emphasis on community conflicts and tensions.[63] As the conflict-provoking "works of the flesh" according to 5:21 constitute a practice (*prassontes*) that excludes people from the kingdom (or empire) of God, they are tantamount to the "works of the law" as a social practice that in our reading is equivalent to the combat order of Caesar's empire.

This becomes even more tangible in the following sentences. Concluding his catalogue of *sarx*-related vices and *pneuma*-based virtues, Paul demands a "crucifixion" of the self-obsessed and self-driven flesh (5:24) and a life entirely shaped by the spirit (5:25). Mutual provocations and envy need to stop, for they are born out of an inflated sense of self-value (*kenodoxoi*) that always competes with the other for honor and recognition (5:26) and is the basic prerequisite for the honor/shame-based power structures of Caesar's empire. The competitiveness among the Galatians imitates, "incarnates," and reproduces the vertical "combat order" of the conquerors, reinscribing it on the "flesh," the carnal existence (*sarx*) of the conquered. In Paul's language this reinscription is called "boasting" (6:4).

Boasting for Paul, in Galatians as well as in Romans (see Rom 3:27-31), is shorthand for what theologically disqualifies "works of the law"—not specifically "works of *Jewish* law" but rather the working(s) of the imperial *nomos* through "works of the flesh," as Robert Jewett has very perceptively noticed.[64] Boasting draws on the self-obsession and other-neglect that in Paul's terminology mark the sphere of flesh as the territory of sin and godlessness. "Good works"—or to use the Latin version, benefactions—are not done simply for the sake of the other but are used as a vehicle for self-advancement in the pyramid of honor and power, to gain an advantage *over* the other, not in solidarity *with* the other.[65]

Paul explicitly addresses this problem when he urges the Galatians to stop contemplating individually the importance of oneself (6:3). In an up-front attack on the competitive system of euergetism/benefactions, which, as we have seen, is a key feature of imperial order in a Roman province like Galatia, "works" are declared to be no longer the showcase of the self in the public race for status. With an ironic undertone, the Galatians are admonished to "boast" only in front of oneself rather than in front of the other, which practically annuls what boasting as a vehicle of social distinction is all about.

> Everybody should evaluate the work of himself or herself [*heautou*] and then will have the boast in front of himself or herself alone [*eis heauton monon to kauchēma*], rather than in front of the other [*eis heteron*]. (6:4)

We might speculate whether this emphasis on "boasting competitions," together with the mentioning of drunkenness, carousing, and magic drugs (*pharmakeia*) among the vices in 5:20-21 (the latter occurring elsewhere in the New Testament only in Rev 18:23 and 9:21), has a specifically Celtic ring (see chapter 4). At any rate, it is clear that more is at stake than just internal rivalries and cultural patterns of honor/shame with a particularly Galatian ethnic flavor. The circumcision campaign of Paul's opponents is described as boast-driven and flesh-oriented. The latter possibly implies a pun on the flesh both as the foreskin and as the sphere of sin. In the sinful realm of *sarx,* the self feeds its own "fleshly" desire for recognition and distinction on the "flesh" of the other, either by making this other the "same" (circumcised) and thus publicly presentable as "us," or by insisting on difference as a signifier of otherness that again boosts the self (see 4:17).

> See what large letters I make when I am writing with my own hand! It is those who want to make a good showing in the flesh [*euprosōpēsai en sarki*] that try to compel you to be circumcised—only that they may not be persecuted for the cross of Christ. Even the circumcised do not themselves obey the law, but they want you to be circumcised so that they may boast about your flesh. (6:11-13)[66]

It is against this false law observance, which is driven by "fleshly" needs of public conformity (*euprosōpēsai*), thus obscuring the proper obedience of law as Torah, that Paul puts up the "law of Christ" as the law of the crucified *one* who is *other* (6:2, 14). It builds community not through trying to gain advantage over one another, but through "bearing one another's burdens" (6:2). What counts is neither circumcision nor foreskin, nor any other of the publicly recognized status markers of distinction, honor, and shame, but rather "faith working through love" (5:6) as the works of peace that signal a new creation (6:14-15). Apart from the works of imperial law, these faith works of love for Paul are indispensable, an insight that has been obscured by the abstract Protestant antithesis of faith versus works. Love of "your neighbor as your self" as the complete fulfillment of Torah (5:14) and the "new" law of Christ (5:6; 6:2) does not abandon

Jewish law as such but rather the competitive and combative hierarchy of self and other that is at the core of Roman imperial *nomos*.

Gaia and the Cosmic Ecology of New Creation

We have to take yet another look at the Great Frieze. The confrontation between Athena and Gaia that unfolds to the left of father Zeus is one the most heartbreaking scenes of the Pergamene combat panorama. (See fig. 20.) In stark contrast to the immovable "pitilessness of Athena" above, the earth goddess below begs for mercy, as Peter Weiss has noted.[67] The goddess of wisdom is enchanted by the outstretched hand of winged Nikē that is about to crown her with victory; Gaia meanwhile cries out for her son Alkyoneus, who is dying in Athena's unrelenting grip. Holding to her doomed child with the deadly wound between his ribs, the earth goddess appears as an ancient *Pietà*.

Gaia is the only deity of the whole Pergamene pantheon who displays the vulnerability of love. None of the fighting gods and goddesses above, frozen forever and inescapably trapped in their own confrontation with the deadly enemy-other, can show mercy to Gaia. For the battle of civilization must go on, victoriously led by Athena as goddess of city, combat, and rationality. It must follow its own—Athena's—irresistible logic, which does not allow for gestures of peacemaking and reconciliation, signifiers of weakness and self-defeat.

And again the messianic intervention breaks into this petrified hopelessness that ties both losers and winners together in the agony of eternal fight. The *one* imageless God who cannot be depicted at the Great Frieze and who is not bound by the logic of its images cuts the Gordion knot of the deadly confrontation. Unlike father god Zeus, God the Father of Jesus, and *our* Father (Gal 1:1-3), can actually hear the groaning of Gaia, the Earth (see Rom 8:21-22). Unlike all the numerous deities assembled and worshiped at the Great Altar, *this* God sees the Earth's despair and cares about her slaughtered sons.[68] When God raises Jesus "from the dead"—the convict whose death, like the death of Gaia's giant sons, was meant to testify to the omnipotence of imperial law and ordering—this is not only a divine border transgression on a cosmic scale, a betrayal of the heavenly alliance, but by implication also an act of solidarity with Gaia/Earth, the wailing goddess who remains half-buried on the underside of the East Frieze. (See image on p. 168.)

A single mother of fatherless, aberrant sons, she and her offspring represent a stark contrast to father Zeus's seemingly intact and triumphant heavenly family. She is the one divine deviancy of the Great Altar, not accidentally represented as a woman. On the wrong side of the battle, a rebel against the heavenly tyrant Uranus whom she herself brought forth, she lacks the powerful male father figure on her side that the deities on the upper side of the Frieze share. The Pergamene depiction presents her as literally cut off from her womb. When he leaves his position of divine invulnerability to raise Jesus "from the dead," God the Father, *our* Father, shows that he is other than the Olympic gods, most notably other than *pitiless* Athena, the motherless goddess in the likeness of Zeus. Acting out of compassion, God the Father becomes a companion of

Gaia and establishes a new order of (pro)creation not based on imperial masculinity and impenetrability (Gal 4:4-7).

God's intervention changes the lower domain as it has changed the higher. Whatever Jesus and his followers have in common with Alkyoneus and his brothers, they do not share the Giants' drive to revolutionize the cosmos by occupying Mount Olympus themselves. They resist and contradict the dominant order, yet they do not respond to violence with counterviolence but rather with self-giving and love, thus breaking the vicious cycle. If we read Galatians 1:4 and 2:20 together, the self-giving of Jesus "for me" as the other is made explicit as an act of love. It is not an act of law, as self-preservation against the evil other, but rather of self-annihilation on behalf of this evil other as "sinner." This love of the neighbor and love of the enemy make Jesus and all who enter into his orbit dead to the old order of combat; love cuts the umbilical cord tied to the imperial *nomos* and its *cosmos*.

In this new order not based on an archetypal matricide, fratricide, and ecocide, self-giving is no longer a failure and a weakness.[69] It is no longer cursed to reinforce the dominant self that within the imperial order inevitably will exploit the self-giving of an other. On the Great Altar, this is precisely Gaia's curse. Her *cornucopia*, the fruit of her fertility, will be fed into the dominant order, female self-sacrifice consumed by male self-assertion, the other of nature devoured by the ruthless self of an exploitive culture and civilization.[70] Rather, in the messianic order, self-giving creates new life in which both self and other can participate, encountering each other outside the law of combat and competition, sharing the fruits of the earth in a sustainable way, without soaking and destroying the fields with blood and making the earth cry out, as the primeval male Cain did when he slaughtered his brother, Abel (Gen 4:8-10).[71] As the social practice of a new creation (Gal 6:15), Paul's empire-critical theology has a profoundly ecological dimension as well.[72] Combat, competition, and mindless consumption of the other—the other human and the other of the Earth—in Paul's system are the "works of the law" and the signature of the "flesh" (*sarx*) in enslavement to sin, crying out for the liberating transformation of the spirit.

Deconstructing and Reconciling Self and Other (Galatians 1-4)

> ... *thus they clashed with one another, acting at higher behest, dreaming, motionless in insane vehemence, mute in inaudible roaring, all of them woven into a metamorphosis of torture, shuddering, persisting, waiting for an awakening, in perpetual endurance and perpetual rebellion, in outrageous impact, and in extreme exertion to subdue the threat, to provoke the decision.*
>
> —Peter Weiss, *The Aesthetics of Resistance*, 1:3

I am astonished that you are so quickly deserting the one who called you through the grace of Christ and are turning to a different gospel—that is not an other [NRSV: there is not another gospel], but there are some who are confusing you and want to pervert the gospel of Christ. (Gal 1:6-7)

The most intriguing and the most underestimated statement in Galatians is made in 1:6-7, when Paul for the first time talks about the *other* gospel, *eis heteron euangelion ho ouk estin allo*. The relative clause *ho ouk estin allo* has remained an exegetical puzzle. It might well contain in a nutshell the whole paradox of Paul's messianic theology concerning the relationship between self and other, new creation and old imperial order.

Traditionally, the vast majority of translations render the phrase as, "I am astonished that you are so quickly deserting to a different gospel—there is no other (gospel)." This blunt repudiation of the other gospel (*heteron euangelion*) as simply nonexistent, or without any right to exist, has the full weight of the *Anathēma* on its side and always appeared in the Christian tradition as the epitome of the Pauline "status confessionis": *Here I stand!*

Anathēma: The Gospel That Is and Is Not Other (Galatians 1:6-9)

In our interpretation thus far, we have tried to decipher the anathematized counter-message and counter-messengers of 1:6-9 as a reflection not of Jewishness but rather of (imperial) idolatry. The *other* gospel concerns the *other* gods; neither have true "being." In this reading, nonexistence with regard to the false gospel in 1:7 (*ouk estin*) and to the false gods in 4:8 (*mē ousin theois*) correspond to each other.

But on a closer look, Paul says something much more complex and subtle than this seemingly straightforward condemnation of the *heteron*, the other gospel. In a strictly literal translation, the relative clause *ho ouk estin allo* would be "*that* is not other," rather than "*there* is no other." If we take the riddle of this phrase seriously, it may say both that the other gospel is a nonexistent gospel of nothingness, that is, no other *gospel*, and that it is no *other* gospel. We may unfold this highly condensed statement as an expression of two different things that summarize the whole of the Galatian debate:

1. Insofar as the "gospel of circumcision" preached by Paul's opponents in Galatia is a surrender to the law and logic of the imperial order, it is indeed an un-gospel and *Anathēma*. Paul suspects that the Galatian "teachers" require circumcision as an act of conformity with Roman rule and religion. Rome does not accept uncircumcised messianic Galatians who refuse to worship Caesar, as if they were proper Jews. In this regard, circumcision means a return to "Egypt" and its idols. Under the pretense of Torah piety, a demonstration of loyalty or faith toward the imperial order is made. This is probably the context of Paul's furious outcry against "hypocrisy" at Antioch in Gal 2:11-14. The Antiochene table community suddenly broke when the Jews withdrew from eating together with the Gentiles, a "Jewish" gesture in subservience to imperial law.[73] For Paul, this means a reversal of the birth process of the new creation that has set in. But no one can reverse a birth process except by accepting the death of both mother and child. Paul, figuratively staging himself as mother-in-labor in 4:19, knows this only

too well. This is the real-life force of the Anathēma he pronounces in 1:8-9: a return to the cursed logic and "sin" inherent to the imperial order of conquest and colonization has deadly consequences.

2. At the same time, the other gospel, the gospel of circumcision that the Galatians are about to accept, is *not* an other gospel at all. If it were, the old divisions, competitions, and combats between circumcised Jewish self and uncircumcised Gentile/other would still be valid. But they are not. Jews and Galatians have truly become one in Christ, yet this oneness involves *two,* one and the other. It is striking to observe that Christian interpretation has for so long, and quite rightly, emphasized that the gospel of Christ is the *one* gospel that counts and that Paul rejects the gospel of circumcision in Galatia. But that same interpretive tradition has shown a remarkable blindness when it comes to the second half of Paul's statement in 2:1-10: the one gospel of Christ is only intact so long as it comprises *both* gospels, the "gospel of circumcision" *and* the "gospel of foreskin" (2:7)—an astonishingly bold phrase that Paul coins here and uses nowhere else in his letters.[74]

The "true" messianic message thus is the new community between Jews and Gentiles that is embodied in the Jerusalem handshake of community, the collection, and later the short-lived table community at Antioch. Oneness in Christ and the *one* gospel of Christ are not valid unless the *other* is fully present. If oneness in Christ turns into oneness without the other, or against the other, it mutates back into the likeness of the imperial *euangelion.* Then the *other* gospel of circumcision indeed becomes an other *gospel,* namely, the all-pervasive idolatrous message that prompts everyone, Paul's fellow Jews and the Galatians alike, to worship the imperial god(s) of the self: power and status. The alternative between curse and blessing in 1:6-9 is not an either-or of Judaism or Christianity, but rather of one-*against*-another versus one-*with*-another.

Fig. 46. Imperial Gospel as *Anathēma*

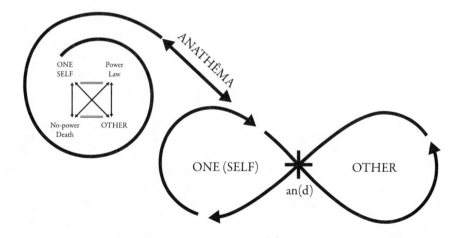

In this diagram (fig. 46), the *Anathēma* Paul pronounces is targeting the lethal consequences of apostasy: slavery and exile imposed by the imperial order—a birth process reversed. It functions as a kind of protective shield that guards the messianic practice of mutuality and solidarity *with one another* against the permanent invasion by the imperial battle construct of *one versus other* that is incorporated in the idols of empire and that keeps both Jews and nations enslaved. Paul, while rejecting the otherness of the imperial world religion and world order, simultaneously deconstructs the category of otherness itself that is at its core. It is an otherness that, in the light of the Christ-event, is nonexistent, an artificial otherness created for the sake of power alone that prompts "me" to see my fellow human as competitor, inferior, enemy. It makes us, in Weiss's words, continuously "clash with one another," always "at higher behest," weaving ever one and other into a "metamorphosis of torture, shuddering, persisting, waiting for an awakening."

Arguably, the most concise formula for this deconstruction of the established self–other antagonism is Paul's summarizing of the law in its *one* and first commandment (*en heni logō*) as "love of your (br)*other*/neighbor as your *self*" (5:14). Yet the rethinking of self and other not only shapes the final part of Galatians in chapters 5–6 but also underlies the whole argument in the preceding chapters 1–4, which we will briefly outline.

Damascus, Jerusalem, Antioch: Messianic Self-transformation (Galatians 1–2)

The starting point of Galatians is the pre-Damascus Paul himself, a blameless holy warrior for God, competing with his fellow Jews, merciless in persecuting the dissident or Gentilizing other of the Jesus-movement or other "liberal" Jews. He uses militant language that clearly situates him within the "combat order" of law, that is, in its Jewish version:

> You have heard how I once practiced my Jewishness [*en tō Ioudaismō*]. I was ahead of everybody in persecuting the church/assembly [*ekklēsian*] of God and made havoc of it. I was at the forefront of Judaism [*en tō Ioudaismō*], outstripping many contemporaries of my people [*en tō genei mou*], as I was far more zealous [*zēlōtēs*] for the traditions of my forefathers [*patrikōn mou paradoseōn*]. (Gal 1:13-14, my translation)

Self and other, right and wrong at this stage for Paul are clearly defined within a strictly antithetical and hierarchical framework that entitles the law-abiding self to feel aligned with God in the holy battle against the sinful, godless, lawless other of the Gentiles/nations. Robert Jewett has pointed out that the problem of Paul's pre-Damascus self-construct is not just a wrong and self-righteous (or works righteous) relationship to God, as traditional interpretation has assumed, but the implied downgrading and contempt of the other as well. Theological and social dimensions are inseparable. The passion for the law and for "coercing compliance with its norms," according to Jewett, is motivated by the "flesh" as the desire to gain superior status and to "surpass others in honor, which engaged a highly religious person to enter into sinful opposition to God's will."[75]

Damascus and the Dis-location of Self, Other, and God (Galatians 1:10-24)

This allows a more comprehensive understanding of Paul's so-called Damascus experience, leading beyond the debate of Damascus as "call" or "conversion."[76] Damascus first and foremost was a world-shattering annihilation and reconfiguration of Paul's concept of both self and God.

> But when God who had set me apart before I was born and called me through his grace, was pleased to reveal [*apokalypsai*] his son in me so that I might proclaim him as gospel [*euangelizōmai auton*] among the Gentiles/nations [*en tois ethnesin*]. . . . (1:15-16)

Paul, who had perceived himself as distinguished custodian of God's Torah and the collective Jewish self, is all of a sudden pushed into the very Gentile otherness and ungodliness he had tried to fend off. God's apocalyptic revelation (*apokalypsai*, 1:16) drops him into a devastating threefold self-alienation that entirely distorts his image of himself, of God, and of the other:

- The divine self becomes other if an accursed crucified is indeed "God's son" (1:16).
- Paul becomes other when God makes him the messenger of precisely this divine otherness as "good news" (*euangelion*) among the lawless and ungodly others, that is, the non-Jewish nations (*en tois ethnesin*, 1:16).
- The world becomes other when both the divine and the human self plunge from their supreme position of oneness/selfhood into the inferiority of otherness, subverting the imperial order that cannot integrate a God who is aligned with a crucified other, nor a human self that sacrifices itself on behalf of the "evil" other (see 1:1, 4).

As Paul is sent to the nations with the messianic message of a divine son *other* than Caesar, he becomes the counter-messenger who contradicts the imperial "good news" among the colonized others of Rome. He embodies and proclaims the "messianic revolution" that demotes both God and self from their established place at the top of the symbolic order and sends them spinning down toward "nonlocations" where nothingness and otherness reside. The combat square crumbles, and the antithetical hierarchies of the imperial cosmos are disordered. At the same time, everything in Paul's own perception of law and God is turned upside down and inside out. He becomes incapacitated as the virtuous self, the crusader of the righteous God among the unrighteous others. Except for a brief visit "after three years" (1:18), this "Damascus experience" for more than a decade keeps him away from Jerusalem, the location of his former self (2:1).

Jerusalem: The Messianic Relocation of Self, Other, and God (Galatians 2:1-10)

Paul could have stayed away from Jerusalem and declared the former others, his uncircumcised non-Jewish sisters and brothers, as his new "Christian" self. Then he would indeed have been the founder of Christianity as the new world religion of "foreskin" in opposition to the Judaism of the circumcised. But this is exactly what Paul refuses. He sees it as vital to reintegrate foreskin and circumcision. The institution of Christianity as the separate religion of the uncircumcised happened long after Paul. It created new boundaries, exclusive identities as well as hierarchical polarities and thus gave up what Paul himself defended as the essence of the messianic event: the eschatological disruption of established selves and others in a continuous liminal movement of border transgression and inclusion.[77] Ironically, Christianity as the reestablished law and order of (Christian) self versus (Jewish) others, which so much claims to be a Pauline foundation, is located more on the side of Paul's opponents than of Paul himself.

It is a symptom of this displaced reading of Paul that, compared to the broad attention his "Damascus experience" found, his second apocalyptic revelation, which makes him "again go up to Jerusalem" (*palin anebēn – anebēn de kata apokalypsin*, 2:1-2) is theologically widely neglected. After many years of living, working, and preaching among the Gentiles, God calls Paul back to the *ones* he once boasted to represent but has left behind when he turned to the Gentile others. Paul, in a way, has become other to his own former self now. Yet, in an astonishing divine revelation of self-insufficiency he is compelled to acknowledge that a collective gesture of consensus is needed. It regards his *other* gospel of "foreskin," which he has independently preached among the Gentiles so far (1:16-19; 2:2). In the messianic order of things, it is not yet sufficient to make the former others one's new self; rather, self and other must be reconciled if the antagonistic combat pattern is to be overwritten.

The way Paul sets up this crucial encounter at Jerusalem is revealing. Apart from the circumcised Jew Barnabas, he is taking the uncircumcised Greek Titus along, apparently to present to his fellow Jews as living proof that both circumcised and uncircumcised bodies are being transformed into messianic oneness and community (2:1).[78] The stormy visit to Jerusalem indeed refrains from enforcing physical sameness, as certain agents of a more conformist infiltration in Paul's congregations were urging, the pseudobrothers and spies (2:3-5). Titus stays "officially" uncircumcised and thus oneness-in-difference is established. The *one* gospel of Christ is recognized as two different gospels, the gospel of the self, which is circumcised, and the gospel of the other, which keeps foreskin[79]:

> On the contrary, when they saw that I had been entrusted with the gospel of the foreskin, just as Peter had been entrusted with the gospel of the circumcision . . . they gave to Barnabas and me the right hand of fellowship, so that we should go to the Gentiles, but they to the circumcision. They asked only one thing, that we remember the poor. (2:7-10)

The mutual trust/faith between self and other (*pistis Christou*) is the messianic signature of this diverse community and reconciles two previously irreconcilable and exclusive identities. It becomes embodied from the side of the Jerusalem leaders in the handshake of community (2:9), and from the side of the Gentiles materializes through solidarity with the "poor" in Jerusalem (2:10). Oneness in the image of the one God other than Caesar is established as horizontal community and mutuality that transforms both oneself and the other into a new body of one-an(d)-otherness; its practice represents conformity with the new creation and nonconformity with "this present evil age"(see 1:4).

The prominent position of the poor in Jerusalem in this context is noteworthy. Paul here refers to the collection, the emblematic trademark of his Gentile mission mentioned in almost all his major epistles. In the context of Galatians 2, material solidarity with the poor is the seal of "being in Christ," the social embodiment of the "handshake of community" between Paul and the Jerusalem leaders. In a world plagued by systematic impoverishment of the colonized nations, by famines, destitution, and desperate survival struggles, the categories of other and self for Paul are not simply spiritual but fundamentally economic terms as well. They need to be considered on an international scale, far beyond the established pattern of individual almsgiving and outside the official institutions of euergetism and patronage, which were vital to inscribe Roman order on the provincial body of Galatia (see chapter 4 above). The economy, politics, and spirituality of the collection, as Dieter Georgi, Sze-Kar Wan, Justin Meggitt, and others have shown, in manifold ways subverts and contradicts the imperial order. What happens to the poor becomes a vital sign of the well-being or suffering of the collective body of Christ.[80]

Antioch and the Return of the "Combat Order" (Galatians 2:11-14)

Under pressure from outside and inside, this community established at Jerusalem breaks apart. In the much-debated Antiochene incident, Peter and all other Jews, including Barnabas, withdraw from the common table with the Gentiles. The old antagonism is revived, officially in the name of God and law, yet Paul calls it a mockery of God and God's law. "Maccabean" language and zeal pervade the entire dispute between Paul and Peter, indicating that Paul sees the collective "hypocrisy" (*synhypekrithēsan*, 2:13) of the circumcised as an idolatrous act of public window dressing that officially quotes Jewish law but secretly bows to civic religion and order. This hypocrisy is closely related to what Paul criticizes as the merely face-saving activities (*euprosōpēsai*) of the circumcision party in Galatia; those who "do not themselves obey the law" but insist on circumcision (6:13) want to avoid outside sanctions and penalties against the rule-breaking behavior of Paul's uncircumcised "Jews," which inevitably would affect the circumcised Jewish congregation as well (6:12).[81]

A number of terms, some of them rarely or nowhere else used in the New Testament, establish a firm intertextuality with Deuteronomy and the Maccabean literature in terms of anti-idolatrous thrust, as both Roy Ciampa and Stephen Cummins have perceptively noticed.[82] If the "idols" in Galatians indeed are a "coded" reference to imperial worship and allegiance, Paul would perceive Peter's enforced "judaizing" of the Gentiles (*ioudaizein*, 2:14) as in fact a gesture of civic/imperial conformity.

Jews would lose (near except
status of uncircumcised were admitted)

Just one scriptural echo might illustrate the likelihood of this assumption. Paul's enigmatic reference to Peter's "Judaizing," which has "fear of the circumcised" as its motive (2:12), seems to point to the book of Esther as its intertextual decoding.

If you as a Jew live in a Gentilish manner [*ethnikōs*] and not like a Jew [*ioudaikōs*], why do you force the Gentiles to judaize [*ioudaizein*]? (Gal 2:14)

. . . and many of the Gentiles were circumcised and Judaized [*perietemnonto kai ioudaizon*] because of fear of the Jews. (Esth 8:17 LXX)

In Esth 8:17 LXX the narrative of the Jewish heroine has arrived at a stage where for a brief moment the Persian empire aligns itself with the Jews. For the Gentiles under Persian rule in this very specific situation, a "conversion" to Judaism in terms of circumcision[83] becomes a matter of opportunism and civic prudence. In our reading, this episode appears as an intertextual mirror that perfectly illuminates the situation in Antioch (and Galatia). Paul sees that Judaism is defined and upheld in line with the divine Caesar, not the God of Israel. He accuses Peter, Barnabas, and the Antiochene Jews not of a *Jewish* apostasy but of an *idolatrous* apostasy toward a non-Jewish imperial way of life that he calls *ethnikōs*.[84]

With Paul's rejection of a collective hypocrisy (2:13) that misrepresents Judaism and its God, the "other gospel" of Gal 1:8-9 resurfaces and at the same time the concrete situation in Galatia: return to the old combat order of (Jewish) self versus (Gentile) other in the name of God but in subservience to a false god who is not God. This relapse into what in Paul's view is truly a conformity with the prevalent antagonistic world *nomos* establishes the misuse of God's name (see Exod 20:7). To call something God's will and Torah that in reality expresses the law and religion of the idol evokes, in the logic of Deuteronomy, the curse of enslavement under foreign powers (Deut 28:30-33): *Anathēma*.

Justification by Faith and Messianic Koinōnia (Galatians 2:15-21)

The conflict at Antioch is the prefiguration of the Galatian one. In a dense theological statement, Paul summarizes why the practice of messianic oneness as inclusive community between circumcised self and uncircumcised other mirrors the image of the one God as revealed in Christ. Justification by faith is the foundational proclamation that Christ-faith cannot coexist with the old separation between *us*/Jews and *them*/Gentile sinners, which builds up again what was torn down by and in Christ (2:15-18). "Works of the law," mentioned no fewer than three times in opposition to faith and justification, are marked as works of self-righteousness and vertical distinction between self and other; faith, on the other hand, equalizes self and other and puts both into a horizontal relationship of community and solidarity without "boasting."[85] Reestablishing the law and its separations, as happened at Antioch, indeed then in an absurd way would qualify the previous messianic practice of one-an(d)-otherness as transgressive and "sinful" (2:18).

At this point, Paul summarizes his personal experience as "dying to the law" in order to "live to God" (2:19). Reminiscent of Albert Schweitzer's "Christ mysticism" (see below), Paul's entire journey before and after "Damascus" is put under the rubric of co-crucifixion and co-living with Christ. His self has died in being exposed to the *other* of God and the Gentile (br)other. It is not alive anymore; rather, Paul lives now a no longer self-centered life in response to the love of Christ "who gave himself on behalf of me" (2:20; also 1:4). *Faith* emerges as radical trust of and commitment to the other of God-in-Christ, and the other of the neighbor-foreigner.

It is in the most repulsive location of otherness that the true image of humanity in the likeness of God reemerges: God is no longer perceived in the position of the supreme *One* as imperial power, victory, and conquest, but in the image of compassion and reconciliation with the *other*. And the human self abstains from asserting its righteousness and entitlement by trying to be Godlike in alliance with the all-victorious and all-powerful God (as in the archetypal "fall" into sin in Gen 3:5), but reenters the primeval community with God by abandoning its self-righteousness and becoming justified in solidarity with the "unrighteous" other (compare Phil 2:6-11). God's justification in Christ thus "rectifies" both the damaged relation between the human self and God, and between the human self and human other *by grace* (2:21).

The latter dimension of a transformed self–other relation is crucial to the messianic logic of Paul's justification theology and to the overall construct of biblical theology as perceived by Paul. Nonetheless, it has often been absent from Protestant statements on "justification by faith (alone)" that have primarily focused on the faith relationship between God and individual self, irrespective of justice, reconciliation, and peace in the horizontal relationship between self and other on the social level. The next two chapters of Galatians further explore this messianic transformation of self, other, and one through an intertextual reading of the Galatian crisis in light of Genesis.

Genesis and the Nonimperial Pedigree of One Humanity (Galatians 3–4)

The two middle chapters of Galatians are a grand restatement of Genesis that revolves around the themes of *oneness*—the one God who reconciles humanity as one (Jew) and other (Gentiles) into a new oneness as children of God and of Abraham and Sarah, and as siblings of Christ. The overarching narrative themes of Genesis, most notably the pattern of irregular fatherhood, motherhood, and brotherhood, form the theological matrix of Paul's programmatic reconceptualization of God's people as a multitude of many nations.[86]

Father Abraham (Galatians 3)

Galatians 3 is strongly shaped by the motive of Abraham's "fatherhood" and lineage, culminating in a solemn proclamation of the legitimate status of the Galatians ("you") as Abraham's offspring and heirs through Christ (3:29). A crucial aspect of an "Abrahamic identity" is Abraham's monotheism. His turning away from the idols to the *one* true God is widely acknowledged today by Jews, Christians, and Muslims as a key element of Abraham's call away from his country, kindred, and fathers' house (Gen 12:1).

Though not explicitly stated in Genesis itself, this motif is present in Judith, *Jubilees*, Philo, Josephus, the *Apocalypse of Abraham*, and the later midrashic collection of *Genesis Rabbah* from the fourth century C.E.[87] Galatians needs to be added to this list.

The overall importance of the theme of oneness in Galatians 3 can hardly be overlooked; it forms the backbone of the entire intertextuality with Abraham and of the whole argument. No fewer than three times in this passage Paul refers explicitly to *one* and *not-one*, beginning with a rather peculiar claim about the "spermatological oneness" of the messianic seed in 3:16. Paul explicitly establishes the one messianic sperm of Abraham embodied in Christ, as opposed to the "many" sperms. This one sperm is the carrier of the decisive "genetic information," namely, the promise of Abraham's inheritance (3:16, 18), which means concretely the blessing of Abraham being extended to all the Gentiles/nations (3:8, 14). Thus, the one and singular messianic sperm "who is Christ" establishes the legitimate lineage of Abraham among the multitude of nations and Israel.[88]

> Now the promises were made to Abraham and to his offspring [*tō spermati autou*]; it does not say "And to offsprings" [*spermasi*, plural], as of many [*epi pollōn*]; but it says "And to your offspring" [*spermati*, singular], as of one [*eph' henos*], who is Christ. (Gal 3:16, my translation)

This undeniably somewhat forced exegesis of Gen 12:7 makes very clear that Paul takes every effort to emphasize the antagonism between the *one* and the not-one of the *many*. The same opposition underlies the following debate about the law (3:17-25). The original and genuine messianic sperm of Abraham is resistant to the contrary inheritance claims made by the 430 years younger *nomos* (3:16-18), which denies the promise made to the *one* seed of Abraham long before the law was in place. This criticism of law appears as linked to the person who "mediated" (*mesitēs*) this law but who is "not of the one" (*henos ouk estin*), whereas "God is one" (*theos heis estin*) (3:19-20).

As an alternative to the imprisonment under the mediated law of the *not-one* (3:22-25), Paul presents the transformation of Jews and Greeks, slave and free, male and female into the messianic *one* in Christ. This new Abrahamic identity embodies the *one* messianic sperm of 3:16 and thus Abraham's (true) offspring and lineage entitled to inherit (3:28-29), that is, to obtain the blessing to the nations promised in Gen 12:3 (see Gal 3:8-9, 14, 18, 29). This mixed identity reflects the *one* God of Israel (3:20), whom Abraham trusted in a programmatic way; it translates God's radical singularity into messianic-Abrahamic *oneness* and solidarity of Jews and non-Jews alike (3:28).

This strong weight on the legitimacy of the Galatians as members of Abraham's "one" multinational people (3:29)—and, moreover, as children of God (4:6-7)—cannot be seen as an innovation within the Jewish reference system alone, however. It immediately transgresses into public space and interferes with the imperial construct of identity and genealogy that has the Roman ancestor Aeneas hold the very position

Paul attributes to Abraham, and that establishes the unity of the nations under the (not-)one father and divine Caesar as *pater patriae.*[89]

Furthermore, Paul's heavily emphasized oneness discourse bolsters our argument that the imperial contextuality of the Galatian circumcision conflict matters indeed. As legitimate children of Abraham and Abraham's God, the uncircumcised Galatians are indeed fully entitled to practice their faith in the *one God* in the same way as Abraham did in his time. They are not allowed to return to the established idolatrous patterns of civic and imperial religion on which Abraham once and for all turned his back, not even if the "law" defines them as Gentiles and subject to imperial worship (4:8-10), exactly as Abraham was prior to his departure for the promised land in Genesis 12.[90]

Nor are the Galatian children of Abraham to adopt circumcision as the distinctive mark of Jewishness (= "works of the law," 3:2-5), not even if only Jews properly defined as such by the "law" are allowed to practice Abraham's monotheism, without any imperial worship. For they are representing the *nations,* who are now receiving the blessing of Abraham, as opposed to the curse of Roman slavery. The law that condemns and exposes them as unlawful owing to their nonconformist identity is the law that is "mediated" by Caesar, the idolatrous *not-one* in contrast to the *one* God of Israel (3:19-20).[91] Like Abraham under Emperor Nimrod in *Genesis Rabbah,* they will have to endure persecution (4:29; 5:11; 6:12) by the representatives of a law that hypocritically claims God and Mount Sinai but, in fact, leads in the opposite direction of imperial slavery and thus curse.[92] Slavery marks precisely the cursed reality of "Jersualem now" (4:24-25). This requires a brief look at Galatians 4.

Mother Sarah and Mother Paul (Galatians 4)

If chapter 3 is shaped by fatherhood, chapter 4 focuses on the mothers and their children—the mother of Jesus (4:4), Sarah and Hagar as the mothers of Israel and not-Israel (4:21-31), and, most surprisingly, "mother Paul" in 4:19. The Genesis patterns of irregular motherhood and irregular succession are reactivated to tell the birth narrative of a new humanity detached from the patriarchal law of biological reproduction, which "naturally" reproduces the order of social hierarchy and antagonism. The divine (pro) creation out of the nothingness of barren mothers and the otherness of second-born sons consistently shapes the narrative theology of Genesis; Paul draws on this pattern when he tells the messianic narrative of the new (pro)creation as birth of a noncompetitive identity that overcomes the murderous divisions and stratifications between firstborn and second-born ones that have split humanity since Cain and Abel.[93]

Solidarity with a weak and despised *other* embodies the new order of (pro)creation, which begets a new and transformed humanity. As already stated, this is the crucial point in Paul's enthusiastic recollection of his earlier encounter with the Galatians in 4:12-15. He came to them as Jewish other, highly vulnerable and needy, and they could have treated him as an enemy or just let him die, but they took him in as neighbor and brother. In his weakness and repulsiveness, he embodied the dying and crucified Christ for them (4:14), and in their solidarity with him they brought him back to life. Together they became the incarnation of the messianic community that rebirths the self through the other: the body of Christ, where the (pro)creative power of resurrection and life-giving is at work.

In this crucial messianic interaction between Paul and the Galatians, Christ functioned as the "one" seed or "generative body" that brings forth the "children" who then collectively are the heirs of the alternative kingdom/empire of God (3:16, 26-28; 4:1-7; 5:21). This new shape of being human as being one-with-another, truly in the image of the one God, is the Christ-shape that the Galatians are now about to lose, and the essence of "mother" Paul's desperate effort to "rebirth" them. In his messianic labors, Paul tries to metamorphose them back into the conformity with Christ that they are giving up in exchange for conformity with the dominant order (4:19-20).

In the collective body of Christ, oppositional identities are the prerequisite for true messianic identity as continuous reconciliation of self and other. They are the test case of faith that loves the *one* God through loving the *other* of the fellow human. This is the implicit presupposition of the allegory of Hagar and Sarah in 4:21-31. One of Paul's most hard-to-decipher texts, this passage unfortunately has often functioned to substantiate the occidental theology of combat and supersessionism as "genuinely Pauline."[94]

The interpretational model we have developed, however, offers a way to read these ten verses in a different code. The messianic identity as self-with-other is the birthmark of Abraham and Sarah's legitimate children *kata pneuma*. They are born out of multiple modes of "nothingness" in terms of social inferiority (second-born brothers), biological infertility (barren mothers), and desolation (Gal 4:27), as children of God. Self and other are integrated and reconciled in a new global "mother-city" (*metropolis*) of freedom where Jews and Galatians/nations can communicate, associate, and unite other than through Rome and Caesar's body (4:26).

While this "Jerusalem above," as allegorical city of *Sarah* and metropolis of freedom, represents a new international exodus of Jews and nations out of Caesar's empire, *Hagar* in this construct becomes the allegorical representation of the *not-one* (3:19) as one-against-other that has hijacked Torah and leads away from (*apo*) Mount Sinai right into imperial idolatry and slavery.[95] Her "son" acting as persecutor of the other—one enslaved body persecuting other enslaved bodies in a delusionary practice of freedom and "lawful" self-righteousness—embodies the manifold ways of "horizontal violence" that has the conquered reenact and re-reproduce their own conquest among themselves.[96] Hagar thus stands for servile motherhood of the nations and Jews under Roman rule that inevitably *bears children into slavery* (4:23-24).[97]

Sarah and Abraham, on the other hand, embody a new transethnic pedigree of humanity that takes its generative power not from "manly" victory over the other in the image of the Pergamene battle, but from the "unmanly" power of the Messiah; this alternative family tree empowers the weak and vulnerable in their solidarity with one another, which mirrors the image of God.

That Paul had become other at "Damascus" and later in Roman Galatia, that his whole theology and practice are an uncompromising embrace of the other, and that throughout his life, until his death imposed by Roman law he stayed an other of the

Roman order—these constitute an interpretational dimension of Paul and of his gospel that is *other* than traditional Pauline hermeneutics has assumed. Whenever the "apostle to the conquered" has been made the proponent of the conquering Christian self, this other meaning of Paul has become unreadable. Nevertheless, it never ceased to light up in different places and moments throughout the history of interpretation. At the end of our textual exploration, we will thus catch a glimpse of two theologians both of whom in an exemplary way, though quite differently, understood this "other meaning" of Paul.

Postscript: The Mystical Body of Christ— Albert Schweitzer and Dietrich Bonhoeffer

A significant impulse toward unearthing an *other* interpretation of Paul than the Constantinian one was Albert Schweitzer's *Mysticism of Paul the Apostle*.[98] Though he is not usually seen in relation to Dietrich Bonhoeffer, it is interesting to note that the main thrust of Schweitzer's work—a socially embodied and embedded concept of faith as genuinely Pauline—coincided with Bonhoeffer's turn to the "real-life implications" of faith around his time at Union Theological Seminary in New York.[99] Operating in different theological disciplines, both theologians have nevertheless radically redefined the concepts of self, other, and one "in Christ," and in both a life practice and lived testimony rigorously interpret, apply, and validate theological inquiry.[100]

When Schweitzer's book on Paul appeared in English (1931), Bonhoeffer had just spent a year of postdoctoral studies at Union Theological Seminary in New York (1930–31), intensely immersed in issues of racial and social justice, as well as peacemaking, which would subsequently involve him in antiwar activism in Europe and in the resistance to Hitler's regime.[101] At that time Schweitzer was already working in West Africa (today Gabon), where he founded the Lambaréné hospital in 1913. He had left his promising career as a New Testament professor and retrained as a physician. Schweitzer was far ahead of his time in his relentless criticism of colonial realities, and his practice of love and "reverence for life" as well as his later interventions into the Cold War and the debate on nuclear armaments won him the Nobel Peace Prize in 1953.

Schweitzer's turn to the ethics of Paul is one of the most important moves in twentieth-century Pauline scholarship. *The Mysticism of Paul the Apostle* is thoroughly academic and conventional in style, yet breathtakingly innovative in its core statement that symbolically marks the end of its author's university career as a theologian.[102] The transition into a life practice of radical commitment as a physician in the African jungle in many ways appears as the "second volume" of his book. This "second volume" is spoken in a different mode, however—not through writing but through actions of solidarity and "true humanity," which Schweitzer saw as an "atonement for the crimes of violence done in the name of Christianity."[103]

This in turn is strongly reminiscent of a concept Dietrich Bonhoeffer would later sketch out in his prison cell, namely, the "nonreligious interpretation" of religious terms. "Praying and righteous action" for Bonhoeffer became the two most essential things that will eventually rebirth all "Christian thinking, speaking, and organizing" and bring forth "a new language, perhaps quite non-religious, but liberating and redeeming."[104] One might see, in a way, Schweitzer's entire work, including his famous philosophy of reverence for (other) life, as a move toward a "nonreligious interpretation" of Paul; at any rate it is deeply embedded in Paul's theology of mystical unity in the body of Christ or, to use our term, one-an(d)-otherness.

In *The Mysticism of Paul the Apostle*, Schweitzer rethinks Paul categorically in terms of embodiment and social practice. The essence of (Pauline) Christianity for him is the mystical integration of the baptized into the body of Christ, where they share the "resurrection mode of existence," losing their previous individual existence (self) to become "a manifestation of the personality of Christ." Being physically interdependent with Christ and with one another in the same new corporeity, they enter into a "reciprocity of relations" where "the one [that is, existence] can pass over into the other."[105]

This again echoes Bonhoeffer, who around that same time preached that the "other person, this enigmatic, impenetrable You, is God's claim on us; indeed, it is the holy God in person whom we encounter" (1928). And a year later we read in a letter to Detlef Albers: "Doubt and temptation . . . will not cease as long as we remain focused on ourselves, as long as in one form or another 'the other' does not step into our lives. Only then, in *panta rei*, in the flux of everything, do we find the stability that receives its potential and strength from elsewhere."[106]

Schweitzer, as is well known, represents a rigorous turn to the apocalypticism of Paul. The new sphere where the "powers manifest in the dying and rising again of Jesus are now at work" is the beginning transformation of the world and of humankind as a whole—merely a peak in the ocean of the old world so far, but with the new creation actually rising from "beneath the waves." Schweitzer here in a bold move reintegrates Jesus and Paul, who, he thinks, have been kept separate for too long and to the detriment of Christian authenticity. He sees Paul's being-in-Christ as the "original" location of justification and righteousness; it corresponds to the resurrection state of existence proper to the messianic kingdom proclaimed by Jesus.[107]

Schweitzer's basic criticism is that Paul's mystical doctrine of redemption through collective being-in-Christ was not adopted into church dogma, but rather the narrower and somewhat secondary concept of atonement through the sacrificial death of Jesus. This in turn is expressed in the doctrine of justification by faith, which focuses on the individual alone. As it lacks the essential connection to ethics and to the kingdom of God, it is merely a "subsidiary crater" within the "main crater," that is, the mystical doctrine of redemption through being in Christ.[108] For Schweitzer, the mystical body of Christ brings Jesus and Paul back together, reuniting the teaching of the kingdom of God with redemption and justification by faith, which both have been detached from one another since the times of primitive Christianity. He wants to reactivate this "extinct volcano" by overcoming the detrimental juxtaposition of an "inauthentic gospel of Christ" with an "inauthentic gospel of Paul," demanding a return to "funda-mental Christianity," where the belief in redemption through Christ is an "integral part of a living belief in the Kingdom of God."[109]

> The great weakness of all doctrines of redemption since the Primitive Christianity is that they represent a man as wholly concerned with his own individual redemption, and not equally with the coming of the Kingdom of God.[110]

For Schweitzer, until this reintegration of God's kingdom and justification by faith, of Jesus and Paul, is accomplished, Christianity "will stand before the world like a wood in the barrenness of winter."[111] His theology of Christ mysticism is very close to the concept of redeemed selfhood through messianic one-an(d)-otherness that we have developed in this study so far.[112] There is some disagreement to be voiced, though, regarding Schweitzer's perception of justification by faith as "subsidiary crater." This perception, however, substantially changes if Paul's theology is no longer read within an exclusively Jewish and Torah-centered framework of "works righteousness" (as Sch-weitzer does). In light of the overarching Roman contextuality of imperial "works" and "law," the fundamental importance and thrust of "faith" and "faith justification" as messianic counter-reality gains new importance.

Conclusion: Messianic Faith versus Imperial Idolatry

Read before the Great Altar of Pergamon and in the scriptural code of Exodus and Deuteronomy, Galatians emerges as a passionate plea to resist the idolatrous lure of imperial religion and social ordering. The six chapters spiral in several movements around the basic juxtaposition of God versus idols, and the clash of two different self/other-constructs that are implied. The entire letter is the "coded" theological manifesto of the nations under Roman rule pledging allegiance to the one God who is other than Caesar; this "semi-hidden transcript" contradicting and resisting the dominant order is embodied in a new horizontal and international community practice of mutual support.

This core dynamic is present in Galatians 1–2 as the foundational messianic intervention of the divine "other One" at the outset of Paul's missionary journey. It shapes chapters 3–4, which offer a renarration of Genesis as the counter-imperial pedigree of one humanity under one God who is other than Caesar. Further, it pervades Galatians 5–6, where Paul focuses on the practical implications of oneness as one-an(d)-otherness within a worldwide practice of transnational solidarity. Already Paul's opening statement in Gal 1:1-9 evokes the Deuteronomic antithesis of blessing and curse, *Amēn* and *Anathēma,* and rotates around the big alternatives of God or non-gods, freedom or slavery, faith or un-faith—locating the whole letter in the symbolic in-between topology of Mount Ebal or Mount Garizim. What Paul rediscovers and radically restates are the exodus foundations of biblical monotheism in the global age of Caesar—and in the new age of the worldwide Jewish Messiah.

The "idols" as the intolerable other of Israel's God according to the first and second commandments (Exod 20:1-6) for Paul may have no longer appeared as simply the equivalent of "other religions" and "paganism" as such. At a time when Roman imperial religion congeals the polytheism of the vanquished nations in a quasi-monotheistic top, Paul "sees" how behind the manifold false and forbidden images of other gods, and even in the imageless worship of Israel's one God, the "Egyptian" *eidōlon* of imperial idolatry and ideology pops up everywhere, *divus* Caesar and *diva* Rome. Like the biblical arch-idol of the golden calf, which was manufactured by the exodus people themselves right at Mount Sinai, the idolatrous image is hailed as God of freedom while it represents the "false gods" of slavery. Monotheism and syncretism get a new meaning. A novel type of a hybrid "monotheistic syncretism from below" based on justice and survival, ruptures the imperial web of power and its "imperial-syncretistic monotheism from above."[113]

Worshiping the deceptive and false other of the imperial idol as god is the core prohibition of Torah. Yet if it marks the boundary between Israel and Gentiles, self and other, in Paul's view it also fundamentally challenges this "dividing wall." For in the biblical narrative, the first and foundational transgression of the core commandment is a transgression not by the pagan others but by Israel itself (Exodus 32). Criticism of idolatry as criticism of imperial ideology is deeply inscribed on the prophetic message, not only as criticism directed toward the outside but also as criticism from within. God's and Moses's wrath at Israel's flirtation with idolatry (Exod 32:10, 19) is tied to the very origin of Torah. As it would be an absurdity to perceive this wrath as "anti-Jewish," it is an absurdity to declare Paul's wrestling with the ongoing infiltration of Torah by the idols as his breaking away from Judaism.

The idol itself is not simply other, but represents the imperial perception, or perversion, of self and other. Rather than representing human and fellow human in the image and likeness of God (Gen 1:26-27), it creates God in the image and likeness of human. The disastrous consequence of such human image making is not that God therefore appears as human; rather, God is molded into the mask of the self that profoundly distorts the face of the human. For as the bull imagery of sexual, social, and military power "naturally" took shape when Aaron melted an image of God for Israel at Mount Sinai (Exod 32:4), what "naturally" turns out as image of god-in-the-likeness-of-human is the image and likeness of the self in its power over the other. The idol as the "desirable" image of the self-turned-into-God thus in reality represents not the human but the inhuman face of God, the life-devouring *moloch* that orders infants to be killed (see Exodus 1). The godlike image of the self on its reverse inevitably bears the image of the other as godless, lawless, enemy, inferior—the "lawful" object of rule and exploitation, of conquest and consumption in accordance with imperial *nomos*.

Yet Paul does not exclusively and not even primarily target the negative of the imperial idol and its order; rather, at the center of his argument is the new messianic community. His insistence on the oneness of God is the claim of human self and human other becoming one in Christ again, through the "birth-canal" of divine self-othering at the cross. It envisions the rebirth of creation, when human is made (again) in the image of God, not as a human self that consumes the other as commodity, but as commonality of one and other, male and female, Jew and Greek, free and slave (Gen 1:26-27; Gal 3:28). Only in this messianic community that embodies the *other* law can God be truly worshiped and served as the singular one God who is other than Caesar and thus reconciles self and other in a noncompetitive and nonhierarchical body of "new life."

A fallen snake-legged Giant is attacked by Artemis's hunting dog from behind. Wild hair, snake legs, distorted face, and armpit hair signal his repulsiveness and Barbarian nature. Detail from the scene on the East Frieze of the Great Altar of Pergamon shown on p. 100. Photo: Erich Lessing/Art Resource, N.Y.

EPILOGUE

Dying Gauls, Jews, and Christians and Rome's Three Great Fires (60–75 C.E.)

At the end of our journey into the cityscapes and mindscapes of ancient Galatia, we will turn back once again to the point of its departure: the uprising of Vindex. The monumental sculpture of a defeated Gaul/Galatian that Nero encountered on his harried journey from Naples to Rome in 68 C.E.[1] reassured him, according to Suetonius, that the gods must be on his side. They had always sided with Rome in the four and a half centuries since the Gallic barbarians had attacked the city for the first time. Indeed, the insurgence in Gaul was quelled and its leader, in the obstinate way of the Celts, killed himself. Yet Nero's victory over Gaius Julius Vindex in 68 C.E. did not become a triumph. Instead it precipitated the downfall of the conqueror himself.

Gaul, Judea, Rome: Empires Competing

The rebellious Gaul bore the typical Celtic marker of the suffix -ex in his last name. He belonged to the indigenous aristocracy of Aquitania, which had been affiliated with the Roman pedigree of power for several decades: Vindex's first two names, Gaius Julius, linked him to Gaius Julius Caesar and to Gaius Octavianus, alias Augustus, Caesar's divine son, and thus signaled the "adoption" of his family into the *gens* of the Julii going back to Venus and Mars.[2] Vindex had lived in Rome for a while and had inherited his senatorial rank from his father, who was made senator when the emperor Claudius allowed Gauls to be admitted to this highest level in the Roman power pyramid in 48 C.E. (Tacitus, *Ann.* 11.23–25). Vindex himself became governor of Gallia Lugdunensis (Lyons, in central France) under Nero. The motives behind his uprising are not entirely clear. There were unbearable tax burdens, on the one hand, while at the same time, according to Cassius Dio (*Roman History* 63.22.1–6), Vindex proclaimed the liberation of Rome from the yoke of Nero as his true cause and thus declared his allegiance to Galba, the provincial governor of

Hispania Tarraconensis (Spain/Portugal) as the new emperor.[3] At this stage, the empire started to descend into ever greater turmoil, and Nero was forced to commit suicide in 68 C.E. (Suetonius, *Nero* 47–49). With his death, the Julio-Claudian dynasty, which had shaped the world of Jesus and Paul, came to a violent end.

It is noteworthy that the Julio-Claudians, in a way, perished where they triumphantly had risen to power roughly a hundred years earlier: in Gaul. Yet the trouble spot was not Gaul alone. While Vindex was beginning to make war against the Roman Empire in Gallia, the Jewish rebellion in Judea had been going on already for two years. In 69 C.E., only a few months after the rebellious Gallo-Roman governor declared Galba the new emperor, another powerful man was hailed as Caesar by his troops in Judea: Vespasian, the commander-in-chief of the military operations against the insurgent Jews.[4] It was in the midst of both upheavals, Gallic and Jewish, that the Roman civil war unfolded and no fewer than three emperors rose and fell within a single year. At last Vespasian seized power in 69 C.E. The synergy of all these simultaneous events is rarely noticed in New Testament scholarship, although they mark a watershed not only in the history of the Roman Empire but also of the New Testament. In terms of external history, the ten years between 60 and 70 C.E. separate the time of the Pauline letters from the time of the Gospels and later writings. This was a formative decade, reshaping everything that was said about Jesus the Messiah after Paul and also what was said about Paul himself.[5]

Tacitus illustrates the point. His infamous excursus about the perversions of Judaism in book 5 of the *Histories* is widely quoted by theologians. Yet, as D. S. Levene states, it is treated mostly as a "self-contained piece, in isolation from the rest of the work." Tacitus's statement on the otherness of the Jews is indeed "the most substantial surviving treatment of Jewish history and religion by a pagan writer of the ancient world."[6] Read in its overall literary context, however, the excursus contributes to a much more comprehensive historical panorama. It is embedded in the overarching framework of the major Gallic and German uprisings against Rome in 68–69, the main topic of the surviving books of the *Histories* in 1–4 and 5.14–26. Without any transitional marker, Tacitus moves from Titus and the last preparations for the storming of Jerusalem (5.13) to the city of Trier in the West (5.14), in which unfolds the narrative of Petillius Cerialis's fight against the Batavian rebel leader Gaius Julius Civilis, another son of the *gens* Julii, who, like Gaius Julius Vindex, was unfaithful to his adoption by the imperial father.

Tacitus repeatedly reports that the Gallic/Galatian insurgents under Civilis took an oath of allegiance to an "empire of all Gaul" that was expected to do away with the Roman Empire (4.58–60).[7] The perception that Rome was coming to an end was fueled by the fact that during the fights of the civil war in 69 C.E., the Capitol with the temple of Jupiter Optimus Maximus went up in flames. The innermost bastion of Roman power, which the Gauls had not been able to take in 387 B.C.E., had finally fallen, destroyed by the Romans themselves. With this fatal fire, the Celtic Druid priests announced, heaven's anger had at last come upon Rome, and the Transalpine tribes were now destined to rule the world (*Hist.* 4.54).[8] The German seer and prophetess

Veleda foretold the destruction of the Roman army (*Hist.* 4:61). In Judea, meanwhile, the air was filled with prophecies and visions of a new empire that would begin from the Jews. As Tacitus notes, these foolish tales encouraged desperate resistance in the Jewish capital, which would soon be razed to the ground.[9]

All of this is important for understanding the background and meaning of Vespasian's eventual victory and rise to power, achieved with the help and unfaltering loyalty of his son Titus, who conquered Jerusalem and burned the temple in 70 C.E. The Roman Empire was consolidated in triumph over the rebellious nations of *both* the Gauls and the Jews, crushing the subversive Druidic religion as well as the superstitious worship of the Jewish God—both unsuccessful rivals of the Roman god(s) in the battle for world rule.[10] According to his own testimony, Flavius Josephus, a Jew-turned-Roman, was the first to announce this victory with prophetic entitlement: In 67 C.E., Josephus, who until that point had been a successful rebel leader against Rome, declared in a dramatic performance at conquered Jotapata in Galilee that the new ruler to emerge from Judea was not meant to be any Jewish or Oriental Messiah but rather the Roman Vespasian, who would become the new emperor:

> You will be Caesar, Vespasian, you will be emperor [*autokratōr*], you and your son here.... For you, Caesar, are master [*despotēs*] not of me only, but of land and sea and the whole human race. (Josephus, *B.J.* 3.401–2, trans. Thackeray, LCL).[11]

The very fact that Josephus was a Jew himself and an ex-insurgent gave his prophecy, made two years before Vespasian actually ascended to power, particular value for the Romans. It allowed him to "rise" from among the dead bodies of his fallen soldiers and fellow Jews at Jotapata to a privileged position of honor and status as a Roman citizen, a truly "imperial resurrection" and co-optation of the type we have already studied in Roman Galatia.[12] He changed his name into *Flavius* Josephus and became a faithful client of the new Flavian dynasty, which after the debacle of the Julio-Claudians was in dire need of ideological and military credentials.[13]

Flavius Josephus proved himself a worthy "son." During the siege of Jerusalem in 70 C.E., he would publicly urge the Jews to surrender to Rome: It was God who had given the worldwide rule over the nations to Italy. A basic law (*nomos*) firmly established both among animals and humans requires the weaker to "yield to the stronger" and to acknowledge that power and rule belong to "those pre-eminent in arms." It is necessary to submit to Rome, because God is on Rome's side and therefore the Jews "are warring not against the Romans only, but also against God" (*B.J.* 5.367–68, 378).[14]

All these events took place after Paul's death. But the basic historical configurations were already there in the 40s and 50s C.E., shaping Paul's time and the context of his interaction with the Galatians. In light of Josephus's speech to his besieged fellow Jews in Jersualem, the dissident nature of the Pauline communities becomes again obvious. They practiced and proclaimed a peacemaking between Jews and Gentiles— one defeated nation and another—that did not yield to the worship of military might and goddess Victory, nor to the "natural law" of the supremacy of the strongest. The peace and grace of their Messiah Christ were neither mediated by the divine Caesar nor defined by the self/other-construct inherent in Roman law and religion.

Yet there was another problem. What probably aggravated the situation was that of all the conquered nations gathered in the Pax Romana under the eagle's watchful gaze; the un-Roman association of Jews and Gauls/Galatians in particular must have evoked one of the worst nightmares of empire. Both Judea and Gaul were notorious hotbeds of insurrection and, according to Tacitus's report, breeding grounds for ideologies of new, anti-Roman empires. Both shared an ambiguous status as allies of the Roman order as well as enemies. Both Jews and Celts were "international" in that they inhabited more than one country and could communicate with one another across provincial boundaries in a language other than Greek or Latin. Both had intellectual elites able to maintain a non-Roman ideology with deep and powerful roots in their native populations. When Claudius, for example, in 49 C.E. expelled from Rome the Jews who "constantly made disturbances at the instigation of Chrestus," he simultaneously turned against the Druids, obviously not for the first time: "He utterly abolished the cruel and inhuman religion of the Druids among the Gauls, which under Augustus had been merely prohibited to Roman citizens" (Suetonius, *Claudius* 25).[15]

Again, William M. Ramsay had a clear understanding of the underlying problem:

> The success of the Imperial Government in the provinces rested greatly on its power of accommodating itself to the ways and manners and religions of the subjects; it accepted and found a place in its system for all gods and all cults. Religious intolerance was opposed to the fundamental principles of the Imperial rule, and few traces of it can be discerned. It proscribed the Christians and it proscribed the Druids. In these two cases there must have seemed to the Imperial Government to be some characteristic which required exceptional treatment. In both cases there was present the same dangerous principle: both maintained an extra-Imperial unity, and were proscribed on political, not on religious grounds.[16]

In Paul's time, then, there was nothing innocent about gathering Galatians and Jews around the table of a crucified "emperor/king [*basileus*] of the Jews," as the Gospels have Pontius Pilate describe Jesus' offense (Mark 15:26 parr.).[17] It is even more scandalous that Paul allowed no libation to the Roman emperor or to the Roman gods at that table, either by circumcised Jews or uncircumcised Galatians, effectively estranging them both from the established patterns of conformity to the civic religion and uniting them into a sort of hideous, barbarian abnormality. Note that in Tacitus, the people who proclaim a world empire of Gaul or Galatia and those who trust the world rule of the Jewish God never talk to one another, although their revolts against Rome happen simultaneously. Yet their segregation and mutual ignorance or contempt is vital for Roman rule. The vanquished, from a Roman perspective, are unable to make peace among themselves, unless the heavy hand of Rome is upon them.[18] This is the Roman pattern of "divide and conquer" and the only reason why in 68–69 Rome could prevail.

Gauls (Galatians) and Jews *did* talk to one another, however. They did declare peace; they did support each other and sit at one table—in the Pauline communities. And this is where they clashed with Roman law and Roman rule. Historically, the earliest clearly marked occasion of such a major conflict between Rome and the Christian movement was the Neronian persecution.

The Neronian Persecution as Reenactment of Pergamon (64 C.E.)

As Suetonius's episode (*Nero* 41) about the anti-Gallic victory monument on the road to Rome shows, Nero obviously had a strong sense of images of power—and of the power of images. Throughout his career he used and manipulated this power with great skill to imprint the normative order, and his own position at its apex, on both hearts and minds. He not only "collected" images in a large-scale operation from Delphi, Olympia, Pergamon, and elsewhere, to have them displayed in his Golden House—one of the grand state-sponsored art robberies of history,[19] but he also had them performed as "living images" in theatres and arenas and was passionate about cultivating his own image as a talented actor on various stages.

Probably the most famous "performance" Nero ever staged was the Great Fire of Rome in 64 C.E. For the imperial biographer Suetonius, the guilt of Nero in committing this devastating crime is beyond any doubt (*Nero* 38). He reports that Nero wanted to see how "earth [*gaia*] mixes with fire [*pyri*]"[20] and moreover felt aesthetically offended by the sight of old houses and narrow streets. He thus ordered his servants to set fire to the city. Rome burned for six days and seven nights and the *plebs* of Rome were forced to seek shelter in underground spaces like tombs and vaults. Meanwhile, the emperor stood high on the tower of Maecenas's palace to oversee the conflagration, marveling at the beauty of the flames. He had put on his theater costume and sang of the "Conquest of Troy."

Dio Cassius adds another important note: the capture of Troy was, in the eyes of Roman spectators, the capture of Rome, and people recalled that only once before had the city thus been laid waste—by the Gauls/Galatains (*hypo Galatōn*). Never before and never since had such a calamity befallen the city—that is, except for the Galatian (*Galatikōn*) invasion (*Roman History* 17.3; 18.2). The conflation of images is interesting: Rome—Troy—Gauls (Galatians). What Nero saw in reality was a large swath of Rome aflame, reduced to ashes. In his imagination, however, the picture before his eyes was transmuted into the defeat of Troy by the Greeks and the attack on Rome by the Gauls in 387 B.C.E. As we saw in chapter 3, these two historically unconnected events had already been interwoven in the mythopoietic fabric of Virgil's *Aeneid,* in particular on the Shield of Aeneas. They established the deep grammar in the foundational myth of Rome as the city destined to rule the world. All the elements of this Roman myth of origin—the new city, the new ruler, and the new creation—would subsequently materialize together in Nero's Golden House, an *imago mundi* erected out of the ruins of the burned "old city" and the "old world."[21]

One piece, however, was still missing to make this image of the world "real." The manifold artwork assembled in the Domus Aurea, all the architectural and spatial ingenuity of its builders, could not replace the life blood of the enemy/other. If sculptures of Dying Gauls in all likelihood had a prominent place in the Golden House, the blood dripping from their open wounds would have been carved in bronze or marble. But a proper sacred foundation for a new city required a *real* sacrifice. It seems that Nero, with his clear instinct for performed images and mass effects, found an ideal substitute: the *Christiani*. As Tacitus states, he offered them to the Roman public as culprits for the Great Fire and had them publicly crucified, burned, or torn to death by wild dogs.

> But neither human help, nor imperial munificence, nor all the modes of placating Heaven, could stifle scandal or dispel the belief that the fire had taken place by order. Therefore, to scotch the rumour, Nero substituted as culprits, and punished with the utmost refinements of cruelty, a class of men, loathed for their vices, whom the crowd styled Christians [*Christianos appelabat*]. Christus, the founder of the name, had undergone the death penalty in the reign of Tiberius, by sentence of the procurator Pontius Pilatus, and the pernicious superstition [*superstitio*] was checked for a moment, only to break out once more, not merely in Judaea, the home of the disease, but in the capital itself, where all things horrible or shameful in the world collect and find a vogue. First, then, the confessed members of the sect were arrested; next, on their disclosures, vast numbers were convicted, not so much on the count of arson as for hatred of the human race [*odio humani generis*]. And derision accompanied their end: they were covered with wild beasts' skins and torn to death by dogs; or they were fastened on crosses [*aut crucibus adfixi*], and, when daylight failed were burned to serve as lights by night. Nero had offered his Gardens for the spectacle [*spectaculo*], and gave an exhibition in the Circus [*circense ludicrum edebat*], mixing with the crowd in the habit of a charioteer, or mounted on his car. Hence in spite of a guilt which had earned the most exemplary punishment, there arose a sentiment of pity, due to the impression that they were being sacrificed not for the welfare of the state but to the ferocity of a single man.[22]

The question for our investigation at this point is not the precise legal foundations of this first official persecution of the Jesus groups in Rome,[23] but what Nero and the Romans saw in these groups that made it possible for the emperor to present them as potential perpetrators of so brutal a crime against the city—indeed, against humanity as a whole. Our earlier exploration of the Roman enemy construct suggests that the Christians must have appeared as the ideal substitute players for the role of the primeval Giants/Galatians/barbarians that Nero needed for his "show." They of all peoples could be most plausibly imagined as the "new Gauls," that is, as yet another assimilation of contemporary enemies to the old lineage of Giants, Amazons, Persians, Galatians, Orientals, Egyptians—that is, barbarians.[24] Dio Cassius's comment (above) on the "Galatian" reminiscences of the Great Fire and Tacitus's remark that the Christians' guilt was fabricated so that they might be punished as culprits of the crime, clearly point in this direction.[25]

These observations make possible a hypothetical reimagination of the Neronian persecution against a broader imaginary background. If Nero saw himself as a refounder and rebuilder of Rome, did his dramatically performed executions of Christians function in part as the theatrical performance of a gruesome ancient Roman tradition, the triple life sacrifice of Galatians and Greeks to safeguard the city's survival in times of crisis (as described in chapter 1)? Or does his action fuse subconsciously or even consciously with Romulus's bloody slaughter of the primordial transgressive *other* who disrespected the city's walls and its laws (see chapter 3)? When he ordered the crucifixion of members of this "disorderly" and anti-civic Jewish sect, was Nero thus in a way reenacting the punishment of "wall-jumping" Remus by his brother Romulus, Rome's founder father and builder of both walls and laws?[26]

Alison Futrell has argued, as we saw in chapter 3, that the Romulus–Remus fratricide at the root of Rome might be seen as a foundational sacrifice for the city. In her opinion, that sacrifice was then reinvented and restaged on a large scale by Augustus in the bloody games of the arena.[27] In a similar way, I ask, were the torture, crucifixion, burning, and "hunting down" of the *Christiani* Nero's creative reimagination of the primeval sacrifice and spectacle? Does it represent a foundational act of law reestablishment by a symbolic deed of "wall reinforcement" that marks the beginning of his new age, destined to offer a truly "golden" image of the world?

We may superimpose yet another image onto Nero's actions. When Nero executed the *Christiani* before everyone's eyes as arsonists, himself visibly present, did he also take on the noble role of brave Manlius? On Virgil's Shield of Aeneas, Manlius "high up" defends the Capitol, the state temple of the imperial world god Jupiter, against the barbarian assault of the Gauls, who reduced the city to ashes but could not conquer the citadel and the innermost sanctuary of power (see chapter 3). Is this imagery part of the heroic play Nero performed on the tower of Maecenas and later in his gardens? Behind this Manlius, as we saw in chapter 1, stood another, Titus Manlius, who in courageous single combat captured a blood-splashed torque from the Gallic enemy in Italy (Livy 7.9–10); and yet a third Manlius, who finally liberated Asia Minor from the marauding hordes of lawless Gauls (to use the ancient stereotype), the direct ancestors of Paul's Galatians (Livy 38.17). Does Nero symbolically take on their mantle as well?

None of this can be known for certain, but it is tempting to hypothesize a mythopolitical connection between Nero's performance on the tower of Maecenas and the scenes in his gardens afterwards. If he staged the Great Fire as a "Trojan war" against Galatians/Gauls attacking Rome, was the execution of *Christiani* then the corresponding reenactment of their fate as Dying Gauls/Galatians/Giants in a truly "Giant" life performance? Their transgression of civic order, their transnational character, their "conquest" of Rome and blasphemous neglect of its god(s), and their origin from a man whom Rome had publicly exihibited as a Dying Jew and disposed of as a Dead Jew—all this undoubtedly brought the *Christiani* into close symbolic proximity with the ancient Giants, the sons of the rebellious Earth goddess.

Whether these images were consciously in Nero's mind or not, the way he staged the dying of the Christians has a "Pergamene" touch to it. There are visual echoes that strongly resemble the dying of the mythological Giants/Galatians as depicted at the Great Altar. This applies in particular to the scenes at the southeast corner of the Great Frieze, scenes that appear almost like a marble model of the gruesome performance in Nero's gardens. Like the Giants/Galatians at Pergamon, some of the Christians, Tacitus reports, were presented in beastly disguise, wrapped in animal skins and then devoured by ferocious hunting dogs—a representation of their subhuman or antihuman nature and their location outside culture and civilization. Others, again according to Tacitus, were burned as torches to light up the night. This is reminiscent of the three goddesses, linked in myth to the nocturnal sphere, who appear on the East and South Frieze of Pergamon, attacking their Giant foes with great flaming torches: the Titan Phoebe, her daughter Leto (the mother of Artemis and Apollo), and her grand-daughter Hekate, the goddess of witchcraft, magic, sacrifices, crossroads, and doorways. Two of these flame-throwing goddesses, Leto and Phoebe, are accompanied by fighting dogs; as is Leto's daughter Artemis, the Olympian moon goddess and divine huntress who fights with her bow, framed by two torch-bearing goddesses (see chapter 2).

Thus, the Pergamene Frieze reassures, light defeats darkness, safeguarding the cosmic and elemental order against a "giant" assault of darkness and chaos. Before the backdrop of these images the nightly burning of Christians at Rome appears as a variation on the theme, and Nero, erect in his chariot, might have represented the sun god Apollo, Artemis's brother, as counterpart of the night-related goddesses with their torches.

One should note that this configuration mirrors exactly the juxtaposition of day and night, sun and moon that is depicted at the Prima Porta statue of Augustus. Here the sun god Sol (corresponding to Apollo) drives his chariot over the canopy of the heavens toward the two goddesses Luna (Moon) and Aurora (Dawn). Luna, who corresponds to Artemis/Diana directly below her, is bearing a torch; so is Artemis, who holds it alongside her quiver—quite uncharacteristically, as Paul Zanker notes.[28] Both goddesses thus are represented as light-bearing and lighting up the night (Latin *lucifera* or *noctiluca*). This once again illuminates the cosmic connotations of the Neronian "spectacle." Tacitus explicitly mentions the polar presence of day and night as part of Nero's "script." The torture and execution of the Christians as living torches who "when daylight failed were burned to serve as lights" might well be a mythological reenactment of the primeval victory of light over darkness, won by the triumphant power of the divine creator and sun god Nero.

The crosses that Nero uses do not have a direct visual counterpart at the Pergamene Frieze. Crucifixion was a peculiarly Roman "reimagination" of the slaughter portrayed at the Great Altar. But the reason given for the execution of the "Christians" is again close to the crime of the Giants. Like the Giants, the *Christiani* are crucified, torn to pieces, and burned because they are the archenemies of civic and civilized law, imperial and divine cosmic order. Their crime, like the crimes of the Jews and the Gauls, is their "hatred of the human race" and their "superstitious" character, that is, their status as outsiders and foes of human and divine law. This is the reason why they are the most ostensible candidates for committing the crime of arson: As the Giants attacked the seat of the Olympians, the Christians have symbolically attacked the heavenly and earthly order, the core of civilization, the metropolis of Rome at the heart of the empire.[29]

That Nero can so easily portray the Christ-followers—alone of all the varied religions and nations dwelling in Rome—as enemies and destroyers of the imperial city confirms the politically charged atmosphere that has been a central aspect of our reimagination of earlier events in Galatia. On the symbolic level, the Roman *Christiani* die as lawless Galatians or Gauls. In all likelihood, Paul was among them.[30] Ten years earlier, when he had written the Galatians his letter, he had urged them to become like him (Gal 4:12): human beings created, reborn, and resurrected from death not in the likeness of Caesar but in the image of Christ crucified, the image of a Dying Jew calling the Dying Gauls back to life—the very image that Paul himself in his weakness (*astheneia*) had embodied among them (Gal 4:13-14). In his death, however, he became "like them," taking the symbolic place of a Dying Gaul.[31]

Jewish Torah and the Grip of Empire

We have already talked about the civil war that broke out after Nero's suicide. Three emperors were announced, then killed, in a single year, and in the final violent showdown in 69 c.e. between Vitellius and Vespasian, eventually and accidentally, the Capitol with the sanctuary of the state god Jupiter went up in flames. It was thus, ironically, not destroyed by a "foreign" Gallic, Jewish, or Christian attack, but by Romans themselves and through the self-destructive forces of competition, war, and violence inherent in empire itself. A Capitol in ruins, however, is a poor symbol to advertise the beginning of the new Flavian dynasty. Vespasian and, later, his sons Titus and Domitian needed a new image to restore the battered imperial worldview, an image even more powerful than the image of Dying Gauls that Nero so theatrically represented (in the bodies of Dying Christians) in 64.

The image that made it possible to imagine the Roman Empire again as all-powerful and victorious was provided by Titus, Vespasian's son and commander-in-chief of the Roman troops who besieged Jerusalem. The city and its sanctuary went up in flames. This was the third great fire of the decade 60–70, and it was meant to reinforce the impression of the first, while overwriting the image of the second. In 70 c.e. Titus conquered Jerusalem and killed or sold into slavery hundreds of thousands of inhabitants and refugees.[32] He had the Jerusalem temple, the dwelling place of the rebellious Jewish God, razed to the ground. In front of the still burning sanctuary, before the Holy of Holies, the soldiers performed a sacrifice, possibly of pork, to the legionary standard of the Roman eagle and hailed Titus as *imperator* (Josephus, *B.J.* 6.316).[33]

This was tantamount to a symbolic rape of the Jewish body, foreshadowing the triumphal imagery on subsequent coinage of "Judea Capta" as a crouching and mourning woman underneath the masculine figure of a Roman soldier.[34] The sexual connotation of imperial conquest is captured in a variation of this story told in the Babylonian Talmud where Titus desecrates and violates the Holy of Holies with a prostitute on a Torah scroll. Subsequently, in an act of symbolic penetration, he also cuts the sacred curtain and robs all temple vessels (*b. Git.* 56b). Titus's eagle sacrifice in the burning temple mirrors Pompey's sacrilegious intrusion into the Holy of Holies in 63 B.C.E., at the beginning of Roman domination over Judea (see chapter 5 above). No image could be more repulsive and traumatizing to the vanquished Jews, inscribing their defeat lastingly on the innermost location of their self-respect and pride.

At last, the Roman eagle again dominated the most contested civic space in the Roman *oikoumenē*, a place from which it had been excluded before. The attributes of the Jewish cult, of the Jewish God's now defeated power, and of Jewish law—golden showbread table, Menora (lampstand), and Torah scroll—were carried from Jerusalem to Rome. They were presented in Vespasian's and Titus's triumph in 71 C.E., followed by numerous images of Victory (*Nikē*) in ivory and gold, which immediately preceded the triumphal chariot of Vespasian and Titus (Josephus, *B.J.* 7.148–50).[35] This scene of restored Roman world power was depicted at the Arch of Titus, erected about ten years later by Domitian. The image of the imageless Jewish God—or rather, as close as one could get to it—had arrived in Rome as a trophy of war, ready for display among the other conquered gods reduced to subservience to Rome.

With their own temple in ruins never to be rebuilt, Jews all over the Mediterranean Diaspora now had to pay their former Jerusalem temple tax to the temple of Jupiter Capitolinus in Rome, supporting its restoration and thereby in a new way being forced to demonstrate their submission to the Roman world god.[36] The defeat of Israel's God and his insurrectionist people by the supreme god and ruler of the universe, Jupiter, could not have been made more plainly visible, and with it, the unfaltering support of Jupiter for the Flavians, who had so obviously atoned for the damage to the Capitoline state sanctuary.[37]

Fig. 47. *Roman soldiers carry away the golden lampstand from the Jerusalem temple in a relief on the Arch of Titus in Rome (81 C.E.) Photo: Wikimedia Commons.*

From the spoils of the Jewish triumph paraded through Rome, Vespasian personally chose the Torah scroll, as Josephus reports, alongside the purple hangings of the sanctuary, to keep in his own palace (*B.J.* 7.162). In light of our deliberations thus far, the symbolic significance of this act needs to be emphasized. The disputed object in the Jewish, Gallic, civil, and "Christian" wars of 60–70 C.E. was the concept of law, *nomos*. Torah scroll and temple curtain more than anything else symbolized the alternative space *other* than the Roman order claimed by the Jewish God. When Vespasian in an ostentatious gesture took the Torah scroll and the purple hangings as supreme trophies into his royal quarters, the Roman emperor's battered *oikos* (house), in a way, was symbolically restored to its proper function as normative space of order and role model of law/*nomos* for the entire *oikoumenē*, that is, the universal household under the Roman *pater patriae*.

The image is powerful and revealing. Jewish law, since Persian times a precarious "allowance" by the various foreign empires holding the Jews under their power,[38] was now visibly on display in the hands of Caesar, the supreme giver of law and order. This applied not only to the Jews, however, but also to the Gauls and Christians, who had been dying in vain for a law and order other than Rome's. The brutality of this political and theological statement in particular vis-à-vis the vanquished Jews can be hardly overlooked; Vespasian gripping the Torah was part of a public ritualization and calculated propagandistic effort to imprint conquest and defeat on the core of the vanquished.

In this context, Gal 3:19-20 emerges as a flash of prophetic (re)imagination that has Paul almost anticipate Vespasian's sacrilegious grabbing for the Torah scroll. Jewish law, the law of God, is publicly administered and ordained (*diatageis*) through the hand of a "mediator" who does not represent the one God of Israel (*henos ouk estin*) but rather the Roman imperial system with its idolatry, which is as destructive as it is seductive. The emperor indeed is posing as a new Moses.[39] This leads to the unbearable paradox of Peter's apparently impeccable Jewishness at Antioch. Peter clearly can quote the letter of Jewish law for breaking up table community with the Gentiles, yet Paul, in an act of prophetic and apocalyptic-messianic criticism, reveals that in the concrete here and now this established notion of Jewishness covers up something profoundly un-Jewish. At a time when everything is overdetermined and colonized by civic religion and imperial religion, nothing, not even Jewish law and Jewish identity, can escape the all-pervading grip of the idol—and of sin.

Behind the Antioch scene, Paul thus already in the 40s had seen something that Vespasian would publicly disclose only in 71 C.E.: that ultimately the divine Caesar draws the strings of any law observance, hijacking and manipulating even Jewish law and its letter in order to inhale his own spirit into it—the spirit of *divide and rule* that makes it illegal for the vanquished Jews and Galatians/Gentiles to sit at one and the same table without sacrificing to Caesar. For Paul, it is to preserve, not to abandon, the core of Torah that God has made the crucified and resurrected Messiah the new interpreter of God's Torah for Jews and Gentiles. To reiterate what we said in chapter 6: Paul at Antioch and in Galatia therefore does not criticize his antagonists from a "Christian" perspective because of their "Judaizing" apostasy. Rather, he criticizes them from the Jewish-messianic viewpoint of an idolatrous Gentilizing apostasy.

Contesting Vespasian's Temple of Imperial Peace

In 75 C.E., Vespasian finally managed to produce an image that would bring the imperial grammar of Roman peace and the iron rules of "proper" association among the conquered nations of Jews, Galatians, and others into plain sight. In his newly built Temple of Peace, both the trophies from the Jersualem temple and the images of Dying Gauls/Galatians were conspicuously gathered. The goddess of peace was placed in the central chamber of the U-shaped temple that had a sacrificial altar standing in front of it. She was posssibly surrounded by the Jewish trophies, while the sculptures of the Dying Gauls/Galatians might be imagined as flanking the sacrificial altar in the open courtyard, leading into the inner part of the hexastyle temple. Many other famous sculptures were exhibited that probably came to Rome during Nero's wholesale art robbery in the East and were now transferred from his Golden House to be "returned" to the Roman public.[40] With the prominent display of Jewish and Galatian trophies, some of the most significant and powerful images of Roman world order and world religion were assembled. It is assumed that the Romans planted roses in front of the temple: Gallic roses.[41] They made the temple look sufficiently "peaceful," and they covered the graves, the blood, the tears, and the despair at the underside of this peace.

Gallic roses, Dying Gauls, the golden table of Jewish showbread and the candlestick with the seven branches: thus in Vespasian's Temple of Peace they were now symbolically together, Rome's vanquished Jews and Gauls/Galatians, finally in accordance with Roman law, forced forever into compliance with Roman religion and order under goddess Victoria/Nikē posing as peace. At last they were pacified and united, immortalized and immobilized as dying, dead, and conquered under the eagle's laws and claws. Their death and defeat represented a foundational rock of Roman power and rule—in other words, of "Roman Peace" (Pax Romana).

Yet deep within and without the imperial order, the Pauline groups moved on and reminded each other of a different peace. In their messianic practice of one-an(d)-otherness as mutual life-giving and solidarity, they proclaimed the power of resurrection, insisting that a *koinōnia* between Jews and Galatians was possible *other* than either collectively dying as transgressors or living in conformity with the imperial law of segregation, competition, and combat. They shared the bread and a new corporeality that symbolized and celebrated the life, rather than the death, that came from the resurrected body of a crucified Jew. Profoundly nonviolent yet unconquerable, this was the negation and abrogation of the idolatrous *eidōlon* of triumph and defeat: Messianic peacemaking in the image of the One God *other* than Caesar, and of the Messiah Jesus.

Paul's letter to the Galatians thus is an apocalyptic critique of the dominant ideology and idolatry that are inseparably intertwined. To reveal the true image of reality and of God one needs to pull away the veil of ideological and idolatrous deception that blurs everyone's vision. Framing his whole theological argument throughout Galatians, Paul's discourse of messianic monotheism implies an appeal to see and to think both critically and faithfully.

Notes

Introduction

1. This topological inconclusiveness of the Greek terms *Galatai* and *Galatia* goes far beyond the traditional debate about a South or North Galatian location of Paul's addressees. In order to signal the more comprehensive Greek and Latin connotation, in contrast to *English* "Galatians" and "Gauls," I will frequently use the form Galatians/Gauls and Gaul/Galatia. This topic will be more extensively discussed in chapter1 below.

2. Most closely related to my own work is Davina C. Lopez, *Apostle to the Conquered: Reimagining Paul's Mission,* Paul in Critical Contexts (Minneapolis: Fortress Press, 2008), who creatively applies its methodology to the image and concept of "nations" (*ethnē*) in Galatians, integrating gender criticism and empire criticism in a highly refined manner. Her study reflects our memorable collaboration on Paul and critical re-imagination during her time as a Ph.D. student at Union Theological Seminary and is a most valuable cross-reference throughout this work, even where not explicitly quoted. As regards the Pauline letters in their entirety, an innovative parallel endeavor has been undertaken by John Dominic Crossan and Jonathan L. Reed, *In Search of Paul: How Jesus's Apostle Opposed Rome's Empire with God's Kingdom. A New Vision of Paul's Words and World* (San Francisco: HarperSanFrancisco, 2004), who in a productive and illuminating way combine expertise on images, architecture, and archeology with textual exploration from an empire-critical perspective. In general, use of Roman images and architecture to reconstruct the background of the New Testament owes abundant insight and inspiration to the foundational study of art historian Paul Zanker, *The Power of the Images in the Age of Augustus,* Jerome Lectures, 16th Series (Ann Arbor: University of Michigan Press, 1988). On the use of images in New Testament interpretation, see also Annette Weissenrieder et al., eds., *Picturing the New Testament: Studies in Ancient Visual Images,* WUNT 2/193 (Tübingen: Mohr Siebeck, 2005).

3. The breadth of this interdisciplinary scope has proven itself both as an inexhaustible source of stimulating insights and as a tremendous challenge, most notably to my own scholarly criteria. I am well aware that in all areas I engage I would need further study. I still hope that the overall picture can verify itself and that it may contribute to a more open dialogue across disciplinary boundaries that are highly artificial and restraining, in departments of religion as well as in those of history and art.

4. The start of my own work with Galatians dates back to the 1970s: Brigitte Kahl, *Traditionsbruch und Kirchengemeinschaft bei Paulus: Eine exegetische Studie zur Frage des "anderen Evangeliums,"* Arbeiten zur Theologie 60 (Berlin: Evangelische Verlagsanstalt, 1976).

5. The term "kyriarchy" was coined by Elisabeth Schüssler Fiorenza to highlight the multiple and interrelated aspects of domination in terms not only of gender (patriarchy/sexism) but also of racism, classism, ethnocentrism, colonialism, nationalism, and militarism. This is a most important analytical clarification and amplification to which the empire-critical re-imagination of Paul presented here is conceptually profoundly indebted, despite some disagreement about the actual position of Paul himself in the multilayered system of domination and war making of his time; see Elisabeth Schüssler Fiorenza, *Rhetoric and Ethic: The Politics of Biblical Studies* (Minneapolis: Fortress Press, 1999), 5–6. For Paul-critical readings, see, for example, Sheila Briggs, "Galatians," in *Searching the Scriptures,* volume 2, *A Feminist Commentary,* ed. Elisabeth Schüssler Fiorenza (New York: Crossroad, 1994),

218–36; Daniel Boyarin, *A Radical Jew: Paul and the Politics of Identity* (Berkeley: University of California Press, 1994); Elizabeth A. Castelli, *Imitating Paul: A Discourse of Power* (Louisville: Westminster John Knox Press, 1991); Elisabeth Schüssler Fiorenza, "Paul and the Politics of Interpretation," in *Paul and Politics: Ekklesia, Israel, Imperium, Interpretation. Essays in Honor of Krister Stendahl*, ed. Richard A. Horsley (Harrisburg, Pa.: Trinity Press International, 2000), 40–57. For a survey of feminist, postcolonial and empire-critical Pauline interpretations and their interconnections, or lack thereof, see Joseph A. Marchal, "Imperial Intersections and Initial Inquiries: Toward a Feminist, Postcolonial Analysis of Philippians," *Journal of Feminist Studies in Religion* 22, no. 2 (2006): 5–32.

6. For a pungent criticism of how Romans 13 was used to substantiate the dominant "state theology" of the apartheid system and its concept of law and order, see, for example, the South African *Kairos Document* (1985).

7. The "liberation of books" (*Délivrez les livres*) from dominant reading paradigms was a famous slogan of the French student movement in 1968 and widely applied to the *relectura* of biblical books by base communities in Latin America and Europe in the 1970s and '80s. This dynamic is reflected in a study that reopened and substantially redirected the debate on Paul for the American context: Neil Elliott, *Liberating Paul: The Justice of God and the Politics of the Apostle* (Maryknoll, N.Y.: Orbis, 1994; republished with a new preface, Minneapolis: Fortress Press, 2006).

8. For an informative summary of some of the transformations that occurred when the emperor Constantine started to act as "universal bishop" of the church and reframed the imperial "theology of victory" within a Christian framework, see David L. Dungan, *Constantine's Bible: Politics and the Making of the New Testament* (Minneapolis: Fortress Press, 2007), 113–18.

9. Most notably Elisabeth Schüssler Fiorenza, in line with Elizabeth Castelli, Sheila Briggs, and Antoinette Clark Wire, has argued for a feminist deconstructive critique of Paul and voiced strong criticism against any effort to "save the liberating voice of Paul" or toward "an emphatic understanding of Paul" that she sees represented by Luise Schottroff, evangelical feminist approaches, and also by myself; see Schüssler Fiorenza, *Rhetoric and Ethic,* 165. The German school around Luise Schottroff (for example, Luzia Sutter Rehmann, Claudia Janssen, Marlene Crüsemann, Beate Wehn) has reconstructed Paul from a feminist-liberationist, sociohistorical perspective; see Claudia Janssen, Luise Schottroff, and Beate Wehn, *Paulus: Umstrittene Traditionen—lebendige Theologie* (Gütersloh: Chr. Kaiser/Gütersloher Verlagshaus, 2001). Roman contexts were considered relatively early, for example, with regard to sin as "structural sin" that made the proper fufillment of law impossible; see Luise Schottroff, "'Law-Free Gentile Christianity'—What about the Women? Feminist Analyses and Alternatives," in *A Feminist Companion to Paul,* ed. Amy-Jill Levine (Cleveland, Ohio: Pilgrim, 2004), 192; Luzia Sutter Rehmann ("To Turn the Groaning into Labor: Rom 8:22–23," in Levine, *Feminist Companion to Paul,* 78) explicitly refers to "the daily reality of life in the Roman Empire, the *imperium romanum,*" as background for Paul's concept of sin and "groaning." A pioneering approach to Paul's justification theology from a third-world perspective and with explicit reference to the Roman imperial background has been presented by Elsa Tamez, *The Amnesty of Grace* (Nashville: Abingdon Press, 1993). Justin J. Meggitt (*Paul, Poverty and Survival* [Edinburgh: T&T Clark, 1998]) has undertaken a major historical reconstruction of Paul's congregations in a Roman context of poverty, pointing to economic mutuality as survival strategy.

10. The charge of neo-orthodoxy was originally directed against Rosemary Radford Ruether, Letty Russell, and Phyllis Trible in Elisabeth Schüssler Fiorenza, *In Memory of Her: A Feminist Theological Reconstruction of Christian Origins* (New York: Crossroad, 1985), 14–21. Conversely, Schüssler Fiorenza's own hermeneutic model with its polarity of "hermeneutics of suspicion" and "historical reconstruction" has drawn criticism for its "apologetic" and even "biblicistic" strands; see Lone Fatum, "Women, Symbolic Universe and Structures of Silence," *ST* 43 (1989): 61–63; and Brigitte Kahl, "Reading Luke against Luke: Non-Uniformity of Text, Hermeneutics of Conspiracy and the 'Scriptural Principle' in Luke 1," in *A Feminist Companion to Luke,* ed. Amy-Jill Levine (London: Sheffield Academic, 2002), 71.

11. Richard A. Horsley, ed., *Paul and Empire: Religion and Power in Roman Imperial Society* (Harrisburg, Pa.: Trinity Press International, 1997); idem, ed., *Paul and Politics.*

12. Robert Jewett, *Romans: A Commentary,* Hermeneia—A Critical and Historical Commentary

on the Bible (Minnesota: Fortress Press, 2007). In general, empire-critical studies are more advanced with regard to Romans than with regard to Galatians, especially through the work of Neil Elliott; see his *The Arrogance of Nations: Reading Romans in the Shadow of Empire,* Paul in Critical Contexts (Minneapolis: Fortress Press, 2008).

13. See Bruce W. Winter, *Seek the Welfare of the City: Christians as Benefactors and Citizens* (Grand Rapids: Eerdmans, 1994), 124–43; Mark D. Nanos, *The Irony of Galatians: Paul's Letter in First-Century Context* (Minneapolis: Fortress Press, 2002), 257–71.

14. Paul's universalism, traditionally understood as his "Christian" signature and pitted against "Jewish particularism," is a highly contested term. Yet, as Daniel Boyarin has shown from the perspective of a Jewish cultural critique, it can also point toward the necessity of human solidarity on a global scale; see Boyarin, *Radical Jew,* 235. Alain Badiou, a leading contemporary French philosopher, has explored Paul as the seminal figure and "new militant" of an "alternative universalism" that today might counteract the hegemonic universalism of global market capitalism. Addressing the dilemma of postmodern identity politics, which rejects the "universal" in the name of the particular, thus keeping each victimized identity apart from the other and isolated in its resistance, Badiou sees in Paul the prototypical reversal of this "particularist" pattern, which tends to empower the powerful rather than the powerless. "Ultimately, it is a case of mobilizing a universal singularity both against the prevailing abstractions (legal then, economic now), and against communitarian or particularist protest." Alain Badiou, *Saint Paul: The Foundation of Universalism,* Cultural Memory in the Present (Stanford, Calif.: Stanford University Press, 2003), 15.

15. Friedrich Wilhelm Nietzsche, "The Antichrist," in *The Portable Nietzsche*, ed. Walter Kaufmann (New York: Penguin, 1976), 565–656; as there is no complete critical edition of Nietzsche's works in English available yet, I subsequently quote by the number of the aphorism.

16. Interestingly, Nietzsche has a clear sense of the essentially antipatriarchal nature of Paul's theology. Its "feminine" and "antivirile" character is linked to the cross as the most radical subversion of a basic building block in the ideological construction of empire: imperial masculinity. This aspect of Roman imperial gender constructs and the depiction of conquered nations as female has been explored by Davina Lopez in *Apostle to the Conquered.*

17. "Obviously Nietzsche is capable, through the lens of his hostility, to perceive or sense some specific qualities of resistance in Paul's theology." Jan Rehmann, "Nietzsche, Paul, and the Subversion of Empire," *USQR* 59, no. 3–4 (2005): 155.

18. Jacob Taubes, *The Political Theology of Paul,* Cultural Memory in the Present (Stanford, Calif.: Standford University Press, 2004), 23–24.

19. See chapter 6 and Brigitte Kahl, "Reading Galatians and Empire at the Great Altar of Pergamon," *USQR* 59, no. 3–4 (2005): 31–34.

20. Taubes, *Political Theology of Paul*, 24.

21. Badiou, *Saint Paul,* 15. See n. 14 above. Like Boyarin, Badiou does not consider Roman universalism and its godlike, idolatrous embodiment in Caesar as the counterpart of Paul's messianic universalism, but rather still thinks in the older Protestant and New Perspective paradigm of Christian universalism versus Jewish particularism/ethnocentrism.

22. Taubes, *Political Theology of Paul,* 24.

23. The New Perspective is based on the work of Krister Stendahl and E. P. Sanders in the early 1970s and currently has James D. G. Dunn as one of its most prominent representatives. It marked a decisive departure from the older Protestant paradigm as it substantially reframed the scope of Paul's law criticism. Judaism was no longer perceived to be the religion of self-justification and self-salvation through meritorious "works of law" (Sanders). Paul was and stayed a Jew himself, and the gist of his argument was not about Judaism versus Christianity, nor about the individual's standing before God but about the community of Jews and non-Jews, that is, the inclusion of Gentiles in the church (Stendahl). Paul does not criticize Judaism or Jewish legalism/Torah per se but only the law in its exclusivism and boundary-marking aspects (circumcision, food laws, Sabbath) that make the divide between Jews and non-Jews impenetrable (Dunn). For a collection of essays that mark the development of the New Perspective since

Dunn's seminal article of 1983, see James D. G. Dunn, *The New Perspective on Paul: Collected Essays,* WUNT 185 (Tübingen: Mohr Siebeck, 2005); see chapter 1 below.

24. Drawing on the anthropological research of Bruce Malina and Philip Esler and J. E. Lendon's work on the "Empire of Honor" (1997), Robert Jewett in his commentary on Romans has taken a fundamental step in redefining *nomos* as the *general* law that requires competition for honor and superiority of status as a universally spread social, rather than simply individual (or Jewish), practice. In this reading "sin" and "boasting" drive, or are driven by, "perverted systems of honor and shame, leading captives into lives of unrelenting competition to gain advantage over other persons and groups." Jewett, *Romans,* 436. That the terms "law," "sin," and "boasting" are essentially reflecting a hierarchical, competitive, and consumptive relationship between Self and Other is a most crucial point of departure for rereading justification theology in Galatians as well.

25. See Brigitte Kahl, "Acts of the Apostles: Pro(to)-Imperial Script and Hidden Transcript," in *In the Shadow of Empire: Reclaiming the Bible as History of Faithful Resistance,* ed. Richard A. Horsley (Louisville: Westminster John Knox Press, 2008), 137–56; also Brigitte Kahl, *Armenevangelium und Heidenevangelium: "Sola Scriptura" und die ökumenische Traditionsproblematik im Lichte von Väterkonsens bei Lukas* (Berlin: Evangelische Verlagsanstalt, 1987).

26. "Acts of Paul: Martyrdom of the Holy Apostle Paul," in Wilhelm Schneemelcher, ed., *New Testament Apocrypha,* 2 vols., Eng. trans. ed. R. McL. Wilson (Cambridge: James Clarke; Louisville: Westminster John Knox Press, 1992), 2:260–63. The martyrdom of Paul is alluded to already in a document from the end of the first century C.E. *1 Clement* 5–6.1 refers to the death of Peter and Paul, stating that Paul after sevenfold imprisonment, exile, stoning, and becoming a herald to the East and West "won the noble renown which his faith merited. To the whole world he taught righteousness and reaching the limits of the West he bore witness [*martyrēsas*] before rulers." Church historian Eusebius in the fourth century mentions the martyrdom of both Peter and Paul in Rome in *Eccl. Hist.* 2.25 and 3.1-2.

27. Luther's fondness for Galatians as his "Katy von Bora" (that is, his wife) is well known and often quoted; see Martin Luther, *Luther's Works,* vol. 54, *Table Talk,* ed. J. J. Pelikan, H. C. Oswald, and H. T. Lehmann (Philadelphia: Fortress Press, 1999, ©1967), 20.

28. Martin Luther, *Luther's Works,* vol. 26, *Lectures on Galatians 1535, Chapters 1–4,* ed. J. J. Pelikan and W. A. Hansen (Saint Louis: Concordia, 1963), 9–10. For a brief summary of Luther's anti-Judaism as anti-legalism, coupled with his rejection of other "opponents of God" such as heretics, popes, and Turks, see Mary C. Boys, *Has God Only One Blessing? Judaism as a Source of Christian Self-Understanding* (New York: Paulist Press, 2000), 67–70; for a more comprehensive treatment, see Heiko A. Oberman, *The Roots of Anti-Semitism in the Age of the Renaissance and Reformation* (Philadelphia: Fortress Press, 1984).

29. See Kathy Ehrensperger, *That We May Be Mutually Encouraged: Feminism and the New Perspective in Pauline Studies* (New York/London: T&T Clark International, 2004), 53–57. Ehrensperger summarizes the triple effect of Platonism and Aristotelianism on biblical interpretation: "The dualistic perception of the world resulted in a general devaluation of the concrete, material world in Christianity, with its devastating impacts, not exclusively but particularly on women and Jews, who as such were associated with this concrete, material, and 'fallen' world. One of the central Christian interpretative axioms was based on this perception, the letter/spirit distinction, which contended that truth and ultimate meaning can only be found in the realm of the Spirit and never in the particularity of the letter of the biblical text. . . . Christians used this dualistic pattern to affirm dogmas and to extract universal statements from biblical texts. . . . Since in accordance with the Aristotelian principle there could be only one true univocal reality behind the text, the true reading of a text had to be unambiguous and without any kind of contradictions. . . . The church enforced this claim with power, oppressing divergent readings once it became affiliated with power" (ibid., 56–57).

30. Boyarin, *Radical Jew,* 17.

31. Womanist theologian and ethicist Emilie M. Townes explores both the "interior life of evil" and the complex social relationships underlying its "production" from an African American perspective. This implies "to see myself through the eyes of those whom I would and do reject." "Exploring evil as a cultural production highlights the systematic construction of truncated narratives designed to support and

perpetuate structural inequities and forms of social oppression." The term "truncated narrative" aptly applies to Paul. See Emilie M. Townes, *Womanist Ethics and the Cultural Production of Evil,* Black Religion, Womanist Thought, Social Justice (New York: Palgrave Macmillan, 2006), 4.

32. See chapter 6 below.

33. The terms "idolatry" and "idolatrous" in this context are not used to vilify "other religions" per se, but rather to mark the theological protest against imperial and conquest religion that in my reading is at the center of Paul's law criticism; the terms categorically apply to the religion of the Self before they apply to any "other religion."

34. See Sister Prudence Allen, *The Concept of Woman: The Aristotelian Revolution 750 BC–AD 150* (Grand Rapids: Eerdmans, 1985), 19–20.

35. In a next step the "light" is divided into cold (air) versus hot (fire), and the "heavy" into wet (water) versus dry (earth); see J. Louis Martyn, *Galatians: A New Translation with Introduction and Commentary,* Anchor Bible 33A (New York: Doubleday, 1998), 403–4.

36. See Algirdas Julien Greimas, *On Meaning: Selected Writings in Semiotic Theory,* Theory and History of Literature 38 (Minneapolis: University of Minnesota Press, 1987); for an application of Greimas's structural semiotics to biblical texts, see Daniel Patte, *The Religious Dimensions of Biblical Texts: Greimas's Structural Semiotics and Biblical Exegesis,* Semeia Studies 19 (Atlanta: Scholars Press, 1990). Neil Elliott in his recent book on Romans uses the Greimasian semiotic square in its adaptation through Fredric Jameson as a "cognitive map" of ideological critique, with particular emphasis on "ideological closure" and "ideological constraint" as reflected in Paul's theology; see Elliott, *Arrogance of Nations,* 54–56. My own use of structuralism as a reading tool goes back to formative encounters with the "deep structures" of Noam Chomsky's Generative Grammar, on the one hand, and with Fernando Belo's and Michel Clévenot's "Lecture matérialiste," on the other; see Brigitte Kahl, "Towards a Materialist-Feminist Reading," in *Searching the Scriptures,* vol. 1, *A Feminist Introduction,* ed. Elisabeth Schüssler Fiorenza (New York: Crossroad, 1994), 225–40. I am well aware of the criticism voiced by post-structuralist approaches with regard to binary thought structures. This is precisely the reason why I consider the semiotic square a most useful analytical tool; it not only helps map and disclose patterns of "ideological constraint" (Elliott) to which Paul and his time were subjected but also the "semiotic labor" of the messianic age in birthing a new, nonbinary creation; see below and chapter 6.

37. Greimas's original semiotic square would arrange the elements as follows:

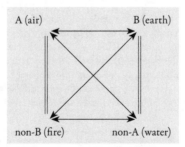

To install A == B as "top" complementarity instead, as I do, is a modification that has emerged over decades of working and experimenting with this pattern and in particular when I proceeded from the analysis of texts to the analysis of spaces and images; it reflects the hierarchical nature not only of the occidental binaries as such but also of space and spatial order. In my own basic semiotic square ONE/SELF is therefore linked to HIGH (and IN) and placed on the upper level, whereas OTHER is aligned to LOW (and OUT) and appears at the bottom. We will return to this in chapter 2 with regard to the spatial and mythological semiotics of the Great Altar, where Earth/Gaia is singled out as the representative of the Below and Out; see also Kahl, "Reading Galatians and Empire," 21–43. A most insightful use of this modified Greimasian pattern for analyzing the concept of the "nations" in Galatians, as well as the ancient imagery relevant for it, has been made by Lopez, *Apostle to the Conquered.*

38. See Boyarin, *Radical Jew,* 18.

39. See Ehrensperger, *That We May Be Mutually Encouraged.*

40. Aristotle *Politics* 1252a–1253b; for the Greek construct of the "barbarian," and most notably Celts as prototypical barbarians , see chapter 1 below.

41. "Paul takes for granted the widespread tradition in which pairs of opposites are themselves identified as 'elements of the cosmos.'" In Gal 3:28; 6:14-15; and 4:1-11, Martyn argues, he applies them to the "elements of religious distinction. These are the cosmic elements that have found their termination in Christ." Martyn, *Galatians,* 405–6; see also idem, "Apocalyptic Antinomies in Paul's Letter to the Galatians," *NTS* 31 (1985): 410–24.

42. Martyn, *Galatians,* 571.

43. Ibid, 560.

44. Even when referring to clearly socially constructed and relevant opposites like Jew/Greek, slave/free, male/female (Gal 3:28), Martyn tends to group them under the rubric of *religious* pairs of opposites, for example: "Citing an early baptismal tradition, Paul emphatically says that the cosmos, founded as it was on religious pairs of opposites, does not any longer exist" (*Galatians,* 570). As our cursory remarks on the tablet of opposites have shown, and as specifically the analysis of the Pergamene battle imagery will demonstrate, the religious, social, and political spheres are inseparably intertwined in the ancient construct of binaries. On the other hand, I believe that Martyn's consistent plea to understand Paul's apocalyptic theology as a radical challenge to "religion" in its established modes and divisions, is more than timely (see, e.g., ibid., 37). In this I draw, like Martyn , on the heritage of Ernst Käsemann, as well as on Dietrich Bonhoeffer's "Church for Others" (see n. 50 below).

45. Krister Stendahl, *Paul among Jews and Gentiles and Other Essays* (Philadelphia: Fortress Press, 1976), 12; see chapter 1.

46. See chapter 6. The juxtaposition of *eleutheria* (freedom) with *douleia* (slavery) runs through the whole letter.

47. In this point I disagree both with Elisabeth Schüssler Fiorenza (see n. 10 above) and Neil Elliott (*Arrogance of Nations,* 15).

48. Even Martyn at times imposes on Paul's discourse an exuberant rhetoric of war, a discourse that seems to be drawn more from the lexicon of the old cosmos than from that of the new creation; see for example Martyn, *Galatians,* 100–102.

49. Ibid., 571.

50. My use of the terms Self and Other is significantly shaped by formative impulses I received from Dietrich Bonhoeffer's prison letters that were very influential in the East German experience of church as "other." Bonhoeffer's sketchy notes on Jesus' "being for others" as true transcendence, on God in the image of the "human being for others" and therefore God crucified, and on "church for others" as the only valid expression of being church became elements of an informal creed in a situation where the church had (involuntarily) lost its affiliation with the dominant societal self and become marginalized within a rigorously atheist state. See Dietrich Bonhoeffer, *Letters and Papers from Prison* (New York: Macmillan, 1971), 380–83.

51. I am grateful to Elisabeth Schüssler Fiorenza that she has consistently challenged me in this most crucial point, where both our agreement and disagreement are condensed. See Schüssler Fiorenza, *Rhetoric and Ethic,* 163–65.

52. See Brigitte Kahl, "No Longer Male: Masculinity Struggles behind Galatians 3:28?" *JSNT* 79 (2000): 43–46.

53. It is noteworthy that in an existential situation close to Paul's, Bonhoeffer in his prison cell thought about a fundamental reconceptualization of religion from the perspective of the unreligious as the "Other" of religion, referring specifically to the circumcision issue in Galatians. See Bonhoeffer, *Letters and Papers,* 281, 329.

54. In a way somewhat reminiscent of Bonhoeffer, Emmanuel Levinas has rethought the idea of Self and of God through a radicalized concept of the Other. God is encountered in the alterity of the other person; the Other reconditions the I/Self as subjectivity-for-the-other that recognizes itself as murderous

and the Other as vulnerable. See Emmanuel Levinas, *Time and the Other* (Pittsburgh: Duquesne University Press, 1987), 17.

55. A strong pledge to restore Paul's letters to their original messianic context and adequate status as "fundamental messianic texts for the Western tradition," as well as the "oldest and most demanding messianic texts of the Jewish tradition" has been voiced by Giorgio Agamben, *The Time That Remains: A Commentary on the Letter to the Romans* (Stanford, Calif.: Stanford University Press, 2005), 1–3.

56. "Symptomatic reading" is a term coined by Louis Althusser and implies a mode of seeing that deciphers the "unseen" (*bévue*) in the "seen," or the unknown in the strongest evidences of the supposedly "known." It reads the fissures and gaps of a text as "symptoms" of a second, latent text; see Louis Althusser and Etienne Balibar, *Reading Capital* (London: Unwin Brothers Limited, Gresham, 1977), 28–33. See also Jan Rehmann, *Einführung in die Ideologietheorie* (Hamburg: Argument, 2008), 142.

57. The term "ideology" was introduced 1796 by Destutt de Tracy as a neologism analogous to "ontology." It is interesting that he explicitly referred to images (*eidos*) as the reality underlying ideas and ideology; see Rehmann, *Einführung*, 20–21. From a theological perspective, the concept of "idol," that is the idolatrous *eidos* (shape, form), adds another critical dimension to the analysis of ideology in light of images.

1. Remapping Galatia

1. Piotr Bienkowski's two standard reference works from 1908 and 1928 on the representations of the Celts/Gauls in Greco-Roman art still serve as an excellent guide to the dramatically violent world of ancient Galatian imagery: *Die Darstellungen der Gallier in der hellenistischen Kunst* (Vienna: A. Hölder, 1908); and *Les Celtes dans les arts mineurs gréco-romains, avec des recherches iconographiques sur quelques autres peuples barbares* (Krakow: Université des Jagellons, 1928); see also Bernard Andreae, "The Image of the Celts in Etruscan, Greek and Roman Art," in *The Celts*, ed. Sabatino Moscati et al. (Venice: Bompiani, 1991), 61–69; Ursula Höckmann, "Gallierdarstellungen in der Etruskischen Grabkunst des 2. Jahrhunderts vor Christus," *Jahrbuch des Deutschen Archäologischen Instituts* 106 (1991): 199–230. As Höckmann shows (p. 223), in particular the motif of a victorious Roman horseman and a fallen dying or dead Gaul that Nero encountered in 68 c.e. was widespread already in third- and second-century Etruscan funerary art in Italy that strongly reflected Roman perspectives.

2. On Large and Small Gauls, see R. R. R. Smith, *Hellenistic Sculpture: A Handbook* (London: Thames & Hudson, 1991), 99–104.

3. David L. Balch, "Paul's Portrait of Christ Crucified (Gal 3:1) in Light of Paintings of Suffering and Death in Pompeiian Houses," in *Early Christian Families in Context: An Interdisciplinary Dialogue*, ed. David L. Balch and Carolyn Osiek (Grand Rapids: Eerdmans, 2003), 105.

4. Philip R. Hardie, *Virgil's Aeneid: Cosmos and Imperium* (Oxford: Clarendon, 1986), 142 n. 56.

5. Balch, "Paul's Portrait of Christ Crucified," 100; see Epilogue.

6. A survey of the previous research on the North and South Galatian hypothesis is given by James M. Scott, *Paul and the Nations: The Old Testament and Jewish Background of Paul's Mission to the Nations with Special Reference to the Destination of Galatians*, WUNT 84 (Tübingen: Mohr Siebeck, 1995), 187–201; for a brief introduction by two of the most prominent commentators see also Hans Dieter Betz, *Galatians: A Commentary on Paul's Letter to the Churches in Galatia*, Hermeneia (Philadelphia: Fortress Press, 1979), 3–5; and J. Louis Martyn, *Galatians: A New Translation with Introduction and Commentary*, AB 33A (New York: Doubleday, 1998), 15–16, both in favor of a North Galatian location.

7. As Paul's letter presupposes interaction with Jewish representatives, a North Galatian location may be challenged by the fact that no significant epigraphic or other traces of Jewish settlements have been found in the North, nor evidence of any significant pre-Constantinian Christianization; see Cilliers Breytenbach, *Paulus und Barnabas in der Provinz Galatien: Studien zu Apostelgeschichte 13f.; 16,6; 18,23 und den Adressaten des Galaterbriefes* (Leiden/New York: E. J. Brill, 1996), 147. Breytenbach presents a

modified version of the provincial hypothesis, assuming that both the northern territory and the southern part of the Roman province of Galatia were ethnically mixed and that particularly after the last Galatian king, Amyntas, had established his power in the South, Galatians lived there next to Greeks, hellenized Phrygians, Isaurians, Pisidians, Lycaonians, Italian settlers, and Roman colonists (p. 159). Ethnically Galatian inhabitants of Antioch, Iconium, Derbe, and Lystra thus could have been the people addressed by Paul as "Galatians" in Gal 1:2 and 3:1.

8. For an extensive philological and topological analysis, see Breytenbach, *Paulus und Barnabas,* 113–19.

9. Susan M. Elliott's book on the linkage between a pro-circumcision attitude among the Galatians and the castration of the Galli-priests and eunuchs in the popular cult of the Anatolian mother goddess Cybele represents a refreshingly new approach that draws attention to the "real-life" context of Paul's Galatians and their circumcision debates as part of popular religiosity. Not surprisingly, Elliott drops the question of north and south altogether and remaps Galatians "somewhere in west central Anatolia," without, however, further exploring the Roman contextuality of this location. Susan M. (Elli) Elliot, *Cutting Too Close for Comfort: Paul's Letter to the Galatians in Its Anatolian Cultic Context,* JSNTSup 248 (London/New York: T&T Clark, 2004), 11; and eadem, "Choose Your Mother, Choose Your Master: Galatians 4:21–5:1 in the Shadow of the Anatolian Mother of the Gods," *Journal of Biblical Literature* 118, no. 4 (1999): 661–83.

10. Robin Scroggs writes, "To some it has seemed that too often the discipline of the theology of the New Testament (the history of *ideas*) operates out of a methodological docetism, as if believers had minds and spirits unconnected with their individual and corporate bodies. Interest in the sociology of early Christianity is no attempt to limit reductionistically the reality of Christianity to social dynamic; rather it should be seen as an effort to guard against reductionism from the other extreme, a limitation of the reality of Christinity to an inner-spiritual, or objective-cognitive system. In short, sociology of early Christianity wants to put body and soul together again." Robin Scroggs, "The Sociological Interpretation of the New Testament: The Present State of Research," *NTS* 26 (1980): 165, cf. 179.

For social-scientific investigations that have recently focused on various aspects of socio-anthropological reality in Galatia(ns), see, for example,John H. Elliott, "Paul, Galatians, and the Evil Eye," *Currents in Theology and Mission* 17 (1990): 262–71; Susan Eastman, "The Evil Eye and the Curse of the Law: Galatians 3:1 Revisited," *JSNT* 83 (2001): 69–87; Clinton E. Arnold, "I Am Astonished That You Are So Quickly Turning Away! (Gal 1:6): Paul and the Anatolian Folk Belief," *NTS* 51 (2005): 429–49; Atsuhiro Asano, *Community-Identity Construction in Galatians: Exegetical, Social-Anthropological and Socio-Historical Studies,* JSNTSup 285 (London/New York: T&T Clark, 2005); for a comprehensive sociological commentary on Galatians, see Philip F. Esler, *Galatians,* New Testament Readings (London/New York: Routledge, 1998).

11. I have addressed the complexities of reading Acts, which shows a pro-Roman and anti-Jewish Paul on the surface but which, upon a deeper reading, serves to deconstruct just that pro-imperial thematic, in "Acts of the Apostles: Pro(to)-Imperial Script and Hidden Transcript," in *In the Shadow of Empire: Reclaiming the Bible as a History of Faithful Resistance,* ed. Richard A. Horsley (Louisville: Westminster John Knox, 2008), 137–56.

12. William M. Ramsay, *A Historical Commentary on St. Paul's Epistle to the Galatians* (London: Hodder & Stoughton, 1899); see also the extensive work on Asia Minor in idem, *The Church in the Roman Empire before A.D. 170,* Mansfield College Lectures 1892 (London: Hodder & Stoughton, 1893); idem, *St. Paul the Traveller and the Roman Citizen* (London: Hodder & Stoughton, 1896); and the posthumously published *The Social Basis of Roman Power in Asia Minor,* prepared for the press by J. G. C. Andersen (Aberdeen: Aberdeen University Press, 1941).

13. Ramsay, *Historical Commentary,* 320–21.

14. Ibid., 322.

15. Ibid., 195–96, emphasis mine. Because of their "western" origin, Ramsay saw the ethnic Galatians/Celts in a relatively positive light. "It has never proved easy to eliminate the national genius of

a Celtic race; and the Celtic element in North Galatia, though numerically inferior,was immeasurably superior in practical strength to the older Phrygian element" (ibid., 129). To what extent this evaluation reflects Ramsay's own Scottish background or—a question raised by Neil Elliott—*contemporary* political references to Turks not welcoming "Western barbarian" influence (but welcoming the British), would need further exploration.

16. Edward Said, *Orientalism* (New York: Vintage Books, 1978). For Ramsay, the truly Occidental religion—that is, non-Judaistic and non-Oriental—that Paul was offering to the Province of Galatia was also the future religion of the Roman Empire as a whole, although the empire at this point still failed to recognize that religion's potential for unifying the diverse nations it had conquered. Ramsay, *Church in the Roman Empire before A.D. 170,* 190–93.

17. For an introduction to postcolonial biblical criticism, see R. S. Sugirtharajah, *Postcolonial Criticism and Biblical Interpretation* (New York: Oxford University Press, 2002); Musa W. Dube, *Postcolonial Feminist Interpretation of the Bible* (St. Louis: Chalice Press, 2000); Fernando F. Segovia, *Decolonizing Biblical Studies: A View from the Margins* (Maryknoll, N.Y.: Orbis Books, 2000); Stephen D. Moore and Fernando F. Segovia, eds., *Postcolonial Biblical Criticism: Interdisciplinary Intersection,* Bible and Postcolonialism (New York: Continuum, 2005); a collection of key authors in the general area of postcolonial studies is conveniently accessible in Patrick Williams and Laura Chrisman, eds., *Colonial Discourse and Post-Colonial Theory: A Reader* (New York: Columbia University Press, 1994).

18. See n. 16 above.

19. Ramsay, *Historical Commentary,* 478.

20. Krister Stendahl, *Paul among Jews and Gentiles and Other Essays* (Philadelphia: Fortress Press, 1976), 5. Stendahl fundamentally criticizes the "spiritualizations of Pauline theology" that lost "Paul's primary focus on Jews and Gentiles" (rather than Jews versus Christians) and portrayed the Jews "as God-killers and as stereotypes for wrong attitudes toward God." Thus "Justification no longer 'justified' the status of Gentile Christians as honorary Jews, but became the timeless answer to the plights and pains of the introspective conscience of the West" (ibid.). It might be worth mentioning that the term "honorary Jews" echoes ancient perceptions of Romans as "honorary Greeks"; see Kathryn Lomas, "Greeks, Romans, and Others: Problems of Colonialism and Ethnicity in Southern Italy," in *Roman Imperialism: Post-Colonial Perspectives*, ed. Jane Webster and Nicholas J. Cooper (Leicester: School of Archaeological Studies, University of Leicester, 1996), 135–44, esp. 136.

21. Stendahl, *Paul among Jews,* 14. Based on Phil 3:6, Stendahl sees the pre-Damascus Paul as a "very happy and successful Jew" who experiences "no troubles, no problems, no qualms of conscience, no feelings of shortcomings. He is a star pupil, the student to get the thousand dollar graduate scholarship in Gamaliel's Seminary" (ibid., 12–13).

22. Ibid., 16–17 and 78–96. For Stendahl the "introspective conscience," with its thrust on "self-examination" and the "innermost individual soul" where "man became more and more clever in analyzing his ego," is a "Western development and a Western plague" that developed in the Middle Ages. Paul himself, however, "was never involved in this pursuit" (ibid., 16–17).

23. Coming from a Lutheran background myself, this interpretation of Luther's scriptural principle (*sola scriptura*) in terms of a church that needs constant reformation—Luther's famous *ecclesia semper reformanda*—to me has emerged as one of the most valuable assets of Lutheran tradition for scriptural hermeneutics. See Brigitte Kahl, *Armenevangelium und Heidenevangelium: "Sola scriptura" und die ökumenische Traditionsproblematik im Lichte von Väterkonflikt und Väterkonsens bei Lukas* (Berlin: Evangelische Verlagsanstalt, 1987); eadem, "Reading Luke against Luke: Non-Uniformity of Text, Hermeneutics of Conspiracy and the 'Scriptural Principle' in Luke 1," in *A Feminist Companion to Luke,* ed. Amy-Jill Levine (London: Sheffield Academic, 2002), 70–88.

24. "And, furthermore, it is obvious that Paul remains a Jew as he fulfills his role as an Apostle to the Gentiles. . . . The 'I' in his wiritngs is not 'the Christian' but the 'apostle to the Gentiles'" (Stendahl, *Paul among Jews,* 12). The doctrine of justification by faith "was hammered out by Paul for the very specific and limited purpose of defending the rights of Gentile converts to be full and genuine heirs to the promises of God to Israel. Their rights were based solely on faith in Jesus Christ" (ibid., 2).

25. E. P. Sanders, *Paul and Palestinian Judaism: A Comparison of Patterns of Religion* (Philadelphia: Fortress Press, 1977).

26. For a brief introduction to the New Perspective see Kathy Ehrensperger, *That We May Be Mutually Encouraged: Feminism and the New Perspective in Pauline Studies* (New York/London: T&T Clark International, 2004), 27–39; and Daniel Boyarin, *A Radical Jew: Paul and the Politics of Identity* (Berkeley: University of California Press, 1994), 39–56. More comprehensive is James D. G. Dunn, *The New Perspective on Paul: Collected Essays,* WUNT 185 (Tübingen: Mohr Siebeck, 2005).

27. Sanders, *Paul and Palestinian Judaism,* 75.

28. Rosemary Radford Ruether's seminal work on the theological roots of anti-Semitism appeared in 1974: *Faith and Fratricide: The Theological Roots of Anti-Semitism* (New York: Seabury Press, 1974). Ruether argued that the foundations of anti-Semitism are embedded within Christian Scriptures and named anti-Judaism as the "left hand" of Christology from the very beginnings of Christianity. See also Ruether, *To Change the World: Christology and Cultural Criticism* (New York: Crossroad, 1981), 31; on the topic of Christian anti-Judaism, see also Mary C. Boys, *Has God Only One Blessing? Judaism as a Source of Christian Self-Understanding* (New York: Paulist, 2000).

29. Lloyd Gaston, "Israel's Enemies in Pauline Theology," *NTS* 28 (1982): 400–423; John Gager, *The Origins of Anti-Semitism: Attitudes towards Judaism in Pagan and Christian Antiquity* (New York: Oxford University Press, 1983), 207.

30. As Dunn states, "Paul's own teaching on justification focuses largely if not principally on the need to overcome the barrier which the law was seen to interpose between Jew and Gentile." Paul thus targets the law as a "boundary-marking ritual" and "source of ethnic pride for the typical devout Jew . . . ; and circumcision as the focal point for this sense of privileged distinctiveness." Dunn, *New Perspective on Paul,* 15, 140.

31. Sanders, *Paul and Palestinian Judaism,* 552. Paul's "criticism of his own former life is not that he was guilty of the attitudinal sin of self-righteousness, but that he put confidence in something other than faith in Jesus Christ." E. P. Sanders, *Paul, the Law and the Jewish People* (Minneapolis: Fortress Press, 1983), 44.

32. For a discussion of the argument see Boyarin, *Radical Jew,* 52, who for himself accepts Paul's anti-ethnocentrism (Dunn's position) as a legitimate version of Jewish cultural criticism directed toward human solidarity, at the same time pointing to its pervasive anti-Judaistic/racist/colonizing potential in terms of a "coercive universalism" that suppresses difference in a "coercive sameness" (ibid., 235–36).

33. Scott, *Paul and the Nations,* 155.

34. Ibid., 203.

35. A standard introduction to these issues is Claude Nicolet, *Space, Geography, and Politics in the Early Roman Empire,* Jerome Lectures, 19th Series (Ann Arbor: University of Michigan Press, 1991). Nicolet is quoted by Scott (*Paul and the Nations,* 103), but not employed in his ideological-critical thrust. The hermeneutical relevance of this new approach toward mapped space and political geography in the context of Roman world rule for Pauline studies is just being discovered; see, for example, Davina C. Lopez, *Apostle to the Conquered: Reimagining Paul's Mission,* Paul in Critical Contexts (Minneapolis: Fortress Press, 2008).

36. As a result of his investigation, Scott simply restates the South Galatian hypothesis (*Paul and the Nations,* 215, 218).

37. As Hall states, the oppositions of "civilization against primitivism, order against chaos, observance of law and taboo against transgression" are not only basic to the definition of barbarians as "anti-Greeks," but they also "lie at the heart of the archaic thought world, for the struggle to conceptualize the nature of civilization is as old as civilization itself." Edith Hall, *Inventing the Barbarian: Greek Self-Definition through Tragedy,* Oxford Classical Monographs (Oxford: Oxford University Press, 1989), 51; see also 50–54, 187.

38. For Galatian lawlessness, see also, for example, Polybius, *Hist.* 3.3.5; 21.40.1; *Anth. Gr.* 7.492; *Sib. Or.* 3.599–600.

39. Another example of such a lost work is the seven books of a *Galatika* by Erastothenes of Cyrene

the younger, dating from the second or first century B.C.E.; see *FGH* 745; for a convenient general introduction into ancient sources about Galatians/Gauls/Celts, see Gerhard Dobesch, "Ancient Literary Sources," in *The Celts,* ed. Sabatino Moscati et al. (Venice: Bompiani, 1991), 35–41.

40. Karl Strobel, *Die Galater: Geschichte und Eigenart der keltischen Staatenbildung auf dem Boden des hellenistischen Kleinasien,* Untersuchungen zur Geschichte und historischen Geographie des hellenistischen und römischen Kleinasien 1 (Berlin: Akademie, 1996–), 18–21.

41. Felix Stähelin, *Geschichte der kleinasiatischen Galater* (Leipzig: Teubner, 1907; repr. Osnabrück: Zeller, 1973).

42. Even a foundational study like Stephen Mitchell's standard two volumes on the Galatians in Asia Minor may reflect this: " The history of the Gauls for a century and a half after the invasion of Asia Minor is not an inspiring one . . . ; the Galatians lived on the margin of civilized life, plundering temples, sacking cities, and inspiring fear, well-merited, among the defenceless population of the Asian countryside. The damage they caused far outweighed the contribution they provided: an unceasing supply of mercenary soldiers; and a series of assassins responsible for the murder of several Hellenistic kings." (*Anatolia: Land, Men, and Gods in Asia Minor,* 2 vols. [Oxford: Clarendon Press, 1993], 1:42). For a critique, see Strobel, *Galater,* 31–32.

43. Strobel, *Galater,* 27–32.

44. Rodney S. Young, *Gordion: A Guide to the Excavations and Museum* (Ankara: Ankara Turizmi, 1968).

45. Mitchell, *Anatolia,* 1:vi.

46. See n. 16 above.

47. Postcolonial studies in the broadest sense aim at deconstructing Eurocentric categories of knowledge, in particular the "knowledge" about the colonial Other and the ways it was produced. Postcolonial studies analyze and critique the binary models of the West—self versus other, metropolis versus colony, center versus periphery—as discursive forms of occidental self-definition and self-justification, focusing in particular on the interrelation between power and knowledge in the representation/production of the colonial Other. Although modern Western and ancient Roman imperialism/colonialism are not the same, the perceptions of the Galatian/Celtic Other throughout history are profoundly embedded into both Roman and Western conceptualizations of the dominant imperial/colonial Self. The empire-critical deconstruction of prevalent theological discourses on Paul's Galatian letter offered in this study, therefore, are part of the postcolonial endeavor, and vice versa. For a most helpful introduction to the impact of postcolonial theory on the study of the Roman Empire, see Jane Webster, "Roman Imperialism and the 'Post Imperial Age,'" in *Roman Imperialism: Post-Colonial Perspectives,* ed. Jane Webster and Nicholas J. Cooper (Leicester: School of Archeological Studies, University of Leicester, 1996).

48. Without explicitly using the label *postcolonial,* Strobel clearly locates his work "after the end of the era of colonialism" and at a time when Europe is confronted with large-scale immigration from non-European cultures without being able to resume the old Eurocentric pattern of white Western-occidental superiority (*Die Galater,* 23); see further below.

49. Sabatino Moscati et al., eds., *The Celts* (Venice: Bompiani , 1991).

50. For the overall issue of ancient non-Greek and non-Roman ethnicities as topic of a dominant "discourse of the conqueror," the stereotypes shaping it, and the problem of European scholarship since the Renaissance treating Greek and Roman accounts as essentially "objective" information about these people, see Peter S. Wells, *The Barbarians Speak: How the Conquered Peoples Shaped Roman Europe* (Princeton: Princeton University Press, 1999), 99–106.

51. Hall, *Inventing the Barbarian,* 5–6. According to Hall, the new "discourse of barbarism" constitutes a "complex system of signifiers denoting the ethnically, psychologically, and politically 'other': terms, themes, actions, images. Many of these were to be of lasting influence on western views of foreign cultures, especially the portrait of Asiaitic peoples as effeminate, despotic, and cruel" (p. 2).

52. Maud W. Gleason, *Making Men: Sophists and Self-Presentation in Ancient Rome* (Princeton: Princeton University Press, 1995); also H. D. Rankin, *Celts and the Classical World* (London: Croom Helm, 1987), 53.

53. Hall, *Inventing the Barbarian*, 121.

54. Aristotle in his *Nicomachean Ethics* discusses fear and courage, naming the Celts as examples of extreme rashness: "Anybody would be mad or completely bereft of sensibility if he feared nothing; neither earthquake nor wave of sea, as they say of the Celts" (*Eth. Nic.* 3.5b.28); Celts (along with Scythians, Persians, Iberians, Thracians, Carthaginians) as hard drinking and warlike are mentioned in Plato, *Laws* 637d. For a discussion of fourth-century B.C.E. sources on the Celts, see Rankin, *Celts and the Classical World*, 45–48.

55. James C. Scott, *Domination and the Arts of Resistance: Hidden Transcripts* (New Haven: Yale University Press, 1990), xii–xiii.

56. This consideration goes far beyond the question that has been traditionally asked with regard to Gal 3:1 as potential trace of anti-barbarian/anti-Galatian polemics. Whether Paul uses, maybe ironically or sarcastically, an element of colonial discourse when he scolds his addressees as "you stupid [*anoētoi*] Galatians" can be answered in a meaningful way only after stating that he communicates with the Galatians as a member of another vanquished nation, not as representative of the colonizing self. On "hidden transcripts" in Galatians, see further chapter 6.

57. The history of Galatia in Asia minor is told in Strabo 12.4.5. Strabo here uses the term *Galatia* and mentions only briefly that it may also be called *Gallo-Graecia*, again using a Latin loanword. He also points out the linkage between the Galatian tribe of the Tectosages in Asia Minor and in Europe, which he had already explained with much detail at the beginning of his report on Transalpine Gaul in 4.1.13. There Strabo told how a part of this tribe, in his time living in the Pyrenees, together with other tribes migrated to Asia Minor and that the Tectosages also took part in the attack on Delphi. For the two other Galatian tribes of Asia Minor, the Trocmi and Tolistobogii, Strabo is unable to give the precise place of origin in Transalpine Gaul, but makes sure to state that "the fact of their racial kinship with the Tectosages indicates that they emigrated from Celtica." That means that Strabo's excursus on the European Gauls/Galatians in book 4 is, in a way, inclusive of the Gauls/Galatians in Asia Minor from the outset.

58. The problems linked to these terminological issues are substantial, as the collective terms Gauls/Galatians/Celts, as well as Germans, might be more of a Roman construct than a rendering of how the different tribes perceived themselves; see Maureen Carroll, *Romans, Celts & Germans* (Stroud: Tempus, 2001). For Caesar's division between Germans and Gauls and its power aspects in terms of a "divide and rule," see, for example, *Bell. Gall.* 1.31, where Rome claims to protect Rome-friendly Gauls from an overpowering Germanic threat, thus justifying military intervention.

59. For a concise historical introduction that gives an overall view of the Celts in Italy, Greece, and Asia Minor, see Rankin, *Celts and the Classical World*; the standard reference works on Asia Minor are Mitchell, *Anatolia;* and David Magie, *Roman Rule in Asia Minor to the End of the Third Century after Christ,* 2 vols. (Princeton: Princeton University Press, 1950); see also the earlier works by W. M. Ramsay (n. 12 above).

60. Rankin, *Celts and the Classical World,* 114.

61. Other explanations are that the Etruscans already had an established ritual of sacrificing Greeks and Gauls together which had to be left intact; or even that "Gallus et Galla, Graecus et Graeca" need to be read as "Gallograecus and Gallograeca." For more extensive discussion, see Heinz Bellen, *Metus Gallicus, Metus Punicus: Zum Furchtmotiv in der römischen Republik,* Abhandlungen der Geistes- und Sozialwissenschaftlichen Klasse 3 (Mainz: Akademie der Wissenschaften und der Literatur, 1985), 13–14.

62. Emma Dench, *Romulus' Asylum: Roman Identities from the Age of Alexander to the Age of Hadrian* (Oxford: Oxford University Press, 2005), 276.

63. " . . . das Gallierpaar (,) vertrat den Gegner in seiner Gesamtheit. Die Überantwortung dieser Repräsentanten an die Unterwelt und ihr Tod dortselbst sollten dem gegnerischen Volk, den Galliern, das gleiche Schicksal bereiten" (Bellen, *Metus Gallicus, Metus Punicus,* 15).

64. Bellen, *Metus Gallicus, Metus Punicus,* 21 n. 76.

65. Mary Beard, John North, and Simon Price, *Religions of Rome* (Cambridge: Cambridge University Press, 1998), 1:80–82. Another most fascinating detail about the religious development at the time

of the Second Punic War is the transferral, at the suggestion of the Sibylline books, of the cult of the Magna Mater Cybele from Asia Minor to Rome in 204 B.C.E., and the erection of a temple for her on the Palatine; for discussion, see ibid., 1:96–98 and chapter 2, p. 120 below. This development is noteworthy not only because of Pergamon's assistance but also because the major sanctuary of Cybele was located at Pessinus, that is, in Galatian territory in Asia Minor.

66. Bellen, *Metus Gallicus, Metus Punicus*, 8, 44–45. Whether this supports the assumption that the nature of Roman imperialism was basically "defensive," as Bellen states (45 n. 185; see also 8), is another matter. On this question, see William V. Harris, *War and Imperialism in Republican Rome, 327–70 B.C.* (New York: Oxford University Press, 1979); and Wells, *Barbarians Speak*, 74–75.

67. Strobel, *Die Galater,* 19: "Die Niederlage an der Allia, die einzige Einnahme Roms durch ein fremdes Heer und die Kette der militärischen Auseinandersetzungen zwischen Römern und Galliern, die sich über die ausserordentlich lange Zeitspanne von 387 bis 50 erstreckt, liessen die Kelten zu 'Angst-gegnern' Roms schlechthin werden … und man entfaltete für sie ein krasses Feind-und Schreckbild, wie es die Römer für kein anderes Volk entworfen hatten." Similarly Rankin: "The impact of frequent Celtic invasions was a powerful factor in the formation of the attitude with which the Romans apprehended real or imagined menace from foreign peoples" (*Celts and the Classical World*, 103); see also Jean-Luc Des-nier, "Le Gaulois dans l'Imaginaire Monétaire de la République Romaine. Images plurielles d'une réalité singulière," *MEFRA* 103 (1991): 605–54. The image of the Celts in its political context as represented by Livy, Cicero, Caesar, Diodorus, Strabo, and Dionysius of Halicarnassus has been thoroughly explored by Bernhard Kremer, *Das Bild der Kelten bis in augusteische Zeit: Studien zur Instrumentalisierung eines antiken Feindbildes bei griechischen und römischen Autoren,* Historia Einzelschriften (Stuttgart: Franz Steiner, 1994).

68. Cicero (*Phil.* 8.3) derives the term *tumultus* from *timor multus* ("great fear"); Bellen points out that tumultus means an acute state of emergency, a sudden outbreak of a war that threatens Rome and thus creates great fear (*timor multus* or *metus*), thereby justifying extraordinary military measures (*Metus Gallicus, Metus Punicus*, 10–11). Sallust (*Hist.* 1 frg. 11) sees the fear of Carthage as precondi-tion for Roman achievement; when Carthage was destroyed, Rome fell into decadence; see also, Bellen, 1–5.

69. Diodorus 5.32.3–6; Plutarch, *Mar.* 11. See also Strobel, *Die Galater,* 20–21; and Bellen, *Metus Gallicus, Metus Punicus*, 37–40. About the construct of the northern barbarian in ethnography see Christine Trzaska-Richter, *Furor teutonicus: Das Römische Germanenbild in Politik und Propaganda von den Anfängen bis zum 2. Jahrhundert n. Chr.,* Bochumer Altertumswissenschaftliches Colloquium 8 (Trier: Wissenschftlicher, 1991), 25–35, also 48–52; and Rankin, *Celts and the Classical World,* 56.

70. Trzaska-Richter, *Furor teutonicus*, 62.

71. Richard Miles, "Rivalling Rome: Carthage," in *Rome the Cosmopolis*, ed. Catharine Edwards and Greg Woolf (Cambridge: Cambridge University Press, 2003), 123–46, here 129.

72. See Miklos Szabo, "The Celts and Their Movements in the Third Century B.C," in *The Celts,* ed. Sabatino Moscati et al. (Venice: Bompiani, 1991), 303–13.

73. See the considerations about Galatian fearlessness and "hidden transcripts" in Galatian speech in this chapter above.

74. However, they obviously had enough diplomatic shrewdness to appear in Babylon together with other nations in 323 B.C.E. to honor the godlike power and worldwide achievement of the returning conqueror-king. See Rankin, *Celts and the Classical World,* 85.

75. Mitchell, *Anatolia,* 1:14.

76. Rankin (*Celts and the Classical World,* 88) states that he became the "first arguably Greek leader to die at the hands of the Celts."

77. For an in-depth investigation, see Georges Nachtergael, *Les Galates en Grèce et les Sôtéria de Del-phes: recherches d'histoire et d'épigraphie hellénistiques,* Mémoires de la Classe des lettres (Brussels: Palais des Académies, 1977).

78. Rankin, *Celts and the Classical World*, 88.

79. Ibid., 99.

80. According to Rankin the Celtic attack and Brennus in particular posed "a genuine menace to the survival of Greek civilization in the peninsula of Greece" (*Celts and the Classical World,* 101).

81. See Karl Strobel, "Keltensieg und Galatersieger: Die Funktionalisierung eines historischen Phänomens als politischer Mythos der hellenistischen Welt," in *Forschungen in Galatien,* ed. Elmar Schwertheim, Asia Minor Studien 12 (Bonn: Rudolf Habelt, 1994), 97–103, 77 nn. 69–70.

82. See, for example, Pausanias 10.22.12 and Herodotus 8.35–36 for the motif of Apollo himself taking over Delphi's defense against the Celts under Brennus and the Persians under Xerxes, respectively. See Rankin, *Celts and the Classical World,* 94.

83. Strobel, "Keltensieg," 69.

84. Ibid., 72, 83.

85. Callimachus, *Hymn to Delos* 4.171–88; see Rankin, *Celts and the Classical World,* 98, for the poem's text; and Strobel, "Keltensieg," 78–79, for discussion.

86. Strobel, *Die Galater,* 236–38.

87. Ibid., 44.

88. Strobel, "Keltensieg," 73–74.

89. Mitchell, *Anatolia,* 1:15.

90. Ibid., 16–25.

91. "Conquerors' accounts . . . are notoriously biased. But if we can understand, and deconstruct, the biases, then we can make fruitful use of the texts. Texts are cultural constructs, and we need to treat them as such. To make sense of the Roman and Greek accounts, we must determine which of the assertions constitute stereotypes or tropes, then separate those and focus on the significant details left." Wells, *Barbarians Speak,* 99–100.

92. Strobel, "Keltensieg," 74.

93. The date of the battle at the Caicus sources is much debated and sometimes also given as 230 B.C.E.; see Magie, *Roman Rule,* 2:735.

94. See ibid., 1:7. As Magie states about Attalus I: "Like Antioch I after his victory over the Celts, he was hailed as 'Saviour.' This title meant even more than the assumption of formal sovereignty, for it signified that he had become the champion of Hellenism against barbarism." It is noteworthy that Attalus's successor, Eumenes II, similarly acquired the title Savior in 184 after another victory won over the Galatians.

95. See Smith, *Hellenistic Sculpture,* 99–104.

96. Strobel ("Keltensieg," 81) lists archaic war rituals, the manner of fighting, head hunting, and sacrifice of prisoners as particularly abhorrent.

97. On hybridity and resistance in the assimilation of Celtic to Roman religion in Britain, and especially the role of Druidism, see Jane Webster, "A Negotiated Syncretism: Readings on the Development of Romano-Celtic Religion," in *Dialogues in Roman Imperialism: Power, Discourse, and Discrepant Experience in the Roman Empire,* ed. D. J. Mattingly, Journal of Roman Archaeology Supplement Series 23 (Portsmouth, R.I.: Journal of Roman Archaeology, 1997), 165–84.

98. On Gallic human sacrifice with regard to its archeological evidence and ideological valency within a colonial discourse, see Jane Webster, "The Just War: Graeco-Roman Texts as Colonial Discourse," in *TRAC 94: Proceedings of the 4th Annual Theoretical Roman Archaeology Conference,* ed. Sally Cottam et al. (Durham: University of Durham, 1994), 1–10.

99. According to Strobel (*Die Galater,* 139), up to the sixth century C.E. Strabo (12.5.1) mentions that the three tribes spoke the same language; Jerome in his commentary on Galatians in the fourth century (preface to book 2) states that the Galatians speak Greek but that "their own language is almost identical with that of the Treviri" in the West. See Strobel, *Die Galater,* 140–42.

100. Jane Webster, "Ethnographic Barbarity: Colonial Discourse and the 'Celtic Warrior Societies,'" in *Roman Imperialism: Post-Colonial Perspectives,* ed. Jane Webster and Nicholas J. Cooper (Leicester: School of Archaeological Studies, University of Leicester, 1996), 111–23, here 117.

101. Ibid., 120.

102. Bellen, *Metus Gallicus, Metus Punicus,* 18–19; Strobel, "Keltensieg," 77–78.

103. For the spatial ubiquity of the Gauls/Galatians, see John R. Marszal, "Ubiquitous Barbarians:

Representation of the Gauls at Pergamon and Elsewhere," in *From Pergamon to Sperlonga: Sculpture and Context*, ed. Nancy T. de Grummond and Brunilde S. Ridgway, Hellenistic Culture and Society (Berkeley: University of California Press, 2000), 191–234.

104. For an overall account of the historical events in second-century Asia Minor and a more comprehensive report on the ancient sources, see Magie, *Roman Rule*, 1:16–33; Mitchell, *Anatolia*, 1:23–26; Peter Berresford Ellis, *Celt and Greek: Celts in the Hellenic World* (London: Constable, 1997), 142–84.

105. Marszal, "Ubiquitous Barbarians," 202.

106. Mitchell sees Manlius's march as "a bold and successful attempt to impress cis-Tauric Asia with the seriousness of Roman intentions" and "to rid the cities of Asia of an ever-present threat," while admitting "that there was much to be deplored in the conduct of Manlius and his troops" (*Anatolia*, 1:23). In a similar vein Magie states: "It was probably necessary to show the turbulent tribesmen that the Romans were now masters of Asia Minor, but Manlius's methods resembled those practiced by the Galatians themselves too closely to be worthy of Rome. After defeating them in two battles, he plundered their country cruelly, and his army returned laden with booty" (*Roman Rule*, 1:21).

107. See Mitchell, *Anatolia*, 1:25–26. It has been speculated that some of these ambiguities in Pergamene–Roman relations might be reflected in the representation of the Great Altar that probably was created around this time; see chapter 2 below.

108. Rankin believes that the Romans used the Galatians deliberately to counterbalance Pergamene influence and therefore were not interested in hellenizing them, as this would potentially have strengthened Pergamon. "Rome's manoeuvres in this episode are not untypical of an intrusive power anxious to secure its own interests by manipulating local sources of instability. For these purposes, the Galatians were ideal material and convenient instruments." Rankin, *Celts and the Classical World*, 99. "The Romans found the alien character of the Galatians in relation to the rest of Asia Minor potentially advantageous to themselves" (ibid., 201). Mitchell, on the other hand, is more reluctant to see the agreement of 165 as a "tacit support for the Galatians and a negation of Eumenes' effort in the recent fighting." He admits, however, that the Roman desire to maintain the status quo of 188 (that is, the peace of Apamea) is "tempered by a certain mistrust of Eumenes" (*Anatolia*, 1:26).

109. Rankin, *Celts and the Classical World*, 118.

110. *Bell. Gall.* 1.29. For a description of the Helvetian and other campaigns of the Gallic War, see Adrian Goldsworthy, *In the Name of Rome: The Men Who Won the Roman Empire* (London: Weidenfeld & Nicolson, 2003), 181–212.

111. For an ideological-critical reading of the *Gallic War*, see Andrew M. Riggsby, *Caesar in Gaul and Rome: War in Words* (Austin: University of Texas Press, 2006).

112. Goldsworthy, *In the Name of Rome*, 212. As Jane Webster notes, Caesar's *Gallic War*, "perhaps the most influential Classical account of the Celts of Gaul," portrays the downfall of the Helvetians and other tribes as a result of perpetual interfactional conflict and intertribal fights among the Celts. According to Caesar, thus "innate Gallic aggression (rather than Roman territorial aggression) was the key causational factor in Roman intervention." Webster, "Ethnographic Barbarity," 118–19.

113. For the events, see Goldsworthy, *In the Name of Rome*, 213–30.

114. Rankin, *Celts in the Classical World*, 124.

115. As Webster states ("Ethnographic Barbarity," 117), Livy's account "was compiled at some point between c 36 BC–AD 4 (ie, in the aftermath of the annexation of non-Mediterranean Gaul)." Its description of the early Roman–Celtic contacts reflects the later colonial context.

116. It should be noted, however, that Vulso's great ancestor Marcus Manlius later was executed for stirring up the plebs of Rome and aspiring to kingship (*ad regni crimen*), which is probably the first case of a Gallic victory being used to substantiate imperial claims (Livy 6.18–20).

117. For example, "such terror they inspired in all the peoples on this side of the Taurus" (Livy 38.16.10) or: "Tall bodies, long reddish hair, huge shields, very long swords, in addition, songs as they go into battle and yells and leapings and the dreadful din of arms as they clash shields according to some ancestral customs—all these are deliberately used to terrify their foes [*ad terrorem*]" (Livy 38.17). See Kremer, *Das Bild der Kelten*, 64–65.

118. How much Manlius Vulso has become emblematic of the Roman state myth of empire building as a "just war" in legitimate self-defense against Galatian and other barbarian assaults shows in the famous imagery used by Virgil in the *Aeneid* to describe the "shield of Aeneas." We will return to this topic in chapter 3 below. On the instrumentalization of Gallic and other enemy constructs to justify Rome's "defensive imperialism" and "just wars," see Philip de Souza, "'They Are Enemies of All Mankind': Justifying Roman Imperialsim in the Late Republic," in *Roman Imperialism: Post-Colonial Perspectives*, ed. Jane Webster and Nicholas J. Cooper (Leicester: School of Archaeological Studies, University of Leicester, 1996), 125–33; and Webster, "Just War," 1–10.

2. Dying Gauls/Galatians Are Immortal

1. For a description and historical contextualization, see Marina Mattei, *Il Galata capitolino: uno splendido dono di Attalo* (Rome: "L'Erma" di Bretschneider, 1987); eadem, "The Dying Gaul," in *The Celts*, ed. Sabatino Moscati et al. (Venice: Bompiani, 1991), 70–71; and Bernard Andreae, "The Image of the Celts in Etruscan, Greek and Roman Art," in *The Celts*, ed. Moscati et al., 61–69, esp. 63–66.

2. R. R. R. Smith, *Hellenistic Sculpture: A Handbook* (London: Thames & Hudson, 1991), 158.

3. Davina C. Lopez, *Apostle to the Conquered: Reimagining Paul's Mission,* Paul in Critical Contexts (Minneapolis: Fortress Press, 2008), 28.

4. Francis Haskell and Nicholas Penny, *Taste and the Antique: The Lure of Classical Sculpture, 1500–1900* (New Haven: Yale University Press, 1981), 225. For a brief history of the two "large" statues of the Dying Trumpeter (often also referred to as Capitoline Gaul) and of its twin sculpture, the Suicidal Galatian Chieftain Killing His Wife and Himself (often referred to as the Ludovisi group), see ibid., 224–27, 282–84. Both are first recorded in 1623 in an inventory of the Ludovisi family of Rome. See also Kim J. Hartswick, *The Gardens of Sallust: A Changing Landscape* (Austin: University of Texas Press, 2004), 107.

5. See Diodorus 5.27–31. According to Smith (*Hellenistic Sculpture,* 101), these features became "legible iconographic signs" denoting Gauls within the official circulation and signification system of the images, no matter whether "real Gauls" were employing them for themselves. As John R. Marszal states, . markers such as a large oval shield, long sword, long or limed hair, mustache, and nudity except for torque, belt, and scabbard are "easily communicated features that quickly come to stereotype the foreigner" and usually are sufficient to identify a Galatian. John R. Marszal, "Ubiquitous Barbarians: Representation of the Gauls at Pergamon and Elsewhere," in *From Pergamon to Sperlonga: Sculpture and Context*, ed. Nancy T. de Grummond and Brunilde S. Ridgway, Hellenistic Culture and Society (Berkeley: University of California Press, 2000), 191–234, here 200. For the "semiotics of images" in general, see Tonio Hölscher, *The Language of Images in Roman Art* (Cambridge: Cambridge University Press, 2004).

6. The "trumpet" is a disputed object, though. It might indicate that this sculpture is indeed the "Trumpeter" (*tubicen*) of the Pergamene court sculptor Epigonos mentioned by Pliny in his *Natural History* (34.88), together with another sculpture, an "Infant Miserably Caressing Its Slain Mother," which is lost. But both the authorship of Epigonos and the identity of the Dying Gaul/Galatian as Pliny's Dying Trumpeter are hypothetical; the two titles are used interchangeably for this sculpture. See Smith, *Hellenistic Sculpture*, 101. For the Galatian use of trumpets (*salpinx*) that "are of peculiar nature and such as barbarians use, for when they are blown upon they give forth a harsh sound, appropriate to the tumult of war," see Diodorus 5.30 (LCL).

7. For a comprehensive overview of visual depictions of Gauls/Galatians all around the Mediterranean world and their historical backgrounds, see Marszal, "Ubiquitous Barbarians," 191–234.

8. A rare exception is the most insightful essay by David L. Balch, "Paul's Portrait of Christ Crucified (Gal 3:1) in Light of Paintings of Suffering and Death in Pompeiian Houses," in *Early Christian Families in Context: An Interdisciplinary Dialogue*, ed. David L. Balch and Carolyn Osiek (Grand Rapids: Eerdmans, 2003), 84–108.

9. See Marszal, "Ubiquitous Barbarians," 212. Marszal contends that the "priority of Pergamon in

the representation of Gauls is no longer maintained" (p. 197). Rather, it is the Romans who "eventually become the most frequent representers of the Gauls, and for good reasons. Rome was the only major Mediterranean city ever to be captured and sacked by the Gauls, but in the end the Romans were very successful against them, conquering and incorporating most of the Gallic nation into their empire" (p. 223).

10. See Brigitte Kahl, "Gender Trouble in Galatia? Paul and the Rethinking of Difference," in *Is There a Future for Feminist Theology*, ed. Deborah F. Sawyer and Diane M. Collier, Studies in Theology and Sexuality 4 (Sheffield: Sheffield Academic, 1999), 57–73, here 57.

11. For this term, see Marszal, "Ubiquitous Barbarians," 195. As Marszal states, scholars are in disagreement whether the concept of "victory dedications without victors" is meant to offer "a treatment of the defeated that is strangely sympathetic," or whether "that sympathy is seen only by modern eyes." See also Tonio Hölscher, "Die Geschlagenen und Ausgelieferten in der Kunst des Hellenismus," *Antike Kunst* 28 (1985): 120–36.

12. For the Roman provincial system as "blood-sucking" and the identification of the provinces "with a wounded and bleeding man who is prone to death," see Warren Carter, *Matthew and Empire: Initial Explorations* (Harrisburg, Pa.: Trinity Press International, 2001), 154.

13. Suetonius, *Nero* 46.1; see also Lopez, *Apostle to the Conquered*, 1.

14. For a comprehensive introduction to the scholarly debate on Paul's Galatian "opponents"— variously called Judaizers, proselytizers, troublemakers, agitators, rivals, teachers, influencers—see Mark D. Nanos, *The Irony of Galatians: Paul's Letter in First-Century Context* (Minneapolis: Fortress Press, 2002), 110–92.

15. For a general introduction to Pergamon, see Helmut Koester, ed., *Pergamon, Citadel of the Gods: Archaeological Record, Literary Description, and Religious Development*, Harvard Theological Studies 46 (Harrisburg, Pa.: Trinity Press International, 1998); and Wolfgang Radt, *Pergamon: Geschichte und Bauten einer antiken Metropole* (Darmstadt: Wissenschaftliche Buchgesellschaft, 1999); the comprehensive work of Esther V. Hansen, *The Attalids of Pergamon*, 2nd ed. (Ithaca, N.Y.: Cornell University Press, 1971) is still unsurpassed.

16. Erich S. Gruen, "Culture as Policy: The Attalids of Pergamon," in *From Pergamon to Sperlonga: Sculpture and Context*, ed. Nancy T. de Grummond and Brunilde S. Ridgway, Hellenistic Culture and Society (Berkeley: University of California Press, 2000), 17–31, esp. 17. As Gruen states, Philetairos, the founder father of the Attalid dynasty (283–263 B.C.E.) had "seized power by confiscating the vast sum entrusted to him at Pergamon by the Diadoch Lysimachos, betraying his overlord, and taking control of the garrison."

17. Radt, *Pergamon*, 171.

18. For a brief history of its excavation and transport to Berlin, see Max Kunze, *The Pergamon Altar: Its Rediscovery, History and Reconstruction* (Mainz am Rhein: Staatliche Museen zu Berlin, Verlag Philipp von Zabern, 1995), 5–16.

19. For a succinct description of and introduction to the state of research and more literature on the Great Altar, see Volker Kästner, "The Architecture of the Great Altar of Pergamon," in *Pergamon, Citadel of the Gods: Archaeological Record, Literary Description, and Religious Development*, ed. Helmut Koester, Harvard Theological Studies 46 (Harrisburg, Pa.: Trinity Press International, 1998), 137–62; and Andrew Stewart, "*Pergamo Ara Marmorea Magna:* On the Date, Reconstruction, and Functions of the Great Altar of Pergamon," in *From Pergamon to Sperlonga: Sculpture and Context*, ed. Nancy T. de Grummond and Brunilde S. Ridgway, Hellenistic Culture and Society (Berkeley: University of California Press, 2000), 32–57.

20. For the historical events of these decades, see chapter 1 above.

21. Stewart, "Great Altar," 34, 37–38.

22. Kästner, "Architecture of the Great Altar," 137–39.

23. Radt, *Pergamon*, 170.

24. For example, Stewart, "Great Altar," 46–47.

25. See Ann Kuttner, "'Do You Look Like You Belong Here?' Asianism at Pergamon and the Makedonian Diaspora," in *Cultural Borrowings and Ethnic Appropriations in Antiquity*, ed. Erich S. Gruen,

Oriens et Occidens 8 (Stuttgart: Franz Steiner, 2005), 137–206, esp. 175–84; Mary C. Sturgeon, "Pergamon to Hierapolis: From Theatrical 'Altar' to Religious Theater," in *From Pergamon to Sperlonga: Sculpture and Context*, ed. Nancy T. de Grummond and Brunilde de Ridgway, Hellenistic Culture and Society (Berkeley: University of California Press, 2000), 58–77, esp. 66, 71–75.

26. The idea that works of art, like texts, are semiotic systems that may indeed speak in their own language and thus can be read has been pioneered most notably through the work of Paul Zanker (*The Power of Images in the Age of Augustus*, Jerome Lectures, 16th Series [Ann Arbor: University of Michigan Press, 1988]) and Tonio Hölscher, who stated programmatically already in 1987: "My project is to explore the language of imagery in Roman art as a semantic system. This 'semantic system' functions according to a sort of grammar, on the basis of certain specific structures, like a language." See the English translation of his "Römische Bildsprache als semantisches System" (1987) in idem, *Language of Images*, 2. Jaś Elsner in his foreword declares this essay to be "one of the most important and least well-known books (at least to an English-speaking readership) to have been published on Roman art in the past thirty years" (ibid., xv).

27. Stewart, "Great Altar," 37, 49. In contrast to this broad accessibility, the neighboring terrace of the Athena temple belonged within the walls of the royal and palatial quarter and was much more secluded as the most decisive political sanctuary of the Pergamene kings. See Erwin Ohlemutz, *Die Kulte und Heiligtümer der Götter in Pergamon* (Darmstadt: Wissenschaftliche Buchgesellschaft, 1940), 42.

28. This reception-oriented and semiotic approach to "reading" the Great Altar, in my own experience, owes initial impulses to almost three decades of living, studying, and teaching in the immediate vicinity of this unique monument in its contemporary Berlin environment. In terms of scholarship, a seminal question of reader-response criticism was posed by Andrew Stewart in the early 1990s: What kind of model reader/spectator does the Great Altar construct? See Andrew Stewart, "Narration and Allusion in the Hellenistic Baroque," in *Narrative and Event in Ancient Art*, ed. Peter J. Holliday (Cambridge/New York: Cambridge University Press, 1993), 130–74, here 132.

29. In New Testament studies, taking works of art seriously as "texts" and "intertexts" (rather than simply illustrations) of biblical texts is a fairly new approach; see, for example, John Dominic Crossan and Jonathan L. Reed, *In Search of Paul: How Jesus's Apostle Opposed Rome's Empire with God's Kingdom; A New Vision of Paul's Words and World* (San Francisco: HarperSanFrancisco, 2004); Annette Weissenrieder et al., eds., *Picturing the New Testament: Studies in Ancient Visual Images*, WUNT 2/193 (Tübingen: Mohr Siebeck, 2005); for the New York project of "critical re-imagination" at Union Theological Seminary, see Brigitte Kahl, "Reading Galatians and Empire at the Great Altar of Pergamon," *USQR* 59, no. 3–4 (2005): 21–43; Davina C. Lopez, "Epilogue: Beyond the Threshold," *USQR* 59, no. 3–4 (2005): 177–86; and eadem, *Apostle to the Conquered*.

30. On the semiotics of space, see the groundbreaking study by Henri Lefebvre, *The Production of Space* (1974; Malden, Mass.: Blackwell, 1991); see further David Harvey, *Spaces of Hope*, California Studies in Critical Human Geography 7 (Berkeley: University of Caifornia Press, 2000); Claude Nicolet, *Space, Geography, and Politics in the Early Roman Empire*, Jerome Lectures, 19th Series (Ann Arbor: University of Michigan Press, 1991); for a brief introduction, see Halvor Moxnes, *Putting Jesus in His Place: A Radical Vision of Household and Kingdom* (Louisville: Westminster John Knox, 2003), 1–21.

31. For an introduction to structural semiotics in general, see Daniel Patte, *The Religious Dimensions of Biblical Texts: Greimas's Structural Semiotics and Biblical Exegesis*, Semeia Studies (Atlanta: Scholars Press, 1990). A very helpful condensed summary on the semiotic square is given on pp. 14–16. As already outlined above in the introduction, my own model of the semiotic square represents a modified version that emerged from using the square to analyze not only texts but also spaces, images, and architecture.

32. On these categories, see Patte, *Religious Dimensions*, 15.

33. As noted in the introduction, this version of the semiotic square differs from the standard version in two ways: It places the two complementary relations (A == B, non-A == non-B) on the horizontal level rather than vertically on top of each other (A == non-B, B == non-A). Thus, the spatial (and social) hierarchy between the four terms is expressed more adequately and visually in a way that conforms both to the structure of the Great Altar and the socio-spatial codes of our culture: the preferred and desirable terms

(A==B) are on top, the undesirable ones on the bottom. For the same reason, the two complementary positive terms are given as A and B and the two negative terms on the bottom as non-B and non-A (rather than A ==non-B and B==non-A). The relations of contrariety thus are trans-located from A versus B and non-B versus non-A in the traditional version to A versus non-B and B versus non-A in my version. The two axes of the (main) contradiction A versus non-A and B versus non-B stay the same, however.

34. Up and down as "fundamental spatial metaphors"of the Great Altar are, for example, mentioned by Stewart ("Narration and Allusion in the Hellenistic Baroque," 159), whereas Kuttner ("'Do You Look Like You Belong Here?'" 179) speaks of "an enormous machine for ascent and descent." She pays close attention also to the "ritual of movement" and the interaction between monument and visitor: "The images prescribed encounter: come up, survey the outside, ascend, scan the inside, turn around, ceremoniously come out and down" (ibid.). Though the linkage of inside–outside to the up–down axis is explicitly stated here, Kuttner does not further explore this aspect of the altar's spatial semiotics.

35. With the plates of the Great Frieze being duplicated around the walls of the Berlin exhibition hall in order to make them fully accessible, the original outside has been turned into an inside. In addition, as one enters now on the west side rather than the east side of the altar, facing immediately the Great Staircase, a spontaneous sense of interiority is communicated, while at Pergamon exteriority would be experienced first. The original tension between inside and outside is thus somewhat obscured.

36. The "evidence for thrones of gods and heroes cut into the rock of mountains in Asia minor" is mentioned by Adela Yarbro Collins, "Pergamon in Early Christian Literature," in *Pergamon, Citadel of the Gods: Archaeological Record, Literary Description, and Religious Development,* ed. Helmut Koester, Harvard Theological Studies 46 (Harrisburg, Pa.: Trinity Press International, 1998), 163–84, here 170. Kuttner ("'Do You Look Like You Belong Here?," 179) refers particularly to the fact that in Anatolia "ancient symbolic staircases were carved into mountain heights for Cybele markers." Sturgeon ("Pergamon to Hierapolis," 73–74) suggests that the Great Altar might have indeed contained a "throne" or seat with a monumental statue of Zeus on it. The linkage between these altar–throne connections and the famous passage in Rev 2:13 about the "throne of Satan" at Pergamon will be explored below.

37. For the idea of such a text existing parallel and in correspondence to the visual narrative of the Great Altar, see Philip R. Hardie, *Virgil's Aeneid: Cosmos and Imperium* (Oxford: Clarendon Press, 1986), 86, 128–29; Smith, *Hellenistic Sculpture,* 164.

38. I am well aware that in the original setting the scene directly at the center, today only preserved in fragments and therefore visually more or less absent, might have been equally impressive. It featured Zeus's consort Hera with four winged horses/winds and three fallen enemies run over by her powerful quadriga. The role of Hera and the strong visual dominance of goddesses in the Great Frieze in general is one of its most striking features and highly controversial in its interpretation. See, for example, Wiltrud Neumer-Pfau, "Die kämpfenden Göttinnen vom grossen Fries des Pergamonaltars," *Visible Religion: Annual for Religious Iconography* 2 (1983): 75–90, who points to the strong presence of mother goddesses in the Anatolian environment of Pergamon, and the decisive role of the queen mothers in the Attalid dynasty (p. 86). For the role of mother goddesses and their potential influence on Paul's Galatians, see also Susan M. (Elli) Elliott, *Cutting Too Close for Comfort: Paul's Letter to the Galatians in Its Anatolian Cultic Context,* JSNTSup 248 (London/New York: T&T Clard, 2004).

39. On the construct of self and other, identity and alterity in twentieth-century psychoanalytic theory and structuralist anthropology (Jacques Lacan, Claude Lévi-Strauss) and its reception in art history and classical scholarship, see Beth Cohen, ed., *Not the Classical Ideal: Athens and the Construction of the Other in Greek Art* (Leiden: Brill, 2000), 3–12. The phenomenon of polarity and oppositions in Greek thought and its role as a self-defining construct was explored already in the 1960s by G. E. R. Lloyd, *Polarity and Analogy: Two Types of Argumentation in Early Greek Thought* (Cambridge: Cambridge University Press, 1966). A semiotic analysis of ancient Greek imagery is developed in Claude Bérard et al., *A City of Images: Iconography and Society in Ancient Greece* (Princeton: Princeton University Press, 1989).

40. For a depiction and brief description of the key images, see Kunze, *Pergamon Altar,* 21–47.

41. Erika Simon, *Pergamon und Hesiod,* Schriften zur antiken Mythologie 3 (Mainz am Rhein: Philipp von Zabern, 1975). We do not know exactly which version of the Gigantomachy is underlying the

Great Frieze. The *Library* of Apollodorus (1.6.1–2) renders a different version much later than Hesiod but may be in part based on the Great Frieze, as Simon has suggested (p. 43). The names of the Giants are mentioned not by Hesiod but by Apollodorus.

42. The different versions are hard to reconcile. While in Hesiod only the Titans and Typhoeus are fighting against the gods, Apollodorus has added an actual Giant battle, much closer to the Pergamene imagery. At the Great Altar, on the other hand, the Titans appear as allies of the gods in the universal battle against the Giants as cosmic troublemakers (Simon, *Pergamon und Hesiod*, 58). Following Hardie (*Virgil's Aeneid*, 85) and a well-established ancient pattern, I will use Gigantomachy/Giant battle as a general term covering all three types of primeval battles for world rule.

43. For an extensive description, see Katherine Anne Schwab, "The Parthenon Metopes and Greek Vase Painting: A Study of Comparison and Influences" (Ph.D. diss., Institute of Fine Arts, New York University, 1989), 24–75; for the vases, see 7–16.

44. Wolfgang Speyer, "Gigant," *Reallexikon für Antike und Christentum* 10 (1978): 1247–76; see also Francis Vian, "Gigantes," *LIMC* 3 (1988): 191–270; and idem, *La Guerre des géants* (Paris: Librairie C. Klincksieck, 1952); Gerhard Kleiner, *Das Nachleben des pergamenischen Gigantenkampfes* (Berlin: Walter de Gruyter, 1949).

45. For a brief overview, see Yarbro Collins, "Pergamon in Early Christian Literature," 176–77. More comprehensively, see Adela Yarbro Collins, *The Combat Myth in the Book of Revelation,* Harvard Dissertations in Religion 9 (Missoula, Mont.: Scholars, 1976).

46. For text of the *Enuma Elish* and an introduction, see Alexander Heidel, *The Babylonian Genesis, The Story of Creation* (Chicago: University of Chicago Press, 1951); for the bestowal of "kingship over the totality of the whole universe" on Marduk in return for his victory over Tiamat, see Tablet IV,14. A brief summary and reflection are given by Rosemary Radford Ruether, *Gaia and God: An Ecofeminist Theology of Earth Healing* (San Francisco: HarperSanFrancisco, 1992), 16–19. As Ruether suggests, Marduk's creation of the cosmos out of the dead body of the mother goddess, and of humanity out of the blood taken from the dead body of her consort Kingu, signals a new absolutizing type of male domination over nature/Earth, female, and fellow humans (king over subjects, master over slaves) (pp. 18, 200). We will return to this subject in chapters 3 and 6 below.

47. Yarbro Collins ("Pergamon in Early Christian Literature," 176) summarizes succinctly: "The combat myth is a genre that emerged in ancient Mesopotamia and provided imagery and a conceptual framework for explaining divine rule over the world as well as human kingship. The major office of divine governance was kingship. A god could win kingship over other gods by resolving a crisis or defeating a threat to cosmic order. Divine kingship mirrored human kingship.... The king was the regent of the gods and represented divine order on earth, on the one hand, and the people before the gods, on the other." See also Henri Frankfort, *Kingship and the Gods, a Study of Ancient Near Eastern Religion as the Integration of Society & Nature* (1948; repr., Chicago: University of Chicago Press, 1978). We will return to this topic in chapter 3 below.

48. Stewart, "Great Altar," 33.

49. As is well known, Zeus had devoured Athena's mother, Metis, when she was pregnant, fearing the power of her child; he then gave birth to his daughter himself through his head. For Athena as a male-identified woman, see Catherine Keller, *From a Broken Web: Separation, Sexism, and Self* (Boston: Beacon, 1986), 56–58.

50. Edith Hall, *Inventing the Barbarian: Greek Self-Definition through Tragedy,* Oxford Classical Monographs (Oxford: Oxford University Press, 1989), 51–55, 68.

51. Ibid., 67–69.

52. All quotations from ibid., 71.

53. Ibid, 52.

54. Ibid, 53.

55. Ibid, 51.

56. Ibid, 52–53; on Heracles' confronting cannibalism and human sacrifice as abominations of the extreme outsider/other in the Bousiris myth, see Margaret C. Miller, "The Myth of Bousiris: Ethnicity

and Art," in *Not the Classical Ideal: Athens and the Construction of the Other in Greek Art*, ed. Beth Cohen (Leiden: Brill, 2000), 413–43.

57. Hall, *Inventing the Barbarian*, 48.

58. Ibid., 49; for Greek colonization, see also Irad Malkin, *Religion and Colonization in Ancient Greece*, Studies in Greek and Roman Religion 3 (Leiden: Brill, 1987); Carol Dougherty, *The Poetics of Colonization: From City to Text in Archaic Greece* (New York: Oxford University Press, 1993); for the Odyssey specifically, see Irad Malkin, *The Returns of Odysseus: Colonization and Ethnicity* (Berkeley: University of California Press, 1998).

59. Hall, *Inventing the Barbarian*, 50. On the profound influence of Greek thought on European attitudes toward non-Europeans, see also John E. Coleman and Clark A. Walz, eds., *Greeks and Barbarians: Essays on the Interactions between Greeks and Non-Greeks in Antiquity and the Consequences for Eurocentrism* (Bethesda: CDL, 1997).

60. On the constitution of the colonial subject as Other, see Gayatri Chakravorty Spivak, "Can the Subaltern Speak?" in *Colonial Discourse and Post-Colonial Theory: A Reader*, ed. Patrick Williams and Laura Chrisman (New York: Columbia University Press, 1994), 66–111, esp. 76; on the deconstruction of binary models as a core concern of postcolonial theory, see Jane Webster, "Roman Imperialism and the 'Post Imperial Age,'" in *Roman Imperialism: Post-Colonial Perspectives*, ed. Jane Webster and Nicholas J. Cooper (Leicester: School of Archeological Studies, University of Leicester, 1996), 1–18, esp. 6–8. On the role of fifth-century B.C.E. Greece and classical Athens in modeling the opposition between "us" and "them," occident and Orient, see Edward Said, *Orientalism* (New York: Vintage, 1978), esp. 2–3, 54–57, 332.

61. The "lesser Attalid dedication" is commonly linked to the sculptures of dying and dead figures two-thirds of life size (presumably "two cubits high") of Giants, Amazons, Persians, and Gauls (the "small Gauls") found in Rome and elsewhere, about "thirty pieces in various collections of appropriate size and subject," as Smith states (*Hellenistic Sculpture*, 102). As Pausanias gives only "Attalos" as donor of this dedication, we cannot know whether this was Attalus I (241–197) or Attalus II (158–138). For a summary of the discussion, see Marszal, "Ubiquitous Barbarians," 191–97.

62. Michael Pfanner, "Bemerkungen zur Komposition und Interpretation des grossen Frieses von Pergamon," *Archäologischer Anzeiger* (1979): 46–57.

63. As Smith (*Hellenistic Sculpture*, 163) observes, the entire middle section of the North Frieze is hard to interpret because inscriptions are missing and the iconography is unfamiliar. However, "[a]ttractive recent interpretations see here various dark forces—Erinyes (Furies), Moirai (Fates), Graiai—who would make up themes of blood revenge, fate and destiny, which were of course all useful and familiar elements in the Olympian armoury."

64. This overall emphasis on heavenly alliance and cooperation rather than focusing on Zeus alone has led Pfanner to conclude that the altar was dedicated to all the gods and not to Zeus or Athena exclusively; see Pfanner, "Komposition," 56.

65. Smith (*Hellenistic Sculpture*, 159) notes that the signatures of the master sculptors responsible for each section were inscribed below the frieze, which was unusual for architectural sculpture. Sixteen fragments of these names have been found. There must have been one designating architect/artist, however, who oversaw the whole project.

66. Stewart, "Narration and Allusion in the Hellenistic Baroque," 160. As the Great Frieze has not often been visually read in conjunction with the overall spatial construct of the Great Altar, the intimate linkage between *Down==Out* has gone mostly unnoticed. As we will see in our analysis of the Great Staircase, the terminal parts of the Great Frieze left and right of the stairs make clear that the Giants' downturn is also their *outcasting and expulsion*—they are not granted access into the citadel of the gods.

67. On lack of self-control and display of emotions as markers of otherness in ancient Greek iconography, see Timothy J. McNiven, "Behaving Like an Other: Telltale Gestures in Athenian Vase Painting," in *Not the Classical Ideal: Athens and the Construction of the Other in Greek Art*, ed. Beth Cohen (Leiden: Brill, 2000), 71–97; on the connection between beastlike features, deformity, and ugliness as signs of barbarian alterity and inferiority in opposition to true humanity as Greek, male, beautiful and "good"

(*kalos kagathos*), see François Lissarrague, "Aesop, Between Man and Beast: Ancient Portraits and Illustrations," in *Not the Classical Ideal: Athens and the Construction of the Other in Greek Art*, ed. Beth Cohen (Leiden: Brill, 2000), 136.

68. That gods can never show emotions in their facial expressions, in stark contrast to the strong *pathos* of pain and despair that marks the depictions of Celtic barbarians and Giants, has been emphasized by Karl R. Krierer, *Sieg und Niederlage. Untersuchungen physiognomischer und mimischer Phänomene in Kampfdarstellungen römischer Plastik* (Vienna: Phoibos, 1995), 53.

69. Hans-Joachim Schalles, *Der Pergamonaltar: Zwischen Wertung und Verwertbarkeit* (Frankfurt am Main: Fischer Taschenbuch, 1986), 81.

70. Peter Weiss, *The Aesthetics of Resistance,* vol. 1 (Durham, N.C./London: Duke University Press, 2005) appeared in German in 1975 and was only recently translated into English; quotation from 1:9–10.

71. Ibid., 1:5.

72. Because of this emotional intensity, the Great Altar has usually been categorized as "Hellenistic baroque." See Smith, *Hellenistic Sculpture*, 99–154, for other baroque groups that also include the Dying Gauls/Galatians. Smith sees Hellenistic baroque as a style designed to characterize "the elevated, tumultuous world of epic heroes." He also points out "that the baroque may have been in some sense a royal style, a grand manner for royal deeds and heroes" (p. 99). For a cautionary remark on the reductive nature of the Great Altar's common characterization as baroque, see Stewart, "Great Altar," 49–50.

73. On the political utilization of the Great Altar and the Attalid tradition within the nationalistic, colonial, and militaristic framework of the German Empire founded in 1871—the same year the excavation of the altar was initiated—and eager to compete with the collections of the French Louvre and the British Museum, see Kunze, *Pergamon Altar,* 5–16; and Schalles, *Der Pergamonaltar,* 6–15. On the reception of the Pergamene prototype in monumental fascist architecture, see Schalles, 88–91.

74. For an exhaustive introduction, see Renée Dreyfus and Ellen Schraudolph, eds., *The Telephosfrieze from the Great Altar* (San Francisco: Fine Arts Museums of San Francisco, 1996–97); a more recent comprehensive rereading of the Telephos myth and the function of the colonnaded room has been presented by Kuttner, "'Do You Look Like You Belong Here?'" 137–206.

75. As Gruen ("Culture as Policy," 22) observes, the "ingenuity of the Attalids" is perhaps best exemplified in "the creation of a mythology. The dynasts fabricated a genealogy and fashioned legendary connections not only to give themselves an illustrious pedigree but to claim links with tradition and history that associated them with a range of Greek states and principalities."

76. Holger Schwarzer, "Untersuchungen zum hellenistischen Herrscherkult in Pergamon," *Istanbuler Mitteilungen* 49 (1999): 249–300; for the assertion that the Great Altar is not primarily dedicated to the gods nor a victory monument, rather a monument of Attalid ruler cult, see p. 292 (". . . dass wir auch den Pergamonaltar als ein Monument für den Herrscherkult der Attaliden zu verstehen haben").

77. Kuttner, "'Do You Look Like You Belong Here?'" 137; for a more detailed description of these monuments, especially the Mausoleum of Halikarnassos, which, similar to the Pergamene Gigantomachy, had an Amazonomachy frieze running around its base, see Sturgeon, "Pergamon to Hierapolis," 59–63.

78. Kuttner, "'Do You Look Like You Belong Here?'" 175, 177. When moving to the west side of the Great Altar one would face the "enormous courtyard" that, according to Kuttner, resembled a "royal heroon" at least as much as a "great altar." "This squared peristyle with ornamental gate, walls covered with historical and mythological relief [the Telephos frieze], is the single most important form of the composite. . . . Imagine the whole top courtyard sliced from the podium and set down elsewhere: it turns into a recognizable monumental type, that of the Lykian royal heroa which were walled compounds whose inner as well as outer surfaces were veneered with myth and history about great kings and the fate of cities" (pp. 176–77).

79. Ibid., 179.

80. There is a heated debate as to whether the lioness in this scene was meant to send a signal of superiority to Rome, whose founder fathers Romulus and Remus were suckled only by a she-wolf; see,

for example, Schwarzer, "Pergamon," 293 (pro) and Kuttner, "'Do You Look Like You Belong Here?'" 147 (contra).

81. On the Telephos myth, see Huberta Heres, "Der Telephosmythos in Pergamon," in *Der Perga-monaltar: Die neue Präsentation nach der Restaurierung des Telephosfrieses*, ed. Wolf-Dieter Heilmeyer (Tübingen: Ernst Wasmuth, 1997), 99–120.

82. In a profound and brutal irony, in Diodorus's Celtic excursus (5.24), Heracles also fathers Galates, the ancestor of his Galatian enemies. During his travels in the western lands of the Celts, Hera-cles encounters the ruling king's daughter, who is enchanted by his prowess and bodily superiority, and is of exceptional strength and beauty herself. Yet the city where this happened, and that he founded himself as he put an end to the "lawlessness" of the country (4.19), is Alesia—in Caesar's *Gallic War* (7.33–56) the scene where Gallic resistance finally collapses and Vercingetorix surrenders to Rome, to be publicly strangled during the victor's triumph. The Galatians thus are destined to be defeated already through their birth myth, and their own "father," as loyal ally of gods, Pergamenes, and Romans is instrumental in this defeat. As Jane Webster notes, the setting of Alesia suggests that Diodorus's *Bibliotheke*, "begun in c 56 BC and not circulated until the reign of Augustus, . . . was compiled during the early years of Roman occupation of northern Gaul. Diodorus uses the trope of Heracles as civilizer to suggest a much older claim to Gaul." Jane Webster, "The Just War: Graeco-Roman Texts as Colonial Discourse," in *TRAC 94. Proceedings of the 4th Annual Theoretical Roman Archaeology Conference*, ed. Sally Cottam et al. (Dur-ham: University of Durham, 1994), 4. In her view, to frame Heracles as forefather of the Gallic race "enables colonialist discourse to allegorize a personal relationship between the coloniser and the colo-nised. At the same time . . . the sexual opposition of male:colonizer, female:colonized embedded in the allegory affirms the power asymmetries structuring the colonial relationship itself" (p. 6). On Heracles, see also François Hartog, *The Mirror of Herodotus: The Representation of the Other in the Writing of His-tory* (Berkeley: University of California Press, 1988), 26–27.

83. Kuttner, "'Do You Look Like You Belong Here?'" 188–92.

84. Ibid., 199.

85. Ibid., 184. Asian kingship thus is endowed with "superior moral stature": "Noble, generous, pious Teuthras of Mysia holds the center [of the Telephos Frieze], bracketed by Greeks of dubious moral status, the hubristic, savage Aloeus of Arkadia, and the unjust and vacillating Agamemnon" (p. 191).

86. About Attalid court protocol, see Kuttner, "'Do You Look Like You Belong Here?'" 195 n. 133, 196.

87. As Kuttner points out (ibid., 195), "Greek textual tradition praises the Attalids as kings who were not power-crazed. Royal self-distancing could even favor the demos' freedom. The polis apart was not necessarily subjugated, but rather spared armed presence in its streets—or so an Attalid apologist for Greek subjects' *eleutheria* would have put it."

88. Whether and to what extent the Great Altar represents already imperial concepts and ideas is a question that has been raised by Krierer, *Sieg und Niederlage*, 172: "'. . ob und inwieweit hier nicht bereits 'imperiales Gedankengut' in das künstlerische Konzept eingeflossen ist."

89. Note the observation of Schalles (*Der Pergamonaltar*, 81) that the power of the Great Altar over its visitors in part derives from how it integrates the architecture into the events of the Great Frieze, making the boundary between images and reality vanish. The battle of the frieze appears like a battle at the altar itself, especially as the bodies of the combatants frequently move beyond the spatial framework set by the frieze and enter the outside space, as at the staircase (pp. 64–65). On stone throwing as a ste-reotypical feature of Giants and centaurs, representing unrestrained anger and lack of self-control, see Krierer, *Sieg und Niederlage*, 132.

90. See Johan C. Thom, *Cleanthes' Hymn to Zeus: Text, Translation, and Commentary*, Studien und Texte zu Antike und Christentum 33 (Tübingen: Mohr Siebeck, 2005).

91. Ibid., 40.

92. Ibid., 86.

93. Cf. Simon's thesis that the philosophical background of the Great Altar is shaped by Stoic think-ing, represented, for example, by Crates of Mallos, the head of the Pergamene library at the time the Great

Altar was built. Simon, *Pergamon und Hesiod,* 54–58. For Simon, the fourfold presence of the eagle at the altar signals the omnipresence of Zeus; the victory of the gods is his victory (p. 6).

94. Louis Althusser, "Ideology and Ideological State Apparatus," in idem, *Lenin and Philosophy, and Other Essays* (New York: Monthly Review, 2001), 122–23.

95. The strongly monarchic structure of the Pergamon Altar and Pergamene art in general has been frequently observed; it was one of the reasons why it was so enthusiastically received in the newly founded monarchy of the German Kaiserreich in the 1870s and '80s. According to Schalles (*Der Pergamonaltar,* 14–15), at an exhibition in Berlin in 1886 a replica of the Great Altar, with a model of the temple to Zeus at Olympia at its top, was prepared. Around it a triumphal procession of "King Attalos" unfolded, with fifteen hundred people posing as Pergamenes and their prisoners in historic costumes. In the presence of the German crown prince, a herald proclaimed, "Barbarians have threatened empire and country; the king defeated them with a strong hand; now he is returning home, adorned with victory; his people are hailing him with delight." This is, in a nutshell, the core ideological program of the Great Altar; after the Attalids, the Romans knew how to utilize it, and so did the Germans millennia later.

96. "One might just be able to drive a herd of frightened and reluctant oxen up this steep stairway, but who would want to force them, horns and all, through a gap less than four feet wide—especially given the damage they would do to the building in the process?" Stewart, "Great Altar," 47.

97. Ibid.

98. Wolfram Hoepfner, "Modell des Pergamonaltars im Masstab 1:20," in *Der Pergamonaltar: Die neue Präsentation nach der Restaurierung des Telephosfrieses,* ed. Wolf-Dieter Heilmeyer (Tübingen: Ernst Wasmuth Verlag, 1997), 171–76, here 175.

99. Stewart, "Great Altar, " 48–49.

100. Kuttner, "'Do You Look Like You Belong Here?'" 195–96.

101. Stewart, "Great Altar," 49–50.

102. On this "bequest" of Attalus III, who ascended the Pergamene throne in 138 B.C.E. and at his death named the Roman people heir to all his possessions, thus transitioning the Pergamene kingdom into the Roman province of Asia, see David Magie, *Roman Rule in Asia Minor to the End of the Third Century after Christ,* 2 vols. (Princeton: Princeton University Press, 1950), 1:31–33; on the subsequent revolt of Aristonicus, an illegitimate son of Eumenes who was able to mobilize considerable resistance to the Roman takeover, see ibid., 148–54; also Frank Daubner, *Bellum Asiaticum: Der Krieg der Römer gegen Aristonikos von Pergamon und die Einrichtung der Provinz Asia,* Quellen und Forschungen zur antiken Welt 41 (Munich: Tuduv, 2003).

103. Ann Kuttner ("Republican Rome Looks at Pergamon," *Harvard Studies in Classical Philology* 97 [1995]: 157–78) has voiced her frustration that Roman reception of Pergamene art is a vastly under-explored topic, as "the indexes of most Republican and Augustan studies lack 'Attalid' or 'Pergamon,' including, alas, every major Augustan project of the last fifteen years" (p. 158). A seminal contribution to the Pergamene–Roman connection was made by Philip R. Hardie (*Virgil's Aeneid*).

104. More recently, this "geographic discrimination" (and the related "discrimination against the so-called copies"), which attributes all artistic originality to Greece and Pergamon rather than Italy has been strongly challenged by de Grummond and Ridgway: "Thus the very real Gallic Wars that took place on Italian territory are disregarded as possible topics within the visual repertoire of Italic and Etruscan artifacts, in favor of the more remote Celtic encounters in Greece and Asia Minor." Nancy T. de Grummond and Brunilde S. Ridgway, "Introduction," in *From Pergamon to Sperlonga: Sculpture and Context,* ed. Nancy T. de Grummond and Brunhilde S. Ridgway, Hellenistic Culture and Society (Berkeley: University of California Press, 2000), 4. On the proximity between Pergamon and Rome, see also Krierer, *Sieg und Niederlage,* 157, who states that Pergamon was at every stage of its history more comparable to the Roman state than Greece at any time.

105. See the broad range of evidence listed, if briefly, by Kuttner, "Republican Rome Looks at Pergamon."

106. Gruen ("Culture as Policy," 26–28) states that the Romans at that time had already adopted the Trojan legend(s). For more background information on the "Advent of the Magna Mater" at Rome,

see his treatment in idem, *Studies in Greek Culture and Roman Policy,* Cincinnati Classical Studies n.s. 7 (Leiden: Brill, 1990), 5–33. The Trojan myth made Aeneas the Roman founding father who escaped from the city of Troy in Asia Minor, which was laid waste by the Greeks because of Helen, the abducted queen of Sparta. This is the narrative setting where Virgil's *Aeneid* will pick up the story some two hundred years later and develop it into the monumental imperial state myth of the Augustan age.

107. The Antigonids and the Attalids, according to Kuttner, "enjoyed a strong Roman reputation, respectively as the most noble enemy and the most noble friend." This "unique friendship with Rome . . . recognized Pergamon's crucial role in Rome's Eastern expansion and its benevolent influence on Rome's national religion (the Magna Mater cult)." Kuttner, "Republican Rome Looks at Pergamon," 159.

108. As a grammarian, he and his followers "promulgated the rhetorical neo-Atticism which men like Cicero would invest with moral overtones," in contrast to rival "Asiatic" modes. Kuttner, "Republican Rome Looks at Pergamon," 162.

109. Ibid.

110. Ibid., 166, citing Klaus Tuchelt, *Frühe Denkmäler Roms in Kleinasien: Beiträge zur archäologischen Überlieferung aus der Zeit der Republik und des Augustus,* Istanbuler Mitteilungen 23 (Tübingen: E. Wasmuth, 1979).

111. Steven J. Friesen, *Imperial Cults and the Apocalypse of John: Reading Revelation in the Ruins* (Oxford: Oxford University Press, 2001), 32.

112. The main sources are Tacitus, *Ann.* 4.37.3 and Cassius Dio 51.20.6–9. The overall arrangement included, in fact, four temples, reflecting different attitudes and sensitivities with regard to the ruler cult among Greeks and Romans. While the Romans living in the provinces of Asia and Bithynia received two temples, in Ephesus and Nicaea, to honor the goddess Roma and the divinized Caesar as the adopted father of Augustus (that is, not the living Augustus himself), the Greeks were allowed to worship Augustus directly, together with the city of Rome in Pergamon and in Nicomedia. The request to erect a temple to Rome and Augustus in Pergamon was made through the provincial assembly (*koinon*); the actual location of the temple is currently unknown. For a more detailed outline, see Friesen, *Imperial Cults,* 25–32.

113. Schwarzer, "Untersuchungen zum hellenistischen Herrscherkult in Pergamon," 294–95. Schwarzer points out that the preservation of the Great Altar in Roman times suggests its active use into late antiquity, up to the beginning of the sixth century C.E. (". . . dass der hier praktizierte Kult wenigstens bis in die späteste römische Kaiserzeit gepflegt wurde"). Furthermore, the Roman imperial cult at Pergamon tended to be installed in places that had previously served the Attalid ruler cult. His argument, however, that this precludes the interpretation of the Great Altar as a victory monument, as the Romans would not celebrate the memory of an outdated victory, needs reconsideration. The victory in the Giant battle for Rome was never outdated.

114. The "great dragon" that is trying to devour the newborn child of the heavenly woman in Revelation 12 and subsequently provokes a huge battle is identified as "Satan" or "Devil" in 12:9 and gives its power and "throne" and great authority to a "beast" rising out of the sea, which is then worshiped by the whole earth, together with the dragon (13:2–4). The "beast" evidently represents Roman imperial power, and the "throne" of Satan/beast/emperor and its worship are closely related. See Yarbro Collins, "Pergamon in Early Christian Literature," 166–67.

115. Adolf Deissman, *Light from the Ancient East* (1910; repr., Peabody, Mass.: Hendrickson, 1995), 281 n. 3.

116. Yarbro Collins, "Pergamon in Early Christian Literature," 174–75, here 171.

117. *IvP* 381.

118. Sturgeon, "Pergamon to Hierapolis," 73.

119. On the Pergamene imperial temple of Trajan and Hadrian, see Radt, *Pergamon,* 209–20.

120. Zanker, *Power of Images,* 183–88.

121. Radt, *Pergamon,* 162–63; *IvP,* 383 (dedication to Augustus); *IvP,* 301 (dedication by Augustus). See also Hans-Joachim Schalles, *Untersuchungen zur Kulturpolitik der pergamenischen Herrscher im dritten Jahrhundert vor Christus,* Istanbuler Forschungen 36 (Tübingen: Ernst Wasmuth, 1985), 54–56;

and S. R. F. Price, *Rituals and Power: The Roman Imperial Cult in Asia Minor* (Cambridge: Cambridge University Press, 1984), 56, 137.

122. Kuttner, "Republican Rome Looks at Pergamon," 176–77.

123. "The emperor was often brought into close relationship with the traditional gods of the city, in joint dedications, in assimilations and in identifications." Price, *Rituals and Power,* 103. Traditional festivals often had an imperial title added to them, and joint cults could emerge that showed piety to both the god and the emperor.

124. According to Price (*Rituals and Power,* 147), the emperor could in various ways be integrated into traditional Greek temples where often different gods and mortals shared the same space. But statues of emperors were generally not set higher than the existing statues. In light of this, the replacement of the Athena statue appears to be a rather blunt act. It is important to note that it was initiated by the Pergamenes themselves. Schalles has looked for an explanation in terms of a diplomatic crisis between Rome and Athens at the time when Augustus traveled through the East; this would make the removal of Athena a diplomatic move on the side of Pergamon. Schalles, *Untersuchungen,* 55.

125. "Attalos I had made the Agora [of Athens] Pergamene, framing it with an enormous portico backing his portrait to mirror the smaller fifth-century Stoa and image of Zeus Eleutherios straight across the square. Augustus made Zeus' stoa now 'talk back' to Attalos' monument, adding to it a Hellenistic ruler-cult exedra extension partitioned to make twin cellas for himself and Roma." Kuttner, "Republican Rome Looks at Pergamon," 177.

126. *IvP* 385.

127. See the ritual calender of the Pergamene "*hymnodes*" of the divine Augustus and goddess Rome conveniently reconstructed by Friesen, *Imperial Cults,* 112. On the imperial choirs of the *hymnodes,* see 104–13.

128. Ibid., 31–32.

129. The quotations are from provincial inscriptions of the new calendar edict: *OGIS,* 458. For a fuller translation of the text, see Friesen, *Imperial Cults,* 32–36.

130. Radt, *Pergamon,* 210, 209–20.

131. For the eagle scepter and the Attalus exedra see Radt, *Pergamon,* 210, 215.

3. Creating the World Out of Dead Gauls

1. For a description of the images listed, see Paul Zanker, *The Power of Images in the Age of Augustus,* Jerome Lectures, 16th Series (Ann Arbor: University of Michigan Press, 1988); and John Dominic Crossan and Jonathan L. Reed, *In Search of Paul: How Jesus's Apostle Opposed Rome's Empire with God's Kingdom. A New Vision of Paul's Words and World* (San Francisco: HarperSanFrancisco, 2004).

2. For the Shield as a "virtual monument" that with its "vertiginous richness of images clearly evokes a whole complex of representations," see Alessandro Barchiesi, "Learned Eyes: Poets, Viewers, Image Makers," in *The Cambridge Companion to the Age of Augustus,* ed. Karl Galinksy, Cambridge Companion to the Classics (Cambridge: Cambridge University Press, 2005), 294.

3. For a summary of the twelve books of the *Aeneid,* see David R. Wallace, *The Gospel of God. Romans as Paul's Aeneid* (Eugene, Ore.: Pickwick, 2008), 72–75.

4. For an insightful description of the Shield in connection with the Jupiter prediction in book 1 and the underworld prediction in book 6, see Davina C. Lopez, *Apostle to the Conquered: Reimagining Paul's Mission,* Paul in Critical Contexts (Minneapolis: Fortress Press, 2008), 73–86.

5. Philip R. Hardie, *Virgil's Aeneid: Cosmos and Imperium* (Oxford: Clarendon, 1986); on the Shield of Aeneas, see esp. 120–25, 336–76.

6. Ibid., 352.

7. Ibid., 123–24.

8. As we have already seen in chapter 1, Titus Manlius (Torquatus) and the Capitoline Marcus

Manlius are both evoked in Livy's speech of Manlius Vulso as belonging to his *gens* when he addresses his soldiers before the decisive Galatian battle in Asia Minor in 189 B.C.E. (Livy 38.17; for the imperial aspirations of the first Manlius see also 6.18–20).

9. On Gigantomachy themes in the *Aeneid* in general, see Hardie, *Virgil's Aeneid,* 85–156.

10. "The elemental conflict at Actium is finally elevated to the divine plane. The ultimate vindication of the Roman right to conquer and the preservation of natural order are matters for the Olympian gods; the physical struggle of the elements is superseded by a theological affirmation of the superiority of the gods of light over the monstrous and demonic idols of Egypt." Finally, "Apollo simultaneously restores Olympian order and establishes Roman world empire." Hardie, *Virgil's Aeneid,* 110.

11. Hardie, *Virgil's Aeneid,* 356–57, here 356. As Hardie also notes, the whole description of the Shield is shaped by the opposition of dark (cave of Mars, nightly attack of the Gauls, gloom of the underworld, murky burial ground of the vanquished Egyptians) and light (flames of war at the sea battle, dazzling brightness shining from the Palatine temple after Augustus's *adventus*).

12. Traditionally in antiquity, Homer's Shield of Achilles with its abundance of images was seen as depicting the universe and the whole cosmos (*Iliad* 18.478–608). This same idea, according to Hardie, also underlies Virgil's Shield of Aeneas. "The Shield of Aeneas is also an image of the creation of a universe, but of a strictly Roman universe." Homer's "universalism" and Virgil's "nationalism" are perfectly blended as Virgil has cosmos and imperium merge. As "cosmic icon," the Shield of Aeneas is "the true climax and final encapsulation of the imperialist themes of the *Aeneid*" (Hardie, *Virgil's Aeneid,* 339). For the Homeric context of the *Aeneid* and its character as both continuation and integration of *Iliad* and *Odyssey,* see Wallace, *Gospel of God,* 56–59.

13. In Livy 1.7, Remus "leaped over the new walls in mockery of his brother"; cf. Dionysius 1.87.4; Plutarch describes in *Romulus* 10–11 how Remus, deceitfully tricked by his brother Romulus, jumps over the trench marking the future city wall and is therefore killed. After his burial, the center of the city and the course of the city wall are marked in a sacred ceremony. The sacredness of the walls and Remus's death as a consequence of his violation are also told by Ovid, *Fasti* 4.818–44; see also Plutarch, *Romulus* 11.3 ("they regard the wall as sacred").

14. Zanker, *Power of Images,* 102–3, here 102.

15. Bravery, clemency, justice, and piety (*virtus, clementia, justitia, pietas*) are the four virtues for which Octavian in 27 B.C.E., according to his own report in *Res Gestae* 34, received a golden honorary shield (*clipeus virtutis*), which was displayed in the *Curia Iulia.* See Zanker, *Power of Images,* 92, 96; italics added. For an incisive and comprehensive ideological reconstruction of Paul's Roman context through the lens of these four terms, see Neil Elliott, *The Arrogance of Nations: Reading Romans in the Shadow of Empire,* Paul in Critical Contexts (Minneapolis: Fortress Press, 2008).

16. As such they correspond to the laurel decoration, symbolizing victory and Jupiter, that Augustus received for the doorposts of his own house from the senate in 27 B.C.E. (*Res Gestae* 34).

17. Zanker, *Power of Images,* 51.

18. Wolfram Hoepfner, "Die Architektur von Pergamon," in *Der Pergamonaltar: Die neue Präsentation nach der Restaurierung des Telephosfrieses,* ed. Wolf-Dieter Heilmeyer (Tübingen: Ernst Wasmuth Verlag, 1997), 38; cf. Zanker, *Power of Images,* 51.

19. Julus/Ilus as cognomen of Ascanius is mentioned in 1.267–68; the lineage Julus/Ascanius → kings of Alba Longa → royal priestess Ilia (pregnant through Mars) → Romulus and Remus (nursed by the she-wolf) → Romulus → Rome is drawn out in 1.267–77. Finally, Caesar Augustus is envisioned as a Trojan descendant of Julian origin derived from the great Julus/Ascanius (1.286–88).

20. See Zanker, *Power of Images,* 34–35; the deified Julius Caesar was officially admitted into the state cult in 42 B.C.E.

21. Zanker, *Power of Images,* 50.

22. The slaying of the children of Niobe on the one door of the Apollon temple and the Gauls driven out of Delphi on the other (Propertius 2.31.12–14) were most likely "veiled metaphors for the defeat of Antony." Zanker, *Power of Images,* 85.

23. On the "conglomeration of symbolism" that has Roman imagination link the Giant battle, the

miraculous preservation of the Capitol from the Gauls in 387 B.C.E., the defeat of the Gauls at Delphi in 279 B.C.E., and the Battle of Actium, see also Hardie, *Virgil's Aeneid*, 124–25.

24. S. R. F. Price, *Rituals and Power: The Roman Imperial Cult in Asia Minor* (Cambridge: Cambridge University Press, 1984), 209–10, 232–33.

25. Steven J. Friesen, *Twice Neokoros: Ephesus, Asia and the Cult of the Flavian Imperial Family*, Religions in the Graeco-Roman World 116 (Leiden/New York: Brill, 1993), 149.

26. Philip A. Harland, *Associations, Synagogues and Congregations: Claiming a Place in Ancient Mediterranean Society* (Minneapolis: Fortress Press, 2003), 122–23, 127–28.

27. Ibid., 116.

28. Price, *Rituals and Power*, 233.

29. It is important to keep in mind that, different from the Latin *divus*, the Greek term *theos/god* was a very fluid category that primarily signaled supreme rule and power and the adequate worship, veneration, and submission (*eusebeia*) on the side of those subjected to this power. See S. R. F. Price, "Gods and Emperors: The Greek Language of the Roman Imperial Cult," *JHS* 104 (1984): 92; and Thomas Witulski, *Kaiserkult in Kleinasien: Die Entwicklung der kultisch-religiösen Kaiserverehrung in der römischen Provinz Asia von Augustus bis Antoninus Pius,* Novum Testamentum et Orbis Antiquus/Studien zur Umwelt des Neuen Testaments (Göttingen: Vandenhoeck & Ruprecht; Fribourg: Academic, 2007), 35–36, esp. nn. 177–78. If this is the case, the factual position of the emperor as single world ruler after Actium must almost automatically have projected the status of the "highest god" on him, at least in Greek perception.

30. See *Res Gestae* 34; and Zanker, *Power of Images*, 91–92.

31. Zanker, *Power of Images*, 98.

32. As Price ("Gods and Emperors," 82–84) has pointed out, different from the Greek *theos/god* the Latin *divus*/divine was attributed to former emperors and members of the imperial family, as well as to the current emperor as "son of the divine" according to a strict protocol; it more clearly maintained the distinction of the deified emperor and his son from the traditional gods. One may ask, however, how much of this distinction remained if the Greeks then addressed living emperors as both God and son of God (*theou hyios theos*). See Witulski, *Kaiserkult*, 36 nn. 179–80.

33. For a lack of interest in ontological questions, see Friesen, *Twice Neokoros*, 152: "Questions of ontological status were not unknown in the Roman world, but they were relatively unimportant in imperial cultic contexts."

34. See chapter 2 above.

35. Justin K. Hardin has pointed out that the amalgamation of local pagan, Greek, and Roman religion in the Greek East, including the province of Galatia, in reality implied a "*de facto* replacement theology" and the hegemony of the imperial cult: "The imperial cult was significant in that it most commonly superseded traditional religious worship with a uniform system of religious devotion." Justin K. Hardin, *Galatians and the Imperial Cult: A Critical Analysis of the First-century Social Context of Paul's Letter*, WUNT 2/237 (Tübingen: Mohr Siebeck, 2008). This applies, for example, to Ephesus, where the temple of Augustus is erected in the upper square as new centerpiece of the city and "notwithstanding the connubial relationship between the emperor Claudius and Artemis, we can observe the priority of the imperial cult over the city's goddess."

36. Zanker, *Power of Images*, 104–10.

37. Ibid., 110.

38. Thus Johan C. Thom, *Cleanthes' Hymn to Zeus: Text, Translation, and Commentary*, Studien und Texte zu Antike und Christentum 33 (Tübingen: Mohr Siebeck, 2005), 45, 48: "Stoic theology tends toward monotheism, although it does not exclude the existence of other gods in addition to Zeus." Further, "Zeus is a natural choice to represent the active and rational principle in Stoic cosmology: he is the supreme and strongest deity of the Greek pantheon, whom all others address as father; he represents the union of power and wisdom; he is closely associated with law, the preservation of order and justice."

39. Walter Burkert, *Greek Religion* (Cambridge, Mass.: Harvard University Press, 1985), 131.

40. Rufus Fears, "The Theology of Victory at Rome," in *ANRW* 17.2 (1981): 59.

41. Zanker, *Power of Images*, 188–91.

42. John Pollini, "The Gemma Augustea: Ideology, Rhetorical Imagery, and the Creation of a Dynastic Narrative," in *The Origins of Roman Historical Commemoration in the Visual Arts*, ed. Peter J. Holliday (Cambridge/New York: Cambridge University Press, 2002), 262, 260. Pollini, however, emphasizes that Augustus is shown not *as* Jupiter but in a subordinate position that is signaled through the absence of the thunderbolt and the *lituus* (staff) he holds in his hand instead: the "crooked staff of the augur defines Augustus's role as interpreter of Jupiter's will on earth and mediator between gods and man" (p. 262). One might wonder, however, in light of the active and militant role the eagle plays at the Pergamene Staircase, acting de facto in lieu of Zeus's thunderbolt, whether it could visually function as a kind of thunderbolt substitute on the Gemma, which would make the demarcation line between Augustus and Jupiter less clear.

43. Pollini, "Gemma Augustea," 266–67; see also Rufus Fears, "Jupiter and Roman Imperial Ideology," in *ANRW* 17.1 (1981): 58.

44. Fears, "Jupiter and Roman Imperial Ideology," 69.

45. Ibid., 70–71; for Caligula (37-41), who put his own head on the statue of Zeus at Olympia, see Suetonius, *Gaius* 22, and Cassius Dio 59.26-28. It is important to imagine that the early years of Paul's mission to the nations were thus shaped by two major conflicts involving emperor religion under Caligula: the clashes between Jewish monotheism and imperial deification in Alexandria and in Jerusalem, where Caligula had tried to install his statue in the temple (Philo, *In Flaccum* 6.41–43; *Legatio ad Gaium* 30.203).

46. See chapter 6 below.

47. For a concise summary, see Harland, *Associations*, 119–21.

48. Price, *Rituals and Power*, 7.

49. Ibid., 248.

50. Ibid., 8.

51. Ibid., 247–48.

52. see Harland, *Associations*, 132–35, on the role of ritual in establishing coherent worldviews regarding the order of cosmos and society.

53. Louis Althusser, "Ideology and Ideological State Apparatus," in idem, *Lenin and Philosophy, and Other Essays* (New York: Monthly Review, 2001), 115–24; see chapter 2 above.

54. See Elliott, *Arrogance of Nations*, 38, who notes that *fides*/faithfulness is a "watchword of the Augustan age" and a "potent euphemism by means of which Rome represented to subject peoples . . . that their subjection and willing obedience would be rewarded by the protective care of their conquerors." For faith/*fides* as a key term of the Roman ideological order, see also Jan Rehmann, "Nietzsche, Paul, and the Subversion of Empire," *USQR* 59, no. 3–4 (2005): 158, who observes that "*fides* is the formula for all kinds of 'vertical' relations of dependency, trust and loyalty: between the Roman emperors and his subjects, between the Roman empire and the subjugated provinces, between military commanders and simple soldiers, patrons and clients, husbands and wives, parents and children. It functions as a sort of ideological lubricant for different types of domination." For an overall investigation of the term faith/*fides*, see Christian Strecker, "Fides-Pistis-Glaube: Kontexte und Konturen einer Theologie der 'Annahme' bei Paulus," in *Lutherische und neue Paulusperspektive: Beiträge zu einem Schlüsselproblem der gegenwärtigen exegetischen Diskussion*, ed. Michael Bachmann and Johannes Woyke, WUNT 182 (Tübingen: Mohr Siebeck, 2005), 221–48.

55. The designation "father of the fatherland" (*pater patriae*), which reminds us of Zeus as "father of gods and men," including the profoundly patriarchal underlying concept of order, was added to Augustus's titles in 2 B.C.E.; see *Res Gestae* 35.

56. For grain deliveries from the provinces to Rome and the role of Egypt in particular, see Peter Garnsey and Richard Saller, *The Roman Empire: Economy, Society and Culture* (Berkeley/Los Angeles: University of California Press, 1987), 83–85, 98–100.

57. The fact that after both the Galatian and the Egyptian triumph, the "mothers" play a key role in the ritual performances on the Shield (8.665 and 718)—again strongly reminiscent of the powerful

role of the "mothers" on the Pergamene Great Frieze—underlines not only the unity of fight–victory–worship but also once again the parallel nature of Galatomachy and the Battle of Actium in Virgil. This also raises the question whether the scene in the underworld (8.666–70) and the march of the vanquished nations are to be perceived as correspondent, turning the conquest and slavery of the others into an inevitable fate representing a superior righteousness of the conquering and enslaving self, which would once more mirror the Pergamene prototype.

58. For the ritual of hunt as practiced by ancient Near Eastern rulers as a symbol of social domination and domination over animals/nature, see Thomas E. J. Wiedemann, *Emperors and Gladiators* (London: Routledge, 1992), 62.

59. The Latin term *munus* or its plural *munera* (gladiatorial combat) literally means "duty" or "obligation" and originally referred to the responsibility of the living to the deceased; it later became the duty owed by the people of Rome to its politicians. The first known *munus* took place in Rome in 264 B.C.E. with three pairs of gladiators; the next in 216 B.C.E., possibly at the Forum Boarium. See Alison Futrell, *Blood in the Arena: The Spectacle of Roman Power* (Austin: University of Texas Press, 1997), 19–24. Futrell notes that these dates are not coincidentally linked to the First and Second Punic Wars as times of impending danger and crisis (p. 23). For our exploration, it is of great interest to observe also a linkage to the first and second Galatian sacrifices of 228 and 216 B.C.E., which shared the same context of the Carthagian threat and the Forum Boarium as its location. (See chapter 1 above, and Futrell, *Blood in the Arena*, 197–203).

60. See Futrell, *Blood in the Arena,* 9–44.

61. The word *arena* is derived from Latin *harena,* "sand."

62. Wiedemann, *Emperors and Gladiators,* 55.

63. Futrell, *Blood in the Arena,* 45.

64. Based on around three hundred epigraphic and monumental sources, Louis Robert already in 1940 pointed out that gladiatorial games as a Roman innovation obviously were highly popular in the Greek East and were inseparably linked to the imperial cult. He observes the highest frequency of gladiatorial contests in regions most densely urbanized, such as in Asia Minor, where every city had its own imperial priest. Louis Robert, *Les Gladiateurs dans l'Orient Grec* (Paris: Librairie Ancienne Honore Champion, 1940), 15, 243, 270–71. For the Roman West, Jean-Claude Golvin estimates the number of amphitheaters at 252, compared to twenty in the East. Jean-Claude Golvin, *L'Amphithéâtre Romain* (Paris: E. de Boccard, 1988). Futrell counts seventy-two amphitheaters in all Gaul (*Blood in the Arena*, 66), thirty of them in the province of Lugdunensis. This compares to twenty-two in Spain and Lusitania (p. 55) and nineteen in Britannia (p. 58).

65. For the construction, see Futrell, *Blood in the Arena,* 154–61; based on the reconstruction by G. Alföldy of an overwritten "ghost" inscription, Louis Feldman suggests that the Colosseum was financed with the spoils from the Great Jewish Revolt against Rome in 70 C.E. in Louis H. Feldman, "Financing the Colosseum," *Biblical Archeology Review* 27, no. 4 (2001): 22–31. For the common notion that thousands of Judean prisoners of war were used to build the Colosseum, see Feldman, "Financing," 311; and Futrell, *Blood in the Arena,* 288 n. 194.

66. K. M. Coleman, "Fatal Charades: Roman Executions Staged as Mythological Enactments," *JRS* 80 (1990): 60–73.

67. See, for example, Ludwig Friedlaender's description of this overwhelming experience, which created a sense of belonging and unity in common "adherence to a nation that appeared so grand even in its decline" ("Das Bewusstsein, einer Nation anzugehoeren, die auch in ihrem Sinken noch so gewaltig erschien"). Ludwig Friedlaender, *Darstellungen aus der Sittengeschichte Roms in der Zeit von Augustus bis zum Ausgang der Antonine,* 4 vols. (Leipzig: S. Hirzel, 1922), 2:98.

68. The "good works" (benefactions) and "gifts" of ancient euergetism thus were, like the games, not as politically innocent as they might seem. They were firmly integrated into vertical power constructs as well as horizontal demarcations between self (in this case the "consumers" of the games) and other (the victims), and part of the social ritual that was in place to establish status and honor, law and order. In this sense, they are "works of (imperial) law," as, for example, the donation that Titus made to the provinces

in 70 C.E. when he presented them with multitudes of Jewish prisoners of war as a "gift" (*diedōrēsato*) in order to have them publicly exterminated by sword or wild beasts in the theaters (Josephus, *B.J.* 7.418). Robert Jewett's argument that Paul's criticism of "works of the law" might not target Jewish works and Jewish law but rather this competitive, combative, and consumptive logic of euergetism dramatically changes the way one reads the core texts of "justification by faith." See Robert Jewett, *Romans: A Commentary*, Hermeneia (Minneapolis: Fortress Press, 2007), for example, 295–303 on Rom 3:27–31. We will return to this in chapters 4 and 6 below.

69. Futrell, *Blood in the Arena*, 46. For an in-depth exploration of the relationship between emperor and the Roman *plebs urbana* during the Julio-Claudian dynasty, considering both the political disempowerment and the relative power of the urban masses in Rome, see Zvi Yavetz, *Plebs and Princeps* (London: Oxford University Press, 1969); for the political dynamics of the games in particular, see 18–24.

70. Futrell, *Blood in the Arena*, 45. Note also the famous words of Juvenal 10.77–81: "There was a time when the people bestowed every honor—the governance of provinces, civic leadership, military command—but now they hold themselves back, now two things only do they ardently desire: bread and games."

71. The cognomen *pater patriae* for Augustus, according to Suetonius, had originally been urged on the emperor by the plebs of Rome during the spectacles (*Aug.* 58). To show his willingness to mix with the people, Augustus tried to attend every performance and even would apologize for absences; see Yavetz, *Plebs and Princeps*, 22, 100–101.

72. Futrell (*Blood in the Arena*, 5–6) states with regard to the provinces: "The Imperial goal of assimilating provincials made use of the arena as a sacred space. When religion is understood as a functional means of unifying a community and providing the individual with a sense of corporate identity, we can view the amphitheater as a setting for public ritual for the provincial populace. . . . Augustus made clearest use of the amphitheatre as an integral part of the Imperial Cult, in the earliest phase of emperor worship. The amphitheater encouraged a large number of participants to join in the celebration of the central authority, thereby confirming the divine status of the emperor and legitimizing his rule."

73. This aspect of seeing as participating is stressed, for example, in the *Passion of Perpetua and Felicity* 21.7, where the crowds demand to see the bodies of the two female delinquents "so that their eyes could participate in the killing as the sword entered their flesh."

74. As Wiedemann observes (*Emperors and Gladiators*, 65–66), the Roman emperor symbolically fulfilled the duty of controlling the wild not by hunting but by "presiding over the artificial venatio in the arena." The symbolism of hunting as domination over nature also links the emperor to the mythical hunter figure of Heracles.

75. As we have already seen for Augustus and Titus, the numbers of animals used must have been enormous, for example, eleven thousand when Trajan celebrated his triumph over the Dacians in 107 C.E. (Cassius Dio 66.25). See Friedlaender, *Darstellungen*, 2:81–83, who also discusses in some detail the problems of the large-scale hunting and long-distance transportation of these animals. While this led obviously in antiquity to the extinction of certain species, Friedlaender apologetically stresses the supposedly beneficial impact of "cleansing" formerly unsafe lands for farming by eradicating lions, elephants, and hippopotami.

76. Wiedemann (*Emperors and Gladiators*, 103) notes that defeated enemies were either sold as slaves or executed, often by being forced to kill each other; some of them, however, were trained as gladiators to fight in the arena. The "crime" of prisoners of war was their refusal to accept "the benefits of subjection to Roman order"—their fight against Rome had turned them into outcasts and nonparticipants in the "community of civilized peoples," and they therefore deserved death. This logic applies, for example, to a substantial number (*pleistous*) of the ninety-seven thousand Jewish prisoners of war mentioned by Josephus in *B.J.* 7.420. Their disposal in provincial arenas (7.418) served as a public performance and celebration of Roman law and order (see n. 68 above).

77. Gladiators, like prostitutes and actors, were socially dead. They lost their full legal status as citizens and suffered *infamia*; see Wiedemann, *Emperors and Gladiators*, 28–30, 105–10.

78. A few very successful gladiators in fact had a chance to be freed and reintegrated into society; see

Wiedemann, *Emperors and Gladiators,* 105: "the criminal condemned *ad ludos* was a socially 'dead man' who had a chance of coming alive again."

79. It is noteworthy that the ethnic category of Gauls/Galatians (*gallus*) itself had become firmly integrated into the "dictionary" of the arena, namely, as a specific class of gladiators whose helmets had a fishlike crest. By the time of Augustus, however, the *gallus* is renamed *murmillo.* According to Wiedemann, this conveys the integration of the Gauls/Galatians into the empire. In a similiar way, *Samnites* became *secutors;* see Wiedemann, *Emperors and Gladiators* 41.

80. Friedlaender, *Darstellungen,* 2:97: "die Scheidung der Menschheit in eine berechtigte und unberechtigte Hälfte." Friedlaender explains the unbridgeable gap between these two halves of humanity in antiquity by the lack of concepts of human rights and international law, as well as the institution of slavery, all of which encouraged a habitual contempt for certain groups of human beings whose suffering and destruction in the arena were watched without compassion because they were either irrelevant or damaging for society: enemies of the country, barbarians, criminals, slaves, or outcasts.

81. Such an adverse reaction "would have signified an undue sympathy toward the disorderly elements of the Roman world or an unwillingness to exercise one's right as a citizen to participate in the maintenance of civic law." Michael Pucci, "Arenas," in *Dictionary of New Testament Background,* ed. Craig A. Evans and Stanley E. Porter (Downers Grove, Ill.: InterVarsity, 2000), 113. Futrell (*Blood in the Arena,* 49) notes that the viewers identify with the perpetrators of violence if the victim is "demonized or alienated from the empathy of the audience." Thus, they "were meant to participate in the 'punishment' of the performer; they were his judges, inflicting the fate he merited, both by his marginal status and by his actions in the arena."

82. Coleman, "Fatal Charades," 58) emphasizes that it was vital for the functioning of the games that the sympathies of the spectators were not going into the wrong direction, that is, toward the objects displayed in the arena, as happened once in 55 B.C.E. when the spectators expressed sympathy for the elephants (Cicero, *Fam.* 7.1.3).

83. For the games as surrogate war, see Futrell, *Blood in the Arena,* 50.

84. Paul Plass observes that the "ritually disciplined violence done to outsiders was reconstituted as the security of insiders who could return home safe, sound, and victorious, as those who witnessed a triumphal spectacle did." Paul Plass, *The Game of Death in Ancient Rome: Arena Sport and Political Suicide,* Wisconsin Studies in Classics (Madison: University of Wisconsin Press, 1995), 37.

85. See Yavetz, *Plebs and Princeps,* 19: "At the circus, however, the masses had a feeling of confidence which they experienced nowhere else, it being the one place where they had authority over people's lives through 'vertere et premere pollicem.'" For details, see Friedlaender, *Darstellungen,* 2:74.

86. Suetonius, *Aug.* 44; see also Futrell, *Blood in the Arena,* 161–62.

87. Suetonius, *Aug.* 40; see Zanker, *Power of Images,* 162–65.

88. Plass, *Game of Death,* 43.

89. Yavetz (*Plebs and Princeps,* 19–20) notes: "Seeing the poor enslaved wretches who fought in the arena, the spectators were animated by a sense of superiority denied to them everywhere else."

90. For Martial and the staging of the Laureolus scene, see Coleman, "Fatal Charades," 64–65, who also describes other such scenes where capital punishment is set in a dramatic (often mythological) context involving role-play.

91. An explicit reference to Prometheus's hanging on the rock as a "crucifixion" is made in Lucian, *Prometheus* 1–2; see Martin Hengel, *Crucifixion in the Ancient World and the Folly of the Message of the Cross* (Philadelphia: Fortress Press, 1977), 11–12.

92. Ibid., 86–87.

93. Ibid., 87.

94. Ibid., 59; and Yavetz, *Plebs and Princeps,* 29–30, 35. The incident reported by Tacitus (*Ann.* 14.42–45) from the time of Nero in 61 C.E. involves the four hundred slaves belonging to the household of a city prefect who was murdered by one of them. The argument that ultimately decides the case is noteworthy: As the slave members of Roman households recently have grown more and more multinational (*nationes in familiis habemus*), multicultural (*quibus diversi ritus*) and alien or nonidentifiable in their

religious affiliation (*externa sacra aut nulla sacra sunt*), the only way to keep such a mishmash (*conluviem*) at bay is through terror (*non nisi metu coercueris*). This gives an interesting background against which to understand the challenges that Paul's mixed and diverse communities from the "nations" faced.

95. See Coleman, "Fatal Charades," 56, 65. In addition to Laureolus, she quotes two more examples: (1) An inscription from Pompej (*CIL* IV.9983a) announces crucifixions (*cruciarii*) in the amphitheater during the ordinary spectacles, together with wild beasts (*venatio*) and awnings (*vela*). (2) The Christian martyr Blandina in Lyons (1.41; see Herbert Musurillo, *The Acts of Christian Martyrs: Introduction, Texts, and Translations* [Oxford: Clarendon, 1972], 5) is "hung on a post as bait for the animals in a posture that is explicitly likened to crucifixion."

96. For the need of public visibility, see Hengel, *Crucifixion*, 50.

97. Another part that belonged to the arena spectacles but for practical reasons often had to be performed outside the amphitheater, was mock naval battles.

98. Coleman ("Fatal Charades," 47) observes with regard to the crucifixion of Jesus that already the soldiers' mockery of Jesus as king and god (Mark 15:16-20; Matt 27:27-31), symbolized in the purple cloak and the crown of thorns (reminiscent of the radiate crown of divine rulers), was part of the standard repertoire of capital punishment. Public humiliation aimed at alienating and self-distancing the onlookers from the other of the transgressor/usurper and his messianic claims.

99. Cassius Dio reports that immediately before the inauguration of the Colosseum in 80 C.E. (66.25), Mount Vesuvius erupted. The catastrophe was preceded by the appearance of Giants (66.22); some people thought that a new revolt of the Giants was taking place, while others believed that the whole universe was being resolved into chaos and fire (66.23). Furthermore, another fire devastated Rome (66.24). All this must have contributed to the perception of the one-hundred-day-long inaugural show of the Colosseum as a reestablishment of order and security against a Giant threat.

100. Hengel, *Crucifixion*, 88.

101. See chapter 6 below.

102. For Nero's persecution of the "Christiani" as an reenactment of the Great Frieze, see the epilogue below.

103. Futrell, *Blood in the Arena*, 7.

104. The emperor in this setting is deep down, that is, close to the site where chaos and the enemy are symbolically confronted and defeated. He is shown as directly and vicariously exposed to the threat, sometimes even blood from the arena splashing over him. He poses as the invincible general leading the legions, the insuperable royal hunter fighting wild beasts and chaotic nature, the highest law enforcement officer supervising lawful torture and execution. In this arrangement, Caesar has a position that resembles the role of Heracles, the supreme human helper and co-combatant of the deities, on the Great Frieze and at the forefront of the primeval battle of civilization.

105. Plass, *Game of Death*, 26.

106. Wiedemann, *Emperors and Gladiators*, 46.

107. Ibid., 46.

108. See the conclusion of this chapter and chapter 6 below.

109. For the text and a summary of the *Enuma Elish*, see Alexander Heidel, *The Babylonian Genesis: The Story of Creation* (Chicago: University of Chicago Press, 1951), 1–60. As the rise of Marduk and of Babylon to supremacy reflects the historical background of the First Babylonian Dynasty (1894–1595 B.C.E.), Heidel assumes that the creation epic in its present form was composed during this time.

110. Heidel (*Babylonian Genesis*, 9) states that the vanquished gods who had been fighting with Tiamat "were made the servants of the victors, for whose sustenance they had to provide. However, their menial task proved so burdensome that they asked Marduk for relief. As Marduk listened to the words of the captive gods, he resolved to create man and to impose on him the service which the defeated deities had to render." Victor Maag points out that the enslavement of the defeated gods by their victors was justified by (martial) law. On the other hand, the permanent enslavement of gods would have threatened the cosmic order with dangerous tensions. Victor Maag, "Sumerische und babylonische Mythen von der Erschaffung des Menschen," in *Kultur, Kulturkontakt und Religion: Gesammelte Studien zur allgemein*

und alttestamentlichen Religionsgeschichte. Victor Maag zum 70. Geburtstag, ed. Hans Heinrich Schmid and Odil Hannes Steck (Göttingen: Vandenhoeck & Ruprecht, 1980), 57–60. For the designation of humankind as substitute workers in place of the gods and the alternative concept of the biblical creation account, see Brigitte Kahl, "Fratricide and Ecocide: Re-Reading Genesis 2–4," in *Earth Habitat: Eco-Justice and the Church's Response,* ed. Dieter Hessel and Larry Rasmussen (Minneapolis: Fortress Press, 2001), 55.

111. For the Babylonian New Year festival and the reciting of the creation epic (or rather its actual performance in the manner of a "medieval mystery play"), see Svend Aage Pallis, *The Babylonian Akîtu Festival* (Copenhagen: A. F. Host, 1926); and Joan Oates, *Babylon* (London: Thames & Hudson, 1991), 175; also 169, 172. The Babylonian king played a crucial role in this ceremony (Oates, 176), which represented the creation of cosmic order out of chaos and restarted a new cycle of natural and social life. This links to the position of Caesar as most prominent "editor" of imperial games, which, similar to the *Enuma Elish,* were an ongoing performance of the imperial creation myth. Major cycles of games in Rome were thus linked to the transitional celebrations of the New Year and Spring Festivals; see Pucci, "Arenas," 112. One might wonder whether the "inverted order" of the arena, which places the emperor "deep down," could be linked to the particular ritual in the Babylonian ceremony where the king was stripped of his royal insignia, humiliated, and forced to crouch before Marduk, in order subsequently to be restored to his power (Oates, *Babylon,* 176). Does Caesar enter into a similar liminality where his power is symbolically at stake?

112. For the *Enuma Elish* as the mythic combat paradigm of Western culture, which posits the (female) other as object, opponent, alien, subhuman, and monstrous in order to establish the patriarchal self and the logic of warfare, see the insightful analysis in Catherine Keller, *From a Broken Web: Separation, Sexism, and Self* (Boston: Beacon Press, 1986), 73–88, as well as Rosemary Radford Ruether, *Gaia and God: An Ecofeminist Theology of Earth Healing* (San Francisco: HarperSanFrancisco, 1992), 15–31, for a comparison of the Babylonian, biblical, and Greek creation narratives from an ecofeminist perspective.

113. As Maag ("Sumerische und babylonische Mythen von der Erschaffung des Menschen," 58) points out, the slaughtering of Kingu as leader of Tiamat's chaotic rebel army has a propitiatory function. Kingu has to give his life as ransom for the rehabilitation of his comrades—that is, for the creation of humans liable for compulsory service to their superiors, the gods. In other words, he is the primeval vicarious sacrifice on which the existence of humanity depends. On the other hand, because of this origin, humanity also embodies the bloodline of uproar and lawlessness. It is inseparably linked to the female arch-rebel Tiamat. ("Eine Sühne aber hatte dennoch sein müssen. In diesem Sinne war *Kingu* dazu verurteilt worden, sein Leben gleichsam als Lösegeld für die Freilassung seiner Gefolgsleute—und das heisst eben für die Erschaffung dienstpflichtiger Menschen herzugeben. So führt denn der Mensch nach diesem klassisch gewordenen Verständnis babylonischer Mythologie das Blut des antikosmischen, lichtfeindlichen, chaossüchtigen Widersachers in seinen Adern.")

114. As shown in chapter 2 above, the same logic underlies Wolfram Hoepfner's proposal to imagine the sculptures of Dying and Dead Giants, Persians, Amazons, and Galatians as actually being placed on the surface of the sacrificial site at the Great Altar.

115. Again we are reminded of the role of the mothers in Virgil's Shield—the "good mothers" of the city engaged in civic/imperial worship of victory, as opposed to the "bad mother" Cleopatra, the defeated barbarian enemy queen and dishonorable lover of Roman Antony. The "bad mother" is reminiscent both of Tiamat in *Enuma Elish* and of Gaia on the Great Frieze, whereas Augë on the Telephos frieze and the fighting goddesses at the Gigantomachy frieze represent the "good mothers/females" compliant with Zeus's patriarchal order.

116. Georges Ville defines the *munera* as agonistic, not sacrificial. Georges Ville, *La gladiature en Occident des origines à la mort de Domitien,* Bibliothèque des ecoles françaises d'Athènes et de Rome 245e (Rome: Ecole française de Rome, 1981), 17. Wiedemann (*Emperors and Gladiators,* 34–35) rejects any notion of sacrifice or scapegoat rituals linked to gladiatorial combat, which he wants to perceive not so much as killing, but rather as "a demonstration of the power to overcome death." (*Emperors*

and Gladiators, 34, and quoting 35). Futrell (*Blood in the Arena,* 169–210, esp. 205) and Plass (*Game of Death,* 58–59), on the other hand, see noticeable parallels between *munera* and human sacrifice or scapegoat rituals.

117. Keith Hopkins, *Death and Renewal,* Sociological Studies in Roman History 2 (Cambridge: Cambridge University Press, 1983), 5.

118. Coleman, "Fatal Charades," 44–73, here 70.

119. Plass, *Game of Death,* 38–39, 59.

120. Ibid., 23.

121. Ibid., 22–23.

122. Futrell, *Blood in the Arena,* 171.

123. Ibid., 207–8.

124. Ibid., 209.

4. Roman Galatia

1. *Pace* Justin K. Hardin, who contends that Augustus had to build "Galatia basically from scratch." Justin K. Hardin, *Galatians and the Imperial Cult: A Critical Analysis of the First-century Social Context of Paul's Letter,* WUNT 2/237 (Tübingen: Mohr Siebeck, 2008), 49.

2. According to David Magie, this act of violence was followed in Galatia itself by another massacre of all remaining members of the Galatian nobility. David Magie, *Roman Rule in Asia Minor to the End of the Third Century after Christ,* 2 vols. (Princeton: Princeton University Press, 1950), 1:223.

3. See ibid., 1:216–17.

4. On another occasion Mithridates, in order to win allegiance, is reported to have proclaimed cancellation of debts, right of citizenship to all sojourners, and freedom to slaves so that "the debtors, sojourners and slaves would consider their new privileges only secure under the rule of Mithridates" (Appian, *Hist. rom.* 12.48).

5. The degeneration and hybridity of the Gauls of Asia Minor is mentioned also by the opponents of Manlius Vulso, who refuse him a triumph—they claim that there was not much glory in defeating these Gallograeci, whose bodies and minds have been mixed and corrupted (Livy 38.46, 49), a topic that Livy will develop further in book 39 in terms of Roman corruption through Hellenistic influences. The fact that both Manlius Vulso and his adversaries work with self-contradictory elements of the Celtic stereotype has been observed by Bernhard Kremer, *Das Bild der Kelten bis in augusteische Zeit: Studien zur Instrumentalisierung eines antiken Feindbildes bei griechischen und römischen Autoren,* Historia Einzelschriften (Stuttgart: Franz Steiner, 1994), 59.

6. Though Livy believes that Chiomara did not act as a woman should, her action seems to be in accordance with Celtic custom, which accorded women a highly independent role even as warriors. Plutarch (*Mor.* 258) describes her as a model of fidelity (*pistis*), intelligence (*synēsis*), and determination (*phronēma*). He also mentions the Celtic women of Italy, who were so successful in arbitrating and mediating controversies that they were regularly consulted in matters of war and peace and disputes with Hannibal (*Mor.* 246). For Celtic women in the classical world, see H. D. Rankin, *Celts and the Classical World* (London: Croom Helm, 1987), 245–58.

7. Stephen Mitchell, *Anatolia: Land, Men, and Gods in Asia Minor,* 2 vols. (Oxford: Clarendon, 1993), 1:43.

8. Ibid., 1:27.

9. Ibid.

10. Ibid., 1:29.

11. Ibid., 1:27.

12. Ibid., 1:37.

13. Ibid., 1:40.

14. William M. Ramsay, *The Social Basis of Roman Power in Asia Minor,* prepared for the press by J.

G. C. Anderson (Aberdeen: Aberdeen University Press, 1941), 4. Ramsay's statement also supports our notion of a functional imperial monotheism as vital for the integration of the conquered nations. See chapter 3 above.

15. Ibid.

16. Helmut Halfmann, *Die Senatoren aus dem östlichen Teil des Imperium Romanum bis zum Ende des 2. Jahrhunderts n. Chr.*, Hypomnemata 58 (Göttingen: Vandenhoeck & Ruprecht, 1979), 48; for Julia Severa, see chapter 5 below.

17. Halfmann, *Senatoren*, 43; see nos. 62, 17, and 19 in the prosopographic section. For the Ancyran inscription dedicated to C. Julius Severus around 114 C.E., see *OGIS* 544, and Emin Bosch, *Quellen zur Geschichte der Stadt Ankara im Altertum* (Ankara: Türk Tarih Kurumu Basimevi, 1967), nos. 105–6.

18. Plutarch mentions her together with Chiomara. While he does not refer to her Pergamene descent, he confirms the importance of the dynastic principle. What he finds worth mentioning among his examples of virtuous women is that Stratonike was unable to bear children and thus provided a surrogate mother for Deiotaros to produce the dynastic offspring he desired in order to guarantee the succession to his throne (*Mor.* 258).

19. Halfmann, *Senatoren,* 48.

20. Mitchell, *Anatolia* 1:33, 35.

21. Ibid., 1:37. The assassination of Castor Tarcondarius is not the only dynastic murder committed by Deiotaros, whose story in this and several other respects resembles that of Herod the Great in Judea.

22. The speech *Pro Fonteio* belongs to a time two decades earlier. Fonteius, a praetor of newly found Gallia Narbonesis in the West was accused by Gallic provincial emissaries of brutal exploitation in 69 B.C.E. Cicero's defense is based mostly on the depravity of the Gauls, who therefore are not trustworthy witnesses. He raises the question whether even the most honorable native of Gaul is "to be set on the same level with even the meanest citizen of Rome, let alone with the highest men of our commonwealth? Does Indutiomarus [the chieftain of the Allobroges demanding justice] know what is meant by giving evidence? When he is brought into the witness-box, is he affected by that sense of awe from which none of *us* is exempt?" (*Pro Font.* 27). Implicitly referring to the ineradicable otherness of the Gauls/Galatians and the blasphemy of their warfare as Giant battle against heaven, including the attacks at Delphi and the Roman Capitol, Cicero continues: "Or do you think that nations like that are influenced, when they give evidence, by the sanctity of an oath or by the fear of the immortal gods, differing so widely from all other nations as they do in habits and in character? Other nations wage wars in defence of their religion, they do so against the religion of every people; others in waging war entreat the favour and the pardon of the immortal gods, they wage war against the immortal gods themselves"(30).

23. Mitchell, *Anatolia*, 1:72.

24. See Strabo 12.6.5; and Magie, *Roman Rule*, 1:453, 2:1303.

25. See Mitchell, *Anatolia*, 1:77.

26. Magie, *Roman Rule*, 1:461, 2:1322.

27. According to Mitchel (*Anatolia* 1:136), in particular III *Cyrenaica*, XXII *Deiotariana*, and VII *Macedonica*. Bosch (*Ankara*, no. 49) renders the fragmentary list of thirty-six soldiers of the Legio III *Cyrenaica* and Legio XXII (subsequently *Deiotariana*) stationed in Egypt toward the end of the first century B.C.E.; ten of them are recorded as natives of Ancyra and ten come from other places (formerly) under Galatian rule, such as Tavium, Sebastopolis in Pontos, Pompeiopolis or Gangra in Paphlagonia. It is interesting to note that two soldiers come from Lugdunum, the capital of the Gallic province in the West.

28. Mitchell, *Anatolia,* 1:136. Mitchell assumes that the name *Deiotariana* dates from the time of Emperor Claudius, while Lawrence Keppie sees it attested only since the Flavian period. Lawrence Keppie, *Legions and Veterans: Roman Army Papers 1971–2000* (Stuttgart: Franz Steiner, 2000), 227.

29. Mitchell, *Anatolia*, 1:141.

30. Ibid., 1:140.

31. For the organization of the Roman army, see Adrian Keith Goldsworthy, *The Roman Army at War, 100 BC–AD 200*, Oxford Classical Monographs (Oxford/New York: Clarendon, 1996), 12–38.

32. Soldiers in the auxiliary forces entered as noncitizens and got their Roman citizenship only after the end of their active service. For the army as instrument of Romanization and integration (including legal, social, and cultural norms, Latin and Greek language, imperial worship), see Werner Eck and Hartmut Wolff, eds., *Heer und Integrationspolitik: Die römischen Militärdiplome als historische Quelle,* Passauer historische Forschungen 2 (Cologne: Bohlau, 1986), 3–7.

33. Ramsay, *Social Basis,* 8.

34. Goldsworthy (*Roman Army at War,* 68) mentions the ease with which former enemies were assimilated into the Roman army and how auxiliary units cooperated "highly effectively against opposition with whom they had more in common than with their Roman leaders." This holds true also for the civil wars that created the empire: "The Republic fell, and the Principate was created, in a series of wars made possible by the willingness of professional Roman soldiers to fight each other" (ibid., 1).

35. In terms of images, this ambiguous process of subjection and imperial identity formation recalls a magnificent mausoleum that the Gallic Julii in the West had erected for themselves at Glanum, today's Saint-Rémy-de-Provence in France. In this eye-catching building, the elevated and superior position of the Galatians/Gauls, appearing in Roman toga high up at the top of a tripartite structure, is literally "built" on a substructure that proudly presents their own defeat. In battle-scenes that appear at the altar-like base of the monument, Galatian warriors are depicted. While this points to the Galatomachy as the foundational triumph of order over chaos, the uppermost part of the mausoleum features a round temple where the Galatian/Gallic Julii in the costume of the master race display their successful way *up.* The message is clear: victory belongs to Rome. If Rome grants to some of the Galatians/Gauls (in return for their pro-Roman collaboration and reidentification) a chance to ascend to a more privileged status, most of their fellow tribespeople would be exploited as new subjects, soldiers, and taxpayers of the empire. Galatian ascension and integration presuppose Galatian defeat and sacrifice. For the monument, see Paul Zanker, *The Power of Images in the Age of Augustus,* Jerome Lectures, 16th Series (Ann Arbor: University of Michigan Press, 1990), 17–18; and John R. Marszal, "Ubiquitous Barbarians: Representation of the Gauls at Pergamon and Elsewhere," in *From Pergamon to Sperlonga: Sculpture and Context,* ed. Nancy T. de Grummond and Brunilde S. Ridgway, Hellenistic Culture and Society (Berkeley: University of California Press, 2000), 217–18, who points to the contrast between Romanized and barbarian Gaul as pictorial program. This contrast is expressed also by the proximity of the monument to the famous triumphal arch of Glanum/Saint-Rémy, which shows Gallic men and women beneath trophies, either bound or chained. They are juxtaposed to a female figure in a fringed cloak, seated atop a pile of weapons, and a man, similarly clothed, both of them showing the pose of the victor and probably representing "the good Gallia," who participated in the Roman victory over itself (ibid., 217).

36. Magie (*Roman Rule,* 2:1304), however, doubts that Amyntas made a proper will. Mitchell (*Anatolia,* 1:61–63) discusses bequests of indigenous rulers as a legal mode of power transfer to Rome in the second and first centuries B.C.E. He believes that Amyntas might have wished to protect both the life of his son from rival pretenders to the throne and his own hard-won—though fragile—power position in the Taurus from his opponents. He therefore handed over his kingdom to Rome, which "showed no sign of embarrassment or reluctance to take control" (ibid., 63).

37. Magie, *Roman Rule,* 1:454.

38. See R. K. Sherk, "Roman Galatia: The Governors from 25 B.C. to A.D. 114," in *ANRW* II 7.1 (1980): 954–1052; for the duties of the provincial governors, who held primary responsibility for judicial and military matters, and the provincial procurators, who were appointed to look after taxes, finances, and compulsory services, see Mitchell, *Anatolia,* 1:63–69. As Mitchell points out, the power of this comparatively small body of Roman administration to intervene in public life was "virtually unlimited" (p. 68). Nevertheless, the immense changes brought to the newly annexed land were caused not primarily by direct administrative interventions but by "the new social, economic and political conditions" in general, which resulted in a monetarized economy, growth of urban settlements, and new forms of exploitation of provincial land (p. 69).

39. Magie, *Roman Rule,* 2:1311.

40. For a description of these territories, see Strabo 12.5–7.

41. On the provincial boundaries in Asia Minor from 25 B.C.E. to 235 C.E., see Mitchell, *Anatolia,* 1:151–57, Appendix 1.

42. *CIG* 3991, and *ILS* 9499; see James M. Scott, *Paul and the Nations: The Old Testament and Jewish Background of Paul's Mission to the Nations with Special Reference to the Destination of Galatians,* WUNT 84 (Tübingen: Mohr Siebeck, 1995), 190–91.

43. Jürgen Deininger, *Die Provinziallandtage der Römischen Kaiserzeit: Von Augustus bis zum Ende des 3. Jahrhunderts n. Chr.,* Vestigia 6 (Munich/Berlin: Beck, 1965), 66–69. In addition, coins that were minted under Nero show the name Nero *Sebastos* or that of his wife Poppaea *Sebaste* on the front and *TO KOINON GALATON* on the reverse (*BMC* I, p. 547, nos. 3563 and 3564). Pliny (*Nat.* 5.27.32), Tacitus (*Ann.* 13.35; 15.6; *Hist.* 2.9), and, in the New Testament, 1 Pet 1:1 refer to the whole province as "Galatia." This, however, does not preclude the use of the term also for the smaller tribal area. See Cilliers Breytenbach, *Paulus und Barnabas in der Provinz Galatien: Studien zu Apostelgeschichte 13f.; 16,6; 18,23 und den Adressaten des Galaterbriefes* (Leiden/New York: Brill, 1996), 151. Breytenbach also points out that Paul had a preference for using provincial names—Macedonia (Phil 4:15; 1 Cor 16:5; 2 Cor 1:16; 2:13; 7:5; 8:1; 9:2; 11:9; Rom 15:26), Achaia (1 Cor 16:15; 2 Cor 1:1; 9:2; 11:10; Rom 15:26), Asia (2 Cor 1:8; Rom 16:5), Illyricum (Rom 15:19), and Spain (Rom 15:24).

44. Mitchell, *Anatolia,* 1:76.

45. Ibid., 1:77; for an extensive treatment, see Barbara Levick, *Roman Colonies in Southern Asia Minor* (Oxford: Clarendon Press, 1967).

46. Mitchell, *Anatolia,* 1:70.

47. *CIL* III, 6974.

48. Mitchell, *Anatolia,* 1:63

49. For colonization and roads as the reconfiguration of landscapes and space, see Emma Dench, *Romulus' Asylum: Roman Identities from the Age of Alexander to the Age of Hadrian* (Oxford: Oxford University Press, 2005), 164–65: "The roads themselves alter forever the ways in which individual areas interconnect, while defying what would seem to be topographical constraints, such as rivers and even mountains." A road "refigures the connection between ethnically diverse peoples and symbolizes in a very visible way the power of the rulers."

50. On "communication" as a core strategy of Rome to create consensus among its subjects, see Clifford Ando, *Imperial Ideology and Provincial Loyalty in the Roman Empire,* Classics and Contemporary Thought 6 (Berkeley: University of California Press, 2000); on images as a crucial part of this communication, see 206–76; on coins in particular, see 215–28. As Ando states, "There can be no question that the medium that reached the widest audience on the most continuous basis was the coinage" (p. 215).

51. Ramsay is inclined to see the three tribes of North Galatia as culturally not very different from those of the Taurus region to the south. Owing to the "European Gallic descent," they were "anti-Roman by racial instinct and still more through the natural antipathy of the Gallic tribal feeling and system to the more highly articulated form of city government. Rome felt that the 'tribe,' with all that it implied, was hostile. With the tribe persisted the Gallic language, in some small degree the Gaulish religion, the spirit of freedom and the reluctance to comply with alien custom." William M. Ramsay, "Studies in the Roman Province Galatia," *Journal of Roman Studies* 12 (1922): 150.

52. Mitchell, *Anatolia,* 1:87.

53. Bosch, *Ankara,* 54, who also gives the proper Greek as *Sebastēnoi,* rather than the Latinized *Sebastēni.*

54. Mitchell, *Anatolia,* 1:87.

55. See n. 22 above for Cicero's reference to the Galatians/Gauls as warriors "against the religion of every people" and "against the immortal gods themselves" (*Pro Font.* 30).

56. On Augustus as "father of the human race," see Ando, *Ideology,* 398–405.

57. For the overall plan and detailed description, see Zanker, *Power of Images,* 193–215.

58. For an interpretation of this statement and the question how exactly the vanquished nations were represented in the Forum of Augustus, see Claude Nicolet, *Space, Geography, and Politics in the Early Roman Empire,* Jerome Lectures, 19th Series (Ann Arbor: University of Michigan Press, 1991),

42–43; see also Davina C. Lopez, *Apostle to the Conquered: Reimagining Paul's Mission,* Paul in Critical Contexts (Minneapolis: Fortress Press, 2008), 52.

59. Zanker, *Power of Images,* 214.

60. Nicolet, *Space, Geography, and Politics,* 43. Horace (*Carm.* 1.12.49–60) and Ovid (*Fasti* 2.127–32) strongly support this linkage between Augustus's earthly and Jupiter's heavenly rule/fatherhood. While Horace addresses Jupiter as "father and guardian of the human race" and Caesar "next in power" (*Carm.* 1.12.49–52), Ovid invokes Caesar with the following acclamation: "Holy Father of thy Country [*sancte pater patriae tibi*], this title has been conferred on thee by the people, by the senate, and by us, the knights. But history has already conferred it, yet didst thou also receive though late, thy title true; long time hadst thou been the Father of the World [*pater orbis eras*]. Thou bearest on earth the name which Jupiter bears in high heaven: of men thou art the father, he of the gods" (LCL). See also Ando, *Ideology,* 400.

61. Ando (*Ideology,* 403) points out that the role of Augustus as "father" was not restricted to Rome but was also claimed by the provinces, for example, in Asia minor, as several inscriptions demonstrate. To show the universal relevance of this title, the *koinon* of Asia, for example, rendered it as "father of his fatherland and of the entire human race."

62. Maria H. Dettenhofer states that Augustus as *pater patriae* turns his house into the all-comprising Roman "super-domus," where he as the "father" has unrestricted patriarchal/imperial power (*patria potestas*) over all his subjects, who owe him piety (*pietas*) as sons owe it to their father. Maria H. Dettenhofer, *Herrschaft und Widerstand im augusteischen Principat: Die Konkurrenz zwischen res publica und domus Augusta,* Historia, Einzelschriften 140 (Stuttgart: Franz Steiner, 2000), 172–76.

63. Andrew Wallace-Hadrill, *Augustan Rome* (London: Bristol Classical, 1993), 68.

64. See chapter 2 above.

65. Bosch, *Ankara,* no. 49. See n. 27 above.

66. Ramsay, "Studies," 181.

67. Bosch, *Ankara,* 32.

68. The overall construct again points to a "functional imperial monotheism." The universal fatherhood and universal divinity of *Augustus alone* intersect through his assimilation to the highest "father" Zeus/Jupiter and through his role as sole benefactor and savior of the whole human race, both paternal and divine. If Augustus thus "endowed the Roman empire with its only universally shared deity," as Ando states (*Ideology,* 392), he is also the only father common to all Roman subjects.

69. Ramsay, "Studies," 154; Magie, *Roman Rule,* 1:459. The *council* of the three Gallic provinces in the West, which had its chief seat in Lugdunum, is called "Concilium Galliarum."

70. Bosch, *Ankara,* no. 56.

71. Deininger, *Die Provinziallandtage,* 66–69 (the *koinon* of Galatia), 99–107 (the three Gallic provinces); a concise summary is given on 189–94.

72. Mitchell, *Anatolia,* 1:103.

73. According to Mitchell (*Anatolia,* 1:107), the entrance to the imperial sanctuary at Pisidian Antioch, which was probably the last element of the whole complex to be completed, is marked by a triple-arched propylon dedicated to emperor Claudius in 50 c.e.; on Antioch, see also Hardin, *Galatians and the Imperial Cult,* 58–63, 71–78.

74. Mitchell, *Anatolia,* 1:107.

75. Hardin, *Galatians and the Imperial Cult,* 64–65, 79.

76. Alison Futrell, *Blood in the Arena: The Spectacle of Roman Power* (Austin: University of Texas Press, 1997), 80–84.

77. On the sixty images of the Gallic tribes at Lugdunum and the remarkable transformation of "an image intimately informed by the iconography of defeat into one celebrating unification," see Ando, *Ideology,* 313. On the somewhat parallel depiction of defeated nations in general at Aphrodisias in Asia Minor, see Lopez, *Apostle to the Conquered,* 42–49.

78. Hardin, *Galatians and the Imperial Cult,* 79–80.

79. While a vast group of giants at the Great Frieze have Gallic/Galatian facial features and hair,

others combine "Makedonian armor with conventional Greek faces," or "reference Seleukid Mesopotamia and North Syria," next to ancient Near Eastern motifs of lion-monster or man-bull. See Ann Kuttner, "'Do You Look Like You Belong Here?' Asianism at Pergamon and the Makedonian Diaspora," in *Cultural Borrowings and Ethnic Appropriations in Antiquity*, ed. Erich S. Gruen, Oriens et Occidens 8 (Stuttgart: Franz Steiner, 2005), 185.

80. See chapter 2 above.

81. Ando, *Ideology*, 46.

82. Ramsay, "Studies," 60; see also Peter Garnsey and Richard Saller, *The Roman Empire: Economy, Society and Culture* (Berkeley/Los Angeles: University of California Press, 1987), 26: "The secret of government without bureaucracy was the Roman system of cities."

83. As Mitchell (*Anatolia*, 1:81) points out, though, effective power and political autonomy had slipped away from the cities to kings and commanders already in the Hellenistic period and was now firmly in the hands of the emperor. City pride, status, and identity were thus manifested especially in public building that "remained one of the few forms of independent political expression open to the cities."

84. Strabo 12.5; Mitchell, *Anatolia*, 1:81–82.

85. Mitchell (*Anatolia*, 1:87) assumes that all three cities were founded by Augustus simultaneously in 22 or 21 B.C.E. The redistribution of tribal territory probably was not without political considerations. Mitchell states that Pessinus and the Tolistobogii (the tribe of Deiotaros) had to give up much territory to the colony of Germa and to the Sebastēni Tectosages of Ancyra, which became the seat of the provincial governor and thus the capital city of the province.

86. Ramsay ("Studies," 150) states that the cities to the south of the Galatian province minted coins earlier, showing their advanced civilization: "Coinage is the test, for the people that coins money binds itself to trade and order, which were of the essence of the Hellenic system."

87. Mitchell, *Anatolia*, 1:113; cf. Ramsay, "Studies," 57, who links the slow development of Ancyra into a proper Greco-Roman polis to the strong "tribal Gallic feeling." Still around 80 C.E. Ancyra appears more as a "tribal centre" than as a self-governing Hellenic city.

88. Mitchell (*Anatolia*, 1:197) points to the often underestimated role of policing forces (*diōgmitai*) in subduing the countryside to the law of the city: "But police activity extended beyond the repression of banditry to cover many aspects of keeping order in rural areas. In particular eirenarchs, *paraphylakes*, and their small forces of armed men were in the last analysis the only means available to compel the peasant inhabitants of city territories to make their material contribution to the administration and prosperity of the community, and to the taxes imposed by Rome."

89. Mitchell, *Anatolia*, 1:244.

90. Ibid., 1:245.

91. Ibid., 1:256.

92. Ibid., 1:254–55. Mitchell assumes that about 50 percent of the overall agricultural produce that also included wool, meat, timber, and garden products would go into taxes to Rome (10 percent or more), rent in kind paid to city-based landlords (20 percent) and seed (20 percent).

93. Ibid., 1:249.

94. Galen, *On the Wholesome and Unwholesome Properties of Foodstuffs* 6.749ff., as quoted by Garnsey and Saller, *Roman Empire*, 97. Although Garnsey and Saller point out that Galen talks here about the special situation during a famine, the tension and imbalance between city consumption and countryside seems obvious. Despite their "resourcefulness" in making ends meet, the country folk had to survive months with very little food . This gives us a concrete impression of situations that Paul and his Galatians probably encountered too.

95. Sherk, "Roman Galatia," 972–74.

96. *OGIS* 533. Text and commentary in Bosch, *Ankara*, no. 51 (Greek and German). Greek text also in Louis Robert, *Les Gladiateurs dans l'Orient Grec* (Paris: Librairie Ancienne Honore Champion, 1940), no. 86, p.135. Mitchell (*Anatolia*, 1:107–12) gives a comprehensive English summary and commentary. For images and the precise placement of the list at the temple, see Daniel Krencker and Martin

Schede, *Der Tempel in Ankara,* Archäologisches Institut des Deutschen Reiches, Denkmäler antiker Architektur 3 (Berlin: de Gruyter, 1936), plates 43, 44a.

97. Bosch, *Ankara,* 48.

98. Ibid., 49 identifies seventeen families of provincial nobility from Ancyra and Pessinus, eight of which are clearly of Galatian ethnicity, seven with hellenized names that point to "Anatolian" background in general (for example, Phrygian or Pamphylian). Two of the Latin names are unclear with regard to ethnic origin. Mitchell (*Anatolia,* 1:109), on the other hand, assumes that "most if not all of the priests were Celts or had strong Celtic connections," as the "heading of the list designates the office holders as Galatians." For our purposes the analysis of the names reveals three decisive points: (1) A strong, even predominant Celtic element both with regard to names that are Celtic (Albiorix, Ateporix) or linked to Galatian nobility (Castor, Pylaemenes, King Brigatus, King Amyntas); (2) Hellenization and assimilation of Galatians and other ethnicities: Aristokles has a Greek name, his father Albiorix a Celtic one. Metrodoros, (adopted) son of Menemachos, born as son of Dorylaos has strong Phrygian links, as his name means "gift of the Mother," probably pointing to the mother goddess Cybele as chief deity of Pessinus, and Dorylaos was the mythic founder of the Phrygian city Dorylaeion. His Celtic affiliation is unclear. (3) Romanization that makes ethnicity widely unrecognizable: Q. Gallius Pulcher of Pessinus, according to Mitchell (ibid.), owes his name and the Roman citizenship of the family to the Roman quaestor Q. Gallius, who was active in Cilicia in 47 b.c.e. On the whole, the names point to a society of diverse ethnic backgrounds (though with a strong Celtic element) in transition toward Roman assimilation.

99. In a Latin version only, reflecting the language and cultural environment of a Roman colony, the *Res Gestae* have been found also in Pisdian Antioch (*Monumentum Antiochenum*). A Greek fragment has been retrieved from the hellenized city of Galatian Appolonia (*Monumentum Apolliniense*); see Jaś Elsner, "Inventing Imperium: Texts and the Propaganda of Monuments in Augustan Rome," in *Art and Text in Roman Culture,* ed. Jaś Elsner, Cambridge Studies in New Art History and Criticism (Cambridge: Cambridge University Press, 1996), 32–56; and John Dominic Crossan and Jonathan L. Reed, *In Search of Paul: How Jesus's Apostle Opposed Rome's Empire with God's Kingdom: A New Vision of Paul's Words and World* (San Francisco: HarperSanFrancisco, 2004), 405–7; for the location of the *Res Gestae* at the Ancyran temple, see Krencker and Schede, *Tempel,* 33.

100. Deininger, *Die Provinziallandtage,* 68–69, 173.

101. The visual and material dimension of the *Res Gestae* as text/inscription that develops its meaning in interaction with the building and environment where it is placed has been emphasized by Elsner, "Inventing Imperium," 35–38. Elsner also points to the "sacredness" of the Ancyran inscription: "In the context of Ankara, the *Res Gestae* was a sacred text—as it was indeed in Rome as soon as the Mausoleum before which it stood became the tomb of a god" (p. 50). Elsner, however, does not consider the intertextuality with the priest list that in my opinion is an essential part of the monumental quality and "scripturality" of the *Res Gestae.*

102. The Greek term *praxeis,* derived from *prasso* ("do, accomplish, act"), is the same term that is used for the Lukan "Acts of the Apostles" (*praxeis tōn apostolōn*) in the New Testament. The Greek headline, like the Latin one, in addition points to the original location of the inscription at Rome on "two bronze pillars."

103. As pointed out by Elsner, "Inventing Imperium," 49.

104. Mitchell (Antaolia, 1:111) finds it significant that the Greek entry for Amyntas, son of Gaezadosiastes, not only uses the Latin word *modii* rather than the Greek *medimni,* but also gives exactly "the monthly total allocated to members of the *plebs frumentarii* in Rome in the late Republic. . . . It thus appears that, for one year at least, a Galatian magnate, presumably the owner of extensive grain lands, chose to imitate the Roman corn dole in his native city."

105. Bosch (*Ankara,* 35) assumes altogether five governors, the name of the first at the beginning of the list having been lost. Both Bosch (ibid., 41) and Mitchell (*Anatolia,* 108) think that the name of the first priest on the list is missing as well. Bosch (ibid., 48) dates the list between 10 and 34 c.e.; Mitchell

between 19 and approximately 40 C.E., which takes us very close to Paul's Galatian encounter. The overall number of priests was probably more than twenty, as several fragmentary lines at the end indicate.

106. For a succinct introduction to the primitive and Greco-Roman systems of gift exchange, patronage and benefactions/euergetism, see Stephan Joubert, *Paul as Benefactor: Reciprocity, Strategy and Theological Reflection in Paul's Collection*, WUNT 2.124 (Tübingen: Mohr Siebeck, 2000), 17–72; for an analysis of honor and shame as driving political forces under Roman rule, see J. E. Lendon, *Empire of Honour: The Art of Government in the Roman World* (Oxford: Clarendon Press, 1997); for an in-depth, source-based study of the ancient benefaction culture as interpretive framework for Paul's concept of "grace" (*charis*), see James R. Harrison, *Paul's Language of Grace in Its Graeco-Roman Context*, WUNT 2.172 (Tübingen: Mohr Siebeck, 2003).

107. Seneca's essay was written between 56 and 64 C.E., that is, chronologically close to Galatians; for a more detailed analysis, see Joubert, *Paul as Benefactor*, 40–51.

108. Peter Garnsey and Richard Saller, "Patronal Power Relations," in *Paul and Empire: Religion and Power in Roman Imperial Society*, ed. Richard A. Horsley (Harrisburg, Pa.: Trinity Press International, 1997), 97. For a discussion of similarities and dissimilarities between the ancient systems of patronage and euergetism as systems of social control, both constituting basic forms of social exchange and obligation between unequals throughout the Roman era, see Joubert, *Paul as Benefactor*, 62–69; for the role of Augustus as supreme patron of the Roman world, see ibid., 26.

109. Richard Gordon, "The Veil of Power," in *Paul and Empire: Religion and Power in Roman Imperial Society*, ed. Richard A. Horsley (Harrisburg, Pa.: Trinity Press International, 1997), 135.

110. Hecatomb means the sacrifice of a great number of victims at one time (literally, a hundred oxen); the question whether this reflects a Celtic tradition of vast sacrifices is briefly discussed by Mitchell, *Anatolia*, 1:109–10.

111. Joubert, *Paul as Benefactor*, 43.

112. Olive oil, usually needed for the gymnasium, is mentioned twelve times on the list and was a standard feature of Greek euergetism. Mitchell (*Anatolia*, 1:109) sees it as a "foreign luxury in Galatia" that indicates a remarkable degree of hellenization.

113. Joubert, *Paul as Benefactor*, 57; this is one of the differences Joubert sees with regard to the benefit exchange within the Pauline collection. It did care about the needs of the poor, rather than status of the donors or Paul's role as benefactor (p. 217).

114. Gordon, "Veil of Power," 134.

115. Ibid.

116. See ibid., 132.

117. Harrison (*Paul's Language of Grace*, 349) states that for Paul God's grace/benefaction "subverts the dynamic of the Graeco-Roman reciprocity system" and thus creates new social relations and fellowship among the believers. Racial, geographical, and religious boundaries are transgressed; honorific titles and privileges "are to be absent from the body of Christ"; and the "hierarchical structure of the honour system is radically overturned."

118. Robert Jewett has written the first major commentary on a Pauline letter that programmatically switches the interpretational focus of "works" and works-righteous "boasting" from its traditional (anti-)Jewish lens to the wider framework of imperial status and honor competition, including Rome as the "boasting champion of the ancient world, filled with honorific monuments and celebrations of imperial glory." Robert Jewett, *Romans: A Commentary*, Hermeneia (Minneapolis: Fortress Press, 2007), 295–96.

119. Heightening the pleasure of the table through exhibiting or imposing cruel suffering in the context of a meal was not as unusual as it might seem. Caligula had torture and capital punishment carried out at banquets (Suetonius, *Caligula* 32.1); Alexander Jannaeus is reported to have had eight hundred captives crucified in Jerusalem, butchering their wives and children before their eyes while he looked on, drinking and reclining with his concubines (Josephus, *B.J.* 1.98). Wall paintings and mosaics depicting gladiators were found in Roman dining rooms, according to Thomas Wiedemann, *Emperors and Gladiators* (London: Routledge, 1992), 24. For affinity between arena and banquet, see also Paul Plass, *The*

Game of Death in Ancient Rome: Arena Sport and Political Suicide, Wisconsin Studies in Classics (Madison: University of Wisconsin Press, 1995), 43.

120. See the extensive treatment of this issue as key to a reinterpretation of Galatians in Lopez, *Apostle to the Conquered,* for example, 4–6, 22–25.

121. Mitchell, *Anatolia,* 1:110.

122. Strabo 4.2.3; and Athenaeus 4.37.152; see Mitchell, *Anatolia,* 1:43–44; and Futrell, *Blood in the Arena,* 107–10.

123. Mitchell, *Anatolia,* 1:110.

124. Dennis E. Smith, *From Symposium to Eucharist: The Banquet in the Early Christian World* (Minneapolis: Fortress Press, 2003), 11. For an overview of the social dynamics of Hellenistic meals, see Hal Taussig, *In the Beginning Was the Meal: Social Experimentation & Early Christian Identity* (Minneapolis: Fortress Press, 2009), 26–32; and Matthias Klinghardt, *Gemeinschaftsmahl und Mahlgemeinschaft: Soziologie und Liturgie frühchristlicher Mahlfeiern,* Texte und Arbeiten zum neutestamentlichen Zeitalter 13 (Tübingen: Francke, 1996), 153–73.

125. For seating order and reclining at Greco-Roman banquets, see Smith, *Symposium,* 14–18; and Taussig, *Meal,* 23–26. For seating order and merit-based food distribution at Celtic meals, see Athenaeus (quoted from Posidonius) 4.36.151e–2d; 4.40.154a–c.

126. Futrell, *Blood in the Arena,* 109.

127. Ibid., 108–9.

128. Mitchell, *Anatolia,* 1:112.

129. "For early Christians, the experience of an alternative societal model, the bonding in community, and the many evocations of Jesus' resistance on the cross at the meals made clear to them that they belonged to a counterimperial entity." Taussig, *Meal,* 140.

130. In Galatians, this issue is of particular interest regarding the programmatic meal conflict at Syrian Antioch (Gal 2:11-14), which is crucial for the argument of the letter and for Paul's justification theology. It is possible that the famous clash between Paul and Peter was not so much fueled by "Jewish sensitivities" per se, but rather by the question of how Caesar was to be adequately honored through cultic acts at a public meal involving non-Jews. We will deal with this more extensively in chapters 5 and 6. For an empire-critical reading of the Antiochene incident before the background of Pergamon, see Brigitte Kahl, "Reading Galatians and Empire at the Great Altar of Pergamon," *USQR* 59, no. 3–4 (2005): 39–41.

131. Mitchell (*Anatolia,* 1:108) translates it as gladiatorial spectacles, whereas Bosch (*Ankara,* 41) assumes that this word in the context of the list means theater performances, as the other categories such as hunts and races are explicitly mentioned. *Theas* is the last readable word of the overall inscription, which is fragmentary in its final entry about Iulius Aquila.

132. Robert (*Les Gladiateurs,* 14–15) came to the conclusion that the enthusiasm for gladiators was not a mark of the raw nature of the Celts in particular but was shared very much by the Greek populations of Asia Minor.

133. Futrell, *Blood in the Arena,* 103.

134. Ibid., 81–83; see the plan of the imperial cult complex in fig. 19 (ibid., 84).

135. On amphitheaters in rural Gaul, see Futrell, *Blood in the Arena,* 93–94. For Roman Galatia we know that the imperial temple at Pessinus that superseded the temple to Cybele as new civic center had a theater attached to it where gladiatorial contests took place; see Marc Waelkens, "The Imperial Sanctuary at Pessinus: Archeological, Epigraphical and Numismatic Evidence for Its Date and Identification," *Epigraphica Anatolica* 7 (1986): 37–73; and Mitchell, *Anatolia,* 1:103–4, also Hardin, *Galatians and the Imperial Cult,* 69–71. On a festival that was sponsored in a temporary wooden amphitheatre at Pisidian Antioch and included hunts and gladiatorial fights together with a public feast, see Hardin, 75–78.

136. Futrell, *Blood in the Arena,* 70–71; see also Jean-Claude Golvin, *L'amphithéâtre Romain: Essai sur la théorisation de sa forme et de ses fonctions* (Paris: E. de Boccard, 1988), 225–36.

137. See Futrell, *Blood in the Arena,* 103–4.

138. Ibid., 93.

139. Ando, *Ideology,* 338. Ando's exploration of the ideological mechanisms of consensus-production is helpful and illuminating in many ways. For a criticism, however, that he takes the official language of consent too much at face value and understates the nonconsensual aspects of coercion and violence that were as vital for the maintenance of Roman power, see Neil Elliott, *The Arrogance of Nations: Reading Romans in the Shadow of Empire,* Paul in Critical Contexts (Minneapolis: Fortress Press, 2008), 39.

5. Messianic Insurrection among Dying Gauls and Jews

1. This point has been made convincingly by James C. Scott, *Domination and the Arts of Resistance: Hidden Transcripts* (New Haven: Yale University Press, 1990).

2. According to Josephus, *Ant.* 12:148–53, Antiochus wrote a letter to Zeuxis, his governor of Lydia, with instructions concerning the settlement of two thousand Jewish families there. As Paul R. Trebilco points out, Jews from Mesopotamia and Babylonia were known for their effectiveness as soldiers and their loyalty to Antiochus and thus were expected to maintain a pro-Seleucid presence. Paul R. Trebilco, *Jewish Communities in Asia Minor,* SNTSMS 69 (Cambridge: Cambridge University Press, 1991), 6.

3. Trebilco, *Jewish Communities in Asia Minor,* 7. Note the places mentioned in a circular letter by the Roman senate, quoted in 1 Macc 15:16-23, in support of Jews in Asia Minor.

4. For Jewish population in northern Galatia, see Emil Schürer, *The History of the Jewish People in the Age of Jesus Christ (175 B.C.– A.D. 135),* rev. ed. by Geza Vermes, Fergus Millar, Fergus, and Martin Goodman, 3 vols. (Edinburgh: T&T Clark, 1973–87), 3:34–35, who sees "some indication of a Jewish presence, or at least Judaising influences" there; for Antioch and Iconium in the south, see ibid., 32 and 34.

5. Trebilco (*Jewish Communities in Asia Minor,* 184) states: "We can thus suggest that in many cities of Asia Minor a tradition of tolerance and positive interaction was established between the city and its Jewish community."

6. On Jewish antiquity as a positive value, especially in the eyes of the Romans, who lacked ancient origin, see Louis H. Feldman, *Jew and Gentile in the Ancient World: Attitudes and Interactions from Alexander to Justinian* (Princeton: Princeton University Press, 1993), 177–200. A programmatic statement is made by Augustus in his *Res Gestae* 6, when he is offered by senate and people of Rome the position of sole guardian of law and order (*curator legum et morum summa potestate solus*) in 19, 18, and 11 B.C.E.; he declines this offer as inconsistent with the ancestral custom (*contra morem maiorum*). See Walter Eder, "Augustus and the Power of Tradition," in *The Cambridge Companion to the Age of Augustus,* ed. Karl Galinsky, Cambridge Companion to the Classics (Cambridge: Cambridge University Press, 2005), 14.

7. On Jewish identity markers in a Diaspora setting, see John M. G. Barclay, *Jews in the Mediterranean Diaspora: From Alexander to Trajan (323 BCE–117 CE)* (Edinburgh: T&T Clark, 1996), 399–441.

8. On the polarity between separation and integration, see Barclay, *Jews in the Mediterranean Diaspora,* 82–124, 320–35. Mary Smallwood states about the Jews of the Diaspora: "Their exclusiveness bred the unpopularity out of which anti-Semitism was born. The Jew was a figure of amusement, contempt or hatred to the gentiles among whom he lived." E. Mary Smallwood, *The Jews under Roman Rule: From Pompey to Diocletian,* Studies in Judaism in Late Antiquity 20 (Leiden: Brill, 1981), 123.

9. Josephus and other ancient authors repeatedly report that non-Jews challenge Jewish irreverence toward the gods of the community of which they wish to be members. Jewish monotheism is seen as a kind of antisocial attitude, for example, in Alexandria: "Why then, if they want to be citizens, do they not worship the same gods as the Alexandrians?" (Josephus, *Ap.* 2.66; see also *Ant.* 4.137–38, 12.125–26).

10. Cicero's remarks in *Pro Fonteio* 30 (quoted above in chapter 4) that the Gauls make war against the religions of all other people (*contra omnium religiones*) is obviously almost identical to Tacitus's critique of Mosaic Judaism as a new cult "opposite of all other mortals" (*novos ritus contrariosque ceteris mortalibus*) (*Hist.* 5.4). And if Tacitus complains that the Jews consider profane "all that we hold sacred" and allow "practices which we abominate," the same holds true for the Gauls, who are criticized for

"un-Roman" practices like human sacrifice, divination and head hunting (Strabo, *Geogr.* 4.4.5); see Peter Garnsey and Richard Saller, *The Roman Empire: Economy, Society and Culture* (Berkeley/Los Angeles: University of California Press, 1987), 168–69, who argue that the problem reflected in these assaults on both Celtic Druidism and Judaism is essentially of a political nature. Both Jews and Gauls/Galatians were resistant to Roman rule in particular ways that were linked to their religion.

11. On Jewish otherness in general and ancient perspectives on Jews, see Peter Schäfer, *Judeophobia: Attitudes toward Jews in the Ancient World* (Cambridge, Mass.: Harvard University Press, 1997); Shaye J. D. Cohen, *The Beginnings of Jewishness: Boundaries, Varieties, Uncertainties,* Hellenistic Culture and Society 31 (Berkeley: University of California Press, 1999). Much less of a conflict between Jewishness and Greco-Roman attitudes or interests is seen by Erich S. Gruen, *Diaspora. Jews amidst Greeks and Romans* (Cambridge, Mass.: Harvard University Press, 2002), 41–53.

12. As Barclay (*Jews in the Mediterranean Diaspora,* 411) notes, circumcision in pratical terms had the function of preventing intermarriage by singling out those male partners with whom Jewish women were, or were not, allowed to have sexual intercourse. On intermarriage, see ibid., 410–12.

13. On circumcision as a distinctive mark of Jewish otherness and its generally negative connotation among non-Jews, see Feldman, *Jew and Gentile in the Ancient World,* 153–58. For a general introduction to the debate on circumcision in its Pauline context, see, from a vast amount of literature, especially Paula Fredriksen, "Judaism, the Circumcision of Gentiles, and Apocalyptic Hope: Another Look at Galatians 1 and 2," *Journal of Theological Studies* n.s. 42 (1991): 532–64; and Daniel Boyarin, *A Radical Jew: Paul and the Politics of Identity,* Contraversions 1 (Berkeley: University of California Press, 1994), 13–38.

14. As Gruen (*Diaspora,* 44) observes with regard to *Hist.* 5.5, "Tacitus here excoriates apostates, but suggests no Jewish menace." While I fully concur with the first statement, I find the second part less agreeable, especially in the overall literary context of Tacitus's Jewish excursus, namely, the Roman siege and imminent destruction of the rebellious Jerusalem; see below. For a comprehensive evaluation of proselytism, see Shaye J. D. Cohen, "Crossing the Boundary and Becoming a Jew," *Harvard Theological Review* 82 (1989): 13–33.

15. There were, however, discussions among Jews about the extent to which circumcision indeed was a mandatory prerequisite of Jewishness. Philo's debate of circumcision in its broad allegorical significance, yet nonetheless also to be performed literally and physically (*Migr. Abr.* 89–94; compare *Spec. Leg.* 1:1–11), is usually understood as an indication that some Jews in Alexandria gave up practicing circumcision. See John J. Collins, *Seers, Sibyls and Sages in Hellenistic-Roman Judaism,* Journal for the Study of Judaism Supplement 54 (Leiden: Brill, 1997), 219–22. Another story that shows controversies about the necessity of proselyte circumcision is the conversion to Judaism of the royal house of Adiabene recounted by Josephus (*Ant.* 20.2–4). The crown prince Izates, out of concern for his public image among his subjects, initially refrained from circumcision and was told that full devotion to the ancestral customs of the Jews was more important than circumcision. Later, however, another Jew who interpreted the law more strictly, convinced Izates that he needed to be circumcised; see Collins, *Seers,* 225–28; and Terence L. Donaldson, *Paul and the Gentiles: Remapping the Apostle's Convictional World* (Minneapolis: Fortress Press, 1997), 275–78.

16. On the aniconic cult of the Jews and the debate whether the prohibition included only the use of images in worship, or images in general, see Barclay, *Jews in the Mediterranean Diaspora,* 433–34. Barclay points to the "well-known disparities between the rabbinic ban on images and the frequent use of paint and mosaic images in later synagogues (especially in Galilee and Dura Europos); these may in fact represent variant interpretations of this command" (p. 433).

17. Josephus, *B.J.* 1.648–55; 2.4–13; *Ant.* 17.149–67. On the eagle episode, see Richard A. Horsley, *Jesus and the Spiral of Violence: Popular Resistance in Roman Palestine* (San Francisco: Harper & Row, 1987), 71–77. Smallwood (*Jews under Roman Rule,* 99, 105–6) assumes that the offensive connotation of the temple eagle might have been linked to its identity with the legionary emblem as the symbol of Roman might.

18. Josephus, *B.J.* 2.184–203; see Horsley, *Jesus and the Spiral of Violence,* 110–16; Smallwood, *Jews under Roman Rule,* 174–78.

19. As Barclay (*Jews in the Mediterranean Diaspora,* 55 n. 18) assumes, the images could eventually be taken out only under Caligula's successor, Claudius; for a comprehensive analysis of the Alexandrian riots, see ibid., 48–71; see also Neil Elliott, *The Arrogance of Nations: Reading Romans in the Shadow of Empire,* Paul in Critical Contexts (Minneapolis: Fortress Press, 2008), 93–96; John Gager, *The Origins of Anti-Semitism: Attitudes toward Judaism in Pagan and Christian Antiquity* (New York: Oxford University Press, 1983), 43–54.

20. On the nexus between imperial iconography and ideology, see Clifford Ando, *Imperial Ideology and Provincial Loyalty in the Roman Empire,* Classics and Contemporary Thought 6 (Berkeley: University of California Press, 2000), 210–15. As Barclay (*Jews in the Mediterranean Diaspora,* 434) states, "the refusal to include cultic images was potentially of the greatest political embarrassment in relation to the imperial cult."

21. According to Monika Bernett, the aim of Caligula was probably not to replace the Jewish God and entirely rededicate the Jerusaem temple to himself but to install his image there (in the Holy of Holies) to be worshiped next to the Jewish God. Monika Bernett, "Der Kaiserkult in Judäa unter herodischer und römischer Herrschaft: Zur Herausbildung und Herausforderung neuer Konzepte jüdischer Herrschaftslegitimation," in *Jewish Identity in the Greco-Roman World,* ed. Jörg Frey et al., Ancient Judaism and Early Christianity 71 (Leiden: Brill, 2007), 241.

22. B. Wardy, "Jewish Religion in Pagan Literature during the Late Republic and Early Empire," in *ANRW* II.19.1 (1979): 629–31; again Gruen (*Diaspora,* 44) substantially minimizes the potential for conflict.

23. The declaration of King Agrippa II in 66 c.e. in a speech to discourage the Jews from their anti-Roman uprising is paradigmatic: "The only refuge, then, left to you is divine assistance [*tou theou symmachian*]. But even this is ranged on the side of the Romans, for, without God's aid, so vast an empire could never have been built up" (*B.J.* 2.390–91, LCL). God is now on the side of Rome, and the Jews have to submit to the "supreme law" (*nomon ischyrotaton*), which is universally established both among animals and humans: "Yield to the stronger" and "The mastery is for those preeminent in arms" (*B.J.* 5.367). For Josephus's relation to the Roman Empire, see Menahem Stern, "Josephus and the Roman Empire as Reflected in *The Jewish War,*" in *Josephus, Judaism, and Christianity,* ed. Louis H. Feldman and Gohei Hata (Detroit: Wayne State University Press, 1987), 71–80; on Philo and Josephus as models of "convergence," see Barclay, *Jews in the Mediterranean Diaspora,* 158–80, 346–68.

24. Zeal for God's law, which required God's sole rule over his people and land, was the decisive theological thrust behind the resistance of the Zealots, who regarded any recognition of imperial rule as idolatry and apostasy and were ready to embark on a holy war against the foreign domination by Rome. See Martin Hengel, *The Zealots: Investigations into the Jewish Freedom Movement in the Period from Herod I until 70 A.D.* (Edinburgh: T&T Clark, 1989), 149–228. Zeal for the law as God's cause, however, in different ways also characterized the movements of the Essenes and Pharisees, that is "the whole of Palestinian Judaism in general from the time of the Maccabees" (ibid., 224). For the development of the Zealot movement, see ibid., 313–76. For a brief introduction to the variegated forms of violent and nonviolent Jewish resistance at the time of Jesus and Paul, see Richard A. Horsley, *Jesus and Empire: The Kingdom of God and the New World Disorder* (Minneapolis: Fortress Press, 2003), 35–54.

25. Technically, the Jerusalem Sanhedrin under the presidency of the high priest was the supreme legal and administrative authority for local Jewish affairs, which enabled Jews to live according to their own law. But as the high priest was appointed by the Roman governor (who also kept the high priestly ceremonial vestments in the Antonia fortress and retained the power of capital punishment), this was an autonomy under tight Roman control. See Smallwood, *Jews under Roman Rule,* 148–49.

26. For Asia Minor, a series of Roman decrees, rendered by Josephus in *Ant.* 14 and 16, are of importance in showcasing Rome's role as protector of Jewish ancestral rights and privileges within an often hostile Greek environment. See Miriam Pucci Ben Zeev, *Jewish Rights in the Roman World: The Greek and Roman Documents quoted by Josephus Flavius,* Texte und Studien zum antiken Judentum 74 (Tübingen: Mohr Siebeck, 1998); Trebilco, *Jewish Communities in Asia Minor,* 7–12; Gruen, *Diaspora,* 84–104.

27. For the prevalent neglect of emperor worship as a dominant feature of Herod the Great's reign

and the customary scholarly arguments that have played down its importance and problematic aspects in the period leading into the Jewish War, see the critical evaluation by Bernett, "Der Kaiserkult in Judäa," 205–14. As Bernett maintains, King Herod was among the first who, after Actium (31 B.C.E.) expressed their subservience to the new power figure Augustus in cultic forms and thus played a decisive role in the symbolic structuring of imperial rule. Herod established games honoring Caesar already in 28 B.C.E. and a year later the new polis Sebaste (that is, the old Samaria) with an imperial temple. Sebaste-Samaria was probably the first city in the Roman Empire named after Augustus/Sebastos, followed a few years later by Caesarea, again named after Caesar, with its monumental temple to Rome and Augustus (ibid., 205–6).

28. Josephus, *Ap.* 2.75–77; *B.J.* 2.197, 409–16; Philo, *Leg. Gai.* 157, 317. For a more detailed discussion, see Stefan Krauter, "Die Beteiligung von Nichtjuden am Jerusalemer Tempelkult," in *Jewish Identity in the Greco-Roman World*, ed. Jörg Frey et al., Ancient Judaism and Early Christianity 71 (Leiden: Brill, 2007), 61–63.

29. See Mark D. Nanos, *The Irony of Galatians: Paul's Letter in First-century Context* (Minneapolis: Fortress Press, 2002), 262–63.

30. Smallwood (*Jews under Roman Rule*, 135) had assumed that Caesar issued a "charter of Jewish rights, which formalized and legalized what had apparently been an unwritten convention that the Jews in the empire could have religious liberty and replaced *ad hoc* enactments by permanent, universal legislation," thus in effect "establishing Judaism as *religio licita*, an incorporated body with an authorized cult, throughout the empire. . . ." This notion of a permanent legislation rather than individual ad hoc settlements has been widely challenged; see, for example, Tessa Rajak, "Was there a Roman Charter for the Jews?" *Journal of Roman Studies* 74 (1984): 107–23. In particular, the exemption from imperial cult as a firm, legally established empire-wide privilege obviously cannot be maintained; see Ben Zeev, *Jewish Rights*, 471–81; and Alfredo Mordechai Rabello, "The Legal Condition of the Jews in the Roman Empire," in *ANRW* II.13 (1980): 662–762: "It can be definitely stated that from the strictly legal point of view no such exemption existed"(p. 703). In a slightly more positive way, Nanos (*Irony of Galatians*, 260–61) points to the legal weight that Caesar's ruling on behalf of the Jews had as precedent that "obliged future rulers to recognize the legitimacy of Jewish ancestral religion, regardless of the precise legal definitions of their voluntary associations in each civic context." He assumes that the Jewish communities in Galatia in all likelihood enjoyed an exemption from civic and imperial worship.

31. Ralph Martin Novak, Jr., *Christianity and the Roman Empire: Background Texts* (Harrisburg, Pa.: Trinity Press International, 2001), 246.

32. "I argue that imperial support for the central national institutions of the Jews, the Jerusalem temple and the Pentateuch, helps explain why these eventually became the chief symbols of Jewish corporate identity." Seth Schwartz, *Imperialism and Jewish Society, 200 B.C.E. to 640 C.E.*, Jews, Christians, and Muslims from the Ancient to the Modern World (Princeton: Princeton University Press, 2001), 14; also 52.

33. Ibid., 20.

34. Ibid., 21.

35. Ibid., 64.

36. On the impact of oppressive imperial regimes in the ancient Near East as a formative element in the development of the First Testament as resistant (hi)story telling, see Richard A. Horsley, ed., *In the Shadow of Empire: Reclaiming the Bible as a History of Faithful Resistance* (Louisville: Westminster John Knox, 2008), 6, and the contributions in this volume by Norman K. Gottwald, "Early Israel as an Anti-Imperial Community," 9–24; Walter Brueggemann, "Faith in the Empire," 25–40; and Jon L. Berquist, "Resistance and Accommodation in the Persian Empire," 41–58.

37. Seth Schwartz, *Imperialism*, 56: ". . . that the Roman authorities could be expected to punish violators of the Torah"

38. As Bernett ("Der Kaiserkult in Judäa," 245–46) points out, an important element of anti-Roman resistance in the period before 66 C.E. was—apart from the severe socioeconomic burdens of Roman rule—the increasingly conspicuous presence of Caesar as god in the land, among the people, and even in

the temple of Israel's God. The imperial cult as a clear transgression of Jewish law offered a Torah-based opportunity to delegitimize and resist Roman domination and its local Jewish puppet-regimes.

39. The "anomalous" combination in Paul of rigorous Torah adherence and at the same time Torah transgression, that is, a strictly nonaccommodationist and culturally antagonistic Jewish stance, together with and a high degree of "universalist"assimilation in integrating the non-Jewish other, has been noticed by Barclay, *Jews in the Mediterranean Diaspora*, 381–95. I would describe this "anomaly" as an uncommon hybridity that refuses, in the name of Israel's exodus-God and Torah, to assimilate Torah and Roman *nomos* or the universal claim of Roman law to hold supreme authority over both Jews and non-Jews alike. While Paul, in a way, shares with his fellow Jew Philo of Alexandria (for example, *Vit. Mos.* 2.17–24) the perception of Torah as universal law for all of humanity, his interpretation of this Torah represents a perspective "from below" that is markedly different from Philo's upper-class position. On Philo's universalism, see Jutta Balzer-Leonhardt, "Jewish Worship and Universal Identity in Philo of Alexandria," in *Jewish Identity in the Greco-Roman World*, ed. Jörg Frey et al., Ancient Judaism and Early Christianity 71 (Leiden: Brill, 2007), 29–53.

40. This is a bold claim. Certainly Paul's movement after 70 c.e., as already Luke/Acts and the deutero-Pauline literature show, became the object of efforts to control and domesticate it. But this might also demonstrate that there was a power at work that had activated a significant counter-hegemonic practice. It is my contention that this power subsequently could be misrepresented, perverted, and denied in multiple ways, but at its core never entirely be assimilated or stamped out.

41. See Tacitus, *Hist.* 5.11; as Jonathan L. Reed states, the Antonia from a topographical perspective stood on the highest point of the bedrock on the temple mountain and enabled surveillance of the activities in the temple itself. "In the architectural hierarchy of the Temple Mount, Rome was on top." Jonathan L. Reed, *The HarperCollins Visual Guide to the New Testament* (New York: HarperCollins, 2007), 90. Consequently, at the outbreak of the great Jewish rebellion in 66 c.e., the insurgents cut down the porticoes that linked temple and Antonia, which, according to King Agrippa, constituted an act of war against Rome. See Josephus, *B.J.* 2.403–4.

42. For the broad variety of attitudes and practices among ordinary Jews with regard to civic gods and sacrifices, food laws and table community, administrative positions and military service (which usually would include an obligation to worship "other" gods), attendance at gymnasia, theaters or arenas, religious festivals and banquets (where idolatrous activities would take place), see Peder Borgen, "'Yes,' 'No,' 'How Far?': The Participation of Jews and Christians in Pagan Cults," in *Paul in His Hellenistic Context*, ed. Troels Engberg-Pedersen (Minneapolis: Fortress Press, 1995), 30–59; Peter J. Tomson, *Paul and the Jewish Law: Halakha in the Letters of the Apostle to the Gentiles,* Compendium rerum Iudaicarum ad Novum Testamentum, Section 3, Jewish Traditions in Early Christian Literature 1 (Minneapolis: Fortress Press, 1990); and the detailed description of "high," "low," and "medium" assimilation among the Jews in Alexandria and elsewhere in Barclay, *Jews in the Mediterranean Diaspora,* 82–124, 320–35. It is evident that also with regard to imperial cult observances a wide range of different forms of participation and nonparticipation was practiced, not least owing to the great attractiveness of benefactions, festivals, and public meals among the population; see Bernett, "Der Kaiserkult in Judäa," 228–29, 245.

43. Josephus, *B.J.* 2.409–17; see Krauter, "Die Beteiligung von Nichtjuden," 69–70.

44. On Paul's clash, or at least Luke's version of it, with images and idols in Greece and Asia Minor, see Halvor Moxnes, "'He Saw the City Full of Idols' (Acts 17:16): Visualizing the World of the First Christians," in *Mighty Minorities? Minorities in Early Christianity: Positions and Strategies*, ed. David Hellholm et al. (Oslo: Scandinavian University Press, 1995), 107–31. The extent to which Jewish prohibition of images according to the second commandment indeed functions as image *criticism* as well is an intriguing question. If we take the work of Paul Zanker, Tonio Hölscher, and others on the "power of images" seriously, it is a basic contention of our "critical re-imagination" that the two cannot be separated. Images are representations of dominant ideologies and power constructs that are under critical scrutiny in Paul's "aniconic" messianic countervision of everything "in heaven above, or on the earth beneath or in the water under the earth." (Exod 20:4). From this perspective, Jewish image prohibition can indeed be perceived as a form of ideological criticism.

45. Bruce W. Winter, *Seek the Welfare of the City: Christians as Benefactors and Citizens,* First-century Christians in the Graeco-Roman World (Grand Rapids: Eerdmans, 1994), 123–43; Thomas Witulski, *Die Adressaten des Galaterbriefes: Untersuchungen zur Gemeinde von Antiochia ad Pisidiam,* Forschungen zur Religion und Literatur des Alten und Neuen Testaments 193 (Göttingen: Vandenhoeck & Ruprecht, 2000); Nanos, *Irony of Galatians;* Justin K. Hardin, *Galatians and the Imperial Cult: A Critical Analysis of the First-century Social Context of Paul's Letter,* WUNT 2/237 (Tübingen: Mohr Siebeck, 2008); see also Thomas Witulski, *Kaiserkult in Kleinasien: Die Entwicklung der kultisch-religiösen Kaiserverehrung in der römischen Provinz Asia von Augustus bis Antoninus Pius,* Novum Testamentum et Orbis Antiquus/Studien zur Umwelt des Neuen Testaments (Göttingen: Vandenhoeck & Ruprecht; Fribourg: Academic, 2007).

46. See David G. Horrell, "Idol-Food, Idolatry and Ethics in Paul," in *Idolatry: False Worship in the Bible, Early Judaism, and Christianity,* ed. Stephen C. Barton, T&T Clark Theology (London/New York: T&T Clark, 2007), 120–40. For imperial religion and idolatry as crucial background of the Christ hymn in Philippians see Erik M. Heen, "Phil 2:6–11 and Resistance to Local Timocratic Rule: *Isa Theō* and the Cult of the Emperor in the East," in *Paul and the Roman Imperial Order,* ed. Richard A. Horsley (Harrisburg, Pa.: Trinity Press International, 2004), 125–54; for Thessalonians, see James R. Harrison, "Paul and the Imperial Gospel at Thessaloniki," *Journal for the Study of the New Testament* 25 (2002): 71–96.

47. Because of the still predominant focus of Galatian studies on Judaism as the primary "opponent," the most common interpretation has been to read 4:10 in line with the circumcision demands of the "agitators" as a reference to the Jewish calendar and its celebration of the Sabbath, new moons, Passover, and other Jewish festivals (see Hardin, *Galatians and the Imperial Cult,* 118–21, for a summary of scholarship). Hans Dieter Betz takes a position that reflects a broad general consensus: Paul did not really mean to say that the Galatians wanted to return to their former *pagan* worship, but that they were about to do something equally objectionable by trying to become followers of Jewish Torah, namely, resubmitting themselves to the enslavement by the "elements of the world" (*stoicheia tou kosmou*), that is, a wrong concept of religious works righteousness common among both Jews and Greeks. In this reading, Paul represents an "enlightened" concept of religion "which is free from cultic and ritual requirements and observances," thus standing against Judaism and paganism alike. Hans Dieter Betz, *Galatians: A Commentary on Paul's Letter to the Churches in Galatia,* Hermeneia (Philadelphia: Fortress Press, 1979), 217–18. It needs to be stated that in this view there is no significant difference between strict Torah observance and pagan idolatry. This is undoubtedly as apt a summary of occidental Pauline interpretation as a complete revocation of how Paul himself saw his relationship to Judaism, Torah, and idol worship.

48. The imperial cult and calendar as backdrop for Gal 4:8-10 was already assumed by Stephen Mitchell, *Anatolia: Land, Men, and Gods in Asia Minor,* 2 vols. (Oxford: Clarendon Press, 1993), 2:10. More recently Witulski (*Die Adressaten des Galaterbriefes,* 158–68) and Hardin (*Galatians and the Imperial Cult,* 122–27) have strongly argued this case; see below.

49. See Hardin, *Galatians and the Imperial Cult,* 126. In a similar vein, Bruce Winter (*Seek the Welfare of the City,* 132) has decoded 1 Cor 8:4-6 as referring to deified emperors and living members of the imperial family as "so-called gods" who were "popularly but erroneously called gods."

50. For Jews as "licensed atheists" and the various acts of "religious misbehavior" committed by the Christians in terms of community sensitivities and Roman state religion, see G. E. M. de Ste. Croix, "Why Were the Early Christians Persecuted?" in *Church and State in the Early Church,* ed. Everett Ferguson, Studies in Early Christianity 7 (New York: Garland, 1993), 35–36.

51. Harrison ("Paul and the Imperial Gospel at Thessaloniki," 80 n. 33) refers to Josephus, *Ant.* 19.285 as evidence that "the Romans would only continue to uphold the rights of the Jews 'while they abide by their own customs.'" And indeed, the edicts of Emperor Claudius for Alexandria and other parts of the *oikoumenē* (41 C.E.) quoted in *Ant.* 19.280–91 draw a clear demarcation line between Jews and non-Jews with regard to law observance. While the Jews and their privilege to follow their ancestral customs, including the right not to call an emperor god (19.284), are confirmed and protected—an important gesture of peacemaking in the aftermath of the Alexandrian riots—Claudius also urges the Jews "in

all the world under us" to use his kindness "with moderation, and not to show a contempt of the superstitious observances of other nations, but to keep their own laws only" (19.290). In the context of the Galatian controversy, one could read this as an implicit prohibition against doing exactly what Paul is doing, namely, including "other nations" under the first Mosaic commandment and making them renounce the "superstitious observances" of imperial or idolatrous worship. Interestingly, in the letter of Claudius to the Alexandrians preserved in *P.Lond.* 1912 (A. S. Hunter and C. C. Edgar, eds., *Select Papyri,* LCL [London: Heinemann, 1932–34], 212; *CPJ* 153), such an unlicensed worldwide missionary expansion seems to be an issue indeed. The emperor threatens the Jews of Alexandria "not to bring in or admit Jews who come down the river from Syria or Egypt, a proceeding which will compel me to conceive serious suspicion; otherwise I will by all means take vengeance on them as fomenters of what is a general plague (*koinēn noson*) infecting the whole world." [Quoted after C. K. Barrett, *The New Testament Background: Writings from Ancient Greece and the Roman Empire That Illuminate Christian Origins* (San Francisco: HarperSanFrancisco, 1987), 49.] As Smallwood (*Jews under Roman Rule,* 214) notes, it is unlikely that already at this early date Christ-followers were seen as a worldwide "common plague." Nevertheless, the overall argument is highly relevant for understanding the uproar created by Paul's border-transgressive outreach to the non-Jewish nations in Galatia.

52. Paula Fredriksen, *Jesus of Nazareth, King of the Jews: A Jewish Life and the Emergence of Christianity* (New York: Knopf, 1999), 132–33.

53. On nations and their restoration with Israel, see Daniel Smith-Christopher, "Between Ezra and Isaiah," in *Ethnicity and the Bible,* ed. Mark G. Brett, Biblical Interpretation Series 19 (Leiden: Brill, 1996), 117–42; James M. Scott, ed., *Restoration: Old Testament, Jewish and Christian Perspectives,* Journal for the Study of Judaism Supplement 72 (Leiden: Brill, 2001).

54. See Davina C. Lopez, *Apostle to the Conquered: Reimagining Paul's Mission,* Paul in Critical Contexts (Minneapolis: Fortress Press, 2008), 153–63.

55. Fredriksen, *Jesus of Nazareth,* 135. From a slightly different viewpoint, the problem of social dislocation and precarious identity of Paul's Galatian converts has been strongly emphasized also by John M. G. Barclay, *Obeying the Truth: Paul's Ethics in Galatians* (Minneapolis: Fortress Press, 1991), 58–60: "To dissociate oneself from the worship of family and community deities would entail a serious disruption in one's relationship with family, friends, fellow club member, business associates and civic authorities" (p. 58).

56. See Collins, *Seers, Sibyls and Sages,* 228–33. As Collins states, the "evidence shows beyond reasonable doubt that Judaism in the Roman Diaspora did win adherents who stopped short of circumcision." However: "What we find is a broad range of attachment, not a class with specific requirements or with a clearly defined status in the synagogue" (p. 232).

57. Nanos, *Irony of Galatians,* 257–71.

58. *P.Lond.* 1912, see n. 51 above.

59. Winter, *Seek the Welfare of the City,* 129–31. See also Duncan Fishwick, *The Imperial Cult in the Latin West: Studies in the Ruler Cult of the Western Provinces of the Roman Empire,* 3 vols., Etudes préliminaires aux religions orientales dans l'Empire romain 108 (Leiden: Brill, 1987–92), II, 1:585–88. On the social pressure linked to the observance of emperor cult, see S. R. F. Price, *Rituals and Power: The Roman Imperial Cult in Asia Minor* (Cambridge: Cambridge University Press, 1984), 107–14.

60. As a sociohistorical case study for Roman Philippi, Peter Oakes has tried to imagine in concrete terms how the transition into the Pauline community would affect the social standing of, for example, a baker's family, with relatively insignificant acts of withdrawal from the civic networks (such as staying away from a burial society one had belonged to, or the removal of a little pagan shrine that used to be placed in the bakery) having massive economic consequences. Peter Oakes, *Philippians: From People to Letter,* SNTSMS 110 (Cambridge: Cambridge University Press, 2001), 89–91.

61. For the possibilities of the *non-Jewish* community challenging the Gentile converts of the Jesus movement with regard to their participation in observances of imperial religion, see Winter, *Seek the Welfare of the City,* 135.

62. If Paul's initial encounter with the Galatians happened toward the end of the 40s C.E., this would

be roughly simultaneous with Claudius's eviction from Rome in 49 C.E. of the Jews "who constantly made disturbances at the instigation of Chrestus" (Suetonius, *Claudius* 25; cf. Acts 18:2). As Smallwood (*Jews under Roman Rule,* 210–16) contends, the term "Chrestus" refers to Christ and the arrival of Christian missionaries among the Jewish community in Rome (ibid., 215). According to Smallwood, the Jews in Rome were under severe pressure, as Claudius had suspended their right of assembly already in 41 C.E. This means that the Jewish right to follow their religion, which simultaneously was confirmed by Claudius in his Letter to the Alexandrinians (see n. 51 above), could never be taken for granted; it could be rescinded in a particular location because of a misdemeanor of any kind. Thus, "the Jews' retention of their privileged position within the empire was conditional on their behaving in a responsible fashion," as Smallwood states (ibid., 215). This sheds significant light on the pressures that must have been felt also among the Jews in Roman Galatia, who were faced with Paul's transgressive and "disorderly" missionary practice.

63. This is the model of Acts 13–14, where Paul during his stay in Roman Galatia is confronted by an alliance between nonbelieving Jews and civic authorities; see Winter, *Seek the Welfare of the City,* 135; Hardin, *Galatians and the Imperial Cult,* 145. On the affiliation of the Jewish community in Asia Minor with the social and political establishment, see Mitchell, *Anatolia,* 2:9.

64. Nanos (*Irony of Galatians,* 258) points out that "claiming protection under the synagogue exemption from participation in the imperial cult (or other local cult) practices," the nonproselyte (that is, non-circumcised) Galatians would "implicate the entire Jewish community, and perhaps jeopardize the legitimation to which it appeals for exemption." The nonparticipation of the Jewish communities in the "local citizen expressions of worship, not least the imperial cult," always could raise the question of Jewish antipatriotism and antisocial behavior. Therefore, the "synagogue's social control agents would be on guard to ensure that their practices conformed to the policies governing this nonconformist behavior" (ibid., 261, 263).

65. That both circumcision and return to the observances of emperor cult are two equivalent options to again "normalize" the social position of the Galatians and reassimilate them, though in different ways, to the civic community and their normative practices is maintained by Nanos, *Irony of Galatians,* 257–71; and Hardin, *Galatians and the Imperial Cult,* 140–42. Witulski (*Die Adressaten des Galaterbriefes,* 71–72, 222–23), on the other hand believes that the circumcision demands and the pressure to return to imperial worship (Gal 4:8-10) reflect two different moments in Paul's missionary work in Galatia and were originally the subject matter of two separate letters that were integrated by a post-Pauline redactor. This means that Galatians in its present form targets two different antagonists, namely, Judaism ("judaistische Agitation" or "judaistische Eindringlinge" [p.72]) and those who want to return to pre-Christian paganism. This does not significantly modify the established anti-Judaistic reading pattern of Galatians, as again Jewish religion and imperial cult—as a paradigm for all pagan cults in general—are de facto equated with regard to the impossibility of gaining salvation through them.

66. Nanos, *Irony of Galatians,* 261.

67. Apart from Mitchell, Nanos, Witulski, and Hardin, this observation has been made also by Dieter Georgi, *The City in the Valley: Biblical Interpretation and Urban Theology,* Studies in Biblical Literature 7 (Atlanta: Society of Biblical Literature, 2005), 89, who states that "Jewish legal piety does not provide the right parallels, is actually foreign to what is described here . . . (namely) the religion and the piety around the Caesar cult." See also Ben Witherington III, *Grace in Galatia: A Commentary on St. Paul's Letter to the Galatians* (Grand Rapids: Eerdmans, 1998), 298.

68. Mitchell, *Anatolia,* 2:10.

69. See Gal 5:3; 6:13. For an overview of different scholarly interpretations of the anti-Pauline circumcision demands in Galatia, see Barclay, *Obeying the Truth,* 45–52.

70. This character of the circumcision project as an "evasive action" caused by external pressure within the framework of imperial cult and in an effort to find "a way around the vexed problem of this civic obligation" has been proposed by Winter, *Seek the Welfare of the City,* 141–42. "There was, in the end, a clear way for the Christian community to escape the obligation of the imperial cult *viz.* by appearing to be wholly Jewish" (p. 136).

71. In a similar vein, Winter (*Seek the Welfare of the City*, 137–40) has read Gal 6:12 as decisive key for understanding the Galatian circumcision party, pointing in particular to the legal connotation of the term *euprosōpeō*. What matters is a "good legal face" for the Galatian converts, who at that time have "no status at all" (p. 138). They have to look like Jews physically in order "to make their Jewish identification absolutely unmistakable" (p. 136). A similar issue might be seen behind Peter's and other Jews' collective "hypocrisy" at Antioch, as recounted by Paul in Gal 2:13.

72. It is indicative of this suppression that usually the phrase *henos ouk estin* (not of the One) in 3:20, which exegetically offers the climactic disclosure of the "mediator's" true identity, has been given little attention in exegetical literature with regard to its anti-idolatrous implications: Betz (*Galatians*, 171–72), for example, simply sees it as referring to a "plurality" that is linked to the concept of a "mediator" of Torah (rather than its direct, unmediated revelation). As "anything that stands in contrast to the oneness of God is inferior," this by implication also "renders the Torah inferior." J. Louis Martyn more carefully considers the theological complexity of this "rather cryptic sentence" when he notices the tension between the "mediator" and the Shema Israel, which affirms the oneness of God. He assumes that Paul confronts the Galatians with "the vision of a godless Law," without noticing, however, that this much more aptly might describe the situation under Caesar as "mediator of the Sinaitic Law," rather than Moses. J. Louis Martyn, *Galatians: A New Translation with Introduction and Commentary*, Anchor Bible 33A (New York: Doubleday, 1998), 357–58.

73. On law in captivity and enslavement under Rome as underlying conflict of the Sarah-Hagar-allegory in Gal 4:21-31, see Brigitte Kahl, "Hagar between Genesis and Galatians: The Stony Road to Freedom," in *From Prophecy to Testament: The Function of the Old Testament in the New*, ed. Craig A. Evans (Peabody, Mass.: Hendrickson, 2004), 219–32; Lopez, *Apostle to the Conquered*, 159–60.

74. The term *Christianus*, mentioned by only two New Testament authors (Acts 11:26; 26:28; 1 Pet 4:16), belongs to the same linguistic matrix as *Sebastēni* or *Augustianoi*, but with an opposite connotation. As E. A. Judge has stated, the suffix *–ianus* "implies the word was coined by speakers of Latin" and "constitutes a political comment. It is not used of the followers of a god. It classifies people as partners of a poltical or military leader, and it is mildly contemptuous." E. A. Judge, "Judaism and the Rise of Christianity: A Roman Perspective," *Tyndale Bulletin* 45 (1994): 355–68. Therefore, the term "Christians" was probably coined by Romans and reflects an outside perspective, more precisely a (potential) disturbance of law and political order. See also Winter, *Seek the Welfare of the City*, 134.

75. Associations and *collegia* in general were under close observation and tight control; see Wendy Cotter, "The Collegia and Roman Law: State Restrictions on Voluntary Associations, 64 BCE–200 CE," in *Voluntary Associations in the Greco-Roman World*, ed. John S. Kloppenburg and Stephen G. Wilson (London/New York: Routledge, 1996), 74–89. A much more positive relationship between associations and imperial power structures, however, is assumed by Philip A. Harland, *Associations, Synagogues, and Congregations: Claiming a Place in Ancient Mediterranean Society* (Minneapolis: Fortress Press, 2003), who strongly downplays evidence for conflict. (see, for example, 137–60).

76. In a contemporary context of colonization, some of these mechanisms have been very similarly described as "horizontal violence" by Paulo Freire: "Submerged in reality, the oppressed cannot perceive clearly the 'order' which serves the interests of the oppressors whose image they have internalized. Chafing under the restrictions of this order, they often manifest a type of horizontal violence, striking out at their own comrades for the pettiest reasons." Paulo Freire, *Pedagogy of the Oppressed* (New York: Continuum, 1986), 62. Freire quotes Frantz Fanon, *Wretched of the Earth* (New York: Grove, 1968): "The colonized man will first manifest this aggressiveness which has been deposited in his bones against his own people. This is the period when the niggers beat each other up, and the police and magistrates do not know which way to turn when faced with the astonishing waves of crime in North Africa. . . . While the settler or the policeman has the right the livelong day to strike the native, to insult him and to make him crawl to them, you will see the native reaching for his knife at the slightest hostile or aggressive glance cast on him by another native; for the last resort of the native is to defend his personality vis-a-vis his brother" (Freire, 62).

77. For a similar reconceptualization of "boasting" and "works" in Rom 3:27 within the Roman imperial context, see Robert Jewett, *Romans: A Commentary*, Hermeneia (Minneapolis: Fortress Press, 2007), 295–98.

78. On the structural proximity between Greco-Roman law and strict Torah observance, see Brigitte Kahl, "Reading Galatians and Empire at the Great Altar of Pergamon," *USQR* 59, no. 3–4 (2005): 28–31. This constitutes a complex dialectic. On the one hand, Roman law and Torah were somewhat compatible with regard to their ordering principles of in/out and self/other. On the other hand, from the Roman perspective circumcision as rigorous Torah obedience could be seen in direct opposition to keeping Roman law, as most explicitly stated in Juvenal's fourteenth satire, where he talks about the bad example of parents for their children: If the father leans toward Judaism and is idle on every seventh day for Sabbath observance or abstains from pork, then the son not only does the same but also may get circumcised, despising Roman law and instead studying Jewish law handed down from Moses (Juvenal, *Sat.* 14, 96–106). This confirms once again that there were different degrees of Torah observance and affiliation with Judaism, and that both were seen as contrary to a Roman way of life. For the Galatian example this simply implies a kind of worst-case scenario: neither proper Torah observance nor adequate behavior according to Roman law.

79. For a brief introduction, see Smallwood, *Jews under Roman Rule*, 2–7.

80. See Jonathan A. Goldstein, *I Maccabees: A New Translation, with Introduction and Commentary,* Anchor Bible 41 (Garden City, N.Y.: Doubleday, 1976); idem, *II Maccabees: A New Translation, with Introduction and Commentary,* Anchor Bible 41A (Garden City, N.Y.: Doubleday, 1983).

81. This includes the conquest of Spain from Carthage in the Second Punic War (218–201) reported in 8:3 and the bloody Roman conquest of Greece, with the brutal destruction of Corinth in 146 B.C.E. and the enslavement of its population "down to the present day" (8:10), an event that happened, however, long after Judas's death. Adopting the Roman point of view, Judas portrays the Greeks and all other enemies of Rome as rightfully punished. As Goldstein states: "Our author accepts the Romans' dubious claims, that in every case the Hellenistic monarchies were the aggressors" (*I Maccabees,* 351).

82. Goldstein, *I Maccabees,* 350; James M. Scott, *Paul and the Nations: The Old Testament and Jewish Background of Paul's Mission to the Nations with Special Reference to the Destination of Galatians,* WUNT 84 (Tübingen: Mohr Siebeck, 1995), 210.

83. The treaty between Judas and Rome was eventually concluded in 161 B.C.E., three years after the Maccabeans had won their decisive victory over Antiochus's forces and reconsecrated the Jerusalem Temple. Apart from the symbolic capital it provided, the practical results of the alliance in terms of concrete Roman support for the Jewish cause were, however, insignificant; as Smallwood (*Jews under Roman Rule,* 6) states, Rome used the Jews merely "as a pawn in her diplomatic game with Syria."

84. Günter Stemberger sees 1 Maccabees 8 also as a deliberate attempt to gloss things over and present Rome in a positive light, in view of inner-Jewish debates whether an alliance was theologically and politically acceptable. Günter Stemberger, *Die römische Herrschaft im Urteil der Juden,* Erträge der Forschung 195 (Darmstadt: Wissenschaftliche Buchgesellschaft, 1983), 9.

85. Daniel R. Schwartz assumes that this "tribute still owed to the Romans" (2 Macc 8:10, 36) probably refers to the Seleucid debts imposed by the Treaty of Apamea in 188 B.C.E. that had not yet been paid. Nicanor had invited slave dealers from the coastal cities and plans to sell off the defeated Jewish victims at a bargain price of sixty-seven drachmas per slave, which is less than the price of an animal. Daniel R. Schwartz, *2 Maccabees,* Commentaries on Early Jewish Literature (Berlin/New York: de Gruyter, 2008), 333, 544–45.

86. As Daniel Schwartz (*2 Maccabees,* 337) notes, this miraculous intervention is frequently quoted, for example, 2 Macc 15:22; 1 Macc 7:41-42; 3 Macc 6:5; Sir 48:21; Josephus, *B.J.* 5.388.

87. This mismatch is even heightened if one considers that in the parallel account of these same events given in 1 Macc 2:1—4:23, Judas quotes the archetypal exodus miracle of Pharaoh's defeat at the Red Sea to encourage his soldiers (1 Macc 3:9).

88. On various options for locating this battle, see Scott, *Paul and the Nations,* 210; Daniel Schwartz, *2 Maccabees,* 337–38; and the appendix by Menahem Stern in ibid., 546–48; see further B. Bar-Kochva,

"On the Sources and Chronology of Antiochus' I Battle against the Galatians," *Proceedings of the Cambridge Philological Society* n.s. 19 (1973): 1–8.

89. See Stemberger, *Die römische Herrschaft*, 10.

90. On the structural similarity between Roman law and Paul's pre-Damascus Torah rigorism, see Kahl, "Reading Galatians and Empire at the Great Altar of Pergamon," 28–31.

91. Josephus, *B.J.* 1.152–53. In contrast to Josephus, the report on these events in the first-century B.C.E. *Psalms of Solomon* is much more critical of Pompey's ruthless act (*Pss. Sol.* 2:22-30). For the historical events around Pompey's conquest of Jerusalem and the temple, see Smallwood, *Jews under Roman Rule*, 21–27; for their reflection in the *Psalms of Solomon*, see Schürer, *History of the Jewish People in the Age of Jesus Christ*, 3:192–95.

92. Josephus, *B.J.* 1.284 mentions the service or "good works" (*euergesia*) of his father as well as his own "goodwill" (*eunoia*) toward the Romans as reason. According to Josephus, *Ant.* 15.379–89, the ceremony included a procession to the Capitol, where a sacrifice was made to Jupiter; see Smallwood, *Jews under Roman Rule*, 55; for the political background of Herod's enthronement, see 44–59.

93. Josephus, *Ant.* 15.187–94; *B.J.* 1.386–92; Smallwood, *Jews under Roman Rule*, 69–70.

94. Josephus, *B.J.* 1.397; *Ant.* 15.217; see Peter Richardson, *Herod: King of the Jews and Friend of the Romans*, Studies on Personalities of the New Testament (Columbia: University of South Carolina Press, 1996), 173; see also Israel Shatzman, *The Armies of the Hasmonaeans and Herod: From Hellenistic to Roman Frameworks*, Texte und Studien zum antiken Judentum 25 (Tübingen: Mohr, 1991), 184.

95. See Josephus, *Ant.* 15.217; for the rivalry between Herod and Cleopatra, who had tried to muster Antony's support in order to oust Herod and secure his territories for herself, see Smallwood, *Jews under Roman Rule*, 61–63. As Smallwood contends, "Herod hated and feared Cleopatra for the rest of her life" (p. 63).

96. On the decree and this kind of request-response communication between rulers and subjects as a diplomatic practice "in which synagogues, like some other associations, could be involved," thereby "replicating the activities of civic and provincial communities," see Harland, *Associations, Synagogues, and Congregations*, 219–20. Harland sees this interaction as "part of the glue that held the empire together" (p. 220). On Josephus's collection of official documents attesting Roman protection for Jewish minority rights within the Greek cities of Asia Minor (*Antiquities* 14 and 16), see n. 30 above.

97. On the symbolic significance of "monumentalizing" such an exchange between emperor and provincials as a way to claim a place for oneself within cosmos and society, see Harland, *Associations, Synagogues, and Congregations*, 158–60: "Those who set up a monument were in a concrete manner, literally set in stone, attempting to preserve symbolically a particular set of relations within society and the cosmos for passersby to observe" (p. 158). This would be especially conspicuous and relevant within a sacred space of imperial religion like the Ancyran temple.

98. "Ancyra" therefore is widely supposed to be "no more than a conjecture on the part of Scaliger. The manuscripts all have *argurē*," as Schürer (*History of the Jewish People in the Age of Jesus Christ*, 3:34–35) states. See also Scott, *Paul and the Nations*, 212.

99. Harland, *Associations, Synagogues, and Congregations*, 200–210. As already stated, Harland strongly rejects the notion that the Jewish groups of the Diaspora were "isolated and introverted communities living in hostile environments, largely alien to the institutions, conventions, and values of society in the Roman Empire" (p. 200).

100. See note 111 below.

101. See Trebilco, *Jewish Communities in Asia Minor*, 58–60, for a succinct summary of Julia Severa's relationship to the Jewish community, her Roman background, and her role as an imperial priestess and influential citizen of Acmonia. Trebilco does not mention her Galatian origin, however, nor does Cilliers Breytenbach, *Paulus und Barnabas in der Provinz Galatien: Studien zu Apostelgeschichte 13f.; 16,6; 18,23 und den Adressaten des Galaterbriefes*, Arbeiten zur Geschichte des antiken Judentums und des Urchristentums 38 (Leiden/New York: Brill, 1996), 46–47. Conversely, Barbara Levick focuses exclusively on the Galatian and Roman background of Julia Severa. Barbara Levick, *Roman Colonies in Southern Asia*

Minor (Oxford: Clarendon Press, 1967), 106–7. All three dimensions are discussed by Harland, *Associations, Synagogues, and Congregations*, 140–41, 227–28.

102. *IGR* III.173; see Emin Bosch, *Quellen zur Geschichte der Stadt Ankara im Altertum* (Ankara: Türk Tarih Kurumu Basimevi, 1967), nos. 105–6, for the text and a comprehensive commentary; see also Levick, *Roman Colonies in Southern Asia Minor*, 106–7.

103. Bosch, *Ankara*, 125.

104. See Harland, *Associations, Synagogues, and Congregations*, 140–43.

105. One coin from Acmonia issued "under" (*epi*) her and her husband Servenius Capito shows the head of "*Sebastē* Agrippina" on the obverse. Another coin has the image of Poppaea Sabina, the mistress of Nero, and an inscription referring to Acmonia and the goddess Roma on the obverse, while the reverse shows goddess Victory/Nikē with a palm branch and a laurel wreath and once more mentions Servenius Capito and Julia Severa, this time explicitly as high priests (*epi archiereōn*). Another coin with a similar reference to the high priesthood of Severa and her husband has the head of emperor Nero as *Nerōnkaisar Sebastos* on the obverse, and an image of Zeus enthroned on the reverse. See Barclay V. Head, *Catalogue of the Greek Coins of Phrygia* (London: Printed by order of the Trustees of the British Museum, 1906), xxii and 6.9–11, plates II and III; conveniently summarized in Breytenbach, *Paulus und Barnabas*, 188–89. For the epigraphic evidence, for example, the inscription referring to Julia Severa as imperial high priestess and sponsor of games (*archiereia kai agōnothetis* [MAMA 6.263]), see Helmut Halfmann, *Die Senatoren aus dem östlichen Teil des Imperium Romanum bis zum Ende des 2. Jahrhunderts n. Chr.*, Hypomnemata 58 (Göttingen: Vandenhoeck & Ruprecht, 1979), no. 5a.

106. On Severa's son L. Servenius Cornutus, see Halfmann, *Senatoren*, no. 5 (p. 102) and pp. 31–32, 78; on her relative C. Antius A. Julius Quadratus from Pergamon, senator in 94 and 105 c.e., see ibid., no. 17 (pp. 112–13) and 78; on C. Julius Severus from Ancyra, senator under Hadrian, see ibid., no. 62 and pp. 31, 79; see also Harland, *Associations, Synagogues, and Congregations*, 142.

107. MAMA 6.264; see Schürer, *History of the Jewish People in the Age of Jesus Christ*, 3:30–32; A. R. R. Sheppard, "Jews, Christians and Heretics in Acmonia and Eumeneia," *Anatolian Studies* 29 (1979): 169–80; Trebilco, *Jewish Communities in Asia Minor*, 58–60 (text and translation). Trebilco dates the inscription in the 80s or 90s of the first century c.e., as it also mentions three other donors who later, presumably a few decades after its erection in the 50s or 60s, helped to restore the synagogue (p. 59).

108. Trebilco (*Jewish Communities in Asia Minor*, 59) sees her as a "Gentile sympathizer"; Nanos (*Irony of Galatians*, 261) emphasizes that she was a friend of the Jewish community "and most likely not a Jewess or even a proselyte candidate" nor "held accountable to lead a Jewish way of life." Schürer (*History of the Jewish People in the Age of Jesus Christ*, 3:31) simply describes her as non-Jewish and a patron of the Jews.

109. She apparently held that office repeatedly; see Trebilco, *Jewish Communities in Asia Minor*, 59.

110. Sheppard, "Jews, Christians and Heretics," 170.

111. Harland, *Associations, Synagogues, and Congregations*, 260. As already stated, Harland strongly emphasizes the "moderate stance" of Christianity in Asia Minor with regard to empire, an attitude he sees confirmed not only by Luke-Acts and 1 Peter but also by Paul (pp. 235–36, curiously giving a full quotation of Rom 13:1-7 rather than mentioning Galatians in any way). Only Revelation challenges this generally positive relationship to the Roman Empire with its "sectarian outlook" and somewhat unrealistic, impractical position of withdrawal and noncompliance (ibid. 262–63). This appears as a biased and significantly oversimplified perspective, especially as Harland addresses the situation in Galatia only in a footnote, where he labels Bruce Winter's proposal "an unconvincing attempt to see imperial cult as an important factor in Paul's letter to the Galatians"—without, however, giving any reason for this blunt statement (ibid., 307 n. 23).

112. William M. Ramsay, *The Church in the Roman Empire before A.D. 170*, 2nd ed. (London: Hodder & Stoughton, 1893), 356.

6. *Amēn* and *Anathēma*

1. Peter Weiss, *The Aesthetics of Resistance,* vol. 1 (Durham, N.C./London: Duke University Press, 2005), 1:3–4. As was mentioned in chapter 2, this historical novel of Peter Weiss, which appeared in Germany in three volumes in 1975–81, is one of the towering works of twentieth-century German literature and historiography. It is a "novel" without plot line and chapters that in a continuous flow of reflections on art, activism, parties, and politics contemplates the history of European resistance to fascism in Germany, Spain, and the cities of exile. The opening passage on the Great Altar of Pergamon, seen through the eyes of three young working-class students determined to resist the Nazi regime, is set in Berlin in 1937 and becomes a leitmotif to which the author returns several times throughout the three volumes. For an introduction, see Inez Hedges, *"The Aesthetics of Resistance:* Thoughts on Peter Weiss," *Socialism and Democracy* 20 (2006): 69–77, as well the foreword by Fredric Jameson in the volume itself.

2. Kjell Arne Morland states that curses in Paul's Greek and Jewish environment were seen as an *"evil, poisonous substance which occupies humans,* destroys them from inside, and makes them a threat to their environments. In short: Curse is a negation of life." As a normal reaction this person would be expelled from the community. Kjell Arne Morland, *The Rhetoric of Curse in Galatians: Paul Confronts Another Gospel,* Emory Studies in Early Christianity 5 (Atlanta: Scholars, 1995), 158.

3. The gender-inclusive NRSV translation of *adelphoi*/brothers as "all the members of God's family" renders this aspect well.

4. Morland (*Rhetoric of Curse,* 16) recalls the pioneering work of John L. Austin, *How to Do Things with Words* (Cambridge: Clarendon, 1962) and draws on speech act theory, especially the concept of performative utterances to explain the function of Paul's *Anathēma.* He does not, however, consider the corresponding *Amēn,* which also belongs to the category of the "powerful words" that create a new reality.

5. A. Jepsen, "'āman," in *Theologisches Wörterbuch zum Alten Testament* (Stuttgart: Kohlhammer, 1973), 1:348.

6. J. Louis Martyn, *Galatians: A New Translation with Introduction and Commentary,* Anchor Bible 33A (New York: Doubleday, 1997), 92.

7. All terms that are not mentioned explicitly by Paul in Gal 1:1-9 (for example, *circumcision* and *justification by faith*) or constitute prevailing interpretational assumptions (for example, *Judaism* versus *Christianity*) are put in brackets.

8. Visual art frequently depicts Paul as holding a sword, often explained as a symbol of his eloquence and rigor in preaching the gospel. The image is sometimes attributed to the letter to the Hebrews—a letter once assigned to Paul—where the word of God is described as "sharper than any two-edged sword" (4:12). Alternatively, the sword is seen as the symbol of Paul's martyrdom in Rome under Nero.

9. For this wider understanding of intertextuality, which sees texts in dialogue not only with other texts but also with other aspects of their surrounding culture, for example, "a ritual or a work of art," see Sylvia C. Keesmaat, *Paul and His Story: (Re)Interpreting the Exodus Tradition,* JSNTSup 181 (Sheffield: Sheffield Academic Press, 1999), 50. Such a broadened definition, which includes "cultural codes" and "archetypal story lines," is vital for our intertextual work with the Great Altar and its underlying mythological combat imagery. Although Keesmaat specifically traces the exodus intertextuality in Paul's letter to the Romans, she also locates his writings more generally "within certain 'cultural codes'.... Sometimes these can be traced to specific texts, but more commonly he is drawing on a matrix of ideas which cannot be linked to any specific text but which is shaped by a number of texts (and traditions) within his culture." In our reading, the Pergamon Altar is a representation of this common "matrix of ideas" that shaped both Paul's context and his text.

10. Richard B. Hays, *Echoes of Scripture in the Letters of Paul* (New Haven: Yale University Press, 1989), 15; for an introduction to the foundational works of Mikhail Bakhtin, Julia Kristeva, and Roland Barthes, who widely shaped contemporary theories of intertextuality, see Graham Allen, *Intertextuality* (London/New York: Routledge, 2000).

11. Jonathan D. Culler, *The Pursuit of Signs: Semiotics, Literature, Deconstruction* (Ithaca, N.Y.: Cornell University Press, 1981), 103.

12. Curiously, while intertextuality is currently expanded toward the inclusion of images, images are increasingly read as semantic systems and "texts" themselves; see chapter 2, nn. 26 and 30 above. For our project of a *critical re-imagination* both approaches work synergistically.

13. Keesmaat (*Paul and His Story*, 49) states that earlier literary theorists like Kristeva and Barthes "stressed the unintentionality of intertextuality," whereas it is currently more common to speak of intertextuality in terms of authorial intention.

14. For a broad introduction to the current research on Pauline literature and scriptural intertextuality, including bibliographic references of more recent literature, see Thomas L. Brodie, Dennis R. MacDonald, and Stanley E. Porter, eds., *The Intertextuality of the Epistles: Explorations of Theory and Practice* (Sheffield: Sheffield Phoenix, 2006).

15. See the informative introduction in Hays, *Echoes*, 1–33.

16. John Hollander, *The Figure of Echo: A Mode of Allusion in Milton and After* (Berkeley: University of California Press, 1981).

17. Hays, *Echoes*, 29. Again this possibility of nonintentionality on the side of the author, and of the incapacity on the side of the reader actually to realize the intertextual potential, is important for our intertextual re-imagination. To explore the relevance of scriptural and Pergamene intertextuality for the interpretation of Galatians does not require Paul or his addressees actually to have stood at the foot of the Great Altar or to have been aware of every scriptural allusion.

18. Ibid., 20. This, again, is important for our intertextual investigation, which studies the triangular interplay of Scripture, Pergamon Altar, and Galatians within the broader framework and matrix of imperial law and cosmic order.

19. On subordinate discourse as "public" and "hidden transcript, " the latter taking place "offstage" and "behind the back" of power, see James C. Scott, *Domination and the Arts of Resistance: Hidden Transcripts* (New Haven: Yale University Press, 1990), 5–6; for hidden transcripts as *practices* (rather than speech acts alone), see 14–15. For the application of Scott's work to New Testament interpretation, see Richard A. Horsley, ed., *Hidden Transcripts and the Arts of Resistance: Applying the Work of James C. Scott to Jesus and Paul,* Semeia Studies 48 (Leiden/Boston: Brill, 2004); for a convenient summary of Scott's thesis within a Roman framework, see Neil Elliott, *The Arrogance of Nations: Reading Romans in the Shadow of Empire,* Paul in Critical Contexts (Minneapolis: Fortress Press, 2008), 30–41. For "coded" messages of freedom and liberation from Roman yoke within the New Testament texts, see also Norman A. Beck, *Anti-Roman Cryptograms in the New Testament: Symbolic Messages of Hope and Liberation,* Westminster College Library of Biblical Symbolism 1 (New York: Peter Lang, 1997).

20. In Scott's classification system, this would be equivalent to a "third realm of subordinate group politics" that lies between an official political discourse of conformity and acquiescence, on the one hand, and its sharply contrasting rebellious, though hidden transcript, on the other. Nor does it represent the rupture of the "political *cordon sanitaire,*" when the content of the hidden transcript bursts into the public realm and speaks truth in undisguised form. Rather, where we might locate Paul's discourse is in what I call the semi-hidden transcript. Scott (*Domination and the Arts of Resistance,* 18–19) describes this hybrid discourse as "a politics of disguise and anonymity that takes place in public view but is designed to have a double meaning or shield the identity of the actors. . . . I argue that a partly sanitized, ambiguous, and coded version of the hidden transcript is always present in the public discourse of subordinate groups. Interpreting these texts which, after all, are designed to be evasive is not a straightforward matter. Ignoring them, however, reduces us to an understanding of historical subordination that rests either on these rare moments of open rebellion or on the hidden transcript itself, which is not just evasive but often altogether inaccessible. The recovery of nonhegemonic voices and practices of subject people requires, I believe, a fundamentally different form of analysis than the analysis of elites, owing to the constraints under which they are produced."

21. "Hermeneutics of conspiracy" in this context means an interpretational strategy that deliberately takes into account the difference between the public transcript of discourse "beneath the eagle's eye" and

the at least partially hidden transcript of the dominated. Embedded within the overall framework of a critical re-imagination, it uses intertextuality—both with the images of the Great Altar and with Hebrew Scripture—to make the "hidden text" visible and readable again by intentionally listening to echoes, resonances, and dissonances that point to an "other" meaning. On censorship, "bilingual" texts, and "reading between the lines" within a Freudian framework and against the background of the East German experience, see Brigitte Kahl, "Reading Luke against Luke: Non-Uniformity of Text, Hermeneutics of Conspiracy and the 'Scriptural Principle' in Luke 1," in *A Feminist Companion to Luke,* ed. Amy-Jill Levine (London: Sheffield Academic, 2002), 71–73.

22. In Deut 27:11-26, Israel has to respond to the curse formula (*epikataratos*) attached to twelve concrete transgressions of the commandments with twelve times Hebrew *Amēn* = Greek *genoito,* "Let it be." This act of self-anathematizing will play a crucial role in Paul's christological argument in Gal 3:10, 13.

23. Roy E. Ciampa, *The Presence and Function of Scripture in Galatians 1 and 2,* WUNT 2/102 (Tübingen: Mohr Siebeck, 1998).

24. For a summary of Ciampa's thesis, see ibid., 295.

25. Morland, *Rhetoric of Curse,* 92.

26. Helmer Ringgren supports this link of "quickly" and readiness to apostasy/doing evil. Helmer Ringgren, "*mhr,*" in *Theological Dictionary of the Old Testament,* ed. Helmer Ringgren (Grand Rapids: Eerdmans, 1974–), 4:714. The Hebrew *mhr* is translated as *tachy* in Exod 32:8; Deut 9:12, 16; Judg 2:17 and as *etachynan* in Ps 105:13 LXX (106:13 NRSV) or *tachinoi* in Isa 59:7.

27. Ciampa, *Presence and Function,* 72.

28. By far the densest compilation of *euangelion/euangelizesthai* terminology anywhere in the New Testament.

29. See N. T. Wright, "Paul's Gospel and Caesar's Empire," in *Paul and Politics: Ekklesia, Israel, Imperium, Interpretation. Essays in Honor of Krister Stendahl,* ed. Richard Horsley (Harrisburg, Pa.: Trinity Press International, 2000), 160–83.

30. *OGIS* 458, l.32–42; translation from Steven J. Friesen, *Imperial Cults and the Apocalypse of John: Reading Revelation in the Ruins* (Oxford: Oxford University Press, 2001), 34.

31. Adolf Deissman, *Light from the Ancient East: The New Testament Illustrated by Recently Discovered Texts of the Graeco-Roman World* (London: Hodder & Stoughton, 1910), 338.

32. Ibid., 342.

33. *Euangelizein:* Isa 40:9; 52:7; 60:6; 61:6. That the term "gospel," for Paul, involves a conflict between biblical monotheism and Israel's messianic hope, on the one hand, and contemporary imperial propaganda, on the other, has been perceptively stated by N. T. Wright ("Paul's Gospel and Caesar's Empire," 165): "Despite the way Protestantism in particular has used this phrase—making it refer, as Paul never does, to a supposed proclamation of justification by faith—for Paul the term 'gospel' is the announcement that the crucified and risen Jesus of Nazareth is Israel's Messiah and the world's Lord. It is, in other words, the thoroughly Jewish (and indeed Isaianic) message that challenges the royal and imperial messages abroad in Paul's world."

34. Brigitte Kahl, "Hagar between Genesis and Galatians: The Stony Road to Freedom," in *From Prophecy to Testament: The Function of the Old Testament in the New,* ed. Craig A. Evans (Peabody, Mass.: Hendrickson, 2004), 230.

35. Hays (*Echoes,* 29–32) lists seven such criteria for testing the probability of a scriptural echo, among them the question of the availability of a certain intertext, the volume and recurrence of the allusion in the overall discourse of Paul, the thematic coherence with the concrete Pauline text and context that "echoes" it, and the historical plausibility of an allusion. All of these would support our intertextual reading of Gal 1:1-9 as described above.

36. "Paul an apostle not from men [plural] nor through (one) man [singular]" (*ouk ap' anthrōpōn oude di' anthrōpou*) as the very first words of Galatians bear some weight. The NRSV translates "sent neither by human commission nor from human authority" and thus erases the switch from plural to singular in the Greek original that might, however, be focal as Paul's self-distancing from the *one*

man and "god" who also used to send his messengers and messages to Roman Galatia and all the other provinces.

37. For the Artemis scene described by Weiss, see the image on p. 290 above.

38. For the symbolic relevance of cross, sword, victory, and scripture in the events surrounding Constantine's "conversion" and the subsequent establishment of a new imperial *Christian* cult, see David L. Dungan, *Constantine's Bible: Politics and the Making of the New Testament* (Minneapolis: Fortress Press, 2007), 98–125; see also James Carroll, *Constantine's Sword: The Church and the Jews. A History* (Boston: Houghton Mifflin, 2001).

39. *Ek* and *ex* in Greek are two variations of the same preposition "out of" or "from." The parallelism of the two *ek*-phrases in 1:1 and 1:4 from a merely textual point of view supports the notion that Paul speaks about resurrection in the terminology of exodus, the foundational "way *out of* Egypt" (Greek: *ex hodos*); we will further explore this notion from an intertextual perspective below.

40. J. Christiaan Beker, *Paul the Apostle: The Triumph of God in Life and Thought* (Philadelphia: Fortress Press, 1980), 152.

41. Ciampa, *Presence and Function,* 46: "The fact that God (the Father) is described as 'the one who raised him from the dead' suggests that this new climactic act of salvation has displaced deliverance from Egypt, the house of bondage, as the defining act which identifies God's redemption." While I strongly agree with the linkage between resurrection and exodus, it needs to be stated that the term "displaced" in this statement is somewhat troublesome, as it has a supersessionist flavor. It adequately reflects, however, the dominant Christian hermeneutical pattern that turned the exodus out of Egypt into an exodus out of Judaism.

42. Ciampa, *Presence and Function,* 40.

43. See chapter 3 above for the establishment of this patriarchal "genetic code" already in the *Enuma Elish*.

44. For this reading of Gal 3:19-20 as a confrontation between the *one* God of Israel and the imperial idol that is "not of the one," see chapter 5 above.

45. Ciampa, *Presence and Function,* 52–53.

46. Ibid., 59. Other potential sources for this christological formula of self-sacrifice are the (prevented) sacrifice of Isaac by his father Abraham in Genesis 22 (Akedah) and the Maccabean "martyr theology" (2 Macc 6:18-31; 7:1-42; 4 Maccabees 5–7; 8–18); Ciampa suggstes that these sources are not mutually exclusive and are part of a "developing stream of thought" (ibid., 58).

47. On works of imperial law versus works of messianic law, see also further below in this chapter in the section on Galatians 5–6.

48. François Bovon, "Une formule prépaulienne dans l'épître aux Galates," in *Paganisme, judaïsme, christianisme: Influences et affrontements dans le monde antique. Mélanges offerts à Marcel Simon* (Paris: E. de Boccard, 1978), 97–98.

49. It is noteworthy that in Dan 3:29 [3:96 LXX] Nebuchadnezzar confirms the unique power of God with a phrase close to Gal 1:7 that "there is no other god [*ouk estin theos heteros*] who is able to deliver [*exelesthai*] in this way." Another echo may be heard in the doxology of 3:88 LXX where God as in Gal 1:5 is praised for his deed of deliverance (*exaireō*) "into the ages" (*eis tous aiōnas*).

50. Bovon, "Formule," 100; Ciampa, *Presence and Function,* 61–62.

51. Horst Heilmann is one of the three protagonists of Weiss's novel; as a member of the resistance group of Harro Schulze-Boyson, he was executed in 1942 at the age of 19. For the Gaia-Alkyonens-Athena scene on the East Frieze of the Pergamon Altar, see fig. 20 and the image on p. 168.

52. Weiss, *The Aesthetics of Resistance,* 1:6, 9.

53. For the "Jerusalem conference," collection, and the dialectic in Paul's language of an "other gospel" in 1:6 and 2:7—an otherness that he embraces in terms of Jewish–Gentile pluriformity but fiercely rejects when the construct of the "other" represents imperial idolatry—see below.

54. Weiss, *Aesthetics of Resistance,* 1:4. For the different aspects of the Heracles legends in ancient sources, see the excellent summary by David E. Aune, "Heracles and Christ: Heracles Imagery in the Christology of Early Christianity," in *Greeks, Romans, and Christians: Essays in Honor of Abraham J.*

Malherbe, ed. David L. Balch et al. (Minneapolis: Fortress Press, 1990), 4–11. Weiss , on the other hand, retells the Heracles narrative as the story of a powerful liberator on whom the hopes of the oppressed are pinned. Heracles is tricked into compliance and subservience to the dominant order; he toils among common mortals as he accomplishes his twelve labors, and he eventually cages up Zeus's eagle, who represents the "system of coercion and menace," thus inspiring new thoughts about an age of justice. For Weiss's protagonists Heilmann, Coppi, and the narrator, Heracles becomes a role model to engage the battle against fascism (*Aesthetics of Resistance,* 1:14–20).

55. Hera was the great antagonist of Heracles, who had been born from her husband's extramarital liaison with the mortal Alcmene.

56. Weiss has his protagonist Coppi call it "an omen that Heracles, our equal, was missing, and that we now had to create our own image of this advocate of action" (*Aesthetics of Resistance,* 1:7).

57. Walter Benjamin, "Über den Begriff der Geschichte," in *Gesammelte Schriften,* 7 vols. (Frankfurt am Main: Suhrkamp, 1972–89), 1.2:691–704, here 704: "Bekanntlich war es den Juden untersagt, der Zukunft nachzuforschen. Die Thora und das Gebet unterweisen sie dagegen im Eingedenken. Dieses entzauberte ihnen die Zukunft, der die verfallen sind, die sich bei den Wahrsagern Auskunft holen. Den Juden wurde die Zukunft aber darum doch nicht zur homogenen und leeren Zeit. Denn in ihr war jede Sekunde die kleine Pforte, durch die der Messias treten konnte." (It is well known that the Jews were forbidden to look into the future. Torah and prayer instruct them, by contrast, in remembrance. This disenchanted for them the future, to which those fall prey who seek advice from the soothsayers. Nevertheless, the future did not turn into a homogenous and empty time for the Jews. For in it every second was the narrow gate, through which the Messiah could enter" [my translation]).

58. The intertextuality between Heracles themes and New Testament texts is not an unfamiliar topic in New Testament Studies, but had its focus on the similarities between Heracles and Christ; see Aune, "Heracles and Christ," 11–13.

59. On the Christ-hymn as a hidden transcript that sets Christ over against the emperor, see Erik M. Heen, "Phil 2:6-11 and Resistance to Local Timocratic Rule: *Isa theō* and the Cult of the Emperor in the East," in *Paul and the Roman Imperial Order,* ed. Richard A. Horsley (Harrisburg, Pa.: Trinity Press International, 2004), 125–53.

60. On the concept of Christ mysticism according to Albert Schweitzer, see below.

61. For a substantial group of interpretations that see the "moral exhortations" of Gal 5:13—6:10 as an "appendix" more or less unrelated to the theological argument in chapters 1–4, see John M. G. Barclay, *Obeying the Truth: Paul's Ethics in Galatians* (Minneapolis: Fortress Press, 1991), 7, 9–16.

62. *Sarx* occurs ten times in Galatians 5–6; *pneuma* twelve times, as compared to eight and six times, respectively, in the preceding four chapters.

63. Whereas strife (*eris*) and jealousy (*zēlos*) occur a few times elsewhere, hatred (*echthrai*), dissensions (*dichostasiai*), and factions (*haireseis*) are not mentioned in any other Pauline catalogue of vices; and fits of rage (*thymoi*), selfish ambition (*eritheia*), and envy (*phthonoi*) turn up only in 2 Cor 12:20-21 and Rom 1:29. Among the "fruits of the spirit" it is joy (*chara*), goodness (*agathosynē*), and self-control (*enkrateia*) that stand out, next to the more common love (*agapē*), peace (*eirenē*), and patience (*makrothymia*); see the comparison of Gal 5:19-23 with ten other New Testament catalogues of vices and virtues in Cilliers Breytenbach, *Paulus und Barnabas in der Provinz Galatien: Studien zu Apostelgeschichte 13f.; 16,6; 18,23 und den Adressaten des Galaterbriefes,* Arbeiten zur Geschichte des antiken Judentums und des Urchristentums 38 (Leiden/New York: Brill, 1996), 138–40.

64. As already stated, Robert Jewett's insight that not Judaism but rather imperial Rome was the "boasting champion of the ancient world" shifts the entire paradigm for interpreting justification by faith from an exclusively (anti-)Jewish focus to the complexities of the Roman imperial context. Flesh, associated with sin, passions, law, and death is the power that "drives perverted systems of honor and shame, leading captives into lives of relentless competition to gain advantage over other persons and groups." Within this overall system also Torah had become "traduced into an instrument of gaining honor;" Jewish religious norms were misused "as vehicles to triumph over other persons and groups." Yet the passions of the flesh (*pathēmasin,* Gal 5:24) as the drive to gain superiority are socially destructive and therefore sinful "because they inevitably damage others and challenge the surpassing honor of God." Robert Jewett, *Romans: A*

Commentary, Hermeneia (Minneapolis: Fortress Press, 2007), 436–37. For an extensive source-based argument that Paul's treatment of boasting, honor, and benefactions "would have cut against the cultural grain" of his contemporary Greco-Roman environment, see also James R. Harrison, *Paul's Langugage of Grace in Its Graeco-Roman Context,* WUNT 2/172 (Tübingen: Mohr Siebeck, 2003), 219.

65. See chapter 4 above.

66. On the interpretation of this crucial passage, see chapter 5 above.

67. Weiss, *Aesthetics of Resistance,* 1:6, quoted above.

68. It is tempting to draw a parallel to Gen 4:10, where God actually hears the outcry of Abel's blood from the *'ădāmâ*/earth and "raises" another son for Eve, in place of the slaughtered victim (4:25). Seth-Abel, not Cain, subsequently is listed as the firstborn of Adam/humanity in the genealogy of Genesis 5 (5:3). Protest against the destruction of human and earth life is firmly linked in Genesis 1–11; see Brigitte Kahl, "Fratricide and Ecocide: Re-Reading Genesis 2-4," in *Earth Habitat: Eco-Justice and the Church's Response,* ed. Dieter Hessel and Larry Rasmussen (Minneapolis: Fortress Press, 2001), 53–70.

69. On the nonimperial relationship between God, Adam (human), and *'ădāmâ* (Gaia, Earth) in Genesis, the background text for Paul in Galatians 3–4, see Kahl, "Fratricide and Ecocide"; also chapter 3 above, on the imperial representation of creation in the *Enuma Elish.*

70. It is symptomatic of this subjugation of Gaia-Earth that in imperial representations she is firmly linked to the masculinity, fertility, and power of the emperor (for example, on the Prima Porta statue, where she is placed in Augustus's groin area) and set in parallel to (female) representations of imperial conquest (for example, on the Altar of Peace, where goddess Roma sits on a pile of weapons, resembling goddess Athena at the Great Altar); see fig. 37, ch. 4. In these images, however, the original brutality of the Gaia scene at the Pergamon Frieze—Earth being subdued by the imperial order of civilization—is masked with an air of "happiness" and bucolic fertility.

71. For a "re-imagination" of the Pergamene Gaia-Athena-scene in terms of ecojustice and inclusive, sustainable table community between gods and Giants, earth and city/civilization, see Brigitte Kahl, "Reading Galatians and Empire at the Great Altar of Pergamon," *USQR* 59, no. 3-4 (2005): 39–40.

72. On this point, Paul again resonates with Revelation, where Earth also plays a significant role as a victim and at the same time noncompliant subject of imperial domination (see Rev 12:16); see Barbara Rossing, "Alas for Earth! Lament and Resistance in Revelation 12," in *The Earth Story in the New Testament,* ed. Norman Habel and Shirley Wurst, Earth Bible 5 (Sheffield: Sheffield Academic, 2002), 180–211.

73. This appears to be the most plausible background of Paul's clearly accusatory statement in Gal 2:14 that Peter, though being a Jew, now lives as a Gentile (*ethnikōs*), that is, conforming to Rome, and thus has no right to "Judaize" the Gentiles/nations; see below.

74. For the two gospels being *different* indeed, a difference that is not merely a difference of audiences, see below. For the highly unusual terms *gospel of foreskin/circumcision,* see n. 80 below.

75. Jewett, *Romans,* 436.

76. For the argument, foundational to the New Perspective, that Paul's Damascus experience was not his "conversion" to Christianity but rather a prophetic call within Judaism, see Krister Stendahl, *Paul among Jews and Gentiles and Other Essays* (Philadelphia: Fortress Press, 1976), 7–23. While Stendahl rightly challenged the idea of a radical discontinuity between the "Jewish Saul" and the "Christian Paul," which is at the center of the traditional Protestant understanding, it was Alan Segal's achievement to reassert and reframe the transformation and discontinuity implied in Paul's transition—not from Judaism to Christianity but from one form of Judaism to another one. See Alan F. Segal, *Paul the Convert: The Apostolate and Apostasy of Saul the Pharisee* (New Haven: Yale University Press, 1990). The interaction between this new type of Judaism and its Roman context, however, was not considered.

77. For a stimulating reconceptualization of Paul's theology within the framework of cultural anthropology, especially Victor Turner's concepts of liminality, transformation, community, and antistructure, see Christian Strecker, *Die liminale Theologie des Paulus: Zugänge zur paulinischen Theologie aus kulturanthropologischer Perspektive,* Forschungen zur Religion und Literatur des Alten und Neuen Testaments (Göttingen: Vandenhoeck & Ruprecht, 1999).

78. Difference thus *did* matter for Paul and was at the core of his theology. This is an argument against Daniel Boyarin's thesis that Paul is driven by a "Hellenistic desire for the One" that, within the dominant framework of Christian occidental civilization, would inevitably lead into a "coercive sameness"; see Daniel Boyarin, *A Radical Jew: Paul and the Politics of Identity,* Contraversions 1 (Berkeley: University of California Press, 1994), 7, 236. For oneness-in-difference as vital for the events in Jerusalem and Antioch, see also Jae Won Lee, "Justification of Difference in Galatians," in *Character Ethics and the New Testament,* ed. Robert Brawley (Louisville: Westminster John Knox, 2007), 191–208.

79. The terms *gospel of the foreskin (euangelion tēs akrobystias)* and *(gospel) of the circumcision (. . . tēs peritomēs)* in 2:7 are unique in the New Testament and highly unconventional; traditional translations such as "gospel for the Gentiles" and "gospel for the Jews" blur the fact that for Paul not just the recipients are different, but also the gospels themselves; see Brigitte Kahl, "Gender Trouble in Galatia? Paul and the Rethinking of Difference," in *Is There a Future for Feminist Theology?* ed. Deborah F. Sawyer and Diane M. Collier (Sheffield: Sheffield Academic, 1999), 57–73.

80. See Dieter Georgi, *Remembering the Poor: The History of Paul's Collection for Jerusalem* (Nashville: Abingdon, 1992); Sze-kar Wan, "Collection for the Saints as Anticolonial Act," in *Paul and Politics: Ekklesia, Israel, Imperium, Interpretation. Essays in Honor of Krister Stendahl,* ed. Richard Horsley (Harrisburg, Pa.: Trinity Press International, 2000), 191–215; Justin J. Meggitt, *Paul, Poverty and Survival,* Studies of the New Testament and Its World (Edinburgh: T&T Clark, 1998), 158–61.

81. See chapter 5, n. 78.

82. For example, *anthistanai kata prosōpon,* "oppose somebody right into his face" (2:11), *hypostellō,* "withdraw," and *phoboumenos,* "for fear" (2:12), *hypokrinesthai* and *hypokrisis,* "hypocrisy" (2:13); for the LXX-intertextual significance of these terms see Ciampa, *Presence and Function,* 157–67; and Stephen Anthony Cummins, *Paul and the Crucified Christ in Antioch: Maccabean Martyrdom and Galatians 1 and 2,* SNTSMS 114 (Cambridge: Cambridge University Press, 2001), 161–88, who assumes an intertextual linkage between Galatians 2 and the story of the faithful martyr Eleazar (2 Macc 6:18-31; 4 Macc 5:1—7:23). Neither Ciampa nor Cummins, however, considers their findings within a Roman imperial context of enforced idolatry.

83. Interestingly, Esth 8:17 LXX renders the Hebrew *hitpael* of *yhd* (to present oneself as a Jew) by two Greek verbs: not only "Judaize" but also "get circumcised," which exactly matches the situation in Antioch.

84. The term *ethnikōs* (translated as "in a Gentile manner, pagan") has a negative connotation in each of the four other New Testament occurrences (Matt 5:47; 6:7; 18:17; and 3 John 1:7). In Gal 2:14, this negative ring is supported by the immediately following reference to "Gentile sinners" (*ex ethnōn hamartōloi*) in 2:15. For the term "Gentile" in the "pagan" Roman imperial context, see Warren Carter, "Matthew and the Gentiles: Individual Conversion and/or Systemic Transformation," *Journal for the Study of the New Testament* 26 (2004): 259–82.

85. The logic of Gal 2:15-21 is very close to Rom 3:27-31, where also the oneness of God is quoted to equalize the relationship between Jews and Gentiles through faith. Works of the law are attached to "boasting" as self-distinction over and against the other. As Jewett (*Romans,* 298) notes, Paul's rejection of "works of law" in Rom 3:28 "drives home the separation between the new honor system in Christ and the traditional achievement of honor through performance or social privilege."

86. For a reflection on the narrative "deep structures" of Genesis and their impact on the genealogical, social, and theological identity construct of Galatians 3–4, see Kahl, "Hagar between Genesis and Galatians," 219–32.

87. James L. Kugel, *The Bible as It Was* (Cambridge, Mass.: Belknap Press of Harvard University Press, 1997), 135–38.

88. Pamela Eisenbaum has made a compelling case that Paul himself saw his call and mission among the nations in analogy to Abraham; I strongly support her argument that Paul wants to establish effective kinship relations, not just a metaphorical faith lineage. See Pamela Eisenbaum, "Paul as the New Abraham," in *Paul and Politics: Ekklesia, Israel, Imperium, Interpretation. Essays in Honor of Krister Stendahl,* ed. Richard Horsley (Harrisburg, Pa.: Trinity Press International, 2000), 130–45.

89. See chapter 4 above. On the intertextuality between Paul and Virgil's *Aeneid* and specifically the relationship between Father Abraham and "Father Aeneas"/Caesar Augustus, see David R. Wallace, *The Gospel of God: Romans as Paul's Aeneid* (Eugene, Ore.: Pickwick, 2008), 150–51.

90. This is explicitly stated in the midrashic retelling of the Abraham story in *Genesis Rabbah* 38:13. Abraham, in an act of prophetic iconoclasm, destroys the idols he has to sell in his father's idol store. In a mock apology he subsequently claims that the idols started to fight each other as to who was entitled first to eat from the food sacrificed to them; the biggest idol then overpowered and crushed all the smaller idols. See Julius Theodor and Chanoch Albeck, *Midrash Bereshit Rabbah* (Jerusalem: Wahrmann, 1965). This midrash reads like a parable on the imperial takeover of traditional religions; it voices an interesting perspective on idolatry as embodiment of imperial power politics and combat law. Though the midrash is a later text than Galatians, the interpretation itself goes back to earlier stages and thus may corroborate our thesis of an "imperial monotheism" in conflict with Jewish monotheism as the subtext of Paul's Abraham intertextuality.

91. See chapter 5 above for our reading of this most cryptic statement in Gal 3:19-30 about the *not-of-the-one* mediator of the law (*henos ouk estin*) as a coded reference to Caesar, somewhat similar to the puzzling reference to the *"singular anthropos"* in 1:1. Expressed in guarded language, it evokes the core conflict of the entire letter as the idolatrous claim of the Roman emperor as supreme guardian and grantor of law vis-à-vis the subject nations, including Jewish law, and the enslaving powers unleashed through his false promises and decrees of "law-mediation." See also the Epilogue. Both imperial "monotheism" and messianic monotheism claim Torah/law/*nomos,* yet with very opposite effects.

92. In *Genesis Rabbah* 38:13, after Abraham has destroyed the idols, he is interrogated and tortured by Nimrod; see Kugel, *Bible as It Was,* 143–44. Interestingly, in the canonical account of Gen 10:8-12, Nimrod is introduced as the first ruler of a primeval Mesopotamian super-empire comprising, among others, Babylon and Assyria. This again matches perfectly our contextual construct for Galatia and the "persecution" of the Christ-followers there because of their reluctance to worship the emperor.

93. For these Genesis patterns, see Kahl, "Hagar between Genesis and Galatians," 224–26; for the narrative of Cain and Abel as intervention into the imperial "genealogy of power" and archetypal story of an alternative motherhood, fatherhood, and brotherhood, see Kahl, "Fratricide and Ecocide," 53–70.

94. The Galatian antithesis of Hagar and Sarah in Christian visual art was often represented as juxtaposition of a triumphant "Ekklesia" and a mourning "Synagogue." On Hagar in Genesis 16 and 21 as symbol of oppression and otherness, see the two classic feminist-critical explorations in Phyllis Trible, *Texts of Terror: Literary-feminist Readings of Biblical Narratives* (Philadelphia: Fortress Press, 1984), 28; and, from an African American womanist perspective, Delores Williams, *Sisters in the Wilderness: The Challenge of Womanist God-talk* (Maryknoll, N.Y.: Orbis, 1993), 15–33. In line with the traditional interpretation of Paul, Williams reads the Galatian story of Hagar as the Christian reinscription of the inferiority and exclusion of the slave, female, poor, ethnically and socially vulnerable: "Hagar and her descendants represent the outsider position par excellence" (p. 5). For a different reading model, see Kahl, "Hagar between Genesis and Galatians"; and Davina C. Lopez, *Apostle to the Conquered: Reimagining Paul's Mission,* Paul in Critical Contexts (Minneapolis: Fortress Press, 2008), 153–63.

95. Paul's emphasis on the "allegorical" nature of his Hagar construct (4:24) is vital, as it creates a distance between "real" and "allegorical." In both Paul's *Galatian* Hagar and Sarah, the identities of the *Genesis* Hagar and Sarah are merged and amalgamated. This allows for the hybrid allegorical Hagar of Galatians to represent the antagonism and irreconcilable fight between the two women and their sons, whereas the hybrid allegorical Sarah embodies their messianic reconciliation and solidarity. See Kahl, "Hagar between Genesis and Galatians," 221–29.

96. See chapter 5 above on Paulo Freire's term *horizontal violence.*

97. For a more detailed argument on Gal 4:21—5:1, especially in light of imperial representations of conquered lands as women who "naturally" bear children into slavery, like the allegorical Hagar, see Lopez, *Apostle to the Conquered,* 26–55, 153–63.

98. Albert Schweitzer, *The Mysticism of Paul the Apostle* (London: A.&C. Black, 1931).

99. On this, see the introduction by Clifford J. Green to volume 10 of the English Bonhoeffer

edition, as well as the contribution of Hans Christoph von Hase ("Turning away from the Phraseological to the Real: A Personal Recollection") in this same volume: Dietrich Bonhoeffer, *Barcelona, Berlin, New York: 1928–1931,* English edition edited by Clifford J. Green. *Dietrich Bonhoeffer Works* (Minneapolis: Fortress Press, 1996–), vol. 10 (2008), 43, 591–604.

100. For Bonhoeffer's turn to the other and a "church for others," see the introduction above, nn. 50 and 53; he criticizes a church merely fighting for "self-preservation" and sees "being there for others" in the image of Jesus as true experience of transcendence. See Dietrich Bonhoeffer, *Letters and Papers from Prison. The Enlarged Edition,* ed. Eberhard Bethge (New York: Macmillan, 1972), 381–82. This somewhat mirrors Schweitzer's disparagement regarding the superiority claims of Western civilization. From the perspective of the colonized other, Western countries for him look like a bunch of "robber states" committing every crime in the name of "the German God, or the American God, or the British God." For Schweitzer, being a disciple of Jesus fundamentally contradicts the separation of human beings into civilized/deserving self and uncivilized/undeserving other. "But our culture divides people into two classes: civilized men, a title bestowed on the persons who do the classifying; and others , who have only the human form, who may perish or go to the dogs for all the 'civilized men' care. Oh, this 'noble' culture of ours! It speaks so piously of human dignity and human rights and then disregards this dignity and these rights of countless millions and treads them underfoot, only because they live overseas or because their skins are of different color or because they cannot help themselves." Albert Schweitzer, *Essential Writings* (Maryknoll, N.Y.: Orbis, 2005), 75–77.

101. See n. 99 above.

102. It is noteworthy that *The Mysticism of Paul the Apostle* was written over two decades between 1911 and 1930, traveling with Schweitzer from Europe to Africa and back twice. Following the unwritten rules of scholarly publication at the time, however, the book itself does not reveal its concrete "setting in life," which clearly shaped, and has been shaped by, Schweitzer's "other" vision of Paul. For a still excellent general introduction to Schweitzer's theological, philosophical, and missionary biography, see George Seaver, *Albert Schweitzer: The Man and His Mind* (New York/London: Harper & Brothers, 1947).

103. Schweitzer, *Essential Writings,* 77–79.

104. Bonhoeffer, *Letters and Papers from Prison,* 300; it is important to note that Bonhoeffer in his turn to the "other" of established religion repeatedly refers to the circumcision debate in Galatians (ibid., 281, 329).

105. Schweitzer, *Mysticism of Paul the Apostle,* 110, 125, 127.

106. Bonhoeffer, *Barcelona, Berlin, New York ,* 495; 190.

107. Schweitzer, *Mysticism of Paul the Apostle,* 112, 205.

108. Ibid., 225.

109. Ibid., 383.

110. Ibid., 384.

111. Ibid.

112. For a thorough reevaluation and repositioning of Paul's theology in the context of first-century Jewish apocalyptic mysticism, see Segal, *Paul the Convert,* 34–71. Segal clearly frames Paul as a Jewish mystic, yet pays less attention to the "horizontal" social and ethical dimension of this mysticism.

113. I tentatively use the term *monotheistic syncretism from below* in order to signal that the Pauline communities of the Jesus movement were, strictly speaking, not a new religion but a border-transgressive movement marked by the coexistence of foreskin and circumcision, that is, inclusive of the *other* of each individual religious identity involved. This is a focal yet widely neglected feature of Pauline theology. Peoples of the "foreskin" had to learn how to live with the people of the "circumcision" and vice versa. The unifying entity was the one God of Israel, who had broken down the law and order of exclusive religious affiliation, including Israel's own, to create a new inclusive community. This hybrid monotheistic liminality with syncretistic features partially resembles the pattern that had been established among the multireligious nations of the first century C.E. by the unifying imperial world

religion under the divine Caesar (see chapter 3). Yet the social location and theological thrust were entirely opposite. Paul's global network of communities functioned horizontally rather than vertically, and on the basis of mutual support rather than competition. To reopen the debate on the meaning of "circumcision" and "foreskin" in a twenty-first-century context would be a vital contribution of Pauline studies to interfaith dialogue and solidarity in a global age of worldwide challenges facing multi-religious humanity as a whole.

Epilogue

1. See introduction above.

2. See H. D. Rankin, *Celts and the Classical World* (London: Croom Helm, 1987), 144–45; Alison Futrell, *Blood in the Arena: The Spectacle of Roman Power* (Austin: University of Texas Press, 1997), 74.

3. Martin Goodman wonders "whether an apparently national rebellion was in fact an action by a Roman aristocrat whose provincial origin was held against him by his enemies." The boundaries between a peasant protest against taxation, brigandry, and "a full-scale war aimed at recovery of liberation from Roman rule" were often unclear. Martin Goodman, "Opponents of Rome: Jews and Others," in *Images of Empire*, ed. Loveday Alexander, JSOTSup 122 (Sheffield: Sheffield Academic, 1991), 225; see also P. A. Brunt, "The Revolt of Vindex and the Fall of Nero," *Latomus* 18 (1959): 531–59; S. L. Dyson, "Native Revolt Patterns in the Roman Empire," in *ANRW* II.3 (1975): 158–61; Vasily Rudich, *Political Dissidence under Nero: The Price of Dissimulation* (London: Routledge, 1993), 210–12.

4. Josephus, *B.J.* 4.601–17; Suetonius, *Vespasian* 6. See Helmut Schwier, *Tempel und Tempelzerstörung: Untersuchung zu den theologischen und ideologischen Faktoren im ersten jüdisch-römischen Krieg (66–74 n.Chr.)* (Freiburg: Universitätsverlag, 1989), 23.

5. See Brigitte Kahl, "Acts of the Apostles: Pro(to)-Imperial Script and Hidden Transcript." In *In the Shadow of Empire: Reclaiming the Bible as History of Faithful Resistance,* edited by Richard A. Horsley, 137–56 (Louisville: Westminster John Knox, 2008), 137–56.

6. Tacitus, *The Histories*, ed. D. S. Levene (Oxford: Oxford University Press, 1997), xvii.

7. In 4.18 Tacitus states that, had his project prospered, Civilis would have been king of Gaul and Germany, which would then have been the strongest and wealthiest country in the world.

8. The preservation of the Capitol even during the conquest of Rome by the Gauls, in contrast to its self-inflicted destruction by rival emperors in 69 C.E., is also mentioned in 3.72. For the involvement of Druids in subversive activities and the political threat they constituted, see Futrell, *Blood in the Arena,* 74; also Nora K. Chadwick, *The Druids* (Cardiff: Wales University Press, 1966), 41–50.

9. "Most people held the belief that, according to the ancient priestly writings, this was the moment at which the East was fated to prevail: men would now start forth from Judaea and conquer the world" (Tacitus, *Hist.* 5.13). See also Suetonius, *Vespasian* 4.5; and Josephus, *B.J.* 6.312–13: "But what more than all else incited them to war was an ambiguous oracle, likewise found in their sacred scriptures, to the effect that at that time one from their country would become ruler of the world" (trans. Thackeray, LCL). See also Schwier, *Tempel und Tempelzerstörung,* 238–45.

10. A connection between the destruction of the Druidic sanctuaries on the island of Mona in Britain in 61 C.E. (Tacitus, *Ann.* 14.30; *Agr.* 14.3) and the conquest of the Jerusalem temple in 70 C.E. has been pointed out by Schwier, *Tempel und Tempelzerstörung,* 314.

11. The Jewish oracle about the world ruler emerging from Judea (see n. 9 above) thus in reality was talking about Vespasian "who was proclaimed emperor on Jewish soil [*epi Ioudaias autokratoros*]" (*B.J.* 6.313). See Tessa Rajak, *Josephus, the Historian and His Society* (Philadelphia: Fortress Press, 1984), 185–94.

12. See chapter 4 above. The Roman conquest of Jotapata in 67 C.E., according to Josephus, *B.J.* 3.336–37, cost the lives of forty thousand people (a number that Mary Smallwood, however, thinks is too big for a town of the size of Jotapata; E. Mary Smallwood, *The Jews under Roman Rule: From Pompey*

to Diocletian, Studies in Judaism in Late Antiquity 20 [Leiden: Brill, 1976], 308 n. 59). Twelve hundred were made prisoners and sold as slaves. Josephus, who had led the heroic resistance of the city against the Roman troops, is personally invited by the victors to surrender. He watches the suicide of his last forty soldiers, who trust that he will join them, and then goes over to the Romans (*B.J.* 3.340–98). Brought before Vespasian, he predicts Nero's demise and Vespasian's and Titus's rise to power. Josephus, however, is eager to present himself not as a traitor but as an interpreter of God's own move away from the Jews and toward the Romans (*B.J.* 3.354). On Josephus's role during the war in Galilee and at Jotapata, see Rajak, *Josephus,* 144–73.

13. Josephus spent the rest of the Jewish War in "honourable detention with the Roman army" (Smallwood, *Jews under Roman Rule,* 308). He later was rewarded with "Roman citizenship, together with the Flavian name that was its conventional accompaniment; he was given a house, a pension, new estates in a fertile part of Palestine" (Rajak, *Josephus,* 194–95).

14. This core theological assumption that God must be on the side of the victorious is later echoed by Titus, who exclaims at the sight of conquered Jerusalem with its powerful fortifications that "God indeed has been with us in the war. God it was who brought the Jews from these strongholds" (*B.J.* 6.411).

15. See also Pliny, *Nat.* 30.13; and Futrell, *Blood in the Arena,* 262–63 nn. 78–79.

16. William M. Ramsay, *The Church in the Roman Empire before A.D. 170* (London: Hodder & Stoughton, 1893), 354.

17. Again it is important to state that the Greek term *basileus* can mean both "king" and "emperor."

18. In a speech to the Treviri and Lingones, Cerialis states, for example, "Tyranny and warfare were always rife throughout the length and breadth of Gaul, until you accepted Roman government. Often as we have been provoked, we have never imposed upon you any burden by right of conquest, except what was necessary to keep peace. Tribes cannot be kept quiet without troops" (Tacitus, *Hist.* 4.74).

19. Pliny, *Nat.* 34.84; Dio Chrysostom, *Orationes* 31.148; Pausanias 10.7.1, who reports that Nero robbed Delphi alone of five hundred bronze statues. According to David Balch, Nero placed sculptures of Dying Galatians/Gauls—for example, the sculpture of the Galatian chieftain killing himself and his wife—in the Octagonal Room of his Golden House. See David L. Balch, "Paul's Portrait of Christ Crucified (Gal 3:1) in Light of Paintings of Suffering and Death in Pompeiian Houses," in *Early Christian Families in Context: An Interdisciplinary Dialogue,* ed. David L. Balch and Carolyn Osiek, Religion, Marriage, and Family (Grand Rapids: Eerdmans, 2003), 100, citing Filippo Coarelli, *Da Pergamo a Roma: I Galati Nella Città Degli Attalidi* (Rome: Quasar, 1995), 15.

20. This phrase is quoted in Greek by Suetonius; it is used in Seneca, *De Clementia* 2.2 as an expression of extreme brutality and ruthlessness. Yet Nero boasts also of having power over the entire creation. The mixing up of earth and fire has cosmic dimensions as an annihilation of the elemental order. As we have shown in the introduction, the separation and juxtaposition of fire and earth are primeval acts of creation that Nero implicitly claims to undo.

21. See Suetonius, *Nero* 31; on the Golden House, see Larry F. Ball, *The Domus Aurea and the Roman Architectural Revolution* (New York: Cambridge University Press, 2003).

22. Tacitas, *Annals,* 15.44.

23. On this, see the still illuminating debate between A. N. Sherwin-White and G. E. M. de Ste. Croix, conveniently accessible in Everett Ferguson, ed., *Church and State in the Early Church,* Studies in Early Christianity 7 (New York: Garland, 1993), 1–59.

24. Interestingly, this exactly corresponds to a "pro-barbarian" bias in early Christian sources of the second to fourth centuries. As Stamenka E. Antonova states, "It is remarkable that the overwhelming majority of apologists who write in this period accept the charge of barbarism rather than denying it." Stamenka E. Antonova, "Barbarians and the Empire-wide Spread of Christianity," in *The Spread of Christianity in the First Four Centuries: Essays in Explanation,* ed. William V. Harris, Columbia Studies in the Classical Tradition 27 (Leiden/Boston: Brill, 2005), 69.

25. The close linkage between Galatians/Gauls and Christians as archenemies of empire and Roman religion has been observed by L. F. Janssen, "'Superstitio' and the Persecution of the Christians," in

Church and State in the Early Church, ed. Everett Ferguson, Studies in Early Christianity 7 (New York: Garland, 1993), 96–104. Janssen quotes the un-Roman *fides*-relation of the Christians to a person who was not the emperor, their refusal of sacrifice and the denial of the Roman gods, as well as the alternative concept of a "Kingdom of Heaven" and concludes: "To a non-Christian all this bore a striking resemblance to the speculations of the Gauls about the end of the Roman empire," adding in a footnote: "As a working hypothesis I would suggest that the Early Church was all too readily associated and even identified with the traditionally subversive Galatians and Gauls" (p. 101).

26. On Romulus and Remus in relation to the foundation of the city, see also Davina C. Lopez, *Apostle to the Conquered: Reimagining Paul's Mission*, Paul in Critical Contexts (Minneapolis: Fortress Press, 2008), 63–66.

27. Futrell, *Blood in the Arena*, 208–10.

28. Paul Zanker, *The Power of Images in the Age of Augustus*, Jerome Lectures, 16th Series (Ann Arbor: University of Michigan Press, 1988), 190–91.

29. For the linkage between eschatological ideas and incendiarism, see Janssen, "Superstitio," 101–2.

30. On the martyrdom of Paul, either through trial and decapitation under Nero (as stated in the second-century *Acts of Paul*), or anonymously during the Neronian persecution, see the introduction above, n. 26; and John Dominic Crossan and Jonathan L. Reed, *In Search of Paul: How Jesus's Apostle Opposed Rome's Empire with God's Kingdom. A New Vision of Paul's Words and World* (San Francisco: HarperSanFrancisco, 2004), 400–403, here 401: "Our best historical guess, then, is that Paul, and presumably Peter as well, died among those many Christians martyred by Nero in 64 c.e."

31. The connection between "Christ crucified" and the images of Dying Gauls as a challenge to "key Roman ideological values" has been most perceptively argued by Balch, "Paul's Portrait of Christ Crucified," 108.

32. Josephus (*B.J.* 6.420) gives the number of ninety-seven thousand prisoners and 1.1 million that perished during the siege. Of the survivors, those over seventeen years old were either sent in chains to Egypt, possibly into the mines, or "presented by Titus to the various provinces, to be destroyed in the theatres by the sword or by wild beasts." The tallest and most handsome of the youth were selected for the triumph at Rome (6.418).

33. See Schwier, *Tempel und Tempelzerstörung*, 315, who observes that this is an act of cultic conquest. As the legionary eagles are the sanctuary of the Roman army, symbolizing the rule of Jupiter Optimus Maximus and the Roman people, the sacrifice signals the victory of the Roman god(s) over the Jewish God, and of Romans over Jews.

34. For the "Judea Capta" coinage, see Lopez, *Apostle to the Conquered*, 35–38; for the linkage between military conquest and sexual violence, see ibid., 108–10.

35. In *B.J.* 5.216, Josephus notes that the lampstand, table, and altar of incense were most wonderful works of art, universally renowned. The seven branches of the lampstand represented the planets; the twelve loaves on the table, the Zodiac and the year; and the altar with the fragrant spices "from sea and land, both desert and inhabited," signified "that all things are of God, and for God." It is precisely this assertion of God as the supreme creator and ruler of the cosmos that is powerfully denounced when these objects are publicly exhibited as Roman trophies.

36. Josephus, *B.J.* 7.218: "On all Jews, wheresoever resident, he imposed a poll-tax of two drachms, to be paid annually into the Capitol as formerly contributed by them to the temple at Jerusalem." Dio Cassius 66.7.2 mentions that the recipient is "Jupiter Capitolinus." The amount to be paid equals the previous temple tax.

37. That the destruction of the Jerusalem temple and the exhibition of its key images in Rome on the level of ideology and public representation served as a "compensation" for the destroyed Capitol and that the Flavian triumph was a carefully orchestrated show of legitimation by virtue of victory over the Jewish God is an argument that has been convincingly made by Schwier, *Tempel und Tempelzerstörung*, 334; also 280–81; Schwier also maintains a linkage between the three fires.

38. On this phenomenon, see Seth Schwartz, *Imperialism and Jewish Society, 200 b.c.e. to 640 c.e.*,

Jews, Christians, and Muslims from the Ancient to the Modern World (Princeton: Princeton University Press, 2001), 55–58, and chapter 5 above.

39. For this interpretation of Gal 3:19-20, which also relates to the critical reading of "Mount Sinai" in the Sarah-Hagar allegory (Gal 4:21-31), see chapter 5 above.

40. For a recent reconstruction and description of the temple, see Maria Paola Del Moro, "The Temple of Peace," in *The Museums of the Imperial Forums in Trajan's Market*, ed. Lucrezia Ungaro (Milan: Electa, 2007), 171–75.

41. Ibid., 173.

Bibliography

Agamben, Giorgio. *The Time That Remains: A Commentary on the Letter to the Romans*. Stanford, Calif.: Stanford University Press, 2005.

Allen, Graham. *Intertextuality*. London/New York: Routledge, 2000.

Allen, Sister Prudence. *The Concept of Woman: The Aristotelian Revolution 750 BC–AD 150*. Grand Rapids: Eerdmans, 1985.

Althusser, Louis. "Ideology and Ideological State Apparatus. (Notes towards an Investigation)." In idem, *Lenin and Philosophy and Other Essays*, 85–126. New York: Monthly Review, 2001.

Althusser, Louis, and Etienne Balibar. *Reading Capital*. London: Unwin Brothers Limited, Gresham, 1977.

Ando, Clifford. *Imperial Ideology and Provincial Loyalty in the Roman Empire*. Classics and Contemporary Thought 6. Berkeley: University of California Press, 2000.

Andreae, Bernard. "The Image of the Celts in Etruscan, Greek and Roman Art." In *The Celts*, edited by Sabatino Moscati et al., 61–69. Venice: Bompiani, 1991.

Antonova, Stamenka E. "Barbarians and the Empire-wide Spread of Christianity." In *The Spread of Christianity in the First Four Centuries: Essays in Explanation*, edited by William V. Harris, 69–85. Columbia Studies in the Classical Tradition 27. Leiden: Brill, 2005.

Appian. *Wars of the Romans in Iberia: With an Introduction, Translation, and Commentary by J. S. Richardson*. Translated by J. S. Richardson. Warminster: Aris & Phillips, 2000.

Arnold, Clinton E. "I Am Astonished That You Are So Quickly Turning Away! (Gal 1:6): Paul and Anatolian Folk Belief." *NTS* 51 (2005): 429–49.

Asano, Atsuhiro. *Community-Identity Construction in Galatians: Exegetical, Social-Anthropological and Socio-Historical Studies*. JSNTSup 285. London/New York: T&T Clark, 2005.

Auget, Roland. *The Roman Games*. Frogmore, St. Albans, Herts: Panther, 1975.

Aune, David E. "Heracles and Christ: Heracles Imagery in the Christology of Early Christianity." In *Greeks, Romans, and Christians: Essays in Honor of Abraham J. Malherbe*, edited by David L. Balch et al., 4–11. Minneapolis: Fortress Press, 1990.

Austin, John L. *How to Do Things with Words*. Oxford: Clarendon, 1975.

Badiou, Alain. *Saint Paul: The Foundation of Universalism*. Cultural Memory in the Present. Stanford, Calif.: Stanford University Press, 2003.

Balch, David L. "Paul's Portrait of Christ Crucified (Gal 3:1) in Light of Paintings of Suffering and Death in Pompeiian Houses." In *Early Christian Families in Context: An Interdisciplinary Dialogue*, edited by David L. Balch and Carolyn Osiek, 84–108. Grand Rapids: Eerdmans, 2003.

Ball, Larry F. *The Domus Aurea and the Roman Architectural Revolution*. New York: Cambridge University Press, 2003.

Balsdon, J. P. V. D. *Life and Leisure in Ancient Rome*. New York: McGraw-Hill, 1969.

Balzer-Leonhardt, Jutta. "Jewish Worship and Universal Identity in Philo of Alexandria." In *Jewish*

Identity in the Greco-Roman World, edited by Jörg Frey et al., 29–53. Ancient Judaism and Early Christianity 71. Leiden: Brill, 2007.

Barchíesí, Alessandro. "Learned Eyes: Poets, Viewers, Image Makers." In *The Cambridge Companion to the Age of Augustus*, edited by Karl Galinksy, 281–305. Cambridge Companion to the Classics. Cambridge: Cambridge University Press, 2005.

Barclay, John M. G. *Jews in the Mediterranean Diaspora: From Alexander to Trajan (323 BCE–117 CE)*. Edinburgh: T&T Clark, 1996.

———. *Obeying the Truth: Paul's Ethics in Galatians*. Minneapolis: Fortress Press, 1988.

Bar-Kochva, B. "On the Sources and Chronology of Antiochus' I Battle Against the Galatians." *Proceedings of the Cambridge Philological Society* n.s. 19 (1973): 1–8.

Barrett, C. K. *Essays on Paul*. London: SPCK, 1982.

———, ed. *The New Testament Background: Writings from Ancient Greece and the Roman Empire That Illuminate Christian Origins*. San Francisco: HarperSanFrancisco, 1987.

Barton, Stephen C., ed. *Idolatry: False Worship in the Bible, Early Judaism and Christianity*. London: T&T Clark, 2007.

Beard, Mary, et al., eds. *Religions of Rome*, volume 1. Cambridge: Cambridge University Press, 1998.

Beck, Norman A. *Anti-Roman Cryptograms in the New Testament: Symbolic Messages of Hope and Liberation*. Westminster College Library of Biblical Symbolism 1. New York: Peter Lang, 1997.

Beker, J. Christiaan. *Paul the Apostle: The Triumph of God in Life and Thought*. Philadelphia: Fortress Press, 1980.

Bellen, Heinz. *Metus Gallicus, Metus Punicus: Zum Furchtmotiv in der römischen Republik*. Abhandlungen der Geistes- und Sozialwissenschaftliche Klasse 3. Mainz: Akadamie der Wissenschaften und der Literatur, 1985.

Benjamin, Walter. "Über den Begriff der Geschichte." In *Gesammelte Schriften*, 1.2:691–704. 7 volumes. Frankfurt am Main: Suhrkamp 1991.

Bérard, Claude, et al., eds. *A City of Images: Iconography and Society in Ancient Greece*. Princeton: Princeton University Press, 1989.

Bernett, Monika. "Der Kaiserkult in Judäa unter herodischer und römischer Herrschaft: Zur Herausbildung und Herausforderung neuer Konzepte jüdischer Herrschaftslegitimation." In *Jewish Identity in the Greco-Roman World*, edited by Jörg Frey et al., 205–51. Ancient Judaism and Early Christianity. Leiden: Brill, 2007.

Berquist, Jon L. "Resistance and Accommodation in the Persian Empire." In *In the Shadow of Empire: Reclaiming the Bible as a History of Faithful Resistance*, edited by Richard A. Horsley, 41–58. Louisville: Westminster John Knox, 2008.

Betz, Hans Dieter. *Galatians: A Commentary on Paul's Letter to the Churches in Galatia*. Hermeneia. Philadelphia: Fortress Press, 1979.

Bienkowski, Piotr. *Les Celtes dans les arts mineurs gréco-romains, avec des recherches iconographiques sur quelques autres peuples barbares*. Krakow: Université des Jagellons, 1928.

———. *Die Darstellungen der Gallier in der hellenistischen Kunst*. Vienna: A Hölder, 1908.

Bonhoeffer, Dietrich. *Barcelona, Berlin, New York: 1928–1931*, English edition edited by Clifford J. Green. *Dietrich Bonhoeffer Works*, volume 10. Minneapolis: Fortress Press, 2008.

———. *Letters and Papers from Prison*. New York: Macmillan, 1971.

———. *Letters and Papers from Prison*. The Enlarged Edition, edited by Eberhard Bethge. New York: Macmillan, 1972.

Borgen, Peder. "'Yes,' 'No,' 'How Far?': The Participation of Jews and Christians in Pagan Cults." in *Paul in His Hellenistic Context*, edited by Troels Engberg-Pedersen, 30–59. Minneapolis: Augsburg Fortress, 1995.

Bosch, Emin. *Quellen zur Geschichte der Stadt Ankara im Altertum*. Ankara: Türk Tarih Kurumu Basimevi, 1967.

Bovon, François. "Une formule prépaulienne dans l'épître aux Galates." In *Paganisme, judaïsme, christianise: Influences et affrontements dans le monde antique. Mélanges offerts à Marcel Simon*, 91–107. Paris: E. de Boccard, 1978.

Boyarin, Daniel. *A Radical Jew: Paul and the Politics of Identity*. Contraversions 1. Berkeley: University of California Press, 1994.

Boys, Mary C. *Has God Only One Blessing? Judaism as Source of Christian Self-Understanding*. New York: Paulist Press, 2000.

Breytenbach, Cilliers. *Paulus und Barnabas in der Provinz Galatien: Studien zu Apostelgeschichte 13f.; 16,6; 18,23 und den Adressaten des Galaterbriefes*. Leiden/New York: Brill, 1996.

Briggs, Sheila. "Galatians." In *Searching the Scriptures*, volume 2, *A Feminist Commentary,* edited by Elisabeth Schüssler Fiorenza, 218–36. New York: Crossroad, 1994.

Brodie, Thomas L., Dennis R. MacDonald, and Stanley E. Porter, eds. *The Intertextuality of the Epistles: Explorations of Theory and Practice*. Sheffield: Sheffield Phoenix, 2006.

Brown, Alexandra R. *The Cross and Human Transformation: Paul's Apocalyptic Word in 1 Corinthians*. Minneapolis: Fortress Press, 1995.

Brueggemann, Walter. "Faith in the Empire." In *In the Shadow of Empire: Reclaiming the Bible as a History of Faithful Resistance*, edited by Richard A. Horsley, 25–40. Louisville: Westminster John Knox, 2008.

Brunt, P. A. "The Revolt of Vindex and the Fall of Nero." *Latomus* 18 (1959): 531–59.

Buchanan, David. *Roman Sport and Entertainment*. Aspects of Roman Life. London: Longman, 1976.

Burkert, Walter. *Greek Religion*. Cambridge, Mass.: Harvard University Press, 1985.

Carroll, James. *Constantine's Sword: The Church and the Jews*. Boston: Houghton Mifflin, 2001.

Carroll, Maureen. *Romans, Celts & Germans*. Brimscomb Port, Stroud: Tempus, 2001.

Carter, Warren. *Matthew and Empire: Initial Explorations*. Harrisburg, Pa.: Trinity Press International, 2001.

———. "Matthew and the Gentiles: Individual Conversion and/or Systemic Transformation." *Journal for the Study of the New Testament* 26 (2004): 259–82.

Castelli, Elizabeth A. *Imitating Paul: A Discourse of Power*. Louisville: Westminster John Knox, 1991.

Chadwick, Nora K. *The Druids*. Cardiff: Wales University Press, 1966.

Ciampa, Roy E. *The Presence and Function of Scripture in Galatians 1 and 2*. WUNT 2/102. Tübingen: Mohr Siebeck, 1998.

Coarelli, Filippo. *Da Pergamo a Roma: I Galati Nella Città Degli Attalidi*. Rome: Quasar, 1995.

Cohen, Beth, ed. *Not the Classical Ideal: Athens and the Construction of the Other in Greek Art*. Leiden: Brill, 2000.

Cohen, Shaye J. D. *The Beginnings of Jewishness: Boundaries, Varieties, Uncertainties*. Hellenistic Culture and Society. Berkeley: University of California Press, 1999.

———. "Crossing the Boundary and Becoming a Jew." *Harvard Theological Review* 82 (1989): 13–33.

Coleman, John E., and Clark A. Walz, eds. *Greeks and Barbarians: Essays on the Interactions between Greeks and Non-Greeks in Antiquity and the Consequences for Eurocentrism*. Bethesda: CDL, 1997.

Coleman, K. M. "Fatal Charades: Roman Executions Staged as Mythological Enactments." *JRS* 80 (1990): 44–73.

Collins, Adela Yarbro. *The Combat Myth in the Book of Revelation*. Harvard Dissertations in Religion 9. Missoula, Mont.: Scholars, 1976.

———. "Pergamon in Early Christian Literature." In *Pergamon, Citadel of the Gods: Archaeological Record, Literary Description, and Religious Development*, edited by Helmut Koester, 163–84. Harvard Theological Studies 46. Harrisburg, Pa.: Trinity Press International, 1998.

Collins, John J. *Seers, Sibyls and Sages in Hellenistic-Roman Judaism*. Journal for the Study of Judaism Supplement 54. Leiden: Brill, 1997.

Cotter, Wendy. "The Collegia and Roman Law: State Restrictions on Voluntary Associations, 64 BCE–200 CE," in *Voluntary Associations in the Greco-Roman World*, edited by John S. Kloppenburg and Stephen G. Wilson, 74–89. London/New York: Routledge, 1996.

Crossan, John Dominic, and Jonathan L. Reed. *In Search of Paul: How Jesus's Apostle Opposed Rome's Empire with God's Kingdom. A New Vision of Paul's Words and World*. San Francisco: HarperSanFrancisco, 2004.

Culler, Jonathan. *The Pursuit of Signs: Semiotics, Literature, Deconstruction*. Ithaca, N.Y.: Cornell University Press, 1981.

Cummins, Stephen Anthony. *Paul and the Crucified Christ in Antioch: Maccabean Martyrdom and Galatians 1 and 2*. SNTSMS 114. Cambridge: Cambridge University Press, 2001.

Daubner, Frank. *Bellum Asiaticum: Der Krieg der Römer gegen Aristonikos von Pergamon und die Einrichtung der Provinz Asia*. Quellen und Forschungen zur antiken Welt 4. Munich: Tuduv, 2003.

Davies, W. D. *Jewish and Pauline Studies*. Philadelphia: Fortress Press, 1984.

Deininger, Jürgen. *Die Provinziallandtage der Römischen Kaiserzeit: Von Augustus bis zum Ende des 3. Jahrhundert n. Chr*. Vestigia 6. Munich: Beck, 1965.

Deissman, Adolf. *Light from the Ancient East*. 1910. Reprint, Peabody, Mass.: Hendrickson, 1995.

Dench, Emma. *Romulus' Asylum: Roman Identities from the Age of Alexander to the Age of Hadrian*. Oxford: Oxford University Press, 2005.

Desnier, Jean-Luc. "Le Gaulois dans l'Imaginaire Monétaire de la République Romaine: Images plurielles d'une réalité singulière." *MEFRA* 103, no. 2 (1991): 605–54.

Dettenhofer, Maria H. *Herrschaft und Widerstand im augusteischen Principat: Die Konkurrenz zwischen res publica und domus Augusta*. Historia Einzelschriften 140. Stuttgart: Franz Steiner, 2000.

Dobesch, Gerhard. "Ancient Literary Sources." In *The Celts*, edited by Sabatino Moscati et al., 35–41. Venice: Bompiani, 1991.

Donaldson, Terence L. *Paul and the Gentiles. Remapping the Apostle's Convictional World*. Minneapolis: Fortress, 1997.

Dougherty, Carol. *The Poetics of Colonization: From City to Text in Archaic Greece*. New York: Oxford University Press, 1993.

Dreyfus, Renée, and Ellen Schraudolph, eds. *The Telephosfrieze from the Great Altar*. San Francisco: Fine Arts Museums of San Francisco, 1996–97.

Dube, Musa W. *Postcolonial Feminist Interpretation of the Bible*. St. Louis: Chalice Press, 2000.

Dungan, David L. *Constantine's Bible: Politics and the Making of the New Testament*. Minneapolis: Fortress Press, 2007.

Dunn, James D. G. *The New Perspective on Paul: Collected Essays*. WUNT 185. Tübingen: Mohr Siebeck, 2005.

Dyson, S. L. "Native Revolt Patterns in the Roman Empire." In *ANRW* II.3 (1975): 138–75.

Eastman, Susan. "The Evil Eye and the Curse of the Law: Galatians 3:1 Revisited." *Journal for the Study of the New Testament* 83 (2001): 69–87.

Eck, Werner, and Hartmut Wolff, eds. *Heer und Integrationspolitik: Die römischen Militärdiplome als historische Quelle*. Passauer historische Forschungen 2. Cologne: Bohlau-Verlag, 1986.

Eder, Walter. "Augustus and the Power of Tradition." In *The Cambridge Companion to the Age of Augustus*, edited by Karl Galinsky, 13–32. Cambridge Companion to the Classics. Cambridge: Cambridge University Press, 2005.

Ehrensperger, Kathy. *That We May Be Mutually Encouraged: Feminism and the New Perspective in Pauline Studies*. New York/London: T&T Clark International, 2004.

Eisenbaum, Pamela. "Paul as the New Abraham." In *Paul and Politics: Ekklesia, Israel, Imperium, Interpretation. Essays in Honor of Krister Stendahl*, edited by Richard A. Horsley, 130–45. Harrisburg, Pa.: Trinity Press International, 2000.

Elliott, John H. "Paul, Galatians, and the Evil Eye." *Currents in Theology and Mission* 17 (1990): 262–71.

Elliott, Neil. *The Arrogance of Nations: Reading Romans in the Shadow of Empire*. Paul in Critical Contexts. Minneapolis: Fortress Press, 2008.

———. *Liberating Paul: The Justice of God and the Politics of the Apostle*. Maryknoll, N.Y.: Orbis, 1994.

Elliott, Susan M. (Elli). "Choose Your Mother, Choose Your Master: Galatians 4:21—5:1 in the Shadow of the Anatolian Mother of the Gods." *Journal of Biblical Literature* 118, no. 4 (1999): 661–83.

———. *Cutting Too Close for Comfort: Paul's Letter to the Galatians in Its Anatolian Cultic Context*. JSNTSup 248. London/New York: T&T Clark, 2004.

Ellis, Peter Berresford. *Celt and Greek: Celts in the Hellenic World*. London: Constable, 1997.

Elsner, Jaś. "Inventing Imperium: Texts and the Propaganda of Monuments in Augustan Rome." In *Art and Text in Roman Culture*, edited by Jaś Elsner, 32–56. Cambridge Studies in New Art History and Criticism. Cambridge: Cambridge University Press, 1996.

Esler, Philip F. *Galatians*. New Testament Readings. London: Routledge, 1998.

Fatum, Lone. "Women, Symbolic Universe and Structures of Silence." *ST* 43 (1989): 61–80.

Faust, Eberhard. *Pax Christi et Pax Caesaris: Religionsgeschichtliche, traditionsgeschichtliche und sozialgeschichtliche Studien zum Epheserbrief.* Novum Testamentum et Orbis Antiquus. Göttingen: Vandenhoeck & Ruprecht; Freiburg, Switzerland: Universitätsverlag, 1993.

Fears, Rufus. "Jupiter and Roman Imperial Ideology." In *ANRW* 17.1 (1981): 3–141.

———. "The Theology of Victory at Rome." In *ANRW* 17.2 (1981): 736–826.

Feldman, Louis H. "Financing the Colosseum." *Biblical Archaeology Review* 27, no. 4 (2001): 22–31.

———. *Jew and Gentile in the Ancient World: Attitudes and Interactions from Alexander to Justinian*. Princeton: Princeton University Press, 1993.

Ferguson, Everett, ed. *Church and State in the Early Church*. New York: Garland, 1993.

Foucault, Michel. *Discipline and Punish: The Birth of the Prison*. Translated by Alan Sheridan. New York: Vintage, 1979.

Frankfort, Henri. *Kingship and the Gods: A Study of Ancient Near Eastern Religion as the Integration of Society & Nature*. Chicago: University of Chicago Press, 1978.

Fredriksen, Paula. *From Jesus to Christ*. New Haven: Yale University Press, 1988.

———. *Jesus of Nazareth, King of the Jews: A Jewish Life and the Emergence of Christianity*. New York: Knopf, 1999.

———. "Judaism, the Circumcision of Gentiles, and Apocalyptic Hope: Another Look at Galatians 1 and 2." *Journal of Theological Studies* n.s. 42 (1991): 532–64.

Freire, Paulo. *Pedagogy of the Oppressed*. New York: Continuum, 1986.

Frey, Jörg, et al., eds. *Jewish Identity in the Greco-Roman World*. Ancient Judaism and Early Christianity. Leiden: Brill, 2007.

Friedlaender, Ludwig. *Darstellungen aus der Sittengeschichte Roms in der Zeit von Augustus bis zum Ausgang der Antonine*. 4 volumes. Leipzig: Hirzel, 1920–22.

Friesen, Steven J. *Imperial Cults and the Apocalypse of John: Reading Revelation in the Ruins.* Oxford: Oxford University Press, 2001.

———. *Twice Neokoros: Ephesus, Asia and the Cult of the Flavian Imperial Family.* Religions in the Graeco Roman World 116. Leiden/New York: Brill, 1993.

Futrell, Alison. *Blood in the Arena: The Spectacle of Roman Power.* Austin: University of Texas Press, 1997.

Gager, John. *The Origins of Anti-Semitism: Attitudes toward Judaism in Pagan and Christian Antiquity.* New York: Oxford University Press, 1983.

Garnsey, Peter, and Richard Saller. "Patronal Power Relations." In *Paul and Empire: Religion and Power in Roman Imperial Society,* edited by Richard A. Horsley, 96–103. Harrisburg, Pa: Trinity Press International, 1997.

———. *The Roman Empire: Economy, Society and Culture.* Berkeley/Los Angeles: University of California Press, 1987.

Gaston, Lloyd. "Israel's Enemies in Pauline Theology." *NTS* 28 (1982): 400–423.

Georgi, Dieter. *The City in the Valley: Biblical Interpretation and Urban Theology.* Studies in Biblical Literature 7. Atlanta: Society of Biblical Literature, 2005.

———. *Remembering the Poor: The History of Paul's Collection for Jerusalem.* Nashville: Abingdon Press, 1992.

Goldstein, Jonathan A. *I Maccabees: A New Translation, with Introduction and Commentary.* Anchor Bible 41. Garden City, N.Y.: Doubleday, 1976.

———. *II Maccabees: A New Translation, with Introduction and Commentary.* Anchor Bible 41A. Garden City, N.Y.: Doubleday, 1983.

Goldsworthy, Adrian Keith. *In the Name of Rome: The Men Who Won the Roman Empire.* London: Weidenfeld & Nicolson, 2003.

———. *The Roman Army at War 100 BC–AD 200.* Oxford/New York: Clarendon Press, 1996.

Golvin, Jean-Claude. *L'Amphithéâtre Romain.* Paris: E. de Boccard, 1988.

Goodman, Martin. "Opponents of Rome: Jews and Others." In *Images of Empire,* edited by Loveday Alexander, 222–38. JSOTSup 122. Sheffield: Sheffield Academic, 1991.

Gordon, Richard. "The Veil of Power." In *Paul and Empire: Religion and Power in Roman Imperial Society,* edited by Richard A. Horsley, 126–37. Harrisburg, Pa.: Trinity Press International, 1997.

Gottwald, Norman K. "Early Israel as an Anti-Imperial Community." In *In the Shadow of Empire: Reclaiming the Bible as a History of Faithful Resistance,* edited by Richard A. Horsley, 9–24. Louisville: Westminster John Knox, 2008.

Greenspahn, Frederick E. *When Brothers Dwell Together: The Preeminence of Younger Siblings in the Hebrew Bible.* New York: Oxford University Press, 1994.

Greimas, Algirdas Julien. *On Meaning: Selected Writings in Semiotic Theory.* Theory and History of Literature 38. Minneapolis: University of Minnesota Press, 1976.

Gruen, Erich S. "Culture as Policy: The Attalids of Pergamon." In *From Pergamon to Sperlonga: Sculpture and Context,* edited by Nancy T. de Grummond and Brunilde S. Ridgway, 17–31. Hellenistic Culture and Society. Berkeley: University of California Press, 2000.

———. *Diaspora: Jews amidst Greeks and Romans.* Cambridge, Mass.: Harvard University Press, 2002.

———. *Studies in Greek Culture and Roman Policy.* Cincinnati Classical Studies n.s. 7. Leiden: Brill, 1990.

Grummond, Nancy T. de. "Gauls and Giants, Skylla and the Palladion: Some Responses." In *From Pergamon to Sperlonga: Sculpture and Context,* edited by Nancy T. de Grummond and Brunilde S. Ridgway, 255–77. Hellenistic Culture and Society. Berkeley: University of California Press, 2000.

———. "Introduction." In *From Pergamon to Sperlonga: Sculpture and Context*, edited by Nancy T. de Grummond and Brunhilde S. Ridgway, 1–16. Hellenistic Culture and Society. Berkeley: University of California Press, 2000.

Grummond, Nancy T. de, and Brunilde S. Ridgway, eds. *From Pergamon to Sperlonga: Culture and Context*. Berkeley, Los Angeles, and London: University of California Press, 2000.

Habicht, Christian. *2. Makkabäerbuch*. Gütersloh: Gerd Mohn, 1979.

Halfmann, Helmut. *Die Senatoren aus dem östlichen Teil des Imperium Romanum bis zum Ende des 2. Jahrhunderts n. Chr.* Hypomnemata 58. Göttingen: Vandenhoeck & Ruprecht, 1979.

Hall, Edith. *Inventing the Barbarian: Greek Self-Definition through Tragedy*. Oxford Classical Monographs. Oxford: Oxford University Press, 1989.

Hansen, Esther V. *The Attalids of Pergamon*. 2nd ed. Ithaca, N.Y.: Cornell University Press, 1971.

Hardie, Philip R. *Virgil's Aeneid: Cosmos and Imperium*. Oxford: Clarendon, 1986.

Hardin, Justin K. *Galatians and the Imperial Cult: A Critical Analysis of the First-Century Social Context of Paul's Letter*. WUNT 2/237. Tübingen: Mohr Siebeck, 2008.

Hardy, E. G., ed. *The Monumentum Ancyranum*. Oxford: Oxford University Press, 1923.

Harland, Philip A. *Associations, Synagogues and Congregations: Claiming a Place in Ancient Mediterranean Society*. Minneapolis: Fortress Press, 2003.

Harnack, Adolf von. *Marcion: Das Evangelium vom fremden Gott*. Leipzig: J. C. Hinrichs Verlag, 1924.

Harris, William V. *War and Imperialism in Republican Rome, 327–70 B.C.* New York: Oxford University Press, 1979.

Harrison, James R. "Paul and the Imperial Gospel at Thessaloniki." *Journal for the Study of the New Testament* 25 (2002): 71–96.

———. *Paul's Language of Grace in Its Graeco-Roman Context*. WUNT 2/172. Tübingen: Mohr Siebeck, 2003.

Hartog, François. *The Mirror of Herodotus: The Representation of the Other in the Writing of History*. Berkeley: University of California Press, 1988.

Hartswick, Kim J. *The Gardens of Sallust: A Changing Landscape*. Austin: University of Texas Press, 2004.

Harvey, David. *Spaces of Hope*. California Studies in Critical Human Geography 7. Berkeley: University of Caifornia Press, 2000.

Hase, Hans Christoph von. "'Turning away from the Phraseological to the Real': A Personal Recollection." In Dietrich Bonhoeffer, *Barcelona, Berlin, New York: 1928–1931. Dietrich Bonhoeffer Works*, volume 10, 591–604. Minneapolis: Fortress Press, 2008.

Haskell, Francis, and Nicholas Penny. *Taste and the Antique: The Lure of Classical Sculpture, 1500–1900*. New Haven: Yale University Press, 1981.

Hays, Richard B. *Echoes of Scripture in the Letters of Paul*. New Haven: Yale University Press, 1989.

Head, Barclay V. *Catalogue of the Greek Coins of Phrygia*. London: Printed by order of the Trustees of the British Museum, 1906.

Hedges, Inez. "*The Aesthetics of Resistance*: Thoughts on Peter Weiss." *Socialism and Democracy* 20, no. 2 (2006): 69–77.

Heen, Erik M. "Phil 2:6-11 and Resistance to Local Timocratic Rule: *Isa Theō* and the Cult of the Emperor in the East." In *Paul and the Roman Imperial Order*, edited by Richard A. Horsley, 125–54. Harrisburg, Pa.: Trinity Press International, 2004.

Heidel, Alexander. *The Babylonian Genesis: The Story of Creation*. Chicago: University of Chicago Press, 1951.

Hellholm, David, et al., eds. *Mighty Minorities? Minorities in Early Christianity—Positions and Strategies*. Oslo: Scandinavian University Press, 1995.

Hengel, Martin. *Crucifixion in the Ancient World and the Folly of the Message of the Cross.* Philadelphia: Fortress Press, 1977.

———. *The Zealots: Investigations into the Jewish Freedom Movement in the Period from Herod I until 70 A.D.* Edinburgh: T&T Clark, 1989.

Heres, Huberta. "Der Telephosmythos in Pergamon." In *Der Pergamonaltar: Die neue Präsentation nach der Restaurierung des Telephosfrieses,* edited by Wolf-Dieter Heilmeyer, 99–120. Tübingen: Ernst Wasmuth, 1997.

Höckmann, Ursula. "Gallierdarstellungen in der etruskischen Grabkunst des 2. Jahrhunderts vor Christus." *Jahrbuch des Deutschen Archäologischen Instituts* 106 (1991): 199–230.

Hoepfner, Wolfram. "Die Architektur von Pergamon." In *Der Pergamonaltar: Die neue Präsentation nach der Restaurierung des Telephosfrieses,* edited by Wolf-Dieter Heilmeyer, 24–55. Tübingen: Ernst Wasmuth, 1997.

———. "Modell des Pergamonaltars im Masstab 1:20." In *Der Pergamonaltar: Die neue Präsentation nach der Restaurierung des Telephosfrieses,* edited by Wolf-Dieter Heilmeyer, 171–76. Tübingen: Ernst Wasmuth, 1997.

Hollander, John. *The Figure of Echo: A Mode of Allusion in Milton and After.* Berkeley: University of California Press, 1981.

Hölscher, Tonio. "Die Geschlagenen und Ausgelieferten in der Kunst des Hellenismus." *Antike Kunst* 28 (1985): 120–36.

———. *The Language of Images in Roman Art.* Cambridge: Cambridge University Press, 2004.

Hopkins, Keith. "Taxes and Trade in the Roman Empire (200 B.C.–A. D. 400)." *Journal of Roman Studies* 70 (1980): 101–25.

Horrell, David G. "Idol-Food, Idolatry and Ethics in Paul." In *Idolatry: False Worship in the Bible, Early Judaism and Christianity,* edited by Stephen C. Barton, 120–40. T&T Clark Theology. London: T&T Clark, 2007.

Horsley, Richard A., ed. *Hidden Transcripts and the Arts of Resistance: Applying the Work of James C. Scott to Jesus and Paul.* Semeia Studies 48. Leiden/Boston: Brill, 2004.

———, ed. *In the Shadow of Empire: Reclaiming the Bible as a History of Faithful Resistance.* Louisville: Westminster John Knox, 2008.

———. *Jesus and Empire: The Kingdom of God and the New World Disorder.* Minneapolis: Fortress Press, 2003.

———. *Jesus and the Spiral of Violence: Popular Resistance in Roman Palestine.* San Francisco: Harper & Row, 1987.

———, ed. *Paul and Empire: Religion and Power in Roman Imperial Society.* Harrisburg, Pa.: Trinity Press International, 1997.

———, ed. *Paul and Politics: Ekklesia, Israel, Imperium, Interpretation. Essays in Honor of Krister Stendahl.* Harrisburg, Pa.: Trinity Press International, 2000.

Janssen, Claudia, Luise Schottroff, and Beate Wehn. *Paulus: Umstrittene Traditionen–lebendige Theologie.* Gütersloh: Chr. Kaiser/Gütersloher Verlagshaus, 2001.

Janssen, L. F. "'Superstitio' and the Persecution of the Christians." In *Church and State in the Early Church,* edited by Everett Ferguson, 79–108. New York: Garland, 1993.

Jepsen, A. "'āman." In *Theologisches Wörterbuch zum Alten Testament,* 1:313–48. Stuttgart: Kohlhammer, 1973.

Jewett, Robert. *Paul, the Apostle to America: Cultural Trends & Pauline Scholarship.* Louisville: Westminster John Knox, 1994.

———. *Romans: A Commentary.* Hermeneia. Minnesota: Fortress Press, 2007.

Joubert, Stephan. *Paul as Benefactor: Reciprocity, Strategy and Theological Reflection in Paul's Collection.* WUNT 2/124. Tübingen: Mohr Siebeck, 2000.

Judge, E. A. "Judaism and the Rise of Christianity. A Roman Perspective." *Tyndale Bulletin* 45 (1994): 355–68.

Kahl, Brigitte. "Acts of the Apostles: Pro(to)-Imperial Script and Hidden Transcript." In *In the Shadow of Empire: Reclaiming the Bible as History of Faithful Resistance*, edited by Richard A. Horsley, 137–56. Louisville: Westminster John Knox, 2008.

———. *Armenevangelium und Heidenevangelium: "Sola Scriptura" und die ökumenische Traditionsproblematik im Lichte von Väterkonflikt und Väterkonsens bei Lukas*. Berlin: Evangelische Verlagsanstalt, 1987.

———. "Fratricide and Ecocide: Re-Reading Genesis 2–4." In *Earth Habitat: Eco-Justice and the Church's Response*, edited by Dieter Hessel and Larry Rasmussen, 53–70. Minneapolis: Fortress Press, 2001.

———. "Gender Trouble in Galatia? Paul and the Rethinking of Difference." In *Is There a Future for Feminist Theology*, edited by Deborah F. Sawyer and Diane M. Collier, 57–73. Studies in Theology and Sexuality 4. Sheffield: Sheffield Academic, 1999.

———. "Hagar between Genesis and Galatians: The Stony Road to Freedom." In *From Prophecy to Testament: The Function of the Old Testament in the New*, edited by Craig A. Evans, 219–32. Peabody, Mass.: Hendrickson, 2004.

———. "Reading Galatians and Empire at the Great Altar of Pergamon." *USQR* 59, no. 3–4 (2005): 21–43.

———. "Reading Luke against Luke: Non-Uniformity of Text, Hermeneutics of Conspiracy and the 'Scriptural Principle' in Luke 1." In *A Feminist Companion to Luke*, edited by Amy-Jill Levine, 70–88. London: Sheffield Academic, 2002.

———. "Towards a Materialist-Feminist Reading." In *Searching the Scriptures*, volume 1, *A Feminist Introduction*, edited by Elisabeth Schüssler Fiorenza, 225–40. New York: Crossroad, 1994.

Kästner, Volker. "The Architecture of the Great Altar of Pergamon." In *Pergamon, Citadel of the Gods: Archaeological Record, Literary Description, and Religious Development*, edited by Helmut Koester, 137–62. Harvard Theological Studies 46. Harrisburg, Pa.: Trinity Press International, 1998.

Keesmaat, Sylvia C. *Paul and His Story: (Re)Interpreting the Exodus Tradition*. JSNTSup 181. Sheffield: Sheffield Academic, 1999.

Keller, Catherine. *From a Broken Web: Separation, Sexism, and Self*. Boston: Beacon Press, 1986.

Keppie, Lawrence. *Legions and Veterans: Roman Army Papers 1971–2000*. Stuttgart: Franz Steiner, 2000.

Kleiner, Gerhard. *Das Nachleben des pergamenischen Gigantenkampfes*. Berlin: de Gruyter, 1949.

Klinghardt, Matthias. *Gemeinschaftsmahl und Mahlgemeinschaft: Soziologie und Liturgie frühchristlicher Mahlfeiern*. Texte und Arbeiten zum neutestamentlichen Zeitalter 13. Tübingen: Francke, 1996.

Kloppenburg, John S., and Stephen G. Wilson, eds. *Voluntary Associations in the Greco-Roman World*. London/New York: Routledge, 1996.

Koester, Helmut, ed. *Pergamon, Citadel of the Gods: Archaeological Record, Literary Description, and Religious Development*. Harvard Theological Studies 46. Harrisburg, Pa.: Trinity Press International, 1998.

Krauter, Stefan. "Die Beteiligung von Nichtjuden am Jerusalemer Tempelkult." In *Jewish Identity in the Greco-Roman World*, edited by Jörg Frey et al., 55–74. Ancient Judaism and Early Christianity. Leiden: Brill, 2007.

Kremer, Bernhard. *Das Bild der Kelten bis in augusteische Zeit: Studien zur Instrumentalisierung eines antiken Feindbildes bei griechischen und römischen Autoren*. Historia Einzelschriften. Stuttgart: Franz Steiner, 1994.

Krencker, Daniel, and Martin Schede. *Der Tempel in Ankara*. Archäologisches Institut des Deutschen Reiches, Denkmäler antiken Architektur 3. Berlin: de Gruyter, 1936.

Krierer, Karl R. *Sieg und Niederlage: Untersuchungen physiognomischer und mimischer Phänomene in Kampfdarstellungen römischer Plastik*. Vienna: Phoibos, 1995.

Kugel, James L. *The Bible as It Was*. Cambridge, Mass.: Belknap Press of Harvard University Press, 1997.

Kunze, Max. *The Pergamon Altar: Its Rediscovery, History and Reconstruction*. Mainz am Rhein: Staatliche Museen zu Berlin, Verlag Philipp von Zabern, 1995.

Kuttner, Ann. "'Do You Look Like You Belong Here?' Asianism at Pergamon and the Makedonian Diaspora." In *Cultural Borrowings and Ethnic Appropriations in Antiquity*, edited by Erich S. Gruen, 137–206. Oriens et Occidens 8. Stuttgart: Franz Steiner, 2005.

———. "Republican Rome Looks at Pergamon." *Harvard Studies in Classical Philology* 97 (1995): 157–78.

Lee, Jae Won. "Justification of Difference in Galatians." In *Character Ethics and the New Testament*, edited by Robert Brawley, 191–208. Louisville: Westminster John Knox, 2007.

Lefebvre, Henri. *The Production of Space*. Malden, Mass.: Blackwell, 1991.

Lendon, J. E. *The Empire of Honour: The Art of Government in the Roman World*. Oxford: Clarendon Press, 1997.

Levick, Barbara. *Roman Colonies in Southern Asia Minor*. Oxford: Clarendon, 1967.

Levinas, Emmanuel. *Time and the Other*. Pittsburgh: Duquesne University Press, 1987.

Levinson, Jon D. *The Death and Resurrection of the Beloved Son: The Transformation of Child Sacrifice in Judaism and Christianity*. New Haven/London: Yale University Press, 1993.

Lissarrague, François. "Aesop, Between Man and Beast: Ancient Portraits and Illustrations." In *Not the Classical Ideal: Athens and the Construction of the Other in Greek Art*, edited by Beth Cohen, 132–49. Leiden: Brill, 2000.

Lloyd, G. E. R. *Polarity and Analogy: Two Types of Argumentation in Early Greek Thought*. Cambridge: Cambridge University Press, 1966.

Lomas, Kathryn. "Greeks, Romans, and Others: Problems of Colonialism and Ethnicity in Southern Italy." In *Roman Imperialism: Post-Colonial Perspectives*, edited by Jane Webster and Nicholas J. Cooper, 135–44. Leicester: School of Archaeological Studies, University of Leicester, 1996.

Lopez, Davina C. *Apostle to the Conquered: Reimagining Paul's Mission*. Paul in Critical Contexts. Minneapolis: Fortress Press, 2008.

———. "Epilogue: Beyond the Threshold." *USQR* 59, no. 3–4 (2005): 177–86.

Luther, Martin. *A Commentary on St. Paul's Letter to the Galatians*. London: James Clark, 1956.

———. *Luther's Works*, volume 26, *Lectures on Galatians 1535, Chapters 1–4*. Edited by J. J. Pelikan and W. A. Hansen. Saint Louis: Concordia, 1963.

———. *Luther's Works*, volume 54, *Table Talk*. Edited by J. J. Pelikan, H. C. Oswald, and H. T. Lehmann. ©1967. Philadelphia: Fortress Press, 1999.

Maag, Victor. "Sumerische und babylonische Mythen von der Erschaffung des Menschen." In *Kultur, Kulturkontakt und Religion: Gesammelte Studien zur allgemeinen und alttestamentlichen Religionsgeschichte. Victor Maag zum 70. Geburtstag*, edited by Hans Hinrich Schmid and Odil Hannes Steck, 38–59. Göttingen: Vandenhoeck & Ruprecht, 1980.

MacMullen, Ramsey. *Enemies of the Roman Order: Treason, Unrest, and Alienation in the Empire*. Cambridge, Mass.: Harvard University Press, 1966.

Magie, David. *Roman Rule in Asia Minor to the End of the Third Century after Christ*. 2 volumes. Princeton: Princeton University Press, 1950.

Malkin, Irad. *Religion and Colonization in Ancient Greece*. Studies in Greek and Roman Religion 3. Leiden: Brilll, 1987.

———. *The Returns of Odysseus: Colonization and Ethnicity.* Berkeley: University of California Press, 1998.

Marchal, Joseph A. "Imperial Intersections and Initial Inquiries: Toward a Feminist, Postcolonial Analysis of Philippians." *Journal of Feminist Studies in Religion* 22, no. 2 (2006): 5–32.

Marszal, John R. "Ubiquitous Barbarians: Representation of the Gauls at Pergamon and Elsewhere." In *From Pergamon to Sperlonga: Sculpture and Context,* edited by Nancy T. de Grummond and Brunilde S. Ridgway, 191–234. Hellenistic Culture and Society. Berkeley: University of California Press, 2000.

Martin, Troy. "Apostasy to Paganism: The Rhetorical Stasis of the Galatian Controversy." *Journal of Biblical Literature* 114 (1995): 437–61.

Martyn, J. Louis. "Apocalyptic Antinomies in Paul's Letter to the Galatians." *NTS* 31 (1985): 410–24.

———. *Galatians: A New Translation with Introduction and Commentary.* Anchor Bible 33A. New York: Doubleday, 1997.

Mattei, Marina. "The Dying Gaul." In *The Celts,* edited by Sabatino Moscati et al., 70–71. Venice: Bompiani, 1991.

———. *Il Galata Capitolino: uno splendido dono di Attalo.* Rome: "L'erma"di Bretschneider, 1987.

McNiven, Timothy J. "Behaving Like an Other: Telltale Gestures in Athenian Vase Painting." In *Not the Classical Ideal: Athens and the Construction of the Other in Greek Art,* edited by Beth Cohen, 71–97. Leiden: Brill, 2000.

Meggitt, Justin J. *Paul, Poverty and Survival.* Studies of the New Testament and Its World. Edinburgh: T&T Clark, 1998.

Miles, Richard. "Rivalling Rome: Carthage." In *Rome the Cosmopolis,* edited by Catherine Edwards and Greg Woolf, 123–46. Cambridge: Cambridge University Press, 2003.

Miller, Margaret C. "The Myth of Bousiris: Ethnicity and Art." In *Not the Classical Ideal: Athens and the Construction of the Other in Greek Art,* edited by Beth Cohen, 413–43. Leiden: Brill, 2000.

Mitchell, Stephen. "Amyntas in Pisidien—Der letzte Krieg der Galater." In *Forschungen in Galatien,* edited by Elmar Schwertheim, 97–103. Bonn: Rudolf Habelt, 1994.

———. *Anatolia: Land, Men, and Gods in Asia Minor,* volume 1, *The Celts in Anatolia and the Impact of Roman Rule,* volume 2, *The Rise of the Church.* Oxford: Clarendon Press, 1993.

———. "Requisitioned Transport in the Roman Empire: A New Inscription from Pisidia." *Journal of Roman Studies* 66 (1976): 106–31.

Mitchell, Stephen, and Marc Waelkins, eds. *Pisidian Antioch: The Site and Its Monuments.* London: Duckworth with the Classical Press of Wales, 1998.

Moltmann, Jürgen. *Der Gekreuzigte Gott: Das Kreuz Christi als Grund und Kritik christlicher Theologie.* Munich: Chr. Kaiser, 1972.

Moore, Stephen D., and Fernando F. Segovia, eds. *Postcolonial Biblical Criticism: Interdisciplinary Intersections.* Bible and Postcolonialism. New York: Continuum, 2005.

Morland, Kjell Arne. *The Rhetoric of Curse in Galatians: Paul Confronts Another Gospel.* Emory Studies in Early Christianity 5. Atlanta: Scholars, 1995.

Moro, Maria Paola Del. "The Temple of Peace." In *The Museums of the Imperial Forums in Trajan's Market,* edited by Lucrezia Ungaro, 171–75. Milan: Electa, 2007.

Moscati, Sabatino, et al., eds. *The Celts.* Venice: Bompiani, 1991.

Moxnes, Halvor. "'He Saw the City Full of Idols' (Acts 17:16): Visualizing the World of the First Christians." In *Mighty Minorities? Minorities in Early Christianity—Positions and Strategies,* edited by David Hellholm et al., 107–31. Oslo: Scandinavian University Press, 1995.

———. *Putting Jesus in His Place: A Radical Vision of Household and Kingdom.* Louisville: Westminster John Knox, 2003.

Murphy, Thomas. *The Messages to the Seven Churches of Asia: Being the Inaugural of the Enthroned King, a Beacon on Oriental Shores.* Philadelphia: Presbyterian Board of Publication and Sabbath-School Work, 1895.

Nachtergael, Georges. *Les Galates en Grèce et les Sôtéria de Delphes: recherches d'histoire et d'épigraphie hellénistiques.* Mémoires de la classe des lettres. Brussels: Palais des Académies, 1977.

Nanos, Mark D., ed. *The Galatians Debate: Contemporary Issues in Rhetorical and Historical Interpretation.* Peabody, Mass.: Hendrickson, 2002.

———. *The Irony of Galatians: Paul's Letter in First-Century Context.* Minneapolis: Fortress Press, 2002.

Neumer-Pfau, Wiltrud. "Die kämpfenden Göttinnen vom grossen Fries des Pergamonaltars." *Visible Religion. Annual for Religious Iconography* 2 (1983): 75–90.

Nicolet, Claude. *Space, Geography, and Politics in the Early Roman Empire.* Jerome Lectures, 19th Series. Ann Arbor: University of Michigan Press, 1991.

Nietzsche, Friedrich Wilhelm. "The Antichrist." In *The Portable Nietzsche*, edited by Walter Kaufmann, 565–656. New York: Penguin, 1976.

Novak, Ralph Martin, Jr. *Christianity and the Roman Empire: Background Texts.* Harrisburg, Pa.: Trinity Press International, 2001.

Oakes, Peter. *Philippians: From People to Letter.* SNTSMS 110. Cambridge: Cambridge University Press, 2001.

Oates, Joan. *Babylon.* London: Thames & Hudson, 1991.

Oberman, Heiko A. *The Roots of Anti-Semitism in the Age of the Renaissance and Reformation.* Philadelphia: Fortress Press, 1984.

Ohlemutz, Erwin. *Die Kulte und Heiligtümer der Götter in Pergamon.* Darmstadt: Wissenschaftliche Buchgesellschaft, 1940.

Patte, Daniel. *The Religious Dimensions of Biblical Texts: Greimas's Structural Semiotics and Biblical Exegesis.* Semeia Studies 19. Atlanta: Scholars, 1990.

Pfanner, Michael. "Bemerkungen zur Komposition und Interpretation des grossen Frieses von Pergamon." *Archäologischer Anzeiger* (1979): 46–57.

Plass, Paul. *The Game of Death in Ancient Rome: Arena Sport and Political Suicide.* Wisconsin Studies in Classics. Madison: University of Wisconsin Press, 1995.

Pollini, John. "The Gemma Augustea: Ideology, Rhetorical Imagery, and the Creation of a Dynastic Narrative." In *The Origins of Roman Historical Commemoration in Visual Arts*, edited by Peter J. Holliday, 258–98. New York: Cambridge University Press, 2002.

Price, S. R. F. "Gods and Emperors: The Greek Language of the Roman Imperial Cult." *JHS* 104 (1984): 79–95.

———. *Rituals and Power: The Roman Imperial Cult in Asia Minor.* Cambridge: Cambridge University Press, 1984.

Pucci, Michael. "Arenas." In *Dictionary of New Testament Background*, edited by Craig A. Evans and Stanley E. Porter, 111–14. Downers Grove, Ill.: InterVarsity, 2000.

Pucci Ben Zeev, Miriam. *Jewish Rights in the Roman World: The Greek and Roman Documents Quoted by Josephus Flavius.* Texte und Studien zum antiken Judentum 74. Tübingen: Mohr Siebeck, 1998.

Rabello, Alfredo Mordechai. "The Legal Condition of the Jews in the Roman Empire." In *ANRW* II.13 (1980): 662–762.

Radt, Wolfgang. *Pergamon: Geschichte und Bauten einer antiken Metropole.* Darmstadt: Wissenschaftliche Buchgesellschaft, 1999.

Rajak, Tessa. *Josephus, the Historian and His Society.* Philadelphia: Fortress Press, 1984.

———. "Was there a Roman Charter for the Jews?" *Journal for Roman Studies* 74 (1984): 107–23.

Rakob, F. "The Making of Augustan Carthage." In *Romanization and the City: Creation, Transformations and Failures*, edited by E. Fentress, 73–82. Portsmouth, R.I.: Journal of Roman Archaeology, 2000.

Ramsay, William Mitchell. *The Church in the Roman Empire before A.D. 170*. Mansfield College Lectures 1892. London: Hodder & Stoughton, 1893.

———. *A Historical Commentary on St. Paul's Epistle to the Galatians*. London: Hodder & Stoughton, 1899.

———. *The Social Basis of Roman Power in Asia Minor*. Prepared for the press by J. G. C. Andersen. Aberdeen: Aberdeen University Press, 1941.

———. *St. Paul the Traveller and Roman Citizen*. London: Hodder & Stoughton, 1896.

———. "Studies in the Roman Province Galatia." *Journal of Roman Studies* 12 (1922): 147–86.

Rankin, H. D. *Celts and the Classical World*. London: Croom Helm, 1987.

Rapin, Andre. "Weaponry." In *The Celts*, edited by Sabatino Moscati et al., 321–31. Venice: Bompiani, 1991.

Reed, Jonathan L. *The HarperCollins Visual Guide to the New Testament*. New York: HarperCollins, 2007.

Rehmann, Jan. *Einführung in die Ideologietheorie*. Hamburg: Argument, 2008.

———. "Nietzsche, Paul, and the Subversion of Empire." *USQR* 59, no. 3–4 (2005): 147–61.

Richardson, Peter. *Herod: King of the Jews and Friend of the Romans*. Studies on Personalities of the New Testament. Columbia: University of South Carolina Press, 1996.

Richardson, Peter, and Stephen Westerholm. *Law in Religious Communities in the Roman Period: The Debate over Torah and Nomos in Post-Biblical Judaism and Early Christianity*. Studies in Christianity and Judaism. Waterloo, Ont.: Wilfrid Laurier University Press, 1991.

Riggsby, Andrew M. *Caesar in Gaul and Rome: War in Words*. Austin: University of Texas Press, 2006.

Robert, Louis. *Les Gladiateurs dans l'Orient Grec*. Paris: Librairie Ancienne Honore Champion, 1940.

Rordorf, W. "Die neronische Christenverfolgung im Spiegel der apokryphen Paulusakten." *NTS* 28 (1982): 364–74.

Rossing, Barbara. "Alas for Earth! Lament and Resistance in Revelation 12." In *The Earth Story in the New Testament*, edited by Norman Habel and Shirley Wurst, 180–211. Earth Bible 5. Sheffield: Sheffield Academic, 2002.

Rudich, Vasily. *Political Dissidence under Nero: The Price of Dissimulation*. London: Routledge, 1993.

Ruether, Rosemary Radford. *Faith and Fratricide: The Theological Roots of Anti-Semitism*. New York: Seabury Press, 1974.

———. *Gaia and God: An Ecofeminist Theology of Earth Healing*. San Francisco: HarperSanFrancisco, 1992.

———. *To Change the World: Christology and Cultural Criticism*. New York: Crossroad, 1981.

Said, Edward. *Culture and Imperialism*. London: Chattu & Windus, 1993.

———. *Orientalism*. New York: Vintage, 1978.

Sanders, E. P. *Paul and Palestinian Judaism. A Comparison of Patterns of Religion*. Philadelphia: Fortress Press, 1977.

———. *Paul, the Law and the Jewish People*. Minneapolis: Fortress Press, 1983.

Sandnes, Karl Olav. *Paul—One of the Prophets? A Contribution to the Apostle's Self-Understanding*. WUNT 2/143. Tübingen: Mohr Siebeck, 1991.

Schäfer, Peter. *Judeophobia: Attitudes toward Jews in the Ancient World*. Cambridge, Mass.: Harvard University Press, 1997.

Schalles, Hans-Joachim. *Der Pergamonaltar: Zwischen Wertung und Verwertbarkeit.* Frankfurt am Main: Fischer Taschenbuch, 1986.

———. *Untersuchungen zur Kulturpolitik der pergamenischen Herrscher im dritten Jahrhundert vor Christus.* Istanbuler Forschungen 36. Tübingen: Ernst Wasmuth, 1985.

Schmitt Pantel, Pauline. "Public Feasts in the Hellenistic Greek City: Forms and Meaning." In *Conventional Values of the Hellenistic Greeks,* edited by Per Bilde et al., 29–47. Åarhus: Åarhus University Press, 1997.

Schneemelcher, Wilhelm, ed. *New Testament Apocrypha,* volume 2. English translation edited by R. McL. Wilson. Cambridge: James Clarke; Louisville: Westminster John Knox, 1992.

Schottroff, Luise. "'Law-Free Gentile Christianity'—What about the Women? Feminist Analyses and Alternatives." In *A Feminist Companion to Paul,* edited by Amy-Jill Levine, 183–94. Cleveland, Ohio: Pilgrim, 2004.

Schürer, Emil. *The History of the Jewish People in the Age of Jesus Christ (175 B.C.– A.D. 135).* Rev. ed. by Geza Vermes et al. 3 volumes. Edinburgh: T&TClark, 1986.

Schüssler Fiorenza, Elisabeth. *In Memory of Her: A Feminist Theological Reconstruction of Christian Origins.* New York: Crossroad, 1985.

———. "Paul and the Politics of Interpretation." In *Paul and Politics: Ekklesia, Israel, Imperium, Interpretation. Essays in Honor of Krister Stendahl,* edited by Richard A. Horsley, 40–57. Harrisburg, Pa.: Trinity Press International, 2000.

———. *Rhetoric and Ethic: The Politics of Biblical Studies.* Minneapolis: Fortress Press, 1999.

Schwab, Katherine Anne. "The Parthenon Metopes and Greek Vase Painting: A Study of Comparison and Influences." Ph.D. diss., Institute of Fine Arts, New York University, 1989.

Schwartz, Daniel R. *2 Maccabees.* Commentaries on Early Jewish Literature. Berlin/New York: de Gruyter, 2008.

Schwartz, Seth. *Imperialism and Jewish Society, 200 B.C.E. to 640 C.E.* Jews, Christians, and Muslims from the Ancient to the Modern World. Princeton: Princeton University Press, 2001.

Schwarzer, Holger. "Untersuchungen zum hellenistischen Herrscherkult in Pergamon." *Istanbuler Mitteilungen* 49 (1999): 249–300.

Schweitzer, Albert. *Essential Writings.* Maryknoll, N.Y.: Orbis, 2005.

———. *The Mysticism of Paul the Apostle.* London: A. & C. Black, 1931.

Schwertheim, Elmar, ed. *Forschungen in Galatien.* Asia Minor Studien. Bonn: Rudolf Habelt, 1994.

Schwier, Helmut. *Tempel und Tempelzerstörung: Untersuchung zu den theologischen und ideologischen Faktoren im ersten jüdisch-römischen Krieg (66–74 n.chr.).* Freiburg: Universitätsverlag, 1989.

Scott, James C. *Domination and the Arts of Resistance: Hidden Transcripts.* New Haven: Yale University Press, 1990.

Scott, James M. *Paul and the Nations: The Old Testament and Jewish Background of Paul's Mission to the Nations with Special Reference to the Destination of Galatians.* WUNT 84. Tübingen: Mohr Siebeck, 1995.

———, ed. *Restoration: Old Testament, Jewish and Christian Perspectives.* Journal for the Study of Judaism Supplement 72. Leiden: Brill, 2001.

———. "Restoration of Israel." In *Dictionary of Paul and His Letters,* edited by Gerald F. Hawthorne and Ralph P. Martin, 796–805. Downers Grove, Ill.: InterVarsity, 1993.

Scroggs, Robin. "The Sociological Interpretation of the New Testament: The Present State of Research." *NTS* 26 (1980): 164–79.

Seaver, George. *Albert Schweitzer: The Man and his Mind.* New York/London: Harper& Brothers, 1947.

Segal, Alan. *Paul the Convert: The Apostolate and Apostasy of Saul the Pharisee.* New Haven: Yale University Press, 1990.

Segovia, Fernando F. *Decolonizing Biblical Studies: A View from the Margins*. Maryknoll, N.Y.: Orbis, 2000.

Shatzman, Israel. *The Armies of the Hasmoneans and Herod: From Hellenistic to Roman Frameworks*. Texte und Studien zum antiken Judentum 25. Tübingen: Mohr Siebeck, 1991.

Sheppard, A. R. R. "Jews, Christians and Heretics in Acmonia and Eumeneia." *Anatolian Studies* 29 (1979): 169–80.

Sherk, R. K. "Roman Galatia: The Governors from 25 B.C. to A.D. 114." In *ANRW* II.7.2 (1980): 954–1052.

Sherwin-White, A. N. *Roman Foreign Policy in the East: 168 B.C. to A.D. 1*. Norman: University of Oklahoma Press, 1984.

Simon, Erika. *Pergamon und Hesiod*. Schriften zur antiken Mythologie 3. Mainz am Rhein: Pilipp von Zabern, 1975.

Smallwood, E. Mary. *The Jews under Roman Rule: From Pompey to Diocletian*. Studies in Judaism in Late Antiquity 20. Leiden: Brill, 1976.

Smith, Dennis E. *From Symposium to Eucharist: The Banquet in the Early Christian World*. Minneapolis: Fortress Press, 2003.

Smith, R. R. R. *Hellenistic Sculpture: A Handbook*. London: Thames & Hudson, 1991.

Smith-Christopher, Daniel. "Between Ezra and Isaiah." In *Ethnicity and the Bible*, edited by Mark Brett, 117–42. Biblical Interpretation Series 19. Leiden: Brill, 1996.

Snyder, Graydon F. *Irish Jesus, Roman Jesus: The Formation of Early Irish Christianity*. Harrisburg, Pa.: Trinity Press International, 2002.

Souza, Philip de. "'They Are Enemies of All Mankind': Justifying Roman Imperialism in the Late Republic." In *Roman Imperialism: Post-Colonial Perspectives*, edited by Jane Webster and Nicholas J. Cooper, 125–33. Leicester: School of Archaeological Studies, University of Leicester, 1996.

Speyer, Wolfgang. "Gigant." *Reallexikon für Antike und Christentum* 10 (1978): 1247–76.

Spivak, Gayatri Chakravorty. "Can the Subaltern Speak?" In *Colonial Discourse and Post-Colonial Theory: A Reader*, edited by Patrick Williams and Laura Chrisman, 66–111. New York: Columbia University Press, 1994.

Stähelin, Felix. *Geschichte der kleinasiatischen Galater*. Leipzig: Teubner, 1907.

Ste. Croix, G. E. M. de. "Why Were the Early Christians Persecuted?" In *Church and State in the Early Church*, edited by Everett Ferguson, 16–48. Studies in Early Christianity 7. New York: Garland, 1993.

Stemberger, Günter. *Die römische Herrschaft im Urteil der Juden*. Erträge der Forschung 195. Darmstadt: Wissenschaftliche Buchgesellschaft, 1983.

Stendahl, Krister. *Paul among Jews and Gentiles, and Other Essays*. Philadelphia: Fortress Press, 1976.

Stern, Menahem. "Josephus and the Roman Empire as Reflected in *The Jewish War*." In *Josephus, Judaism, and Christianity*, edited by Louis H. Feldman and Gohei Hata, 71–80. Detroit: Wayne State University Press, 1987.

Stewart, Andrew. "Narration and Allusion in the Hellenistic Baroque." In *Narrative and Event in Ancient Art*, edited by Peter J. Holliday, 130–74. Cambridge/New York: Cambridge University Press, 1993.

———. "*Pergamo Ara Marmorea Magna:* On the Date, Reconstruction, and Functions of the Great Altar of Pergamon." In *From Pergamon to Sperlonga: Sculpture and Context*, edited by Nancy T. de Grummond and Brunilde S. Ridgway, 32–57. Hellenistic Culture and Society. Berkeley: University of California Press, 2000.

Strecker, Christian. "Fides-Pistis-Glaube: Kontexte und Konturen einer Theologie der 'Annahme' bei Paulus." In *Lutherische und neue Paulusperspektive: Beiträge zu einem Schlüsselproblem der gegenwärtigen exegetischen Diskussion*, edited by Michael Bachmann and Johannes Woyke, 221–48. WUNT 182. Tübingen: Mohr Siebeck, 2005.

———. *Die liminale Theologie des Paulus: Zugänge zur paulinischen Theologie aus kulturanthropologischer Perspektive*. Forschungen zur Religion und Literatur des Alten und Neuen Testaments. Göttingen: Vandenhoeck & Ruprecht, 1999.

Strobel, Karl. *Die Galater: Geschichte und Eigenart der keltischen Staatenbildung auf dem Boden des hellenistischen Kleinasien*. Untersuchungen zur Geschichte und historischen Geographie des hellenistischen und römischen Kleinasien 1. Berlin: Akademie, 1996.

———. "Keltensieg und Galatersieger: Die Funktionalisierung eines historischen Phänomens als politischer Mythos der hellenistischen Welt." In *Forschungen in Galatien*, edited by Elmar Schwertheim, 97–103. Asia Minor Studien 12. Bonn: Rudolf Habelt, 1994.

Stupperich, Reinhard. "Zur Beschreibung einer galatischen Villa im 20. Brief Gregors von Nyssa." In *Forschungen in Galatien*, edited by Elmar Schwertheim, 97–103. Bonn: Rudolf Habelt, 1994.

Sturgeon, Mary C. "Pergamon to Hierapolis: From Theatrical 'Altar' to Religious Theater." In *From Pergamon to Sperlonga: Sculpture and Context*, edited by Nancy T. de Grummond and Brunilde de Ridgway, 58–77. Hellenistic Culture and Society. Berkeley: University of California Press, 2000.

Sugirtharajah, R. S. *Postcolonial Criticism and Biblical Interpretation*. New York: Oxford University Press, 2002.

Sutter Rehmann, Luzia. "To Turn the Groaning into Labor: Rom 8:22-23." In *A Feminist Companion to Paul*, edited by Amy-Jill Levine, 74–84. Cleveland, Ohio: Pilgrim, 2004.

Szabó, Miklós. "The Celts and Their Movements in the Third Century B.C." In *The Celts*, edited by Sabatino Moscati et al., 303–13. Venice: Bompiani, 1991.

———. "Mercenary Activity." In *The Celts*, edited by Sabatino Moscati et al., 333–36. Venice: Bompiani, 1991.

Tacitus. *The Histories*. Edited by D. S. Levene. Oxford: Oxford University Press, 1997.

Tamez, Elsa. *The Amnesty of Grace*. Nashville: Abingdon, 1993.

Taubes, Jacob. *The Political Theology of Paul*. Cultural Memory in the Present. Stanford, Calif.: Stanford University Press, 2004.

———. *Die politische Theologie des Paulus*. Munich: Wilhelm Fink Verlag, 1993.

Taussig, Hal. *In the Beginning Was the Meal: Social Experimentation & Early Christian Identity*. Minneapolis: Fortress Press, 2009.

Theodor, J., and C. Albeck, eds. *Midrash Bereshit Rabba*. Jerusalem:Wahrmann, 1965.

Thom, Johan C. *Cleanthes' Hymn to Zeus: Text, Translation, and Commentary*. Studien und Texte zu Antike und Christentum 33. Tübingen: Mohr Siebeck, 2005.

Tombs, David. "Crucifixion, State Terror, and Sexual Abuse." *USQR* 53, no. 1–2 (1999): 89–109.

Tomson, Peter J. *Paul and the Jewish Lae: Halakha in the Letters of the Apostle to the Gentiles*. Compendia rerum iudaicarum ad Novum Testamentum, Section 3, Jewish Tradition in Early Christian Literature 1. Minneapolis: Fortress Press, 1990.

Townes, Emilie M. *Womanist Ethics and the Cultural Production of Evil*. Black Religion. New York: Palgrave Macmillan, 2006.

Trebilco, Paul R. *Jewish Communities in Asia Minor*. SNTSMS 69. Cambridge: Cambridge University Press, 1991.

Trible, Phyllis. *Texts of Terror: Literary-feminist Readings of Biblical Narratives*. Philadelphia: Fortress Press, 1984.

Trzaska-Richter, Christine. *Furor teutonicus: Das Römische Germanenbild in Politik und Propaganda von den Anfängen bis zum 2. Jahrhundert n.Chr.* Bochumer Altertumswissenschaftliches Colloquium 8. Trier: Wissenschftlicher Verlag Trier, 1991.

Tuchelt, Klaus. *Frühe Denkmäler Roms in Kleinasien: Beiträge zur archäologischen Überlieferung aus der Zeit der Republik und des Augustus.* Istanbuler Mitteilungen 23. Tübingen: E. Wasmuth, 1979.

Vian, Francis. "Gigantes." *LIMC* 3 (1988): 191–270.

———. *La guerre des géants.* Paris: Librairie C. Klincksieck, 1952.

Ville, Georges. *La gladiature en Occident des origines à la mort de Domitien.* Bibliothèque des écoles françaises d'Athènes et de Rome 245e. Rome: Ecole française de Rome, 1981.

Waelkens, Marc. "The Imperial Sanctuary at Pessinus: Archeological, Epigraphical and Numismatic Evidence for Its Date and Identification." *Epigraphica Anatolica* 7 (1986): 37–73.

Wallace, David R. *The Gospel of God: Romans as Paul's Aeneid.* Eugene, Ore.: Pickwick, 2008.

Wallace-Hadrill, Andrew. *Augustan Rome.* London: Bristol Classical, 1993.

Wan, Sze-kar. "Collection for the Saints as Anticolonial Act." In *Paul and Politics: Ekklesia, Israel, Imperium, Interpretation. Essays in Honor of Krister Stendahl,* edited by Richard A. Horsley, 191–215. Harrisburg, Pa.: Trinity Press International , 2000.

Wardy, B. "Jewish Religion in Pagan Literature during the Late Republic and Early Empire." In *ANRW* II.19.1 (1979): 592–644.

Weber, Carl W. *Panem et Circenses: Massenunterhaltung als Politik.* Düsseldorf/Vienna: Econ, 1983.

Webster, Jane. "Ethnographic Barbarity: Colonial Discourse and 'Celtic Warrior Societies.'" In *Roman Imperialism: Post-Colonial Perspectives,* edited by Jane Webster and Nicholas J. Cooper, 111–23. Leicester: School of Archaeological Studies, University of Leicester, 1996.

———. "The Just War: Graeco-Roman Texts as Colonial Discourse." In *TRAC 94: Proceedings of the 4th Annual Theoretical Roman Archaeology Conference,* edited by Sally Cottam et al., 1–10. Durham: University of Durham, 1994.

———. "A Negotiated Syncretism: Readings on the Development of Romano-Celtic Religion." In *Dialogues in Roman Imperialism: Power, Discourse and Discrepant Experience in the Roman Empire,* edited by D. J. Mattingly, 165–84. Portsmouth, R.I.: Journal of Roman Archaeology, 1997.

———. "Roman Imperialism and the 'Post Imperial Age.'" In *Roman Imperialism: Post-Colonial Perspectives,* edited by Jane Webster and Nicholas J. Cooper, 1–18. Leicester: School of Archaeological Studies, University of Leicester, 1996.

Weiss, Peter. *The Aesthetics of Resistance,* volume 1. Translated by Joachim Neugroschel. Durham, N.C./London: Duke University Press, 2005.

Weissenrieder, Annette, et al., eds. *Picturing the New Testament: Studies in Ancient Visual Images.* WUNT 2/193. Tübingen: Mohr Siebeck, 2005.

Wells, Peter S. *The Barbarians Speak: How the Conquered Peoples Shaped Roman Europe.* Princeton: Princeton University Press, 1999.

Wiedemann, Thomas. *Emperors and Gladiators.* London: Routledge, 1992.

Williams, Patrick, and Laura Chrisman, eds. *Colonial Discourse and Post-Colonial Theory: A Reader.* New York: Columbia University Press, 1994.

Winger, Michael. *By What Law? The Meaning of Nomos in the Letters of Paul.* Society of Biblical Literature Dissertation Series 128. Atlanta: Scholars, 1992.

Winter, Bruce W. *Seek the Welfare of the City: Christians as Benefactors and Citizens.* First-century Christians in the Graeco-Roman World. Grand Rapids: Eerdmans, 1994.

Witherington, Ben, III. *Grace in Galatia: A Commentary on St. Paul's Letter to the Galatians.* Grand Rapids: Eerdmans, 1998.

Witulski, Thomas. *Die Adressaten des Galaterbriefes: Untersuchungen zur Gemeinde von Antiochia ad Pisidiam*. Forschungen zur Religion und Literatur des Alten und Neuen Testaments 193. Göttingen: Vandenhoeck & Ruprecht, 2000.

———. *Kaiserkult in Kleinasien: Die Entwicklung der kultisch-religiösen Kaiserverehrung in der römischen Provinz Asia von Augustus bis Antoninus Pius*. Novum Testamentum et Orbis Antiquus/ Studien zur Umwelt des Neuen Testaments. Fribourg: Academic; Göttingen: Vandenhoeck & Ruprecht, 2007.

Wright, N. T. "Paul's Gospel and Caesar's Empire." In *Paul and Politics: Ekklesia, Israel, Imperium, Interpretation. Essays in Honor of Krister Stendahl*, edited by Richard Horsley, 160–83. Harrisburg, Pa.: Trinity Press International, 2000.

Yavetz, Zvi. *Plebs and Princeps*. London: Oxford University Press, 1969.

Young, Iris Marion. *Justice and the Politics of Difference*. Princeton: Princeton University Press, 1990.

Young, Rodney S. *Gordion: A Guide to the Excavations and Museum*. Ankara: Ankara Turizmi, 1968.

Zanker, Paul. *The Power of Images in the Age of Augustus*. Jerome Lectures, 16th Series. Ann Arbor: University of Michigan Press, 1988.

Ziegler, Konrat. *Das hellenistische Epos*. Leipzig: Teubner, 1966.

Indexes

Subject Index

Modern Authors

Ancient Literature

PAUL IN CRITICAL CONTEXTS

Other Titles in the Series

call 800-328-4648

fortresspress.com